THE LETTERS OF
FREDERICK PHILIP GROVE

Frederick Philip Grove. *Courtesy Leonard Grove*

Edited with an introduction
and notes by Desmond Pacey

The Letters of Frederick Philip Grove

UNIVERSITY OF TORONTO PRESS
TORONTO AND BUFFALO

Printed in Canada

Library of Congress Cataloging in Publication Data

Grove, Frederick Philip, 1879–1948.
The letters of Frederick Philip Grove.

Includes index.
1. Grove, Frederick Philip, 1879–1948 – Correspondence.
PR9199.3.G77Z53 1975 813'.5'2[B] 74-75828
ISBN 0-8020-5311-4

This book is dedicated to
the memory of
Frederick Philip Grove
and to that of his wife
Catherine
and to their son
Leonard,
his wife, Mary, and their
children.

Desmond Pacey — 1917-75

Desmond Pacey published his first work on Frederick Philip Grove, an article in the *Manitoba Arts Review*, in 1943. This was followed by a monograph, *Frederick Philip Grove* (1945), which for many years stood alone in Grove criticism, *Frederick Philip Grove* (1970) in the Critical Views on Canadian Writers series, and *Tales from the Margin* (1971), a scholarly edition of Grove's short stories. In his classes at the University of New Brunswick, in public lectures in various parts of Canada and abroad, and in numerous publications, Dr Pacey maintained that Grove was a major writer. Nor was this commitment a light one: this edition of the letters – in preparation for over ten years – constitutes an impressive tribute to his research and scholarship.

Dr Pacey never apologised for Canadian literature, nor did he view it from the point of view of a myopic nationalism. Not content merely to add to the stock of opinions or to engage in literary sophistry, he established, during more than thirty-five years of dedication to Canadian literature, a firm foundation for the study of that literature. His works include books on the history of English-Canadian literature, on Ethel Wilson, on Canadian poets, on Canadian criticism, articles on almost every major Canadian author, contributions to the *Literary History of Canada*, and several anthologies; he was instrumental in the establishment of many journals as well.

Dr Pacey did not live to see this book take its final shape; he died on July 4, 1975 while it was still in production. At the time of his death, he was preparing definitive editions of the collected poems and letters of Sir Charles G.D. Roberts and planning no end of literary work.

J.C. Mahanti
University of New Brunswick
Fredericton, NB, July 8, 1975

Contents

Illustrations

Preface

Editing the letters of any man or woman is a difficult and delicate task. Unlike essays or novels or poems, letters may be expected to be the spontaneous, unrevised expressions of a writer's feelings and thoughts, and reading them often gives the uneasy feeling that we are trespassing upon the private domain of their author. On the other hand, nothing can give such a sense of immediacy as a letter, and when that letter is written by a professional writer we are apt to get from it a glimpse into his personality and purposes which no other medium can so fully afford.

The usual difficulties associated with editing letters are compounded in Frederick Philip Grove's case because he was such a mysterious and enigmatic figure. Although there was, during his lifetime and immediately afterwards, a good deal of controversy about the merit of his work, there now seems to be general agreement that he was one of the most skilful Canadian novelists of his generation. Controversy about Grove's life and personality, however, has increased rather than diminished with the passage of time. The fact is that until recently we have known nothing definite about Grove's life prior to his settling in Manitoba as a teacher late in 1912. Some people have always regarded Grove's accounts of his early life in Europe as purely fictional, and recent scholarly analyses of the many inconsistencies in his various autobiographical accounts of it have certainly demonstrated that none of them can be accepted as unvarnished statements of fact.

Indeed, Professor D.O. Spettigue's assiduous research seems now to have established beyond a reasonable doubt that Frederick Philip Grove of Canada was, prior to 1910 or 1912, Felix Paul Greve of Germany. If this is true, Grove was born in 1879 rather than in 1871 or 1872, was brought up in eastern Germany rather than in southwestern Sweden, and came to North America around 1910 rather than, as Grove himself always maintained, in 1892 or 1893. Apart from these differences of time and place, however, the identification of Grove with

Greve does not seriously invalidate the story of his early life which Grove gives in his autobiography, *In Search of Myself* (1946). If Grove was Greve, he *was* educated at leading schools in Hamburg and at great German universities, he *was* a young writer of promise who associated with such persons as Stefan George and André Gide, and he *had* written a considerable body of work (including two novels, two plays, some poems, and a great many translations of such writers as Swift, Wilde, Browning, and Wells) before emigrating to North America shortly before World War I.

The letters here presented, however, apart from the samples of Greve's correspondence printed in Appendix A, are those of Frederick Philip Grove, the Canadian novelist and essayist, and it is for the light they shed on Grove's Canadian career that they are chiefly important.

The history of this collection may, in a sense, be said to go back to the year 1941, when my own correspondence with Grove began. Several years later, Dr Watson Kirkconnell was kind enough to send me his letters from Grove, and to suggest that I should undertake to edit a collection of them. I broached the idea to Grove's widow, the late Mrs Catherine Grove, and after some years of hesitation she eventually gave the project her warm blessing and vigorous co-operation.[1] I have also enjoyed the strong support of Grove's son, Mr A. Leonard Grove, and of Leonard's wife, Mary. To them, and the many others who have helped in the task, I extend my deep thanks. As a result of the co-operation so freely extended to me, I have managed to assemble a much larger collection of the letters than had once seemed possible. No doubt other letters will turn up as the years go by, but I have printed below all the letters that I have been able to locate thus far: the attempt has been to produce a *collected*, rather than a *selected*, edition.

To attempt to mention by name all those who have played a part in making this collection possible would be a task of almost insurmountable difficulty. The list would include all of Grove's known surviving friends and many of his relatives, dozens of librarians and archivists across Canada and in the United States, France, Germany, Scotland, England, and Sweden, and many colleagues at the University of New Brunswick and other universities in many parts of the world. I must, however, single out for special mention the following:

David Wilder, John Muchin, and Margaret Mackenzie of the Elizabeth Dafoe Library, University of Manitoba; H. Pearson Gundy, John H. Archer, and Rose Mary Gibson of the Douglas Library, Queen's University; Edward Phelps of the Regional History Library, University of Western Ontario; Keith Crouch, Peggy Carroll, and Kate Lewis of the McGill University Library; Mary Percival, Marion E. Brown, Anne Fabbro, and Katherine Wales of the University of Toronto Library; Mrs L.B. Martyn and K.R. Macpherson of the Ontario Department of Public Records and Archives, and Mary Harland of the Ontario Department of Education; James Anderson of the Perth County Archives, Stratford, Ontario; Elizabeth Spicer of the London (Ontario) Public Library and Art Museum; Autar K. Ganju and Linda Shellington of the Simcoe Public Library; Mary Leppan of the North Bay Public Library; Marian Childs of the Thunder Bay Public Library; The Rev. Glenn Lucas of the Archives of the

United Church of Canada, Victoria University, Toronto; Honor Buttars of the McLaughlin Public Library, Oshawa, Ontario; H.N. Brachen, Archivist, The Incorporated Synod of the Diocese of Toronto, Anglican Church of Canada, Toronto, Ontario; Ruth Vukadinov of the Windsor Public Library, Windsor, Ontario; Mary Fry and Chris Fox of the Metropolitan Toronto Central Library; R.S. Gordon of the Public Archives of Canada, Ottawa; W. Kaye Lamb and Guy Sylvestre of the National Library of Canada, Ottawa; Erik J. Spicer of the Library of Parliament, Ottawa; George Stacey, Cheryl A. Ranson, and Kenneth M. Glazier of the University of Calgary Library, and Mrs Georgeen Barrass of the Glenbow-Alberta Institute in Calgary; W.B. Kelly, Secretary, The Law Society of Alberta, Calgary; Marjorie Morley and Barry Hyman of the Manitoba Provincial Library and Archives; W.E. Ireland of the British Columbia Provincial Library and Archives; Robyn Robertson of the Prince Rupert Library, Prince Rupert, BC; Allan R. Turner of the Saskatchewan Archives Board; the staff of the Harriet Irving Library, University of New Brunswick, especially Nan Gregg, Patricia Ruthven, and Sylvia Guidry; Frank Brown of Winkler, Helen Rempel of Steinbach, J.M. Young of Neepawa, Mr and Mrs Norman Basher and Mrs W. Taylor of Rapid City, Edith Gunn of Winnipeg, and Kaye Rowe of the Brandon *Sun*; Ralph B. King, A.E. Birkinshaw, and R.B. Inch of Brandon University; John Gray, Gladys Neale, and Isobel Syme of the Macmillan Company of Canada; Frank Flemington of McGraw-Hill Ryerson Limited; Graham Spry and Wilfrid Eggleston of Ottawa; C.J. Eustace of Willowdale, Ontario, and formerly of J.M. Dent and Sons of Canada; Francess G. Halpenny of the *Dictionary of Canadian Biography*, University of Toronto Press, and Jean Jamieson, Jean Wilson, and Prudence Tracy of the Editorial Department of the Press; W.E. Collin of the University of Western Ontario; Roy and Laurenda Daniells of the University of British Columbia; Trevor Lloyd of McGill University; Watson Kirkconnell of Wolfville, NS; Jean Hubener, Robert Cattley, Leonard Smith, Abram Friesen, Alfred G. Bailey, Harry Lusher, Franz Eppert, Karl Kuepper, Inge Pataki, Laszlo Szabo, John Brebner, Harold Sharp, and Sister Beverley Mitchell of the University of New Brunswick; and Dr William L. Webster of Shediac, NB; the Canada Council, which gave me several grants in aid of research and the Humanities Research Council of Canada, which has given a grant in aid of publication, using funds provided by the Canada Council; the Publications Fund of the University of Toronto Press; my two successive research assistants, Alastair Robertson and J.C. Mahanti; the chief typist of the text of the letters, Janett Kieley of Fredericton; and my own secretary, Mrs Vera Downing.

Without these persons, and the cheerful forbearance of my wife Mary, this book would never have seen the light of day. The many imperfections which that light will reveal are the results wholly of my own inadequacies, not of theirs.

The University of New Brunswick
Fredericton, NB
June 10, 1974

DESMOND PACEY

1 She did, however, make some minor excisions in some of the letters from her husband to herself.

Introduction

According to his own accounts of his early life, now, as the preface mentions, partially discredited, the man whom Canadians know as Frederick Philip Grove was born in a place east of the River Vistula of an Anglo-Swedish father and a Scottish mother. His childhood was spent on the parental estate of 'Castle Thurow,' supposedly situated on the southwest coast of Sweden.[1] He claims to have received his formal education, however, in Germany, first at a Realschule and then at a famous but unnamed Realgymnasium in Hamburg, which German scholars quickly identified for me from his description as the Johanneum. Later he attended university to study archaeology, classical philology, and, briefly, law and medicine. But much of his time he spent in associating with young men who were, or were soon to be, famous literary personalities, such as Stéphane Mallarmé, André Gide, and Stefan George, and in travelling across Europe, to the Far East, Africa and, eventually, the Americas. His ostensible reason for staying on in North America was that he found himself stranded in Toronto in 1892 when news reached him that his father had died, and had died in heavy debt. In the descriptions of his subsequent travels as a hobo and farmhand in the western United States and Canada, which in some versions of his own life story covered a period of twenty years and in others merely two, he portrays himself as an aristocratic youth, idealistic in temperament, who rejects American materialism or, as he says in one of the earliest letters extant, 'the aristocracy of grocerdom.' His idealism eventually led him to settle as a teacher in rural Manitoba, to build, in his words, 'a domestic island' in the prairie wilderness.

To rehearse here all the evidence which now suggests that this is a considerably distorted version of the early life of Grove would be to attempt – and vainly at that – to steal Professor D.O. Spettigue's thunder.[2] I shall therefore content myself with indicating briefly how Grove has cunningly interwoven fact and fiction in his autobiographies. If Frederick Philip Grove was indeed Felix Paul Greve, his mother's name was in fact Bertha, but her maiden name was Reichentrog rather than Rutherford and she was German, not Scottish.[3] His father's name was Charles Edward, or at least, Carl Eduard – but the father also was German, not Anglo-Swedish. There was, as the autobiography suggests, a considerable discrepancy in the ages of his parents – Carl Eduard was born in 1847, Bertha in 1855 – and they did eventually separate. The father did, during Felix Paul's early boyhood, run an agricultural estate at Thurow, but it was situated near Schwerin in eastern Germany rather than near Lund in southwestern Sweden. Instead of continuing as a farmer, Greve's father became a minor official in Hamburg, where the son did indeed attend the Realgymnasium Johanneum, but in the late eighteen-nineties rather than the late eighteen-eighties. And so it goes – in very broad outline the Grove version is correct, but he has so altered names, places, and dates as to make the Greve-Grove identification extremely difficult to establish.

We can only speculate on the motives which led Grove to create his elaborate disguise. One almost certain motive is that Felix Paul Greve was arrested for fraud in Bonn in 1903, and spent several months in jail – presumably Grove wished to dissociate himself from this criminal record. As for the pretence that he was Anglo-Swedish rather than German, this is not hard to understand in one who was attempting to start a new life in Canada immediately prior to World War I, when anti-German feeling was running high.

All this, of course, is of somewhat dubious relevance to the present book, which collects the letters of Grove's Canadian period – and for this reason I have dealt with it very summarily, rather than in detail. What obviously *is* relevant, however, is the degree to which the Grove letters shed light on his European past. And here the fact must be faced that the light is very dim indeed. Unlike the letters of most persons, Grove's are seldom the products of a man with his guard down. In references to his age, for example, he is always scrupulously careful to date his birth in 1871 or 1872, rather than in 1879.[4] Only when challenged about dates, as when Carleton Stanley questioned the date of Furtwaengler's tenure as professor at Munich or I tried to sort out some of the inconsistencies of dating in writing my biographical and critical study published in 1945, did Grove reveal some defensiveness and evasiveness, taking refuge in pleas that all this had happened many years ago and that he could no longer be sure of the facts.

The early letters to Isaak Warkentin, with which his volume opens, certainly make clear that Grove was at home in the German language and knew a good deal about the state of contemporary German society – but this might be explained by Grove's German education and by his acknowledged residence there as a youth. And when Grove, late in 1925, tells E.J. Moore of Ryerson Press that he has *always* had twelve free copies of his own books, and we remember that he had by this time only published two small books of essays in Canada, it does rather suggest that he had previously published other books, presumably under another name – but it suggests only, and does not prove. A mere month later, indeed, Grove solemnly assures Moore that he was born in Sweden in 1872 and came to Canada in 1892, although he does truncate the usual twenty years of American hobo-dom to two and refers, for the only time that I can recall, to having taught in private schools before becoming a public school-teacher in Manitoba. Perhaps the most revealing comment in these earlier letters is Grove's correction, in the April 30, 1926 letter to the *Canadian Bookman*, of Watson Kirkconnell's attribution to him of the first complete edition of *Gulliver's Travels*, and his counter-claim of merely being 'instrumental ... in bringing about the publication of two, perhaps three continental editions.' Now of course there is no record of Frederick Philip Grove having had anything to do with editions of *Gulliver's Travels* – but Felix Paul Greve did indeed edit Swift in German translation, and for once Grove seems to have let his guard slightly down.

The guard has been raised again by November 11, 1927, when Grove in a letter to Kirkconnell refers to the nineties as the decade when he lived in France – whereas if he was Greve he was in that decade merely a schoolboy in Hamburg. Whatever the degree of Grove's acquaintance with the French poets he mentions in that letter, the following letters to Kirkconnell make clear that his knowledge of German literature at the turn of the twentieth century was very detailed indeed – far more detailed, in fact, than his knowledge of English literature of the same period, since we find him asking who 'Sassoon or Sasson' is. Another revealing reference in this sequence of letters to Kirkconnell is contained in that of December 14, 1927, in which Grove admits to knowing the work of Gide only up to *La Porte étroite* – which was published in 1909, the very year in which Spettigue believes Greve to have left Europe for America.

There are a number of references in the letters written to Grove's wife during the triumphant lecture tours of 1928 and 1929 to the way in which the deferential manner in which he was treated during those tours by the wealthy and powerful reminded him of the splendours of his European past. The irony is that, if indeed Grove was originally Greve, his wealthy phase was that escapade with someone else's wife and someone else's money which led to his jail sentence in 1903! Although Greve's parents seem to have been financially comfortable, there is nothing to suggest that they were truly aristocratic, powerful, or wealthy. The boyish excitement with which Grove relays to his wife his appearance in the Ottawa 'Society News,' in the letter of March 20, 1928, tends to confirm the suspicion that Grove was not really accustomed to moving in high society.

But if, as now seems certain, Grove was something of a liar, he was very clever at appearing to be an ingenious one. Nothing could excel the apparent frankness with which he answered my enquiries about his life and work in the early months of 1941. Casually he tells me that 'Among my Parisian friends of 1889 to 1891 were Mallarmé, Verlaine, Heredia, Henri de Régnier, Jules Renard, André Gide,' and then, with becoming modesty, goes on: 'Since some of them are still living, I should, however, prefer to leave them in twilight.' In the next letter the modest mask is still very much in evidence: 'though both Maupassant and Zola were still living at the time, I had no contact with them except, perhaps, a social one; I don't remember.' That 'perhaps' is beautifully in tone! Very quickly, however, the apparent ingenuousness could change to what, in retrospect at least, seems like the height of ingenuity – in case I might be rash enough to investigate his knowledge of Swedish, he assures me that he had almost forgotten his 'native Swedish' even during his Parisian days.

If the letters, then, shed only a dim and intermittent light upon Grove's European years, they are much more revealing about his life in Canada. On arriving in Winnipeg in 1912, Grove sought and was granted an interview with Robert Fletcher, then Deputy Minister of Education. Grove was an impressive-looking man; Manitoba had scattered German-speaking, Mennonite communities; and bilingual teachers were especially hard to come by. Thus Grove, who could be extremely articulate on his own behalf, had little difficulty in obtaining an 'interim' teacher's certificate from Fletcher. In January 1913, he was hired to teach in Haskett, a rural outpost on the border between Canada and the USA. Thus began a decade during which Grove taught in several rural or small-town schools in succession – Haskett, Winkler, Virden, Gladstone, Leifur, Ferguson, Eden – qualified for his permanent teacher's certificate, became a naturalized Canadian citizen, and graduated in arts from the University of Manitoba as an extramural student (1922). He seems to have found an outlet for his idealism in teaching; and also during this time he found the 'domestic island' he had been seeking to establish in the wilderness, for on August 2, 1914, when he was Principal of the Intermediate School at Winkler, he married Catherine Wiens, a teacher in the same school, and a year later, on August 5, a daughter christened Phyllis May was born.

In the summer of 1922, the Groves moved to Rapid City, he as Principal of the high school and she as a teacher in the public school. *Over Prairie Trails* and *The Turn of the Year*, two books of essays, appeared in 1922 and 1923 respectively, and encouraged by this success Grove gave up teaching after the 1923–4 school year. His first novel, *Settlers of the Marsh*, was published in 1925, followed by *A Search for America* (1927), *Our Daily Bread* (1928), *The Yoke of Life* (1930), *Fruits of the Earth* (1933), and another book of essays, *It Needs to Be Said* (1929). These must have been days of furious literary activity, although they lacked the drama and the excitement of the adventures Grove claimed to have undergone in his youth. But the move to Rapid City not only marked the emergence of the author, thus removing him from his self-imposed obscurity; it also brought him into contact with Canadian intellectuals such as Arthur L. Phelps and Watson Kirkconnell, both then professors at Wesley College, Winnipeg, Professors A.S.P. Woodhouse and W.F. Osborne of the University of Manitoba, and Lorne Pierce and Hugh S. Eayrs, the Toronto publishers.

Grove's stay in Rapid City was climaxed by three lecture tours in 1928 and 1929, which were perhaps the most exciting events in his life in Canada. These tours, sponsored by the Association of Canadian Clubs, brought him into public notice across the country, plunged him into a whirl of social activities and receptions which were attended by men prominent in Canadian letters, education, business, industry, in politics, and while they lasted made him a national celebrity. Grove was never to enjoy such popular success again. In fact, he was not to achieve publication after *Fruits of the Earth* (1933) until 1939, and then five more years were to elapse before his next book appeared.

However, encouraged by the success of the lecture tours, and the prospect of employment in the east, the Groves left Rapid City in the fall of 1929. This move was no doubt partially motivated by the tragic death of their daughter in 1927, which had made Rapid City a place of unhappy memories. December 1929 saw Grove in Ottawa, as an employee of Graphic Publishers Limited, the same firm which had published in 1927 his *A Search for America*. His direct involvement in the publishing business did not last very long, although he continued to act as a publisher's reader until almost the end of his life. The Graphic company was already in financial difficulties, and the Depression made new risk capital impossible to obtain. Although the control of Graphic did not pass on to the trustee until May 1932, Grove left the firm in the fall of 1931, bought a farm near Simcoe, and settled on it with his wife and one-year-old son Leonard. This was the final move. In 1944 he suffered a stroke which left him partially paralysed, and he died at Simcoe after prolonged illness on August 19, 1948.

Although 'The Seasons,' intended as his *magnum opus*, remained incomplete at the time of his death, and several of his manuscripts did not find publishers,[5] four other books were published in his life-time: *Two Generations* (1939), *The Master of the Mill* (1944), the autobiography *In Search of Myself* (1946), and *Consider Her Ways* (1947). *Tales from the Margin*, a collection of his short stories selected and edited by me, was published in 1971.

Grove was, in spite of his complaints against lack of recognition in Canada, one of the most honoured Canadian novelists of his generation. The Royal Society of Canada awarded him the Lorne Pierce Medal in 1934 and elected him a Fellow in 1941; the University of Manitoba conferred the honorary D.LITT. on him, Mount Allison University, the LL D, and the Canadian Authors Association, honorary membership, all in 1946. He also attracted considerable critical attention: many reviews and articles, a graduate thesis, and two book-length studies of his life and works were written during his lifetime. Yet neither the honours, the critical recognition of his merit as a writer, nor the financial rewards from his writings were quite commensurate with his expectations. Grove continued to regard himself as a victim of powerful forces against which he must wage war even though the best he could hope for was a momentary, Pyrrhic victory; and he died avowedly with the sense of having failed, the veil over his past still intact, and his personality, even to those who knew him well, still an enigma.

The letters document these events in Grove's Canadian experience to a considerable degree, although it must be admitted that there are gaps in the correspondence which make the documentation far from complete. The 1913–14 letters to Warkentin and to Catherine Wiens show us something of the zeal and dedication with which Grove addressed himself to the profession of teaching in rural Manitoba. Unfortunately, there is then a long gap in the correspondence – by the time the letters resume in 1925 (with the single exception of the curious letter to Dr William Reid in 1923) Grove has had his first two Canadian books published, and we miss all the excitement of the acceptance by McClelland and Stewart of *Over Prairie Trails* and *The Turn of the Year*. If we could recover the letters which Grove must have written to McClelland and Stewart in the early nineteen-twenties, and his early correspondence with Arthur L. Phelps, we should have a much clearer picture of the years during which Grove was establishing himself as an author in Canada. It may well be that the letters to McClelland and Stewart will finally come to light – the present owner of the firm,

Mr Jack McClelland, tells me that they may be among the many boxes of the firm's papers stored in a Toronto warehouse – but Professor Phelps assured me, not long before his recent death, that he had destroyed his letters from Grove.

From 1925 onwards, however, the correspondence is fairly continuous, and provides a quite detailed record of Grove's dealings with his various publishers, of his lecture tours in the late twenties, of his brief stint in publishing in Ottawa, and of the extensive writing and reading which he did during the last years of his life in Simcoe. No doubt some letters are missing – there is evidence to suggest that Grove also wrote to the critic William Arthur Deacon,[6] to the historian Lawrence Burpee, to the poet E.J. Pratt, and to the scholars A.S.P. Woodhouse, Maurice Hutton, and Gilbert Norwood, although the correspondence has not come to light – but the letters which have survived are plentiful and varied.

Perhaps the chief value of the correspondence is the insight it provides into Grove's complex and often contradictory personality. Many passages in the letters, for example, suggest that Grove was an arrogant and authoritarian figure. In the December 6, 1913, letter to Warkentin he writes: 'I made it plain to him that *I* was running this school, not he. ... Well, I conquered along the whole line.' To Miller of Graphic Press, on November 14, 1926, he asserts: 'I write my books for a public which is not yet born.' In his letters to Mrs Grove he is often contemptuous of those persons whom he encountered during the lecture tours. On October 23, 1928, for example, he dismisses a lawyer and a newspaper man as not having an idea in their heads, and goes on: 'I was quite rude at last, saying that, if those were their opinions, we were on opposite poles of the world: learn something, I said, before you try to preach.' Again, he tells Mrs Grove on January 27, 1929, that 'They consider me the leading man in Canada at last,' and that 'A word from me placed Regan's book with them [Carrier and Co.].'

But these and the many other examples of arrogance that might be cited are balanced by passages of apparently genuine humility. 'Maybe I really lack philosophical training,' he tells Watson Kirkconnell on January 30, 1927, and 'I am just a dilettante,' he writes to the same person on March 7 of that year. To W.J. Alexander on September 4, 1937, he confesses: 'I am always so uncertain about my own work unless I have had it lying about for many years,' and to Lorne Pierce, on February 2, 1940, he admits that he may be overestimating his work and that he has always been diffident. He makes the same point to Carleton Stanley in a letter of January 16, 1946: 'You probably know that I am very diffident and cannot imagine why anyone should want to read what I have written. Who am I? It is quite true that on rare occasions I am seized with megalomania, mostly after I have been dreaming of something I have done. ... What nonsense, all this talk of great art. ...' Again, he dismisses his alleged erudition in another letter to Stanley, dated February 8, 1946, asserting that his learning 'is so small that I spread it out thinly and husband it.' Was, then, Grove arrogant or humble? The truth seems to be that like most human beings he alternated between the two moods, but that because of his intense sensitivity the swings of mood were more extreme than is customary. Grove was never a moderate man.

Similar inconsistencies confront us at every turn. For example, Grove was obviously proud of the strong sexual appeal he exercised over women, and yet he was in many respects a prude. Just as he boasts in his autobiography of his many sexual conquests, so in his letters to his wife during the lecture tours does he revel in the number of lonely women who pursued him. At the same time he expresses disgust when the photograph of a skimpily clad girl appears on the front page of the Edmonton newspaper, and deplores the short skirts of the twenties which, as he quaintly puts it, revealed when the girls bent over 'the whole differential.'

Again, Grove is almost always loud in his condemnation of the relentless quest for material possessions which he sees as the main feature of American society, and yet his own dealings with his publishers reveal that he was extremely interested in getting the maximum material return from his own books. Grove claimed to be a great admirer of Thoreau, and often dreamed of retreating like Thoreau to a hut in the wilderness, and yet he patiently saved up the fees from his lecture tours, bought new models of the then fashionable Essex car, and eventually purchased a large house and an extensive farm near Simcoe.

The mask which Grove wears most frequently is that of the tragedian, who sees the world as a bitter and frustrating place. The outlook which dominates his novels and his letters is a grim one, far more alert to the ironies and misfortunes of existence than its occasional joys. And yet a strong vein of boyish excitement co-exists with that grimness, and persists to the very end, or almost to the very end, of his life. This enthusiasm shines through when he writes to Mrs Grove of the triumphs of the lecture tours (see, for example, the letters of March 3, 14, 17, 20, and 31, 1928), when he writes jubilantly to Willard Holliday about his election to the Royal Society of Canada, and when he exults in 'the sudden burst of fame' which followed the publication of *The Master of the Mill* (see the letter to Ellen Elliott, December 7, 1945).

There is also, again in spite of the prevailing grimness and the frequently uttered charge that Grove lacks humour, a sprinkling of laughter in the letters – as there is, indeed, in the short stories. Writing to his wife on September 12, 1928, he describes his Wolseley audience as consisting of fifteen persons, among whom were two male infants, two female flappers, three sheiks, four beef-eaters, and four old ladies come out of cold storage. On June 5, 1939, writing to Lorne Pierce about his novel for juveniles, 'The Adventures of Leonard Broadus,' serialized in *The Canadian Boy* but never published as a book, he says that if Pierce likes the story he will 'murder a local druggist to get the necessary paper, and the principal of the business college to get the carbon and the ribbons needed.'

It would be quite misleading, however, to exaggerate these lighter elements. There are far more letters in which Grove reveals his loneliness, his frustration, his sense of hope eclipsed, and his withering sense of failure, than those in which he enjoys a momentary triumph. It would be difficult to surpass the depth of depression reached in the letter of May 30, 1940, to Lorne Pierce, in which Grove writes: 'most of the time I feel that, if I were my dog, I'd sit down on my haunches and howl with my pains.' Even at this low point, however, Grove's remarkable strength of will asserts itself, and he goes on: 'The strange thing is that I am convinced I have not yet done my best work. Five minutes ago, since it is raining, I finished re-reading Part I of 'The Seasons.' As a novel, it might well rank among the great works of the age; provided I had leisure and the bare essentials to finish it.' And although Grove wrote to Lorne Pierce on April 25, 1941, that 'I begin to feel that I am just a dead burden on this earth which, to me, is barren,' he continued to seek publication of his manuscripts all through the remaining seven years of his life. For all the occasional despair, there was at work in Grove an indomitable will.

This indomitable will dwelt, however, in an increasingly frail body. Grove complains of illness as early as October 20, 1913, and on July 19, 1914, tells Catherine Weins that he is 'overworked and tired.' In 1926–7 he suffered for months with a back ailment which confined him to bed for long periods – on November 25, 1926, for example, he tells Watson Kirkconnell that he has now been laid up for twelve weeks, on February 25, 1927, he expresses doubt as to whether he will be well enough to make the trip to Winnipeg at Easter, and as late as March 29, 1927, he describes himself as 'crawling about, but full of pains.' He had still not fully recovered from this back trouble when, in November 1927, he had 'two severe acute attacks of appendicitis' and had to be taken to the Bigelow Clinic in Brandon, where an operation was prescribed. On December 7, 1927, he writes to Kirkconnell that he is 'absolutely in bed, suffering pain, and unable to rise,' and states that he has not eaten anything solid since November 11. During the trans-Canada lecture tours of 1928–9 he had to be continually on the alert about his health, dosing himself with thermogene and consulting doctors at various points along the route. He was still having acute abdominal pains in May 1929, and his hearing, which had been failing all through the nineteen-twenties, was by now only one-third of normal and people had to shout to make him hear (letter to Watson Kirkconnell, May 15, 1929).

The deafness continued to bother him throughout the rest of his life, and to that trouble was soon added failing eyesight, a chronic cough and sore throat, and arthritic pains. By October 24, 1938, he is ready to tell Richard Crouch that he feels 'that the time remaining to me is very short indeed; and so I work feverishly.' After delivering three lectures in one afternoon at University College, Toronto, in January 1939, he broke down and was in bed for several days (letter to Crouch, January 30, 1939), and on April 5, 1940, he writes to Lorne Pierce, in a memorable phrase, that he was 'feeling menaced with a cessation of things,' mentioning as evidence his chronic arthritis and a 'suspicion of cancer of the throat.' There are frequent references to colds and sore throats in the letters of his declining years, and to a growing sense that he is soon to 'lie down for the long rest' (to Barker Fairley, December 12, 1943). On April 14, 1944, he suffered a stroke, and for the remaining four years of his life he was a continual invalid.

The remarkable thing is, of course, that in spite of this physical weakness and suffering Grove continued to work at his books, and to be intellectually alert, almost to the last. Within two months of the 1944 stroke he writes to Barker Fairley (June 11, 1944) that in spite of being paralyzed on his right side he is continuing to write (type) with one finger of his left hand and that his mind is as active as ever, and shortly afterwards he tells Lorne Pierce that he is 'meanwhile planning no end of literary work' (June 26, 1944). During the four years that remained to him he solicited subscriptions for the limited edition of *The Master of the Mill* and saw that novel through the press, continued to appraise manuscripts for Macmillan, made final revisions to *Consider Her Ways*, reread all of his unpublished works, read parts of my monograph on him, read Carleton Stanley's *Roots of the Tree*, his *Matthew Arnold*, and the manuscript of his unpublished book on Grove, put the final touches to his autobiography *In Search of Myself* and saw it through the press, read Duhamel's *Défense des lettres*, tutored his son Leonard in algebra, read George Meredith's *Beauchamp's Career*, conducted an animated discussion with Carleton Stanley about the dates and whereabouts of Dr Furtwaengler, read Franz Werfel's *Star of the Unborn*, Leslie Gordon Barnard's *So Near is Grandeur*, Matthew Arnold's *On Translating Homer*, and Daniel McCowan's *A Naturalist in Canada*, negotiated a contract for the school edition of *A Search for America*, and wrote (or dictated to Mrs Grove) eighty-seven letters that have been traced and probably another twenty or so that have not been traced. Grove, it is clear, did 'not go gentle into that good night.'

As a correspondent, Grove was at his most attractive in his letters to his wife and to such literary friends as Watson Kirkconnell, W.J. Alexander, Carleton Stanley, and Richard Crouch, and at his most unattractive in his letters to publishers. The tone in the latter group runs from arrogant bullying to self-pitying whining, but in his letters to his wife he is unfailingly gentle and solicitous. His relationship with her does not seem to have been one of passionate love – at least the letters are sparing of endearments and avowals – but he obviously respected her, cherished her, and felt a great dependence upon her. Apart from her, it is with Kirkconnell, Alexander, Stanley, and Crouch that Grove seems to have felt most at ease. He writes to them of books and writers knowledgeably, modestly, wittily, and pungently. Any lingering notion of Grove as an untutored peasant will quickly be dispelled by these sequences of letters, which prove beyond all doubt that Grove was a highly educated man, steeped in the traditions of classical and European literature. He can write knowledgeably of Sappho, Sophocles and Simonides, Homer and Horace, Dante, Milton and Shakespeare, Swift, Goethe, and the English Romantics, and of most of the leading nineteenth- and twentieth-century writers of Germany, France, Italy, England, and America. Although he was obviously more interested in the ideas of literary works than in their more purely aesthetic qualities, he shows himself to be an acute critic of both style and substance. His comments on other writers, in fact, are so perspicacious that one wonders why Grove was not more aware of the flaws in his own work.

Of special interest to Canadians among these literary letters will be those in which Grove comments shrewdly on the works of his Canadian contemporaries such as Martha Ostenso, W.O. Mitchell, Mazo de la Roche, Raymond Knister, and Hugh MacLennan. There is perhaps a certain amount of jealousy involved, for example, in his quite destructive analysis of Martha Ostenso's *Wild Geese*, but on the whole his comments are just and have been upheld by subsequent criticism.

Grove's interests and erudition, however, extend far beyond literature in the limited sense of that word. Informed allusions and discussions in the letters make clear that he had a more than superficial knowledge of mathematics, music (particularly that of Wagner), philosophy (Nietzsche, Croce, Pascal, Bergson, T.H. Huxley, Boethius, and Plato), ancient and modern history (Zimmern, J.A. Spender, C.P. Scott, Chambers, Spengler, and Thucydides), politics and economics (Proudhon, Dean Inge, Graham Wallas, Karl Marx, Alexis Carrel, Harold Laski, J.S. Haldane, Sir Thomas More, and Henry George), and natural history and science (Bates, Belt, Raymond Pearl, Samuel Butler, and Daniel McCowan). Although it might be objected that many of these are allusions merely to books he was currently reading, the fact is that when he does pause to discuss them he does so as one who has already pondered the ideas concerned and has reached at least tentative conclusions of his own. It seems to me that there is quite sufficient evidence in these letters to indicate that Grove was by far the most erudite Canadian novelist yet to appear.

Another source of intense scholarly interest in the letters will be the light they shed on the composition of Grove's own books. Even to summarize here the large amount of evidence they provide would be to take more space than would be proper, and would be to deprive other scholars of a task that I have no doubt they will tackle with enthusiasm. To choose but one example, it is clear that the book which was finally published as *Consider Her Ways* in 1947 had been many years in preparation. If we are to believe the first reference to this book in the correspondence, it was originally written about 1907 – for on January 11, 1927, Grove writes to Kirkconnell: 'I don't know whether you've ever heard of my "Ant-Book" which for 20 years or so I used to consider *the* book of mine.' We can at least be sure that he was working on it in 1933, for on March 20, 1934, Grove writes to Henry Button of Dent as follows: 'You know that I slaved on that "Antbook" at least partly, last year, because you told me not to worry about that $251.04. … ,' and it is apparent from the letter to Button of March 22, 1934, that Dent had offered the book to Doran in the USA, who had rejected it. He was again at work on *Consider Her Ways* in 1939, for on August 7 of that year he writes to Lorne Pierce: 'The moment I have *The Master* off my mind and fingers, I shall start once more rewriting "Go to the Ant."' By September 15, 1939, however, he tells Pierce that 'In view of the outbreak of the war I have once more abandoned work on the "Antbook."' He must have resumed work on it shortly afterwards, however, for on March 25, 1940, he informs Pierce that he is sending him the manuscript in four parts entitled 'Go to the Ant,' and gives the following information about the history of its composition: 'This is the Ant-book so often mentioned on which I have been at work since the fall or early winter of 1919. It has had even more rewritings than *A Search for America* or the "Life"; in fact, I believe it is the most laboriously produced book of mine, the plan of which reaches back to 1892 or 1893.' That the original draft was indeed written in or about 1919 is confirmed by his letter to me of January 20, 1945, in which he says 'It was finished in 1920, and I found only one word which I wished other,' and by his letter to me of January 30, 1945, in which he says 'The "Ant-book," however, was, after 20 years of study, written in 1920.' He was still tinkering with the book, however, as late as December 1945. By that time Macmillan had agreed to publish the novel, and Grove writes to Ellen Elliott: 'I'll send the "Ants" in two or 3 days. I had cancelled the preface; and I want to add, instead, an appendix. ... ' He writes to her again on December 31, 1945, saying: 'I want to cancel the appendix of the ant-book and replace the first 23 pages with a few changes, for which I need another few days.' He was, thus, quite accurate in at least the latter part of this sentence written to Carleton Stanley on February 8, 1946: '"Ants" was finished during the winter 1920–21 but has, as is my custom, repeatedly been nibbled at since.'

To come now to the more technical points involved in the editing of these letters, one source of difficulty has been Grove's casualness about the spelling of proper names and the correct identification of other people. His letters to his wife during the three lecture tours posed some of the more difficult and frustrating problems. He was, by this time, quite hard of hearing, and in the confusion of travel and receptions such errors occur rather frequently. Many of the people he mentions he met for the first time and very briefly, with no thought of ever seeing them again. Yet a casual inaccuracy in stating the position a man held or the misspelling of his name has often sent me on elaborate, but false, trails. In a letter from Ottawa, of March 10, 1928, for example, Grove describes his meeting with 'Geo. Gardiner, head of the Royal Bank system.' Enquiries to the Royal Bank of Canada revealed that they did not have, in 1928, a Gardiner on their staff, not even in a subordinate position. However, a Frank George Gardiner of the firm Gardiner and Mercer, Vancouver architects, built several branches of the Royal Bank. The present owner of the architectural firm, now renamed Mercer and Mercer, wrote me that although the Gardiner of the firm was usually known as Frank G. Gardiner, 'his middle name could have been used and emphasized if a distinction was thought to be necessary as between he and his brother, Mr W.F. (William Frederick) Gardiner, who was also an architect, and a keen competitor.' [Jack Mercer to DP, March 12, 1971] To complicate matters further, there was a George C. Gardner (without the middle 'i') who was, in 1928, a manager of the Bank of Toronto in Ottawa. In either case, both the name and the designation are inaccurate, and we cannot be sure which of the two, if either, is referred to.

A few names, indeed, have defied all attempts at identification. 'The German cowboy Lipke,' referred to in the letter of September 18, 1928, could not be traced, although the Saskatchewan Provincial Archives, the Govenlock Post Office, and even the RCMP joined me in the hunt. In a few instances, however, a slight alteration in spelling a name has led me to the right person. For example, in a letter from Nanaimo, BC, Grove refers to a Dr Ri*dd*ington. I am reasonably certain that the reference here is to John Ri*d*ington, who was then a lecturer in English and librarian at the University of British Columbia. These are, of course, familiar, indeed routine, problems in annotating letters, made more difficult by the fact that many of the people mentioned in Grove's letters were his casual acquaintances, people he met by chance and sometimes for less than an hour during three very hectic lecture tours.

In preparing the letters for publication, I have been guided by the two overriding considerations of preserving the accuracy of the text and promoting its readability, but have always given primary emphasis to the former. Many of the editorial decisions evolved as the work progressed, as new letters were added creating new situations. Thus many decisions had to be revised, some scrapped, and in their place new ones introduced. Inevitably, it meant starting all over again. But, for the sake of readability, I have tried to present the letters in a uniform format without, however, seriously interfering with the text.

Most of the letters are either in Grove's holograph or in typescript; only a few are written by a scribe, usually Mrs Grove. Grove wrote with a flourish so that his *time* may look like *Prime*, and often his small *h* and small *t* are interchangeable. Among his other peculiarities, his *e*'s and *o*'s, *m*'s and *w*'s, *n*'s and *r*'s are often confused with each other. His small *g* sometimes looks like a capital *S*. Some of the letters are in pencil, some were written in bed or moving trains, and these are somewhat more difficult to decipher. Occasionally, I have had to guess at a word or two, and one word in particular – in a letter of February 6, 1928 – has proved indecipherable. Mrs Grove's handwriting, fortunately, is clear, legible, and presents no difficulty.

I have chosen the chronological arrangement over grouping letters according to their recipients because the primary interest is Grove himself, his life, personality, and works rather than his relationship with other persons. Besides, students of Grove's works will find the chronological system best suited to their needs, for it facilitates the placing of his work in his lifespan, and permits appreciation of the development in his point of view and craftmanship.

Almost all the letters are either on Grove's own stationery or that of the hotels he stayed in. The latter contain, in addition to the name and address of the hotel concerned, the name of the proprietors and, frequently, some advertising slogan. I have, for the sake of consistency and readability, followed a uniform format: the name of the addressee at the top left-hand corner; slightly below it but at the top right-hand corner, the name of the place, the province in standard abbreviation, and then the date. If the letter is on hotel stationery, the name of the hotel is provided above the name of the place, but the proprietor's name and advertising slogans have been dropped. I have, again for the sake of consistency, followed a uniform practice in transcribing dates on letters: month fully spelled out, date, and year – in that order. Grove, as one might expect, followed different systems at different times, such as the use of Roman numerals to indicate the month, abbreviation of the year to its last two digits, and so on. A few letters are without dates, and in such cases I have supplied the date from the postmark where this evidence exists, and conjectured from the context where no such evidence is available. All such interpolations have been indicated in the notes. Two or more letters of the same date have been arranged in the sequence in which they appear to have been written, and to facilitate reference their order is indicated in Roman numerals after the date.

I have put all marginal writings at the end of the letters, following Grove's signature. *Lacunae*, consisting exclusively of Mrs Grove's excisions, have been indicated in the text, at the point where they occur, by inserting a remark to that effect in square brackets. This is done to facilitate reading, so that the reader does not have to refer to the notes too frequently. In some letters in typescript, following Grove's paralytic stroke in 1944, he often neglected to release the lever for capital letters, so that for no apparent reason a word or several words are typed in capital letters. These inadvertent errors as well as misspellings and occasional Americanisms – Grove's spelling is usually standard British – have been silently emended. Abbreviations, in most cases, have been fully spelled out, and additions here and elsewhere, as is the custom, have been indicated by the use of square brackets. In the original letters, titles of books were expressed in a variety of ways: in block letters, within inverted commas, underlined, or with no indication whatsoever. To avoid confusion, I have italicised all titles of books and put titles of short stories, poems, essays, and unpublished manuscripts within inverted commas.

Grove's peculiarities in punctuation have been retained, as well as his occasionally awkward syntax. For example, he often used the dash where a comma or colon is called for, and sometimes after a period to indicate lapse of time or for no apparent reason at all. He also put words he considered slang or colloquial within inverted commas, as he did in his short stories and novels, and these punctuation marks have been retained since they indicate something of his stiffness of character. All foreign words and phrases have been italicised in letters written in English, and translations have been provided for the two letters originally written in German. Where Grove used a line of periods in letters to indicate separation, I have standardized this line to six periods only.

In providing notes on Grove's correspondents, I have tried to give concise outlines of their careers; for most other persons mentioned, however, merely their dates are recorded and the briefest identification is made. Generally speaking, well known public figures have received shorter notices than people less well known. In annotating books, journals, and literary and topical allusions, my usual practice, in the case of books, has been to give the name of the author and the date of publication; in the case of journals, volume and year are given, and the context in the case of allusions. Where an allusion has resisted research, this fact has been acknowledged in the notes.

In making interpretative comments, I have tried to meet the needs of an average reader who has some acquaintance with Grove's life and works, but who possesses no specialized knowledge of the subject. The volume is primarily intended for the student of Grove, however, who will read it for biographical and bibliographical information, for Grove's views on his own works and on literature and society in general.

Having been involved in the study of Grove intermittently for over thirty years now, I find it difficult to be completely objective about him and his work. When I first read his novels, my overwhelming impression was of his complete and sometimes truculent honesty. Now it seems almost certain that about his early life he was deliberately dishonest. And yet that knowledge, or that suspicion, does not fundamentally alter my impression of the man. It is apparent from the 1913–14 letters to Warkentin that as early as that he had defined for himself the role he was to play for the remainder of his life, and he played the role with remarkable consistency from that point forward. In changing his name and disguising his early circumstances he was only doing, if in somewhat more extreme form, what many other immigrants to North America had done before and have done since. If he had been guilty of criminal behaviour in Europe, he more than compensated for it by the thirty-five or more years of exemplary living which ensued in Canada. He almost certainly left a wife behind him in Europe; one of the letters to Warkentin suggests that there may have been another wife in the United States; but from 1914 onwards he was a completely faithful and devoted husband to Catherine Grove.

But Grove, even the Canadian Grove, was certainly no saint. He could be arrogant and opinionated, snobbish and rude, egotistical and self-seeking. There are times when he takes on the characteristics of a bully, and others when he closely resembles a spoiled child. When things were going well for him, as when he was being lionized on the trans-Canada lecture tours, he was usually at his worst – condescending to his hosts, contemptuous of his audiences, rude to those who served him. It was in adversity that his overriding virtues were called forth – his resilience, his indomitable will-power, his determination to survive and to create art out of his own frustrations.

Of Grove the writer it is still much too early to make a definitive assessment – only time will determine whether he or someone else or no one will be remembered as the great Canadian novelist of this century. Grove's writing is certainly flawed – flawed by fairly frequent infelicities of style, by didactic intrusions, by faulty structure, and by uncertain taste. On the other hand his work is powerful, massive in its strength and cumulative effect. He may be depreciated, but he cannot be ignored. My own conviction is that his novels, essays, and short stories will continue to be read for many decades, and that more and more readers will become aware of the complexity and profundity which they contain. I hope that the publication of these letters will make the reading of Grove's creative prose more informed and more enjoyable.

1 For some evidence that Grove may at least have been familiar with a similar castle in this area of Sweden, see my article 'In Search of Grove in Sweden,' *Journal of Canadian Fiction* I (Winter 1972) 69–73.

2 See D.O. Spettigue, *FPG: The European Years* (Oberon Press 1973).

3 He may have obtained the name Rutherford, and the idea of the alleged Scottish connection, from the fact that Lord Andrew Rutherfurd Clark (1828–99), the eminent Scottish jurist, was the grandfather of Greve's friend in Bonn, Herman F.C. Kilian. It should also be noted that when Grove thought of publishing *Over Prairie Trails* under a pseudonym, the name he suggested to McClelland & Stewart was Andrew Rutherfurd.

4 He almost made a slip in one letter, that to Watson Kirkconnell on November 30, 1927. It appears from one holograph that he originally wrote: 'That's all I've done in a life of 50 yrs.' If he was born in 1879, he would then have been almost 49 years old. However, a '6' is imposed over the '5' in the holograph: presumably Grove caught himself just in time.

5 Particularly regrettable is the loss of the manuscript, 'Felix Powell's Career,' which was destroyed by Mrs Grove. 'Powell' is phonetically very close to the German 'Paul,' and presumably the novel (which, according to Lorne Pierce, was 'a champion portrait of a

cad') dealt with the adventures of Felix Paul Greve. The other unpublished novels are 'Heart's Desire,' or, 'Two Lives' (alternative titles: 'Mortgages,' 'Is It Business?'), 'Jane Atkinson,' 'The Lean Kine,' 'Murder in the Quarry,' 'The Canyon' (alternative title: 'The Poet's Dream'), and 'The Weatherhead Fortunes.'

6 In his weekly column, 'The Fly Leaf,' in the Toronto *Globe and Mail* (February 17, 1945, p 8), Deacon quotes from a letter he received from Grove on *The Master of the Mill*. Since the letter is presumably no longer extant, the extract as printed in the *Globe and Mail* is reproduced here: 'I was trying to make clear two strains in the old man's revisualizations. In one he thinks and remembers; in the other, he relives the past. In the latter he is the young man; and he is absolutely accurate, though he slips out of this rebirth of himself every now and then.'

Chronology

A FELIX PAUL GREVE IN EUROPE

February 14, 1879 Birth of Felix Paul Berthold Friedrich Greve
1881 The Greve family settled in Hamburg
Easter 1886 Enrolled in Realschule St Pauli in Hamburg
Easter 1895 Graduated from Realschule St Pauli and enrolled in the Realgymnasium der Johanneum in Hamburg
February 2, 1898 Passed 'Entlassungsprufung' (school final examination)
Fall 1898 Enrolled in the University of Bonn
December 1900 Withdrew from the University
1901–2 In Munich: travelled extensively – Rome, Paris, Berlin, and Palermo
1902 Published *Wanderungen* (verse), *Helena und Damon* (verse drama), and *Lehren und Sprüche von Oskar Wilde* (compilation)
1903 Published *Oscar Wilde* (essay) and *Randarabesken zu Oscar Wilde* (essay)
May 29, 1903 Sentenced to one year's imprisonment in Bonn
Summer 1904 Visited André Gide in Paris; Married (?) Frau Else Hildegard (née Ploetz) Endell
1905 In Wollerau, Switzerland; published *Fanny Essler* (novel)
1906 Settled in Berlin; published *Maurermeister Ihles Haus* (novel)
1907 Published (?) *Der Heimliche Adel* (comedy)
July 1, 1908 Travelled (?) in Scandinavia
September 1909 Disappeared; allegedly committed suicide

B FREDERICK PHILIP GROVE IN CANADA

1912–29: In Manitoba

December 1912 Arrived in Winnipeg, Manitoba
January to June 1913 Taught in Haskett

Summer 1913 Attended Normal School in Morden
September 1913 Became Principal of the Intermediate School in Winkler
August 2, 1914 Married Catherine Wiens
July 1915 Began teaching in the High School in Virden
August 5, 1915 Daughter, Phyllis May, born
September 1915 Enrolled in the University of Manitoba as an extramural student
August 1916 Became Principal of the High School in Gladstone
July to August 1917 Taught in Leifur
December 1917 Resigned from the High School in Gladstone
March 1918 Began teaching in Ferguson School while staying with family in Falmouth
August 1919 Became Principal of the Consolidated School in Eden
November 1919 Resigned from the Consolidated School in Eden
January 1920 In Ashfield; prolonged illness
August 1921 Rejoined the Consolidated School in Eden as Principal
December 1921 Became naturalized Canadian citizen
May 18, 1922 Received the degree of Bachelor of Arts from the University of Manitoba, majoring in French and German
Summer 1922 Resigned from the Consolidated School in Eden and became Principal of Rapid City High School
October 1922 Published *Over Prairie Trails*
November 1923 Published *The Turn of the Year*
December 1923 Resigned from the High School but continued to live in Rapid City
January 1924 Rejoined the High School in Rapid City until June 1924
October 1925 Published *Settlers of the Marsh*
July 20, 1927 Daughter, Phyllis May, died
October 1927 Published *A Search for America*
February 27, 1928 First day of the first Canadian Club lecture tour in Ontario (until April 1928)
September 9, 1928 First day of the second Canadian Club lecture tour in western Canada (until November 1928)
October 1928 Published *Our Daily Bread*
January 1929 Associate Editor, *The Canadian Nation* (until June 1929)
January 22, 1929 First day of the third Canadian Club tour in eastern Canada (until March 1929)
March 1929 Published *It Needs to be Said*

1929–48: In Ontario

September to December 1929 Left Rapid City and moved to the east, staying in Canton, Ont. (October) and Bobcaygeon, Ont. (November)
December 1929 Joined Graphic Publishers Limited in Ottawa
October 14, 1930 Son, Arthur Leonard, born
October 1930 Published *The Yoke of Life*
October 1931 Left Graphic Publishers Limited and settled near Simcoe, Ont.

January 1933 Published *Fruits of the Earth*
June 1934 Awarded the Lorne Pierce Medal of the Royal Society of Canada
January 1939 Published *Two Generations* (limited edition; trade edition in July)
April 7, 1940 Published 'The Adventures of Leonard Broadus' serially in *The Canadian Boy* (April 7 to June 23, 1940)
April 1941 Elected a Fellow of the Royal Society of Canada
August 1943 Defeated as a Co-operative Commonwealth Federation candidate for the Haldimand-Norfolk seat in the Ontario provincial election
April 14, 1944 Suffered a stroke and was paralysed on the right side
December 1944 Published *The Master of the Mill*
July 1945 Publication of Desmond Pacey's *Frederick Philip Grove*
May 1946 Awarded the D. Litt. by the University of Manitoba
June 1946 Made an Honorary Member of the Canadian Authors' Association
Fall 1946 Awarded the LLD by Mount Allison University
October 1946 Published *In Search of Myself*
January 1947 Published *Consider Her Ways*
July 1947 Received the Governor-General's Award (non-fiction) for *In Search of Myself*
August 19, 1948 Died in Simcoe after prolonged illness

A

Into the Wilderness: The Manitoba Years 1913-28

'Only the robust thick skinned people ever could endure active life: the rest of them went to the wall or into the wilderness. I am of the latter.'

TO ISAAK J. WARKENTIN,
FEBRUARY 10, 1914

TO ISAAK J. WARKENTIN

Winkler, Man.
September 7, 1913

Lieber Herr Warkentin,

Ich bin so froh, jemanden in D[eu]tschl[an]d zu haben der mir vielleicht behilflich sein kann, dass ich Ihnen möglicherweise lästig fallen werde. Vielleicht wird es Ihnen zur Genugtuung gereichen dass Sie ja schliesslich Ihrer Heimat helfen.

Ich habe 3 weitere Büchertitel über die ich gern Auskunft hatte:

Fitzga, *Die Leitenden Grundsätze für den Elementarunterricht in Rechnen und Geometrie* (Wien 1897)
Knilling, *Die Naturgemässe Methode des Rechenunterrichts* (München 1899)
Rein Pickel, *Volksschulunterricht* (Leipzig 1889)
Petersen, *Methoden und Theorien für die Lösung geometrischer Konstruktionsprobleme* (Kopenhagen 1879)

Wenn sie noch nicht bankrott ('broke') sind, kaufen Sie mir doch, bitte, den *Rein Pickel*; ich werde Ihnen, sowie ich Nachricht über den Preis erhalte, den Betrag schicken.

Vielen Dank im voraus
Ihr
F. Grove

N.B. Wir erregen Aufsehen hier durch die Neuerungen, die ich in Winkler eingeführt habe. Sie werden wohl davon hören. A.W. ist starr und sieht trauernden Auges zu.

TO ISAAK J. WARKENTIN[1] *translation*

Winkler, Man.
September 7, 1913[2]

Dear Mr. Warkentin,

I am so happy to have someone in Germany who may be able to help me, that I may possibly become a nuisance to you. Perhaps it would be of some satisfaction to you that you are, after all, helping your country.

I have got 3 more books, about which I would like to get some information:

Fitzga, *Die leitenden Grundsätze für den Elementarunterricht in Rechnen und Geometrie* (Wien 1897)[3]

Knilling, *Die Naturgemässe Methode des Rechenunterrichts* (Munchen 1899)[4]
Rein Pickel, *Volksschulunterricht* (Leipzig 1889)[5]
Petersen, *Methoden und Theorien für die Lösung geometrischer Konstruktionsprobleme* (Kopenhagen 1879)[6]

If you are not yet bankrupt ('broke'), please buy Rein Pickel for me; I'll send you the money as soon as I know the amount.

Many thanks in advance,
yours
F. Grove.

N.B. We are causing a sensation here with the innovations I introduced in Winkler. You surely will hear about it. A.W.[7] is shocked and looks at it sadly.

1 Isaak J. Warkentin was born in the Mennonite farm village of Hoffnungsfeld, Manitoba, on November 27, 1885. His parents came to Manitoba from South Russia in the great Mennonite migration of the 1870s.

After teaching in rural schools in Manitoba for three years, he attended Wesley College (now the University of Winnipeg), graduating (BA) in 1912. In 1912–13 he taught in Winkler, holding the position of Principal of the Intermediate School, and then went to Germany, in 1913, to study at Leipzig University. He was interned in the Ruhleben Prison Camp shortly after the outbreak of World War I (for an account of this camp see J.D. Ketchum, *Ruhleben: A Prison Camp Society*, 1965). On his return to Canada in 1918, he attended Normal School in Winnipeg, and then resumed his teaching career once more, serving various Mennonite communities in rural Manitoba. He retired as Principal of the Steinbach School System in 1951. He died on October 6, 1971.

Grove came to Winkler in 1913 to succeed Warkentin as Principal of the Intermediate School, and they only met briefly in the spring and summer of that year before the latter left for Europe. This was their only contact, apart from the correspondence.

For Grove's account of his years in Winkler (1913–15), see *In Search of Myself* (Toronto: Macmillan 1946) 262ff. All subsequent references to the book are to this edition.

2 The month is specified in Roman numeral (IV); however, in a note Warkentin says, 'The IV is probably meant for a IX?' Warkentin was still in Winkler in April 1913.

3–6 The titles, in translation, read, respectively, as follows: The Fundamental Principles of Teaching Elementary Arithmetic and Geometry; Natural Methods of Teaching Arithmetic; Teaching in Elementary School; and Methods and Theories of Solving Problems of Geometrical Construction.

7 Andrew Weidenhammer (afterwards Willows) (1863–1925), then Inspector of Schools in charge of the Mennonite schools in Manitoba with headquarters in Morden. Although *Canadian Men and Women* (1912) gives Heidelburg, Ontario, and a 1925 obituary article Elmira, Ontario, as his birthplace, he may have been born and educated in Germany. He taught school in Ontario from 1883 to 1903, and then seems to have entered public life as a platform speaker, municipal councillor, and as an official of the Waterloo County

Teachers' Association. Also in Waterloo, he edited and managed the German newspaper *Canadischer Bauernfreund*.

Sometime between 1909 and 1912, he joined the Manitoba Department of Education as an Inspector of Schools, for in 1912 he was in Morden in that capacity. Later he changed his name to Willows, took an Arts degree from the University of Manitoba and, in 1924, obtained his MA in history from the same university. He died suddenly from cerebral hemorrhage while on his way home from a teachers' convention.

TO ISAAK J. WARKENTIN

Winkler, Man.
October 20, 1913

Dear Mr. Warkentin,

Thanks for your letter. It sounds a little homesick? Now you, too, want money! You'll have to wait till next Saturday. Did I want the 8 vol[ume]s of Rein Pickel? You bet I did. So slide them along, please, as soon as I send the money.

As far as our innovations go there is not much to report. The sewing works fine. Miss Wiens[1] is a very good teacher, at that and in her room, too. The boys – I had to take them myself. I have given both P.H.[2] and Enns[3] a chance at it. Enns simply cannot manage them. And P.H. fooled away his time: never got started. Enns is glad that *I* start it now. P.H. is mad. He thinks I am the most interfering fellow he has ever met with.

You see, one of the worst troubles here is undue and rash promoting. When a kid does a little good work for once – swish, up he or she goes into the next grade. Nobody really masters the course. I have ruthlessly retransferred about 50 pupils since I started. P.H. has not the faintest idea of teaching. *Er salbadert*, as we used to say in Germany – *er seift*.[4] If I stay here next year, 14 years will be the age limit for entrance. Why, we have kids of 13 in the 3rd class! Getting permanently hurt by cramming. For what else is it? So far I have the trustees on my side. I had to fight a little. But it seems they trust me and believe that I know what I am doing. – Bench work will be started this week with a class of 6. The rest of the boys do raffia and reed work – basketry, in short.

I think I told you that 2nd class work has started. My teaching day is 9 h[ou]rs long – besides 3 times a week 2 h[ou]rs in the evening (Full matriculation). We need 2 more students for 2nd class, in order to get high school standing. I wrote a letter to your sister – but it seems she does not think it worth her while to answer. Quite apart from the personal affront it is a little disheartening to see *Winkler* students go to Gretna instead of helping their home cause. Unless we get the high school grant we shall not be able to put in the laboratory. Also your brother Peter[5] does not turn up! Nor your brother Cornelius![6]

As for the exhibition – the gov[ernmen]t – as always –

was prompt to promise and is slow to act. I have a splendid collection of books, though. All the big American publishers came to the front with exhibits of educational literature. Personally I make an exhibit of 'Books that every teacher ought to have' – and 'a model outfit for teaching plant biology.' – For the library I have bought a flora that costs $15. (Britton-Brown – you may know it). The Museum grows slowly but steadily. – Moths and butterflies that do not fly any longer are being hatched in a home-made pupa incubator. The aquarium is transformed into a terrarium – full of caterpillars, beetles, frogs etc.

Now for you: what are you hearing, whom? Let me know some details, please. If I cannot have those things myself, give me a *farbiges Abbild*[7] (*Im farbigen Abbild haben wir das Leben, sagt Goethe.*)[8] You will probably say 'there speaks old age!' – yes, or experience! I wish I could get the *Insel-Verlag Taschen-Ausgabe von Goethe's Werken*[9] in soft leather! I wish I could get a decent critical edition of Homer's *Odyssey*. The older a man gets the more he wants to be left alone with the 2 or 3 companions that he has found worth while – Goethe's *Westöstlicher Divan, The Odyssey* and Shakespeare's 2 *Richards, Lear, Timon* and *Midsummer Night's Dream*! Give me those and a life sentence and I will rest content. I tell you I get mighty tired fighting stupidity – *Mit der Dummheit kampfen Gotter selbst vergebens*.[10] – Well, well – catch me complaining!

Our friend A.W.[11] is my stoutest ally – I knew it. You know he is not a bad fellow. I doubt whether his influence is *all* to the bad. Seeing those young students of his now I sometimes wonder whether a really good normal class – theoretical – would not dislocate their joints, disintegrate their self-sufficiency to such an extent that there would be nothing left except shreds and rags. Of course, the right thing to do would be to drop the theory completely and give nothing but the practical part. But A.W. sees that himself, and he really likes me. You know I have avoided knocking him – and *he appreciates that*. Fletcher[12] told me that I could not have a better advocate than him, and that his recommendation had been such that I could command any position that I might wish to get next year. I told him if Winkler went along I might wish to stay right here so as to carry through what I had started.

But enough for today.
Cordially
Fred Grove

I have been sick – 4 days in bed; now I am crawling about with very little 'vim.'

1 Catherine Wiens who, in 1914, became Mrs Grove. See note 1 to letter of June 26, 1914. She was born on February 11, 1892, and died on January 9, 1972.

2 Peter H. Neufeld (1874–1941), who taught in Winkler from 1904 to 1917. Mr Frank Brown, who has provided me with information about Grove's colleagues in Winkler, suggests that a possible explanation for the evident lack of cordiality between the two men could be found in the fact that 'Mr Neufeld was a Mennonite Brethren Church preacher and Mr Grove had been touched by Indian mysticism or philosophy.' But the actual reason

had probably less to do with their differing beliefs than with their clashing personalities. Neufeld must have resented Grove as an outsider who was thrust upon him. And Grove's inability to take kindly to any criticism, even if well meant, may have aggravated the situation.

3 John J. Enns, who taught in Winkler from 1913 to 1919; see also letter of June 29, 1914, note 1.

4 He babbles ... he blathers.

5 Peter Warkentin, who became a teacher, is now a resident of Nanaimo, BC.

6 Cornelius Warkentin, who became a graduate engineer, now lives in retirement in Sarnia, Ontario.

7 A coloured picture

8 In a coloured picture there is life, says Goethe

9 The Insel-Verlag (a Leipzig publishing company) 'pocket edition' of Goethe's works

10 Even the gods fight in vain against stupidity.

11 Andrew Wiedenhammer; see letter of September 7, 1913, note 7.

12 Robert Fletcher (1873–1963), then Deputy Minister of Education in Manitoba; for an account of Grove's first meeting with him, see *In Search of Myself* 278f. He is remembered for his services in the cause of education in Manitoba, and for his kindness to many teachers. The University of Manitoba conferred an honorary doctorate on him in 1922.

TO ISAAK J. WARKENTIN

Winkler, Man.
November 1, 1913

Dear Mr. Warkentin,

Enclosed please find 17 M[arks] which will cover what you paid out so far. I hope to send you the balance for the rest of the vol[ume]s on Dec[ember] 1st so I will then have the complete work (Rein Pickel, I mean). I have very little time at present. We have now 5 2nd class students, 1 full matric. I have bought chem[istry] & phy[sic]s outfit to the tune of $300 out of my pocket and we have not yet what we need. Manual outfit also was insufficient, and I had to throw in another $35 (Total cost now $136.65). That sounds pretty, does it not? Well, somebody has got to start things, or they will never get started. I will write more fully soon.

Very cordially yours
F.G.

und dennoch hab ich harter man die Liebe.[1]

1 ...and yet I, a hard man, have love...The line is not in Grove's handwriting. In a note Warkentin says, 'The word *Mann* is misspelt. the m should be capitalized and Mann (meaning man) is spelled with 2 n's ... It is not in my handwriting either. How did it slip in? The line is from a German folk song ["*Ich schiess den Hirsch*"].'

1 Isaak J. Warkentin. *Courtesy John Warkentin*

TO ISAAK J. WARKENTIN

Winkler, Man.
December 6, 1913

Dear Mr. Warkentin,

Your letter amused me immensely – chiefly because I had expected something of the kind. You American people are funny: preferring the destructive downpour to the slow, penetrating, fruitful drizzle. And when things are not done in a hurry you think they are not being done at all. Those boys who seem old to you have it in them to go far. You live faster, but do you make faster progress? Has not good, staid, old Germany gone to the front, slowly, but surely? Who is beating out the English on the South American market? Whose trade in Canada grows double as fast as that of old Engl[an]d? I was much interested in the report about your curriculum. Only regret: I do not see any exact sciences nor the classical languages represented. I am teaching J.R. Wolkof[1] full matric now. With our friend P.H.[2] it is fight, I am afraid. It looks as if the issue will soon be: he or I. Well, I am ready. I believe, when the question comes up as it is bound to do within a month or so, I can at least say: look what I have done! The fight has sometimes exasperated me, sometimes galled me, but my dander is up, and as long as I can get living wages here I am going to stick it out and to refuse better offers of which I have four since Fletcher[3] gave out his interview about our school – of which you probably have heard. The Dep[artmen]t anyway is sitting up. But I am bleeding. The things said about me here are sometimes funny, sometimes they hurt because there is a kernel of truth in them. I cannot afford to pay any attention to that. *I have got* to win out. I am remodelling the whole arrangement:

Room I	Grades	I & junior II
" II	"	Sen[ior] II, III, IV
" III	"	V, VI, VIII
" IV	"	IX, X, XI.

This was my last fight. P.H. opposed me again although I did it because *he* proved incapable of handling the 4 grades. – The open war broke out on this ground. Some people had come to the school to see if we could take outsiders. P.H. caught them and told them: impossible (enrollment 160). For several days I did not hear about it; but when I did I went straight up and asked him whether he was the principal? I made it plain to him that *I* was running this school, not he. That if I assigned pupils to him he had to take them, whether he liked it or not. I went after those people again – poor farmers whose only chance is with us. And I told the trustees that if they did not think it worth their while to discuss the school affairs with their principal instead of with one of the assistants, said principal would not think it worth his while to go on with his work beyond next pay day. Well, I conquered along the whole line. Old man Wiebe[4] stood by me at last. The assistant teachers are my assistants now, not hidden bosses. – I have put in physical & chemical equipment out of my pocket (cost close to $300) – a botanical outfit (cost close to $200) – manual training (cost $139.65), and we are going to have a flag or a banner that will cost about $68 in materials alone – and all that has not cost the district one red cent. – I believe I deserve a little credit, if it comes to that, instead of being run down as I am, don't you think so? Besides we have a collection of insects, mounted by yours truly, a large collection of weed-seeds – a nice number of dried plants – a series of microscopical slides (mounted by myself) – a pond vivarium – culture chamber for bacteria – 200 or more glass jars filled with all the farm seeds of Canada – specimens of chief manufactures in all stages of manufacturing – and a large collection of minerals. It is true that for some of these things I got the co-operation of the gov[ernmen]t, but who *got* it? Nobody ever even offered to help me write the hundreds of letters. My postage account foots up to $59 at present. – My expressage account shows an expenditure of $63. – If money counts, well, I think these figures tell. –

But enough, it goes against my grain to give vent to my indignation.

Will you do me *a big favour*? I would like to get 2 piano selections: the one: *Das* PREISLIED *aus den Meistersingern von Nürnberg*,[5] the other one: *Am stillen Herd, zur Winterzeit* ... (Stolzing's first song) *aus derselben Oper*.[6]

If you possibly can slide them along – or if the store can ship C.O.D. (I not knowing the price) – you would oblige me immensely. – – Did I tell you that I am going to get married soon?[7]

Cordially yours
F.G.

1 J.R. Wolkof, who became, in 1916, the Principal of Schools in Winkler, retiring in 1940.

2 Peter H. Neufeld

3 Robert Fletcher

4 Gerhard Wiebe, who was at this time a trustee on the Winkler School Board. Born in Russia, he came to Canada in 1888 to assume the leadership of the Mennonite Brethren Church in Burwalde, some four miles north-west of Winkler. After farming for a few years in Burwalde, he moved to Winkler, where he owned a lumber yard. He was active in civic duties, and was Mayor of Winkler in 1910.

5 The 'Preislied' from *The Mastersingers of Nürnberg* – an opera (1868) by Richard Wagner (1813–83)

6 From the same opera

7 Grove married Catherine Wiens on August 2, 1914. See also the following letter, note 9.

TO ISAAK J. WARKENTIN

Winkler, Man.
February 10, 1914

Dear Mr. Warkentin,

Thanks for your letter which I received yesterday. I am glad you wrote me a little more fully because I see now where the hitch is. Of course, in many things you are dead right. Also, of course, I hate Germany. I hate America, too, but probably a trifle less because I am here. Excuse me for saying what I am going to say, but you know, I am quite a trifle older in y[ea]rs and maybe still a little older in life. I was anxious for you to get your trouble's worth out of this undertaking. I did not at all want you to like Germany – but I did want you to like the experience you are going through. To every question there are so many sides, and very few people see more than a fraction of their own side. I have very little patience with narrow-mindedness. My father was a Swede, my mother a Scotchwoman, I was raised in Germany, I have lived in pretty nearly every country of Europe, in N[orth] A[merica] and Canada, I have travelled in Africa, through Asia, in Australia, I know India and China a little, the Islands south of Asia fairly well – so I believe – speaking merely geographically – I can claim a certain 'manysidedness.' Also as far as 'education' goes (the ' ' means that I think very little of what is commonly called education) – I speak English, French, German, Italian, and Arabian – and I have a fair knowledge of Latin, Greek, Sanskrit, Spanish and Swedish with their respective literatures; I believe I have imbued myself with the fundamental principles of modern Science, and I do not know of any corner of Mathematics, where, f[or] i[nstance], I meet difficulties in reading the latest and most advanced treatises. I have travelled a good deal, *mentally* too. And what have I got out of it? Nothing, except a certain broadmindedness – and an extreme fastidiousness in matters of art, literature, and women (excuse me again!). I have one longing: to leave the world, to retire to the little corner just west of Etaples, south of Boulogne, on the French coast that seems to swing in resonance with the vibrations of my inner tuning fork – to live there in absolute seclusion, write a poem now and then and finish a book that I have been working on between times for 20 y[ea]rs. – But there is one thing that I hate: patriotism, which for me is synonym[ous] with ignorance and 'cornerdom' (*Winkeltum* we called it in Bonn). I never can be a 'citizen' – which, after all is merely a translation of *behäbiger Bürger*.[1] You see, there are things in Germany: *Bier, Behäbigkeit, Gemütlichkeit*[2] (!!!!), that smell like a badly aerated room: but do they smell worse than baseball, than divorce scandals of married life, than the abominable religious and moral hypocrisy of America? Take the *sexuelle Frage*.[3] I believe that your figures are correct: they tackle[4] with my own experience. *But*! are you aware that things are just as bad in every densely populated district in the world? The nauseating percentages of sexually diseased are to be found in N[ew] Y[ork] City, Chicago, New England, Cape Town, Canton, *England* above all, just as well. Germany has (as France, too) at least the courage to take the bull by the horns. Now let me make an alarming statement: I do not object to sexual intercourse without marriage – but I object to just those consequences. I also object to premature development of sexual instincts. I have suffered immensely myself from that very cause. I think I was 15 y[ea]rs old when I was 'seduced' by a married woman, the young wife of one of my old professors.[5] If in spite of that I have managed to keep free of sexual infection I owe that to my mother's broadminded advice and to luck, I think (– that first experience resulted in a public scandal, as the lady in question went through a divorce suit with me – 16 y[ea]rs old – as the witness –). I also believe that, since German civilization is essentially a city civilization, these things partly account for the fact that Germany has no aristocracy of the mind or of achievement. *But*: what kind of an aristocracy has America? They *call* it an aristocracy of achievement. It *is* an aristocracy of grocerdom, of mental hollowness, of dollar wisdom. – In America all fortunes are self-made; in Germany all mental achievement is *Parvenutum*.[6] There is only one real aristocracy left in the world: that of lamadom in the Thibet. I do not believe that Germany as a power is declining. It is just the infantile diseases of the country that I loathe. I prefer downright decay. I prefer 'the golden hues that herald and beautify decay,' as somebody, I don't know who, expressed it. – As for the men of science in Germany – Nietzsche said: '*Sie sind wie die Mehlsäcke: klopft sie, und heraus fliegt der Staub der Gelehrsamkeit*.'[7] I love France.

But!: Germany is the one really instructive country where Americans ought to go: just as much in order to learn what to avoid: what they themselves are drifting into, as what to imitate.

Yes, I am afraid, I *am* an American, always was one, sorry to say so. *I* could no longer live in Germany.

Superiority! But do you know that this ridiculous feeling of superiority to the rest of the world is much more prevalent among Americans than Germans? I believe I have been through every representative part of America with the exception of the extreme Northwest of Canada, and everywhere I found the closed mind: 'We are leading the world in everything: we have nothing to learn.' As far as making the best of this poor job that we call life is concerned, I think that we ought to try what works out best – not hastily or rashly but observantly; in any case we must give things a trial. Now take Winkler – quite true, the people are slow to move; but so am I. Only I come with many things that have been tried out. I tell them you have a bunch of 'bad boys' here that *are not* bad. They are being treated wrong. Why is it that I can do *anything* with Willy Neufeld, with Jake Loewen?[8] Even make them work? But the people here condemn me – not because they know anything about my work – nobody has ever been in school! But because they see me introducing a few innovations – slowly, carefully – and because they are pent up in their own ideals – because they listen to the talk of a disgruntled man *who belongs to them* and whom I have shaken up from a 10 years' sleep. They do not see that we have 20 pupils more than ever before; they do not see that by working night and day I give the reserve a chance to raise the standard of their teachers. Counting everything I shall send more than 30 candidates into 3rd and 2nd class examinations. And I should not even mention it if people would only leave me alone. In a way I should like to stay here at least another year. I am open for a proposition: but it seems I am not even going to get the chance – judging from what a few adherents tell me. Of course, I do not care. I know I have done what a man could do – I have even waited till the holidays before I lay down to get rid of the fever I had contracted. Even now I still keep working for the High School Standing which is practically assured to Winkler for next year. – But that, too, is American, I mean the way I am treated here. –

Now just a word about Science and the slow German mind. Yes, Germans are slow – yes, as individuals Germans are thoroughly despicable. But even if they do work slowly – they keep at it. The instances you quote have made me impatient thousands of times. But on the other hand, are they not trifles? Let me say this: I am for education for education's sake. I also am for knowledge for knowledge's sake. In the whole of life I do not see any sense. If I want to be truthful I must say that in our individual effort I can see only a struggle to get over it in the best possible way. *I* stand apart, aloft, if you want to put it that way. It is a horrible thought to me that I am *acting*, 'doing,' at all. Whenever you touch life you make a mess of it. When you are young you don't notice it so much. My love for dogs, pups and all kinds of animals rests in the firm conviction that their life is the only sincere, the only untainted life. On the other extreme stands the contemplative life – the life of the spectator who wants to *know*, not to do. That is my only salvation. (As for my marriage, that has gone to smash: something I have been working for for the last five years. I don't blame the girl – I merely don't understand her. Difference of age was considerable: she was my pupil before she went to college. At Christmas I went down to Arkansas – into the hospital!! And when I came out, after a week of raving fever, I did not know my world any longer! I was so changed. Well, enough of that!)[9] So naturally I value even one tiny little bit of found knowledge immensely much more than all the deeds ever done. You say: 'If we had waited for German philosophy to decide ... where would we be?' But where *are* we!?! Is life one trifling little bit less raw, less cruel to-day than it was 10000 y[ea]rs ago? Only the *robust* thick skinned people ever could endure active life: the rest of them went to the wall or into the wilderness. I am of the latter. I do not see that we have come any nearer to the solution of essential problems. Even Science never explains: it describes; describes more and more minutely – and I enjoy the spectacle. Let the slow, careful German labo[u]rers of the mind work for me, and let the whole city of Leipzig go to smash, let traffic be stopped and the fire department lift trolley cars!!

By the way, you misunderstand the Germans there. Again the dense population accounts for it. Why should anybody dirty his gloves to drag a horse out of the way when there are people specially appointed to do that? It is none of *their* business!! Here, where men are scarce, everybody does everything. *I* should have bought a horse this fall if I could afford as in Germany to hire a man to keep it in tiptop condition and appearance, but I do not care to curry it myself or even to draw a strap tighter when that is needed. It would be different if I thought it my business to *teach* how to saddle a horse. I promised to run this school, and so I do it: do it to the best of my knowledge and ability. But do I like it? I believe if I really wanted to stay I could pull that off, too – but is it worth while? I don't think so, not for myself. Fletcher says: 'You *must* stay there and finish what you have begun.' But why 'must' I? I spent the greater part of my salary on this school – that puts me back one year. Instead of being through [in] 1918 I shall have to work on till 1919 before I can retire: but I believe there ought to be a school somewhere that *suits* me. Selkirk has been offered to me. One school in

Sask[atchewan], one in B[ritish] C[olumbia]. In each case they are willing to let me pick my assistants – so why should I fight for this position? And yet I'd stay if they wanted me to – because I like to be of help – but they don't.

Well, I believe I have wearied you enough!
Yours cordially
F.G.

B. – The *Meistersinger*[10] selections will be heartily welcomed. Thanks ever so much. Give me a chance to 'revenge' myself, will you?

This long letter, Grove's last to Warkentin, outlines, in brief, the argument of *A Search for America*. The correspondence was, no doubt, interrupted by the War and Grove's marriage in 1914, and was not resumed.

1 *Behäbiger Bürger* literally means 'comfort-loving man' – with the additional connotation of being middle-class, conservative, and narrow-minded.

2 Beer, comfort, high spirits. *Gemütlichkeit*, here translated as 'high spirits,' literally means the quality of the good-natured, sanguine, easy disposition.

3 The question of sex

4 An example of Grove's occasional difficulties with the idiom; he probably means 'tally' here.

5 The episode is described, in greater detail, in *In Search of Myself* 134f – the professor, named Dr Broegler in the book, has not been identified.

6 Self-made

7 They are like bags of flour: hit them and scholarly dust flies out.

8 William Neufeld and Jake K. Loewen are now both deceased. William's brother, George W. Neufeld, was also a student of Grove. He remembers an occasion when Grove hit him on the head with a bell to make him toe the line as others were lining up. Jake and William were good friends – 'always together' – and were not much interested in their studies.

9 This is probably a reference to a previous marriage, in the United States, about which nothing is known. In *In Search of Myself*, there is a hint that his coming to Canada had something to do with women – 'I have not for nothing opened the discussion of this section with a mention of women' (p 229). Five months later, in August, Grove married Catherine Wiens, a teacher in Winkler. His marital status then, according to the marriage licence, was that of a widower.

10 See the preceding letter, note 5.

TO CATHERINE WIENS[1]

The Empire Hotel
Winnipeg, Man.
June 26, 1914

My dear Miss Wiens,

I just had a rather prolonged talk with Mr. Fletcher,[2] and it is now practically a certainty that I shall be back at work in Winkler by the middle of August. I say 'practically' – advisedly, for I have fully made up my mind not to go back *unless you are coming back, too*. I shall be in Morden next week, reading papers. Will you let me know whether there is any doubt about that?

The Department[3] has behaved handsomely, in one way. Without waiting for the result of the examinations they have given me collegiate (so called Grade A) standing, which would accord me professional First anywhere in Canada. Also they have assured me that I shall receive a University Degree on submitting my German University credentials. I mention this in order to show that I am under certain obligations with regard to this province. At the same time it was made plain to me that I was expected to remain at Winkler for another year. So, if I jump Winkler the Dep[artmen]t will regard that as a breach of faith though I have not promised anything definite. If I leave I shall have to leave the province. As a matter of fact, I should hardly know where to go. But nevertheless, unless you come back, too, Winkler will have to get along without me. I shall explain later on – when I see you.

I should like to run up into your part of the country and call on you, maybe. But being under rather heavy expense at present, I shall have to forego even that. It has been a little my fate, of late, to have to forego things, and things look rather grey to me.

Please, drop me a line to reassure me about that particular point. Address Morden, Arlington Hotel. I hope you are enjoying yourself better than I am.

Cordially yours
F.P.G.

I have been playing tennis, rowing & swimming ever since. I am just beginning to limber up.

1 See letter of October 20, 1913, note 1.
The four letters in this sequence form a record of the courtship which is slightly at variance with Grove's own account of events leading to the marriage on August 2, 1914. The idea of the visit to Rush Lake, where Miss Wiens' family lived on a farm, seems from these letters to have been Grove's, although in *In Search of Myself* (p 277f) he implies that the invitation came from her.
2 Robert Fletcher, the Deputy Minister of Education
3 ie, the Department of Education. The 'interim certificate' was issued following the interview with Fletcher. Grove began teaching in Haskett in January 1913, and during the summer attended the Normal School in Morden. In September 1913, he was appointed principal of the Intermediate School in Winkler. Inquiries to the Manitoba Department of Education re Grove's in-service training have elicited little information.

2 View of Eden, Manitoba, with Consolidated School on the horizon. *Photo by Desmond Pacey*

TO CATHERINE WIENS

Winkler, Man.
June 29, 1914

My dear Miss Wiens,

In stopping over at W[inkler] on my way from Winnipeg to Morden I find your note. I am glad you are enjoying yourself. Do you know what I got into here? John J. Enns's[1] marriage festivities! He is the limit! I cannot help looking on with some melancholy. Instead of settling down to work and making something out of himself he settles into the rut of mediocre home-life! I must say I do like the Warkentins[2] better, even though they all have got the 'swelled head': at least they have got ambition. – He told me he 'loved the girl.' I told him that's just why he ought not to marry her at this stage. He throws away the only chance of ever getting above the $75 mark. Well, *Des Menschen Wille ist sein Himmelreich*.[3] I hear he also bought the car from his father and they are going to live in it. Alright in summer, but I cannot guarantee the truth of this rumo[u]r.

With best regards
Yours
F.P.G.

1 See letter of October 20, 1913, note 3. Enns was, contrary to Grove's gloomy predictions, a fairly successful man by local standards. In 1922 he became a trustee and chairman of the school district, and functioned in the twin capacities until 1924, and again in 1927. He was, in 1928, elected Mayor of Winkler, an office he held till 1935. Later he operated a grain elevator, and became manager of Winkler Milling Co. He also made an unsuccessful bid for a seat in the Manitoba provincial legislature.

2 The family of Isaak J. Warkentin; see letter of September 7, 1913, note 1. Warkentin's two brothers, Peter and Cornelius, were Grove's students; see letter of October 20, 1913, notes 5 and 6.

3 The wish of man is heaven for him.

TO CATHERINE WIENS

The Arlington Hotel,
Morden, Man.
July 9, 1914

My dear Miss Wiens,

Thanks for your kind letter. I hope you mean what you say; for I nearly think I will take you at your word. In the first place I should like to see you; and in the second place it seems that in leaving the province for a while there is the only chance of my getting any vacation at all. We have just (1/2 hour ago) finished the Entrance papers, and I have been asked to teach a matriculation summer class. If I stay here or go back to Winkler that will be my fate, and I believe that I ought not to work all the time. If I go somewhere else I shall be working for sheer loneliness. I am not 'a mixer.' I shall go east for a week or so and then return to W[inni]peg. Now if I should be unwelcome for any reason, I sincerely hope you will let me know. I suppose word would reach me if you would drop me 2 cards at the same time: one to W[inni]peg, Empire Hotel; one to Winkler. Either one or the other will reach me.

I am overworked and tired. Rest alone cannot help me. If I could have company it would do the trick, I believe. So, unless you beckon off I am apt to turn up in Rush Lake[1] some time next week. If there is a hotel in town it might be just as well to let me stay there, since I do not want to be any trouble. I should consider it just as much as a kindness on your part to have asked me. What I want is merely a little company.

I am glad to hear that you are enjoying yourself, and I feel quite reassured since you told me that you are sure to come back.[2]

Cordially yours
F.P.G.

1 In Saskatchewan, near Swift Current; Miss Wiens' family lived on a farm on the southern outskirts of that town.
2 See letter of June 26, 1914.

TO CATHERINE WIENS

The Empire Hotel,
Winnipeg, Man.
July 11, 1914

My dear Miss Wiens,

Just before starting east to Kenora I receive your very kind note offering again an asylum against work. A man[1] whom I have got to see regarding my next or overnext year's work is at Kenora for the summer, and I have made an appointment with him over the phone for to-night. That will very probably detain me there till the Imperial Limited[2] goes west on Monday. I have no time-table here and shall have to leave in a few minutes. But I shall have to pass through Winnipeg again on Monday about 10 p.m. That train will land me at Moose Jaw about 11 a.m. on Tuesday morning, if I remember right. Also, if I am not mistaken, there is a local train from Moose Jaw west at about 12 noon. But that is the end of my recollection. Probably you know when it gets to Rush Lake. Should I, against inclination and anticipation, be detained, I shall send you a wire and trust that you will let me pay for the delivery which for all I know may cost a small fortune. So, *auf baldiges Wiedersehen.*[3]

Yours
F.P.G.

1 Possibly Robert Fletcher, Deputy Minister of Education in Manitoba, or some other official of the Department

2 Canadian Pacific's first trans-Canada train
3 Till we meet again very soon

TO WILLIAM REID[1]

Rapid City, Man.
January 29, 1923

Dear Sir,

Seeing that you found it worth your while to write to me after having read my little book, I take pleasure in telling you that in another, larger book which I hope will soon see the light of day I have a good deal to say *for* at least one representative of the medical profession. My attitude to this profession is, of course, largely tinged by my personal experience with its exponents; and unfortunately I have been handed about from one to the other for somewhat over fifty years, and that not generally to the benefit of my poor body. But I do not mean to say that the country practitioner is necessarily the worst. It was an eminent city doctor who for two years treated me for diabetes with disastrous results (with meat and coffee – both poisons for me), till at last I took matters into my own hand and by a number of experiments – I am originally a chemist: I don't mean a druggist; I studied medicine myself when I was young – proved conclusively to my own satisfaction that there was no sign of diabetes. Since then I have recovered to a point where I can see a few more years of life ahead.

The particular doctor in the case by whom the remark[2] in *Over Prairie Trails* was provoked once came into the livery stable in the 'One-third-way town' to get a team. 'We're lucky,' he said to the hostler who was to drive him, 'it won't take more than ten minutes. Case of pneumonia. He'll be dead by morning.'

But talking of operations, are you so sure that nine tenths of all operations would not better be left unperformed? I have still kept my appendix and mean to keep it. I believe there are fashions in surgery just as there are fads in education. However, I am quite willing to say that there are at least as many conscientious men among doctors as among other people; unfortunately there are no more among them.

Hoping that you will not feel badly about that little passage, I remain with the assurance of

cordial sincerity yours
F.P. Grove

P.S. – We must have been neighbours in 1895, for I was then teaching somewhere near Toronto; I rack my brain in vain to remember the name of the district.[3]

1 William Reid, a native of Watford, Ontario, was a graduate in medicine of the University of Toronto (MB 1904). Before that he taught school for a few years. He registered with the

College of Physicians and Surgeons of Ontario on June 27, 1905, and began practising medicine at Wyoming, Ontario, in the same year. He died on February 4, 1936.

It is not known if Grove and Reid ever met, or if indeed they were once neighbours; the occasion of this letter was, of course, one from Reid to Grove about *Over Prairie Trails*, which had been published in the previous year.

2 Presumably this remark: 'I was enough of a doctor to trust my ability to diagnose. I knew my wife would in that respect rather rely on me than on the average countrytown practitioner' – *Over Prairie Trails* (New Canadian Library edition, 1957) 117. However, there are other remarks about doctors in the same book.

3 This handwritten postscript to the typed text provides the only evidence we have of Grove teaching in Ontario in 1895, but there is no record of this with the Ontario Department of Education, and the 'evidence' remains unsubstantiated.

TO LORNE PIERCE[1]

Rapid City, Man.
August 28, 1925

Dear Dr. Pierce,

The August *Bookman*[2] came to hand to-night with the first ad of the *Settlers*.[3] That was cheering. But could you give your advertising dep[artmen]t a hint that my name is not Frederick *William* Grove but as above?[4]

I have just returned from 'flowering'[5] in the Rockies and am trying to catch up with accumulated work. So, hurriedly

Yours sincerely
F.P. Grove

1 Lorne Pierce (1890–1960) was born in Delta, Ontario; his parents were third-generation Canadians of Irish descent. After graduating from Queen's University (BA 1912), he attended Union Theological College, New York, obtaining his BD (1916) and concurrently an MA from New York University. Further theological training followed at Victoria College, University of Toronto (BD 1917), and United Theological College, Montreal (TH D 1920). In 1916 he was ordained to the Methodist ministry, and, in the same year, he married Edith Georgina Chown of Kingston, Ontario.

After serving for a while in the Queen's Field Ambulance Service, he was, in 1920, appointed Editor-in-Chief of the Ryerson Press, a post he held until a year before his death in 1960. He founded the Lorne Pierce Medal, awarded by the Royal Society of Canada for outstanding achievement in Canadian literature, on his own election to the Society in 1926. The following year saw the establishment of the Edith and Lorne Pierce Collection of Canadian Literature at Queen's University. The universities of New Brunswick (1930) and Alberta (1955), as well as Emmanuel College, Toronto (1954), were beneficiaries of awards and scholarships given by the Pierces.

Dr Pierce was the author of some eighteen books – religion, biography, and literary criticism – and editor of a good many more, including anthologies of prose and poetry for use in schools.

3 Grove with Rapid City High School students 1923. *Courtesy Leonard Grove*

2 *The Canadian Bookman* began in Montreal as a monthly periodical in 1919. In 1921, after the formation of the Canadian Authors' Association, that Association adopted it as its official organ; but in 1922 the CAA broke off its connection with the *Bookman* and began to issue its own periodical, called at first the *Authors' Bulletin*, later, the *Canadian Author*. Ownership of the *Bookman* found its way into the hands of Lorne Pierce, who later gave it to the CAA. Thereafter, it was issued as the *Canadian Author and Bookman*.
3 *Settlers of the Marsh*, published by Ryerson (Toronto) and Doran (New York) in 1925. A 'cheap edition' was issued in 1927, the New Canadian Library edition (McClelland and Stewart) in 1966.

The advertisement, on p 126 of the August 1925 issue of *The Canadian Bookman*, reads as follows:

> SETTLERS OF THE MARSH
>
> By Frederick William Grove. $2.00
>
> No stronger romance has come from the pen of a Canadian writer. It is a realistic study, outspoken and tellingly powerful, of life in pioneer districts of the Western Plains of Canada. The hero suffers moral disintegration and then fights his way back through the process of regeneration. This book will be widely discussed and it would seem that 'the great Canadian novel' has really been introduced.

4 The letterhead with his full name and address
5 This word, enclosed in quotation marks in the holograph, is dubious; but presumably refers to the collection of botanical specimens.

TO THE CANADIAN BOOKMAN[1]

Rapid City, Man.,
November 3, 1925

Editor *Canadian Bookman*,

You were right in your footnote. It is not possible to let the short article on 'Realism in Canadian Fiction' go without a protest.

In fact, there is nothing in it which should be allowed to go without contradiction except the statement contained in the phrase, 'There being, therefore, no Canadian realism.' There is none – in print.

Two points call for correction; one of literary, the other of historical criticism.

In the article in question Realism – which is a method of literary procedure – is confounded in frankness with matters of sex – which is a thing concerning the choice of subject. They have nothing whatever to do with each other. That, historically, the two have occasionally been associated, is true but irrelevant. With amazement I read the statement that, in Francis Dickie's view, Pierre Louys' *Aphrodite*[2] marks the extremity of realism. Why not mention the 'Smart Set' of today? To me the extremity of realism is marked by Shakespeare, Homer, Goethe.

Historically, it shows very little acquaintance with the currents of thought in France if Flaubert and Zola are classed together. Flaubert defended himself against the imputation that he was the founder of what in France is called *le naturalisme*. Flaubert and Zola were antipodes. Flaubert, indeed, was a realist; he was so whether he dealt with matters of sex or not; *Bouvard et Pécuchet*[3] show[s] very little of the sex taint. Zola was a romantic. With him, a preconceived, presumably scientific theory came first: the picturing of human life as it is came second. In fact, he never hesitated to falsify facts in order to make them conform to his theories. He called his novels 'experiments': his aim was always outside the domain of art. Which does not hinder that Zola was a poet, a great poet sometimes: but he was no realist. It is my firm conviction that Zola will not live, while Flaubert will endure as long as the language endures.

Space forbids that I enter into details. It is not the purpose of this letter to give an analysis of either Flaubert or Zola; nor to investigate the essence of realism; but merely to register a protest against a falsification of facts in literary criticism.

F.P. GROVE.

1 This letter, in response to Francis Dickie's 'Realism in Canadian Fiction' (*The Canadian Bookman* [October 1925] 165), was published in the *Bookman* of November 1925 (p 188). Dickie's paper was prepared for the Winnipeg convention of the Canadian Authors Association, but Dickie was unable to attend and, in the words of the *Bookman*, 'In the crush of matter crying for attention in the too-limited time devoted to the convention session no opportunity afforded itself for reading this paper.'

According to the program of the convention, as published in the *Bookman* of April 1925 (p 69), Augustus Bridle was to give an address on 'Realism in Canadian Fiction' in the morning session on June 27, 1925, which was to be followed by a discussion 'led by F.J. Niven, F.P. Grove, Francis Dickie, Austin Bothwell, G.H. Locke and E.J. Pratt.'

2 A novel (1896) by Pierre Louÿs (1870–1925)

3 The unfinished novel by Gustave Flaubert (1821–80), published in 1881. In André Gide's 'Conversation avec un Allemand,' which records his first meeting with Felix Paul Greve, Greve claims to have translated this novel into German.

TO E.J. MOORE,[1] THE RYERSON PRESS, TORONTO, ONTARIO

Rapid City, Man.
November 10, 1925

Dear Mr. Moore,

Thanks for your letter of Nov[ember] 7.[2]

I am glad you will look after the matter of the author's copies. I look forward to receiving the copy you are sending.

Yes, I should be very glad if you will keep me posted with regard to reviews appearing, etc. Any clippings which you wish to have returned, I shall send them by return mail.

I am delighted with Powell's review.[3] It contains, towards the end, a few sentences that will do well in advertisements, I believe though I know nothing about that sort of thing. As for the folder – whenever you wish to make up a new one, let me know. I can improve it.

Yours sincerely
F.P. Grove

1 E.J. Moore was Advertising Manager at Ryerson in the mid 1920s, and has since moved to the United States. He also did some manuscript reading and evaluation.
2 This letter covered the matters to which Grove refers here. Doran had not provided Grove with author's copies of *Settlers of the Marsh*. Apart from assuring Grove that the matter of the copies was being looked into, Moore wrote about forthcoming reviews of *Settlers*, anticipating a good one from Arthur Phelps in *Saturday Night* and another from Professor W.T. Allison in the *Winnipeg Tribune*. Re the folders, Moore wrote that 'these were prepared rather hurriedly on the basis of the meagre information we had regarding you.'
3 In the *Montreal Star*, a clipping of which Moore had enclosed with his letter of November 7, adding, 'You probably know Morgan Powell's reputation as the dean of Canadian reviewers. We always feel exceedingly pleased when his opinion on any of our books is favourable.' Morgan-Powell's review, as well as those by Arthur L. Phelps and W.T. Allison, is reprinted in my *Frederick Philip Grove* (Critical Views on Canadian Writers 1970) 106–13.

Samuel Morgan-Powell was born in 1867 and educated in England. He began his journalistic career as an office boy with the *Yorkshire Post*, and later studied music under the noted critic, C.E. Thompson. After a number of years of free-lancing and travelling widely all over the world, he came to Canada in 1905. Three years later, he was appointed News Editor of the *Montreal Star*, and later, for many years, was its influential Literary and Dramatic Editor. He died in 1962. He wrote two volumes of verse, *Night Thoughts* (1895) and *Down the Years* (1938), and several volumes of essays such as *Memories that Live* (1929).

TO E.J. MOORE, THE RYERSON PRESS, TORONTO, ONTARIO

Rapid City, Man.
November 17, 1925

Dear Mr. Moore,

I received last night 7 copies of *Settlers*. I do hope you don't mean that as the total allowance. I have already *bought* one extra copy. I have always had 12 and had intended to insist on more this time;[1] but it was overlooked. I use about half my copies – when I have 12 – in the interests of the book itself.

I also wish to correct one copy in case a new edition should become necessary some time or other; for, in spite of my exceeding care in reading proofs, the book swarms with misprints. In one place two whole lines were dropped out; and that at a critical point. In another, one line. Line spaces have repeatedly been put in at the wrong place, etc.

Yours sincerely
F.P. Grove

1 Since Grove had by this time published only two previous books – *Over Prairie Trails* and *The Turn of the Year* – in Canada under his own name, this reference lends some support to the belief that Grove had published books under another name in Europe.

TO AUSTIN M. BOTHWELL[1]

Rapid City, Man.
November 18, 1925

Dear Mr. Bothwell,

On the night of the executive meeting[2] on Oct[ober] 10 you spoke very highly of *Wild Geese*.[3] I had not read the book; so I could say nothing. I have read it since; and I have been tempted by the desire to give you my reaction. In order to get rid of the temptation, I will do so.

(1) The book is deplorably, even unusually immature. I will not, for the moment, speak of Caleb Gare.[4]

There is a teacher, Miss Ostenso, drawn by stencil, pretty, charming, etc., with all the conventional reactions of the NEW WOMAN which exist only in books. There is Mark Jordan, the typical stencil stranger from the 'wider world,' the dream of every 'tame goose.' How he gets into the scene is unspeakably funny. There is the oppressed mother and wife with a past, held in submission by an impossible threat. Only in books is such a threat effective: in life it does not work. There is also a submissive and a rebellious daughter: what could be more stencil work than that rebellion? And there is a comp*lai*sant son and one less comp*lac*ent: the typical dreamer of books, not of life: Laddie personified.

Besides, there are half a dozen outsiders seen from the outside.

Not one of them all is more than a drawing; not one of them lives in space; not one of them *lives*.

Now all this is, of course, only natural when an immature young girl sits down to write a book, not because that book cries in her to be written; but because she has the itch to write. She knows nothing of the grim things of life.

(2) *One* character is *seen*, in glimpses; Caleb Gare. He is not understood; only a Hamsun[5] could understand him. In fact, no attempt is made to understand him. The book is written as a prosecutor's plea against him to ensure conviction. Whenever he *acts*, he forgets who he is. The moment he attempts to make his abstract power concrete it must of necessity collapse; that

was the real tragedy contained in the premises which Miss Ostenso failed to see. His end is twaddle. A man like that does not by mistake run into a slough which he knows. That end, untrue and silly, destroys the one tragic possibility of the book.

A man like Gare does not '*happen*.' He grows. What did Caleb grow from? Do you understand his genesis? If so, you have greater psychologic insight than I have. But, in order to understand him, we must see *his side* of the case.

Yet, in glimpses, the man is seen. Characteristically he is most impressive at his first appearance on the stage of the book. There lies its slender promise. I have observed it to be a common fault with beginners: the interest further on fritters itself away.

(3) Needless to say, the book is reasonably well written, though not unusually so. There are scores of American and even Canadian novels as well written. After all, not a page compels you to go back to it by its graphic representation.

(4) The *petty* 'sexiness' of many passages makes a mature person smile. One cannot avoid the suspicion that that sort of thing was sprinkled in as a spice or with an eye on the 'movies.' In fact, how could a young girl know anything of the fierce antagonisms that discharge themselves in sex? Nobody will accuse me of prudishness. What I object to is the incompetence, psychologic and artistic, in dealing with these things...

VERDICT: immature, but promising. The author will be spoiled by praise such as yours: else she might write *a book* 30 y[ea]rs hence.

It is the old story: only trash wins a prize. That is why, for the last twenty years, I have steadfastly refused, for myself, and disadvised, in the case of other, younger people, submitting anything in competitions.

. . . . . .

Now, my dear Mr. Bothwell, I should not say this in public. I have twice declined to review the book. If I did review it, I should speak sparingly of the faults and appreciatively of the few good points which hold promise – alas, too few.

That was a thing I could not do with *Captain Salvation*:[6] there were no good points, from the point of view of literary art. And, of course, I am not dealing with mere reading matters. Our cheap magazines furnish that to the facile clerk agog for a sensation. That sort of thing has no place in books.

Yours dissentiently, but sincerely,
F.P. Grove.

1 Austin McPhail Bothwell (c1885–1928), was born in Perth, Ontario, where he received his early education. At the age of eighteen, he moved to the North-West Territories, teaching in rural schools during the summer, and attending the Regina Normal School in the winter. He was chosen as the first Rhodes Scholar from the NWT. After his graduation from Oxford, he spent an additional year studying at Heidelberg, Germany. On his return, he joined the staff of (then) Wesley College, Winnipeg, and taught there for seven years. In 1917, he moved to Regina to become the head of the English department at Central

Collegiate Institute. In December 1927, he was appointed Inspector of Public Schools, the position which he held at the time of his death.

He was a prolific writer. In addition to the preparation of a doctoral thesis on Thomas Mann, he was the author of several text books, editor of the *Saskatchewan Teachers' Alliance*, and a regular contributor to a number of Canadian and foreign journals. He attended the executive meeting of the Canadian Authors' Association in his capacity as president of the Saskatchewan branch, which he had helped organize.

2 Of the Canadian Authors' Association

3 By Martha Ostenso, published that year. Martha Ostenso was born in Bergen, Norway, in 1900, and came to North America in 1902. She grew up in Manitoba, being educated at the University of Manitoba and Columbia University. She wrote a book of verse, *In a Far Land* (1924), and some ten novels, of which *Wild Geese* was the first and best known. It won the Dodd-Mead Prize in 1925, and deals with settlers' life in Manitoba – hence, Grove's interest not only in its literary qualities but also in its subject-matter. The book has been praised as unusually realistic for its day.

4 The central figure in the novel, a cruel taskmaster who sacrifices members of his family to the cause of material success

5 Knut Hamsun (1859–1952), the Norwegian novelist, dramatist, and poet. He won the Nobel Prize for literature in 1920. His first novel, *Sult* (1890) – translated into English as *Hunger* (1899) – established him among the pioneers of naturalism in fiction.

6 A romance of the sea by F.W. Wallace (1886–1958), published in 1925. Two reviews of the same novel, one by Grove and the other by Bothwell, appeared in *The Canadian Bookman* of September 1925 (p 148). Bothwell was only slightly critical, saying that the novel required 'a wide capacity of belief in the reader,' but was on the whole highly favourable, praising, among other things, the book's realism: 'Bearing in mind the time, one must pronounce *Captain Salvation* not only a remarkable reconstruction of the physical features of the age of sailing ships, but also a very successful attempt to catch the spiritual.' Grove's much shorter review, which appears to have been editorially reduced, was totally destructive. It began:

> If, while condemned to read the book, one wonders what kind of people may like this sort of thing, one wonders still more, after laying it aside, at the mentality of him who could write it. Two-thirds of it is 'sex slush' of the worst kind; one-third is a watersoup of fourth-hand salvationism. It is awful, awful.

It concluded on the note that if the public wanted books of this kind, 'then ... the public be damned.'

TO E.J. MOORE

Rapid City, Man.
November 21, 1925

Dear Mr. Moore,

I am enclosing a second sheet[1] containing a few authentic notes on the very few facts of interest in my life which has, for the last thirty years, been singularly uneventful, quite in contrast to the preceding ten years or so. If that can be of any service, I shall be glad.

Yours truly,
F.P. Grove

[*The following two enclosures were included with the above letter.*]

[I]

In writing *Settlers of the Marsh*, the author aimed at presenting the reaction of the Western Canadian landscape on the settler, and that of the settler on the landscape. He tried to present circumstances, conflicts, tragedies which do not merely happen but which spring with necessity from character and environment.

At the same time, in depicting the eternal struggle, which forms the background of his work, between man and nature, he aimed at laying the stress, not so much on the external, economic things, on outward failure or success, as on the inner consequences of all happenings for the souls of the men and women involved.

He himself considers as the distinguishing feature of his book the fact that all things are seen, as it were, from the inside, and weighed according as they widen or narrow down the hero's or the heroine's humanity.

[II]

Biographical Facts.

Born 1872 in Sweden, son of Swedish father and Scotch mother. Spent, during childhood and early youth, periods varying from a few weeks to a few years in Sweden, England, Scotland, France, Germany, Austria, Italy, Switzerland. Travelled as a young man in Sweden, Norway, Russia, Siberia, Spain, Asia Minor, Africa; and voyaging.

Came to Canada in 1892, returned to Europe, and again to Canada and the U.S.A. in 1893. Being suddenly left without resources, he lived for two years as a tramp and hobo. When tired of this life, a R[oman] C[atholic] priest suggested to him that he become a teacher. Taught in various private schools and as an independent coach; then as a public school and finally as a high school teacher. While engaged as such, graduated from Manitoba University, as an extra-mural student.[2] Left the teaching profession in 1924 when he was principal of Rapid City High School in Manitoba.

Wrote his first book 1895 to 1898. One copy is still in existence though not in the author's possession. Wrote book after book; but did not attempt to publish till 1915. First publication in book form 1922, *Over Prairie Trails*; next, 1923, *The Turn of the Year*; last, 1925, *Settlers of the Marsh*. The latter book was sketched in its first form in 1917, as a novel in 3 vol[ume]s. Rewritten several times from 1917 to 1924 when it reached its present form.

1 As printed below. It is interesting to note that Grove's own estimate of *Settlers of the Marsh* lays stress, not on those features which are generally thought of as placing him in

the social realist tradition ('the external, economic things'), but on 'the inner consequences ... for the souls of men and women concerned'; and this is reiterated in the final paragraph – 'all things are seen from the inside.'
2 This sentence is inserted in Grove's own handwriting in the typewritten text. He graduated (BA) from the University of Manitoba in May 1922.

TO E.J. MOORE

Rapid City, Man.
November 30, 1925

Dear Mr. Moore,

In reply to your letter of Nov[ember] 25, I beg to say that I have indeed never received any contract from Doran beyond a copy of certain passages contained in a letter from Doran to you, communicated to me under date of June 12, 1925. In this memorandum nothing is said of author's copies. I am sorry that, at the time, I did not call your attention to it. But I was exceedingly busy in June, copying out my next novel in order to have a Ms. which I could take along into my holidays. I had little thought, then, for the *Settlers*. As for the proofs, I read them some time in July, with the greatest possible care. The lines I mentioned were dropped in paging. However, that is beyond remedy for the time being; I only wish a new edition, if it ever becomes necessary, to be better in that respect.

I wish to add that what I have seen of reviews, with the exception of Morgan Powell's, is singularly unintelligent.[1] And without any exception, they seem to me to miss the point. I think of writing a short statement of my side of the matter; if I do, I shall send it to you, to do with as you please. It may serve as the basis of advertisements if you approve of it.[2] In that case, of course, I should prefer not to be mentioned.

Yours sincerely
F.P. Grove

1 See letter of November 10, 1925, note 3. As pointed out in my introduction to *Frederick Philip Grove* (Critical Views on Canadian Writers 1970), while it may be fair to say that critics treated Grove's work superficially, one is impressed, not indeed by any moralistic savagery in reviews of *Settlers of the Marsh*, but by their respectful tone, and their defence of the book's morality. About the banning of the book by public libraries, J.F.B. Livesay, father of the poet Dorothy Livesay, wrote to Grove, 'I am glad to note that "Settlers in the Marsh" [sic] has been banned from the Winnipeg Public Library – the best kind of advertisement for a young author. Toronto Public Library lets it out only to mature people of good character.' (March 19, 1926) The Livesay letter is preserved in the University of Manitoba Grove Collection.
2 There is an amusing reply (December 8, 1925) to this letter. After stating that Grove's proposed riposte 'might be useful in further publicity,' Moore takes the trouble to advise

4 Catherine, Phyllis May, and Frederick Philip Grove 1924. *Courtesy Leonard Grove*

him, at some length – gently and tactfully – against any direct published defence. He goes on to suggest the old trade maxim that all publicity is good publicity, and explains:

> As a matter of fact in most cases in Canada, the people who do this review work do it as a side-line or as an incidental and sit down, we presume, with half a dozen books before them to get through in one or two evenings. ... A year or so ago we had a reviewer on perhaps the leading English paper in Montreal, who was simply taking the blurbs from the jackets on the books we sent him and printed them with a note of his own at the end to the effect that 'being a Ryerson Press book this is of course a good one.'

TO WILLIAM TALBOT ALLISON[1]

325 Vaughan St[reet],[2]
Winnipeg, Man.
December 7, 1925

My dear Dr. Allison,

You have just 'flattened me out' with your Annual Christmas Book page.[3] Let me express to you my most sincere thanks for having given me space beyond my boldest expectations.

You know I do not crave publicity for its own sake. But I do wish very much to relieve my wife of the onerous task of making the greater part of our living. And if this page of yours does not bring the 'filthy lucre,' nothing will.

This is just a note to let you know how much I appreciate your kindness.

Yours most sincerely
F.P. Grove.

1 For Allison, see letter of February 18, 1929 III, note 3.
2 The explanation of this address is not clear. It was not, apparently, the number of the YMCA building, which was situated on Vaughan Street, but of a house then occupied by W.T. Holmes, teamster with Crescent Creamery.
3 In *The Winnipeg Tribune Magazine*, November 21, 1925, p 13. For an extract from this review, see my *Frederick Philip Grove* (Critical Views on Canadian Writers 1970) 110–11.

TO E.J. MOORE

Rapid City, Man.
December 21, 1925

Dear Mr. Moore,

The matter of the agreement[1] has been held up by my being ill. There are two points which I should like to clear up before signing.

1stly. Moving picture rights. I do not expect that there will be a moving picture version; if there were a demand, I do not know whether I should welcome it. Yet it seems best to have a definite understanding. Are the provisions provided for U.S. book rights to apply to it, as outlined in #2? (10% commission?) If so, may I add a line to that effect?

2ndly. #13 provides for my submitting my next novel to the Ryerson Press. I have no objection whatever. But we should fix a time limit beyond which I should not be bound by that offer. I have had trouble before with regard to this point. Shall we say that the Ryerson Press should decide within a month or within six weeks whether to accept or to decline? Further, does this provision include the Doran people? I will frankly say that I am disgusted with the way Doran handled the book in the U.S.A. The jacket killed it. I know for a fact that the 3 leading reviews of what may be called 'literature' ignored the book for the sake of the jacket (Danby,[2] Sherman,[3] Mencken[4]). The buyer of 'North Country Romance,' not getting what he wanted, returned the book to the booksellers. So it fell between two stools. I doubt whether even a few hundred copies were sold.

In addition, Harper Bro[ther]s have repeatedly written to me asking for a novel – which, of course, does not mean that they would accept what I have to offer. But I should like to give them the chance. My new novel is ready. If I had not been ill, you would have had a typescript by now.

I might add that I shall not again be satisfied with 8 free copies. I should have been glad to send you a corrected copy of the *Settlers* if I had one. But I have already bought half a dozen copies, paying the full price, in order to rectify in small part Doran's blunderings; and I cannot, at present, afford to buy any more. After a while I wish to get 4 more copies from you directly.

Awaiting your kind reply on those two points, I am holding the agreement.

Yours very truly
F.P. Grove

1 In a letter to Grove, December 14, Moore enclosed a copy of Ryerson's terms and contract for *Settlers*, although the original question had concerned Doran's. There had 'apparently been some little misunderstanding' between the two companies. Moore's conclusion indicates that arrangements with Doran over US publication were to be handled through Ryerson, who would pay over royalties on US sales to Grove. The actual contract is missing from the collection.

2 Almost certainly an error for Canby, as no Danby seems to have been connected with any leading US journal of reviews. Henry Seidel Canby (1876–1961) was editor of the distinguished *Saturday Review of Literature* (1924–36), and chairman of the board of judges, Book of the Month Club (1926–58).

3 Stewart Pratt Sherman (1881–1927), the American editor and author, who was literary editor of the *New York Herald Tribune* from 1924 until his death.

4 Henry Louis Mencken (1880–1956), the American literary critic and director of Alfred Knopf, Inc., the publishing house. He was co-editor (1914–23) and editor (1924–33) of the *American Mercury*, and contributing editor (1921–32) of the *Nation*.

TO THE RYERSON PRESS, TORONTO, ONT[ARIO]

Rapid City, Man.
January 14, 1926

Dear Sirs,

By the same post and under separate cover I am sending you a Ms. of my novel

Our Daily Bread.[1]

Would you be kind enough to confirm receipt?

I am writing Dr. Pierce simultaneously and at greater length.[2]

Yours sincerely,
F.P. Grove

1 Eventually published (in the USA and Canada) by Macmillan, two years later

2 The letter, if it was written, does not appear to have survived.

TO THE RYERSON PRESS, TORONTO, ONTARIO

Rapid City, Man.
February 15, 1926

Dear Sirs,

Your letter of Febr[uary] 11[1] came to hand to-night, and I see from it that the affair with Harper's has miscarried. I might say that I consider that as no more than what was to be expected if the ordinary publisher's reader had the decision. That was the reason why I wished to send it to Mr. Hartman[2] direct. Only a person predisposed in my favour would really read on after finding out that the book is not the average trash which makes immediate commercial successes.

However, it is useless to worry over spilt beans.

The question for me is, of course, solely whether you wish to publish the book in Canada. The last line of your letter makes me doubtful as to that. If I interpret it correctly as meaning that, Dr. Pierce being away, you do not care to consider the question, then, of course, the sooner I get the Ms. back, the better. I have had a veiled offer from another Canadian publisher who wrote me that in his opinion 'I was now entitled to link up with a publisher who will build me up as an author of succeeding novels.' (I might mention, by the way, that it was Macmillans).[3]

We arrive again at the point where we were last year during Dr. Pierce's absence. The trouble is, I cannot and will not wait beyond the stipulated time unless I am assured that the book will appear in Canada next fall. After this assurance is given, I have no objection whatever to any attempts on your part or my own to secure a U.S.A. publisher, provided it does not affect that assurance.

You would oblige me greatly by letting me know at once if I interpret the last line[4] of your letter correctly; for in that case, of course, I should like to take immediate steps for publication elsewhere.

Yours truly,
F.P. Grove

1 The letter of February 11, signed by Blanche Hume (Lorne Pierce's secretary), dealt with matters relating to USA publication of *Our Daily Bread*. Pierce had sought Harper Brothers' collaboration but they declined, and the idea of Ryerson publishing the novel fell through. It was published two years later, in 1928, by Macmillan.

2 Lee Foster Hartman (1879–1941). A native of Fort Wayne, Indiana, he completed his education at Wesleyan University, Middletown, Connecticut, receiving his BA in 1901. In 1904 he joined the literary department of Harper & Brothers, remaining in that post until 1908, when he transferred to the editorial staff of *Harper's Magazine*. In 1918 he became Associate Editor, and in 1931 Editor, holding the latter post until his death. He was also a vice-president of Harper & Brothers, publishers. Hartman had commented favourably on one of Grove's short stories, which had been submitted to him by Francis Arthur Jones of New York, who was then acting as Grove's literary agent.

3 In a letter of January 19, 1926, which has survived, Hugh Eayrs of Macmillan wrote:

> You have quite a wrong impression of my attitude if you think – as you appear to do – that I bear you a grudge. Nothing could be further from my mind. I should like to say quite frankly to you, that I had a very sincere admiration for *Over Prairie Trails* and it is deepened now that I have read *Settlers of the Marsh*. ... Let me say frankly that you are now entitled to link up with a publisher who will build you up as the author of succeeding novels.

See the letter of November 14, 1926, for a note on Eayrs (note 2), and for a further reference to his letter.

4 Which was: 'Shall we retain the copy of your manuscript when it returns from Harper's?'

TO LORNE PIERCE

Rapid City, Man.
April 8, 1926

Dear Dr. Pierce,

I am sending you, by concurrent mail, a Ms. of my novel 'The Canyon' – alternative titles: 'The Poet's Dream' – 'Frances Montcrieff' – 'The Unending Quest.'[1]

I think I mentioned that I am corresponding with regard to this novel with the Viking Press of New York. I have told them that you would handle the book in Canada. It need in no way interfere with *Our Daily Bread*, since they are in no hurry. I shall let you know as soon as I hear. And, of course, it is just as likely as not that this will lead to nothing. But they have asked me for something that is not strictly Canadian in theme. That is why I sent them this.

Yours truly
F.P. Grove

1 This remains, unpublished, in the University of Manitoba Library collection of Grove's mss.

TO LORNE PIERCE

[no date][1]

Dear Dr. Pierce,

I am glad to hear that 'The Canyon' interests you. Since the Viking Press people betrayed an interest in my work, I do think it best to let them have the reading. It should not take long, for I wrote them that I could not give them more than 2 weeks to decide in. If they want it, it will be for the good, if not, there will still be time. I am sorry, though, that things did not work out so that your Mr. Walker[2] could take the Ms. along. If the V[iking] P[ress] people decline, I shall let you know at once; and you can then do as you see fit.

Meanwhile I have reread a Ms. of 'The Weatherhead Fortunes – A Story of the Small Town'[3] – which I revised some 2 years ago. Like *Our Daily Bread*, it is an old piece of work somewhat modernized by references to the war. I sent a copy of the Ms. to Phelps[4] in 1924; he praised the 'three-dimensionality' of the characters but did not seem to be enthusiastic – which caused me to leave it for a year or so. But, having re-read it now, I do not agree with him. I think it decidedly *good* and very characteristic for the peculiar pseudo-civilisation of the West where economic factors out-rank cultural ones. I shall, therefore, fix a Ms. up for you and send it along – if you are not tired reading my work.

There is another book of mine[5] which is nearly in shape for the press. It, Phelps thinks 'enormous': in its interweaving of human destinies and western lake-landscapes. I am not fully satisfied with its structure. But I shall attack it once more now and see what I can do with it (as it stands it is much too long). It too, I shall send whenever I can if you are willing to read it ... [letter cut here]

1 The only copy I have of this letter was supplied by Mrs Grove – handwritten on the back of a letter from Pierce date April 14, 1926, and doubtless only a draft. The letter is incomplete.
2 Pierce's letter of April 14 acknowledges the ms of 'The Canyon,' and remarks, 'Mr Walker who leaves for New York today is anxious to take it over with him but owing to the fact that you are corresponding with the Viking Press [see Grove's letter of April 8 – ed.] and owing to the further fact that I have not your permission, I am not allowing him to take it.' Ernest W. Walker was in charge of the Wholesale Department of the Ryerson Press.

3 The ms is in the University of Manitoba Grove Collection, in two typescript copies. A note by Mrs Grove reads, 'Never to be published.'

4 Arthur L. Phelps was born in Columbus, Ontario, in 1887. A graduate of Victoria College, Toronto (BA 1913), and an ordained minister of the Methodist (later United) Church of Canada, he became Head of the English Department at Wesley College, University of Manitoba, in 1921, a post he held till 1945, when he became General Supervisor of the CBC's International Service. From 1947 to 1953, he was Professor of English at McGill University, and, after his retirement, he was Special Lecturer in English at the universities of British Columbia and Toronto.

He was also the author of a volume of poems (1921) and several books on current affairs and literature, and was active all his life in broadcasting. He was elected a Fellow of the Royal Society of Canada in 1949. He died on April 27, 1970. His *Canadian Writers* (1951) has a chapter on Grove; he also wrote the foreword in *The Turn of the Year*, and played a key role in securing the publication of *Settlers of the Marsh* by the Ryerson Press.

Phelps wrote frequently to Grove from 1923 onwards, encouraging him to keep on writing. Many of the Phelps letters are in the University of Manitoba Grove Collection, but unfortunately Grove's letters to Phelps appear not to have survived.

5 Most probably *The Yoke of Life* (Toronto: Macmillan; New York: Richard Smith 1930)

TO WATSON KIRKCONNELL[1]

Rapid City, Man.
April 30, 1926

My dear Kirkconnell,

The April *Bookman* came to hand last night; and I wish to thank you for the good will it shows.[2] As you will see from the enclosed copy of a letter of mine[3] to the *Bookman*, it forced a correction from me, on a point which it would neither be safe nor honourable for me to leave uncontradicted.

There are one or two other points which are not entirely accurate; but they do not matter. The scientific expedition to South America was, for instance, really no more than a holiday trip undertaken to see ants of which I had read; it was made by myself alone.

But I do not want to encumber the *Bookman* with a long letter which would savour of self-advertisement; and it seems that such points are irrelevant. The main thing is that people be reminded of my existence and of the existence of my books. That purpose you have well served; and if I felt compelled to set this one thing right, it was chiefly because, you knowing me personally, it might seem as if this information had come from myself directly, as a vain boast.

Yours sincerely,
F.P. Grove

1 Watson Kirkconnell was born in Port Hope, Ontario, in 1895. After graduating from Queen's University (MA 1916) and the Toronto Conservatory of Music, he joined, in 1922,

5 A.L. Phelps. *Courtesy H.E. Duckworth*

the staff of the then Wesley College, Winnipeg (now the University of Winnipeg), becoming in 1934 the Head of the Classics Department. In 1940 he moved east to become Professor of English and Head of the Department at McMaster University. In 1948 he was appointed President of Acadia University, a post from which he retired in 1964, being then appointed Professor of English (1964–8).

He is the recipient of a notable number of chivalric awards and titles, as well as academic and literary honours including the Royal Society of Canada's Lorne Pierce Medal in 1942. He is a Fellow of the Society, and author of a large number of books and articles in many fields. Among his first was *International Aspects of Unemployment* (1923); and those that followed have included original verse and prose, translations from several languages, literary history and criticism, political writing, and an autobiography, *A Slice of Canada* (1967).

He married twice; his first wife, Isabel née Peel, died a year after their marriage in 1924. In 1930 he married Hope Kitchener.

Dr Kirkconnell is still an active scholar, and lives in Wolfville, Nova Scotia.

Kirkconnell and Phelps visited Grove several times in Rapid City, and did much to encourage him in those early and difficult years.

2 It contained a biographical sketch of Grove by Watson Kirkconnell, which in part read:

> Born in Europe in 1872, the son of a wealthy Swede and a Scotchwoman, he lived for years the life of a roving young intellectual; visiting all parts of Europe and most of the world; taking part in a scientific expedition to South America; writing with distinction in French, German, Swedish, and English; actively co-operating in London in the eighteen-nineties with H.G. Wells, Wilde, and their group; and editing personally, at that time, the first complete edition of Swift's *Gulliver's Travels* [see the following letter, note 2 – ed.].
>
> In 1896, family reverses led him to come to Canada as an immigrant. ... He has been married twice and has two sons and one daughter.

Kirkconnell confirms that the article was based on personal conversations with Grove.

3 Which follows

TO THE EDITOR, THE CANADIAN BOOKMAN, TORONTO, ONTARIO

Rapid City, Man.
April 30, 1926 II

Dear Sir,

One error of Mr. W.K.'s,[1] in his biographical notice of myself, contained in the April number of the *Bookman*, I cannot allow to go without correction, seeing that it detracts from the work of others.

I did not, in my non-age, edit the first complete edition of *Gulliver's Travels*: that honour belongs to Mr. Temple Scott.[2] It was he who first saw clearly that the text must have been altered after it had left Swift's hands.

My own work was restricted to a re-collation of early editions and the South Kensington Ford MSS.[3] As a result of these labours I was instrumental (though not directly engaged) in bringing about the publication of two, perhaps three continental editions of *Gulliver's Travels*, my aim being to rescue the work from dying as a literary masterpiece to become a 'children's classic.'

Yours sincerely,
F.P. Grove.

1 Watson Kirkconnell's; see the *Canadian Bookman* (April 1926) 110; and the preceding letter, note 2.

2 Jonathan Swift, *Prose Works*, 12 vols., ed. Temple Scott (London 1897). It is interesting to note that Felix Paul Greve edited Swift's prose works – Jonathan Swift, *Prosa-Schriften* – in 1909/10 (Berlin).

3 The reference is to the Charles Ford manuscripts of Swift material in the Forster Collection, South Kensington. Ford was one of Swift's close friends, and he often received and transcribed Swift's manuscripts. (I am indebted to Professor Denis Donoghue of University College, Dublin, for this note.)

TO THE EDITOR, THE RAPID CITY REPORTER[1]

Rapid City, Man.
June 19, 1926

Sir,

I cannot leave town, even for a holiday, without thanking our many friends for the courageous and effective way in which they have downed the dastardly attack from the dark, and around a corner which has been levelled against a defenceless woman: defenceless because unskilled in the use of underhand weapons; her only crime being that she did her duty unflinchingly and unremittingly with somewhat more than the usual devotion, and therefore, with somewhat more than the usual success.

As to myself, I need no defence. I have been attacked before; I have shrugged my shoulders and gone on doing what I thought was right. The irony of it is that hundreds of teachers in this province and in other parts of the Dominion were once my pupils; if I may believe those of them who have spoken to me, they are spreading seed which, in them, I have planted.

As for my little girl, she does not go to school because I want her to learn more, of course, not less than the public school can teach.

My method of life? I follow Milton's rule: 'To shun delights and live laborious days.'[2] If, on the rare occasions – rare on account of the exacting nature of my work – on which I have mingled with my fellow citizens, I avoided those who launched the attack, does not the very nature of that attack prove that I was right?

We have agreed to return to this town. We have done so under the pressure of public opinion; our own inclinations would have led us to seek greener fields. But we felt that it would be ungrateful indeed not to listen to the plea of those who have shown themselves to be our friends, especially since their number provéd to be so much greater than, in our most optimistic moods, we should have expected.

Yours truly,
F.P. Grove
Rapid City, Man.
June 19th, 1926.

1 A copy of this letter, which appeared in *The Rapid City Reporter* of June 26, 1926 (p 5), was supplied by Dr Margaret Stobie of the University of Manitoba. The matter covered in it refers to the unsuccessful petition to the School Board by a group called the Returned Soldiers' Organization for the termination of Mrs Grove's services as a teacher. For further details, see Margaret Stobie, *Frederick Philip Grove* (New York 1973) 113–16.
2 'Lycidas,' 1:72: 'To scorn delights, and live laborious days.'

TO H.C. MILLER[1]

Rapid City, Man.
November 14, 1926

Dear Mr. Miller,

I have been ill since middle of September; but, though I am still in bed, I am at last able again to look after my business.

Since I did not receive word from you yesterday, I take it that you insist on a reduction of the *Search for America* to 60,000 words. But, if you will for a moment consider that that would mean dropping 2/3 of it, you will understand why I balk. Once before, in the case of the *Settlers*, I have spoiled a good book by cutting it to the bone. As for the *Search*, it is as it stands less than 1/2 of the original work. I do not particularly care for its publication. I offered it under pressure from my friends who are afraid that I do with it what I have done to countless other books of mine, namely burn it. There was a time when it existed in only a single copy and when that single copy was no longer in my possession. As a matter of fact, I have not read the book since 1920. Eayrs,[2] of Macmillan's, read it in 1923 and wrote me that he considered it the best thing of its kind ever written; and yet I did not consent to publish. The book is largely autobiographical; in its older form it was strictly so. I should not like that fact to be exploited; but I also shrink from removing it more and more from that standard and from reducing it to a short story. In fact, I shrink from any further reduction. My friends say, they would rather see it appear in a shortened form than not see it appear at all; they think it will one day be printed in its unabridged form of which there is only one copy extant – that copy being in the vaults of a Canadian publisher. My own idea is to let the Ms. lie as it has lain for nearly 30 years; its interest will be enhanced as my work becomes known. I should like to leave it till after my death. On the other hand, I do want to get a book out; and I feel sure that I shall get one out shortly. My choice lies between two of my novels, one of these being *Our Daily Bread*. The other will probably be published in the U.S.A. I do not much care about publication in the U.S.A. but the book had been offered before I heard of you. If we do any business with each other, I shall, when the time comes, arrange for you to handle that book in Canada.

What makes me rather optimistic is the fact that my work – though only about 1500 copies of the *Settlers* were sold – begins to attract attention. I have two letters before me, both written to me without my having done anything towards getting them. In one of them Mr Arthur Meighen says, 'While writing will you permit me to express my appreciation of the great service you have rendered to Canadian literature, and indeed to Canada?'[3] In the other H.S. Eayrs, of Macmillan's, says, 'I should like to say frankly to you, as I have said about you, that I had a very sincere admiration for *Over Prairie Trails*; and it is deepened now that I have read *Settlers of the Marsh* ... Let me say frankly that you are now entitled to link up with a publisher who will build you up as an author of succeeding novels.'[4]

Having had a rather disagreeable experience with Macmillan, I have not, so far, answered this letter of Eayrs' which I consider as a veiled offer. Meighen I do not know at all, and the letter from which I quoted was his first word to me.

If, then, you care at all to enter into business relation with myself, I would ask you to consider whether *Our Daily Bread* appeals to you. If not, the sooner I know it, of course, the better.

I might say in addition that I consider fall publication of my books a mistake. People are bewildered by the flood of fall books; and, naturally, they reach for such trash as *Wild Geese*[5] which is advertised to sell. But that is a commercial consideration with which I am not primarily concerned. I write my books for a public which is not yet born.

All this I would ask you to take as a mere frank statement of my point of view.

Sincerely yours,
F.P. Grove.

1 This is almost certainly Grove's first letter to Miller, for Grove had been, as he says, ill since the middle of September and unable to look after his business.

Henry C. Miller, originally an Ottawa printer, established in 1923 The Graphic Publishers Limited – 'an all-Canadian Company ... for the purpose of producing and marketing all-Canadian books by Canadian writers,' as the promotion on the jacket of one of their books proclaimed. In a similar vein, he wrote Grove on October 30, 1926, saying, in part, 'In a letter from our mutual friend, W.A. Deacon of Toronto *Saturday Night*, he tells me that you are desirous of connecting with some all-Canadian publishing firm.' Evidently, Mrs Grove replied and sent him manuscripts of *Our Daily Bread* and *A Search for America*. In his reply, Miller offered to publish both the books, adding, 'I would also want the *Search* cut as I have suggested [to 60,000 words], and then *if we produce results*, I want the first opportunity at *Our Daily Bread*.' He also offered to negotiate with Ryerson to take over *Settlers of the Marsh*. However, he published only one book by Grove, *A Search for America* in 1927, although Grove's connection with Graphic was resumed in December 1929, when he joined the firm as reader. It went into liquidation, after eight years of fluctuating fortunes and various managements, in 1932.

2 Hugh Smithurst Eayrs was born in Leeds, England, on March 11, 1894, and educated in that country. He came to Canada in 1912, and after short spells with the *Canadian Courier* as editor and *Maclean's Magazine* as assistant editor he joined the Macmillan Company of Canada, of which he became president in 1921. He was a co-author of *The Amateur Diplomat* (1916) and author of *Sir Isaac Brock* (1917). He died on April 29, 1940 after a heart seizure.

Grove's contacts with Eayrs appear to have begun in 1923, when Grove offered *A Search for America* to Macmillan for publication. Eayrs replied on March 9, 1923: 'Both in my opinion and that of our reader's, this book ought to be published. ... The fact of the matter is that, so far as we are concerned our lists for this spring and fall and indeed for the spring of 1924, are full up. Our directors insist that, during these days of wretched publishing conditions, we should do no more books than are absolutely necessary...' In February 1924, Grove offered *Settlers of the Marsh*, but Eayrs found the novel, in the form it was then, too long: 'In 203 pages of closely written manuscript you set forth a story which we suggest might have been much more effectively presented in two thirds of the space' (February 25, 1924). The negotiations with Eayrs for *Our Daily Bread*, the first Grove book actually published by Macmillan, were initiated by Mrs Grove, and at one stage Grove must have suggested that the contracts should be drawn up in her name, for on April 16, 1928, Eayrs wrote, 'My contract has already gone to you so that I cannot from here alter it, but if you would like it made with Mrs Grove we can arrange it. New York's is not yet made out. I think it might be arranged in their case to make it with Mrs Grove.' These early Macmillan letters are preserved in the University of Manitoba Grove Collection, but those from Grove have not come to light.

3 Arthur Meighen (1874–1960). Born in Ontario and educated in that province (BA, Univ. of Toronto 1892), he moved to Winnipeg and then, in 1901, to Portage la Prairie, Manitoba, where, in the following year, he was called to the Bar. In 1908 he was elected to Parliament, and, in 1913, appointed Solicitor-General in the Robert Borden cabinet. A succession of cabinet posts followed, including those of Secretary of State and Minister of the Interior and Indian Affairs. In 1920 he succeeded Sir Robert Borden as Prime Minister following the latter's retirement, but had to resign in December 1921, after his party's defeat in the general election. In June 1926, he was called upon to form another ministry which lasted until September of that year. He became a Senator in 1932, and served for a while as minister without portfolio in the Bennett cabinet.

He published a collection of his speeches, *Unrevised and Unrepentant*, in 1949.

In addition to writing to Grove himself, as indicated in this letter, Meighen sent a letter to Ryerson congratulating them – in the words of Lorne Pierce – 'on having sufficient literary insight to accept a manuscript like *Settlers of the Marsh* and enough guts (I think that was his phrase) to publish it.' In his letter to me in 1945 (from which the above is an extract), Pierce goes on to say, 'The temperance, prohibition and moral reform agencies all climbed over my back when the book *Settlers* came out. They were especially malignant in my own church. And at the height of it the General Manager of the Publishing House lost his nerve ... That [congratulation], coming from Meighen, made the General Manager very happy, and so far as I was concerned the barrage was lifted.'

4 See letter of February 15, 1926, note 3, for a reference to Eayrs' letter.

5 See letter of November 18, 1925, for Grove's extensive comment on the book. His own book, *Settlers of the Marsh*, was sometimes unfavourably compared with *Wild Geese*, which, as has been noted, won the Dodd-Mead Prize in 1925. Reacting to this comparison, Arthur Phelps, in a 'letter to the editor' in the *Winnipeg Free Press*, said, 'If ever there was a piece of well written and promising immaturity constituting a good story it is the $13,500 prize novel *Wild Geese*. If ever there was a piece of seasoned workmanship foot-fast in the gumbo it is Grove's *Settlers of the Marsh*. The Ostenso book is interesting, romantic, unsatisfying.' Novelist Robert Watson, in a personal letter to Phelps, agreed, 'I noticed the controversy in the *Free Press* and I wish to tell you that you are right. Grove's book is a masterpiece, both as a novel and as a slice out of life.'

TO WATSON KIRKCONNELL

Rapid City, Man.
November 15, 1926

Dear Kirk,

Am returning the best books at last. I have lingered over them. Croce[1] anticipates a good deal which I thought I had to say: on Schiller, Vigny, Balzac, Flaubert, Baudelaire. He is everywhere at least stimulating (Leopardi).[2]

Zimmern's *Greek Commonwealth*[3] is a book *I love*. I have put it down on the long, long list of my *desiderata*. By the way, I have sometimes dreamt of writing 2 historical books – with aims somewhat analogous to, though quite different from, Carlyle's *French Revolution*: one on the Peloponnesian War; one on Thomas Cromwell – the two great historical tragedies to which I have profoundly reacted in my life.

As for *Thais*, I cannot, much as I try, enjoy France.[4] What is it? Is he a *vulgarisateur des sciences philologiques*? [5] As pure fiction it simply does not interest me. As ironic persiflage of church history I find it out-lived and weak. As *satanisme* one line of that part of Baudelaire which I look on with suspicion outweighs whole volumes of this sort of thing. Possibly I am simply too old-fashioned. I turn to Vigny with relief:

Dieu! Que le son du Cor est triste au fond des bois![6]

He[7] quotes that line in the *Red Lily* and confounds himself.

Well, let it go. I wonder whether you've got more, old man?

Don't foget that, though the bed which you had has been taken downstairs for myself, there is still a bed available at any time for you – alone or with A.L., or even two for you with A.L. + Mrs P. and Ann.[8]

Yours
F.P.G.

Watch *Tribune* of Nov[ember] 20 for a slightly bolder touch than the last one.[9]

By the way, the bed is still ἀνέκβατος.[10]

1 Benedetto Croce (1866–1952), the Italian philosopher. His *European Literature in the Nineteenth Century* was published in 1924 (New York).
2 Giacomo Leopardi (1798–1837), the Italian poet-philosopher. *The Poems of Leopardi* (tr. by G.L. Bickersteth) appeared in 1923. Grove seems to imply that he found Croce's critique of Leopardi stimulating.
3 Alfred Eckhard Zimmern (1879–1957), the German classical scholar. His *Greek Commonwealth* went through several editions; the fourth appeared in English in 1924.
4 Anatole France (1844–1924), the French novelist, essayist, and satirist, famed for the perfection of his style. *Thais* (1890) and *Le Lys rouge* (1894) came out of his ill-fated love for Madame Arman de Caillavet.
5 A popularizer of language sciences – *philology*, in French, does not have the narrow technical connotation it has in English, and includes all studies requiring the use and understanding of language.
6 'Ah, God! How sad the sound of the [hunting] horn in the depths of the woods' – a quotation from Alfred de Vigny's poem, 'Le Cor' ('The Horn').
7 ie, Anatole France
8 Arthur Phelps, his wife and their daughter Ann; see letter of April (no date, to Lorne Pierce), 1926, note 4.
9 'Camping in Manitoba' appeared, with a photograph of the Grove family camping, in the *Winnipeg Tribune Magazine* of November 20, 1926. This was the second of the twenty-three short stories and sketches by Grove published in that magaine between October 9, 1926 and April 23, 1927. The 'last one' refers to 'The Gypsy Trail.' It appears from the Phelps correspondence that it was he who suggested to Grove the idea of contributing stories and sketches to the *Tribune*.
10 Literally, 'ungetoutable.' Grove was confined to bed with a back ailment, having slipped on a pile of wood in the back yard of his house in Rapid City.

TO WATSON KIRKCONNELL

Rapid City, Man.
November 10, 1926

Dear Kirk,

Thanks for your plentiful provision towards the occupations of my enforced leisure. I am at present reading the book on Greece.[1] Wassermann's book[2] interested me greatly, chiefly as being symptomatic of latter-day outlook. It is weary, despondent; it does not even dare to strive after the great effect. Strange that these men who have insight and artistic power should take the exceptional for their protagonist: the idealist in an environment of the grotesque. That is why I left Europe: it seemed all that was left.

I have not been able to feel myself into A. France. *The*

Red Lily seems trivial, *conventional* to me (of course, in a French sense).[3] I shall read *Thais*.

Croce is interesting in many ways – though I cannot always agree and find many *lacunae* in the work. I wish I could discuss it in detail. But Deacon,[4] the only one who wants any of my views, does not send me such books for discussion.

Remizov[5] I cannot find anything in.

Lastly your own book:[6] I again admire the enormous *comprehension*. The immense amount of material (quite beyond my own power to collect) is most effectively presented. I wish many Canadians would read it. I wish I could pass a bye-law to make every Rapid Citizen read it. It, too, I should like to discuss with you more fully. For, I cannot but disagree with its fundamental tendencies.

As for myself, I do think I am improving at last. I have twice sat up for 1/2 hour, though not without paying the price afterwards.

By the way, Dr. Mulvey[7] (whom you met here) yesterday crossed this street at 11:45, well and lively. He went home for dinner; rose from table at 12:55 and at 1 o'clock was found *dead* by his wife in the parlo[u]r. Such is our insecurity of tenure.

A reviderci as they say in Italy

F.P.G.

1 Zimmern's *Greek Commonwealth* – see letter of November 15, 1926, note 3 – but more probably another book on Greece

2 Jacob Wassermann (1873–1934), the German novelist. Several of his novels appeared (in English) around this time – *The World's Illusion* (1920, 1926); *Oberlin's Three Stages* (1925); and *Wedlock* (1926).

3 Presumably in the sense of following a *literary* convention. For Anatole France and Benedetto Croce, see letter of November 15, 1926, notes 4 and 1.

4 William Arthur Deacon was born in Pembroke, Ontario, in 1890, and educated in Victoria College, Toronto, and the University of Manitoba (LL B 1918). After a few years of free-lancing, he joined *Saturday Night* as literary editor (1922–8), and then the Toronto *Mail and Empire* (1928–36), and upon its merger, continued in the same capacity with the *Globe and Mail*. He was a syndicated book reviewer to Canadian daily newspapers, and contributor to some prominent American literary reviews, including the *New York Times Book Review, New York Evening Post*, and *Saturday Review of Literature*. He now lives in Toronto in retirement. His publications include books of essays on literature and current affairs.

Grove's indication that Deacon sought his views is not borne out by Deacon's recollection; in a letter to me, Deacon writes, 'He only wrote me when he wished to extract information. ... It was a one-way street. I supplied...' (April 25, 1968). However, Grove is referring here to his review articles in *Saturday Night*, two of which are certain: 'The Living Aztec' in *SN* of October 1, 1927, 15–16 (on D.H. Lawrence's *Mornings in Mexico*), and 'Caveat Emptor' in *SN* of December 3, 1927, 212 (on Nordahl Grieg's *The Ship Sails On*).

5 Alexei Mikhailovich Remizov (1877–1957), the Russian novelist, short story writer, and dramatist, who left Russia in 1924 to live in Paris. He wrote from the experience of his

youth, about society from the worm's-eye point of view – a technique introduced and perfected by Gogol, of whom he was an acknowledged disciple. Which of his several books Grove read, we cannot be certain; a translation of his short stories, *The Clock*, had been published in 1924.

6 *International Aspects of Unemployment* (1923)

7 James T. Mulvey (1872–1926) was born in Wellington, Ontario. After graduating from the medical school in Winnipeg (MD 1899), he practised for six years in Minto, and then moved to Rapid City, where he enjoyed an extensive and lucrative practice as a physician and surgeon. He died of a heart seizure.

TO WATSON KIRKCONNELL

Rapid City, Man.
November 25, 1926

Dear Kirk,

I am returning to you the last shipment of books. At first I was a bit astonished to find Sterne's vol[ume][1] in it. However, I came to the conclusion that you wished to 'show up' the rest. Little as I like Sterne, yet it's 'done' – more so than a score of modern vol[ume]s.

Hassan[2] rather disgusted me. It's crude, isn't it? Beautiful verse, etc. I know, I know. But! Do you know Burton's *1001 Nights*? The real thing.

Angellier[3] and Heidenstam,[4] each in his way, don't get me. The Frenchman's poetry is thin, the Swede's homely; and I have always asserted that poetry to which you can apply any qualifying adjective has hardly any right to exist. It must be 'poetry' – or it is nothing.

Remains Masefield.[5] That interested me very much. But, again, I found only the last 2 acts of *Pompey* and Act II of *Nan* quite up to what I expected. Some of them – the *Sweeps* – are just playlets. *The Campden Wonder* is sheer horror – certainly not tragedy. I have a suspicion that the merely horrible must be pushed through into the grotesque to become subject matter for art. Yet I find a few things in this vol[ume] which seemed to make it worth while to read it – apart from the *fact* that I knew nothing of Masefield's.

A word re your economics.[6] No, it was not really your savagery: though I myself think that the problem of the submerged fraction of humanity – which will always be with us – might be handled differently. But – is not the whole thing an attempt at 'symptomatic treatment'? We remove the pain but leave what caused it? By that I do not mean to detract from the value of the book. Perhaps its author could one day point a way to real remedies? 10 y[ea]rs ago I flattered myself that I could do so myself. I have, since, found my life too short. I have given up. The best I can do is to cut down a few more of my old Mss. to publishable form. But you are so much younger than I am. I firmly believe that the root of the evil lies in our system of exchange values. *La propriété, c'est le vol* – somebody has said.[7] But there is a misunderstanding there. What is *la propriété*? Overproduction should be the greatest blessing: it means getting ahead of our needs. It is a curse. What made it so? As nations we live from 'hand to mouth.' The old Incas of Peru knew better. Credit? But by the very nature of things, nothing can be paid for in the future; at least not by nations, not by humanity. But I'm afraid I can't make clear what I mean. Please tell A.L.P.[8] that you are getting letters while he is not because he is not behaving well; I haven't had a letter from him since he was here – though by coming here he made up for many past sins.

I am making very slow progress. When I sit up, – as I do for an hour a day now, my weight seems gradually to increase till it reaches about 5000 lbs. – and then I have to go back to bed.

I have ruthlessly cut the *Search* to one half its former vol[ume]. I hope, Miller[9] will take it that way. I don't like it a bit any longer. I should have preferred to leave [it] till after my death. But, I feel that I have no right to suppress a book which I can bring out; Mrs. Grove is entitled to anything that may somehow further things towards a solution – especially now that I am laid up. This is the 12th week now.

Thanks for the books. As ever
F.P.G.

1 *Tristram Shandy* by Laurence Sterne (1713–68)
2 *Hassan: A Play in Five Parts*, by James Elroy Flecker (1884–1915), originally published in 1922, was re-issued in 1923 with an introduction by J.C. Squire, and again in 1924, with illustrations by Thomas Mackenzie.
3 Auguste Angellier (1848–1911), the French poet and critic, was best known in the latter field for his *Life and Works of Robert Burns* (1893), written in opposition to the views of Hippolyte Taine. Of his poems, the two major collections were *A l'Amie perdue* (1896) and *Dans la Lumière antique* (1905–11). There is no way of knowing which particular book Grove was reading.
4 Karl Gustav Verner von Heidenstam (1859–1940), the Swedish poet and writer, who won the Nobel Prize for Literature in 1916, and was best known for his lyric poetry, the third and greatest collection of which, *Nya Dikter*, appeared in 1915
5 *Prose Plays* (1925) by John Masefield (1878–1967)
6 In *International Aspects of Unemployment*. See letter of November 10, 1926.
7 'Property is theft' – the dictum of the French moralist, Pierre Joseph Proudhon (1809–65), which occurs in his *Qu'est-ce que la propriété?* (1840).
8 Arthur Phelps
9 Henry C. Miller; see letter of November 14, 1926, note 1.

TO WATSON KIRKCONNELL

Rapid City, Man.
December 9, 1926

Dear Kirk,

This note enjoys a unique distinction. It is the first to be penned with myself sitting in a chair – a rocker, at my desk – the first since Sept[ember] 14.[1]

Thanks for your message, with encl[osure].

No, I have not performed any major operation,[2] but a number of smaller ones; and ca. 20,000 diminutive ones. I've inserted one phrase of 6 words to sidetrack the reader who smells autobiography. If I had been able to handle the typewriter, I'd have recast the whole thing in the *3rd* person. However, Miller has suddenly become hesitant. I was expecting something of the sort: like Julia's betrothal his acceptance was 'too rash, too unadvised, too sudden.'[3] So I may have spent 3 weeks worrying for nothing –

Yes, that's my fundamental objection to economics: it's a defence of that which is instead of a philosophical endeavour to reorient mankind. The latter has been attempted only in Utopias which are ... well, utopian. We have to thank all former economics for every violent revolution that has taken place on earth. 'Vested interests' and economics have been synonyms. Of course, a book on economics based on *reason* – that is, one which would attempt to bridge the gap between the real and the ideal – or to accelerate legislation to the point where it would overtake the needs of mankind and forestall revolution – might however go begging for a publisher. But does that matter? As I said, I haven't the foundations – all my knowledge consists of odd shreds or I'd be at it to-morrow. But you! Young and with a rigorous training!

Well, here goes –

Yours

F.P.G.

Bourget:[4] Many fine observations, *but* !! like Wassermann, thin. I don't mean in *action*. You understand me, I suppose. A vitality worn thin: afraid of big conflicts. Afraid of an emotion which shakes and shatters. What a trite, worn-out thing the plot is. And the minor conflicts: a sister-in-law who is a slave to convention: and the man who cannot fight. Why don't they emigrate together if they are worth a tinker's damn?

Tchekov: One of my favourites. With usual felicity you hit upon a volume which I did not know. Since I needed $20 badly I have shamelessly stolen an idea for a Christmas story[5] from him: the first literary theft I have knowingly committed. I felt, since I value Tchekov so highly I could do it.

Rodò:[6] Interesting as coming from Latin America.

Masefield: Well, I am holding the books on his account. I'll say a little more about him next time.

1 He had been ill and confined to bed with a bad back.

2 Miller had asked Grove to cut *A Search for America* to 60,000 words; see letter of November 14, 1926, note 1.

3 The quotation, from *Romeo and Juliet* (II.ii.118), is Juliet's comment on their precipitous betrothal. There was no hesitation, on Miller's part, in his letters to Grove that I have seen; but they are not the complete correspondence. His acceptance was certainly enthusiastic and showed a shrewd literary judgement. It could hardly be described as rash or ill-advised. Miller was, however, rash and impulsive in business matters.

4 Paul Charles Joseph Bourget (1852–1935). His voluminous output included novels, short stories, plays, poetry, and criticism. The reference here is probably to *L'Emigré*, described by its author as a *roman à idées*.
5 'Christmas in the Bush' appeared in the *Winnipeg Tribune Magazine* of December 18, 1926. The story by Anton Tchekov (1860–1904) was almost certainly 'At Christmas Time' (in *The Tales of Tchekov*, translated from the Russian by Constance Garnet, vol. VI, London 1918).
6 José Enrique Rodò (1872–1917), the Uruguayan philosopher, essayist, and educator. His credo, as set down in a single sentence in his *Motivos' de Proteo* (1909), was 'Reformarse es vivir' ('to reform oneself is to live'). Among his other books, *Ariel* (1900) and *El Mirador de Prospero* (1913) enjoyed European fame. His anti-materialism must have appealed to Grove.

TO WATSON KIRKCONNELL

Rapid City, Man.
December 17, 1926

My dear Kirk,

I hope you are not getting impatient or need any of the books. I have started to do a little work of my own once more and am somewhat absorbed in it. So I am still hanging on to Masefield for a little dipping here and there.

Masefield *has* something, and yet my criticism is almost all negative, reluctantly so. *Salt-water Ballads* should be prose; they are anecdotal. The dramatic things, strangely, I like better here than in the other vol[ume][1] – which perhaps argues that I find them lyrical rather than dramatic. Certain of the narrative poems: 'Reynard,' 'Rosas,' 'Right Royal,' 'King Cole' at times get into an epic stride; then, as in 'Rosas,' a side current disembogues into the river and absorbs the interest. In 'Enslaved,' there are magnificent moments, but the whole thing is *râté*. It's too specially interesting as a story; the magnificent moments even disturb: I resent them where the aim is topical. Etc. etc.

Sometimes I feel that here a minor poet rises to major harmonies. At others I feel convincingly that a major poet goes to seed for lack of an appropriate subject which would assist his powers to unfold themselves.

Yet this man has had an aim and has heard voices. And on the whole I can say of him what he says of a ship. He is

'Made half divine to me for having failed.'[2]

Some little things in the sonnets are almost perfect, so that they become a spiritual experience. But no whole poem is: such as there are half a dozen each in Wordsworth, Shelley, Keats; scores in Milton, hundreds in Shakespeare – though I've never found a single one in Tennyson or Browning. Perhaps I'm dense. I don't know.

Yours
F.P.G.

1 See letter of November 25, 1926. This second volume is presumably the *Collected Poems* (1923), which includes those mentioned here.
2 Masefield's 'The *Wanderer*' I 144

TO WATSON KIRKCONNELL

Rapid City, Man.
January 7, 1927

My dear Kirk,

Received the new parcel. Thanks for still thinking of me. Inge's essays[1] I've long been wishing to read. I don't think I agree with much that he writes but it will be stimulating. Pratt's *Titans*,[2] I should have bought were it not for this illness of mine which still continues. I've had a slight relapse which is rather painful. After having been up, during the holidays, 2/3 of the day I'm spending again 2/3 of it in bed. Worst of all, I ascribe it to the painful and expensive treatment I am receiving: electric vibratory massage. I am struggling hard to keep that *Tribune* business[3] going: it, after all, brings more money to my doctors than any books of mine have ever brought to me. However, I remain reasonably cheerful.

Gosse,[4] by the way, will serve to reconstruct a bridge into the more recondite corners of the French literature for which I did battle when I was young. Mallarmé,[5] what a name that used to be to conjure with – yet, almost forgotten. *Sic transit gloria mundi*.

I don't know yet for sure whether the *Search* is coming or not – nor do I care much. But if it doesn't, it is not my fault. I haven't heard from Miller[6] since second week of Dec[ember] when he promised the contract which has not yet arrived.

If ever you feel like coming, just board the train and send a wire – or simply walk in. It won't take more than a 1/2 hour to get your room ready.

Yours
F.P. Grove

Mrs. G. says, both boys,[7] but especially the one, resemble their father.

1 Dean William Ralph Inge (1860–1954), the English theologian and controversialist. His *Outspoken Essays* (2nd Series), which Grove read first (see letter of January 30), appeared in 1922.
2 Published in 1926. It contained 'The Great Feud' and 'The Cachalot,' the complexity and intensity of which established Pratt's reputation as a major Canadian poet. For Pratt, see letter of March 23, 1928, note 1.
3 Grove contributed twenty-three short stories and sketches to the *Winnipeg Tribune Magazine* between October 9, 1926 and April 23, 1927; for details, see the bibliography in my *Frederick Philip Grove* (Critical Views on Canadian Writers 1970).

4 Edmund Gosse (1849–1928), the English critic. The reference here is probably to *Aspects and Impressions* (1922), which deals with English and French literature.
5 Stéphane Mallarmé (1842–98), the founder of the *Symboliste* movement in France. Grove claimed to have attended, in his youth, Mallarmé's famous Tuesday evening *salons* in Paris. The claim, however, cannot be verified.
6 Henry C. Miller
7 Kirkconnell's twin sons, then two years old

TO WATSON KIRKCONNELL

Rapid City, Man.
January 11, 1927

Dear Kirk,

Well, say, more stimulating than irritating? My opinion of Inge's essays was formed from abstracts and discussions apparently written by fools who, being unable to understand, did the next best thing and misrepresented. I had the biggest surprise I've had for some time: I agree. Not, perhaps, with everything. Not, f[or] i[instance] with his estimate of Tennyson, nor of Dickens. But with his outlook and, above all, with his condemnations (machine-age; 'civilization'; 'religion'; 'God'). I have simply devoured the vol[ume] and shall devour more, if you'll be good enough to let me have it. I have read parts of it to Mrs. Grove who says, 'Sounds as if it were in your "Ant-book"[1]' – I don't know whether you've ever heard of my 'Ant-Book' which, for 20 y[ea]rs or so I used to consider *the* book of mine, till one day A.L.P. knocked the conceit out of me by saying, 'A pretty good sermon, that.' Since then I haven't read any of it.

No, the gap[2] last Saturday arose from the fact that a Ms. was lost in the mails. It was, by the way, the other one[3] of the only 2 stories – 'Lost' being #1 – which I'd ever admit into a book of mine. Of most things they print I feel rather a bit ashamed. The fact is, I offer them good and bad; and they infallibly decline the good. The next one, of Jan[uary] 15, I feel particularly badly about; but $20 is too good to miss. After that, I hope they'll bring 'The Rockies versus the Alps' – just a causerie. And then – 4 stories from a discarded part of *Our Daily Bread*.[4] But I don't think I can keep it up: 'inspiration' does not come fast enough: I am a slow worker; and what I've ready, they don't want.

I'm glad to hear that your *Elegies*[5] are making progress towards publication. I hope Knopf takes them. I'll shortly send you a copy of what I didn't say at the convention[6] in August: 'Literary Criticism and its function in National Economy.' I found, after all, that I wanted to write down what I had gathered in a few notes for the occasion.

As for the relapse, or rather 'set-back,' I am now sure it is the treatment; for whenever I omitted it, the back got better; and after every treatment it was slightly worse than after the previous one. I am, therefore, discontinuing it but feel that it has already put me back for weeks.

Yours
F.P.G.

6 Watson, Jamie, and Tommy Kirkconnell. *Courtesy Leonard Grove*

1 Eventually published in 1947 by Macmillan as *Consider Her Ways*
2 The 'gap' refers to the January 8, 1927 issue of the *Winnipeg Tribune Magazine*, in which Grove's weekly contribution to that magazine did not appear. See the preceding letter, note 3.
3 From what Grove says elsewhere (letter to Carleton Stanley, February 21, 1946), I am inclined to believe this was 'Water,' which was published on March 26, 1927. There are three extant versions of this story: the published *Tribune* text; a holograph ms in the University of Manitoba Grove Collection (Box 21); and a typed ms as part of the typed ms of 'Tales from the Margin,' where, in Grove's ordering, it is No. 1 (University of Manitoba Grove Collection, Boxes 13 and 14). 'Lost' was later entitled 'Snow,' and is the most frequently anthologized of Grove's stories.
4 Three of these are certain, being a series: 'The Agent' (January 22); 'The Sale' (January 27); and 'The Immigrant' (February 5) – published under the general title 'Prairie Character Studies.' The fourth could be any of the three Dave Chisholm stories which follow: 'Dave Chisholm Entertains' (February 12); 'The Flood' (February 19); and 'Dave Chisholm, "The Goat"' (February 26). The dates are those of publication in the *Winnipeg Tribune Magazine* in 1927.
5 *European Elegies*, a book of translations from several languages, published in 1928, by Watson Kirkconnell
6 Presumably, of the Canadian Authors' Association

TO WATSON KIRKCONNELL

Rapid City, Man.
January 30, 1927

Dear Kirk,

Thanks for that last shipment.

Saintsbury[1] at first rather antagonised me. I don't like his style and tone; but the book as such is charming.

The book on French lit[erature] of the second half of the 19th century is somewhat futile, is it not? I was glad to read it, of course. But it is hardly more than a text book in its best parts summarizing the verdicts of French criticism. In the second half – beginning with the symbolist school it goes to pieces. F[or] i[nstance], of Rimbaud it gives nothing but an outline of his life; of Mallarmé, an outline of his principles: in neither case do I get an idea of the work they did. The treatment of Verlaine is singularly inadequate. Neither of the authors 'is somebody' – rather a drawback. Still, as I said, to me who live here without a library, it meant much as a refocalisation of much I used to think and to ponder about.

Strange to say, I find the first series of *Outspoken Essays*[2] less interesting, less far-reaching than the second. It promises, to me, what the other keeps. It presents a powerful intelligence at work on comparatively futile problems. What is the Tractarian movement[3] to us today except a *provincially* Oxonian attempt at *revivals*. Much as I like Newman's *Apologia*, in a literary way; I've done with him as a spiritual factor. I did find the summary of Catholic Modernist criticism marvellous in its precision and was glad to find it. But on the whole, I find the vol[ume] too narrowly Anglican. After all, the problem even of the Anglican church cannot be profitably handled apart from the world-problem of materialistic directions of thought. I could wish that Inge could set himself to treat the great problem of honest *doubt*, quite apart from the schism between Science and religion. After all, doubt is and has been, for many centuries, the besetting sin or virtue of western civilizations: why should Pascal[4] be so emphatic in his demand for faith unless his faith was a mere reaction against doubt?

I don't know, of course; maybe I really lack philosophical training. But I'm greatly troubled.

I'll return the books tomorrow or day after. Thanks again. Can I reciprocate in some way?

Yours
F.P.G.

1 Probably *Last Scrapbook* (1924) by George Saintsbury (1845–1933). His *Collected Essays* also appeared in the early twenties.
2 See letter of January 7, 1927, note 1. The first series of Dean Inge's *Outspoken Essays* appeared in 1919.
3 Led by John Henry Newman (1801–90), who began, in 1833, the series, *Tracts for the Times*, to fight for the doctrine of apostolical succession and the integrity of the *Book of Common Prayer*. His collaborators were William Palmer, R.H. Froude, and A.P. Perceval. His famous *Tract* XC (1841), on the compatibility of the Articles with Catholic theology, brought the official ban on the Tractarian Movement. In 1845, Newman joined the Roman Catholic Church, and his *Apologia pro Vita sua*, which deals with his spiritual history in a language of utmost simplicity and sincerity, appeared in 1864. Its immediate purpose was to reply to Charles Kingsley's accusations against Newman, but its literary qualities have proved enduring. Newman is also remembered for the hymn, 'Lead Kindly Light,' composed in 1833.
4 Blaise Pascal (1623–62), the French thinker, scientist, and writer on religion. His *Pensées* (1670) were fragments of an uncompleted defence of Christianity, directed against the free thinkers.

TO WATSON KIRKCONNELL

Rapid City, Man.
February 7, 1927

My dear Kirk,

I am very sorry to hear of your illness. I'm afraid I'm sometimes selfish in not thinking of such possibilities. Since I am afflicted with a major trouble, I forget that others are worried with the minor ones.

How's your book[1] coming along? Any developments yet?

Mine[2] is supposed to be in the press.

Meanwhile I've revised an old production of mine[3] which, I believe, contains some moving scenes. But it is afflicted again with 'the taint.'

I am always glad when I hear that one of my friends is not in sympathy with the ecclesiastic mind. Yet I cannot entirely rest at ease with any form of rationalism. But I must say that the churches do not satisfy me. All I can make out for sure is that I am troubled. I am likely to remain so. I'm afraid it's our lot.

Well, this is just a brief note to say that I hope you're quite all right again.

Yours
F.P.G.

1 *European Elegies* (1928)
2 *A Search for America*
3 Probably *Our Daily Bread*, which was published in 1928

TO WATSON KIRKCONNELL

Rapid City, Man.
February 25, 1927

Dear Kirk,

The most puzzling of the three vol[ume]s you sent me last I found to be *The New Poetry*.[1] Well, I simply read it all through and then I asked myself what remained. Three things stood out: (1) a mood which is not mine and which was not so completely dissolved or so magically illumined as to remain with me henceforth as a potentiality of my own: Hardy's. I have recently read 6 vol[ume]s of Hardy's prose which I did not yet know. His prose, much as I may rebel at such misdrawn things as Lucetta, f[or] i[nstance] in *The Mayor of Casterbridge* – or the externality of destinies in *Life's Little Ironies* or *A Group of Noble Dames* or *Wessex Tales* – or the shallowness of the characterisation in *A Laodicean* – his prose never fails to 'get' me. But his poetry has never 'got' me yet. (2) There was a glorious failure already known to me: Masefield.[2] (3) One poem as such: 'Resurrection' (Lawrence). All else melted into a huge slush. Is the fault mine or that of the 'New Poetry.' To say, as the editor does, that *The Spoon River Anthology*[3] stands in the great tradition seems to me either a truism (ultimately, of course, all things stand in that tradition, can't help but) or a wilful and inexcusable paradox. That is *extensive* stuff – padding for fiction, at best; such padding I'll admit, as perhaps even the great fiction-writer whom we all long for must use; but poetry is, above all, intensive, isn't it? The great tradition, to me, means, leave space and time and similar fallacies behind and get down to rock-bottom. It means, forget about matter and intellect (to use Bergson's distinction) and use your intuition in order to seize upon the *élan vital*. And it also means, in poetry at least, find the *final* form – whatever that may be. It was one thing for 'The Alexandrian Few' who wrote *Ecclesiastes*;[4] another for Dante, no doubt. But, to me, every verse of the former is as perfect and ultimate as

Lasciate ogni speranza voi ch'entrate.[5]

Well, by this time I'm full tilt in Abercrombie's *Idea of Great Poetry*,[6] with most of which I heartily agree – though there are two points which rouse me: his idea of the tragic hero, which remains vague, and his determination to give Dante the highest place. Dante stands very high for me; but appreciably lower (with, by the way Milton, *Ecclesiastes*, Shelley, Keats, Marlowe, Lucretius, to name a few at random as they come to mind) than, let me say, Homer, Shakespeare, Goethe (the latter in spite of his signal failure to make a tragical hero out of Faust: he failed because he was too comprehensive to stop at mere tragedy; and Abercrombie has not begun to feel his way to Goethe's significance which lies in his totality of a spiritual personality, of such enormous 'envergure' as not to have been measured yet. His greatness, by the way, shows nowhere more clearly – though always fragmentarily – as in *Faust* II. *Am farbigen Abglanz haben wir das Leben*[7] summarises the older Modernity as completely as Shakespeare's *Macbeth, Hamlet, Lear*, the renaissance). As for 'the tragic' I have long been wanting to set my own ideas down in one of those little talks which I've been collecting for the last twenty years and which sound so enigmatical to most of those who've heard one or two; Dr. Crawford,[8] f[or] i[nstance]. If the line of life seen by and large runs thus ______________; the hero's line, juxtaposed to it, runs thus: ______________. But life runs on. And the hero's line must return into its line and does it thus: ______________. There's the catastrophe; and it is terrible only when entirely forced: tragic when accepted, acquiesced in, *gut geniessen*[9] as Nietzsche calls it somewhere. When the return into the line of life, catastrophic though it be, is voluntary, is almost in the nature of atonement for greatness, as if greatness were a sin. To be a hero is to be tragic. To call him a 'tragic hero' is redundant, tautologous. That little humans use Othello's strengths as weaknesses in order to pry him down, is quite in line with that reasoning. But I see, I am not, speaking at random, making quite clear what I mean.

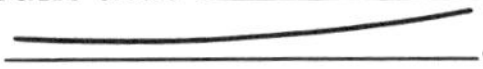

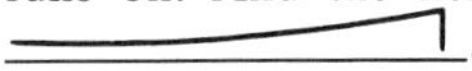

I was going to say more about Bergson; but I have been sitting too long at the desk already and had better lie down again. I'm going to start a second reading of Bergson tomorrow or day after.[10] I'm reading *Paradise Lost* in between. To recover my balance from the shock of *The New Poetry*.

Thanks in any case. I'll return the 3 vol[ume]s as soon as I've reread Bergson. And if I can, I'll say a few words about my reaction to the latter.

How are the 100 elegies coming on? Any publisher's comment yet?

Hope you are quite well again? There's a possibility of

my being (with Mrs. G.) at W[inni]peg at Easter – if I think I can stand so long a trip.

Yours
F.P.G.

1 *The New Poetry*, Harriet Monroe and Alice Corbin Henderson, eds., Macmillan 1917; new and enlarged edition 1926
2 See letter of December 17, 1926, note 2.
3 By Edgar Lee Masters (1869–1915), published in 1921; a 'new edition' was issued in 1925.
4 This book of the Old Testament was once ascribed to King Solomon, but is now thought to be of later date. It exhorts to wisdom, industry, and fear of God; and concludes, as it begins, sombrely, 'Vanity of vanities, saith the Preacher; all is vanity.'
5 The last line of the inscription over the gate of Hell: 'Abandon all hope, you who enter here' ('Inferno,' III.9).
6 Published in 1925
7 'We have life [only] in the colourful reflection [of something greater].'
8 Alexander Wellington Crawford (1866–1933), a Methodist minister who was a Professor of English (1909–30) at the University of Manitoba. He wrote on education and literary criticism, and edited two anthologies of poetry.
9 The phrase literally means 'well enjoyed.' Here it seems to have the sense of 'gladly accepted.'
10 He did reread it: for a long and thorough commentary, see the next letter.

TO WATSON KIRKCONNELL

Rapid City, Man.
March 7, 1927

Dear Kirk,

I hope you haven't been getting impatient over the long delay in returning the books which go out today. That delay – and the character of my reaction to Bergson – is due to the fact that I have read very little post-Kantian philosophy (practically only Schopenhauer; for Nietzsche is no philosopher of the systematic kind) and none at all for the last 15 or 20 y[ea]rs (I mean of new things.)

Now, to me, the value of a philosophic system is largely aesthetic: 'What is *truth*?' But Plato has a value apart from truth. Would you call it wrong if I confess that Plato is 'edifying' to me even where I know him to be in error? I might even go farther and say, for my appreciation of a philosophic system, its inconsistency with other systems is a *sine qua non*. The mystery of this world of ours, as seen with this intellect of mine: that is what I have come to feel at home in: down to Zeno's antinomies of motion.[1] In fact, B[ergson] himself says that pure reason applies only to geometry and logic (essentially playthings even though they have given us the toys of modern civilisation); in other things it 'must be supervised by common sense' – whatever that may be. Well, then, how about letting our needs, or even our wishes supervise it?

I began to read the book[2] with a certain exhilaration; but it soon turned into depression. That may be, of course, because I am just a dilettante – in this as in other things. Yet, in spite of doubts, in spite of the discovery of fallacies, my exhilaration does not turn into depression when I read Aristotle, Plato, Spinoza, Kant.

Now the dictum, 'There are things which intelligence alone is able to seek, but which, by itself, it will never find. These things instinct alone could find, but it will never seek them,'[3] tastes to me of a stage couplet. Is it, on my part, a *parti pris*? How does he know what instinct *seeks*? If it is pessimism I'm after, I prefer an aesthetic pessimism like Schopenhauer's. But perhaps I am simply dense.

Generally speaking, I'm not so sure about instinct. My own, very limited observations – the only ones I have made under scientific conditions were made on ants – lead me to the conclusion that you may just as well ascribe the building of the city hall at W[inni]peg to instinct as, f[or] i[nstance], the careful & scientific fungus-farming of the oecodoma ants of Central America and S[outh] A[merica] north of the Amazons. I have not found anything new, but I have seen observations of Bates,[4] Belt,[5] and others confirmed, and they seem to point to the fact that education, among ants, plays at least the same part as with us – though, as you know, I do not call it education but inducation.[6]

If I am right, the central idea of B[ergson]'s is disposed of: the triple opposition of vegetative, instinctive, & rational life. Yet I believe that the idea of a divergent, instead of a successive evolution seems to me to be a fruitful one, whether true or not. But it is scientific, not philosophic; i.e. essentially useless. What we need is an anti-Baconian *Novum Organum*.[7]

As for the idea of *creativeness* in evolution, I fail to grasp it.

The nervous system as 'a reservoir of indetermination?' My reason refuses. The effect may be disproportionate to the cause (and I am well aware that both words are merely figurative in our use of them), as in the case of the match and the powder-barrel. But without the match the explosion does not occur. Taking the powder-barrel as a mere metaphor, does a vital explosion occur without a match?

But then we are back in frank mechanism; and all things are fore*see*able; for, to a sufficiently comprehensive intelligence the disproportion of the potential explosion is as present as the chain of external events which will bring the match in contact with the powder.

This determinism, contradicted by my *feeling*, I cannot get away from with my reason. B[ergson] wants the *élan vital* to be able to go this way or that way, i.e. as it pleases. But this sort of decision we can study in ourselves; and I have never yet analyzed, with my reason, any decision arrived at, by what I call I, without finding *den zureichenden Grund*[8] – in spite of the fact that, while still in indecision, I had the feeling of freedom.

Feeling & reason are here hopelessly at variance – from which I conclude that either one or the other *must* be wrong: the human dilemma out of which B[ergson] has failed to point the way *for me*. My feeling drives me to the solution of the Schoolmen (*credo quia absurdum*,[9] in a non-religious sense); my reason condemns my feeling because my reason, to itself, seems divine and at one with the *purpose* of creation (even though I deny teleological interpretations). Essentially I stand where we stood before Darwin: and Milton's Satan is I.

Homo faber – I ask myself, in certain sections, whether this book was not, like most economic books, written as a defence of industrial and commercial life. Personally, I believe that a tool invented means a certain amount of physical accomplishment and, therefore, of intelligence, *not gained but lost*. *Homo sapiens* it is, for me: that's what I want to be.[10]

To make the invention of mechanical tools – which to me is a side-issue – the essential characteristic of humanity, seems, to say the least, superficial. Has not human evolution (*true* evolution) stopped the moment invention began? Not even the proof of the Moulin-Quignon quarries holds good. In palaeontological investigations conclusions can, of course, be drawn only from actual finds. And intelligence cannot furnish any other sort of finds but tools, shelters, records.[11]

Oppose to that this consideration: is it the tool-perfection which, in historical times, makes the Parthenon memorable? Or specifically human? Are the Homeric poems primarily interesting to us as testimonies of the degree to which matter had been subdued by 1000 B.C.?

Instinct, on the other hand, as the tool-maker, the *creator* of organised tools is perfectly incomprehensible to me. I can understand the present world as having arisen by a multitude of experiments, all failures being eliminated; but I cannot see how instinct could *create* the eye. That may be because it is a natural antinomy, or because my own intellect is defective. In each case I am back at the point where finalism (teleology) attempts its short-cut: the miracle of creation. But miracles??? I am tempted to subscribe to Weissmann's *Ignoramus et ignorabimus*.[12] In other words, if it is a question of adopting mysticism, I prefer the older one.

However, it has given me pleasure to read the book and to fill a gap in my knowledge; and it has helped me to put in time which has hung heavy on my hands when I had my usual depressions.

This long rigmarole about B[ergson] may make you laugh. I really don't like to speak about such things, for fear of merely exposing my ignorance. Well, if you do laugh, it'll do you good.

How are you? I hope that attack of the 'flu' has left no bad residues? I have, for the last 4 weeks or so, been troubled with a very painful throat.

Yours,
F.P.G.

P.S. I just stumble on to a paragraph which I want to re-read – so I stop in packing the books and postpone it till to-morrow.

1 A series of paradoxes used by Zeno (c500 BC) to discredit the belief in plurality and motion, of which eight survive in the writings of Aristotle and Simplicius. For further details, see H.D.P. Lee, *Zeno of Elea: A Text, with Translation and Notes* (1936).
2 *Creative Evolution* by Henri Bergson (1859–1941) translated by Arthur Mitchell, 1911. The page references, in the following notes, are to the Modern Library edition of that translation (1944).
3 *Creative Evolution* 167
4 Henry Walter Bates (1825–92), the English naturalist, explorer, and author. Grove had probably read his paper, 'Contributions to an Insect Fauna of the Amazon Valley.'
5 Probably Thomas Belt (1832–78); his *The Naturalist in Nicaragua* (1874) was reissued in 1911 (Everyman's Library).
6 In *Consider Her Ways* (frequently referred to by Grove in these letters as the 'Ant-book')
7 *Novum Organum* (1620) by Francis Bacon (1561–1626), a philosophical treatise in Latin, sets forth the method by which knowledge can be universalized. Bacon believed that experience was the source, and induction the method, of knowledge, and by means of knowledge man could extend his control over nature.
8 The sufficient basis (ground)
9 'I believe because it is impossible' – an expression frequently cited out of its context where it appears in a series of paradoxes – Tertullian, *On the Body of Christ*, V.
10 Grove's comments apply to the following passage in Bergson:

> If we could rid ourselves of all pride, if, to define our species, we kept strictly to what the historic and prehistoric periods show us to be the constant characteristic of man and of intelligence, we should say not *Homo sapiens*, but *Homo faber*. In short, *intelligence, considered in what seems to be its original feature, is the faculty of manufacturing artificial objects, especially tools to make tools, and of indefinitely varying the manufacture*. (pp 153–4)

11 The relevant passage in Bergson:

> To what date is it agreed to ascribe the appearance of man on the earth? To the period when the first weapons, the first tools, were made. The memorable quarrel over the discovery of Boucher de Perthes in the quarry of Moulin-Quignon is not forgotten. The question was whether real hatchets had been found or merely bits of flint accidentally broken. But that, supposing they were hatchets, we were indeed in the presence of *human* intelligence, no one doubted for an instance. (pp 151–2)

12 We do not know, and shall not.

It is not clear whether the reference is to the German biologist, August Weissmann (1834–1914). He was noted for his theory of continuity of germ plasm, and for his research in insect embryology.

TO WATSON KIRKCONNELL

Rapid City, Man.
March 11, 1927

My dear Kirk,

I am, today, returning all the books except the Euripides to which I did not get around so far. I liked Mackail[1] much though his treatment of Homer seems inadequate to me, the more so since I've just reread the 1st 3 books of the *Iliad*. I feel flattened out. I can hardly understand how I've been able to read other poetry. I'm going to get myself a complete *Iliad* at once. For over thirty years I've read and reread the *Odyssey* which has always been my favourite. But I am inclined to think that I'll change my mind.

I like Mackail particularly on Sappho, Sophocles, and Simonides. *Ὦ ξειν᾽ ἄγγειλον Λακεδαιμονίοις ὅτι τῇδε κείμεθα τοῖς κείνων ῥήμασι πειθόμενοι.*[2] I agree with him on Pindar who is one of my antipathies.

We still hope to be in W[inni]peg end of the week. I know if we can't go – or the doctors can't do anything for me, I give up. It will be Dante's *Lasciate ogni speranza*.[3] For in spite of my ability to crawl about, fundamentally I am iller than even last fall.

Well, yours
F.P.G.

1 John William Mackail (1859–1945), whose *Lectures on Greek Poetry* appeared in 1910 (new edition, 1926)

2 Simonides' famous epitaph on the Spartans who died defending the pass of Thermopylae against vastly superior Persian forces, in 480 BC:

Go tell the Spartans, stranger passing by,
That here, obedient to their word, we lie.

Grove – or whatever edition he was using, if not memory – appears to read ἄγγειλον, the aorist imperative, instead of the commoner reading, ἀγγέλλειν, present infinitive, which has the very slightly different force of 'you are to tell.' (I am indebted for assistance with this note and translation to Professor R.E.D. Cattley, formerly of the University of New Brunswick.)

3 Already quoted; see letter of February 25, 1927, note 5.

TO WATSON KIRKCONNELL

Rapid City, Man.
March 23, 1927

My dear Kirk,

Thanks for thinking of me again.

I have so far read Wallas' *Great Society*.[1] To me its greatest value lies in the fact that it shows me that others, too, are troubled by the same problems that trouble me; though often it is not the writers themselves of the books I read. You know how reading branches out. For thirty years I've been sitting in my corner and thinking – and the world has gone on. It is pleasant to see that, in spite of all, I've arrived at points where I am not alone; and that, though I can't say what I'd like to say, others perhaps can. Have you any Chesterton[2] or any Belloc?[3]

Yes. I believe that ultimately aesthetics and ethics are at one. They are two roads to one goal. And no cosmogony or theology or metaphysics can help us along the way.

You know, sometimes I feel that I absolutely long to spend another year or two, before I die, in Europe. As I get old, I find the isolation and solitude of this western country almost too much to bear. I have often thought I'd like to go to China or India – but I begin to realise that life is too short for me to assimilate another perfectly strange civilisation. But Europe, since the war, has changed. It seems curious to me that I should, at last, look upon Europe as my true home, at the very time when the *Search* is to appear which is tinged with the violent dislike for Europe of my youth. I can forgive those people, the French, the Italians, the Germans, the Swedes, the Norwegians even their squabbling and fighting when I see how seriously they strive and long after the ultimate things. I am homesick for them.

Yours
F.P.G.

1 *The Great Society* (1919), a critique of the American way of life by Graham Wallas (1858–1932). The title was later to enjoy resurrected fame as the keynote phrase of Lyndon B. Johnson's presidency.
2 Gilbert Keith Chesterton (1874–1936), the essayist, critic, Roman Catholic polemist, biographer, and all-round man of letters
3 J. Hilaire P. Belloc (1870–1953), the French-born English essayist and critic

TO WATSON KIRKCONNELL

Rapid City, Man.
March 29, 1927

My dear Kirk,

Being engaged on a little 'stunt' myself, namely the task of rewriting 2 or 3 of my little sketches in French & German,[1] brings to mind your 'stunt'[2] – as I have heard it called. I do hope most sincerely that Milford[3] will be interested. It would be splendid. But it is, of course, best to preserve a skeptical attitude. Nobody knows that better than I do. On the other hand, it seems, one must never feel discouraged. I don't really know how I should have felt ten years ago if any one had told me that by the end of 1927 I should have 4 vol[ume]s on the market. Sometimes, no doubt, I should have thought, 'Is that all?' But...

It occurs to me that perhaps we may occasionally feel

encouraged by hearing of difficulties that others have gone through. A day or two ago I received a letter from Calgary in which my correspondent told me how much she had felt encouraged by listening to Roberts'[4] talk at the C[anadian] A[uthors] A[ssociation]. Now I don't think I could ever persuade myself to entertain an audience for a whole evening by complaints. But, humorously, a word now and then ... I thought of the nadir of my own discouragements, after 15 y[ea]rs of attempts. I wrote to a publisher, asking whether the offer of such and such a work would be welcome. He replied, 'Ship it along. I've been looking for just that sort of thing.' Now comes the joke. I had no Ms. fit to send out. And I had, in my typewriter, a ribbon which would no longer yield legible print. I might have waited 2 weeks or so, and I'd have had the money to buy a new ribbon. But I was afraid I might lose a possible chance. So I started typing, running line for line three times through the machine. Thus, by the cumulative action of the exhausted ink, I produced a Ms. which could be read, working day & night, for ten days, Sunday included.[5] When Mr. publisher had read the Ms., he returned it with a printed rejection-slip. The Ms. was of the *Search*, by the way. That is now about 10 y[ea]rs ago.

When you do feel discouraged, you should every now and then read the last sentence of Dr. Weeks'[6] opinion on your volume.

Has Knopf had the offer?[7]

I am in my second reading of MacKail.[8] Have you an annotated *Iliad* which you don't need? I am homesick for that sort of thing. I have the *Odyssey* and have long been waiting to get a good text of the *Iliad*; but I haven't the cash.

I am crawling about, but full of pains. Hope to be in W[inni]peg by April 15 at night.

Yours sincerely
F.P.G.

1 No such manuscripts exist in the University of Manitoba Grove Collection. So far as is known, Grove published nothing in French or German – but of course Felix Paul Greve published a good deal.

2 *European Elegies* (1928), a book of translations from several languages

3 Humphrey Sumner Milford (1877–1952), publisher to the University of Oxford. He edited the Oxford Poets editions of Cowper and Leigh Hunt.

4 Charles G.D. Roberts (1860–1943). Born into a distinguished New Brunswick family (Bliss Carman was a cousin of his, and his mother's family traced its lineage back to the grandfather of Ralph Waldo Emerson) and educated in that province, he lived in the Maritimes until 1897, when he went to New York. In 1907, he left America for seventeen years abroad in England and the Continent, which period included war service. He returned to Canada in 1925, and settled in Toronto.

Roberts was a voluminous writer, having edited the first *Canadian Who's Who*, and written guide and travel books as well as original fiction and verse, for which he is best known. His animal stories were immensely popular in their day, and many of them are still in print. Roberts' *Selected Poems*, edited by me, appeared in 1956 and, in a new printing, in 1974, and editions of his *Letters* and *Collected Poems* are in preparation.

5 See *In Search of Myself* (pp 359–61), in which the recalcitrant publisher is named as that of the *Saturday Evening Post*. From time to time critics have dismissed the episode as impossible on the ground that to retype a page, once out of the machine, would be an impossibility. But Grove makes clear here that he meant a line-by-line retyping which, although laborious, is quite possible.
6 Raymond Weeks (1863–1954), then Professor of Romance Languages and Head of the Department in Columbia University. Kirkconnell, in response to an enquiry, offers this explanation: 'He was one of the international panel to which I had submitted all of my originals and translations before I approached a publisher, and he was enthusiastic over the Romance group.' (received March 20, 1972)
7 Kirkconnell's negotiations with Alfred A. Knopf fell through, and *European Elegies* was eventually published in 1928 by Graphic Publishers Limited of Ottawa.
8 *Lectures on Greek Poetry* (1910; 1926) by John William Mackail – see letter of March 11, 1927 for an earlier reference to the same book.

TO WATSON KIRKCONNELL

Rapid City, Man.
August 1, 1927

My dear Kirk,

You will have wondered at not having received word from me for so long. Many things have happened. For various reasons *my* operation was postponed. Instead, my little girl[1] has had to undergo an operation for appendicitis and died under the ether. Since then we have been homeless; and only yesterday had we the courage to face matters here. I am still exceedingly taken up with the various matters arising from her death– they seem to be a last link. Apart from that our own lives seem extinct.

Quis desiderio sit pudor aut modus
Tam cari capitis.[2]

I am sure you will forgive our taciturnity. Nobody can quite understand what this means to us.

Yours
F.P.G.

1 Phyllis May, born August 5, 1915, died on July 20, 1927, in a hospital at Minnedosa while undergoing treatment for acute appendicitis.
2 The first line and a half of Horace, *Odes* I.18, which is a lament on the death of his friend, Quintilius Varus – 'What restraint or limit should there be to grief for one so dear?' The word, *desiderium*, here translated as 'grief,' means literally 'longing' or 'desire,' and connotes deep and intimate affection. (I am indebted for assistance with this note and translation to Professor R.E.D. Cattley.)

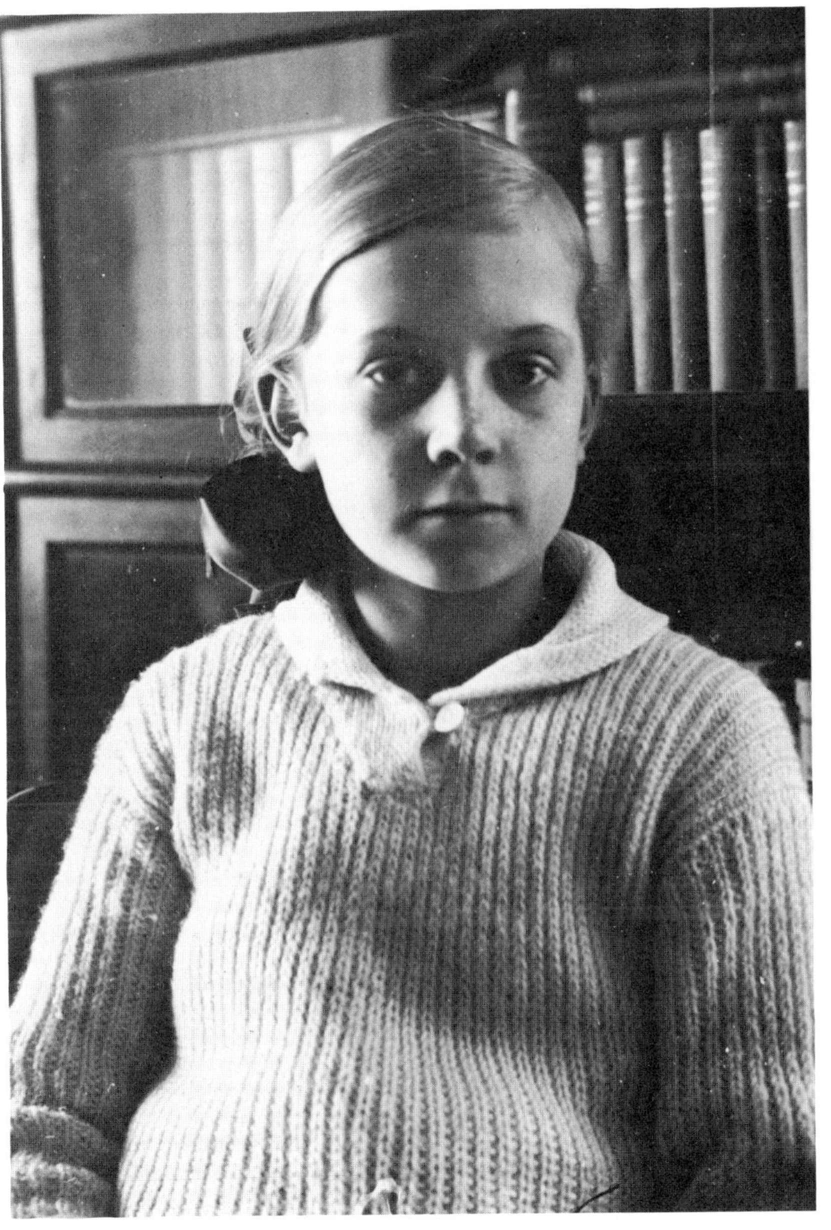

7 Phyllis May Grove 1926. *Courtesy Leonard Grove*

TO GRAPHIC PUBLISHERS, 175 NEPEAN STREET, OTTAWA, ONTARIO

Rapid City, Man.
September 6, 1927

Dear Sirs,

Will you please take notice that, by reason of your failure to bring out an edition numbering at least 2000 copies of my book *A Search for America* on or before May 1st 1927 (See par. 5 of our contract) I consider that contract as cancelled and hereby withdraw the Ms. which I would ask you kindly to return to me at once.[1]

I might add that this withdrawal is [in] no way to prejudice any further action of mine, legal or otherwise, which I may deem necessary to protect my interests.

Yours truly,
F.P. Grove

1 As previously stated (see note to letter of November 14, 1926), the story of Graphic Publishers, and of Grove's relationship with them, is sketchy. Correspondence between Grove and Miller, however, gives some clues.

Miller's letter of January 17, 1927, mentions an audit at Graphic: a hint of trouble to come, which descended in full force on August 31, as Miller recounted four days later:

> You will be receiving a startling communcation some of these days, if you have not already received it, stating that in future Graphic will be handled by Messrs. Davisson and Burland. This is the culmination of several months of wrangling, and I was definitely ousted from any connection with Graphic last Wednesday evening [August 31]. The whole thing started last March, and I have been trying in every possible way to secure control, but when you are up against monied people, and have none yourself, you can be rushed off your feet before you realize it.

Grove's reply (see the following letter) was sympathetic, but he reiterated the cancellation and withdrawal of the ms, citing previous unfulfilled promises in Miller's letters and adding, 'At that time you were in full control.' Miller was hardly defeated, however – he goes on to promise Grove that he would stage a come-back. (By what means, we do not know, but on October 10, 1927, he writes: 'Since my return to the charge of affairs of the company on September 18th...')

Matters were, however, patched up, and *A Search for America* was published late in 1927.

TO H.C. MILLER

Rapid City, Man.
September 8, 1927

Dear Sir,

I cannot, of course, at this distance fully appreciate the details. For your information I might say that I have withdrawn my imprimatur from the Graphic Publishers. All I want out of this unspeakable mess is my copyright. I do not want to see the book appear at all.

But, may I call your attention to the following extracts from the file of my correspondence with yourself?

Nov[ember] 13, 1926. 'We are announcing this for *Spring*.'

(The only thing I had insisted on as essential was spring publication as you may remember. You may not have approved of that. The fact remains that I gave you the Ms. on condition that the book be published in spring.)

Dec[ember] 11, 1926. 'This will acknowledge receipt of the Ms. of the *Search for America which will start on the machines next week*.'

Jan[uary] 17, 1927. 'Type setting *starts this week on it*.'

Contract, dated Jan[uary] 8, 1927.

(5) 'The publisher undertakes to place a first edition of the book of at least 2000 copies on the market by *May 1st, 1927*.'

This I considered too late; but, seeing how things were going, I accepted it as an utmost limit.

At that time you were in full control; the contract, therefore, was broken by yourself. What, in view of the fact that the book is not out today, shall I think of your statements of Nov[ember] 13, Dec[ember] 11, Jan[uary] 17?

Now I do not say that, after further investigation, I may not humanly excuse you and be willing to do further business with you. But the fact remains that I was all along being fed with promises which were not kept. To say nothing of that $500 which apparently you had no right to offer.

As I said, for the moment I am interested in nothing except in regaining absolute control over my book; which means that I shall not sign any of my rights away.

As for the operation, it was not made. In view of the fact that I had a death in my family,[1] my health seems quite irrelevant to me.

Yours truly,
F.P. Grove

1 Grove's daughter, Phyllis May, died on July 20, 1927; see *In Search of Myself* 390–1, and letter of August 1, 1927.

TO GRAPHIC PUBLISHERS, OTTAWA, ONTARIO

Rapid City, Man.
October 4, 1927

Dear Sirs,

Letter after letter of mine re *A Search for America* has remained without answer. On Sept[ember] 6 I gave notice that I consider our contract as cancelled. On Sept[ember] 12 I made an alternative proposal through Mr. Burpee[1] – not to mention several letters previous to these dates.

I beg to say that by Oct[ober] 10 I shall consider further silence on your part *as consent to the cancellation of the contract* as demanded by myself on Sept[ember] 6. There is, naturally, an end to any patience. On that date I shall consider myself at liberty to enter into other arrangements.

Yours truly
F.P. Grove.

1 Lawrence J. Burpee (1873–1946) was one of the directors, and literary advisers, of Graphic Publishers Limited. He entered the Canadian Civil Service in 1890, but remained active in literary circles, having published, in 1904, *A Bibliography of Canadian Fiction*, and, in 1926, *Encyclopaedia of Canadian History*. *The Search for the Western Sea*, his best-known book, appeared in 1907 (reissued in 1935). The letter to Burpee referred to here appears not to have survived.

TO WATSON KIRKCONNELL

Rapid City, Man.
October 7, 1927

My dear Kirk,

Just a suggestion. If A.L.P.[1] and you would rather come together, well and good, of course. But would it not, perhaps, if you wish to come, facilitate arrangements, *for yourselves*, I mean, to come singly, one at a time? Not that to us, at this end, any – even the slightest – inconvenience would arise from the combination of the two visits; but, even as far as we are concerned, their separation would give us something to look forward to on *two* occasions instead of one.

As for Miller, I don't know anything directly. I don't care particularly. He has not answered a letter of mine since May.[2] But I understand he has no money to carry on.

Thanks for the 5th article.[3] Well, yes, I suppose that sort of thing is bound to be tabloid – yet it will help to show up the 'champion nation of the world' as our neighbours call themselves.

Tell A.L.P.,[4] please, I'm sorry to hear he has been ill.

Now, mind, don't debate too long – let the Monday program go and plunge.

Mrs. G. joins me in the repetition of my invitation; and her baby sister[5] who is with us would like to see a living man who has translated poetry from forty or fifty languages. She is doing some 2nd year Arts work with my help.

Yours
F.P.G.

P.S. I liked the Pushkin translation best.[6]

1 Arthur L. Phelps; see letter of mid-April (no date, to Lorne Pierce) 1926, note 4.
2 Miller did write to Grove on September 4, 1927 (see note 1 to letter of September 6, 1927). However, Grove was interested in a reply to his notice of September 6, 1927, that he considered his contract with Graphic as cancelled. Miller's letter was an explanation of his failure to bring out *A Search for America* by May 1927, and dealt primarily with his own situation in the Graphic organization. Clearly Grove did not regard Miller's letter of September 4 as a reply to his repeated request for the return of the ms.
3 Presumably, Kirkconnell's 'Research into Canadian Rural Decay' (in *Eugenics Review*, July 1926)
4 Arthur L. Phelps
5 Amanda Wiens, now Mrs Bert Mather of Calgary, at that time a girl of 16
6 Presumably a reference to Kirkconnell's translation of a poem of Alexander Sergivich Pushkin (1799–1837), the first national poet of Russia. The translation in turn served as a model for Kirkconnell's own 'The Drifting Corpse' (in *The Flying Bull, and Other Tales*, 1940). See Watson Kirkconnell, *A Slice of Canada* (1967) 49.

TO WATSON KIRKCONNELL

Rapid City, Man.
November 11, 1927

Dear Kirk,

This is just a note to tell you that, after two severe acute attacks of appendicitis, I was, yesterday, taken to the Bigelow clinic[1] in Brandon. After an examination, the doctors declared that an operation was unavoidable; but, in the then condition of my abdomen, would have to be postponed till Friday, next, Nov[ember] 18. To their disgust, I insisted on being shipped back home where I am treating myself with starvation. I promised to be in Brandon General Hospital on Thursday, Nov[ember] 17, at 11 a.m. to go under the knife on Friday morning 8 a.m. Thus, you see, the fates are not exactly kind to us. Mrs. G. who was along is greatly upset, of course.

I am returning all books so there will be no trouble about them in case ... As for the French anthology, I have greatly enjoyed it, but find that it suffers from the weaknesses of all anthologies: it gives rather the striking thing than the good or great. To me, outstanding are still the figures that stood out in the nineties when I lived in France: Mallarmé, Verlaine, Verhaeren, Regnier.[2] And even there I find a life in artificial worlds. More than by anything else I was struck by the overshadowing of the present by the past (Louis XIV – Versailles, *les fauves*,[3] etc.) (That is an abominable sentence; but my temperature seems to be too high to write clear English.) Life is lived in figures of speech rather than directly. If that is *symbolisme*, I prefer *Les Parnassiens*[4] who were perhaps sometimes frighteningly direct. But Verlaine, at least, is more than a *symboliste* though he does not appear so in this book. As for the rest of them, *c'est plutôt de la poésie touchante que de grande poésie*.[5]

Rhythm[6] interested me greatly. I see as I have so often seen – for the lack of books and, perhaps, of a formal education, that I had set out to discover things which others had done before me. More than ever I incline to shrug my shoulders at certain modern excrescences. However, *Wenn sich der Most auch ganz absurd geberdet Ergiebt zuletzt doch noch 'nen Wein*.[7]

I understand the *Search* is out. But I have not heard or seen anything about it. Somebody said he had seen a review in *Saturday Night*.[8] Have you?

Well, so much for that. If you should write after Wednesday Nov[ember] 16, please address c/o General Hospital, Brandon.

Since I am not able, just now, to do much writing, and since A.L.P.[9] has not written for an age, I would ask you to let [him] see this sheet. I am glad you were here recently. Mrs. G. will go along to Brandon; taking leave of absence here at the school.

Yours as ever
F.P.G.

1 Probably the first medical clinic in Canada, established by Dr Wilfred Abram Bigelow (1879–1966) in 1900. Bigelow's book of reminiscences, *Forceps, Fin and Feather*, edited by his son Dr Wilfred Gordon Bigelow of Toronto, was published in 1969.

2 Poets of the French *Symboliste* movement, of which Stéphane Mallarmé (1842–98) was the acknowledged leader. Henri de Régnier (1864–1936), who was elected to the French Academy in 1912, was also a significant novelist. Émile Verhaeren (1855–1916), the Belgian poet of the cult of humanity, wrote most of his works in French. Paul Verlaine (1844–96) was distinguished for the musical quality of his verse. For Grove's alleged attendance at Mallarmé's Tuesday evening *salons*, see letter of January 7, 1927, note 5.

3 A short-lived movement in art, ultimately leading to cubism. At the 1905 Salon d'Automne in Paris, a group of artists, led by Henri Matisse (1869–1954), offered the first collective exhibition of their paintings, which were characterized by the use of brilliant pigments instead of light and shade. The movement came to be known as fauvism when Louis Vauxcelles, a French art critic, dubbed the group *les fauves* ('the beasts').

4 A group of French poets, headed by Leconte de Lisle (1818–94) and Théodore de Banville (1823–91). They derived their name from the anthology to which they contributed: *Le Parnasse contemporain* (1866, 1871, and 1876), edited by Xavier de Richard and Catulle Mendès. They turned away from contemporary society towards exotic past

civilizations, notably to ancient Greece and India, and valued impersonality, technical perfection, and pictorial quality in verse.

5 It is sentimental, rather than great poetry. *Touchante*, like the English 'touching,' implies a certain superficiality.

6 Edward Adolf Sonneschein, *What Is Rhythm?* (1925)

7 Even if the must behaves quite absurdly, it finally produces wine. *Geberdet* is archaic; the modern usage is *gebärdet*.

8 The review by W.A. Deacon appeared in *Saturday Night* of December 3, 1927 – see also letter of December 7, 1927, note 1. Grove, it seems, knew about it in advance, presumably through Deacon.

9 Arthur L. Phelps who, as I well know, was an extremely reluctant correspondent

TO WATSON KIRKCONNELL

Rapid City, Man.
November 30, 1927

Dear Kirk,

Thanks for your recent note. You have probably heard that I was once more shipped back home. Things are dragging along. I am suffering; the colon seems to be inflamed throughout its length. But the reason why the operation was postponed is the condition of my chest. That was hard on Mrs. G. because it was, for her, proof positive of the blunder made on July 20.[1] I, of course, had never doubted that. That chest condition is unchanged, so I am not going into Brandon this week.

I am doing nothing, of course. I have done little since you were here except burn mss. But, in putting things into order, I found that there are 4 vol[ume]s which I should want to publish, and 3 more which I should release if there were any demand for my stuff. The balance – some 5 or 6 vol[ume]s more I'd burn if I could. One or two vol[ume]s are still unwritten. That's all I've done in a life of nearly 60 y[ea]rs.

I'm reading Wordsworth's *Prelude* – no very strenuous diet, eh? I have recently reread Masefield – little there, after all, that will endure, though he has some lovely things – too lovely. I believe we should face a pessimistic period in poetry. The mess in which science has left things will have to be cleared up – though I won't deny that it has focussed our eyes on this life here.

By the way, who is Sassoon or Sasson?[2] I ran across a fragment the other day, at the clinic, in Brandon, reading over somebody's shoulder – a fragment that happened to catch my eye.

As ever
F.P.G.

P.S. Should you hear or read anything about the *Search*, will you pass it on?[3]

1 Grove's daughter, Phyllis May, died on that date. See letter of August 1, 1927, note 1.

2 Siegfried Sassoon (1886–1967), the First World War and post-war poet, and author of *Memoirs of a Fox-Hunting Man* (1928)

3 ie, reviews of *A Search for America*, which had just been published

TO WATSON KIRKCONNELL

Rapid City, Man.
December 7, 1927

My dear Kirk,

Thanks for your note. Have you seen Deacon's effusion in the Lit[erary] Sec[tion] of the *S[aturday] N[ight]*?[1] I am most curious to see it; but have been unable to get hold of a copy; and he did not send me any.

The reason why I am curious to see it is that W.A.D.[2] has almost bullied me into (financial) concessions to Miller with talking of what he was going to do for me. I had the impression that, surely, he must be himself interested in the 'Graphic' venture. I, since Burpee[3] who had promised to look after my interest left me in the lurch, had at last no choice, ill as I was, but to let them do as they pleased.

The trouble is, it is 2 mo[nth]s too late. I do not expect anything from the Christmas trade. In fact, I believe it would have been good policy to wait till January now. But it can't be helped.

I am absolutely in bed, suffering pain, and unable to rise. Since it means having myself shipped to Brandon in the express car when I want a doctor's opinion – or paying from $25 to $50 to have one come up, I am entirely in the dark as to what may be proceeding within that abdomen of mine. I have not eaten anything solid since Nov[ember] 11. Yet even a draught of broth brings agony.

However, I am still alive and kicking. If the *Search* had been out in Spring and got into its stride, I should have been able to remain at Brandon when I was there. As it is ... But it's no use complaining. I'm even working feverishly.

Yours
F.P.G.

(I've just sold the least-prized part of my library to buy medicines with the proceeds. The remainder will probably have to follow.)[4]

1 The review appeared in *Saturday Night* of December 3, 1927 and is reprinted in my *Frederick Philip Grove* (Critical Views on Canadian Writers 1970) 119–20.

2 W.A. Deacon; see letter of November 10, 1926, note 4.

3 Lawrence Burpee, who was, at this time, one of the directors of Graphic. See letter of October 4, 1927, note 1.

4 It would be interesting to discover where Grove sold his books. It was not, I am informed, to the most likely purchaser, the University of Manitoba Library.

TO WATSON KIRKCONNELL

Rapid City, Man.
December 13, 1927

Dear Kirk,

Miller acknowledged in Sept[ember] that our contract was void.[1] Asked for a new one when he got back into the saddle. We made a contract, stipulating for advance payment of royalties on copies *printed*, not sold. I considered that I was entitled to that since the book had been delayed through none of my fault. This Deacon induced me to waive – or rather not to object if Miller simply did not act on it.

Mrs. G. will write Irwin.[2] I don't 'cotton' to him.

Thanks for the books. I spent a sleepless night browsing in the German anthology. A few remarks. The three undoubtedly leading poets are missing. Stefan George[3] (whose *Der Teppich des Lebens* I wish you'd read and *buy*, to loan to me. Or *Das Jahr der Seele*); Rainer M. Rilke;[4] and Richard Dehmel[5] ('Schon nascht der Star die rote Vogelbeere'). Instead, Ludwig Fulda[6] (an 'Epigone' of the classic period, facile and shallow), Otto Ernst[7] (vulgar, shallow, sentimental) and others take up the space.

On the whole, however, the *survey* seems good. Preoccupation with mechanics. Vollmoeller[8] (a disciple of George and d'Annunzio[9]) 'Die Riesin'; 'Die *Fabrik* des Herrn' by Ginzkey;[10] even in nature: 'Zwischen Glockenblumen glanzt *Bahn*geleise.' I can't convince myself that the accidentals of our so-called civilization have a legitimate place in lyric poetry. I don't find the accidentals of Greek civilization in Simonides or Sappho. They are, of course, in the epos, but as accidentals: they do not form the theme. The theme is *Man*. Much of this is 'homey,' too, *spiessburgerlich*,[11] I believe they call it, bourgeois to the second power, especially where it tries to be unconventional. The only thing *great* that I've run across – and it, being overloaded with ornament, is not *very* great – is Hugo v. Hofmannsthal's[12] 'Verganglichkeit.' His 'Manche freilich' is pretty, ornate, even stately in places: marvellous in its careful elaboration – but? artificial!

Presber's[13] 'Totenschädel' I find impressive; but I thought of Goethe's 'Im ernsten Beinhaus war's'[14] – and it seemed artificial. There is a young Jew by name of *Bab*[15] who may have something to say, though he seems rather *zerrissen*.[16] Why write of 'Die Dirnen' when you are not a Baudelaire. Yet I liked lines in his 'Deutschland.'

These are random notes. Very interesting to me. Conclusion: there is no genius growing up in Germany, unless the anthologic principle works: genius is excluded. It would jump out of the page; it would disturb the balance.

The other book I have not yet looked at.

I've been reading Saurat's *Milton*[17] – very interesting.

Also Croce's *Aesthetic*[18] which seems to me to deal in futilities, except the fundamental thesis with which I agree: 'intuition' = 'expression' though expression is not necessarily verbal, of course.

I *rather* liked Deacon's review, though it made me smile.

It should help to sell 2 or 3 copies.

Miller's 'list' makes me fully expect that he'll be bankrupt before I get any royalties out of him.

Well, this will have to do for a rambling chat.

Yours

F.P.G.

1 I have seen no letter from Miller to this effect; but the complete correspondence is not available. For a résumé of the correspondence, see previous notes on Graphic in the letters of November 14, 1926 and September 6, 1927.

2 Most probably William Arthur Irwin (b 1898), now publisher of the *Victoria Daily News*. A graduate of the universities of Manitoba and Toronto, he was, in 1925, appointed Associate Editor of *Maclean's Magazine*. In 1943 he became Managing Editor, and, in 1945, Editor; after which he went on to head the National Film Board (1950–3), and Canadian diplomatic missions in Australia, Brazil, Mexico, and Guatemala (1953–64). He is a co-author of *The Machine*, an ice ballet, and is married to the poet P.K. Page.

3 Stefan George (1868–1933), whose *Der Teppich des Lebens* was published in 1899, and *Das Jahr der Seele* in 1897

4 Rainer Marie Rilke (1875–1926), who is considered by many critics to be the greatest lyric poet of modern Germany

5 Richard Dehmel (1863–1920), the German lyric poet. The first collection of his lyrics, *Aber die Liebe*, was published in 1893, and this was followed by *Weib und Welt* (1896) and *Zwei Menschen* (1903).

6 Whose reputation as a poet is not considerable; he translated Molière into German, and wrote *Der Talisman* (1892), one of the most popular plays of the time

7 Pseudonym for Otto Ernst Schmidt (1862–1926), a minor German poet who wrote two successful plays, *Jugend von Heute* (1900) and *Flachsmann als Erzieher* (1901)

8 Karl Gustav Vollmoeller (1878–1948), the pioneer of the film, industrialist, amateur pilot, and world traveller, was born in Stuttgart and educated in Paris, Berlin, Athens, and Bonn. He lived for a while after 1919 in Venice, and then moved to the United States. Noted chiefly for his plays – the most successful being *Das Mirakel*, staged by Max Reinhardt in Berlin – he wrote a volume of verse, *Parcival: Die frühen Gärten* (1903). His hectic reputation as a neo-romantic poet has faded rapidly.

9 Gabriele d'Annunzio (1863–1938), the Italian poet, novelist, and dramatist, who broke with classicism and introduced the new inspiration of foreign writers such as Hugo, Baudelaire, Dostoyevsky, and Nietzsche. In his later years, he abandoned aestheticism and his international reputation and became the national prophet of Italian imperialism.

10 Franz Karl Ginzkey (B 1871), the Austrian poet and novelist. His neo-romantic lyric poetry is remarkable for its interweaving of symbolism and folk-songs (*Das heimliche Läuten*, 1906; and *Befreite Stunde*, 1916).

11 commonplace, bourgeois

12 Hugo von Hofmannsthal (1874–1939), the Austrian poet and playwright. Grove's assessment of his promise has been confirmed by modern scholars. Ernst Rose, in *A History of German Literature* (1960), says, 'During his life-time, only a few poets and artistic friends realized his greatness. ... A more general conception of Hofmannsthal's singularity is emerging only now' (p 291).

13 Rudolf Presber (1868–1935) was born in Frankfurt and in 1889 moved to Berlin, where he published the magazine *Uber Land und Meer*. He wrote novels, plays, poetry, and biographies.
14 Goethe's famous poem, inspired by Schiller's skull
15 Julius Bab (1880–1955), the drama critic (*Chronik des deutschen Dramas*, 1911; *Das Theater der Gegenwart*, 1927) and biographer (*Richard Dehmel*, 1926; *Albert Bassermann*, 1928). He emigrated to the United States in 1933.
16 disorganized, ragged, lacking unity
17 Denis Saurat's *Milton: Man and Thinker* (1925)
18 Presumably in Douglas Ainslie's translation (1909; second edition, 1922)

TO WATSON KIRKCONNELL

Rapid City, Man.
December 14, 1927

My dear Kirk,

I have now, not only browsed, but grazed. And have found nothing to change my view about [the] modern German lyric. I find three currents; apart from the *Epigonen*[1] (like Fulda): (1) the Stefan George circle; but I must say, the disciples are weak mirrorings of the master; (2) the Mombert-Arno Holz circle[2] which I abominate; (3) the ultra-moderns, with Unruh,[3] Hasenclever,[4] Johst,[5] etc. ('Expressionists') who are most remarkable for what they have in them of *Chaos*. Scattered among these, both of older and younger, I find a few physiognomies: Hofmannsthal, Bab,[6] etc. But, come to reflect, God is said to have created the *world* out of Chaos.

As for Boyd:[7] journalism. Immense compilations. Little depth. I'd value it for the information if I could trust it. Of course I can verify very little. His article on *Gide* makes me very little confident; strangely, he discusses Gide just as far as I know him (*La Porte étroite*[8]). Gide's latest work I have not read.

This is characteristic (page 176): 'It will be a thing *without* sound and fury, signifying nothing…'[9] That he got his quotation mixed up, did not strike me till I had puzzled for some time over the non-sense. It is like that. Even were I inclined to trust the man – he has not troubled to *organize* his material. I have rarely read anything that made me so distrustful – in spite of the fact that I sometimes agree with him (Unamuno, Verga – whose *Mastro Don Gesualdo* is, to me, enormous – Papini, Proust, Brandes, Reymont), though I disagree rather more frequently (D'Annunzio, France, two of my antipathies, Spitteler, Bojer, Larsen, etc.).[10]

I'll return the vol[ume]s as soon as I get a chance.

Am a little easier, which may be a good sign and may be a bad sign.

Yours
F.P.G.

1 The plural ending is German, although the word is a pure Greek formation and an

English version (same spelling) does exist. The same word is used, again of Fulda, in the preceding letter. It means a second-rate follower, or imitator.

2 Alfred Mombert (1872–1942), sometimes called the 'German Blake,' wrote lyrics of great power and a strange fantasy. He was, in the words of one critic, 'a distant volcano' who remained 'in the regions of phantasmagoria.' Arno Holz (1863–1929) was a leading figure in the growth of naturalism in German literature, demanding of art 'unswerving consistency in the exact reproduction of nature.' It is odd that Grove should lump two authors, so different from each other, in a single group.

3 Fritz von Unruh (b1885), the Prussian poet, novelist, and playwright, who was converted to pacifism following his experience as a Prussian officer in World War I

4 Walter Hasenclever (1890–1940), the German impressionistic poet and dramatist

5 Hanns Johst (b1890), one of the 'Dichter des heimlichen Deutschlands' – his reputation has suffered since the defeat of the Nazis.

6 See preceding letter, note 15.

7 Ernest Augustus Boyd (1887–1946), *Studies from Ten Literatures*, 1925 (reprint issued in 1968)

8 By André Gide (1869–1951), published in 1909; the German translation by Felix Paul Greve, entitled *Die enge Pforte*, also appeared in the same year (Berlin: Reiss).

9 The sentence, which is the concluding one in Boyd's essay on Giovanni Papini, continues, 'but the fact that Giovanni Papini can "sell" the New Testament story of Christ to a Protestant country which professes to regard the English Bible as one of its priceless possessions and deathless literary heritages.'

10 The authors mentioned here are discussed in Boyd's *Studies in Ten Literatures*:
Don Miguel de Unamuno (1864–1936), the Spanish novelist and essayist, was one of the most influential thinkers of his time. His philosophy is summarized in the only formal exposition he wrote, *The Tragic Sense of Life* (1913).

Giovanni Verga (1840–1922), the Italian novelist, whose *Mastro-Don Gesualdo* (1888) (English translation by D.H. Lawrence) was the second volume of a projected pentalogy, of which only the first two were completed.

Giovanni Papini (b1881), the Italian polemist and editor, who wrote *The Life of Christ* and an autobiography, *The Failure*. His *The Dictionary of a Savage* (written with a collaborator) ruffled many American feathers, including Boyd's.

Marcel Proust (1871–1922), the French novelist

Georg Brandes (1842–1927), the Danish critic and scholar, whose *Main Currents in Nineteenth Century Literature* (1901–5) was, paradoxically, both praised for being cosmopolitan and internationalist in outlook, and condemned for being 'too negatively nationalistic.' His mission, as he conceived it, was to bring Denmark out of its cultural isolation.

Wladyslaw Stanislaw Reymont (1867–1926), the Polish novelist. His four-part novel, *Chlopi* (1902–9; in English translation, *The Peasants*, 1924–5), may have suggested the plan for Grove's 'The Seasons' (unfinished). He won the Nobel Prize in 1924.

Gabriele d'Annunzio; see preceding letter, note 9.

Anatole France; see letter of November 15, 1926, note 4.

Carl Spitteler (1845–1925), the Swiss poet. He won the Nobel Prize in 1919.

Johan Bojer (1872–1959), the Norwegian novelist of naturalism and a contemporary of Knut Hamsun

J. Anker-Larsen (1874–1957), the Danish actor, playwright, and novelist; his best-known work, *The Philosopher's Stone* (translated from the Danish by Arthur G. Chater, New York 1924), is considered to be 'a modern epic of religious unrest.'

TO WATSON KIRKCONNELL

Rapid City, Man.
January 24, 1928

My dear Kirk,

I'm sorry to hear about your teeth. I am going to have 2 out shortly myself.

Thanks for Huxley's book.[1] I'm writing some articles for MacLean's New Magazine for Women!!![2]

I'm glad to say that I have had some easier days. I had a big surprise from Doran. *Settlers* have been reprinted: sale at Christmas 1927 copies – I hope in 1928 they'll sell 1928 copies – or more.

1925: 302 copies in the U.S.A.
1926: 357 "
1927: 1927 "

Total sale (including Canadian) of *Settlers* to-date 3,685 copies – not bad, it seems. But, from what I hear from Toronto, the *Search* is at a stand-still. Did you, by chance, see the big review of it on Jan[uary] 14 in the *N.Y. Times*?[3] I'd like very much to get hold of it.

I hope Miller will bite; but he's a moron.

Glad to hear *Aestus vitae*[4] is on a trip. Good luck to it.

Yours
F.P.G.

1 Probably *Essays New and Old* (1926) by Aldous Huxley (1894–1963)

2 *Chatelaine* was begun in 1928, published by Maclean-Hunter. Nothing identified as by Grove appeared in it during 1928–30, but he may have used a pseudonym. This writing was probably undertaken as a result of his contact with Arthur Irwin (see letter of December 13, 1927).

3 It appeared in the January 15, 1928, issue of the *New York Times Book Supplement* (IV, 2:2), and is reprinted in my *Frederick Philip Grove* (Critical Views on Canadian Writers 1970) 121–2.

4 A literal translation of the title of Kirkconnell's first book of his own verse, *The Tide of Life*, which was not published until 1930.

TO WATSON KIRKCONNELL

Rapid City, Man.
January 31, 1928

My dear Kirk,

We have not heard from you and Phelps for so long that we are worried. Anything seriously wrong? How is A.L.P. taking the thing; and Mrs. P.[1] As I said, we are worrying, knowing how much there is wrong at that end. But also about yourself. How about those teeth. I know a person does not feel like writing when there is anything wrong; but just a line – a postcard. It adds to *our* worries not to hear a word.

I have read Huxley's *Essays*[2] and find a good deal in them that is *good*. But does he not make the fundamental mistake to assume that science *explains*? I also doubt whether I agree with his position re evolution – man as the *conscious* furtherer of the process as traced out for him in the records of the rocks. I have an idea that man's 'evolution' stopped when he transferred his vital energies to *tools*. You may call *that* evolution instead of the organic process, of course; but my suspicion is that with the first tool invented (a club or a stone) a devolution began, organically; and I am much afraid that, with the 'Press,' radio, etc. that devolution has already extended to the brain. Thinking is becoming a lost art, as walking has already become: I mean, of course, among the large substratum of life from which, in the future generations, the thinkers must spring. I have not been able to convince myself that the age of invention either has enlarged or improved man's brains or that it has given evidence of considerable previous growth. Inventing is rather a mechanical thing. Edison is – to my mind – not a great man; the moment he talks of things outside his special sphere, he betrays himself. Just as the 'learned' man of former ages was largely the ant carrying sand grains. He was the owner of many sand grains; but he did not know what to do with them. All mere knowledge has always waited for the philosophic genius to be interpreted: and all previous interpretations have, after a while, been disproved – which did not lessen their value. To me, let me say, Thucydides is still a great man; so is Plato. But, when I look about today, I fail to find one of their calibre.

As usual, I find much in the book overlapping with my own thought. I plan three lectures: Science, Religion, Art. I am very anxious to go out and meet people. But I must make those meetings *pay*. Only, what in the world could I lecture on that will draw people? With the *literary* (?) success of the *Search* the time would perhaps not be ill chosen. Mrs. G. urges me to go east while Amanda[3] is with her. Next year we shall be alone. But I don't know – even if otherwise it were feasible – how to go at that sort of thing. Whenever I think of it, I see myself standing at [the] cor[ner] of Yonge & King St[reet]s[4] offering handbills to the passers-by in which I announce a lecture and solicit attendance.

Well, send us a line, will you.
Yours as ever
F.P.G.

I keep Huxley for rereading.

1 Watson Kirkconnell 'vaguely remembers' that the Phelpses' daughter Ann (now Mrs J.D. Hamilton of Toronto) had contracted a serious contagious disease and had to spend some weeks in an isolation hospital. Grove, in view of his own tragic experience in losing a daughter, would worry even more than the Phelpses did. Arthur Phelps, Kirkconnell adds, 'was the world's worst correspondent, and his silence would intensify Grove's anxiety.'
2 *Essays New and Old*; see note 1 to the previous letter.
3 Amanda (Wiens) Mather
4 A main intersection in the city of Toronto. These sentences are the first hints of the lecture tours to come.

TO WATSON KIRKCONNELL

Rapid City, Man.
February 5, 1928

My dear Kirk,

Well, you have our sympathy, old man. It all sounds like a perfect terror. I hope the worst is indeed over?[1]

Yes, A.L.P. wrote me about that Can[adian] Club business. I'm frankly afraid of it. However, there is no true courage without fear. The rest is foolhardiness.

You say there would be no heavy financial return. Will there be any? Will the thing pay its way, seeing I cannot at present ride the rods, both on account of my health and the season? I hate the publicity which is personal: but I suppose I can't get it for my book in any other way.

Don't bother about the *N.Y. Times* review.[2] Somebody – a lady by name of Mrs. Thomas[3] – sent it to me.

Now do pull up all hidden springs of vitality and recover, will you?

Yours
F.P.G.
I'm still keeping Huxley, unless you need the book?

1 Kirkconnell's letter of February 2 covers the matters referred to here. He was having a rough time with his teeth, and extraction, even limited to three teeth a week, led to heavy suppuration and hemorrhages – 'One tooth in particular broke off deep down the jaw and had to be quarried out; an eight-hour hemorrhage followed, which was finally blocked in desperation in a midnight session at the dentist's; violent internal suppuration followed, but the dentist was afraid to lance for fear of starting another blood-flow; hence I lay about in impotent distress from Friday till Wednesday (yesterday) when the pus-pocket opened up of its own accord and brought relief. ... The worst is now over.'

He then goes on to speak about the proposed lecture tour which Grove undertook, starting February 27: 'By strange coincidence, your letter* suggesting lectures and travel came by the same mail as one (to Art) [Arthur L. Phelps] from Graham Spry, national secretary of the Association of Canadian Clubs, enquiring as to the possibility of getting you to give a series of addresses under their auspices right across Canada. There would be no heavy financial returns from such a trip (or tour) but the publicity value would be very real, likewise the psychic stimulus of meeting people and recognition from Halifax to Victoria.' (*See the preceding letter, paragraph 3.)

2 See letter of January 24, 1928, note 3. Kirkconnell had tried unsuccessfully to secure a copy of that review for Grove.

3 I have been unable to identify Mrs Thomas.

B

A Great Celebrity: The Trans-Canada Lecture Tours 1928-9

'I was introduced at both meetings as the "nationally and internationally outstanding author – a great celebrity."'
TO CATHERINE GROVE,
MARCH 1, 1928

TO CATHERINE GROVE

Hotel Portage
Portage La Prairie, Man.
[February 27, 1928][1]

My dear Tee,[2]

Got here nicely. Club sent taxi to station and had engaged room for me. No bath, though. Chest is clear; nose gives no trouble. That's absolutely all I know unless I am to copy my address out for you. Am going to wear tux[edo].

Bye-bye
Phil

1 Date supplied by Mrs Grove, who adds the note that this was Grove's first day out on his first lecture tour. He started out on crutches, after a long illness in bed with back trouble.
2 This endearment which, Mrs Grove states, her husband told her meant 'mistress' in Chinese, he uses only in letters addressed to her – and, very occasionally in reference to her elsewhere.

TO CATHERINE GROVE

Hotel Portage
Portage La Prairie, Man.
February 27, 1928 II
9 p.m.

My dear Tee,

I'm through with no. 1.[1] Quite a success, I believe. But that blamed address takes 2 hours to deliver. I spoke 1 hour and had to leave half of it out and to hurry through the last quarter.

Of course, I was all in a sweat when I got through. So I have just, very carefully, changed clothes. Am going out to have supper – boiled fish. (Met *Miss Suttis*[2] here who's boiling the fish.)

That's all for tonight.
Bye-bye
Phil

1 ie, his first lecture, this being the second letter of the same date, written after his speech; often Grove would write two (separately mailed) letters in a day; at other times, add a postscript to say how the evening had gone.
2 Of whom nothing more is known; presumably an official of the host club. Mrs Grove adds that she was 'a perfect stranger who, for some reason I cannot remember, offended him.' There are many such references to people Grove met in this way on his tours, who simply cannot be traced, and of whom Mrs Grove had, understandably, little or no knowledge.

TO CATHERINE GROVE

Millers' Lodge,
Keewatin, Ont.
February 28, 1928.
2:30 p.m.

My dear Tee,

Well, I'm in luck. Came down here on the chance of finding this more restful than Winnipeg, and find a most charming little hotel, really homelike where I can take good care of myself. The weather is beautiful, too. Chest is clear, nose open. This by way of a bulletin of health.

Now, my dear, this is important: I want you to find for me in one of the Bulletins of the P.E.N. Club an address. Find a section headed *France*. At the end of it a sub-section '*Traducteurs*.' In it sub-sub-subsection: '*Editeurs et Libraires*' or something to that effect. In it a title like this: *La Nouvelle Revue de France* – or *La Nouvelle Revue Française* or simply *Revue de France* or *Revue Française*. Also *Mercure de France* or *Le Nouveau Mercure de France*.[1] Anything that seems to fit please copy out. Send, at once, addressed to myself c/o Mr. Graham Spry,[2] 55 Metcalfe St[reet], Ottawa.

Besides, please tell me in same letter all you know about Metcalfe.[3]

Miss Suttis[4] came last night at 11 p.m. to fetch me for supper. She found me gone to bed and asleep. I refused to go out. I wasn't hungry. A.L.P.[5] met me at Eaton's this morning, helped me shop, and then rushed off to college, after having put me in a taxi.

I got a nice Gladstone bag for $16.75. You probably have Gardiner's[6] by this time. My 50¢ studs broke the first evening. Had to buy new ones. Local secretary just called. Nice people here, it seems.

Well, bye-bye
Phil

1 If Grove was planning to write or submit some articles or translations for either of these periodicals, nothing, so far as is known, came of it. He had, perhaps briefly, been engaged in rewriting a few of his 'sketches' in French and German; see letter of March 29, 1927. The project was probably interrupted by his uncertain health, the preparation of *A Search for America* for publication, and, above all, by the death of his daughter in July 1927. But with his confidence restored by the success of the lecture tour, he might have been urged to resume it. There is, however, no known publication by Grove in French under his own name.

Le Mercure de France, a literary review founded in 1890, was the rallying ground of the French symbolist school. In 1893 it incorporated a publishing house, which was to issue for many years André Gide's books. *La Nouvelle Revue française* was founded in November 1908, by André Gide and his friends.

2 Graham Spry was born in St Thomas, Ontario, in 1900, and educated at the University of Manitoba (BA 1922), Oxford University (BA 1924), and the Sorbonne (1924). He was, from 1926 to 1932, National Secretary to the Association of Canadian Clubs, and organized, on

behalf of the Association, Grove's three lecture tours. In 1934 he went to England to take up executive appointments with a number of petroleum firms. During World War II, he was a sergeant in the British Home Guard and War Correspondent to the London *Times* and the Ottawa *Citizen*. He served, from 1942 to 1945, as Personal Assistant to Sir Stafford Cripps, then British Minister of Aircraft Production. In 1946, he participated in an economic survey of Turkey. He became, in 1947, Agent-General for Saskatchewan in London, retiring in 1967. He organized, in 1930, the Canadian Radio League, of which he is a Life Member, and has published several articles on broadcasting policy in Canada. He now lives in Ottawa.

3 Presumably Grove was interested in knowing something of the man after whom Graham Spry's Ottawa street was named – Charles Theophilus Metcalfe (1785–1846). He came to Quebec in 1843 as Governor of the Province of Canada and Governor-General of British North America. His term was one of continuous conflict, for the British Colonial Office instructions were firmly against any concession of responsible government, the very principle on which the existing Canadian ministry took its stand. Metcalfe deliberately ignored the legislature, and, despite ministerial resignations, was vindicated in the elections of 1844. He died of cancer.

4 See letter of February 27, 1928 II, note 2.

5 Arthur L. Phelps

6 Edgar Samuel Gardiner (1884–1951), a real estate agent, neighbour of the Groves in Rapid City, and for some years Chairman of the School Board there.

TO CATHERINE GROVE

Millers' Lodge,
Keewatin, Ont.
February 29, 1928

My dear Tee,

Have just spent 10 minutes threading a needle and 5 min[utes] sewing on a button on my gaiters – as I prefer to call them. By calling my new bag a Gladstone bag I proclaim myself as English.[1] Also had a delicious hot bath.

I had not been here long, yesterday, when I was found out. So I had to go for a car-ride through the country: it is *very* beautiful: a place to build in. Then I looked over one of the famous Backus power plants.[2] At night some people wanted to take me to a show (cinema); I wriggled out of it. But 9:30 Dr. Baker, vice-president of the C[anadian] C[lub] fetched me to a reception. I got home at 11 and slept till 6. Then lay in bed till 7. Breakfast at 8. Just now, when I sat in the hot water, more people called. But I couldn't go. It's very amusing, for the circular which I haven't seen yet, apparently proclaims me as the celebrated Mr. so-and-so. Yet they call me 'Groves,' 'Grave' and 'Graves.' Only the 'Frederick Philip' they remember.

By the way, wherever I go, they talk about the Carillon Book Club.[3] Those people surely spend the postage. And it seems, people subscribe. I saw a new circular of the thing last night, with my 'mug' as the doctor called it all over one page.[4] Everybody here is violently anti-U.S.A. So there's a topic with common ground for me.

It's really *very* beautiful here. This afternoon I am going to be taken over the Lake of the Woods Flour Mills.[5] At the hotel, all things are, of course, charged to the C[anadian] C[lub]. I can get what I want. The hotel-keeper has orders to 'take good care of me' – and he does. When I say 'fish' – he has a fresh trout caught for me. Poor fish!

I wish you could be along. Here, too, the women are in rebellion and have simply demanded that they be invited for to-night. I've written to Kirk,[6] asking him to send you *Esther Waters*.[7]

Well, that's all for today, I suppose.

Tonight I speak from 7 to 8. At 9 I take the train to F[or]t William. The car with my berth will be kicked off at F[or]t W[illiam] and I can stay in bed as long as I like.

Yours
Phil

1 Grove, of course, is posing as an English aristocrat on a visit to the colony; hence, the use of the slightly archaic word 'gaiters,' and 'gladstone,' a hold-all bag named after a British Prime Minister (W.E. Gladstone).

2 Edward W. Backus (1863–1934), a native of New York, was the principal developer of the Rainy River country. The Norman Dam, built in 1892 by the Keewatin Power Company, was acquired by Backus and Brooks Company in 1913 and converted for power purposes. Evidently, this was the development Grove saw on February 28.

3 The Club was the idea of Henry C. Miller of the Graphic Publishers Limited (who handled *A Search for America*). C.C. Knight, a personal friend of Miller, was President, assisted by a selection committee of L.J. Burpee, E.W. Harrold (1889–1945) of the *Ottawa Citizen*, and James Pedley (1892–1945), author of *Only This – A War Retrospect* (Graphic 1927). Knight ordered 500 copies of *A Search*, and as of the beginning of February 1928, had mailed half of them. The Grove book was the Club's first selection. See also letters of March 11 and 15 II, 1928.

4 A circular advertising *A Search for America*

5 The town and its flour mill may well have provided Grove with the germinal idea of *The Master of the Mill*. He told W.J. Alexander on August 10, 1939 that he began to write that novel in the summer of 1929.

6 The letter, to Kirkconnell, if it was written, has not survived.

7 A realistic novel of lower class life (1894) by George Moore (1852–1933)

TO CATHERINE GROVE

The Avenue Hotel,
Fort William, Ont.
March 1, 1928

My dear girl,

Yes, I know. It must be lonesome. But not as bad as when

I was in the hospital. I had 3 meetings today. Noon luncheon, Men's. 4:15–5:30 Women's club + F[or]t William Teachers' Association – 150 ladies. It's a roaring success, all right. Had also what is called 'a good press' – but Spry[1] wants that; and I can't procure another copy. I was introduced at both meetings as the 'nationally and internationally outstanding author – *a great celebrity*.' In the evening they lugged me to a Kiwanis meeting. I told these that by my contract I could not speak; but I'd tell them some stories. Kept them laughing for about 20 minutes – they roared. Then I slipped away, taking 'French leave.' It's 8 p.m. now and I'm ready to go to bed.

Too bad I didn't have those passes[2] sooner. I've already spent $30. Well, my dear, I simply cannot get along with my baggage. I'll ship our old suitcase home and must buy myself a larger one. Baggage gets more bulky all the time. Shirts new are nicely folded into small space. But I can't close the darn things any longer. Also, people give me folders and booklets and so on ... I'll send you my underwear[3] tomorrow: that will give a slight relief. Come to think of that, I may try it once more. But the farther I go, the more it will cost to express the suitcase back. However ... Well, I'm dog-tired and 'll go to bed.

Bye bye
Phil

1 Graham Spry

2 Railroad passes, obtained by Grove at Graham Spry's suggestion, to save the Association of Canadian Clubs some money. There is a letter in the University of Manitoba Grove Collection from J.M. Gibbon, General Publicity Agent of the CPR, to Grove, dated June 23, 1928, which in part reads, 'When the time comes, we can fix up transportation over our Lines, in view of your newspaper connections.'

3 In the days before every large town had its laundromats, this presented quite a problem in logistics for Grove, who was seldom in one place long enough to make use of conventional laundries, and was in any case trying to save as much as possible. The result was an intricate series of postal arrangements, as is evident from other letters. How he managed as regards shirts is not so clear – partly by the same method, partly by buying, one gathers.

TO CATHERINE GROVE

Prince Arthur Hotel,
Port Arthur, Ont.
March 2, 1928

Well, my dear, I've got this far now. Am waiting for the lady president of the Women's C[anadian] C[lub] to call on me. Had a half day's absolute rest by pretending in F[or]t W[illia]m that I was leaving early in the morning and telling people here that I should arrive about 3 p.m. That turned the trick.

As far as travel goes, this is the way. Room with bath. Give orders. Taxi when I go out. Call in the stenographer when I write to other people, etc. Shall send my underwear tomorrow morning – by the bell-boy.

Probably I can, before I leave here, give definite directions where to forward it. Montreal Women's Club wired me this morning, asking me to speak to them on Mar[ch] 17. So I shall. The lady who drove me over this morning and who was in the plot about my escaping from the F[or]t W[illia]m crowd, said to me, 'Well, now, Mr. Grove, that you are *rich and famous*, surely you don't mean to go on living in the country? You'll move to Toronto or Ottawa or Montreal, won't you?' I just smiled to myself. It seems such a hollow show. I asked in the bookstore at F[or]t W[illia]m how many copies of the *Search* they had ordered – '6 copies' – 'How many have you sold so far?' – 'THREE.' Marvellous, isn't it?

But late last night a Mr. W.A. Wilson,[1] H[igh] S[chool] Inspector for North-Western Ontario, called on me, saying that farther east I'll set my audiences aflame with my talk. 'Don't change a word,' he said. The people I meet have usually read one or two of my books. He had all four. Which was one for him.

I dropped the Gardiners[2] a line yesterday – thought they'd feel tickled. I'll tell them here I'll leave tomorrow morning. But I'll wait till Sunday morning. This hotel suits me. With my underwear out of the way, my baggage will do me a few laps farther. Till, I suppose, I shall have to buy new underwear. I understand the Teachers' Association of the twin cities which I addressed jointly with the Women's C[anadian] C[lub] will present me with some silver. I'll see. Well, Mrs. Spofford[3] – that's her name – is due. So I'll stop.

Bye-bye.
Phil

Darn my collars! They're all too wide. I'm sorry I spent $4 on them.

1 A graduate of Queen's University (BA 1897), he was Public School Inspector for the cities of Port Arthur and Fort William (now Thunder Bay) from 1925 until his retirement in 1936.

2 E.S. Gardiner and his wife; see letter of February 28, 1928, note 6.

3 Martha Jane Spofford (née Stewart; 1868–1944), a pioneer resident of Port Arthur. Born in Orillia, Ontario, she came to Port Arthur with her father as a young woman, and married Robert G. Spofford, one of Port Arthur's first meat dealers. She was active in church and community work from the early days of the town until her death in 1944 at age 76. During Grove's visit, she was the President of the local Women's Canadian Club.

TO CATHERINE GROVE

Prince Arthur Hotel
Port Arthur, Ont.
March 2, 1928 II

Well, my dear, just had one of the experiences of my life – found out what I can do with an audience when I set my mind to it. For a while I had thundering applause after every sentence.

8 Catherine Grove. *Courtesy Leonard Grove*

The women said they had never lived through anything like that before. A man,[1] inspector of schools said, I gave more in one sentence than any speaker he had ever heard had given in an hour. I'm sure I sold my books here. 'I am no orator as Brutus is'[2] doesn't hold good any longer.

Well – And so to bed.
Phil

1 W.A. Wilson; see preceding letter, note 1.
2 *Julius Caesar* III.ii.221

TO CATHERINE GROVE

Prince Arthur Hotel,
Port Arthur, Ont.
March 3, 1928

My dear Tee,

Have just given orders to mail my underwear. Don't return it till I send further directions. The *next* underwear I'll need, I'll buy at Ottawa, together with another club-bag. Teachers' Ass[ociation] of F[or]t W[illia]m sent me last night a cigarette case – as I expected – as a small token of gratitude for my 'truly inspiring' address. I'm getting into my stride, knowing my address by heart – though I keep remodelling it as I go. I speak now without the ms, though I have it with me.

It is, after all, quite an experience. All these hundreds upon hundreds of people whom I meet and who all insist on shaking my hand when I get through and on whispering their name to me – hoping that they'll be the privileged ones to be remembered. Last night was rather a triumph – I spoke well because they responded. Of course, rumour had preceded me from F[or]t William. Also, the hall was small enough so that I could save my voice for the big effects. I believe I wrote you about this once before, last night. But if I didn't – when I came to the statement of what I found in the west, there was applause after every sentence – then breathless silence, then the thunder again. When I got through, I was exhausted; and they made me rise and thank [them] for the applause by a bow at least a dozen times. It was quite an ovation. I do hope it'll sell the book.[1]

They think I'm gone to Sudbury – only one man knows I'm still here; and I've invited him to have lunch with me today. I'm supposed to leave tonight for Sudbury. But I'll trust to the train's being on time and wait till tomorrow morning 6:09. That will take me there shortly after midnight on Monday morning and I'll have two good nights of rest. I turned my lights out at 11:30 last night and awoke at 5. It's exciting, you know.

I was in hopes of having a letter this morning, from home. But there was nothing. The more I see of this, the more I am convinced that I must go through with it. Financially, I believe, it'll be our salvation. All these people who now know me will want to read my next book, too, when it comes out. And they all want me to come again next fall.

I do hope I'll have a letter from you at Ottawa anyway. I just received my itinerary for next week. I'll speak at Smith's Falls, south of Ottawa, and at Belleville, on Lake Ontario. Shall spend 1 1/2 days at Ottawa: Wed[nesday] and Thurs[day] till 1:35 p.m. The only rush will be at Smith's Falls where I arrive at 2:37, speak at 3:00, leave at 5:00 to reach Belleville where I stay over the Sunday. So, Belleville will be a week-end address for *March 10*.

Well, so long, my dear. Kiss.
Phil

1 ie, *A Search for America* – this was, of course, the main point of the lecture tour which, as Grove later complains, brought him little by way of direct financial return: the fee per lecture was $25.

TO CATHERINE GROVE

The Nickel Range Hotel,
Sudbury, Ont.
March 5, 1928

Just hear that yesterday's storm has been by far the worst of the year; all trains except the one I came on were many hours late. That was luck – for I was shaving time pretty closely by remaining at P[or]t Arthur overnight instead of taking the night train.

One of the towns in which I was to speak this week, Port Hope, burned down to the ground in that gale.[1] The paper says that out of 1000 buildings no more than 6 are left. That will mean a change in my itinerary, I suppose.

This is a mining town, of course. Everywhere you see evidence of it. You listen in where a group of men is talking and it's all about speculation in mining stock. Shall mail this tonight, after my lecture. – –

In between the vice-president of the Club called. She's a dunce. Didn't even know my name. But sat down and talked for an hour, boosting the town. Drat her. – –

Well, I had got that far but no farther when the Rotarians ('service' club as they call themselves; 'booster' club as I call them – like Kiwanis) kidnapped me; and I had to give them a short 20 minute talk – quite informal. It's amusing enough in a way, but tiresome. They wanted me to stay till tomorrow morning; but I refused, saying I *must* get to North Bay tonight which isn't really true. But I'll get my night's sleep anyway if I make the 2 h[ou]rs run tonight.

And now I've got to dress up for the afternoon ladies' meeting. So bye-bye.

Well, it was the least enthusiastic meeting I've had. A bunch of old ladies. It was mostly over their heads. However, I've sold the book I believe.

It's train-time.
So bye-bye
Phil

1 Trinity College School at Port Hope, not the town, was burned down. See letter of March 15, 1928 II.

TO CATHERINE GROVE

Ottawa, Ont.
March 8, 1928

My dear Tee,

In a terrible rush. Got your letters. Return underwear c/o Spry, 55 Metcalfe.

The enclosed notice please give to *Stone*.[1] It's news for you, too, of course. 'It' has started, all right. As for me as a speaker, Senator Hardy[2] said to me, 'You start speaking; and the banquet hall *is a church*!' Quite a compliment, isn't it? I was told that over *100 Million Dollars* were sitting at the board. Have several invitations for the summer. Have, also, contract Coward-McCann, New York, for *Search*.[3] Also offer to open 1929 with speaking tour in New England at *Boston*.[4] Contract with Spry calls for tour Sept[ember] *1st* till Dec[ember] 22. Christmas to be spent at Ottawa, guest of Senator Hardy – you to come down or up. We'll stay here till Jan[uary] *1st*; if money available, you come with me from then on. Had invitations from Vancouver, Calgary, New York. Things are happening fast. Must get down-town for luncheon with the executive of the C[anadian] C[lub]s. Got $50 for short story.[5] Orders for *Search* come in by wire from all points where I have spoken. Miller[6] is not as bad as he is painted. But – – – –

Bye-bye
Phil

Shall write more fully from smaller places. Too much of a rush here.

1 Cooper Stone (1886–1957), owner and editor of the *Rapid City Reporter*. He was born in Melbourne, Derbyshire, and went to school in Derby. In 1900, he went into the book-binding business as a 'glue boy,' and then worked for six months as an apprentice compositor before training as a blacksmith. He came to Canada in 1907, and found work as a blacksmith in Rapid City. Later he took a job on the weekly newspaper. In 1911, he formed a partnership with Henry C. Clay and bought the weekly from C.H. Jackson. He edited the paper, with the help of his son Oswald (who still edits it), until late in life. He was

a member of the school board during the Groves' stay in Rapid City, and later served as Mayor for three years. By all accounts, he was highly regarded by the Groves – Mrs Grove in a letter quotes Carleton Stanley as having said, 'Stone is sterling,' and herself remarks, 'a fine person.'

2 Arthur Charles Hardy, PC, born in 1872, was a barrister and agriculturist. In 1922, he became a Liberal senator. His father was a former Premier of Ontario. He died on March 13, 1962. For Grove's account of their friendship, see *In Search of Myself* 428–9.

3 Coward-McCann did not publish any of Grove's books; see letter of March 14, 1928 II, note 2.

4 Nothing came of it.

5 Presumably for 'Drama at the Crossroads' in the *Canadian Nation* (April 1928) 14–18

6 Henry C. Miller of Graphic; see letter of November 14, 1926, note 1.

TO CATHERINE GROVE

On board train
Ottawa/Smith's Falls
March 9, 1928

My dear Tee,

Will you please mail me at once 1 copy first ed[ition] of *Over Prairie Trails*. My mss. were stolen from me (by press people);[1] and I borrowed a stenographer from the International Joint Commission. She took dictation and typed the whole thing over for me. She's a very intelligent woman and I can't offer her pay. So I told her I'd give her a 1st ed[ition]. Address c/o Spry.

You received my wire I suppose. Signed up London and New York (the latter on 10%, the former on 5% – they will sell at 6 shillings).[2]

Till I write or wire, I shall be back at Ottawa every week-end staying with Spry.

This is hard writing, and I must memorise.

Arrive at Smith's Fall 2:37, have to dress, and speak at 3. Leave Smith's Falls at 7 for Belleville. Return to Ottawa Sunday morning.

Bye-bye
Phil

1 ie, the manuscript of his speech; see also letter of March 14, 1928 II, for another such incident.

2 Since, in a letter of March 10, Grove speaks of *A Search for America* selling in England for 7/6, this may be a reference to the contract with Macmillan in New York and Cape in London for the publication of *Our Daily Bread*. It seems more probable, however, that the reference is to *A Search for America*, but that the price is in error. Arrangements with Coward-McCann fell through; see letter of March 14, 1928 II, note 2.

The telegram to Mrs Grove does not appear to have survived.

TO CATHERINE GROVE

Hotel Quinte,
Belleville, Ont.
March 10, 1928

My dear Tee,

I can't write with that pen. Well, ran down yesterday in the worst blizzard I've seen in many years from Ottawa to Smith's Falls where I arrived about 5 minutes of three. Had to be rushed to the hall where I spoke at 3. Left Smith's Falls at 12:15 midnight. Got here at 3:37 a.m. Of course I had a bed at Smi[th's] F[alls] and a berth in the sleeper, and a bed here. But that was a beastly night. Tomorrow I go back to Ottawa, by day-train, parlo[u]r-car and all the frills. Stay at Ottawa over Sunday and Monday. Leave Ottawa Tuesday to return to a place less than an hour from here. If the fares were at my expense, I should not do so, of course. But what with passes and expenses paid ...

I have many and powerful friends at Ottawa. Senator Hardy[1] (a multi-millionaire) – Geo[rge] Gardiner, head of the Royal Bank System[2] – the 2 speakers of the 2 houses of the Parliament, etc.[3] Ottawa alone took more than 300 copies of the *Search*. I'm going to bring that up to 500 when I speak there (twice) on Saturday. Next week will be my hardest week – 6 addresses in 5 days.

I am having 2 copies of the *Search* bound by a French binder, with our names imprinted.[4] You'll get them some time end of this month – very beautiful, I think. The President of the binding firm – another good friend of mine, will present them to me with his compliments.

I have deposited $225 in the Bank of Montreal, to replace what I drew out. Shall add another $200 to it next week – so as to replace the royalties.

In addition, I expect to have at least another $200 or $300 from my fees.

I have, so far, spent a little over $100 in expenses, all local expenses being paid by the local clubs; + $60 private expenses. I had to buy a new pair of shoes because the old ones looked too shabby. Also, I bought a 3-compartment portfolio which solves the problem of baggage – all my papers, books, etc. + handkerchiefs, and other trifles going into it. Am going to get some shirts, collars, ties, underwear, cap, etc. on Monday. The thaw-up is in full swing here, and it is getting too warm for fur-caps. Don't send the heavy socks back, either. Too hot for this weather.

It is marvellously beautiful here. I am right on the Bay of Quinte. The city a nice, sleepy, south-Ontario town.

I had never realised that Martin Burrell[5] is quite a power in Ottawa. He has access, without knocking, to any place about the Parl[iament] buildings. I listened to the most stupid debate I ever heard on Thursday.[6] Met Woodsworth[7] and the whole left wing of the H[ouse] of C[ommons]. Premier King[8] has promised to come to the C[anadian] C[lub] on Saturday to hear me. I've quite a story about him. I am going to recast my talk for the occasion, so as to make it very, very strong. I never realised quite so forcibly before what a power I am myself in the land. A man like Senator Hardy begs me for *4* autographs in my 4 books.

At North Bay I stayed with the principal of the Normal School for Northern Ontario – delightful people – he of straight German descent, she, of Waterloo Mennonite stock – Mr. & Mrs. A.C. Casselman[9] – if not rich, very well-to-do. They invited you and me to come in the summer and stay with them as long as we like. He's a great talker, I, a good listener. I spoke at the Normal School in the morning on Tuesday, Mar[ch] 6. By noon the local bookstore (5 copies) was sold out and wired for 25 copies more.

I sent you a wire re London and New York – they are in such a hurry that they want to buy the sheets from Miller – the 1st time that has ever happened: usually they insist on selling sheets to Canada. They wanted options on my next 2 books. I refused; but signed contracts yesterday morning. *Coward-McCann* in New York: 10% royalty – price of the book in the U.S.A. to be $3.50; no export rights. In London, *Jonathan Cape*,[10] one of the finest firms; 15c royalty per copy; book to sell at 7s 6d – which is about 10%. On account of the low price I myself proposed a lowered royalty. I do believe, it's beginning. The presses are roaring, though Miller had great difficulty in getting the paper. It will pull the Graphic out of the hole, I believe. But next week they'll be out of stock.

Everywhere *all* my books are selling.

A few people, very few, though, tell me they like *Settlers* better than the *Search*.

As for my return home, I believe I shall get home during Easter week. Nothing is very certain just now. I am *not* going to Montreal; it would be too hard after having spoken twice at Ottawa to take the night-train and speak again when I step off. Besides, I am afraid, it would spoil my audience in the fall. I'd speak to 100 now; in the fall I expect to speak to 500 or more. The biggest audience I've so far had was 450 (at F[or]t W[illia]m). I didn't know there had been that many. I had estimated at 250. But the official report of the Sec[retary] came in yesterday morning to Spry. They reported my address to have been 'inspiring and helpful in the highest degree' and said that for the first time they had realised the value of the National Office at Ottawa. Orders for my book went by wire into Ottawa the night I had spoken.

Spry is charming – a young chap of 27 or 28. I'm going to 'bach it' with him. When I had spoken at the luncheon banquet tendered to me by the big men, – politically, businessly, militarily big – he said to me, 'You are a find for the C[anadian] C[lub]s, Mr. Grove.'

Well, I feel a bit tough from the broken night. So I'll stop and get a 'hot towel' and a facial massage at the barber shop.

Bye-bye
Phil

1 Senator Arthur Charles Hardy

2 Grove's information is at times a little confused as to detail – perhaps understandably, in view of the social whirl into which he appears to have been precipitated in Ottawa, and the

fatiguing amount of travel detailed in these letters. As far as is known, no George Gardiner was ever on the staff of the Royal Bank, certainly not in a senior position. However, a Frank George Gardiner of the firm Gardiner and Mercer, Vancouver architects, built several branches of the Royal Bank. The firm continues under the name of Mercer and Mercer, and Jack Mercer, son of the original partner, suggests that although F.G. Gardiner was usually known by his first name and initial, 'his middle name could have been used and emphasised if a distinction was thought to be necessary between him and his brother, ... William Frederick Gardiner ... also an architect and a keen competitor.' (March 12, 1971)

George C. Gardner, who was then a manager of the Bank of Toronto in Ottawa, may also be considered.

3 The Speaker of the Senate at this time was Hewitt Bostock (1864–1930), and the Speaker of the House of Commons was Rodolphe Lemieux (1866–1932).

4 Leonard Grove confirms that these specially bound copies are still in the family's possession, and are of fine workmanship.

5 Martin S. Burrell (1858–1938) was a Conservative MP from 1908 to 1920, and held various cabinet portfolios during that period. In 1920, he was appointed Parliamentary Librarian, a position he held until his death. Burrell had written to Grove about *Settlers of the Marsh* in March 1926, and was probably the 'M' who wrote the review of that novel in the *Ottawa Journal*, February 20, 1926.

6 The debate in the House of Commons on Thursday, March 8, 1928, was over the budget. The speeches were long and dreary.

7 James S. Woodsworth (1874–1942), the founder of the Co-operative Commonwealth Federation (the predecessor to the New Democratic Party), and an MP from 1921 until his death. In his letter to Grove, of March 1, 1927, he wrote, 'A year ago I read your book *Settlers of the Marsh* with much interest – I regret that it has been so bitterly attacked. As a matter of fact, I sent it on to my daughter...' A Methodist minister and a confirmed pacifist, his deep knowledge of and interest in the plight of prairie immigrant settlers would have provided common ground for conversation with Grove. See also letter of March 12, 1928, and note 1 to that letter.

8 William Lyon Mackenzie King (1874–1950), Liberal Prime Minister of Canada from 1921 to 1930, and from 1935 to 1948.

9 Alexander Clark Casselman (1860–1940) was the first Principal of North Bay Normal School (now Teachers' College) from 1909 until his retirement in 1930. In 1902, he published an edited version of Major John Richardson's *War of 1812* (Brockville 1842).

10 See the preceding letter, note 2.

TO WATSON KIRKCONNELL

Hotel Quinte,
Belleville, Ont.
March 10, 1928 II

My dear Kirk,

I have an idea that I am not so very far from Lindsay now; but I have no map handy on which to look it up.[1] It appears that I am not going to speak there. I have, here, today, given my address for the 10th time. Twice my

Ms. has been stolen from me, after the lecture – by the press people, no doubt. But I am so much at home in the thing by this time that I don't need it any longer. Next week I'll have my hardest week: 6 addresses in 5 days. It will, however, still take 8 more addresses from today to pay for my new clothes. A week from today I shall speak twice at Ottawa where I have more friends than I thought I had. I have, yesterday, signed contracts with Coward-McCann, New York (35c a copy for me); and Jonathan Cape, London (15c a copy for me; the book to retail at 7/6) for the *Search*, I mean.

Miller is pulling himself out of the hole by *my* shoe-strings. Both McCann and Cape, to save time, are buying their first copies in flat sheets from him – 1000 each at 60c a copy. His presses are roaring. He is not as bad as I thought he would be. You know, of course, that the Carillon Book Club,[2] strange to say, is a success? They have actually taken in more than $4000. Your book[3] will be no. 4 or 5. That secures Miller with regard to costs. I've been asked a good many questions about it. E.S. Gardiner,[4] being a 'charter member' of the Club, will get his copy that way. (This is an abominable pen, but the best in this hotel; and I left my fountain pen at Ottawa where I return tomorrow, Sunday, to do a little shopping.)

They entertain me to death. But for tonight I managed to escape. Am reading Murray[5] at last and enjoying it greatly. Gave the same talk that I gave at Wesley[6] at North Bay Normal School. An hour later the local book store (which had 5 copies) was sold out and ordered 25 copies by telegram. Here, they have 1 copy at the public library. And they are going to take turns reading it.

Well, so long.
Yours
F.P.G.

1 Kirkconnell's father was then Principal of the Lindsay Collegiate Institute; presumably Grove had hoped to meet him.
2 See letter of February 29, 1928, note 3.
3 *European Elegies*, published by Graphic in 1928
4 of Rapid City
5 Presumably, *The Classical Tradition in Poetry* (1927) by Gilbert Murray (1866–1957).
6 Wesley College, as it was known then; it later became United College, and is now the University of Winnipeg.

TO CATHERINE GROVE

Hotel Quinte
Belleville, Ont.
March 11, 1928, Sunday

My dear Tee,

Within an hour or so I start once more for Ottawa to do a little shopping tomorrow. There, I shall not have time for anything. So I'll write once more from here. I just figured out the cost of this thing.

Local expenses (paid by local clubs)	per day average ...	$12.00
Train expenses	”	18.00
My fees, average 4¾ lectures per week,	”	19.00
	average daily expense	$49.00

not including advertising, etc. It seems frivolous. Yet...

I take, of course, room with bath where I can get it, etc. I've got to. I had a slight cold when I got here. An Ottawa doctor told me a new way to use Thermogene. Last night I followed his advice; when I got through I was as red as a lobster when boiled; and this morning chest and nose are quite clear again. As for abdomen and back, I have not had a pain for more than a week now. It does seem to work as Hunter[1] said it would.

Funniest thing on earth to me how here, in the east, wherever I go, whether people have read my books or not, I am the 'famous' author, 'Canada's foremost writer,' 'such a celebrity.' Of course, that might not be so if I were travelling as a private person. As it is, I come with the enormous prestige of the C[anadian] C[lub]s; and with the support of *Ottawa*. Everybody bows before me. When I left Ottawa day before yesterday to run down to Smith's Falls, a lieutenant colonel carried one suit-case; the gen[eral] manager of the Royal Bank my club-bag;[2] and a member of the H[ouse] of Commons my portfolio.

And then I suddenly think of little May – – –.

And if I could, I'd annihilate this world.

Am to fly over Ottawa tomorrow.

Looking over my engagements, I don't see how they can keep me busy beyond April 10 or 15. This week I speak 6 times in 5 days. So far I am covering loops from Ottawa going back to Ottawa. Over next week, I suppose, it will be the same with Toronto. I'll wire you in time to change address. At Toronto, if I make it headquarters, it will be '*King Edward Hotel*' – so, if I say Toronto, that's where you must address.

They are, of course, trying to entertain me to death. But I'm a tough customer to deal with. And a person *does* need the rest, of course.

Carillon Book Club,[3] strange to say, is actually a success. It's being talked about everywhere. I am told they have taken in $4000 within 2 months. But it is, of course, a Graphic institution: don't tell E.S.G.[4] Kirk's elegies[5] will be no. 4 or 5. Not bad, eh?

Well, it's time to order my taxi.

Bye-bye, my dear.

Phil

1 Presumably the 'Ottawa doctor' earlier referred to. Dr James Earl Hunter (1900–63), a graduate of the University of Western Ontario, practised in Ottawa in the 1920s.

2 See letter of March 10, 1928, note 2.

3 See letter of February 29, 1928, note 3.

4 E.S. Gardiner

5 Watson Kirkconnell's *European Elegies* (1928)

TO CATHERINE GROVE

Rideau Club,
Ottawa, Ont.
March 11, 1928 II

My dear,

I have nothing to say, except that I am back at Ottawa, after 1/2 day's travel. Am supposed to be baching it with Graham Spry and Phinney,[1] commanding officer of the Can[adian] Air Force. But as it happened, both had engagements for tonight. So I strolled over to the Club[2] (the so-called 'Cabinet Club') of which I have been made a temporary member and where I simply sign my name to the bill after having dined.

Spry, while dressing, told me that my tour was beginning to justify his holding the office he holds. He met three big bankers at lunch – all from the West, all members of their C[anadian] C[lub]s. When he introduced himself, he said, one of them asked, 'Oh yes, then you must be the man who arranges Grove's tour? Best thing we ever had.' It turned out that all three had read my book.

Well, if this letter were written to anyone else, I suppose, it would be mere snobbery. But with regard to you I still feel that the sort of reception I had here justifies at least in part what you've done during the last few years.

I had hardly arrived here this afternoon – and was sitting all alone in Spry's apartment when a man by name of Ainslee Greene[3] called – he's the Sir Augustus Nanton[4] of Ottawa. He has read my book, of course; and he has even bought 10 copies of it to give away. He told me that it is his opinion that the book will 'stagnate' for a year or so and then go around *the world*.

Last night, after my lecture at Belleville, an elderly lady came to shake hands with me and said a good thing. 'You first reassured me by pulling out and arranging a Ms. That showed that you had thought out and prepared what you were going to say to us. Then you stepped to the front, leaving your Ms. behind on the table; and now I felt reassured that you were not going to *read* your address.' Quite clever. So you find a few everywhere here even in the small cities. What a contrast to Brandon or Portage. The western *country* is all right. It's only there that you find the Stanises, the Holms, the Langs, etc.[5] But the western *towns* are a terror.

Well, I think I'll stroll home and go to bed.
Bye-bye.
Phil

1 Lawrence Hudson Phinney (b1892), who was at this time a pilot officer with the RCAF, employed in photographic mapping. Born in Winnipeg, he graduated (LL B 1913) from the Manitoba Law School, and thereafter worked in banking and legal practice. He was called to the bar in 1922, having seen military service from 1915 to 1919. In 1927 he joined the RCAF; he later served in the Manitoba Government Air Force from 1932 to 1936. In July 1944, he was called up, being posted to Air Force HQ on the staff of the Special Commis-

sioner, and thus curiously fulfilling Grove's highly inflated description here. He retired, in 1945, with the rank of Wing Commander.

2 ie, the Rideau Club, on Wellington Street opposite the Parliament Buildings in Ottawa, to which most senior officials of the government belong

3 Ainslie W. Greene (1880–1945), was a partner in the Ottawa law firm of Greene, Johnston and Strike, and later a judge in the Supreme Court of Ontario.

4 Sir Augustus Nanton (1860–1925) was born and educated in Toronto. At the age of thirteen he entered the service of the Toronto brokerage firm of Pellat and Osler, and in 1884, on becoming a partner, represented the firm in Winnipeg. In 1924, on his election as president of the Dominion Bank, he returned to live in Toronto. He was one of the outstanding figures in the financial life of Canada, serving as a director of several Canadian companies, such as Hudson's Bay and Canadian Pacific Railways. He was knighted in 1917.

5 Actual settlers whom Grove knew in rural Manitoba (Mrs Grove's note). This, along with the sentence that follows, sums up and illuminates a deeply-felt attitude on Grove's part, one that permeates his writing, especially where the setting is western – eg, *Settlers of the Marsh*. Mrs Grove adds that she thinks 'Stanises' should be 'Standish' (a Scots name); the Holms and the Langs were of German origin.

TO CATHERINE GROVE

Rideau Club,
Ottawa.
March 12, 1928

My dear Tee,

Have just bought you a hat – a very pretty little thing, but with no wide brim. You simply cannot get anything wide-brimmed at present. I tried 3 or 4 stores. Also, Jersey dresses are all 2-piece dresses. Most of them silk Jerseys – $35 to 50 – nothing I really liked. So I did not buy.

It is hot here. I bought some socks, and a suit of underwear. Shall send my soiled suit tomorrow.

The last definite engagement which I see on my itinerary is for Mar[ch] 29 at Stratford. Of course there may be more arranged for any day. But there is an enquiry from the U.S.A. – New York and Boston. I am not committing myself, for I am getting somewhat tired of all this and wish I could go home soon.

The left wing of the left side of the H[ouse] of Commons has invited me for lunch today at the Parl[iament] B[ui]ld[in]gs.[1] I went in here, after shopping, to rest.

After lunch, if there is time, I am to fly over the city. At 4:30 there is a reception for me where a number of French ladies wish to talk to me.

Next week I'll be at Toronto. But just what the arrangements are is still quite uncertain. In fact, it is impossible to give an itinerary in advance. There are changes from day to day, and sometimes from hour to hour.

So, I suppose, you'd better stick to the Ottawa address, c/o Ass[ociation] of Canadian Clubs, 55 Metcalfe. They'll forward.

I don't think I want to go on into New England now. I'm worried about you. No need for you to worry about me. I'm all right.

Well, I suppose I'd better stroll over to the Houses, as everybody calls them here – viz. of Parliament. I was in at the Graphic awhile ago. They tell me that Brandon stocked up on the *Search* and is now kicking since my meeting there was cancelled.

Bye-bye.
Phil

I forgot to say that I bought the hat on approval. Should you not like it, you must send it back. Bill with address I ordered enclosed. It is slightly more than 22 in[ches] inside measurement. If you return it – as I hope you won't, ask for refund, of course. Next Saturday when I speak here, I arrive at 7 a.m., speak twice, and then leave at 11 p.m. for Toronto; so I can't attend to it. I had to take a chance.

So long.
Phil

1 Presumably at the invitation of J.S. Woodsworth, who then led a small group of the Progressive party in the House of Commons. Following the Regina conference of 1933, the group led by Woodsworth became the CCF (Co-operative Commonwealth Federation), for which party Grove was a candidate near the end of his life, in 1943. The successor to the CCF is the NDP (New Democratic Party), which similarly promotes a policy of moderate socialism.

TO CATHERINE GROVE

Canadian Pacific Railway
En Route
March 13, 1928

My dear Tee,

Am sending you parcel of underwear etc. of which Spry's office took charge. Don't return heavy socks nor shirt. As to underwear itself, I expect to find the first suit here – or rather at Ottawa on Saturday. After that I shall wire you where to address the next parcel. My itinerary is very uncertain. They keep it just a week ahead of my coming.

This is hard writing. So I'll say nothing else. Also, must look matters over for Bowmanville where I speak on arrival.

Bye-bye,
Phil

9 Groves' house in Rapid City, Manitoba. *Photo by Desmond Pacey*

TO CATHERINE GROVE

Balmoral Hotel,
Bowmanville, Ont.
March 14, 1928

My dear,

Got here last night on a straight run from Ottawa and arrived with a wild head-ache. Had it been an ordinary night, I'd have begged off. But they had put bells on: ladies invited; a big banquet; and a meeting of 143 people in a town of 3500. Them, I thought, I could not disappoint. So I went ahead, speaking from 9 till 10:30, the headache petering out. And it was the biggest success I have had yet. Anglican Archdeacon[1] moved the vote of thanks, saying, 'We have heard the most prominent speakers of this country, the U.S.A., and some from Europe (Stanley Baldwin,[2] premier of England, was here last year). And we have always enjoyed it and profited. *But what shall we say tonight?*' He talked for half an hour, prophesying immortality, etc. I did have them going. Everybody was *sweating* before I got through. Then the richest man in town wanted me to come to his house for the night. But I was sweating myself and refused to go out. I slipped upstairs, had a bath, changed my clothes, and came down again. They were still talking. This morning, at breakfast, I heard my name from all sides as I entered the dining room. They were all discussing my address.

Had a really good sleep and feel fine this morning. I wish I could send you some newspaper reports; but I never get to see them. I leave for Port Hope at 10:14. It's 9:30 now. So I'd better pack up. Met here a friend of Phelps' and Kirk's.[3]

Well, so long. In a month I should be home.

Phil

Am anxious to hear from you. Hope to find a letter at Ottawa on Saturday. Speak there 3 times. Arrive 7:45 a.m., speak at Normal School 9:30, at men's club 1 p.m. Women's, 7:15 p.m. Leave for Toronto Sunday 1:15 p.m.

1 The only resident Anglican clergyman in Bowmanville at this time was the Rev. R.J. Shires (c1886–1964) and he was not an archdeacon but rector of Bowmanville from 1925 to 1930. He retired from the ministry in 1955 as a Canon of St James' Cathedral, Toronto.

2 Stanley Baldwin (1867–1947), the Conservative Prime Minister of England during the 1926 general strike and 1936 abdication of King Edward VIII. In all, he was Prime Minister of England three times: 1923 (May-October), 1924–9, and 1935–7.

3 Arthur Phelps' and Watson Kirkconnell's; there is no clue as to who he was.

TO CATHERINE GROVE

Queen's Hotel
Port Hope, Ont.
March 14, 1928 II

Well, my dear, here I am. I wrote once before, this morning, from Bowmanville, but forgot to tell you that it's raining here and has been raining since day before yesterday. The lake is open, huge waves running; and all brooks and rivers are foaming with spring.

There has been a continuous arrival of people here at the hotel since I got here who tell me how much they admire my books – but not *one* had read the *Search*. Which shows that, as far as this district goes, I could have done this tour last year just as well. Here, along Lake Ontario, I've been a name for years. It's different in the industrial centres of the Ottawa Valley. At Ottawa itself, there are literally hundreds of people who have read the *Search* – but, the price being $3, hundreds borrow it. The Library of Parliament has quite a few copies; I enquired 3 times for one; they were always out – and nobody but members can borrow them there.

Twice now my Mss. have been swiped – by newspaper people. Last night a cub reporter, perhaps 17 y[ea]rs old, came to me after the lecture and asked me to loan him my Ms. for an hour. I gave him a talking to! The trouble is, they don't use their shorthand the moment they see a speaker has a Ms. I never use mine; but I want to have it there. At last, however, I relented. He promised high and low I'd have the papers back before I was through with my bath. Well, this morning my young friend hadn't turned up yet. At 9 I started phoning to the paper – but my reporter could not be found. At last I had to go to the station. Well, there he was, waiting for me. I told him it was his good luck for I'd have sent him a bomb by mail and blown him up. He laughed.

By the way, the Toronto *Globe* had sent the nincompoop[1] who reviewed the *Search* to Bowmanville to get an advance report on my lecture. I treated him like a dog. The impertinent puppy! I can afford to.

Coward-McCann[2] wired me yesterday that they make it a point to have options on my two next books. That was a p[oin]t which I refused to sign when their representative met me at Ottawa last Thursday (last Thursday? It seems a year ago). I did not think they would balk at my refusal – though the contract was accepted subject to their acceptance of the change. I have not answered their wire and shall not do so for a few more days. And then I'll repeat my refusal (necessarily, of course, seeing that I want Macmillans for *Our Daily Bread*). I'm utterly indifferent and in no hurry. The *Search* will appear anyway; but, of course, unless it appears this *spring*, I can't let it appear till 1929, or it would interfere with *Our Daily Bread*. I've got them anyway, for nobody dares to interfere and to print without my consent now that I've made a splash. I'm going to get the London market – and without paying British Income Tax – that's the advantage of dealing from Ottawa instead of from Rapid City. I had a copyright lawyer – services free. Miller quotes a price including royalty and pays over royalty as he gets his money – provided that he doesn't go bankrupt first. However, I believe he is pulling himself out of the mire by *my* shoe-strings. Still, Macmillans are going to get the real benefit from all this publicity, for the *Search* suffers from its price. People borrow instead of buying. However ... things have started at the long last.

I hear, Mr. French,[3] of McClelland & St[ewart] wishes to see me and is on the look-out for me. Well, he'll get it.

Am going to speak to the women here at 8 p.m.; and I just heard, over the phone, that they'll have a reception for me at 5 p.m. So I suppose, I'd better get dressed – morning suit and all the bells. It's tiring. But I had a dandy sleep last night.

To-morrow Peterborough. Afternoon lecture at 4:15. Have spent $235 to-date. Have $30 left to get back to Ottawa with. Then I must have another cheque. Have deposited $225 at Bank of Montreal, Winnipeg. In a week or two I'll deposit another $200 – and that will probably be all. It means that we must pay our premium out of current income. For the holidays I'll get another royalty cheque. Then Mandy's[4] needs will be provided for – and as we replace that next fall, we'll pay off the loan.

Meanwhile I'll be making more money by the next tour. U.S.A. agency offers $100 a night at the big centres. But I'm not anxious, for the expenses will be high; and I must look after them myself.

Bye-bye
Phil

1 Who remains unidentified. The unsigned review in the Toronto *Globe* of January 14, 1928 (p 17) was favourable, but rather superficial.
2 The confusion seems to be due to Grove's habit of jumping to conclusions. This is the first indication that negotiations with Coward-McCann were experiencing difficulties. See letters of March 8, March 9 (note 2), March 10, March 10 II, March 19 (note 10), and March 19 II, 1928.
3 Donald Graham French (1873–1945) was Literary Editor for McClelland & Stewart Ltd. and author of *Points about Poetry* (1910), *The Appeal of Poetry* (1923), an anthology, *Standard Canadian Reciter* (1918), and, jointly with J.D. Logan, *Highways of Canadian Literature* (1924).
4 Amanda (Wiens) Mather, Mrs Grove's younger sister, who was staying with her at this time

TO CATHERINE GROVE *post card*

Peterboro[ugh], Ont.
March 15, 1928,
8 P.M.

Just a sign of life today. Too busy to breathe. Am sending

similar cards to everybody I can think of. Am to speak in $1^1/_2$ h[ou]rs and must dress.

Regards to all (inc[luding] Mandy)
Phil
Am very anxious to know how you liked the hat.

TO CATHERINE GROVE

Empress,
Peterborough, Ont.
Wednesday,
March 15, 1928 II

My dear,

This has been, so far, the biggest week I have had. It has been one triumph after the other. Today, I declining all private invitations for supper and receptions, 4 men asked whether they could come to the hotel. They did; and one of them (Anglican clergyman) began to express his feelings. He said at last that all those with whom he had talked had agreed that this afternoon had been the biggest experience of their lives. I did have them sweating.

At Port Hope we have another invitation for the summer. Family of a lawyer by name of McMahon (pron[ounced] McMann).[1] Tomorrow morning I leave here at 7 a.m. and go back there, to Port Hope, one of the prettiest places I have seen along Lake Ontario – by the way it was not the *town*, but the college which had burned down. I wrote about that some time ago.[2] The McMahons insist on my stopping over with them for a few hours between trains. They being very delightful people I am going to do so. There is also the Benson family – she a poetess whose work quite impressed me.[3] By the way, Kirk was born there and went to school there. Old Mr Kirk was a prin[cipal] of schools at P[or]t H[ope].[4] It is a triumphant progress all right; and it *seems* the book must be selling like hot cakes (???). Everybody knows it. I had today an audience of ca. 200 in this little city; and everybody, from the first word to the last, sat still as a mouse, except when they were applauding. I do hope, the royalties will show the result. Most of the success goes through the Carillon Book Club which seems to be a real big success. Knight[5] claims he gets 170 members a week. The statement will show whether it's true or not.

Well, I have a slight headache and all my reports to make out. So I'd better stop, I suppose.

Bye-bye
Phil

1 Mrs Mary Jean McMahon, who now lives in Weston, Ontario, was, at or around this time, President of the local Women's Canadian Club. Grove was billeted, during his stay in Port Hope, in the home of the McMahons. Mrs McMahon recalls that her husband, 'who was really taken with him,' lent Grove a little money, which of course was later repaid. She

assumes, as was the case, that the central office of the Association of Canadian Clubs was paying expenses, 'but I'm sure the poor man never had much extra cash and found incidentals like laundry, taxis, etc., eating up the money he had with him.' (June 27, 1968)

Mrs McMahon also kindly supplied me with a letter from Grove, printed below.

2 Cf. letter of March 5, 1928, note 1.

3 Mrs H.W. Benson, née Mary Josephine Trotter, was born in Port Hope (1887), the daughter of a Baptist minister, and a cousin of Bernard Freeman Trotter (1890–1917), the 'soldier-poet.' She married a local doctor in 1915. A series of war narrative poems, originally published in *Maclean's Magazine*, provided the material for her first book, *My Pocket Beryl* (1921). She also ran for some time the 'Prominent Women' feature in *Everyman's World*, and edited the women's supplement to the *Canadian Courier*.

4 Watson Kirkconnell's father, Thomas Kirkconnell (1862–1934), who was headmaster of high schools in Port Hope (1894–1908) and Lindsay (1908–32). The younger Kirkconnell wrote his biography, *A Canadian Headmaster* (1935).

5 C.C. Knight of the Carillon Book Club; see letter of February 29, 1928, note 3.

TO CATHERINE GROVE

Trenton, Ont.
March 16, 1928

Well, here I am at Trenton on the Trent Valley Canal, feeling a bit tired and blue. This is a place I don't like – a crude industrial sort of thing, centre of the Canadian 'Movie' Industry. Also the cheap jewelry of Eaton's catalog is made here. Also, for the first time the executive[1] is distinctly discouraging. I wish I had stayed at P[or]t Hope where I met many delightful people. They'd have motored me over in time for the talk. I've got a night-ride to Ottawa ahead, and to-morrow *three addresses* (Normal School and 2 C[anadian] C[lub]s). But perhaps it sounds worse than it is.

The McMahons[2] at P[or]t Hope had kept the 2 morning papers for me. So I sent them along awhile ago. I don't know yet whether it has been possible to make a date at Toronto. I know there was some difficulty about it. To make one's living by lecturing would be a dog's life.

But I love this country with its cedars and white pines and apple orchards. This is the real apple country of Ontario. West of Toronto is the grape country. Especially did I like P[or]t Hope which faces the open lake. Living is cheaper here, too, than in the west. They have, of course, no idea here of foreign settlements, etc. (Do you know, by the way, that Ferguson School and Cottage burned down? No doubt set fire to.)[3] But I am the distinguished man who confers a great honour on them. There was a bit of jealousy between Mrs. McMahon and Mrs. Benson[4] over my staying with the former although they call each other by their first names. So I went over to the Bensons at 11 p.m. I had breakfast again this morning with the McMahons, having three hours to wait for a connection at P[or]t Hope – on the way from Peterborough here, by little one-horse trains.

I just came in from a walk to the station where I made sure of my berth in the sleeper – shall leave here at 2:23, a terrible hour to board a train. Get to Ottawa at 7:45 tomorrow morning. Speak at 9:30, 12:30, 8:00 – I wish that were over. Next week west of Toronto – Hamilton, etc. They are plowing there, the papers say. Here it is mud, mud, mud wherever I go. At Ottawa it was snow, snow, snow. My coat is getting to be too hot and heavy.

By the way, whatever I send home in the way of laundry, don't send out again anything but the underwear. It just increases my baggage. Underwear is too expensive to buy it new. I'll know more, of course, after to-morrow. But so far it seems to me I'll be home by middle of April – some time during Easter week. Most clubs cease to meet about then. Well, I guess I better get dressed.

Bye-bye
Phil

1 Of the local Canadian Club
2 See the preceding letter, note 1.
3 The Manitoba Department of Education records contain no history of the fire which destroyed the school and the teacherage – Grove taught there from March 1918 to June 1919.
4 See the preceding letter, note 3.

TO CATHERINE GROVE

Chateau Laurier,
Ottawa, Ont.
March 17, 1928

My dear,

Got the two parcels and three letters. Yes, I know, my dear, it's hard. But I suppose we must go through with it next fall,[1] for, after all, the thing sells the book and the old books, too, and all those to follow.

I am completely exhausted. The noon meeting was enormous. 200 men: 3 cabinet ministers, 1/2 doz[en] Senators, the Speaker of the Senate, Speaker of the H[ouse] of C[ommons], Bishops and Archbishops, Military men, Big business, etc. etc. They had told me it was the most brilliant gathering that had ever assembled for any speaker.

When I at last was called over the phone, I went down. When I entered the banquet hall, the whole Assembly rose and cheered. When I rose to speak, it took five minutes before I was allowed to say a word. Half a dozen times thundering applause during the speech. When I finished, I had to stand fully ten minutes bowing to their applause and their cheering.

The Hon[ourable] Motherwell,[2] minister of I know not what, said: What we need is 100,000 Mr. Groves: thundering applause and cheering. I did not know what to say.

Spry and everybody said there never had been a meeting like that before. While I spoke, you could have heard a pin fall. And I was in my full stride. I knew I could do with them what I pleased.

Most of them said they wanted to hear me again tonight. The women have changed the meeting to the biggest hall they could get.

Spry said, I had put *him* over. I am going to a country estate 80 miles from here to-morrow, to spend the Sunday with the Hon[ourable] E.C. Grant[3] and Martin Burrell[4] and their families. There is not a minute now but somebody calls and leaves his card. I do not receive – advice of Doctor. I have undressed and am going to have a bath; then change underwear. Speak on Wednesday at Hamilton.

The hotel people have placed a table in the lobby: 'Callers for Mr. Grove please leave cards here.'

I simply had to get rest, so as to be ready for the evening. I expect a very big meeting.

Well, I'd better climb in to the tub.

Bye-bye,

Your

Phil

[on the back of the envelope] Have Miller send you the special copies of the *Search*.[5]

1 Another lecture tour, from September 10 to November 4, 1928, which Grove did undertake

2 William Richard Motherwell (1860–1943) was prominent in various agricultural bodies in Saskatchewan. After serving as Minister of Agriculture in the provincial government of Saskatchewan, he was elected, in 1921, to the House of Commons, becoming Minister of Agriculture in W.L. Mackenzie King's cabinet; he continued in the same portfolio in the second King cabinet of 1926, retiring in 1930.

3 Edward C. Grant (1862–1942), a keen sportsman whose interests included polo, golf, and speed-skating. During the First World War, he organised a 'paper scheme' to secure additional funds for the purchase of comforts for Canadian forces overseas from the sale of paper and other wastes. He also designed a mechanical dart for the destruction of Zeppelins and presented his patent to the Air Ministry.

He was active in various civic duties, and in amateur theatricals. He had the distinction of introducing the first automobile, a Dion Bouton, to the streets of Ottawa.

4 Who was the Parliamentary Librarian at that time; see letter of March 10, 1928, note 5.

5 The specially bound copies of *A Search for America* mentioned in letter of March 10, 1928; see also note 4 to that letter.

TO CATHERINE GROVE

Chateau Laurier
Ottawa, Ont.
March 18, 1928

My dear,

Well, I've given my two addresses here, and they were great successes. I'll try to get you that underwear when I get to Toronto. I'm not speaking there just yet. The dates did not suit.

I'll be in Hamilton on Wednesday. Today I'm going to a country seat in the Gatineau hills, north of Ottawa, to spend the time till Tuesday when I run down to Hamilton. *Settlers, Prairie Trails*, and *The Turn* also sell here at present.

I autographed your leather copy of the *Search*,[1] and it will go forward to you. If you like it, write Miller a few words of thanks and ask him also to thank Mr. Keegan, the binder – who *gives* you the binding – Miller gives the book. He is so excited that he brought me a bottle of Hennessey last night.[2]

Had a good sleep after that exertion of two important talks. With the satisfaction that I have put them over; though the first went better than the second. I was fagged.

Just to give you an idea of the appalling expenses here:

room only (with bath and dressing room)	$10.00
breakfast	1.65
lunch	1.60
dinner	4.50
breakfast today	1.75

And I have nothing but what I have at home; nor is it any better; f[or] i[nstance] the bacon. Well, I must pack up to get ready for the millionaires who will send their car for me in an hour.

Last night, by the way, the ladies had rented the 'Ladies Cafe' in this hotel, cost $100. But it would not hold the crowd; so they changed to the 'Salon des Palmes' – cost $175 for an hour and a half. It's *Frivolous*. One amusing feature is that the waiters here know that this nabob called Grove has been a waiter.[3] So they crowd into the doors, etc., when I speak and applaud frantically though they don't understand a word.

Well, bye-bye.
Phil

1 See letter of March 10, 1928, note 4.

2 Relations between the two men appear to have re-established themselves on a friendly basis (cf. letter of March 10, 1928 II: 'He is not as bad as I thought he would be.') – but not for very long.

3 In his 'autobiographies' Grove claims to have worked as a waiter in Toronto shortly after his arrival in Canada.

TO CATHERINE GROVE

24 Blackburn Avenue,
Ottawa, Ont.
[March 18, 1928 II][1]

My dear,

This thing is beginning to be funny. I am here in the house of Sir E.C. Grant, a multimillionaire[2] who has no idea of what life on less than 100,000 a year may be like. And I am invited tonight to dine at the American Ambassador's.[3] Amazing, isn't it? I just keep laughing in my sleeve all the time. Of course, I act as if I took it all for granted. When I stir a finger, three footmen and half a dozen maids jump.

Just had lunch: present 3 senators, his Lordship, President of the Supreme Court of Canada,[4] and 2 Knights. All had read my book and say it's the best yarn ever, but don't for a moment believe I lived through it. Think I'm the most entertaining liar in the world, poke me in the ribs, drink whiskey and laugh and have no idea that I am storing their portraits away in my memory.[5]

Tell you more about this crowd when I get home. My eyes are wide open.

[no signature]

1 No date appears; that given is a reasoned conjecture.

2 See letter of March 17, 1928, note 3.

3 William Phillips (1878–1968), who became, in 1927, the first Minister of the United States to Canada at the American Legation in Ottawa.

4 The reference is probably to the Chief Justice of the Supreme Court at that time, the Rt. Hon. Francis A. Anglin (1865–1933).

5 This may be a reference to Grove's treatment of such characters in *The Master of the Mill* (1944), a novel which he was probably planning as early as this.

TO CATHERINE GROVE

24 Blackburn Avenue,
Ottawa, Ont.
March 18, 1928 III

The astonishing thing about [it] is, you know, that these people *know* my books – to the point where they ask me 'What became of Ray?' 'Did you ever meet Ivan again?' – 'Bobby Lund, I suppose, is largely yourself?'

– 'Poor Mrs. Amundsen! And you say she actually died in life?'[1] – They can't imagine that I may invent things. They are as stupid as can be imagined; but they do read my books which argues that they are accessible.

Poor Miller will, of course be either furious or mortified when he finds I have given *Our Daily Bread* to Macmillans.[2] Of course, I'll say it's all *your* fault. The book is yours.[3]

I am now waiting for a car to fetch me to a reception – I don't know where or in whose house. The only thing I do know is that the U.S.A. Ambassador has asked me for dinner at 8 p.m. and that a Chinese Lord is going to be there.

Half an h[ou]r ago some bigwig in industry dropped in. 'So you've written that book? ... I've heard about it ... Say, E.C.,[4] I'll just slip that in my pocket.' – 'No, you won't.' – 'Why not? What the devil ails you?' – 'Suppose I wanted to sneak a little of...' whatever the man's output was. 'Wouldn't you show me where I get off? No, my dear, if you want to read that book, you'll have to buy it.' – 'All right, I will, to-morrow.'

Etc. etc. It's amusing enough.

Well
Phil

1 Characters in Grove's novels: Ray and Ivan in *A Search for America*; Bobby Lund and Mrs Amundsen in *Settlers of the Marsh*

2 See previous letters of November 14, 1926 (note 1), and October 7, 1927 (note 2). On October 13, 1926, Miller had written to Grove that Graphic would accept *A Search for America* first, and consider *Our Daily Bread* for later publication since two books by the same author in the same time would be injudicious. On January 17, 1927, he wrote that he had 'had splendid report this morning on *Our Daily Bread* and hope that results [of *A Search for America*] will justify us handling this later.'

Perhaps Hugh Eayrs of Macmillan had offered better terms and a more immediate commitment to publish, which Macmillan did in 1928. Possibly also, Grove thought a Macmillan edition would reach a far wider public than one by Graphic.

3 By saying that *Our Daily Bread* is hers, Grove is possibly alluding to the fact that the novel is based upon Mrs Grove's family, the Wiens, in Saskatchewan; but the Macmillan correspondence indicates that Mrs Grove had actually submitted the novel for publication. See letter of November 14, 1926, note 2.

4 Edward C. Grant

TO CATHERINE GROVE

24 Blackburn Avenue,
Ottawa, Ont.
March 19, 1928

My dear,

This is beginning to look serious. Last night I dined with Sir & Lady E.C. Grant, Lady Pope,[1] and Mr. Phillips[2] (American Minister to the

Dominion) in Sir John A. Macdonald's house,[3] now owned by Dr. Charles Harriss[4] – a very wealthy, very strange musician, who was our host. Mr. Phillips had read part of my book and left at 11 in order to finish it through the night, after having extracted a promise from me that I would lunch with him at the Embassy today – *with* Martin Burrell,[5] Grant,[6] and Premier King.[7] Mr Phillips used to be attaché at the London embassy and is thoroughly Anglicised. He was very charming, and wanted to talk with me about American publication. But, of course, we had the ladies and could not very well discuss business. He is, by the way, a friend not only of Premier King's, but of King George as well. On account of Lady Pope, an elderly but still magnificent French Canadian (widow of a, then, young cabinet minister under Sir John A. Macdonald) much of the conversation was in French, though she understands English perfectly. She, by the way, professed herself so 'enchanted' by *myself* that I had to promise to come to tea (5 o'clock) today, for a chat '*deux-a-deux*' (just the two of us). Premier King had expressed his regret at not being able to attend the meeting on Sat[urday]. Phillips seems to wish to win me for the U.S.A.

With all these people bowing before me, it will be a wonder if I don't, like Swift, get the swelled head.[8] However, I am studying, studying and could already write a better book about this world of diplomacy and politics and – yes, wealth and, after all, real culture, too, than the crude *Land of Afternoon*.[9] Phillips, friend of the president, etc. of the U.S.A., himself a multimillionaire, is a remarkable man in many ways; and I only wonder what is going to come of it all.

Coward-McCann wired 'Par[agraph] 4 (relating to an option on my next 2 books) absolutely essential.' I shall wire back today: 'Contract not essential to me. Cancel.'[10] These people here think that I should be entitled to an income of 50 to 60,000 a year!!!

Harriss, by the way – a very eccentric figure – took me aside at some time and told me, in 5 minutes, the very tragic story of his life. I wonder what impelled him. I was almost taken aback.

Well, I'm writing this in bed and I'd better get up, I suppose. The home in which I am must have cost over 100,000 to build: it contains furniture and collections (of china, f[or] i[nstance]) worth at least half a million. All these people are in some strange way queer (Grant collects medieval *barber* plates and insists on showing them: he has, by the way, a villa at Pau in southern France, and a chalet in Switzerland[)]. The fact that I came from Europe, is an asset in this atmosphere.

People, by the way, want to buy my autograph at $25 each. I say, I'll be delighted to do it anyway; but they won't accept.

Well, it's 9 a.m. Breakfast at 10. So I'll rise. A maid has been hovering about the door with a cup of tea for some time. I'll let her come in and then get up.

Bye-bye
Phil

1 Henrietta Pope, the widow of Sir Joseph Pope (1854–1926). Her father, Sir Henry

Taschereau, was a Chief Justice of Quebec, and her husband was the Private Secretary (later biographer) of Sir John A. Macdonald. She died in 1950.

2 See letter of March 18, 1928 II, note 3.

3 Earnscliffe; see below, note 4.

4 Charles A.E. Harriss (1862–1929) was a composer of music and organizer of international music festivals in Ottawa. He was married and lived in considerable splendour in Earnscliffe – apparently his wife had the money. Photographs of the interior of their house appear in Norman Reddaway's *Earnscliffe, Home of Canada's First Prime Minister and Since 1930 Residence of High Commissioners for the United Kingdom in Canada* (London 1955). A good deal of information about his musical activities is contained in Helmut Kallmann's *A History of Music in Canada 1534–1914* (University of Toronto Press 1960). A letter from Harriss to Grove, dated April 3, 1928, survives in the University of Manitoba Grove Collection.

5 Who was the Parliamentary Librarian; see letter of March 10, 1928, note 5.

6 Edward C. Grant; see letter of March 17, 1928, note 3.

7 William Lyon Mackenzie King (1874–1950); see letter of March 10, 1928, note 8.

8 The reference to Swift is a bit too vague for precise identification. It probably refers in a general way to Swift's satire on the swollen-headed Aeolists in Section VIII of the *Tale of a Tub*. (I am indebted to Professor Denis Donoghue of University College, Dublin, for this note.)

9 *The Land of Afternoon*, Graphic's first title, published in 1924 under the pseudonym 'Gilbert Knox,' was the work of Madge Hamilton Lyons MacBeth (1878–1965). A satire on the political and social life of Ottawa, its success was immediate, and it made Miller's (and Graphic's) name. Four other books of Mrs MacBeth were subsequently published by Graphic: *Curiosity Rewarded* (1926) (a further contribution to the 'Gilbert Knox' mystery), *The Long Day* (1926), *Over the Gangplank to Spain* (1931), and *Shackles* (1926). She published several other books, including the autobiographical *Over My Shoulder* (1953) and *Boulevard Career* (1957).

10 See letter of March 14, 1928 II, for the first hint of difficulties in contract negotiations. It was, of course, too late for Grove to agree to the provision for option on his next two books as he had, by this time, accepted Macmillan's offer for *Our Daily Bread* (see letter of March 18, 1928 III, note 2).

TO CATHERINE GROVE

24 Blackburn Avenue
Ottawa, Ont.
March 19, 1928 II

My dear,

Have just, on the advice of Mr. Phillips, U.S.A. Minister to the Dominion, broken off negotiations with Coward-McCann, New York. He advises waiting. There will be U.S.A. publication because the book calls for it.

Had luncheon at the embassy with the Hon[ourable] Mr Forke,[1] minister of colonisation and agriculture, Hon[ourable] Martin Burrell,

Dr. Duncan Campbell Scott,[2] Deputy Superintendent of Indian Affairs, Sir E.C. Grant, and, of course, Mr. Phillips, the host. Premier King was prevented the last minute and begged to have his regrets expressed to me.

Have now an hour's rest before going to Lady Pope's, widow of Sir Joseph Pope, Sec[re]t[ary] of State under Sir John A. Macdonald. I have almost got used again to having 3 foot-men spring for my cane, etc. when I enter a house. It is a life full of reminiscences.

Sent you this morning 4 press notices re my addresses, 2 in each paper and enclose review of *Search* in the *Canadian Forum* of March 1928.[3] It is slow, slow work to sell a book. But it is coming. Mrs. Phillips read it and phoned for 12 copies to send to her friends. Dr. Harriss, the biggest man in music in the British empire, bought it this morning. Am looking forward to a quiet evening. Shall speak only in Hamilton and Wingham this week. Busy week next week. Then, first week of April will be the last as far as I can see. Then home.

Bye bye
Phil

1 Robert Forke (1860–1933); officially his portfolio was Immigration and Colonization – a slight confusion on Grove's part with Motherwell (letter of March 17, 1928). Born in Scotland, Forke came to Canada in 1882, and settled as a farmer in Pipestone, Manitoba. He won his first election to Parliament in 1921, and in 1926 joined the Mackenzie King cabinet. He was appointed to the Senate in 1929.
2 Better known, of course, as a poet. He was born, in 1862, in Ottawa, and educated in Ontario and Quebec. *The Magic House and Other Poems*, his first book of verse, appeared in 1893, and *In the Village of Viger*, a collection of his short stories, in 1896. In 1921–2, he presided over the Royal Society of Canada, to which he had been elected a Fellow in 1899. *Poems of Duncan Campbell Scott* was published in 1926. *The Green Cloister* (1935) and *The Circle of Affection* (1947) were his last two volumes of verse. He died in 1947.
3 This review, by J.F. White, is partially reprinted in my *Frederick Philip Grove* (Critical Views on Canadian Writers 1970) 122.

TO CATHERINE GROVE

En route, Ottawa–Toronto
March 20, 1928

My dear,

Type this out and send to Stone:[1]
From Ottawa papers, 'Society News.'
'On March 19, Frederick Philip Grove, the distinguished author of *A Search for America*, was entertained at luncheon by Mr. William Phillips, Envoy Extraordinary and Minister Plenipotentiary of the United States of America to the Dominion of Canada. Other guests were the Hon[ourable] Mr. Forke, the Hon[ourable] Martin Burrell, Dr. Duncan Campbell Scott, and Sir

Edward Grant. The Hon[ourable] Lyon Mackenzie King was, to his regret, detained at the last minute. In the afternoon, Lady Pope gave a reception in honour of Mr Grove.'

If that does not dazzle them, what will? But if you think it too snobbish, let it go, of course.

When I left Ottawa today, quite a crowd gathered at the sta[tion]. I was told 1/2 doz[en] times, my Ottawa stay had been a triumph. Grant and a few others are working on a scheme of getting me a job in the Dep[ar]t[ment] of Immigration; and, failing that, in a college as professor of moderns or classics. We'll see.[2]

I'll keep this till I get to Toronto.

You might also show Stone the *Journal* (or *Citizen*)[3] in which the list of those is given who sat at the table of honour during the C[anadian] C[lub] men's luncheon. The reception of Lady Pope's which the papers mention was in reality just the other thing. She is about 65 and wanted me absolutely *alone*; I spent a charming 1 1/2 h[ou]rs talking Europe with her; and every now and then she started to scold me for living in the beastly West; we spoke French. She is a terrific sort of woman, dominating, used to giving orders; and she likes me because I laugh at her. I like her tremendously; but she amuses me. She has surely read and re-read my book. She would *so* have liked to ask me to autograph it for her; but Grant had told her that I charge $25 for my signature; and she is too poor (with an income of $30,000 a year) to spend that much on a whim. So I autographed it without her noticing me. She'll find it by chance, I suppose. Dr. Harriss, owner of Sir J.A. Macdonald's house, thinks himself poor with $150,000 a year. He was offered $1,500,000 for the house; but declined to part with it. It is a marvellous thing, full of treasures of art, etc. That's the way to live, all right, if you forget about the poor pioneers, etc. He is a friend of King George. But he called on me yesterday at the Grants. I was quite back in my heyday of Europe at Ottawa. Well, bye-bye.

I enclose a letter of poor old Casselman's.[4] We are going to spend a little time with them in summer when Ottawa society is at Palm Beach or Bermuda or in Southern France.

Well, bye-bye
Phil

1 Cooper Stone, editor and publisher of the *Rapid City Reporter*; see letter of March 8, 1928, note 1.

2 This job did not materialize.

3 The *Journal* and the *Citizen* are the two daily newspapers of Ottawa.

4 The Casselmans were Grove's hosts in North Bay, and had invited him to visit them again in the summer. For Casselman, see letter of March 10, 1928, note 9.

TO CATHERINE GROVE, CANADIAN NATIONAL TELEGRAM

Smith Falls, Ont.
March 20, 1928 11

Mrs. Groves

Rapid City Man

Am worried, are you ill, if so shall come home at once wire answer care MacMillan 70 Bond St Toronto.

Phil

TO CATHERINE GROVE

Royal Connaught Hotel
Hamilton, Ont.
March 22, 1928

My dear,

This was a fizzle. Out of 500 members 76 were there. With them it went big; but there should have been 200 or 300; there was a winter sports carnival on.

To show you how this thing is handled by the local clubs, I enclose the sort of announcement they send out. I am, of course, not responsible for the text. In fact, I hardly ever see that sort of thing.

Re the *Search*, I might say that, waiting for me here, I found 2 wires from U.S.A. firms – numbers 5 and 6. They are competing against each other. The last one read: 'Would be prepared undertake American edition *Search for America. Your own conditions*. Wire if negotiations possible.' Just imagine my not even answering a wire like that. A year ago it would [have] given me a sleepless night. Today I just shrug my shoulders and put the wire in my pocket.

I spoke to New York over the phone yesterday, from Eayrs'[1] office. I believe I shall give the *Search* to Macmillans, N[ew] Y[ork]. They are distinctly interested; and it will mean double publicity if they have 2 books: *Search* and *Daily Bread*.[2] I'll have to decide next week. Eayrs thinks that beginning with 1929 my books will pay a good living. So do I. Did you like the leather-bound copies which I asked Miller to send you?

As usual I did not get to bed till 1 a.m. But I told them I was going to leave on the 6:45 train this morning. Whereas I leave at 3:20 p.m. to make Wingham in time for my next talk. I believe the total will be exactly 24 addresses. Nothing, so far, has gone as big as Ottawa. The cost of this thing is terrific, though. Even to myself. Have to buy collars, shirts, etc. as needed because there is often no time to get laundry done. It's only in the big centres that I can get 24 hour service in laundry – and that sort of thing is terribly hard on the goods. Am sending you a parcel of dirty laundry today. *Don't return*. Have things done by the chink, please.[3] As far as I can see, I shall be home by April 10 or II, but, of course, more clubs may any time ask for me. Spring is here, however; and people are beginning to use their cars. The carnival, here, was held on artificial ice.

Well, there isn't much news. So
Bye-bye
Phil
I have a perfect trail of invitations across Ontario.

1 Hugh S. Eayrs of Macmillan; see letter of November 14, 1926, note 2.
2 Macmillan published *Our Daily Bread*, but the US edition of *A Search for America* was to bear Carrier's imprint; see letter of March 29, 1928 III, note 1. For the result of negotiations with Coward-McCann, see letter of March 19, 1928, and note 9 to that letter.
3 'By the chink'; ie, by the Chinese laundryman. Chinese laundries were to be found all over Canada in the nineteen-twenties and -thirties.

TO CATHERINE GROVE

Hotel Brunswick
Wingham, Ont.
March 23, 1928

My dear,

This is a very small city, and the poorest hotel I have so far seen on this tour. Tomorrow I go back to Toronto where I am going to stay with 'Ned Pratt,'[1] over the week-end. Deacon[2] wants me to see a play. I am sending him a wire declining. I want rest, rest, rest. Next week will be a very busy one, but I believe it is the last busy one. Over next week, I see only 2 or 3 appointments ahead – unless a date can be arranged with Toronto. I hope so; but it seems somewhat doubtful. If no arrangement can be made now, I shall speak there in the fall.

I am dropping a line every now and then to the Gardiners.[3]

I believe I have already mentioned that it seems as if I were going to be in shape about a year from now to make my books pay us a living – a modest one, yet still a living. So I am not committing myself with regard to a job. It would be unwise to bind myself at the very moment when success seems within reach.

Just now the Pres[ident][4] of the local club called; and I am going to be billeted with the postmaster;[5] that will be more comfortable and convenient. As it happens, those people will have to be ready in the morning for the train at 6:40 a.m. I want to get to Toronto in reasonable time. Well, since I am to move, I'd better pack up.

Bye-bye
Phil

10 E.J. Pratt. *Photo by Randolph Macdonald, courtesy Victoria University, Toronto*

1 Edwin ('Ned') J. Pratt (1883–1964), the poet. He was born in Newfoundland, the son of a Methodist minister, and educated at St John's Methodist College and the University of Toronto (BA 1911; MA 1912; BD 1913; PH D 1917). He then joined the staff of the University of Toronto, first as a lecturer in psychology, and in 1920 as a professor of English in Victoria College, retiring in 1953. He is generally regarded as the leading Canadian poet of the first half of this century. *The Collected Poems of E.J. Pratt* (second edition), edited by Northrop Frye, appeared in 1958. He was elected a Fellow of the Royal Society of Canada in 1930.

Grove had read Pratt's *Titans* the previous year (see letter of February 7, 1927); it is not known if this was the first time they met: there are suggestions in the Phelps letters to Grove that the Groves may have met the Pratts at Bobcaygeon before this.

2 William Arthur Deacon

3 E.S. Gardiner and his wife in Rapid City

4 The President of the Canadian Club in Wingham at this time was Dr R. Redmond, MD (1870–1953).

5 A.H. Musgrove (1854–1940)

TO CATHERINE GROVE

25 Tullis Drive, Toronto, Ont.
c/o Dr. Pratt.
March 24, 1928

Well, my dear, I am here at Pratt's, with my Sunday off, of course. Stayed last night with two old maiden ladies at Wingham, and to escape the ordeal of too much entertainment, slipped away this mor[ning] at 6 a.m. Bought you 2 p[ai]rs of silk stockings today at Simpson's. One a very good pair at $3.50. Also 1 p[ai]r for Mandy a $2.50 stocking on special sale (p[ai]d $1.75). Take the label off (no. 8¹/₂). Hope it fits. That will be all I'll buy for M[andy] but I thought I'd like to send her some *small* present.

Found here my itinerary and shall be through by *April 7* in Ontario. Then home. Shall wire you about that (so the tour will have been of 6 weeks, with 25 cities visited).

Also found your letter of Mar[ch] 18, addressed to Ottawa and forwarded by Miss Klotz – the chief clerk of the Ass[ociation]. Well, if I am to believe the people here and at Ottawa, I'm one in 100,000,000. But that does not matter. I have a string of invitations across Ontario, for the summer; and I want you to meet people. Most of them are just plain, everyday people – with the exception of Ottawa where I was lionized by the very highest society. I hope, however, you'll meet a few of those also; though most of them will be in Europe, then.

Carillon Club is a decided success; and on my advice the *next* book will be a Macmillan book.

Have offer after offer from U.S.A. and am glad I broke

with Coward McCann. As for my health, I am eating *anything*, without bad effects. When I struck Ottawa, I had to.

Dr. Alexander[1] called on me here ½ h[ou]r before I arrived. Did not see him, therefore; but shall have lunch with him tomorrow. Tonight they wanted me to speak at the Arts and Letters Club; but I have declined to go out. Caught a slight cold at Hamilton; but the two maiden ladies nursed me beautifully yesterday – put me to bed after lunch, thermogened me by my direction, made a hot brandy toddy and did not permit me to get up till after 5 p.m. Then hot and cold bath, supper, and then the meeting. Chest and nose are quite clear. But I'll stay at home, all alone, tonight; shall take a hot bath and 'so to bed.' Am waiting now for W.A. Deacon.[2]

Shall speak here twice on April 2; next day at Sarnia; then back to Ottawa – then Chapleau – then home. So when you get this, it will be less than 2 weeks till I get there.

Meanwhile I wonder whether you got my wire asking for underwear to be sent here. It's Saturday night; and I have not received it. It's just a trifle embarrassing, for the stuff does get dirty in travelling. However, I'll manage. Please don't return any laundry except underwear. Have things done by the chink there. I keep buying new things because I've got to. Now don't worry. Things *are* breaking. And I've covered only Ontario, so far – one province out of 9. It is, after all, significant that such people as Dr. Alexander think it worth their while to *call on me* when they hear I'm going to be in town. I value that more than the whole Ottawa gov[ernmen]t and society bunch. The only thing that worries me is that you keep saying 'I'm not ill' and then 'I'm better today.' So you were not well, after all.

This is interesting and stimulating, etc. etc., but I'll be glad when it's over. Hope you like the underwear: of the silk I bought the very best – plain, but highest quality. You can pay $50 for a pair of bloomers here: but it's for lace and embroidery you're paying. Never mind about sending money – what's the use? I'm not suffering. Have spent close to $400 by now, not counting R[ail]r[oad] fares and local expenses, except on week-ends – and on week-ends I've mostly got invitations.

Well, I'd better close since Deacon will appear any moment.

So bye, bye, my dear. As to children, I quite agree. And I'd be willing right now – but we must wait till the money's in sight. Eayrs[3] thinks that within a year or two I should be making $8 to 10,000 a year. I've sold him 'Adolescence'[4] – provided he can pull off international publication.

For awhile longer we'll have to remain frugal, though.

Bye-bye

Phil

1 William John Alexander (1855–1944), for whose literary judgement Grove had the highest regard; see the letters to Alexander, the dedication in *The Master of the Mill*, and the letter to me of January 4, 1945.

Born in Hamilton, Ontario, he received his BA (1876) from the University of London, and PH D (1883) from Johns Hopkins University. He was, from 1876 to 1879, an Assistant Master at Prince of Wales College (now merged with the University of Prince Edward Island). In 1884, he was appointed Professor of English at Dalhousie University, and in 1889, at University College, Toronto. Queen's University conferred the LL D on him in 1919. He retired in 1926, but continued to live in Toronto. His *An Introduction to the Poetry of Robert Browning* was published in 1899. The Alexander Lectures at the University of Toronto commemorate his name.

On March 8, 1928, he wrote to Grove praising *A Search for America* for being 'by far the most interesting contribution to so-called Canadian Literature,' and *Over Prairie Trails* for having 'more sheer literary quality than any other prose Canadian book that I have read.' Thus began one of Grove's most satisfying friendships.

2 In 1928, W.A. Deacon left *Saturday Night* and joined the staff of the Toronto *Mail and Empire*.

3 Hugh S. Eayrs of Macmillan

4 Actually published as *The Yoke of Life* (Toronto: Macmillan; New York: Richard Smith 1930)

TO CATHERINE GROVE

En route Toronto–Kitchener, Ont.
March 26, 1928

Now, my dear, listen here. Things are breaking; and I want you to meet me at Winnipeg, probably on Good Friday. I *may* even wire you to meet me at P[or]t Arthur. Now make sure that, in case of need you can board the 5:40 p.m. train #4 from W[inni]peg to P[or]t Arthur (C.P.R.) on Thursday night. If, next week, Tuesday or Wed[nesday] I wire you, meet me at P[or]t Arthur Friday morning, then leave R[apid] C[ity] on Thur[sday] 10:30 a.m. via Minnedosa – borrow a suitcase. Arrive W[inni]peg 4:45; leave W[inni]peg 5:40 (Phone Phelps to meet you for the hour – or Kirk).[1] Take, of course, return ticket. As soon as you arrive at W[inni]peg, go to the 'reservations' wicket and take out a lower berth W[inni]peg – P[or]t Arthur. If I am not at Sta[tion] at P[or]t Arthur, go to *Prince Arthur* Hotel and ask for a *Lake-view* room with bath, stating your husband will be in later. If you see Phelps, ask him whether we can stay with him during Easter week till Sat[urday]. I want to get another suit. You will need to take ca. $50 along for fare and incidentals. Beyond that you don't need to worry about money. We'll stay at P[or]t Arthur for a day or 2 and then return to W[inni]peg – All clear? If not, wire night letter on Tuesday, April 3, to Ottawa – it will reach me on April 4. I *may* have to change the date. Nor is it sure that I can arrange for the stay at P[or]t Arthur. My wire will tell you. If we meet at W[inni]peg, you will probably have to spend a night there before my arrival, I shall *likely* arrive at 10 a.m., though possibly at 8:15 p.m. I should prefer you to go to A.L.P.'s,[2] but if that is repellent to you, go Royal Alexandra. Expense no object.

You ask why itinerary changes. Well, you see it is very difficult to get a date that suits both local clubs and me. Toronto, f[or] i[nstance] $\mp$[3] told I'll be there March 19 – wires back, 'Cannot arrange meeting: will Mar[ch] 21 do?' Answer: 'No, Mar[ch] 21 Grove at Hamilton. Propose Mar[ch] 24.' Answer: 'Saturday meeting would necessarily be small – too many counter attractions. How about Monday 26?' Answer: 'Grove promised to Kitchener Monday 26. Monday April 2 open.' Answer: 'Accept Monday April 2.' Enquiry from Grove: 'Is Monday April 2 for Toronto, 2 meetings, acceptable?' Grove's answer: 'Will depend on whether there is a Tuesday *mor[ning]* train to Sarnia in time for 4:15 meeting.' Ottawa answer: 'There is. Please confirm Toronto men noon women evening April 2.' All right, I confirm. Now that sort of thing is going on simultaneously with perhaps 10 clubs. We've a date made with the men at last. The women hear of it and say, 'we want him, too.' But we've got a University extension lecture on that night, and everything is upset again, etc. etc. See?

Well, I am 'the biggest thing there is in Canada' in Toronto. Same thing as in Ottawa. Only here, the university people dominate. I was introduced at a small meeting as 'perhaps the most significant voice in the English-speaking world of today.'

Can't tell all in letters.

Have 7 offers from U.S.A. Shall make new contract today or tomorrow, Wed[nesday] at latest.[4] All over the wire. Am spending money like water. Can't be helped. Shall spend over $20 in telegrams alone today. Well, bye-bye

Phil

By the way, no underwear reached me. So I'm off in the same suit for the second week.

1 Arthur L. Phelps and Watson Kirkconnell

2 Phelps

3 ie, more or less

4 Presumably, in the light of earlier remarks, for the publication of *A Search for America* in the United States; see letter of March 29, 1928 III, note 1.

TO CATHERINE GROVE

Walper House
Kitchener, Ont.
March 26, 1928 II

Well, my dear, here I am in the heart of the Ontario German district. Opposite my hotel room window is a haberdasher's with the proud name 'Wettläufer'[1] over the whole of the show window. Had a delightful time with Pratt, Fairley,[2] and Alexander in Toronto over the week-end. Shall be back there next week-end when I have consented to attend one big dinner given in my honour where I am to meet Mazo de la Roche.[3] I am sending you her last (prize) novel. When you have read it, please return it to:

Mrs. M.J. McMahon[4]
Port Hope, Ont.

Enclose a visiting card, saying 'With thanks from Mr. & Mrs. F.P. Grove.'

Eayrs[5] said when I confronted him with the misdoings of his firm, 'Yes, I could kick myself. I've simply been mistaken. I have wanted to build up a Canadian novelist and thought Miss de la Roche was a comer. I know today and have known for some time that she has no future. You have. You have written the two biggest books that have come out of America. And European and world-wide recognition will follow.'

At Alexander's one person after the other took me aside (the grand old man himself, too) and said, 'By the side of your work the work of all contemporary America looks dwarfed.' Another man (Prof[essor] Fairley) added, 'You are the only genius living this side of the Atlantic. Even on the other side, in England, people are beginning to wake up to the fact that we have, in Canada, one of the 3 or 4 significant voices of the English-speaking world of today.' Etc. etc. Miss Thompson,[6] a very interesting girl, 'Book Adviser' at Eaton's, said, 'You've got to eat your own words, Mr. Grove. You say we've got only one single, slender vol[ume] on our 3000 mile book-shelf. But we have 5, and 4 of them were written by yourself.'

I am playing a bold game in the U.S.A. but I think I'll win. Am holding out for full royalties and want them to *print* there: to show Miller how the book should have looked. At first (Coward-McCann) wanted to buy 1000 sheets from Miller. But no investment would have meant no pains taken. Last offer from New York – which I am likely to accept was, print 5000 copies first edition; appear *June*; price not less than $3.00 (this to protect Miller); royalties: 10% first 5000; 12½% second 5000; 15% thereafter. Macmillans are among the bidders. Expect a wire from them any moment. It is a race between 3 firms; the rest I don't even answer. Expect to make a definite contract tomorrow or day after.[7]

Wrote you this morning in the train about meeting me about Easter. I can't tell yet whether I'll come via P[or]t Arthur or not. There are one or two talks hanging in the background which are still uncertain. But the week of April 2 will be the last. On April 2 I speak twice at Toronto. Day after at Sarnia. Then back to Ottawa overnight. Then West.

I shall have to speak in 1½ h[ou]rs. So I think I'd better polish my shoes and lie down for an hour.

Bye-bye
Phil

[the bottom of the letter is torn off]

1 A runner. Grove may have meant *Wettlämpfer*, the German word for a 'prize-fighter.'

2 Barker Fairley was born in 1887 in England, and educated in that country and Europe. He came to Canada in 1910 as Professor of German at the University of Alberta, having taught previously at the University of Jena (1907–10). From 1915 to 1932, and again from

1936 until his retirement in 1957, he was Professor of German at University College, Toronto. During the interim, he was Head of the German Department at Victoria University, Manchester (England) (1932–6). He has published books on Goethe, Charles Doughty, Heine, and William Raabe.

3 Mazo de la Roche (1879–1961), the celebrated author of the 'Jalna' novels about the Whiteoak family. Born in Newmarket, Ontario, and a long-time resident of Toronto, she enjoyed great popular success after *Jalna*, the first novel of the series, won the *Atlantic Monthly* Prize of $10,000 in 1927. She published some two dozen novels, many short stories, and several plays and books of non-fiction. Her autobiography, *Ringing the Changes*, was published in 1957. See *Mazo de la Roche* by George Hendrick (New York: Twayne 1970) and *Mazo de la Roche of Jalna* by Ronald Hambleton (New York: Hawthorn Books 1966).

4 Mrs Mary Jean McMahon; see letter of March 15, 1928 II, note 1.

5 Of Macmillan, with whom Grove was negotiating publication of *Our Daily Bread*.

6 Norah Thompson (now Mrs H. Depencier of Owen Sound, Ontario) was Eaton's Book Adviser in the twenties and thirties. She went to London and Paris each year, and bought books for T. Eaton Company, relying largely on British book reviews. In 1928, when the Eaton Book Club was formed, she became a member of the selection committee. Other members of the committee were W.J. Alexander (Chairman), J.F. Macdonald (see letter of September 15, 1928, note 4), C.J. Eustace (who later became President of Dent's in Canada) and Lady Willison (see letter of September 15, 1928, note 2).

7 Grove, it seems, included Louis Carrier's firm in the group of US firms he talks of; see letter of March 29, 1928 III, note 1.

Louis Carrier (1898–1961), was a journalist, lecturer, publisher, and collector of Canadiana. He was born in Lévis, Quebec, and educated in that province. He served in the RAF during World War I, following which he worked as a reporter successively for the Quebec *Chronicle Telegraph* and the Montreal *Gazette* and *Star*. In 1928 he established the Mercury Press and engaged in book publishing under the imprint Louis Carrier and Company, with offices in Montreal and New York. By 1930 the firm seems to have ceased operation, and in the same year Carrier became Special Correspondent to the *New York Times*. Later he was general manager of *Le Canada*, and a consultant for the French-language edition of the *Reader's Digest*.

Known particularly for his research in the history of the arts and crafts of Quebec, Carrier lectured widely on these subjects and organized exhibitions of French art in Canada and the United States. He was a curator of the Chateau de Ramezay, and upon retirement was appointed an honorary curator and consultant. He was a fellow of the Royal Society of Arts and Royal Geographical Society.

TO CATHERINE GROVE

Walper House
Kitchener, Ont.
March 27, 1928

Well, my deah! Drat it all! I can't sleep when I have these ovations. Had 2 in succession last night. Spoke at 4:15 till 5:30. Banquet at 6:30.

Just had time to change; and that was all. Then spoke again at 7:15 till 8:30. 'The Greatest Canadian' I was called. Plup, plup!

But they all know that the rest of Canadian writers are pygmies by my side; and they say so. Alexander, f[or] i[nstance], and Fairley, and others. I believe I've told you so before. Some Toronto people who know they can't hear me on April 2 came out here (Eaton and Simpson book dep[artmen]t managers, f[or] i[nstance][)]. I'm surely stirring up this countryside. Guelph which, so far, had been unable to make a date, wired last night, asking for the one open night this week. I 'confirmed' there, by upsetting a dinner party given by Deacon in my honour. I don't say so to [letter cut here] next year, this time of year, to 'cash in' – nothing big yet; but some $3000 to $4000. And it will *grow* – and in that estimate I discount Miller from whom we'll never get anything, I am pretty sure. However ... Things are moving; and I have touched only 1 province out of 9 so far. I must go through with this. There's no other way. But I worry about you. What about next fall? I see no way except for you to board. I believe that after Christmas you can give up teaching; but till then? While I'm on the tour? On that tour I should make $1000 or so, possibly more. And that money will carry us till royalties come in. Then we'll go east together, to Ontario to live there.

Well, I've nothing else to write. Am expecting some wires. This is my only day off this week. Quite a good hotel here.

Bye-bye
Phil

TO CATHERINE GROVE

Hotel London,
London, Ont.
March 28, 1928

You wonder how the wire came to come from Smith's Falls. I'll tell you. You had assured me so often that you were well that, when in a letter which I received at the moment of leaving Ottawa for Southern Ontario you said, 'I am better this morning,' I became suspicious. And, since people here travel with all modern conveniences – or inconveniences, as in the case of the radio blaring away through the chair-car in which I usually sit (expense no object) – you can send wires from 'En route'; but, as it happened, I handed mine to the conductor at the precise moment before the through train to Toronto came to a stop at Smith's Falls; and he, to save himself the trouble of the wireless, handed it – probably; I don't really know – to the agent there. So that's that.

This is a place I dislike. It's too 'swell' for me – that is the only word that fits. Ottawa is Dukes and Lords; and I'm at home among them. These people here would only like to be Dukes and Lords; and I can't stand them. From the moment I landed here, they've been entertaining me, showing off their material achievements which *are* considerable. But if they dressed a little less perfectly and had a little less money and didn't put on such an air of culture – with nothing below – they'd be more of my kind though I can fence well enough with them. It's only half an hour now that I ceased speaking. No more than 20 came to shake hands with me because they felt moved. At Kitchener, every man and every woman stood around and tried to; and their jaws shook; and when I said, 'Ladies and gentlemen, I'm exhausted and feel all in. Will you permit me to retire and say that I read in your faces all you wish to express?' they sneaked away.

Well, it seems you did not get one wire I sent; for I just now got a suit of underwear which I expected to find at Pratt's – or Eayrs'. But it does not matter except that I felt 'smelly' this afternoon. I'll return the suit I'm wearing to-morrow morning, and hope I'll find another one at Ottawa so I can change.

I can see already, however, that there will be no time for P[or]t Arthur. I believe I shall reach Winnipeg on Saturday, April 7, at 8:15 p.m. Try to bring me another clean suit of underwear there; and if it is very warm, could you bring my spring coat? I had hoped we could spend a day or two at Thunderbay. Cape Thunder is quite a sight.

Here it was almost summer day before yesterday. Yesterday we had a regular blizzard. And today it is cold. Yet I am getting over a slight cold which I caught at Hamilton. Sent you a 'write-up' on my Kitchener speeches this morning.

I am, of course, thinking a great deal of the little girl who is no more.[1] All the more since I see the time coming when finances won't worry us any longer. Am anxiously waiting for the U.S.A. contracts which should have reached me today but didn't. Still, there is time for them to reach me tomorrow morning.

Well, I'm to meet a bunch of University of Western Ontario students tonight, at the house of the Librarian of the Public Library.[2] So I'd better go down for dinner or supper – they call it dinner here and eat my $5. meal. I am no longer dieting, except at breakfast.

Bye-bye
Phil

1 Phyllis May, who died the previous summer

2 Richard Edwin Crouch, who was born in London, Ontario, in 1894, and educated at the Universities of London (1918–19), Western Ontario (BA 1920), and Paris (1921–2). On his return from Paris, he served briefly as a Lecturer in Economics at the University of Western Ontario. In 1923, he was appointed Chief Librarian of London (Ontario), to which post, in 1940, the office of the Director of Public Libraries and Art Museums was added. He died on January 25, 1967. He was the author of a chapter on libraries in *Adult Education in Canada* (1950), and a contributor to several professional and other periodicals.

From the nature of his remarks here, and in the following letter, it is clear that this was Grove's first meeting with a man who was to become a close friend.

TO CATHERINE GROVE

Hotel London,
London, Ont.
March 29, 1928

Had, after all, in spite of my dislike of this town, a delightful time last night. It shows again that the right sort of people gravitate towards me. The librarian of the – rather famous – Public Library here[1] asked me whether I'd come to meet a small group at his house, promising it would be strictly 'stag.' But when, at 11:30 I rose to slip away, I found that some 2 or 3 [the rest of the page is cut off] now, since they see what a reception I had at the women's club, they are trying to set a date. I think it good policy not to cheapen myself by coming back before the fall. So I told them to write to Spry and to see what he can do in October.

I am sending a parcel of soiled laundry. Don't return anything. I expect one more suit of underwear at Ottawa – nothing else. Shall send home, from now on, all soiled things – there will be no other stop to get laundry done. At Toronto I'll arrive Sat[urday] late – too late for getting things washed. Leave on Monday night for the long hop to Sarnia. Then, in one jump, overnight, to Ottawa where I hope to get the cash still coming to me. I have had $525.

Of these $200 were for expenses – which will just about cover them; $225 are in the bank at W[inni]peg; and ca. 100 I have spent – on face massages (which greatly refresh before speaking when I'm tired), tobacco, underwear, ties, collars, shirts, hat for you, underwear for you, stockings for you. It does not [the bottom of the letter is cut off]

1 As previously noted (letter of March 28), Richard Crouch

TO CATHERINE GROVE, CANADIAN NATIONAL TELEGRAM

Stratford, Ont.
March 29, 1928 II

Mrs C Grove
Rapid City Man

Please send Louis Carrier Co thirty three, tenth street New York list of misprints in *Search.*[1]

Phil

1 See the following letter, note 1. For Louis Carrier, see letter of March 26, 1928 II, note 7.

TO CATHERINE GROVE

Stratford, Ont.
March 29, 1928 III
8 p.m.

Well, I've eluded the 'distinguished-guest' hounds and am sitting, in my pyjamas, in an overheated hotel room where I daren't open the windows for fear of catching a cold – at least not before I get into bed.

At London, this morning, I was the victim of that group of last night's – the too kind people who are really very cruel. They want to show the visitor all sorts of things that don't interest him: the public library, and the U[niversity] and the city hall, and the country about the city. You see London is 1/2 the size of W[inni]peg. But I had one satisfaction; I asked, before leaving, to see the manager of that 'crack' hotel. When he came, I said to him, wearily, 'Well, when the stranger lands at this place, he is dazzled. This is a hotel truly American in its splendour of marble and costly woods. But it takes only 24 hours for him to find out that there is nothing first class about the place except the prices; everything else, and above all, the service is at best fifth-rate.' And then I gave him a list of his sins. When I got through, I waved him away, saying, 'And now you can go, Sir. You won't see me again; and I shall spread the report of this hold-up hostelry wherever I go; you know I go to many places. Please leave me alone.' And he did; he was so dumbfounded.

But I signed the American contract[1] as you know from my wire and got $500 *down*. I could have had $1500 from another publisher; but as the payment for 30,000 copies. This 500 is merely part of the 10% for the first 2000 (at $3.50 per copy). The first edition to be of 5000 copies – or to bring us $1750 – payable, the balance, next year in April. Since I believe that the book will sell in 20,000 copies at least, I thought it wise not to sell future profits for a paltry thousand now. Till then we'll worry along.

1st five thousand ...	$1750
2nd " "	2187.50
1000[0] –	2625
Total	$6562.50 for 20,000

copies by my contract. It would be foolish to sell that for $1500 down instead of being satisfied with $500 now – which will pay off our debt to the Life Ins[urance] Co[mpany]. I was out of money, though, and had to take $100 out, being unwilling to wire for money to Spry, for a good deal of the last 100 received from him was spent for ourselves – your underwear and stockings, etc. We'll cash in on magazines, etc., during the year. I also have the advantage of saving the 5% U.S.A. income tax. Things have broken, after all.

Am just now receiving wire after wire of invitations to stay with the wealthiest and most prominent Torontonians. I have, for Monday, accepted the invitation of Major Norsworthy[2] to stay at the *York Club* – the aristocratic Club of Toronto – where I shall escape the women.

Here I did not quite escape – nor the men, either, by the way. They have captured me and exacted a promise to address the Normal School to-morrow morning. Well, I don't mind though I'm pretty hoarse just now.

But I am distinctly the great man of the hour in Ontario.

In London, the swell place, people don't *buy* books; they borrow them.

Here, in little Stratford (size of Brandon, I believe, or a little larger) they buy them.

This was the 21st city today. Tomorrow Guelph. Then Toronto, then Sarnia, then Ottawa, Chapleau, and *home*, I hope.

Well, bye-bye
Phil

1 With Louis Carrier & Co.; see letter of March 26, 1928 II, and letters previous to that. Carrier, of course, would be more naturally considered a Montreal publisher, although he did have a New York office.

2 Major Stanley C. Norsworthy, DSO, was born in Ontario in 1881, and entered the service of the Bank of Montreal in 1898, becoming its Assistant General Manager in 1931 after a distinguished career of managing several branches of the Bank in Canada and overseas. In 1928, when Grove met him, he was in charge of the Ontario Division of the Bank's operations.

TO CATHERINE GROVE

The Windsor
Stratford, Ont.
March 30, 1928

Have just spoken to the Normal School. A smug, self-satisfied bunch (the teaching body, I mean) who felt disquieted, disturbed, *threatened* by my talk (on 'The classical tradition'). The prin[cipal][1] said to me, 'Of course, you can't talk of Greek to us. They don't know Greek. We don't teach it.' 'That,' I said, 'is why I'm going to talk Greek to them.' For that is just the point. Perhaps, though I doubt it, one or two of the students got the p[oin]t; none of the teachers did.

Besides, I am travelling in the wake of that vermin Wilson Macdonald[2] who peddles his own wares. When *he* enters a town, he brings a trunkful of his books along. When he has spoken, he displays them and rakes in the shekels. And these people can't distinguish gold from dross. This oldest part of Ont[ario] is provincial, parochial, self-sufficient, commercial, ignorant, materialistic, impenetrable to ideas – I mean, of course, as a whole; there are exceptions everywhere. But nothing is as discouraging as to listen to the comments made on my talk of which they understand nothing. I'll write a comedy after this. The rank and file is vastly less intelligent than the rank and file in Winnipeg; and I tell them so. [letter cut here] with it for another week or so.

I expect to get home (or to W[inni]peg at least) by Saturday or Sunday of next week. Meet me at W[inni]peg, will you? I'll wire the exact date and hour of arrival from Ottawa.

Well, bye-bye, dear.
Phil

[the bottom of the letter is cut off]

1 Dr Sidney Silcox, who was Principal of the Stratford Normal School from 1909 until his death in 1935. A native of Iona, Ontario, he graduated from the University of Toronto in 1893, specializing in science, and received his D PAED. from the same university in 1903. He was active in the Stratford Historical Society, and presented a number of papers on the settlement of the district. During his principalship, the annual presentation of a Shakespearean play became a feature of life of the Normal School. The Normal School (later Teachers' College) ceased functioning in May 1973.

2 Wilson Pugsley Macdonald (1880–1967) was a Canadian poet who enjoyed great popularity in the nineteen-twenties and -thirties, when his lecture tours, particularly to high schools, brought him to public attention. He fell into relative obscurity in the period after World War II. His flamboyant personality, rhetorical manner of speech, and romantic style of verse would obviously not have appealed to Grove.

TO CATHERINE GROVE

New Hotel Wellington
Guelph, Ont.
March 31, 1928
8 a.m.

Well, and Toronto next. Here I had once more a great triumph. Why? The Guelph Agric[ultural] College.[1] The way those people shook my hands, and then almost carried me home to the hotel!

Major Norsworthy,[2] of the Toronto C[anadian] C[lub] wired me a welcome last night, inviting me to stay at the York Club ('swellest' club of Toronto), and I accepted for Monday. On Tuesday, drat it, I'll have to make the big hop to Sarnia. I'm tired of it and wish I could run east instead of west. I hope I shall be able to catch a night train to Ottawa whence I'll start west and home. I'll heave a sigh of relief. I've been crowding things so as to get through before Easter, and fortunately Toronto, hearing, according to Major N[orsworthy], 'such glowing reports of my addresses at Ottawa,' came to the scratch and made a special effort to have the meetings at a date to suit me.

Well, it's 1/2 h[ou]r till train time. Perhaps I'd better get my baggage ready.

Bye-bye
Phil

1 The Ontario Agricultural College, now part of the enlarged University of Guelph.

2 See letter of March 29, 1928 III, note 2.

TO CATHERINE GROVE

Prince George Hotel,
Toronto, Ont.
March 31, 1928 II

My dear,

It seems this is going to be a big splash here. Newspaper men stood lined up when the train pulled in, to interview me. Photographers clicked their cameras, one of them being lucky enough to catch me when I was taking my cap off to a lady. I hope my hair wasn't looking too disorderly.

At last, to have an hour's rest, I escaped into this out-of-the-way hotel. Have just phoned Eayrs to take me out of this. Am going to stay with him till Monday mor[ning], when I shall transfer to the *York Club* and move back into the light of publicity.

Deacon brought me, from Pratt, the parcel and your letters. I think I'll be home, or rather at W[inni]peg a week from today. Must wire you particulars. I want you to meet me there, you know. Don't send any more underwear, but, if you come to W[inni]peg, bring a suit if you can.

Now listen here, old girl. I ran out of money at London and being utterly unknown there, cashed a cheque for $100, leaving as security a cheque for $500 from my American publishers and my bankbook, with instructions to transfer cheque to Winnipeg and collect my cheque. To the W[inni]peg office I gave instructions to forward bankbook to R[apid] C[ity]. Now bring that bankbook (B[ank] of Montreal) along when you come (I'll have more money to deposit, and we'll pay off our life-insurance loan[)].

Re such items as that about Mr Phillips[1] – use your own judgment. I'll try to get hold of a copy of tonight's Toronto *Star* and mail it to you. You can, if it is at all true to fact, give it to Stone. But I don't care whether you do or not. Monday's 'splash,'[2] I am afraid I won't get, for I'll have to leave on Tuesday very early to make Sarnia. It will depend on what connections I can make from Sarnia to Ottawa, whether I'll get home – or to W[inni]peg – within the next week. I am going to enquire shortly and shall let you know, by wire, when I find out myself.

Well, so long –
Phil

Here I am, just to rest for an hour, taking a hotel room at $4.00. Some extravagance, eh?

But I'm tired of this terrific pace.

1 Grove was the guest of honour at a luncheon given by William Phillips, the American Minister to Canada, on March 19. See letter of March 20, 1928, in which Grove has copied out an item from an Ottawa newspaper describing those present at the luncheon, to be shown, at Mrs Grove's discretion, to Cooper Stone, editor of the *Rapid City Reporter*.

2 The Toronto *Globe* of April 2, 1928 (p 16) carried a biographical article on Grove in

connection with his visit to the city on the following day to address the local Women's Canadian Club on 'Canada – the Spiritual Awakening of an Individual.' The article, presumably based on information supplied by Grove, credited him with nineteen novels 'in manuscript,' and contained still another version of his autobiography. Grove's family fortunes failed, according to this version, when he was twenty-four, which would make 1895/6 the date of his arrival in Canada. On the following day, April 3, the paper carried an enthusiastic review of Grove's address (p 8).

TO CATHERINE GROVE

The York Club
Toronto, Ont.
April 2, 1928

My dear Tee,

Well, this has been a tremendous round so far; and today I shall have to fight my biggest battle. I'm quite keyed up.

This is the most exclusive club in Canada; it looks down upon the 'Cabinet Club' (the 'Rideau') at Ottawa as at the venture of the newly rich. On my arrival 1/2 h[ou]r ago a valet was placed at my exclusive disposal; and he promptly unpacked my baggage, hanging everything up, etc.

The newspapers carry double announcements. The *Search*, of course, is out of print. Too bad. Am wiring Carrier, of Montreal, to try to buy Miller out; for I hear Graphic is on the verge of bankruptcy.[1] But there's nothing to worry about. The thing not only has started; it's rolling irresistibly. I have enjoyed Eayrs and Mrs. Eayrs very much.[2] They are really delightful people.

Well, I must get back to work and study my *short* talk for the men's luncheon – which I have given only twice before. All my friends (Pratt, Eayrs, Edgar,[3] Alexander, Hutton,[4] Fairley, and many others) have been invited to share the table of honour on the platform with me. There will be a press gallery of 12 reporters, etc. etc. It's enormous.

Bye-bye
Phil

[the bottom of the letter is cut off]

1 A premature assumption; bankruptcy officially came in 1932, but things were no doubt very shaky from 1928 onwards.
2 The relationship between Eayrs and Grove was somewhat uneven. But Eayrs retained a life-long faith in Grove's work; and Grove, in his turn, never accuses Eayrs of lack of discernment.
3 Oscar Pelham Edgar (1871–1948), Professor of English at Victoria College, Toronto (1902–38), a distinguished humanist and scholar. He was elected a Fellow of the Royal Society of Canada in 1915, and received the Society's Lorne Pierce Medal in 1936. He was

one of the founders of the Canadian Authors' (later Writers') Foundation, which was to support Grove in his last years. His *A Study of Shelley*, prepared as a doctoral dissertation for Johns Hopkins University, was published in 1899, *Henry James: Man and Author* in 1927, and *The Art of the Novel* in 1933. His memoirs, *Across My Path*, edited by Northrop Frye, were published in 1952.

4 Maurice Hutton (1856–1940). Born in England and educated at Oxford, he came to Canada in 1880 as Professor of Classics at the University of Toronto, becoming Principal of University College in 1901. He became a Fellow of the Royal Society of Canada in 1913. He wrote such books as *The Greek Point of View* (1925), *Many Minds* (1927), *All the Rivers Run into the Sea* (1928), and *The Sisters, Jest and Earnest* (1930), which are notable for their urbanity and wit.

Hutton wrote a letter to Grove on January 29 [1929?] and it is preserved in the University of Manitoba Grove Collection; but if Grove wrote to Hutton the letter does not seem to have survived.

TO CATHERINE GROVE

The York Club
Toronto
April 2, 1928 11

My dear,

This was, at noon, one of the most amazing things I've experienced. Between 4 and 500 men went frantic over my address. And who were they? University men, big business leaders, Doctors, Lawyers, etc.

When I slipped out through the crush, I heard things like this. 'Who is this fellow?' 'Dunno.' 'Most gripping thing I've ever heard. Don't you agree?' 'I do. Fellow's written some books.' 'Well, he's sold them to me.' 'And to me, you bet.'

Elsewhere I heard, 'Magnificent!' 'Enormous!' 'Every sentence went home.' etc. etc. Pratt shook hands with me, tears in his eyes. Alexander, Dr. Grant,[1] the same. The chairman of the board of Directors of Macmillan's[2] came and said, 'I've just congratulated Hughie (Eayrs) on having captured a book of yours.' Merrill Denison[3] had to stenograph the thing for one of the papers. I enclose an advance article which, of course, contains the usual misstatements. It appeared in the Toronto *Star*, the biggest newspaper in Canada.

Well, I must get ready for the evening ordeal. I want a hot bath and a face massage. Winnipeg Friday. Hope you'll be there.

Bye-bye
Phil

1 Presumably, William Lawson Grant (1872–1935). Born in Halifax, Nova Scotia, he was educated at Queen's University, where his father, George Munro Grant, was Principal, and at Balliol College, Oxford. After teaching for a few years at Oxford and Queen's, he

was, in 1917, appointed Headmaster of Upper Canada College, Toronto, a position he held till his death. He was elected a Fellow of the Royal Society of Canada in 1911, and was the author of two historical works, and co-author and editor of several others.

His wife, Maude E. Grant (née Parkin) (1880–1963), a native of Fredericton, New Brunswick, taught history at Manchester University, England, from 1905 until her marriage in 1910. Their son, Professor George Grant of McMaster, recalls, 'Mr Grove and Professor Edgar were often in my mother's house. Generally Mr Grove came alone or with his wife for long solitary talks with my mother. Professor Edgar would often be there for more public gatherings.' (May 30, 1972)

Grove may have drawn on some of these contacts for material in his novel, *The Master of the Mill* (1944). Notice, for example, the name Maude.

A letter to Grove from Grant, dated January 5, 1928, is preserved in the University of Manitoba Grove Collection.

2 John M. Gray, a member of the Board of Directors of Macmillan in Toronto, wrote to me on August 8, 1971:

> We believe there wasn't a Chairman in those days in the sense there now is, but that one of the Macmillans took the chair if the meeting was in London, as it sometimes was, or the President, Hugh Eayrs, took it for the meeting when it was here...
>
> I think that Grove must have been mistaken and that he may have been referring to Mr Johnston, our lawyer at that time, or Mr W. McLaughlin of the same firm. Unfortunately both of these men are dead.

3 Merrill Denison was born in Detroit in 1893, and educated at the universities of Toronto, Pennsylvania, and Paris. A playwright specializing in one-act and radio plays, he has also written books of humour (*Brothers in Arms*, 1923), realistic comedy (*The Unheroic North*, 1923), semi-autobiography (*Klondike Mike*, 1943), and histories of corporations such as Massey-Harris (1946) and Molsons (1955).

TO W.F. AND MARY JEAN MCMAHON[1]

Rapid City, Man.
April 17, 1928

Dear Mr. and Mrs. McMahon,

This is to be not much more than a sign that I have reached home again – for I am still pretty much under the weather. My cold got worse and worse; and, on my return trip, I did not get beyond Winnipeg where my wife met me before I had to give in and go to bed; after nearly a week, however, I could proceed home where I am confined to my house, though no longer to my bed.

The tour was one of the most pleasantly exciting, but also one of the most strenuous experiences of the last thirty years or so of my life; and will you permit me to say with perfect sincerity that the short stay at P[or]t Hope stands out as among the most pleasant ones? Proof of my sincerity is this very letter: for, of course, I cannot write to all the people who have been good to me.

At Trenton, the day of our last meeting, I got to bed at 11:30; at 1:30 I was called: to board the train for Ottawa at 2:33 a.m. Arrived at Ottawa 7:45 on Mar[ch] 17; spoke to the teachers at 9:30; to the men's C[anadian] C[lub] at 12:45; to the Women's C[anadian] C[lub] at 9:00 p.m. That is a fair sample of my life during the second half of my tour.

However, I am back at home where at 10:00 p.m. the house is quiet and dark.

Mrs. G. and I are laying more detailed plans now for a trip east, to begin the last week of June. I am going to have my old coach[2] overhauled and re-painted so as not to scare too many crows. Mrs. G., I assure you, knows as much of P[or]t Hope as I do; and we both wonder whether you will be at home in July and August: it is hard to say in advance just when we'll strike the shores of Lake Ontario. If you are at home at the time, we shall ask for permission to pitch our tent on your back yard for a night or so. I might also say that we shall keep half an eye open for a 'location.' I saw a magnificent building site north of Sarnia, on Lake Huron.

However, all that, so far, is a 'castle in Spain' as the French call it.

May I hope for an occasional line from those whom it is perhaps mere presumption on my part to think of as friends?

Yours sincerely
F.P. Grove

1 See letter of March 15, 1928 II, note 1.
2 'Coach' was a term in use at this period for an automobile with two doors, as against a 'sedan,' which had four doors.

TO CATHERINE GROVE

Moosomin, Sask.
September 10, 1928
10 a.m.

Well, my dear, here I am;[1] and the rain is pouring down outside. When I arrived, committee was waiting, as usual; and I had to allow myself to be 'entertained' till midnight. Speak to-night. This is a large club – 200 members, 3/4 of them farmers. Well...

I hope you got home all right?

I am sending *Disraeli*[2] – read it. The latter half, from the accession to power on, is *very* good. Perhaps a bit superficial, but fundamentally true. A new novel is shaping itself in my head.

Please convey my thanks to the Gardiners[3] for the ride – I am afraid I did not say very much. I was preoccupied with worry about leaving you alone. I am at bottom too old for this sort of thing. I don't want to influence life directly any longer. I want to sit back and look on. However...

It started to rain soon after I arrived; and it has been raining all night. I am glad in a way; they wanted to show me the country in the afternoon. That, at all events, I escape.

Crops here are very heavy; but most of them frozen. I enquired about price of wheat: 90¢ for #1 Northern. 35¢ for frozen wheat – that means quite a loss to the farmer. Tell John[4] if you write. He may not be so very badly off after all. For 35¢ a bu[shel] does not pay for seeding, harvesting, and threshing. Harvest hands cannot get more than $2 a day – in threshing time. Pretty bad.

Well, as I said, keep your spirit up. This has got to be gone through.

Bye-bye
F.P.

1 These letters to his wife were written on Grove's second lecture tour, covering the western provinces, in the fall following the eastern tour. The tour was sponsored, as before, by the Association of Canadian Clubs.
2 Either *Disraeli* (1927) by David Leslie Murray (1888–1962), or *Disraeli: A Picture of the Victorian Age* (tr. Hamish Miles, 1928) by André Maurois (pen-name of Émile Herzog, 1885–1967).
3 E.S. Gardiner and his wife
4 John Wiens, Mrs Grove's elder brother, a farmer

TO CATHERINE GROVE

Moosomin, Sask.
September 11, 1928

Well, old girl, that's that. The first number on the program. Gave the new talk. With the usual success. Audience about 100 – which was astonishing in view of the weather. It stopped raining for about 1/2 hour yesterday in the afternoon; then began again; and it has been pouring ever since. I wish I had rubbers. Must get them at Regina, I suppose. In about an hour I am to speak to the staff and the students of the Collegiate. I am going to give them a bit of a shake up. Well, that's all I've got to write.

No. In order to escape the Wolseley crowd tonight – if there *is* a crowd, I am going to take the midnight train to Regina if I can. Then I can sleep. Last night they kept me up till 2. There were people in the audience who had come from 20 and 30 miles north and east and south and west, in spite of what I should call impassable roads. The prin[cipal][1] of the Coll[egiate], by the way, when asking me to address the school, said with fervour, 'Mr. G., I've lived and taught in Regina and have been a member of the C[anadian] C[lub] for many years; but that was the best address and the best delivered address I have ever heard, barring none. I am the sec[retary] of the Sask[atchewan] Ed[ucation] Association. Would you come next Easter and act as our outside speaker at the convention if you are asked?' Well...

Bye-bye
Phil

Have spent 50¢ so far. Both grey stockings have holes. I can't understand it. Shall send them as soon as I can.

1 The Principal of the Moosomin Collegiate at this time was Gordon Churchill (c1883–1929). The Collegiate is now known as McNaughton High School, named after Gen. Andrew McNaughton (b1887), a native of Moosomin. The present Principal, Mr Frank J. Stoeber, writes that Gordon Churchill 'started out as a United Church minister but switched to teaching after a few years as a minister. His main interest was putting on operettas. He taught mainly Latin.' (November 12, 1973)

TO CATHERINE GROVE

Queens Hotel
Moosomin, Sask.
[September 11, 1928 II][1]

Well, just to let you know a change in schedule. Govenlock just phoned me up to say that, what with the rain, it will be impossible to arrange for the *80 mi[le]* drive to Manyberries. Roads will be impassable for weeks. So I shall speak at Govenlock on Sunday 16th instead and go on to Lethbridge on Monday 17th. Shall, therefore, leave Moose Jaw a day sooner: on *Fri*[day], instead of Sat[urday]. That eliminates all car riding for this time. Should suit you, eh?

Am on the point of going on to Wolseley, waiting for the train.

So bye bye
Phil

1 No date, but postmarked September 12. Since in the previous letter, dated September 11, Grove said he was to speak in Wolseley *tonight*, presumably this second letter was written on the same day.

TO CATHERINE GROVE

Hotel Saskatchewan
Regina, Sask.
September 12, 1928
11 a.m.

My dear girl,

Arrived here last night. At Wolseley it was the biggest and most amusing frost ever. Audience: 15, among whom 2 male infants of p[re] s[chool] age and 2 female flappers; the remainder consisted of 3 'sheiks,' 4 'beef-eaters' (1 a doctor) and 4 old ladies come out of cold storage. They did not know what to make of me. Applause: 3 distinct claps. Quite a contrast to Moosomin where I had to rise 4 times after having sat down. So I got away, out of town, by the next train which brought me here a little after midnight – (the 'beef-eaters,' considering me as a curious sort of insect, wanted to entertain me; and that was more than I would stand for). Had to wait for my baggage till 1:30 a.m.; and since they have daylight time here, it was 2:30 before I could go to bed. However, I slept well and am getting ready for the first battle. I shall leave the envelope unclosed, so as to be able to add how it came off. Most wheat grades #6 here, or 'feed' – killed by frost Aug[ust] 19.

Shall see Mandy[1] this afternoon, I suppose. I shall have an hour's time.

2 p.m.

Well, that's that. Had a very good audience of men. And the usual thing – swamped them off their feet. They do not very often hear that sort of thing. – Like Ottawa or Toronto, you know.

Am sitting here in my underwear, to cool off and rest up for battle #2 – at 4:30. Shall meet Mandy in between, I suppose.

Sent the Moose Jaw people a wire saying I'd come tomorrow morning – so I'll get a good night's rest; having shaken off all invitations etc. Bye-bye.

9 p.m.

Well, through with the day's work. Address #4 came off successfully. Mandy met me at 3, and I took her in. Since she doesn't get enough to eat, I treated her to afternoon tea (which I wanted because when I speak at noon, I don't eat much) and to supper when I gave her so much that she had to beg off. She'll write you about it, I suppose.

I've got my reports to make out. Then for a bath and to bed. I feel honestly tired.

I'll mail this tonight – so as not to leave you too long. Don't forget that as I go west, letters will space themselves by more than the intervening days, especially when I dip south to Govenlock and Lethbridge.

And so,
bye-bye.
Phil

1 Mrs Grove's younger sister, then seventeen, was attending the Regina Normal School.

TO CATHERINE GROVE

The Grant Hall
Moose Jaw, Sask.
[September 13, 1928][1]

Well, my dear, the 1st week's work is done. Got here at 11, was whirled around the district, dressed, spoke at 12:30, got through at 2, was whirled about again till 3, dressed, spoke at 3:30; and there you are. $150 earned.

Above all, I got your letter today. Good if you can keep it up. We must go through with it. Almost everybody seems to read my books; but how few buy them! I see that both C.N.R. and C.P.R. carry the *Search* in their observation car libraries. Damn them! I am going through this with perfect detachment, grinning at it all. Have I achieved 'fame'? 'Fame' – you know Hazlitt's sentence, 'is the recompense, not of the living but the dead.' They don't catch on at all that all I say is tantamount to preaching 'Repent ye!' – as, of course, *I* have repented and am repenting.[2]

My dear, you are living the life heroic; and I am trying to do the same. It isn't a matter of intellect: what does it count for or stand for? 'The erring mind' ... Everywhere they ask me to have my address printed. The fools! It isn't what I say that matters. But for 1/2 h[ou]r I lead them up on a mountain top – and they go home and settle down again in the valley.

To-morrow's a day off. Off? They'll whirl me around again; and in the afternoon I am to address the new Normal School here. Why did Mandy not go here? It was opened a year ago. I did not know of it. Name of the principal Dr Huff.[3] Does that tell you something? Used to be inspector in the Herbert district.

Well, am sending *Precious Bane*[4] home. A pretty little book, but ... well, not my taste.

Bye-bye, am hungry. So I'll go and eat supper.
Phil

1 Date from postmark

2 Repenting, that is, of the frenetic pursuit of material prosperity, which he considered destructive of the 'ideal' America – the theme of *A Search for America*, summed up in 'In Search of Acirema' (*Tales from the Margin*, 1971, pp 298–306).

3 Dr John Samuel Huff (c1885–1959), who was the first Principal of the Moose Jaw Normal School (1927–9), was born in Ontario, and educated in that province and Saskatchewan. He joined the Saskatchewan Education Department in 1910 as Inspector of Schools, later becoming Assistant Principal of Regina Normal School (1915–24), and Principal of Saskatoon Normal School (1924–7). In 1929 he became an official in the Education Department, retiring, in 1934, as Deputy Minister.

4 A novel by Mary Gladys Webb (1883–1927), published in 1926 and a best-seller of the period

TO CATHERINE GROVE

The Grant Hall
Moose Jaw, Sask.
September 14, 1928

Well, my dear, this is my day 'off.' That is, I have nothing to do but ironically to permit myself to be motored about and to address the Normal School this afternoon.

But I have had two good nights of sleep – 10 p.m. to 5 a.m.; and I can face a few more lectures now. No night trip now till Oct[ober] 2nd; then 2 in succession; and no early morning rising till Sept[ember] 26. That's good.

I enclose a few clippings which I ran across. Many of them, of course, I never see. You might let Stone[1] see one or two of them if you care. Or not; just as you think. Everybody here talks of 'fame.' I laugh. Well, to-morrow train all day.

The phone is ringing. That means they want me.
Bye-bye
Phil

1 Cooper Stone, editor of the *Rapid City Reporter*

TO CATHERINE GROVE, CANADIAN PACIFIC RAILWAY TELEGRAM

[September 14, 1928 II]

Moose Jaw Sask Sep 14/28 945am
Mrs. F P Grove,
Rapid City, Man.
Eatons order twenty five hundred copies of *Our Daily Bread*
Phil
12.24 pm

TO CATHERINE GROVE

En route Moose Jaw-Shaunavon
September 15, 1928

My dear,

Well, the day of rest is over, not much of a rest, physically, at that. Gave the Normal S[chool] rather a rousing address. Then again, as in the morning, out on a car ride through the country, with the Huffs (Dr. Huff prin[cipal] of N[ormal] S[chool]);[1] and supper with them. On the whole, a very interesting day, though. Shall tell you about the Huffs when I get home. I surely made a hit in Moose Jaw. Four big newspaper articles about me and my addresses, even about my Regina addresses.

Now about *Our Daily Bread*. The Eaton Selecting Committee consisted of Lady Willison (wife of Sir John, biggest newspaper owner in Canada),[2] W.J. Alexander, Norah Thom[p]son,[3] and Prof[essor] Macdonald,[4] of the Eng[lish] Dep[artmen]t of the U[niversity] of Toronto. Their verdict was unanimous (though hundreds of books were entered) – R.Y. Eaton,[5] senior partner of the Company, stepped in and said, if the book appears anywhere before they are ready to ship, the deal would be off, much to his regret. Was in communication with Eayrs over the wire from Moosomin on. Yesterday, Sept[ember] 14, the agreement was reached in the morning. I agreed to delay; they took 2500 copies to be listed at $2.50. I could have afforded to cut or even to waive royalties; for the advertising value of the thing (they being Eaton's) even exceeds the cash value of this single deal. But I waived nothing. 25c a copy. I understand that other pre-publication sales in Canada run to about 1000, in the U.S.A. to about twice that. So the book is off to a good start at least; and I trust Eayrs as a salesman to follow that start up. At Moose Jaw I let it be known that the scene is laid between M[oose] J[aw] & Swift Current. So they are agog.

Eaton's will do the advertising: they will, of course, use the names of the selecting committee: a big drawing card. Things do seem to look up.

I am *perfectly well*. It has been raining overnight. Marvellous wheat in this district.

Bye-bye
Phil

1 See letter of September 13, 1928, note 3.

2 John Stephen Willison (1856–1927). He entered journalism in 1881 as a reporter on the London (Ontario) *Advertiser*, and afterwards on the Toronto *Globe*, becoming Editor of the latter in 1890. He resigned from the *Globe* in 1903, to found his own paper, the Toronto *News*. He was also the Chief Canadian correspondent of the London *Times*, and founder-editor of *Willison's Monthly* (1925–9). He wrote several books on political questions, the best known being *Sir Wilfrid Laurier and the Liberal Party* (1903). He was elected a Fellow of the Royal Society of Canada in 1900, and knighted in 1913.

The Lady Willison referred to here (and in the letter of March 26, 1928 II) was his second wife, Marjory MacMurchy (?–1938), whom he married in 1926. She was active in feminist causes, having published, in 1916, *The Woman – Bless Her*. She also wrote such novels for girls as *The Child's House* (1923) and *The Longest Way Round* (1937).

3 See letter of March 26, 1928 II, note 6.

4 John Ford Macdonald (b1878), who was, at this time, an Associate Professor of English at University College, Toronto, having previously taught at Queen's University. He became a Professor in 1935, retiring in 1948. He was the author of *William Henry Drummond* (Toronto 1923).

5 Robert Young Eaton (1875–1956), nephew of the founder, Timothy Eaton, was President of the T. Eaton Company from 1922 to 1944.

TO CATHERINE GROVE

Govenlock, Sask.
September 17, 1928

I am waiting for the train to Manyberries where I must spend the night. Had to come in here after all by a 100 mi[le] car ride. We think we know bad roads. But we know nothing compared with what they have here. The Govenlock people had sent a car to meet me at Shaunavon. There is a huge hotel there – a border town hotel. Not a room to be had anywhere. I slept in the office of a lawyer, on a couch. Very good. Even there, 2 people had read my books and thanked me for the honour of talking to them. The car had come with 2 men to alternate in driving. That made me afraid. 'Is it slippery?' I asked. 'Oh,' said one of them, 'I don't mind the slipping. What I mind is that the rear-end is everlastingly getting ahead of me.' Well, both drivers were expert and very, very careful. There was at no time any real danger; but I must say I have had no idea what a car can do and under what circumstances it will still go. They were very considerate; and whenever anything was about to happen, they stopped and warned me. I enjoyed it. They do it all the time and know just how to go at it; and I had absolute confidence in them – which was justified by the fact that in about 6 h[ou]rs we got here. Eden is a metropolis as compared with Govenlock: population 30 souls, all counted. Buildings are 1/4 mi[le] apart. But in its utter bareness it is very beautiful; more beautiful even than the desert west of Medicine Hat. Cypress Hills in the north; Bearpaw M[oun]t[ain]s straight south; east of them the 'Little Rockies,' west, the Sweetgorn M[oun]t[ain]s. Radius of visibility: 80 mi[les].

It is a marvelous fall day.

No place to eat at in 'town.' Dinner on the road yesterday. For supper I was driven 17 mi[les]. For breakfast today I walked 3 mi[les]. For dinner I am going to be fetched 7 or 8 mi[les] out. The train is due at 4:50; they say it rarely gets here before 7. So, where they will take me for supper, I don't know yet. It's very interesting indeed.

The man who drives me around here is a border patrolman[1] who, over the bunch grass prairie, without any road or trail whatever, drives a new Buick Sedan, government-owned, with marvellous expertness, day or night. Last night we came back about 11 p.m. through an inky black night, meteors falling all about. It was exceedingly beautiful.

The only man with an 'education' around here is an old, German cow-boy by name of Lipke.[2]

A very strange country.

Well, to-morrow back to civilisation: Lethbridge.

I hope you are well and keep your spirits up, my dear.

I am quite well and, in a wistful way, enjoying this. But, of course, it is all very primitive.

I see the car coming that's going to take me for dinner to a ranch, the so-called K. Lease.* So bye-bye

Phil

*Land here is leased by the sq[uare] mile from the Dom[inion] gov[ernmen]t for grazing purposes.

1 David Allison Fleming; see the following letter.

2 Who remains untraced. Mr Andy McRae, of Govenlock, in a letter of May 29, 1972, writes:

> I never heard of a Lipke here. There was a Klittke but he was elderly & a homesteader, never rode a horse in his life. He was German.
> Andy McRae
> PS I have been here over *60 years*.

TO CATHERINE GROVE

En route Govenlock-Lethbridge.
September 18, 1928

Well, I'm on the way again. This is a terrible R[ail]r[oad]. It is 11 now; and we are $1^1/_2$ h[ou]rs late – mixed train; you remember the one from Glenella to Portage? I left Govenlock last night 1 h[ou]r 40 min[utes] late. We were supposed to make Manyberries at 7 p.m.; and we reached there by 11. Then a night in a hotel without a grade. This morning boarded train at 6:30. Scheduled arrival at Lethbridge 2:30 p.m. Distance Manyberries to Lethbridge 104 mi[les].

Now, my dear, do me a favour. Somewhere on the *west* book-shelves you will find a small book – size of a school text-book – dark red binding, I believe, entitled, I think, *Mineralogy*. Send it to *David Allison Fleming, Esq., Govenlock, Sask*[atchewan].[1] I unearthed some fossils there, part of a petrified tree, etc. Most of them I left with him; and he promised to box them up and send them on by freight to R[apid] C[ity]. I promised him that book in return; its receipt will remind him and put him under an obligation.

The train jolts so I can't write. But I hope you're well? I am.

Thus the weeks are nibbled off. This is day 3 of week 2.
Bye-bye. This will have to be all for today.
Phil

1 David Allison Fleming (1894–1966) served first with the Border Guard and later with the Royal Canadian Mounted Police in Saskatchewan and Calgary.

TO CATHERINE GROVE, CANADIAN PACIFIC TELEGRAM

Lethbridge, Alta.
September 19, 1928

Mrs. F.P. Grove
Rapid City Man

Address till Monday Palliser Hotel Calgary.
Phil

TO CATHERINE GROVE

Marquis Hotel,
Lethbridge, Alta.
September 19, 1928 II

I'm back in so-called civilization. Olds has cancelled, on account of harvest: many farmer members. So I shall be at Calgary till Monday. I'm afraid the mail service through the pres[idents] of the clubs does not work out. Here, f[or] i[nstance], the pres[ident] is away on a county court circuit; and so my mail, if any, travels after him. I, therefore, sent you a wire re address.

Nothing much to say. Got here yesterday late at 4:30. Terrific wind and dust storm blowing. The crop here is enormous. 40 to 60 bu[shels] to the [acre] [cut]

Speak today at luncheon [cut] last night. Then on at 4:30 to Calgary [the bottom half of the page in the original is cut off]

The papers are full of me. Calgary, Regina, Moose Jaw, Lethbridge announce my Lethbridge lecture today. Enclose one of the announcements.

I think I wrote you that I consented to postpone Can[adian] publication of *Our Daily Bread* till October 1st because Eaton's insisted on it.

This week-end *Calgary*.

Next week-end *Banff* – where you might use address *general delivery*, Banff, Al[ber]ta. If they put me up at the C.P.R. Hotel, I'll phone to the post-office. If down-town, I can go over myself.

Am trying to put an address together for the Ukrainian Club at Calgary.

Have nothing left to read except Thackeray. Shall try to borrow or buy a book or so at Calgary day after tomorrow.

Well, how are you? I wish I had a letter from you here, but there is none. Wired to Ottawa yesterday. Reply said, Confirm [cut] had been wired c/o Judge Jackson[1] who is aw[ay?] [cut] of telegram from telegraph office [cut] though if it has been [the bottom half of this page in the original is cut off]

1 The President of the local Canadian Club mentioned at the start of the letter as being on circuit at the time

TO CATHERINE GROVE

Hotel Palliser
Calgary, Alta.
September 20, 1928

Well, here I am. So the scene shifts. My telephone has been ringing since 8 o'clock. All sorts of queer people want to see me. Probably to get some money for this or that. I am going to give audience after awhile.

This is a terrific place. Telephone again ... It was the Gyro club wanting me to lunch with them. Since it saves money, I'll go.

When on the point of leaving Lethbridge yesterday, a colleague of Judge Jackson's came rushing to the station and brought me your letter of last Friday (Sept[ember] 14). So that is that. Am glad you are all right. I am, too. Though, of course, the pace gets on one's nerves. The weather, thank the Lord, is beautiful. Since Olds cancelled, I shall have the week-end off. But I must compose a talk to the Ukrainians here.

I shall be back here on Tuesday night (Sept[ember] 25) and again on Fri[day] (Sept[ember] 28) when, at night, I leave for Banff* (General Delivery). Thence I leave early on Oct[ober] 1st and after that I shall not count on mail till Oct[ober] 3rd at Vancouver, Hotel Vancouver.

On Sat[urday] I shall despatch underwear.

Last night Eayrs wired me from *Winnipeg*. He goes, from there, straight through to Vancouver; and we shall meet on Sat[urday], Sept[ember] 29, at Banff. He seems very anxious to see me. I don't know why, of course.

Lethbridge was rather a knock-out; though they don't know what I'm talking about. The density of the average mind is astonishing. But they all want to read my books now. That's the main thing. They merely gather that *I* know what I'm talking about. And that's enough.

Dream? So do I. Well,
bye-bye
Phil

Was glad to hear that the gladiolus [sic] are still blooming.

*So I shall expect mail at Banff up to Sat[urday] Sept[ember] 29 only; for on Monday it will be too early for the P[ost] O[ffice].

TO CATHERINE GROVE

Hotel Palliser
Calgary, Alta.
September 20, 1928 II

Well, this was another 'knock-out.' I surely can handle my audiences. By the way, the pres[ident][1] of the women's club phoned me this morning; and having made an appointment, in the lobby of the hotel, asked 'How can I recognise you?' I thought for a moment and answered, 'Look for the tallest man there.' When, at the appointed hour, I was standing there, surrounded by hundreds of women, and a few men, she, having forgotten that I had given her the clues myself, came up to me and said, 'I am looking for Mr. Grove. I have been told to look for the tallest and *most distinguished-looking* man in the lobby. You must be he?'

Did *you* know I was distinguished-looking? Well, well...

I have accepted an invitation at Mrs. Williams'[2] for tomorrow night.

A certain woman called on me this morning trying to get a recipe for becoming a famous author. You can imagine what I told her. But she claims to know you. A Mrs. Edwards, née Johnson,[3] or something, Icelandic by birth, attended the Ira Stratton Summer School *in* 1918, she says.

All day long it was caller after caller. At noon the Gyro Club kidnapped me. I told them stories. *International* Service Club; i.e., a U.S.A. organisation.

I am afraid I shall have to buy myself a new razor. My old one will not do the job any longer. It just scrapes and leaves a stubble behind.

Got your letter. Too bad about Gertie.[4]

Hope to get the underwear here, for it will be difficult to catch me on the wing beyond Calgary or Banff. Here again there was difficulty: Mrs. Glass, the pres[ident], having moved and changed her address. However, I got the letter at last.

This was address #9. $225.

You will have to send the cheque to the Life Ins[urance] Co[mpany] next week. Be sure they get it *before* Oct[ober] 1st; for they will claim another month's interest unless they do. This tour is going all right; and the loan will have to be repaid in any case. If $400 is taken from the bank, it will leave 400 there, if I remember right: of that I shall need $150 more before I get through. But that will be repaid by and by.

Another week, and I shall have earned $125 – more – or total $350 – including Banff.

Well, so long.
Phil

The woman, by the way, who moved the vote of thanks said that my address was going to light her 'like a glowing jewel' when, in the future, she reads my books. They are being inspired to poetry, are they not?

1 Mrs H.G.H. Glass. A native of London, Ontario, she moved to Calgary in 1906, and was active in various civic and literary activities, which included the IODE, YWCA, and the Women's Canadian Club.
2 Mrs Flos Jewell Williams was born in Ontario in 1893, and was educated in Toronto. Her husband, David S. Williams, was a travelling salesman in Calgary, and is now dead. Her first novel, *Judgement of Solomon*, was published in 1925, and was followed by *New Furrows* (1926), *Broken Gods* (1930) – both under Graphic's imprint – and *Fold Home* (1950). She has contributed verse, short stories, and articles to Canadian periodicals.
3 Mrs Margaret Edwards, wife of Gwillym Edwards, who retired in 1958 as Inspector with the Board of Grain Commissioners. Mr Edwards was one of the Governors of the Dominion Drama Festival in 1935, and received the Canadian Drama Award the same year.
4 An obscure reference

TO CATHERINE GROVE

Hotel Palliser,
Calgary, Alta.
September 21, 1928

My dear T.,

As you will see by the enclosed, I am, as usual, all over the papers. The Manager of the second, more important paper, the *Calgary Herald*, called an h[ou]r ago to get material for a big write-up on Monday.[1] I speak here again on Tuesday you know.

I dropped in at the Hudson's Bay and found 1/2 doz[en] copies each of *Search* and *Settlers* there. Not much, but every trifle helps. I let them know of Eaton's order. They had *not* ordered any of *Our Daily Bread*. They will now. People are sluggish here – as throughout the west.

Tonight I am in for a formal dinner – evening clothes and all the frills – at the Williams' – the husband is a 'knight of the grip'[2] as they so beautifully style it. I'm very curious.

Went to bed last night at 9, to sleep at 10, slept till 5. That was not bad, was it?

The tour is, after all, gathering momentum. Just had a letter from Banff welcoming me and promising much.

I think I mentioned that I am going to meet Eayrs there.

Well, that's all I can think of in the line of news.

No, had a haircut and shampoo in this hotel: $2. They won't cut any more of my hair, I'll warrant.

I wonder much about the little plot.[3] I don't think there

will be time for me to write anything on this tour. I can't collect my thoughts sufficiently.

Shall send woollen's to-morrow morning.
Bye-bye, dear.
Phil

1 Which would be September 24, but the *Calgary Herald* of that date does not appear to have contained any reference to Grove. As far as can be ascertained, only two articles on Grove appeared in the *Herald* in the months of September and October 1928 – on September 12, an article on Grove and his forthcoming engagements in the city, and, on September 20, a summary of his address (on 'Nationhood') to the Women's Canadian Club that afternoon.
2 A travelling salesman; see the preceding letter, note 2.
3 Presumably, a reference to Phyllis May's grave in the cemetery at Rapid City; the Groves were probably considering an inscription for the gravestone.

TO CATHERINE GROVE

Hotel Palliser
Calgary, Alta.
September 22, 1928

Well, my dear, this is beginning to pall on me. So I am going to go to Gleichen tomorrow, Sunday, to return here on Tuesday when I am to address the Ukrainian C[anadian] C[lub].

Last night, dinner at the Williams's. I was disgusted. Evening clothes. Mrs. W[illiams] in low cut dress. 2 or 3 more ladies the same. Men in dinner jackets. What for, I couldn't see. An ordinary affair like a meal at Gardiner's.[1] The most amusing thing: Mrs. W[illiams], in evening gown, had to go around the table and collect the soiled plates. The young Williamses came in, one on bare feet, the other in knickers unbuttoned at the knees to fetch their share of the food. No objection, of course, for a family dinner: but laughable when the company sits around fully dressed.

Mr. W[illiams] started to talk of the damn foreigners that were spoiling business, not paying their bills, etc.

I told him he must have mistaken an Anglo-Saxon district for Russian.

Then he talked of 'Canadianisation' – I asked him what he meant by that, saying that I was one of the 'damn foreigners.' 'Well,' he said, 'you have adapted yourself, you wear Canadian clothes, etc...' 'No,' I replied, 'I am wearing the sort of clothes European people wear when they have the money. You Old Canadians are imitating the style.' Then he talked of 'Canadian ideals.' Well, I asked him who was doing more to form Canadian ideals, I, the 'foreigner' – or he, the old Canadian. – The company sided with me, as they plainly showed by asking me to explain all sorts of things to them. – It was highly amusing. I stripped the beef-eater bare, metaphorically speaking. However, they are people who are not worth wasting a breath on. I told Mrs. W[illiams] that she needed to think her books out for a few more decades.

The town is full of the echoes of the C.A.A. convention: Elson[2] lorded it. Roberts[3] was drunk most of the time. Several people called him 'a swine.' I am glad I severed my connections with that crew. I told everybody who gave me a chance that I was *not* a member.[4]

This morning, having nothing to do, I went down to the island where the tourist camp used to be. Then took a sight-seeing street-car (25¢) to go through the city. The same old jokes: free boarding house (jail) – liquor stores, etc. etc.

That's all. I have sent the parcel with underwear this morning. Hope you get it. Yes, if I receive the 1st parcel back at Banff, it will be all right.

After that, try to catch me at Vancouver, Vancouver Hotel.

This is the end of the second week; 7 more ahead. It makes me feel weary to think of it. But I am quite well. No, I don't need hot-water bottles. But I had a head-ache yesterday. Better today. Am hard at work writing an address for the Ukrainian Club. Have bought *Swan Song*[5] – but shall not read it for some time. Shall keep it for the steamer trip etc. Enclose cards. Well, bye-bye, my dear. Walk and keep cheerful.

Phil

1 Of Rapid City; see letter of February 28, 1928, note 6.

2 Presumably, John M. Elson (b1880), the novelist, who in 1928 was President of the Ontario branch, and National Treasurer, of the Canadian Authors' Association. His best known work, *The Scarlet Sash* (1925), is a romance of the old Niagara frontier district.

3 Charles G.D. Roberts, the poet; see letter of March 29, 1927, note 4.

4 An explanation of Grove's hostile attitude towards the Canadian Authors' Association is found in Watson Kirkconnell's *A Slice of Canada* (1967) 293:

> The 1926 convention was held in Vancouver, with a leisurely social epilogue in Victoria. As a matter of fact, the social side of the convention had tended, even in Vancouver, to crowd out the more legitimate activities of the gathering. Thus an afternoon session devoted to the basic business of authorship was simply scrapped in order to give the delegates more leisure to prepare for a tea-party at the new chalet on Grouse Mountain. More indignant even than I was Frederick Philip Grove, who had been asked to prepare a paper for the session and had brought his carefully written manuscript two thousand miles by car only to find it ignored in this cavalier fashion. On returning home, he expanded its ideas to book length, and three years later Hugh Eayrs, of Macmillan, issued it as *It Needs To Be Said.* The first

address in this austerely idealistic volume was entitled 'A Neglected Function of a Certain Literary Association.'

5 By John Galsworthy (1867–1933), published in 1928

TO CATHERINE GROVE

Hotel Palliser
Calgary, Alta.
September 22, 1928 II

Just got your second letter addressed here. Shall be back here twice, so, till Fri[day] send here (except parcel; for on Fri[day] I shall check my baggage through to Banff); I'll pick letters etc. up as I pass through.

You'll have noticed that, after all, I did get the Lethbridge letter. So it was all right. But this president business does not work out.[1] The Banff pres[ident], f[or] i[nstance], wrote me from Regina yesterday. However, I'll get things ultimately, I suppose. Shall add a few words tomorrow morning. Now for a hot bath.

Sunday.

I am going on to Gleichen this afternoon, to escape from the city.

Sure, I think you can simply ask for leave of absence when you want to go to Winnipeg – without furnishing a substitute, though, I believe, I should offer to do that.

Extra money? No, it does not work out very well. When, as at Govenlock, the club as such gets me from Shaunavon (livery tariff: $30), I can't charge it up. However, this long stay at Calgary has saved me the pressing for this week: [cut] expense along that line. Laundry, though, has been $2.10 a week so far. Yet I am still a dollar or two ahead on the R[apid] C[ity] ride.

I'm glad to hear that the gladiolus is still in bloom.

As for letters, I write daily; but as I get farther away, mail will take longer for the road; and there may be odd days without anything reaching you. When I turn back at Prince Rupert, they will come in bunches.

Quite an idea, that about the socks. It never occurred to me. I'll try to remember, though.

Yes, I can imagine that it did not suit Gardiner[2] to cancel that policy. But I think the money in the bank is worth more than the possible protection next summer. I'm outright stingy. Give 20¢ tips in this hotel where most people give 50¢ – As a rule I give a quarter.

Well, that's all, I think. 4 lectures this week: Gleichen, Calgary, Drumheller, Rockyford, Banff – by jingo, that seems to be 5.

But 8 next week. Revelstoke, Kamloops, Vancouver (3), Victoria (2) – no, that's only 7.

At any rate, when I reach Victoria, I'm more than half through – in work, though not time [the rest of the letter is cut off]

1 Grove was having his mail sent care of the local Canadian Club presidents – but, as is clear from previous letters, the presidents were not always at home when Grove arrived; and his own schedule was subject to alteration.
2 E.S. Gardiner was also an insurance agent, and handled the Groves' business.

TO CATHERINE GROVE

Gleichen, Alta.
September 24, 1928

Haven't much time. Am billeted here with private people and can't get away. So, just not to break the rule that I write daily, a few lines. It's glorious weather; I am to visit an Indian reserve this afternoon.

They tell me that there is hardly a day without some papers reporting something about me. They tell me all sorts of strange stories about myself. This thing is bound to pay in the long-run through the sale of my books.

Well, bye-bye.
More to-morrow. I'll write from the train. To-morrow night, the Ukrainians.
Phil

TO CATHERINE GROVE

Gleichen, Alta.
September 25, 1928

My dear T.

Had a very dull meeting last night – in a huge hall where the 55 listeners looked like so many mice in a huge barn. Rather depressing. Yet there are a few interesting people here. Spent the afternoon, yesterday, on the 2nd largest Indian Reserve. Met the Blackfoot chief Joe Crowfoot – very interesting indeed. Am, this morning, to run down to the Bow River to see coal-seams, etc. A distance of about 10 mi[les], I believe. Am staying at a private house – nice people. But it is a dismal, cold day. To-night, Ukrainian Club[,] Calgary. Tomorrow Drumheller – promise myself much from that trip into the Red Deer Valley. Well, my hostess is pulling the car out. So I'd better say bye-bye. It is always hard to find time for writing when I'm billeted.

Bye-bye, then.
Phil

TO CATHERINE GROVE, CANADIAN NATIONAL TELEGRAM

Drumheller, Alta.
September 26, 1928

Mrs. F.P. Grove,
Rapid City Man

Jonathan Cape[1] buys one thousand *Our Daily Bread.*
Phil

1 The London publishing house that handled British distribution of this novel. Cape advertised the novel extensively, but the English reviews were lukewarm at best, and singularly undiscerning. For a selection from these reviews, see my *Frederick Philip Grove* (Critical Views on Canadian Writers 1970) 138–41.

TO CATHERINE GROVE

Drumheller, Alta.
September 26, 1928 II

My dear T.

Small towns are bad places to write from. People monopolise you. But I've snatched a few minutes.

I sent you a wire to say that Jonathan Cape, London, England, has ordered 1000 copies of *Our Daily Bread*. That is, in a way, a small order for a publisher; but with the *Search* and the *Daily Bread* on the English market, a beginning is made. Also, the N[ew] Y[ork] Macmillans have now disposed of 3500 copies, pre-publication sale; and that more than covers the cost of printing 15000 copies or so. I have, therefore, a publisher who is making money on me.

This is a tremendous country. No use trying to describe. But it is strange that we have never gone into it: in its way as stupendous as Marble Canyon or the Washington desert; you remember the crossing of the Columbia River, don't you?

Spoke last night to the Ukrainians. Great meeting. They treated me as if I were the king of England. I expressed the wish to hear some folk-songs. The most stirring thing in music I've ever listened to. Some of the guests, of other C[anadian] C[lub]s were equally amazed. Those people have indeed something to teach us. They should make a tour through the Dominion. If I'd the money, I'd finance it. Well, they are there with the car.

Bye-bye
Phil

TO CATHERINE GROVE

Drumheller, Alta.
September 27, 1928

Well, my dear, that is that. Since I count on $200 as the minimum of my expenses, the $500 I received is earned at last. 12 meetings at $25 each.

A very poor meeting last night. A mining town, you know. Yet, there are a number of interesting people here. Above all the county court judge – an old French-Canadian who, being a bachelor, takes his meals with me. Most of them, however, have no thought except money, claims, etc.

I enclose a letter[1] I got yesterday – which, coming from a widow, shows what the popular lecturer is up against. Tonight, Rockyford: to-morrow nothing to do but to get to Banff. When I reach Victoria, I shall ask the Ass[ociation] for more money, I believe. Or not?

No. The weather has, with the exception of one day, at Gleichen, been glorious. It is so today. It freezes over-night, but it is very nice indeed in daytime. Shall let you know about winter-coat. Probably at Edmonton. Don't need it so far.

Again, this morning, they are waiting for me – I am to take a peep at one of the mines.

Is the gladiolus cut down by frost?
How are you keeping?
Bye-bye, dear,
Phil

1 See the following letter, note 1.

TO CATHERINE GROVE

Drumheller, Alta.
September 27, 1928 II

Well, I was in the mines this morning. Quite interesting. I forgot to enclose the letter of which I spoke. So I do it now.[1] I feel tired. So I'll lie down for a while. It's 3 p.m. My train leaves at 4:45. Rockyford next.

Bye-bye
Phil

1 The letter from Mrs Lavinia Creighton, the widow referred to in the previous letter, provides evidence of the sort of reaction among female audiences of which Grove speaks elsewhere (see letter of October 3, 1928 II):

> Dear Mr Groves [sic],
>
> Out of pure whimsicallity [sic] I am writing you, thinking perhaps it might amuse you.
>
> On Thursday Sept. 20, I sat in the Lounge at the Palliser [Hotel] and watched the men file past. I had just come to the city for the day and did not know of the convention there but thought it was the 'Kiwanis.' I have been out of life for a couple of years having lost my husband and so the throng was strongly interesting to me.
>
> I said to myself here are many men, I will sit and watch them as they pass about me and see if I can discern, any who carry about them anything of the Caste of genius, or of power or of the 'grand manner' as often princes pass this way, and statesmen and men of great wealth. Only one stood out and that was yourself. I marked *you*, and after a while you came down to the end of the room where I sat alone, and began walking up and down before the dining room door. Time and again I looked back at you pacing up and down there and I almost thought you noticed me.

She then goes on to explain how she found out who he was, invites him to lecture in Stettler 'under the auspices of the Church, as I would dearly love to hear it, and meet you personally,' and signs herself 'Yours in search of America also.' The letter is preserved in the University of Manitoba Grove Collection.

TO CATHERINE GROVE

En route, Rockyford–Calgary, Alta.
September 28, 1928

Well, my dear, here I am, travelling again. Had to get up at 6 o'clock. Drumheller was interesting; but the town is dismal. The clothes I wore (my old grey suit) will never be free of dust again. I'm going to have them vacuum-cleaned, though, at Vancouver. Last night, at Rockyford, they introduced me as Frederick Philip *Cook*. It shows how carefully they had prepared for the meeting.

The farming condition is very interesting. Everybody has bought combines; and most people, even in this year of a marvellous fall, uses[1] binders: the investment, or rather debt on the combine is a total loss. That's what the implement manufacturers do to the farmers. I predicted it last year.

Sometimes I ask myself, what in the world do I do all this for? But I suppose it must, in the long run, help the books. Yet – you have no idea how these people are *pestered* here with lectures. I have not been anywhere yet where no lecturer had preceded me by a few days or followed me immediately. Sometimes perfect nincompoops. They always say to me, 'Best ever' – 'Best I ever listened to' – etc. etc. How much of it they mean, I don't know, of course. But...

However, I'm 1/3 through with it, or shall be tomorrow night. Reach Banff tonight at 8:40. Am very curious to know where they will put me up. Banff Springs Hotel is still open – till Sunday. I'd be a bit out of the way there. Next week will be the hardest of all: 7 lectures, 1 night in the train, and once going out (from Revelstoke) at 4 in the morning. After that, things become more leisurely. By the end of next week my earnings will have amounted to $525, all going well.

I am quite all right. No trace, so far, of a cold. But I have given Spry[2] the dooce for taking me at a place like Rockyford – size of Eden, and hotel like the Eden hotel. I wrote him that I don't mind a billet in a farm-house where I am known; but that, at my age, I draw the line at a place like that where they introduce me as Mr. F.P. *Cook*. I'm not a casual lecturer peddling his wares.

I wonder how much of this you can read.
How are you? Hope to find a letter at Calgary.
Bye-bye.
Phil.

1 Thus in the original
2 Graham Spry, the organiser of the tour

TO CATHERINE GROVE

[Calgary, Alta.
September 28, 1928 II][1]

[the beginning of the letter is cut off] When I got to C[algary] [cut] my baggage failed to turn up. I can't wait to [cut] located it by wire; for I surely raised a racket. Nobody knew I was travelling on a pass – or they wouldn't have bothered. If they do what they promised to do, it should catch up with me tomorrow at Banff. *But*! my old grey suit looks about as shabby as anything I have ever worn; dirty, crushed, etc., and I have to give an evening lecture in it. The meeting is at 7; and the train which *may* bring my bags arrives at 8.40. Too bad, too bad. But, can't be helped.

Now I have spent this beastly day (a glorious day, by the way) – from 9 till 5 in Calgary without a room – I wanted to save and I'm through with Calgary – except for the baggage. I walked the streets and sat about at the station. I'll not do it again. Let them pay for a room even when I use it for a few hours.

But I'm as well as can be.
Hurrah! First call...
So I'll stop it but for the time being. –

6.30 p.m.

Well, had my supper. The first m[oun]t[ain]s appear. The streams are the colour of malachite. – I can hardly stand going through here…

There is nothing else to say, I'm afraid.

Shall write again to-morrow when I've seen Eayrs.

By the way, I got parcel #1 at Calgary. But no further letter.

The *Search*, Hudson's Bay book adviser[2] says, is going well. I dropped in to buy Galsworthy's *Silver Spoon*. There was too much of a gap between *The White Monkey* and *Swan Song*. – So I have the two vol[ume]s[3] now and shall read them at the coast.

Shall let you know when my baggage turns up. Wish much we [the rest of the letter is cut off]

1 Assumed from letters before and after

2 Possibly Robert Watson; see letter of October 9, 1928, note 3.

3 *The Silver Spoon* (1926), *Swan Song* (1928) (see letter of September 22, 1928), and *The White Monkey* (1924).

TO CATHERINE GROVE

Banff, Alta.
September 29, 1928

Well, my dear, I had a nice ride through the valley this morning. I had already heard, as it happened, that Roseberry[1] had enquired about openings here – I mean before I got your 2 letters. I am staying with the Lonsdales[2] – people like the Heeneys[3] in Eden of whom they remind me much, apart from the fact that these people, especially the Mrs., have literary pretensions. The four-flusher A.M. Stephen[4] has captivated them. They think him a great poet.

I wrote you a special line or so this morning to tell you that my baggage had turned up.

Eayrs failed to arrive; but there is another train in $^1/_2$ h[ou]r – the Trans-Canada. So I'll go down to the station and take this note. Has the planting been done on the hill? It's high time now. Here the weather up to an h[ou]r ago has been glorious; but it looks threatening now.

No, I haven't bought a razor yet. I mistrust what I can buy here in the extreme West. Tonight lecture #14 – $350. Next week is my hardest week: but it will net $175. So I must be satisfied. Well, as to the strain, I don't know. Physically it is quite a strain, otherwise, were it not for what has happened, I'd rather like it. However…

Have changed underwear and sent a parcel. How about getting one back by Oct[ober] 10 – Vancouver? Have not yet worn the new suit. Shall probably [cut] overcoat which should meet [the rest of the letter is cut off]

1 An obscure reference
2 The Rev. T.H. Lonsdale was born in Lancashire, England, and came, in 1908, to Alberta to work for the Methodist Church. After graduating from the University of Alberta (BA) and Alberta Methodist College (BD), he was appointed minister of the Rundle Memorial Church in Banff, from which he retired in 1957 after serving for thirty-two years. In 1971, the Lonsdales moved to Calgary, where they now live.
3 T.F. Heeney (1867–1951) was a United Church minister and secretary-treasurer of the School Board in Eden, where Grove was Principal (1919–22) of the Consolidated School.
4 Alexander Maitland Stephen (1882–1942) was a rural school-teacher in British Columbia who settled in Vancouver after being severely wounded in World War I. He became actively involved in the social and labour movements of the day, and his writing, which included two novels and four collections of verse, reflects the conflict between his idealism and the harsh realities of political agitation. His best known novel is *The Kingdom of the Sun* (1927). He also edited two anthologies of verse, including *The Golden Treasury of Canadian Verse* (1928).

TO CATHERINE GROVE

Banff, Alta.
September 30, 1928

Well, my dear,

Eayrs arrived on the Trans-Canada, with private secretary, wardrobe trunk, etc., engaging a suite at the Banff Springs Hotel.

The meeting was quite a triumph. Eayrs introduced me as 'Canada's greatest living man' – and more, as 'internationally recognised as one of the great novelists and essayists living.' In the vote of thanks an Englishman said, 'We have never had anything like this before' etc. The astonishing thing was the international character of the small crowd.

Eayrs, in some ways, is not as reliable as he might be.[1] Tell you about that later. I am disgusted with one thing. He has arranged for full page ads in Vancouver and Victoria – with portraits etc., saying that Mr. F.P. Grove will autograph any copy of *Our Daily Bread* bought between Oct[ober] 1st and Oct[ober] 4. I refused at Calgary to do just that.

New York is advertising the book in all leading magazines. Here, people want to read my books. The Lonsdales have been on the waiting list at the Calgary Public Library for 1½ months and are told that their turn will come in about *9 months*. And they wait – rather than pay $3.00. Well, I don't know whether I wouldn't do the same thing. But that rolls up no royalty account.

Well, I want to have a swim. Shall have lunch with Eayrs. Am invited out to dinner. Off tomorrow morning.

Bye-bye
Phil.

1 This probably refers to the negotiations with McClelland & Stewart for the purchase of sheets in stock of *Over Prairie Trails* and *The Turn of the Year* (see letter of November 3, 1928, note 4), in which Grove had sought Eayrs' help. In a letter of September 12, Eayrs explains, 'I purposely had not written to McClelland because he has been away. He will be home tomorrow, however, so I will write to him then.' Perhaps he never did, and hence Grove's disappointment.

TO CATHERINE GROVE

En route Banff–Revelstoke.
October 1, 1928

Well, I'm over the Great Divide. Mrs. Lonsdale,[1] my hostess at Banff, said she'd send you the local sheet. It was interesting there.

It is a dull day; lots of snow last night. All the mountains are hooded; snow even in the valleys.

Our Daily Bread appears today. I'm very curious how it will take; but at bottom unconcerned.

Nothing else to write about. This is the 4th and the hardest week. I'm glad it has started. Once I get over this one, the end of the first half of the tour is near; and things will be more leisurely for awhile.

I'm deucedly hungry just now.

May add a word or two later. So long.

6 p.m.

Well, got to Revelstoke in pouring rain. At 5 p.m. Shall leave here at 4:50 in the morning. That's the worst night I shall have for some time.

However, Time runs e'en through the roughest day.[2] And this week pays well.

Feel tired – speak at 8. So I'll rest an hour or so before supper. Just had a bath.

How are you?
Phil

1 See letter of September 29, 1928, note 2.
2 Grove was probably thinking of these lines from *Macbeth* (I.iii.147–8):

Come what come may,
Time and the hour run through the roughest day.

TO CATHERINE GROVE

Plaza Hotel,
Kamloops, B.C.
October 2, 1928

Well, my dear, this is the hardest day – and I must say I find it hard. Spoke last night at Revelstoke. Got to bed at midnight. Was called at 3:15, left R[evelstoke] shortly after 4 – or rather was to have left R[evelstoke] then; but was dismally delayed by a freight-train derailing just after I had reached the station. My train had to wait outside the yard; had it happened a few hundred feet lower down, I could have occupied my berth. As it was, I did not go to bed again, in the train, till about 6 o'clock – which did not give me much rest; for by half past seven I was too hungry to stay in bed. Got here at 11; was whisked about till 12:30 and, at lunch, succeeded in getting rid of the crowd; so I am now sitting about in my dressing-gown. Speak again at 7 p.m.

At Banff trees were pretty bare; on the west-slope of the Rockies (from Field on – Yoho valley –) they were in full fall colour. Here they are still quite green.

Go on tonight at 9:50 to Vancouver where I shall get to-morrow morning. Trains travel slow over these dangerous tracks. Looked down thousands of feet yesterday, travelling over trestle viaducts. Very beautiful in the rain, though the m[oun]t[ain]s were invisible.

Well, that's all. I must work over a part of my address which I have changed. Made it more effective.

Shall send my underwear from Victoria.
Bye-bye. Kiss
Phil

Am going to enclose Galsworthy's *Silver Spoon* in my parcel.

TO CATHERINE GROVE

Hotel Vancouver,
Vancouver, B.C.
October 3, 1928

Well, my dear, this was #17; and it was the usual triumph. 2 stores have 100 each of *Our Daily Bread*; 2.25 each; it is also on all the news-stands. There is a rush for copies.

Speak again tomorrow morning at the University –[1] Bishops and ministers of state, etc. etc. Had to stand bowing till the tears came into my eyes. Again they said 'there's never been an address like that in this city before.' –

Now, yes, I had one of the new folders; but the chairman, General Odlum[2] borrowed it of me and, though I told him I needed it back, he forgot to return it. It was the first copy I had seen myself: It is headed: 'Lecture-tour throughout Canada, 1928–1929' – so it will go on, I suppose.

To-morrow women's club and North-Shore club. Day after, Victoria. Just bought my berth, etc. I'm devilishly hungry; so shall go down and have afternoon tea. Then shall go out for a little – it's raining as usual here. Shall write more perhaps tonight – but will mail this now, so you'll not miss a day.

I wish I had the *rein-gewaschene*[3] here. Well, the end of the fourth week is near.

The university has surely been set by the ears. Something might come from that.

Bye-Bye
Phil

1 The University of British Columbia.

2 Major-General Victor Wentworth Odlum, CB, CMG, DSO, journalist, soldier, and diplomat, was born in Cobourg, Ontario, in 1880, and, after a childhood in Japan, started as a journalist, and later newspaper-owner, in British Columbia in the early years of the century, went on into investment and insurance business, and was Canadian High Commissioner in Australia, and Ambassador to China and Turkey. His military career was long and distinguished.

3 Presumably, clean underwear. The word is an adjective, meaning 'washed clean.'

TO CATHERINE GROVE

Hotel Vancouver,
Vancouver, B.C.
October 3, 1928 II

Yes, my dear, 2 tulip clusters along the south fence will be nice. As for moss etc., you must decide that. I don't think I would take leaves: they cling too much to the ground in spring. In case of need I would simply use brush (poplar) – so as to hold the snow.

If I get the underwear at Victoria, the next will have to go to Edmonton, I think. There, too, I must expect to find my winter-coat, for the drives in the Peace River district. A parcel to Edmonton will take at least 3 days, by mail or express. If everything goes well, I shall arrive at Edmonton on *Oct[ober] 17 – Macdonald Hotel.* Mark all mail and parcels: 'Please hold for arrival.'

I shall expect further mail here or Victoria. Here I shall leave on Oct[ober] 17 for Prince Rupert. Mail to Prince Rupert you had better address to the President of the Club there, Mrs. F.C. McLennan. After that Edmonton above address.

As for the sale of *Our Daily Bread* (Can[adian] price, by the way $2.00), I am not so optimistic as Eayrs – I have had too many disappointments in counting my chickens before they were hatched. But, undoubtedly, the *advance* sale (pre-publication) has been greater than the total sale of *Settlers* to-date. I counted here today 270* copies in the book-stores, not including the news-stands. Everywhere the book is most prominently displayed.

As for that widow[1] ... I can assure you that a dozen or a score of women *offer* themselves in almost every larger place. The effect of my address seems to be almost erotic. If I did not receive their advances with a disarming but ironic benevolence, they'd mob me.

I am very curious to see the reaction of the press to today's luncheon meeting. I'll try to send you clippings tomorrow.

Banff was nice – very quiet there now. But on the day I left it was snowing. Here

Es regnet und es regnet,
Es regnet seinen Lauf;
Und wenn's genug geregnet hat
Dann hört es noch nicht auf.[2]

I must get money to-morrow. Am down to the last $10 bill.

But what an abominable and utterly senseless jacket on the *Daily Bread*? Here nobody had heard yet of the *Search* till Eayrs told them of it. Spencer ordered 25 copies by wire. They arrived yesterday. I autographed them for the store: just my name, of course.

Just ordered my reservation for the Prince Rupert trip on Oct[ober] 11. A week from to-morrow. Today's address was # 17 – $425.

Well, last spring to-day's meeting would have excited me, and I should have wired. Now it leaves me quite cold – just like Kamloops: there they nearly carried me to the train: nearly everywhere they want me to come again. In moving the v[ote] of thanks, a doctor said: 'This is the first speaker whom the Association has sent us. We have waited for over two years. It was worth waiting for. And if Mr. Spry can promise us, at the end, another man like Mr. Grove, or another visit from Mr. Grove ...' (Thundering applause) '... we shall feel repaid for waiting another 2 years for the next association speaker.' Today, a bishop waited humbly for nearly 30 minutes before he could get through the crowd. Then he took my hand and just squeezed it in his two, saying, 'God bless you! That's all I can say'; and, wagging his snow-white head, he walked away. From the first word, I 'had' them. Others deliver their so-called speeches between waking and sleeping, I sweep them off their feet – men, I mean. With women I proceed differently: I amuse them for awhile; and then I hammer. Not in vain did I go to school with the Greeks and Romans. They knew how and so do I.

Well, since this has become a letter, I'll send it as today's #2. If I don't send any letter tomorrow, it is because I shall speak 3 times. But I'll have a good night's rest if I can – can? Well, yes, things bother me, you know what.

Bye-bye
Phil

*100 David Spencer's Dep[artmen]t Store (oldest store at the coast)
100 Hudson's Bay
25 each in 2 book-stores
20 in one.

1 Mrs Creighton; see letter of September 27, 1928 II, note 1.
2 Literally,

It is raining, and it is raining,
It is raining, pouring;
And when it has rained enough,
(Then) It still does not stop.

TO CATHERINE GROVE

Hotel Vancouver,
Vancouver, B.C.
[October 4, 1928][1]

My dear,

This is a rush day. Spoke this morning at a public meeting called by the University – 1400 people in the audience. One of the most exhausting things imaginable. Just looked in at the ladies' hall and see that they have placed 500 chairs there. Am to address them in 20 minutes.

And again tonight on the North Shore of Burrard Inlet.

There is a rush on *Our Daily Bread*. My name is all over the papers and all over the stores. I shall try to add a few words tonight but don't know whether there will be time.

I prepare this, so can mail it if there isn't. In that case, bye-bye

Phil

No parcel now till Edmonton. I think I explained yesterday.

5.30 Just through with one meeting. No time to write. They are coming for me in 15 min[utes] and I have to dress. It was the biggest triumph I have had.

At night

I shall roll up 2 copies of the *Morning Star* tomorrow and send them to you – one for *Stone*.[2] Tell Mrs. Duncan[3] that a Mrs. Mark spoke to me, having heard my afternoon address.

Well, I must pack up to catch the boat to Victoria.
Bye-bye
Phil

1 No date; that given is a reasoned conjecture.

2 Cooper Stone, the editor and publisher of the *Rapid City Reporter*; see letter of March 8, 1928, note 1.

3 The Duncans were farmers just outside Rapid City.

TO CATHERINE GROVE

Empress Hotel,
Victoria, B.C.
October 5, 1928

Well, here I am on the island for a week. Yesterday surely was a devilishly hard day – ran into Harvey,[1] by the way, and promised to have tea with them next Thursday. There are still tourists here.

Last night I boarded the steamer at 10:15, went to bed at once and slept through till 5 this morning, got up half past six, in dense fog. I never noticed when at 11:45 the steamer started from Vancouver. The sea was so quiet that, when I awoke in the morning, I lay and listened and could not make out whether we were moving or not till I turned the light on and looked at my watch. Shall, some time during the day, go to the post office and get mail. Then, tomorrow morning, I'll mail a parcel. Am enclosing Galsworthy's *Silver Spoon*.

Everything is marvellously green here after all the rain. As usual, I never saw the sky at Vancouver, but here the weather promises to be glorious.

Send you the papers I mentioned yesterday. It's merely a sample. I don't hunt all the reports up. I hate the papers. But, I believe I have [said] that already, there was a rush on my books at the stores. No book-seller had ever heard of my work. Miller had sent them catalogs of his publications; but nobody, of the book-sellers, had ever seen a volume. Interesting, eh?

There should be quite a sale after this. *Our Daily Bread* was, at Vancouver, dominating all book displays – the worst of the photographs hanging over the tables. Huge signs:

OUR DAILY BREAD
by
FREDERICK PHILIP GROVE
\$2 \$2 \$2 \$2 \$2 \$2 \$2

even on the news-stands at the stations.

Many buy it because they think it's another sex-novel. How they'll get left. Will serve them right.

By coming Tuesday 1/2 the trip is over. Thank the Lord. Shall speak twice today.

Yesterday, at the women's meeting, the President rose at last, trying to say something. They shouted her down. I had left the platform. Nothing would do but for me to mount it again and bow and bow. Damn them!

What a fuss! What a fuss! Because a man knows how to give it to them.

Well, I must shave.
So Bye-bye
Phil

1 Presumably Daniel Cobb Harvey (1886–1966), who was a Professor of History in Winnipeg, first at Wesley College (1915–20) and later at the University of Manitoba (1920–8), before moving to Vancouver as Head of the History Department at the University of British Columbia. In 1931, he was appointed Provincial Archivist of Nova Scotia and Special Lecturer in Canadian History at Dalhousie University, retiring in 1956.

A native of Prince Edward Island, he was educated at Prince of Wales College, Dalhousie University, and Oxford University (1910–13). He presided over Section II of the Royal Society of Canada in 1945–6, having been elected a Fellow in 1928. He was the author of several books and articles on Canadian history.

TO CATHERINE GROVE

Empress Hotel,
Victoria, B.C.
October 5, 1928 II

Just received parcel and letter.

In la sua voluntade è nostra pace.[1] (*Italian* – Dante) = In His will is our peace – which means a great deal. I often quote it to prove the impossibility of translation. It is just a sentence in English; in Italian, it is a world.

Telephone keeps ringing. Saw displays, here, too, of *O*[*ur*] *D*[aily] *B*[*read*] in 3 stores. Spencers have a huge display, with an advertisement in large type in their ladies 'afternoon frock' window. She's going, I believe.

No, re cheque. Doran takes half; Ryerson 10% of the balance.[2] Hogs? I should say. But I have different contracts now. The Graphic shipping bill refers to the new edition,[3] I suppose. You'll probably get the books. Well, I don't know about Norah.[4] Maybe it will, maybe it won't work out. But if not, I don't know what can be done.

I'll cash that check – for I have not nearly enough money with the $100 I drew yesterday. Here boats and trains need to be paid for. No C.P. nor C.N. here.

I had intended to change underwear as soon as I got the

parcel. But I have no bath with this room – the hotel being still crowded. With tomorrow ends this most crowded week.

I find the expense of pressing and cleaning clothes very high. I believe I should charge that to the association. At Vancouver it was $3.70 *a day*. It can't be helped; and yet it is a nuisance. Still, even at that, the association expenses have, so far scarcely exceeded $25 a week. But the most expensive parts of the itinerary are still ahead.

Friday; *At night*. Well that was that. #s 20 & 21 – $525 and a day's rest ahead – much needed. C[anadian] A[uthors'] A[ssociation] wanted me to address them – I declined.[5]

Well, I'll lie down for a while. Shall perhaps add another word or two later. If not, Bye-bye.

1 Thus in manuscript. This famous line of Dante ('Paradiso,' III, 85) has at least three variants:

E la sua volontade è nostra pace in *La Divina Commedia*, illustrata di note da Romualdo Zotti (London 1920);

E'n la sua volontate è nostra pace in *The Divine Comedy*, Oxford World's Classics Series, III (London 1929);

E'n la sua volontade è nostra pace in *Le Opere di Dante*, Testo Critico Della Società Dantesca Italiana (Firenze 1960).

2 This remark presumably refers to sales of *Settlers of the Marsh*, which was published by Ryerson, with Doran handling the US sales.

3 Of *A Search for America*, which was reprinted in June 1928

4 Norah Thompson; see letter of March 26, 1928 II, note 6.

5 The local, Victoria, branch of the Canadian Authors' Association, to which Grove did go; an account of the meeting was reported in the *Victoria Daily Times* of October 8, 1928. He spoke, according to that paper, 'at some length upon his experience as a novelist, revealing most amazing industry and courage in the production of his books and in the search of publishers who would give them to the world ... a collection of his inspired verse, unusual examples of which he read to an appreciative audience, will appear in print in 1930.' No such collection of his verse was ever published. For Grove's attitude towards the Canadian Authors' Association, see letter of September 22, 1928, note 4.

TO CATHERINE GROVE

Empress Hotel
Victoria, B.C.
October 6, 1928

This is nice, 2 whole days without work. Shall mail this afternoon parcel with underwear, and a bunch of papers. That the reporting is accurate, I do not, of course, guarantee. I don't read the stuff myself. The only thing that interests me is the amount of space they give; and, therefore, how many books the thing may sell. We *do* need the money. And yet it is all vanity, vanity. Why in the world ... I ask myself. But I can get up in front of an audience and talk and talk and sway them and provoke applause every now and then – in fact, whenever I feel like doing so; and they think they are getting something and never suspect that every word I say condemns every day of their lives.

When I cross the lobby of one of these 'crack' hotels, I sometimes hear remarks, 'That's Grove!' or 'That's the "famous" writer who's speaking here.' The other day I heard it even in the street at Vancouver.

But, 'Gosh!'[1] I wish it were over. I have a slight cold in the head, nothing to worry over; but I went to bed last night at 9 p.m. and had a hot lemonade brought up after I had had my bath and was covered up. It's almost gone today. Still, in the sense of complete relaxation which I enjoyed this morning – with no lecture to give and no train to catch – I had my breakfast brought up to my room and stayed in bed for an hour after that.

Tonight I am to meet some of the 'authors.' Well...

It's raining again. I'm glad I'm not at Vancouver. There, the rain is unbearable.

Yesterday, by the way, a brother of the late Pete McIlvride[2] called on me and told me a great deal of the antecedents of that death: also of the early married life of the R[apid] C[ity] McIlvrides. It's just as I had divined it. Don't mention it to Mrs. McI[lvride]. I'll tell you about it when I get home.

Well, I'll stop now and go down to have lunch...

Darn them! there a crazy woman phoned up just now to tell me how sorry she is that she missed my lecture ... As if I could possibly care.

As for sending moss[3] or so, it can't be done. Apart from this week-end, I'm busier than the d[evil?]; and it rains and rains. Neither do I care to go out car-riding. I do my best to avoid that sort of thing.

As for your father – I'm sending all of the Victoria papers in which my name struck me. So you'll have some more to send him.

Well, bye-bye. Shall send the parcel etc. this afternoon when I go out.

Phil

1 Grove's habit of placing slang expressions within inverted commas is found in his fiction also.

2 The McIlvrides were farmers in Rapid City. Peter McIlvride died on May 10, 1925 after four days of an illness which was thought to be a heavy cold but was actually double pneumonia, and for which no one thought of seeking medical help until it was too late. His wife survived him by some forty years.

3 Presumably peatmoss, for gardening purposes

TO CATHERINE GROVE

Empress Hotel,
Victoria, B.C.
October 6, 1928 II

Evening. – Coming back from a short walk I find my whole room fragrant with the scent of fruit; and, on looking up, discover a magnificent basket of fruit, decorated and ornamented in the most elaborate fashion. The enclosed card[1] was attached – no doubt from one of my yesterday's hearers. I had just been thinking of a little fruit for a laxative.

One more day of rest ahead. The wind is still east – that means more rain. But I managed to take advantage of a break in the weather.

I have cashed that check. I believe it will see me through. They have ordered here the *Search*, this afternoon. Had a chat with the book-adviser at Spencer's. Those meetings for autographing have fallen through. At Vancouver it was advertised for Thursday afternoon – when I was speaking to the women. Here for Friday, when I was speaking again: then the date was changed for today. Only 7 people turned up.[2] Well, it's supper time. I'll go and eat caviar and oysters. Let them pay for it. This is the end of week #4. Shall go on to-morrow. Have mailed underwear etc. By the way, *Swan Song* bores me. Sorry to say so; but it's a fact.

Sunday, Oct[ober] 7

Well, the last day of this week-end. However, I'm much refreshed and improved. Slept from 11 p.m. till past 7 a.m. The cold is as good as gone. *I* could wish it were a bit colder. Too soft altogether. Enclose a bit of a clipping which seems to show that, after all, things *do* seep in.

Somebody is going to call for me for a drive, unless the rain will keep him away. It has been drizzling steadily now for 2 days. Everything, therefore, looks emerald green, with the sweetness of Mr. Donald Frazer,[3] 'poet-laureate' of Victoria whom I met last night and shocked. For, asked to speak or read, I recited 'Science'[4] from my poems. They did not know, of course, what to make of it. However...

Our Daily Bread sells here. I'm all over the show-windows – So, perhaps, it will go.

The coast being too soft for me, I've made up my mind to leave from Prince Rupert on Sunday morning and have my week-end on the train rather than at the port. That way I shall have the extra day at Edmonton to get laundry done, etc. I shall need it by that time. For I shall have no extra time at Saskatoon, as per original schedule, another club – Prince Albert – having asked for me. I shall be there, at Prince Albert, on Tues[day] Oct[ober] 30 – arriving from F[ort]t Saskatchewan. That will, everything going well, give me a total of $975 in fees. Too bad it isn't an even 1000. However...

Tomorrow Nanaimo; then Courtenay. Wednesday back

to Vancouver. Thur[sday] boat to P[rince] R[upert] – another rest; no doubt it will be much needed by then.

I believe, I shall have to get a new coat at W[inni]peg? If not, I shall order the suit – light weight Norfolk jacket, eh?

Well, bye-bye.

I hate this vulgar, shallow authors' and poets' crowd.

Bye-bye. Kiss

P.

Swan Song is excessively tedious. G[alsworthy] attempts what he cannot do. Drivel.[5] But, like stale bread, it will last me longer.

1 A personal calling card of the usual type – 'Miss Agnew. 1322 Rockland Avenue, Victoria, B.C.' printed in a script type; with the following message in a strong clear round-hand: 'For your kind acceptance, compliments of ' and a signature. For further details of the donor, see the following letter.

2 See letter of September 30, 1928. Clearly Grove did go through with the arrangement. For a curious incident regarding autographing, see the following letter.

3 Donald Andrew Fraser (1875–1948), a school-teacher, was the son of an Ontario Presbyterian minister. He was active in the local Canadian Authors' Association branch, and author of a verse collection, *Pebbles and Shells* (1909), some children's verse, *The Potter's Dream* (1928), a work in rhymed dialogue, and *Centenary* (1943). He was also a contributor to a number of periodicals.

4 Presumably at the meeting of the Victoria branch of Canadian Authors' Association; see letter of October 5, 1928 II, note 5. The poem was published in the *Canadian Forum* of March 1929, p 206.

5 The word is hard to decipher. It looks like 'Drivle,' which may be a misspelling of the word supplied here.

TO CATHERINE GROVE

Empress Hotel,
Victoria, B.C.
October 7, 1928

'And thus the days go by, a long, long line...'[1]

I wish I had had that fruit somewhat sooner, I'd have shipped it home. But it's Sunday and nothing can be done. I'm also afraid it would rot. There's nothing to it but to give it away to the chambermaids. What a shame – though, perhaps, they'll enjoy it.

The mania of these people to show their west coast off! They keep telling you, this is very beautiful and almost resent it when you say you wouldn't want to live here. Rain, rain, rain! I prefer the clean snow at home. I also prefer to be away from the publicity. The telephone rings every five minutes. 'Are you free, Mr. Grove?' – 'Could we take you here or there?' – There's especially one woman, a rather faded sort, with a Boer husband trailing around who phoned me 5 minutes after my arrival and has been repeating it half a dozen times a day since. 'What are you going to do tonight, Mr. Grove?' – 'I'm sorry I am engaged.' – 'Where do you go?' – 'Here and there.' – 'I simply must phone and get an invitation, too.' etc. etc.

This afternoon? 'Are you going out for tea, Mr. Grove?' – 'No. I'm resting.' – 'Couldn't we take you to the Butchart gardens?'[2] – 'Oh, I don't know.' 'Now let me tell you. I'll call with the car, let me say at 3 o'clock. If you are busy, all right. But if you are not, I'd love to take you. I'll tell George to put plenty of robes in the car, etc. etc.'

If a man were a cow-bird!...

And why? The 'celebrity' .... Phew!

Some girls – mere kids – stopped me in the street last night. 'Mr. Grove, would you give us an autograph?' – Well, I did. Wrote my name across an envelope.

I've cashed that check.

By the way, do you know what a room *without* bath costs at the Banff Springs Hotel? $14. Eayrs had a suite of 2 rooms with private bath. Whence does it come? Out of the poor authors, of course. I wonder whether you have any copies yet? I hadn't seen the book[3] till I got to Vancouver. I rather like it. I wish, though, that the print on the side cover were gold, not yellow. I don't like the opacity of it. Well, there goes the phone bell...

Sunday night. – Well, as chance would have it, I found out all about Miss Agnew.[4] A bunch of Swedes got hold of me. Her name was mentioned as that of the owner of a place second only to the Butchart place. Enormous wealth: a spinster of 40 or 45. While I was taking all this in, suddenly one of the men turns around and asks me, 'How do you like her, Mr. Grove?' – 'I can't remember her.' Everybody laughs. And one says to another: 'Some return for her devotion, eh? There she's been raving about this man since June – telling everybody that they *must*, they simply must read this or that, above all *Settlers of the Marsh*! And here he is and is introduced to her and doesn't pay enough attention to remember her!'

I didn't say anything about the fruit which I am actually giving away – I couldn't eat it in four weeks and can't carry it along, of course.

Well, I better slip into some evening clothes; for I've promised to go for an hour or so to a reception.

Next letter from Nanaimo.

Bye-bye,

P.

1 An adaptation of the first line in the last stanza of Grove's 'From *The Dirge*,' written after the death of his daughter on July 20, 1927, and published in the *Canadian Forum* XII (April 1932) 257:

Yet still the days go by, a long, long line
Of figures bent beneath their dreary load
Of thus much time; and each ascends the road
From rise to noon, thence nightward to decline.

2 Famous gardens near Victoria, BC
3 *Our Daily Bread*
4 See the preceding letter, note 1.

TO CATHERINE GROVE

Hotel Malaspina,
Nanaimo, B.C.
October 8, 1928

My dear,

I have just delivered the first address here and am all in a sweat. Fortunately I succeeded in getting away from the crowd. Speak again in 2 hours, to the men. Tomorrow Courtenay; then Wednesday, Thursday, Friday off – for the trip to Prince Rupert; and again some days off – trip to Edmonton. I find it devilishly hard work – to key yourself up to the point where you can put things over – again and again. But it's got to be done. When I've covered this country from coast to coast, I should have enough readers here to support us modestly; and that's what we are aiming at. The frills must come from the U.S.A. I do hope they will come.

But I'll be mightily glad when it's over.

This is a nice hotel; and I have a room – with bath – overlooking the Sound. But rain, rain, rain – nothing but rain here. Haven't seen the sun for 3 days now.

This was #22: $550. Now comes the part that doesn't pay so well: too much travelling. Here, I've got to pay fares. I'll go on to Edmonton on Sunday, I believe – provided there's a decent train. That will cost the Ass[ociation] one extra day at Edmonton; but it will give me a chance to get laundry done and to get away from this terrible climate.

I believe, I'll let you, after all, go through to Winnipeg on Wednesday, Oct[ober] 7, to arrive there late in the afternoon; and I shall be at the station to meet you, arriving myself via C.N. in the morning: otherwise I should have to drop off my train at two or three o'clock at night – highly inconvenient – at a place like Gladstone or so. There is no good train from Kamsack to Winnipeg in daytime. But I'll write about that again later on.

Well, bye-bye, I'll lie down for awhile and rest.
Phil

TO CATHERINE GROVE

Hotel Malaspina,
Nanaimo, B.C.
October 9, 1928

That was #23 last night. As to work to do, more than half; as to time 1/2 exactly done. $575; tonight it will be $600. I am waiting for a long distance call I have put in to find just when the meeting of the Comox County Club is tonight; for I have a chance to go by car, with the County Court judge – whose wife is pres[ident] of the women's club here. It is clearing, so it seems; it has been pouring all night long. Tomorrow I go back to Vancouver by boat from here. Shall have supper with the Harveys[1] there. At Victoria, half a dozen people rushed to the train, 9:15 a.m., after having waited for the stores to open at 9 – so as to get me to autograph their copies of the *Daily Bread*. There were 75 copies in the stores – 3 stores 25 copies each: one or two of them will no doubt send in repeat orders at once or very soon. It helps. But I am sometimes quite despondent over the fact that a person has to hammer away in this fashion, hammer and hammer, in order to sell a few copies of books which will be classics after awhile.

Swan Song is decidedly tedious.

At Victoria I ran into a man called Regan[2] who has been writing for 20 y[ea]rs – has had 2 vol[ume]s published in England – got £30 each advance royalties which were never earned. Wife has been in bed for 14 y[ea]rs. 3 kids. No source of income except 'remittance' of £10 a month. Knows no trade – has been farmhand like myself for years on end; is getting old. I took one of his books and promised to see whether I could do anything for him.

A 'poet' also asked me to do something for him. He has a comfortable position. I gave him 5 minutes, his wife being present. Then I said, 'But permit me, that's distinctly fifth-rate. Why in the world do you want to write verse?' His wife nearly scratched my eyes out. By the way, Mrs. Bobbie Watson honestly thinks her husband[3] is the greatest of writers living, barring none. *Me and Peter*, she says, will live when Hardy and Galsworthy have joined the limbo of forgotten things. How does that strike you? I, she thinks, stand more of a chance of making an immediate success: my 'stuff' is 'sensational' and 'spectacular.' I grinned through it all. Dr. Riddington[4] did not remember having taken us halfway up Grouse Mountain.

Temperature here, today, 72°. Hot-house air. People can't understand that I don't like it.

Well, that's all I've to say, I believe. Except perhaps that last night's talk was poorly attended. Yet there was the cream of 'society.' Met, in the afternoon, Miss Honor Austen of Aldenburgh, Suffolk, England, great-granddaughter of Jane Austen – herself on a tour around the world – an interesting spinster. At night Judge, Senator, etc. etc. The demand for having my 'nationhood' address printed becomes general. I believe I'll either propose to Spry to issue it in pamphlet form or give it to *Maclean's*.[5] Have arranged – did I tell you – with Eayrs to bring [out] a small vol[ume] of addresses in 1929 – title 'Addresses not delivered.'[6] Judge Barker [7] said to me last night: 'That's a masterpiece – in close reasoning, expression, and delivery. There's only one thing wrong. It's so condensed that a person wants to have an hour or so to think over each sentence. Why not print it?'

Well, bye-bye, my dear. I must try that long distance once more.

I am well.
Phil

1 Daniel Cobb Harvey and his wife

2 John Hugh Regan (c1879–1954), who had two novels published in London: *Valiant Heart* (1926) and *The End of the Furrow* (1927). He does not seem to have published since that time. That Grove tried to help him is indicated in a letter from Regan to Grove, November 6, 1928:

> *Valiant Heart* and the new Ms. have gone to Louis Carrier as you advised. I mentioned that you had referred to him as 'a comer,' but said nothing of what you thought of the book. I did not feel at liberty to do so without your permission. ... I do not think your criticism 'mere impertinence.' I am complimented that you thought it worth while to make them. ... I am very grateful for the interest you have taken, and for your kindness in helping me in search for a publisher. If *Valiant Heart* should be published and prove successful, it will be owing to you entirely.

'The new Ms.,' apparently never published, was a novel entitled 'The Flesh and the Spirit.'

3 Robert Watson (1882–1948), born and educated in Scotland, was originally an accountant by profession. He came to Canada in 1908 to work with a shipping firm in Vancouver, and later with the Hudson's Bay Company. He wrote a number of historical and adventure novels, such as *My Brave and Gallant Gentleman* (1918), as well as actual historical works. *Me and Peter*, the novel referred to in this letter, was published in 1926. He was also a regular contributor to a number of Canadian periodicals. Later he turned to the cinema, moving to Hollywood in 1932, and wrote screen-plays for a few films there. For Watson's favourable comments on *Settlers of the Marsh*, see letter of November 14, 1926, note 5.

4 Probably John Ridington (1871–1945), whose name is misspelled here. Born in England, he gave up a lectureship at the City College of London, and came to Canada, first as a teacher in Manitoba and later as a reporter with the *Winnipeg Free Press*. In 1911 he moved to British Columbia, working in a variety of jobs until 1915, when he became Head of the University Library, and lecturer in English at UBC. He retired in 1940, but remained active in literary and library circles until his death. The Groves must have met him during their 1926 trip to Vancouver with Arthur L. Phelps to attend the Canadian Authors' Association convention. Grouse Mountain was the venue for a Canadian Authors' Association sponsored tea-party.

5 'The Meaning of Nationhood' appeared in the *Canadian Nation*, II (March-April 1929)

8–16, and was also printed in *It Needs to Be Said* (1929). Only two articles by Grove appeared in *Maclean's Magazine*: 'Canadians Old and New' (March 15, 1928) and 'Assimilation' (September 1, 1929).

6 These addresses were published by Macmillan, in 1929, as *It Needs to Be Said*; an abridged text of 'Nationhood' is reprinted in *Recent Prose* (C.L. Bennett, ed., 1941). See letter of September 22, 1928, note 4.

7 Charles Howard Barker. Born in 1864 in Sheffield, NB, and educated at the University of New Brunswick and Osgoode Hall Law School, he went in 1891 to Nanaimo, BC, where he practised law until 1909, when he was appointed a judge in the County Court there.

TO CATHERINE GROVE

On board Princess Patricia,
Nanaimo-Vancouver, B.C.
October 10, 1928

I did not know that this passage could be rough. But with a strong n[orth] wind blowing, we are being pitched about in great shape. A piece of news: I am not going up to Prince Rupert: Club collapsed the last moment. So I shall have nearly a week off. Too bad. I'd prefer to get through that week sooner. However – I shall stay to-morrow at Vancouver to get my laundry done. Then I shall run up to Glacier National Park – stay a few days, and, perhaps, run down to Wainwright Nat[ional] Buffalo Park, to put in time till I speak at Edmonton. Meanwhile I shall take care to clear nose and chest of the last remnant of that slight cold which I contracted at Vancouver. Shall have dinner to-night at Harvey's. Courtenay, or rather Cumberland was another experience like Rockyford. This morning the driver who was to take me 10 miles to the station arrived at the hotel 12 minutes before train time – and then drove at the rate of 65 mi[les] an hour. Rather gruelling on winding mountain roads. But we got there and I made the train. The boat is beginning to roll too much for me to go on writing.

Bye-bye
Phil

TO CATHERINE GROVE

Hotel Vancouver
Vancouver, B.C.
[October 11, 1928][1]

[the beginning of the letter is cut off] But things will come out all right. In case of need I'll have to let the letter go back. By the way, have you not yet received any copies of the American ed[ition] of the *Search*? If not, drop Louis Carrier & Co., 2055 University St., Montreal, a line asking about it. Enclose 2 letters – the sort I get dozens of.[2]

Harvey just phoned up – I'll have supper with them tomorrow night. Shall leave here 9:30 and promptly go to bed in the train. Get to Jasper next night. Money goes like water from a sieve. But, so far, I am only a little over $10 out on my own account. So, if Canora[3] does not cancel, I hope to have $900 clear at the end.

Have you received your policy yet? It should have reached you by this time, it seems?

Well, it's 8 p.m.; and that is time for a good boy to start having his bath, especially since last night he did not have one. The bed at Cumberland looked a bit suspicious (a mining town) – and I slept with my rain coat on and my dressing gown about my feet. My suspicion was probably unjustified; but I was heartily glad to shake the dust of the island – though the dust was mostly rain. I never opened my baggage [the bottom of the letter is cut off]

1 Date from postmark
2 Cf. the letter from Mrs Lavinia Creighton, referred to in letter of September 27, 1928. The first of these two letters was from Mrs W.G. (Dorothea Lucile) Ross, of Moose Jaw, Saskatchewan – a straightforward and innocuously-worded invitation to address the Moose Jaw Canadian Club, ending with the delightful, if unconscious, humour of 'My husband hopes to shoot a number of ducks for the occasion.' The second letter, from Mary E. Cohnan of Vancouver – no indication of marital status – attempts to strike up an acquaintance on the grounds that the writer herself was 'a Canadian-by-choice' and a poet – an 'enclosed poem' has not survived – and invites Grove and his wife to spend an evening with the writer.
3 In Saskatchewan, north of Yorkton

TO CATHERINE GROVE

En route Vancouver–Kamloops
October 12, 1928

Well, I'm on the homeward run; expect to get to Jasper by to-morrow night – end of the 5th week. I'm making the run up there by day stages. The canyon of the lower Fraser is, to me, one of the most terrifying things: a marble canyon a mile wide or more. Shall stay over at Kamloops for the night.

Spent the evening, yesterday, with the Harveys. He's, after all, one of the oldest Groveans.[1]

At Vancouver, every book-store had the *Daily Bread* in the window – the two big Dep[artmen]t Stores, Spencer and Hudson's Bay, have a whole table or circle given over to my books, with posters calling attention to them. If *that* doesn't help! But I rather expect that from both there will be repeat orders before Christmas. I do hope the book will sell in the U.S.A.

I'll find this long, long trip across the M[oun]t[ain]s to Edmonton tiring before I get through, I suppose. In fact, I'm sick and tired of it already; and I'm still on the first of three 12 h[ou]r legs. I hope I'll find mail at Edmonton.

Well, this is merely a note – the promised daily letter. Can't write much in the moving train.

Sent home *Swan Song* – shall send *The Bridge of San Luis Rey*[2] from Jasper. Tried to buy a present for you at Vancouver; but found by comparison of prices which I happen to know that everything is from 10 to 25% higher than at W[inni]peg. So I let it go.

Bye-bye
Phil

1 See letter of October 5, 1928, note 1. Presumably D.C. Harvey became interested in Grove during the former's tenure as Professor of History at the University of Manitoba.
2 By Thornton Wilder (b 1897), published in 1927

TO CATHERINE GROVE

En route Kamloops–Jasper
October 13, 1928

I'm getting tired of this. Travelling 300 mi[les] a day – in day-coaches, so as to save a little money. The distances are so enormous; and the trains so slow, climbing the mountains. It would all be very interesting and beautiful, could a person look at things with different eyes. As it is ... Yet, at the end of it I hope to have $1000 in the bank – and that, of course, is something.

Yes, it's a good piece of book-making.[1] But, as you say, the cover, with the huge yellow print, is ugly. However...

I'm reading Ludwig's *Napoleon*[2] which I bought at Vancouver. Am revolving a huge new novel – something entirely different from all I have done. But, I believe, I shall first work over the 'Ant-book'[3] now. I'm going to bring a vol[ume] 'Addresses Not Delivered'[4] next. Then 'Adolescence'[5] or the new book I've been working at last.[6]

I see all sorts of things now and then. Strange visions. This travelling over dizzy viaducts affects me: I must be getting old. At Vancouver I could not sleep because my room was on the 12th floor. But it's all nonsense, of course.

I'd be quite satisfied to stay at R[apid] C[ity] – on that hill-side we've been looking at. I suppose I'll have to go east again early next year. The sooner the better – so as to get through with it. Money, money, money!

Don't forget to tell the Zilzes[7] that I'm spending the week-end in Jasper National Park, and that there is *no* motor-road in: and even near it you can get only from the east and by very poor prairie trails. I'd like to run down to Edmonton in daytime, too. But there is no train apart from the night train. The C.N. runs only 1 train between east and west in winter; and *it* isn't crowded.

On the island, I was thrown, for a day or so, with a couple who reminded me of ourselves. The man (County Court Judge Barker)[8] 60 or 65; the woman, 20 y[ea]rs younger. And both still in love with each other – she, not merely his wife, but his mistress. I liked both of them.

Well, next week-end at Peace River.

Cheer up, old girl; 4 weeks from now: home!

Phil

1 *Our Daily Bread*, published by Macmillan

2 By Emil Ludwig (1881–1948), the German biographer, who became internationally known for his penetrating character studies. His *Napoleon* appeared in German in 1925, and in English in 1926.

3 Eventually published, in 1947, as *Consider Her Ways*

4 Published as *It Needs to Be Said* (1929)

5 Published in 1930 as *The Yoke of Life*

6 Grove's next published novel, after *The Yoke of Life*, was *Fruits of the Earth*, but the reference here could be to one of his unpublished novels, or to *The Master of the Mill* (1944) – see letter of February 29, 1928, note 5.

7 An obscure reference

8 See letter of October 9, 1928, note 7.

TO CATHERINE GROVE

Pyramid Hotel,
Jasper, Alta.
October 14, 1928

Here I am once more in the mountains. But this is by no means as beautiful or as imposing as Banff and surroundings. I've just got back from a 6 mi[le] walk. It is, of course, also somewhat too late in the year for the east-slope. On the west slope, right up to the Yellowhead pass, broad-leaved trees are just in full fall colour. Here they are bare.

This hotel is not the acme of comfort. Jasper Lodge is closed for the winter, of course.

We came in here last night by several hours late. Just where the road-bed seemed to be stuck on to the mountain-side, way above the upper Thompson River, a freight-train had been wrecked; and they were clearing the debris away. We had to wait. Rather a ghastly sight – the second time I've seen it this trip.

Now a strange piece of news. All day yesterday, in the train, a certain man drew my attention by buttonholing any one he could and talking and talking in a rather provocative way. I thoroughly disliked him. Late at night, when we were nearing Jasper, I went into the smoker, to have smoke #10; and there he was, soon trying to get into a debate with me. I froze him. But as I was getting off here, he suddenly pounced on me and asked, 'Is your name Grove?' 'It is,' I said. 'I'm your brother-in-law,' he said. 'My name's Friesen.'[1]

Then he said that he had noticed me all day but had not spoken to me because he had been told I was ill; so he had thought he must be mistaken. Well, I took a taxi and was off – and there was the end of that meeting. Isn't it funny?

Again, as I go on with this tour, the futility of it all grows upon me. And the cost of it! It's appalling – in spite of the passes. Well, I'm within 1200 miles of home now; and week #6 has begun. These last 4 weeks won't be very paying weeks. $75 a week on the average. However...

Shall send underwear tomorrow morning. Enclose more 'pokerhands'[2] and a book which won't interest you – one of last year's best sellers. From Edmonton I may send another book which might interest you – Ludwig's *Napoleon*.[3] For me, it is too 'popular.'

I hope I'll find mail at Edmonton. I shall be cut off from communication for quite awhile. You know of course that I shall be at Edmonton twice: Oct[ober] 17 & Oct[ober] 27. *Hotel Macdonald*. I also hope my winter-coat will meet me there. It may be cold before long.

Well, I'll leave this open till towards evening when I shall take it to the station. Now I had better go and eat for 'one does not eat here at all hours' – the place is asleep.

Later. I've eaten. It's a gloomy day; and the mountains are gloomy here: nothing of the exhilaration of Banff. I'm going to lie down and sleep awhile. If the clouds should open up, it will be snow.

Bye-bye
P
I've been sleeping. Now I'll go and mail this.
Bye-bye.[4]

1 In a letter of March 22, 1973, Leonard Grove writes:

> Mr Friesen, whose first name I don't know, was my father's brother-in-law. He married one of my mother's older sisters, Marie. My mother was, at one time, to have married a brother of Friesen's. Whether or not there was an actual engagement seems to be in doubt; however, the rumour at the school where they met was that she was engaged to be married. It was this 'engagement' which she 'broke' in order to marry F.P.G.

2 Probably a cigarette-card series or a premium competition
3 For bibliographical information, see letter of October 13, 1928, note 2.
4 These last phrases are added in pencil.

TO CATHERINE GROVE

Pyramid Hotel,
Jasper, Alta.
Monday, October 15, 1928.
10 a.m.

There is really nothing to write about. This putting in time on the road is the most stupefying occupation on earth. If I'd known what sort of weather I'd have, and how little is accessible here for a poor pedestrian like myself (the more so since I used to be a good one), I'd have gone to Edmonton via Banff and Calgary.

Yesterday, I had another 6 mi[le] walk in the afternoon; and so I feel pretty stiff and knocked up today; it was gloomy and chilly. Then, at 8 o'clock, I went into a hot bath and to bed. I've really nothing to complain of: room with bath. But my room is 8 by 7 f[ee]t; the bath room 6 by 6. It wouldn't be too bad if a person were not all alone. I do hope they'll billet me at Peace River and Grande Prairie. If not, I'll have 9 days of sitting in a train or a hotel room. Yet there is just enough disturbance all the time to keep a man from working. After that, there will be some quick work till I reach Winnipeg.

This is the first day of the 6th week. 3½ weeks now till we shall meet at Winnipeg. I think I have mentioned once before: you will do best to go right through to Winnipeg. There is only one train on the Kamsack Dauphin line – and it a night train. The main line of the C.N. has been transferred to Portage, Rivers, Saskatoon, Edmonton (did you know that?), using, between Winnipeg and Edmonton, the old Grand Trunk track. From Edmonton via Kamloops to Vancouver it is the old Canadian Northern – and the Prince Rupert line (the old main line of G.T.R.) is now a branch.

This whole business of lecturing looks to me like throwing my time away – and, considering that I may not have much time left, it seems rather a shame. Still, I think my books sell; and we shall be a few hundred dollars to the good at the end.

I'm taking my meals at the railway lunch counter – to save money, so as not to be too much out when I get through.

My laundry, at Vancouver, was exactly $5. It's outrageous. But, charging a reasonable amount here for meals, $2.75 a day, I make up for part of it. Meals actually cost me yesterday $1.40; and it won't be any more today. On the train they cost ca. $5 a day – so the association should have nothing to complain of.

I've just mailed a parcel with underwear. I've not yet used the new suit. I'm holding on to it for colder weather. I may need it on the Peace River trip – I know already that I cannot go from Peace River to MacLennan by car. I shall have to go from P[eace] R[iver] to Spirit River, along the north bank of the Peace River – that, they tell me, is a 150 mi[le] trip. I'll see when I get there. If it involves anything that may threaten me with a cold, I simply won't go. In these outlying places there are no people any way that can do more than gape at what I may have to say. I prefer, after all, the big cities where there are always a few people anyway who have sufficient brains. So far, Vancouver was the biggest success – and it was the largest city in which I have spoken.

Well, old girl, I'll stop. It's just rambling along.

Bye-bye. Shall leave this open in case I want to add anything. Shall mail it tonight: the train goes about 10 o'clock.

P.

5 p.m. Since I absolutely did not know what to do with

myself, I had another 8 mi[le] walk to Pyramid Lake. Came back bathed in sweat, had a bath, changed underwear, went to bed, slept for 1/2 hour and now had better pack up, since they charge for the night if the room is occupied after 7 p.m.

Bye-bye

TO CATHERINE GROVE

The Macdonald,
Edmonton, Alta.
October 16, 1928.
11 a.m.

My dear,

Have just arrived here and find your two letters. Strange that thing about the *Search*. Well...

Got here some 4 or 5 h[ou]rs late: another wreck barring the way. But it gave me a chance to sleep. The first 2 h[ou]rs or so out of Jasper I could not go to sleep at all. Then we stopped while the wrecking train was at work; I went to sleep and slept through till about 6 o'clock. Have no room as yet – there was no reservation made here; and the place is 'full up.'

I know there are two parcels here; but, not having a room, I have not taken them out. Am waiting, waiting.

Yes, I know, it must be *almost* as hard for you to be left alone as it is for me to flit about this way. Yet ... It's got to be done. The more I see of this country, the more clearly do I realise that without some such stimulus as this lecture tour[,] it would take decades longer for my books to penetrate the dense resistance of these people. I do believe that *O*[*ur*] *D*[*aily*] *B*[*read*] is selling along the coast. Too bad about that *Mail and Empire* review (written, by the way, by Deacon).[1] How different it would have been were Jacob[2] alive! Lethbridge is not bad;[3] but then Lethbridge is a very small place.

Well, with regard to that Quebec heater, you know that I have been in favour of something like that for some time. It seems ridiculous for the 2 of us to occupy the whole house. Frankly, Tee, I do not think that we can leave R[apid] C[ity] for the winter. I could, of course, get an advance on royalties from Macmillans. *But*! it would mean that *next* year we'd be still uncertain about our own daily bread. I am in favour of not touching any royalties till they are due – we can't tell yet what they may amount to. If the book goes into a second or third printing before Christmas, that will be different. But will it?

We'll be $1000 ahead, all going well, when I get through. That isn't much. I'll have to go east if the call comes – that, however, will bring $600 at the most. I'll do what I can to make a little extra money from newspapers and magazines. But that won't amount to much. That translation business seems to have fallen through.[4] As for McClelland and Stewart, their proposal[5] is out of the question.

Now as for Winnipeg – I'll tell you. I had intended to buy

you one of those hat-boxes here. You speak of an evening dress. To tell you the truth, I don't really think you'll have any use for an evening dress for another year, apart from, perhaps, one eve[ning] in Winnipeg. But I'll not buy that hat-box – and hold onto the money for you. I can, of course, draw money at W[inni]peg if it is needed; but it is my ambition, for the moment, to have $1000 in the bank – for a rainy day. That's what I'm working for. So, if you've got the money for whatever else you need (as I said, I'll hold on to $35 – which I should have spent for that hat-box), better bring it along.

Yes, I know, Mrs. D. and G.[6] must get on a person's nerves; they do, on mine. Mrs D. more, though, than Mrs G. The latter, to me, is merely funny.

But, cheer up, old girl. Time is speeding. I've had a desperately hard week, without work. It's gone. In 3 weeks or so we'll meet at W[inni]peg. No, I shouldn't like to see you rely on making the 3 o'clock connection at Brandon; it's too uncertain. The other way your connection is guaranteed. I'll have to see about the next place to send underwear to. I'll let you know in a day or two.

Well, bye-bye.

1 Presumably the unsigned review of *Our Daily Bread* in *The Mail and Empire*, October 6 1928 – reprinted in my *Frederick Philip Grove* (Critical Views on Canadian Writers 1970) 131. The review, although it calls the novel 'distinguished,' asserts that 'The whole conception is grim, unrelenting, powerful and unlovely.'

2 Probably Fred Jacob (1882–1926), Toronto novelist, dramatist, and critic, author of the novel *The Day Before Yesterday* (1925) and of several one-act plays. Jacob was Deacon's predecessor as literary editor of *The Mail and Empire*.

3 Rather than the town, this is probably an allusion to the review of *Our Daily Bread* in the *Lethbridge Herald* of October 2, 1928; the review is reprinted in my *Frederick Philip Grove* (Critical Views on Canadian Writers 1970) 129–31.

4 Gustav Amann's *The Legacy of Sun Yatsen*, translated from the German by Frederick Philip Grove, was published by Louis Carrier in 1929.

5 The reference here is presumably to the negotiations with McClelland & Stewart for the purchase of the sheets in stock of *Over Prairie Trails* and *The Turn of the Year*; see letter of November 3, 1928, note 4.

6 Mrs Duncan and Mrs Gardiner of Rapid City; see letters of October 4, 1928 and February 28, 1928 respectively.

TO CATHERINE GROVE

The Macdonald,
Edmonton, Alta.
October 16, 1928 II
3 p.m.

Swear about the underwear? You bet I do. It's summer weather here. But the worst of it is: where am I to put it? I'll have to carry it over my arm I suppose. For my suitcases are full to bursting. However...

I'll send one suit of light-weight home on Thursday. Then send *one* suit heavy-weight (but the lightest of them: the newest) to Saskatoon, General Delivery – but I shall be at Saskatoon only a few hours – I am going to *Prince Albert* on Tuesday and arrive at Saskatoon only the last minute. I'll manage somehow to get it. If I know beforehand where I am going to stay there, I'll wire.

Now I'll try to engineer things so as to stop at a hotel in W[inni]peg. Should Phelps write, you say that I have said I must do as the clubs wish me to; and I am declining *all* private invitations.

Well, being so dirty and having had to wait for a room till 5 min[utes] ago, I have not eaten.

My cold is practically gone.

There is not a copy of my book in town, and I dislike the place like anything.

Bye-bye –

The train to Peace River has *sleeper* but no dining car. I'll take a box along.

P.

TO CATHERINE GROVE

The Macdonald,
Edmonton, Alta.
October 16, 1928 III

My dear girl,

I am enclosing a corner of the front page of the *Edmonton Bulletin* which I would ask you to keep for me. That picture, openly flaunted in view of every kid walking the streets is significant and needs exposing.[1]

Have nothing else to report just now. Not a notice in any paper of my coming. This seems to be the deadest of all dead towns. But I'll see tomorrow. I mean, of course, dead to me.

Evening. Well, I don't know, my dear. My letters sound weary? Yes, I suppose they do. I *am* weary of all this. But it has *got* to be done. Whenever I can, I'll quit; but I must go on with it somewhat longer. Till royalties are sufficient. Look at Disraeli, at Napoleon: what tragedies: and Deacon, the fool, complains of the tragedy in *O[ur] D[aily] B[read]*.[2] Only people who do not know life – or who are still young enough to think *they* amount to something can talk such nonsense. I've got to knock them down. [the rest of the letter is cut off]

1 The picture, a two-column spread of a girl scantily clad in a long scarf and slippers, appeared in the *Edmonton Bulletin* of October 16, 1928.

2 See the first letter of this date, note 1. Although quite favourable, the review complained of the book's excessive drabness.

TO CATHERINE GROVE

The Macdonald,
Edmonton, Alta.
October 17, 1928

Am to speak in a couple of hours and don't feel a bit like it. It's raining, raining, raining.

As for the Maritime tour[1] – I must go, my dear. It's the only way I see so far to ensure that you can throw up your job in the near future.

Nice of Kirk to write.[2]

As for your question about the intelligence of women or men, I don't know. I find both equally stupid here in the west, I believe. Not one has ever shown the slightest sign of understanding that I am preaching on the text 'Repent ye.' But I often say that I appeal to the women through their heads, to the men, through their emotions. I'll fix it so that you can hear both my addresses at W[inni]peg – come in at the men's luncheon after the meal. Sit at the door.

It's hot, and I am worried about all that additional baggage. I shall try tomorrow to send home the light top-coat. But not, as yet, the rain-coat. Dr. Broadus,[3] head of the English department at the U[niversity][4] phoned up, asking me to have tea with him and his wife. I have accepted. So I don't know whether I'll have time for another line. Now I must dress; and I shall mail this when I go down to meet the women.

Bye-bye.
P.

I was just told that there is a telegram for me at the president's. I've sent a messenger to fetch it. So I'll wait with[out] closing this. – –

The wire was of no importance except to say that Canora has not yet confirmed. I hope they will, though. It means $25; and I'll be on the road anyway. Might just as well make that money.

Telephone keeps ringing. Newspapers are at last waking up.

My throat does not bother me at all. My head is quite clear. There's a slight cough. But it's subsiding. It was the coast climate that brought it.

Have just made my reservations for tomorrow to Peace River: cost of ticket $24 odd.

Well, bye-bye; I must dress.
P.

Shall send big parcel tomorrow.

1 The last tour he undertook, in the following spring

2 Watson Kirkconnell wrote on October 12, 1928, praising *Our Daily Bread*.

3 Edmund Kemper Broadus (1876–1936) was a native of Alexandria, Virginia, and educated at Washington, Chicago, and Harvard. He came to Canada, in 1908, to become Professor and Head of the English Department at the University of Alberta. He was elected a Fellow of the Royal Society of Canada in 1934. He wrote a number of books – literary studies, essays, and anthologies – and contributed prose and poetry to various scholarly and popular periodicals. His *A Book of Canadian Prose and Verse* was published by Macmillan in 1923.
4 The University of Alberta

TO CATHERINE GROVE

The Macdonald,
Edmonton, Alta.
October 17, 1928 II

Well, another one done – and very successfully. Spry writes 'It will be very difficult for us to secure speakers in the future who will live up to the high standard you have set.' I should say! Everybody tells me that everything else is 'piffle' – the actual word of a woman. I'll say in my answer that it is not necessary to compliment me; I *know* I can speak.

Now, one trifle. I don't know where I am going to stay at Saskatoon – so, please address mail (what cannot reach me by Oc[tober] 28, *here*) c/o Mr. A. Hutcheon, Sec[retary], The Canadian Club, *Prince Albert, Sask[atchewan]*. It must be there by *Oct[ober] 30*. Send *one* suit of heavy-weight (lightest of these) underwear. *Don't* send my fur coat nor heavy-weight socks – nor any more scarfs. I have everything I need in that line.

That, however, by the bye. Apart from that cheer up. Three weeks from today I'll be in Winnipeg; and by this time of the day I shall be at the station (C.P.R.) waiting for you. Cheer up, therefore.

Bye-bye
P.

I'm to go out for supper.

TO CATHERINE GROVE

The Macdonald,
Edmonton, Alta.
October 17, 1928 III
9 p.m.

This is the evening of another day. I am, after all, amazed to realise that the time goes on, on, on. Only 3 more weeks now till we meet – out of $8^1/_2$. Then $^1/_2$ week, and we'll go home. And 2/3 of Canada has been covered.

Spent the afternoon and early evening with the Broadus's – Dr. Broadus, head of the English dep[artmen]t at the U[niversity] of Al[ber]ta.[1] Got away at 8 o'clock, pretexting the need of rest – which is real enough. That week without work was the hardest of all – especially up at Jasper where I stuck for 2 days because it was cheap.

By the way, I expect to find a letter here when I return from the Peace River district. Shall be here Saturday night, Oct[ober] 27 – exactly 10 days from today. Of course, it's no use sending anything that may arrive later than Sat[urday], for I leave here very early on Monday morning for F[or]t Sask[atchewan] – next day Prince Albert. I think I have mentioned before this that my itinerary is somewhat changed. Between now and Oct[ober] 27 you cannot expect much mail. Trains up north are bi-weekly – so you cannot possibly get more than 2 letters a week; and a whole week may pass without since I am not sure how to catch the mail. If this rain turns into snow; or if it has snowed farther north, I may have to cancel Grande Prairie.

By the way, please enclose in your next parcel (to Prince Albert) the *tan* gaiters, will you? They keep my feet warm if it turns cold by then as it is likely to do.

I'll have a hot bath and then to bed. Bye-bye or night-night.

1 See the first letter of this date, note 3.

TO WATSON KIRKCONNELL

The Macdonald,
Edmonton, Alta.
October 17, 1928 IV

My dear Kirk,

Thanks for your letter which I received this morning. Yes, I think myself that the book is good. Deacon has just pushed it aside (in the *Mail and Empire*)[1] as 'drab' and 'grim, unrelenting, powerful, and unlovely.' It seems to me we have all too much of a certain kind of 'loveliness' – I'd call it 'agility and prettiness' rather, especially in verse. What we need is sober power. Well...

As for the success, Eaton's took 2,500 copies. There were 270 copies in Vancouver (in 4 stores) besides the news-stands where I did not enquire. I spoke 4 times at Vancouver, once, at the University – (open meeting) – to an audience of 1,500, on Nationhood (the same address I intend giving to the men at Winnipeg); and, consequently, there was a rush on my books. But most people *borrow* books here in the west. At Banff, 5 people told me that they had been on the waiting list (for the *Search*) at the Public Library for months; they had been told that they would get the book within the coming *year*.

But buy? It never enters their minds as a possibility.

Well, thanks again. So long.
As ever
F.P.

1 See previous references to this review: letters of October 16, 1928, note 1, and of the same date, no. III, note 2.

TO CATHERINE GROVE

The Macdonald,
Edmonton, Alta.
October 18, 1928.
morning

This will be the last note, my dear, before the 10 day break of the Peace River trip. I have the parcel ready – unfortunately I have to part with the light top coat – which means I'll sweat, for it is summer warm: the rain has stopped at last.

I'm much interested in the P[eace] R[iver] trip – but it may not be so simple as it seems.

The women, here, have already written to Spry, so I was told last night, asking to have me again. Well, I can only say that, if I ever go again, it will be for the bigger cities only – with 1 address a day at the most. And that will cost them too much; for I shall want more money, too. The thing does sell books. Yesterday Mrs. Murphy called ('Janey Canuck')[1] – you may never have heard of her: Mrs. McClung[2] #2: judge of the Juvenile Court for the province of Alberta since 1915. She's quite a figure. She wants me to collaborate with her on a book she's writing, says she has 'wonderful material.' How would it sound: 'The Frozen North, by Janey Canuck and Frederick Philip Grove'? 'Wonderful material.' 'You know, Mr. G.,' she said, 'I've read but one book of yours, *Settlers of the Marsh*, but I've always said, that man Grove is the man for me, he's such a *sense of humour*!' I nearly fell off my chair: in *Settlers of the Marsh*! But that is the book I'm known by *here*. The library has 3 or 4 copies. Still, I found a few copies also in the book-stores, at $2.25. There's 1 copy of *Over Prairie Trails* here, 1st ed[ition], much faded, also at $2.25.

Well, now I'll go downtown and send the parcel, buy my tickets for P[eace] R[iver], and a book which I intend taking along.

So bye-bye for the long break. When I get back, it will be a little over a week only to Winnipeg.

P.

1 Emily Gowan Murphy (1868–1933), née Ferguson, who wrote under the pseudonym 'Janey Canuck.' The wife of a missionary, she spent most of her adult years in the prairies, and was one of the leading figures in the struggle for women's rights in Canada. As a result

of her campaigns for a special women's court, she became the first woman magistrate to be appointed – in Edmonton, in 1916 – in the British Empire. She published a number of books, mostly about life in the Canadian west, and a tour diary of her visit to Britain and Germany: *The Impressions of Janey Canuck Abroad* (Toronto 1902).
2 Nellie Letitia McClung (1873–1951), née Mooney, one of the five women, including Emily Murphy, who are particularly remembered for their successful agitation for the appointment of a woman to the Senate. It was rejected by a ruling of the Supreme Court in 1928, but upheld on appeal to the British Privy Council in 1929. She was an ardent temperance advocate, a lecturer, and the writer of a series of novels, all dealing in different ways with the women's rights question and pioneer life in the west. Her best known book is *Sowing Seeds in Danny* (New York 1908).

TO CATHERINE GROVE

The Macdonald,
Edmonton, Alta.
October 18, 1928 II

I thought I had dropped the last line into the mail box: from here, I mean; but lo and behold! along comes another letter from you and one from Mrs. Duncan. Tell her I received it and thank her for it. Truth to tell, there was nothing of any importance in it. However ... I dropped her a few post-cards, of course – for your sake – same as the Gardiners.

Well, as to your finances, don't worry. If you can't make both ends meet, you must draw. But, of course, we'll both be 'near.'[1] I'm so near that I just dickered at a book-store for the price of a book I wanted. I autographed the last copy of the *Search* to be found in this town and, thereby, knocked 25¢ off the price I was to pay.

But it's no use worrying. The devil of it is that we shall have to pay income tax, in spite of the fact that we had to skimp and skimp. I'll make some extra money somehow when I get home. The expense bill will amount to about $300 – rather more, I'm afraid, than less. But I manage pretty well as I intended to do. Have repeatedly succeeded in bucking pressing and laundry on to the local clubs. I don't give a continental whether they consider it shabby or not. I can't afford to carry that expense myself.

Have just bought thermogene, throat pastilles, Lavoris, and a small nasal douche and salt. – Not that I need the stuff; but, going up into the wilderness and not knowing what I can get there, I thought it wise to be prepared *if* I need anything. Spent $2.15 on that and it hurts even though I don't think that *ich zuviel gezahlt habe*.[2] Though 55¢ for thermogene *is* high.

Well, I can account for more money than I've had: that's very strange; but it's a fact nevertheless.

Now I must dress for the noon speech (men) – and then change for the long trip north.

So once more bye-bye.
P.

I had already sealed this, but tear it open again (Hotel stationery doesn't cost me anything – otherwise I'd have been too 'near') to say that the sec[retary] of the men's club just phoned me up to ask whether ladies might come after the lunch – he had had over 100 enquiries: I bet there won't be more than 40 or 50 men. But the women come back to hear me once more: but then there are other reasons, besides intellectual ones.

1 Cf. letter of October 6, 1928, note 1, on Grove's peculiar use of quotation marks. 'Near' is obviously slang for 'frugal.'
2 I've paid too much.

TO CATHERINE GROVE

En route Edmonton–Peace River, Alta.
October 18, 1928 III

Well, I'm en route again, off for Peace River. That men's meeting at Edmonton was a fizzle – a bunch of 'Service Club' people – business men who don't have an ounce of brains, nothing but the low sort of cunning which enables them to levy a tax on an unsuspecting public. But there were some 25 women there; and many, many more went back disappointed because there was not even standing room left. Among the men, there were perhaps 5 or 6 who were not dunces – no more. One of them the Hon[ourable] Mr. Baker,[1] minister of education for the province. He spoke to me at the close of the meeting and even sat down for a talk; but I had to change and pack up. I am firmly convinced that he was on the point of making me some sort of offer; but I had to leave him. I could see he wished to unburden himself: I liked him: the ironical resignation with which he said, 'Too bad! Too bad! I could have wished to speak more personally ... Well, you see, you have "arrived" at last.' I laughed at that word "arrived" – and he joined in in a way which I liked. Well, that's all; except that another day has been nibbled off the last three weeks. I'm beginning to be curious how Winnipeg will turn out for me. University of Alberta has asked me to address them on Saturday night, Oct[ober] 27. Bye-bye.

Oct[ober] 19. Still en route. I'm north of Lesser Slave Lake now. It is a clear, cold day, so it seems. But what a road-bed on this line! Most of the time, at night, it felt as if the train were going to roll over. And now another 4 h[ou]rs to the river valley. It's rather amazing to think that a person isn't quite worn out after such a trip. I actually had to hold on in order not to roll out – as in a ship with a gale blowing. And all the time a person stiffened his muscles to counteract the jolts. And yet I slept a little and feel all right this morning. And it's the last of these extraordinary things, I believe. After this I get to smoother going and quicker work. No 10 days any longer to deliver 2 lectures. And never again, that's sure, unless it is being made worth my while – at the rate of *at least* $100 a week which would give me $150 instead of $50.

Well, I'll close this, so as to drop it in a box when I arrive – then it will go back tomorrow. Next letter will be from Grande Prairie, I think.

Bye-bye! Night-night – no, day-day.

P.

1 Perren Earle Baker, who was born in 1877 in Blenheim, Ontario, educated at McMaster and Chicago universities, and settled as a pioneer farmer in Alberta. Elected to the Alberta legislature in 1921, he was Minister of Education from then till his defeat in the election of 1935.

TO CATHERINE GROVE

Peace River, Alta.
October 20, 1928

That was #27.

This is a marvellous country here: the town at the confluence of 3 rivers – Peace, Smoky, and Harmon (locally called Hart). I am writing in the interval between the meeting and dinner at the house of the President's. For I shall not have an opportunity to write again before Monday or Tuesday. Tomorrow a local man is going to take me on to a farm (some 25 mi[iles] from here) owned by a Mr. Lamont[1] (M.A. of Oxford, pioneer farmer and breeder of Shorthorns[)] – a most interesting man, friend of G.B. Shaw's, whom I met last night. Lamont is going to take me on to Fairview where I shall have to spend the night. On Monday I'll have to hire a car as far [as] Spirit River (25 mi[les]) – the total length of the trip being 150 mi[les] – where again I shall spend a night. Then on to Grande Prairie. I have stipulated that nobody who drives me is to go faster than 25 mi[les] per hour. The number of fatal accidents around here (all from driving 50 or 60 mi[les] per hour over roads fully as dangerous as mountain roads) is appalling. So I declined to go with a man who is going to go right through to Grande Prairie. Lamont has seen several such accidents; it has made him very careful. Lots of moose and deer around here. The river boat – plying from F[or]t St. John (Hudson's Bay post) 200 mi[les] upstream to F[or]t Vermilion, 300 mi[les] downstream – had, a few days before my arrival, sunk in 10 f[eet]t of water. They had to repair the bottom through divers under water and raised it yesterday. It has made its last trip for the year.

I am still wearing my old *light* underwear; but intend changing into the new suit tomorrow morning – possibly I'll even put on, for the big drive, the winter-weight. I don't know yet. I don't want to spoil myself. In closed cars there is really no need to coddle yourself.

I am quite all right, even though the accommodation leaves much to be desired. These people here assure me that my lecture was the greatest hour of their [cut]
who is worth a straw. [cut]
Literary Supplement [cut]

Well, my dear, little [cut]
you were here in the [cut]
By the way, latitude 56° N, longitude 120° W (nearly).

Grande Prairie, Alta. Monday, Oct[ober] 22, 1928

I'm that much farther on the way again. Came over here in 3 relays last night. The train would have been out of the question. So I went blindly, that is, without knowing whether I could complete the journey or not. I had been invited to Lamont's farm for dinner. That was 20 mi[les] from Peace River along the Grande Prairie road. The secretary of the P[eace] R[iver] club offered to take me that far. Thence I went 60 mi[les] with Lamont who offered to take me to a hotel which he said was the best place between P[eace] R[iver] and G[rande] P[rairie]. There we arrived at 6 p.m. For a few hours I kept sitting around. I was just on the point of going to bed, having vainly inquired about a chance to go on when three G[rande] P[rairie] men blew in, heard of my inquiries and came up to offer to take me. I didn't know what they had stopped for. Business? I found out later: to drink. I thought it wise to accept. It was still nearly as far to go as from Calgary to Banff. It was then 10 o'clock. We started: the driver was careful enough. But: when we were in the middle of the Saddle M[oun]t[ai]ns, with precipitous and winding roads (at night), he ran out of gas. We had just passed a little log-house. Now drinking started in earnest. But the driver remained relatively sober: apparently he could stand quite a bit. The other two, fortunately, promptly went to sleep in the car. The driver and I walked back to the log-house. No; the man had no car; and therefore no gasoline. But he told us of a Swede who lived there and there[2] (3 mi[les] away) and who kept a Ford car. The nearest gas-station was 12 or 14 mi[les] away. So we started to go there. We had walked at least 5 mi[les] and hadn't found the place. However, I stuck to the driver so as not to let him go to sleep, too. It was pretty cold; but the walk warmed me up wonderfully; and the night was very beautiful. Suddenly the light of a car appeared. We stopped it. The man had plenty of gas but no way of getting it out of the tank. All right; he went on. And we started to search once more for the Swede. I felt responsible for our getting back to the car, ultimately. Well, we searched for close to another hour and had just located a light in the spruce wilderness to our right – when again a car appeared. We stopped it. Yes, he thought he could let us have a gallon of gas – with that we'd be able to make the next filling sta[tion]. Well ... but we were 4 or 5 mi[les] from our car; and this car was filled to the last place. I described to its driver as well as I could where he'd find our car and trusted that he would do as he promised. We started to walk back to the car. Well, we found it; and the man had actually transferred enough gas for us to make the next sort of town. We got here in the small hours of the night – only to find that no room was to be had in any one of the hotels. Since I had arrived ahead of time, I couldn't blame anybody. I did phone the president of the club up; but, on second thought, told him not to bother. I sat up for the rest of the night and feel quite all right this morning. Just got a room and am going to have some sleep now. It was no worse than riding in a sleeper on a branch line where the road-bed is bad. In fact, the ride was less disagreeable.

Lamont is a very fine man; and we had a long talk on the 60 mi[le) drive – chiefly on what we called 'the new code' among educated young men and women (in the college [the bottom of the page is cut off] about him when I get home. He was one of the most striking men I've met on the tour: a marked man – in a way his acquaintance alone pays for the tour.

Well, bye-bye, old girl. I must have a little walk, to get some fresh air; and then for a sleep!

P.

1 John Murdoch Lamont (1876–1970) was born in Scotland, and was a graduate of the University of Edinburgh, not Oxford. Following his graduation, he attended the University of New York in Syracuse, New York, where he wrote a thesis on 'The Boy in the City.' Later he spent a winter at the University of Marbourg in Germany.

He came to Peace River, Alberta, in 1913, and was very successful in breeding a champion stock of shorthorn cattle. In the thirties, he moved to British Columbia, and experimented with the planting of dwarf fruit trees. He was one of the first orchardists in the Okanagan Valley to recognize their commercial possibilities.

About his friendship with Shaw, Mrs Lamont writes:

> I'm not sure that it would be totally correct to say that he was a friend of G.B. Shaw. Certainly he attended every possible meeting at which Shaw spoke; ushered at some of his meetings, and in later years saw practically every play of Shaw's, in some cases on first-nights when Shaw was present. On one or other of these occasions I believe the young men who ushered were presented to Shaw, and I'm sure I recall John speaking of an occasion when the hall was so packed that seats had to be found for some of them, including my husband, on the platform with Shaw. And I know that I've heard him mention Shaw's charm of manner and kindliness.

2 Thus in the manuscript

TO CATHERINE GROVE

Grand Prairie, Alta.
October 23, 1928

This is pretty terrible indeed. Not that I suffer in the least. But the tedium of it! I arrived here on Sunday night. If those people in Ottawa had known conditions, I could have spoken last night and been out today. Instead, I shall have to wait till Friday. In order to pass the time, I have agreed to address the *Board of Trade* (!) at Wembley, 16 miles west of here, quite near the mountains. Till then, I have nothing whatever to do but wait. Everybody is busy. At night, yesterday, a lawyer and a newspaper man came and wanted to talk: not an idea in their heads. I was quite rude at last, saying that, if those were their opinions, we were on opposite poles of the world: learn something, I said, before you try to preach. Well, it had at least the effect of ridding me from them.

This is a place like Drumheller: pioneer in the worst sense: the boosting sense. Nobody thinks of anything but – to call it by the right name – squeezing the last dollar out of the poor settlers.

I shall speak at the University of Alberta on Saturday night at 8 o'clock. For Sunday I have accepted an invitation to tea with 'admirers' – I hate that sort of thing; but it will help to pass the time. They were pursuing me with telegrams. All right, I agreed. After that, a little over a week. Thank the Lord!

Have you seen that silly review of *O[ur] D[aily] B[read]* in the *Saturday Night*?[1] It is clear at once that the reviewer has not even read the book; or he could not talk such nonsense abou John junior. Still, there were two skillful ads in the same number: Eaton's – saying that my book is the first 'book of the month' – and Macmillan's. Also – a half page picture – Comfort's[2] drawing. It will all help. They tell me there was a big article about my work in the *New York Times*;[3] but I haven't seen it.

Just now I haven't a thought nor an ambition in the world except to make enough money that we can face the future without your teaching and my lecturing. Not, you know, that the latter is without value for myself. A person sees and hears quite a bit of how the world is wagging: but I wish I were younger. In any case, I'll promise not to go out again – after I've covered Canada – except if I get much more money – at least twice as much – or a fixed sum per week: $200 a week – with no more than 5 lectures a week to give. Then you could come along, for the thing could be worked so as to cost no more, for you, than about $15 a day on an average. Half the earnings for your expenses: as it is, your trip would eat up the whole. I find it devilishly hard to keep my own, personal expenses reasonably low.

[letter cut here] it will be all over, as far as I am concerned. I am terribly anxious to have a place of my own where I can stay and work. For I still have work to do: and I can't do anything while I'm on the tour.

Well, I suppose I'd better stop. 3 more days after this one before I'll climb into the train. Then 24 h[ou]rs in the train, Edmonton; and then 10 more lectures! 10! But even that will go by. 2 weeks from tomorrow.

Bye-bye.
P.

1 The review by Raymond Knister in *Saturday Night* of October 13, 1928, is reprinted in my *Frederick Philip Grove* (Critical Views on Canadian Writers Series 1970) 132–3.

Raymond Knister was born in 1900 near Blenheim, Ontario, and educated at the University of Toronto and Iowa State University. He published two novels, *White Narcissus* (1929) and *My Star Predominant* (1931), and edited *Canadian Short Stories* (1928), the first anthology of its kind. His review of *Our Daily Bread* was slightly condescending and a little critical, but on the whole quite favourable. Grove was later to meet and correspond with Knister, and to recognize his merit as a writer. Knister was drowned in 1932 just when his literary reputation was becoming established.

11 Drawing of Grove by Charles Fraser Comfort, RCA, for use on Grove's 1928 lecture tour. *Courtesy Leonard Grove*

2 Which is reproduced as an illustration (p 193). The same drawing was used by the Association of Canadian Clubs in their special folders promoting Grove's lecture tour through eastern Canada.

Charles Fraser Comfort, RCA, was born in Edinburgh, Scotland, emigrating to settle in Winnipeg in 1912. His education in art was in Winnipeg and New York. After serving as official Canadian war artist (1943–6), he was appointed Director of the National Gallery of Canada in 1960, a post he held until 1965, when he retired. He now lives in Hull, Quebec.

3 An unsigned review which appeared in the issue of October 7, 1928 – reprinted in my *Frederick Philip Grove* (Critical Views on Canadian Writers 1970) 131–2.

TO CATHERINE GROVE

Grande Prairie, Alta.
October 25, 1928

That was #28. And thus time drags on. The stupidity of it and the people!

Well, perhaps ... I said the same about Edmonton; and yet, I find in the *Journal* a farewell editorial[1] which perhaps shows that there may be some more lasting effect. Also, I was asked to address the University Saturday night. And the women, of course, pursue me with invitations. Well, well...

At any rate, I'll be heartily glad when this thing is over. I'm getting more than tired of it. 10 more unless Canora cancels. If they are at all decent, it seems to me they should pay me for Prince Rupert even though I did not speak there. For I have now, in more than 2 weeks made only $100.

By the way, I'm perfectly well. I hope you are, too. Tonight I am to speak at Wembley – not C[anadian] C[lub], of course; there is none. I agreed chiefly because it will do away with one more tedious night.

I hope you get my last letter on Fri[day] or Sat[urday], so as not to let the week-end go by without one. This, of course, won't reach you before Tues[day] or Wed[nesday] next week. After that, it will all be easier again: more work for me; more letters for you. Well, I'll go out for a walk. The weather is glorious. I'll leave this open to add to today or tomorrow. Bye-bye.

Oct[ober] 27 That editorial[2] which I enclose should impress Stone if you care to give it to him. It's allee samee me.

This letter, with the postscript of October 27, and the letter of October 26, with added material of October 27, were mailed together from Edmonton on October 27, 1928.

1 In the *Edmonton Journal* of October 19, 1928. Entitled 'Mr Grove's visit,' it concluded: 'He has been accused at times of painting their [western rural pioneers'] existence in too drab colors. But this criticism will only be offered by the careless reader. Beneath the hard conditions that he paints one should be able to see the sterling worth he finds there.'

2 The editorial in the *Edmonton Journal*; in the manuscript letter, Grove links the postscript with the earlier reference to the editorial by drawing a long line on the margin.

TO CATHERINE GROVE

Grande Prairie, Alta.
Friday, October 26, 1928

Thank the Lord, this is the last day here in this god-forsaken town. Went over last night to Wembley to speak there to a small gathering of perhaps 20 – just to kill time. Have an invitation today to go to Beaverlodge Experimental Farm and have dinner with the superintendent; but don't think I'll go. It's 28 miles; and I'm little inclined to take any chance on catching my train. To stay here longer would be death from tedium, unbearable and never to be outlived, with not even hope of the diversions of hell; for nobody here has even the gumption to tempt me to sin. Since I've waited at wayside stations to catch a ride on the rods or bumpers, I've not felt so bored. Nor have I eaten the sort of food I've had to eat here. There's plenty of beautiful country around; but apparently everybody is so engrossed with sense[less]ly[1] rushing about, in this dirty town, that nobody thinks of taking me out at least. Nothing is so hard to bear as loafing about. I've read everything I had along, including time-tables – the latter half a dozen times. If I were better versed in curses than I am, I'd surely curse this place in twenty languages.

As for other people, they seem all so intent on getting away from here that reservations for the sleeper have to be made two weeks ahead. Fortunately, I made mine before leaving Edmonton; and so I'm safe. I have my tickets. I'm astonished, from the rush for every train, that there's a single soul left in the entire Peace River country. Withal, those that are left are much astonished when I ask them in what way this country, according to them, is different from other parts of the rolling prairie – except in as much as their scrub poplar bush here is interspersed with a few spruce trees. Then they say, 'Well you haven't seen much of the country around.' I agree. But, I say, I've seen enough of it not to want to see any more; and they are indignant. They do think they have the most marvellous country: it all boils down to this that, for the American continent, they are reasonably far north. Then I tell them that I've seen wheat mature in Europe north of lat[itude] 70°; and they gape. It seems all such nonsense. However, I'm getting out of it. Manitoba, as far north, is vastly more beautiful. But the weather is glorious: regular Indian summer. If only it did not take 24 hours to get out of here.

Well, there's my laundry. I'll put it away. Leave this open to add to it. Bye-Bye.

P.

Oct[ober] 26

3 p.m. And thus the hours drag on. Train leaves at 7:15 – 4 hours to wait; and one more supper to take. If ever I am to go out again lecturing in the West, *this* place will be skipped, that is certain. Nothing else to say. One gets into a state bordering on sleeping sickness here: a syncope of all faculties. Bye-Bye...

7:20 p.m. Here I am sitting again in the swaying car – the sleeper of the train, I mean. Thank the Lord! Moving homeward at least. I'll be glad if I never see Grande Prairie again! Rapid City is metropolitan in comparison: chiefly as regards cleanliness. And the noise at that hotel! Gramophones blaring away everywhere. I do hope my baggage is on board! Well, it is too hard to write with the train rolling that way. I'm in for 24 h[ou]rs of this. Good night. Good night.

Oct[ober] 27

8:15 a.m. 13 h[ou]rs out of the 24 h[ou]r run are gone. Just had my breakfast. The train is wearily rolling along, through dismal, burnt-over spruce forests. It froze a little overnight; but it is quite mild. Every mile now brings me definitely nearer the end. I can't write. Bye-bye.

4 p.m. And thus the hours drag on. Another 3 of them before I get to Edmonton. I just overhauled my accounts. Total expense, so far $245 or, roughly, $35 a week. I have $50, roughly, left. That will just see me through, I suppose. Sometimes it seems enormous to me that, in spite of my passes, it should cost the Association $300. At other times I say, to h[ell] with them if it doesn't suit them. I'm not going to save for them – though I've done so, staying at a little 5th rate place at Jasper.

I'll close this now, so as to mail it on arrival. I expect *at least* a letter or one letter,[2] possibly more. Haven't heard a thing now for ten days or longer. I wish all those who've been inviting me would forget about it. But they won't.

Well, bye-bye, old girl. 11 days after this one. 2 weeks to home.

P.

1 No doubt a slip of the pen

2 Thus in the manuscript

TO CATHERINE GROVE

The Macdonald,
Edmonton, Alta.
October 27, 1928

Here I am just arrived, still alive, in spite of that Peace River road-bed. But I find only one letter here: and it a week old. How is that?

Now I must explain why I wanted to have the underwear at Prince Albert: my suitcases are full to bursting. *Here* I am only over Sunday – no chance to get rid of the soiled things. I haven't worn the winter-weight yet. I was waiting for the suit you sent: it is lighter than my old ones. Now I'll have to carry a parcel in addition to my baggage. That's why, old horse. Understand now? Railway hotels don't attend to parcels.

Well, I'm glad M[iller] and Carrier[1] made a decent job of the *Search*. Am curious to see the ed[ition]. *I* don't dislike *O*[*ur*] *D*[*aily*] *B*[*read*]. Just the yellow *print*. For a *novel* it's the only correct format. It's a good piece of book-making: better than Miller ever can do. There's substance to the binding. But damn Carrier for not sending the 10 copies stipulated.

During the last five minutes in the train my eye fell on a paper which somebody had dropped. My name struck me. I enclose it. Maybe a person underestimates after all the effect.

Well, I'll drop this in the letter-box. I hope I won't have to go out tonight. There was a big football game on at the U[niversity], and no letter was waiting for me here from the registrar. So I hope that meeting has fallen through. I'd much rather not go out.

Bye-bye
P.

1 Miller (ie, Graphic Publishers Limited) and Louis Carrier (of Montreal and New York). Carrier published the US edition of *A Search for America* in 1928; originally it was published by Graphic in 1927.

TO CATHERINE GROVE

The Macdonald,
Edmonton, Alta.
October 28, 1928.
Noon

My dear,

Just got back from a nice and rather interesting drive of 50 or 60 mi[les] through the country – to find that I am, as usual, beleaguered by telephone calls with invitations. Have accepted one for a reception at 4 o'clock.

No, I shall not need any further underwear now. I intend keeping on what I'm wearing – still summer weight, though with 2 pairs of drawers till Wednesday or Thursday. Then I'll change and send the summer weights home – with my rain coat I suppose. That will leave one suit to put on when I reach Winnipeg.

As for money, I have still ca. $250 in the bank at W[inni]peg, having had the extra cheque, from *Settlers*. So you don't need to worry. We'll draw whatever will be needed. Yes, I was counting on spending ca. $35 on something for you. Too bad, in a way, that you will have to travel with that old patched-up suitcase, though. But my baggage does no longer look so good, either. It's seen considerable wear. So have my clothes, of course. I am going to have my light-grey Norfolk slightly altered in W[inni]peg.

As for my books, they'll sell by and by – within reason, of

course: I have given up the idea of a great rush sale. There is little chance for that.

You know the Peace River country is very nice: if those people had had the sense to billet me; and if at Ottawa they knew how to route a person in the district (so that I could have got out on Tuesday instead of Friday) – it would not have been so bad. But to spend 5 days at Grande Prairie, in an atmosphere of Commercial Travellers, noisy, reeky, dusty, dirty, smelly, and crude, was more than I had bargained for. There's homestead land to be had there. I'm sometimes tempted. I've never used my homestead rights.[1] How would you feel about it? Only trouble is that, where the country assumes some grandeur and beauty, there's no water to be had except from the ice of the river. Where there's water, it's just prairie. And, of course, a person is in absolute isolation.

With this lecture tour as much of a success, after all, as it is, I suppose the eastern tour (Maritimes) is pretty well assured. I *must* make that tour: in the first place, for the sake of what money it can bring; in the second, for the sake of what books it can sell.

The money I make directly will have to carry us till royalties become due – even though you teach to the end of the year.

On the other hand, of course, you are right: I figure on 24 or 25 lectures. Of course, I don't know. But that's what I estimate. That would give me an additional $600 to $625. I also count on getting a little by selling the serial copyright of at least one of my addresses, either to the Association, for a pamphlet, or to *Maclean's*.[2]

I'll write some articles and short fiction besides: they'll be less hard to place now I should think; and I'll put a price on them.

Well, I'd better go down and, *Na, essen!*[3]

That train from Grande Prairie: now and then, if a person knew, he could get out and walk alongside. What remains, is the mental picture of the rivers: Peace and Smoky; and the Athabasca.

Bye-bye – or rather, so long. 1½ weeks now.

Well, I've had my lunch; and that's absolutely all the news there is. Caviar and Goldeyes ($1.70). And there you are. I wish I could eat at 35¢ a meal and *earn* the balance by abstinence. But that sort of thing I haven't learned yet. Have also made my reservation for tomorrow night: last but one of the all-night rides.

Now I'll lie down for 1½ h[ou]rs; then dress and go to that reception. A lady just phoned up to say she'd call for me, to save me the trouble of finding the place by myself. Well, that's all right.

7 p.m. Well, again, I can say that's that. The lieutenant governor honoured me by coming to my reception.[4] If he knew that I did not understand his name and was not sufficiently interested to enquire for it, he'd be pretty indignant, I suppose. But people are reading *O*[*ur*] *D*[*aily*] *B*[*read*]. I

wonder what you are doing this minute and how you got through your last but one Sunday alone?

I'll go down and have supper.
Bye-bye
P.

1 Under the Free Land Homestead Act of 1872, people from the eastern provinces, as well as immigrants from abroad, went west to homestead. A homestead was typically a quarter-section of land (1 section = 1 mile square), and granted to the homesteader on the condition that he improve it (ie, clear the wood growth, or break the sod where the land was open prairie). The homesteader had the right to a second quarter section of land if he met his obligations within a prescribed time limit.
2 Two articles by Grove appeared in *Maclean's Magazine*: 'Canadians Old and New' (March 15, 1928) and 'Assimilation' (September 1, 1929).
3 Well, eat!
4 William Egbert (1857–1936), a physician, was lieutenant-governor of Alberta from 1926 to 1931.

TO CATHERINE GROVE

En route N[orth] Battleford–
Prince Albert, Sask.
October 30, 1928

Yesterday was the first day in the whole tour when I found it impossible to write. They did not leave me a minute's time. Had, in the afternoon, to go back to Edmonton with a party – in a car. They wanted to show me the N[orth] Sask[atchewan] valley, etc. Was invited for lunch and for supper. Spent the night in the train – hardly slept. Was dumped out this morning at North Battleford, at 7 a.m.; no diner on the train. Had to run uptown for a bite of breakfast – for I don't get to P[rince] A[lbert] till 1:40; so I thought I couldn't go without both breakfast and luncheon. In the rush I forgot or lost my cane – well, it doesn't matter.

Shall stay at P[rince] A[lbert] overnight and get to Saskatoon tomorrow 5 minutes before I shall have to speak. It's all rather a rush this week. But I'd rather have a rush than the tedium and lack of hospitality of Grande Prairie. Besides, this is the last full week – with 6 addresses – which really suits me – only the distances are so great – which makes it a bit hard: that, of course, is better in the east.

Well, it's very hard to write in these western trains. This is to be just an extra – to make up for the one you missed yesterday. I suppose the Peace River gap is bridged now and you get letters practically every day. It seems to me, my books must be selling – although, whenever I see a copy, it's a borrowed one.

By the way, I saw the first copies of the larger *Search* – and, sorry to say, don't like it at all. There's no relation between letter press and format of page. The running-head is just as objectionable in itself as before – and, by its detached position, more so. The binding is just as flimsy – gaping wide open on the booksellers' shelves. The cloth of the book is still of the very poorest quality – in fact, it is the same as that used in the 1st ed[ition].

No, no, Miller doesn't know how to make a book.[1] Macmillans do. However...

This is the first dull day I've had for some time. Well, old girl, bye-bye: a week and a day; so cheer up.

P.

9 more addresses now – unless Canora cancels, 1½ h[ou]rs left of this 15 h[ou]r run. It's more than I bargained for.

Well, shall seal this. Bye-bye.

1 In the light of Grove's remarks in letters of March 1928, it seems likely that Miller printed the book, and Carrier bought the sheets and issued it under his imprint – there would be no point in blaming Miller if Carrier handled the printing of *A Search for America*. Macmillan, of course, have always had a reputation for well produced and bound books. See also letter of October 27, 1928, note 1.

TO CATHERINE GROVE

Empress Hotel,
Prince Albert, Sask.
October 30, 1928 II

My dear,

This is a new club, and I am their first speaker. Consequently, they think they must rush me about. I succeeded only in shoving them off for one hour, during which time I changed clothes from skin to tie. Have just donned the 1st suit of winter weight underwear and find it suffocatingly hot. However, I have already mailed the other suits, and I've to put up with it now.

Don't send anything else now. I have all I need. This rush is pretty hard, too. I don't really know which is harder, the rush or the opposite.

However ... There's the man who wants to drive me around. So.

Bye-bye. Kiss.

P.

TO CATHERINE GROVE

En route Prince Albert–Saskatoon, Sask.
October 31, 1928

#30 that was; and it was a good one. Got your letter of Oct[ober] 25/26 last night just before speaking. Big audience – and a very good one. Roaring success. Everybody knew *Settlers* and *Search*. McCl[elland] & Stewart[1] could surely make capital out of my first two books if they were at all alive to their opportunities. I am asked about them all the time; but they can't be procured. Strange to say, I always spot the one or two odd American women in the audience: a little too *décolleté* – showing a little too much of their flesh. Too bad you can't attend an *evening* meeting, so you'd see it, too.

This was a pretty town, with hills and forest – some evergreen, a national Forest Park close by – and the river (two within a few miles), S[outh] and N[orth] Saskatchewan joining below.

Well, a week from today I'll be at Winnipeg this time of day – waiting for you. Only 6 more addresses to give in between – I mean, to C[anadian] C[lub]s; for I had yesterday 3 long-distance phone calls asking me for additional addresses – Service Clubs etc. I declined but promised to visit the Collegiate at Melville.

This is another swaying train – a horror.

Well, good thing that concert is over.

I at last got hold of the enclosed.[2]

Well, I must speak the moment I get off the train – so I'll read my address over – the one on nationhood which I haven't given for some time (since Edmonton).

Bye-bye
P.

1 McClelland & Stewart, the Toronto publishing house, who handled Grove's first two books, *Over Prairie Trails* (1922) and *The Turn of the Year* (1923). *Over Prairie Trails* was reprinted in 1923, and reissued by Macmillan in 1929. It was published in McClelland & Stewart's New Canadian Library series in 1957 with an introduction by Malcolm Ross. *The Turn of the Year* was reissued only once, in 1929 by Macmillan.

As is noted in the introduction, it is a great pity that the earlier Grove letters to McClelland & Stewart have not come to light. The letters from the firm to Grove are preserved in the University of Manitoba Grove Collection. They make clear that the two books of essays sold poorly, especially *The Turn of the Year*, and that the firm turned down *Settlers of the Marsh*. At Phelps' suggestion, Grove then succeeded in interesting Lorne Pierce of the Ryerson Press in the book.

2 The enclosure, whatever it was, is missing from the letter; but in view of the statement in the letter of November 2, 'I enclose another report from Saskatoon,' it was probably a newspaper clipping about one of his addresses.

TO CATHERINE GROVE

King George Hotel,
Saskatoon, Sask.
October 31, 1928 II

Halloween – Yes, I know...

I was as mad as a hatter when I began to speak at noon. Nobody at the station to receive me. I did not know where to go. Had to phone, phone, phone till I hit on the meeting place. And then ... 25 men present. Well, I gave it to them. And the result? Invitation from the University to come in January and give them a series of lectures extending over 3 days.[1]

At the women's meeting? Business transacted – tea served; and the left-overs of their time turned over to me – I spoke for just 1/2 h[ou]r and gave it *to them*. You bet I did. Sarcasm all through. And how they like it!

Well, my dear, a week from now you'll be at W[inni]peg. Canora has not yet confirmed the date. I just wired them, saying that unless I know by tomorrow definitely I shall give them the go-by.

I'm getting to be 'fed up' with these empty-heads. Darn them! I wish I had Shakespeare's cursing vocabulary, sometimes. Melville,[2] on the other hand, welcomes the 'distinguished stranger' to the Canadian West and asks me to address church etc. etc. and, incidentally, enquires whether I, as they hope, am going to speak in English. Of all the......

This is Saskatchewan all right.

Well, old girl, I wish this last week were over. Tomorrow I am going to get to Melville after midnight. Then one more night ride – to Winnipeg.

Night-night.
Phil
Am going to go to bed at 9 o'clock.

1 At the University of Saskatchewan, Saskatoon, from January 10, 1929; see letter of that date.

2 The Saskatchewan town of that name, of course, rather than the American writer

TO CATHERINE GROVE

En route Biggar–Melville, Sask.
November 1, 1928

That was Biggar. #33. 4 or 5 more. I'll be at Melville for 2 or 3 days. That's the last of this week. I'll get there at midnight; a 9 hour run. I'll soon get to Winnipeg now.

I got your two letters at Biggar. Yes, I know. Those

reviewers don't bother me – I'm just curious, that's all. They don't touch the real thing: what they expect me to do is to boost the West. They don't know what literature is: a deepening of the emotional reaction to life. I don't know how Eayrs got the idea that I have the blues. I gave him the dickens because when at Edmonton he had had a good time with the Broadus'es[1] and not called on the one bookseller who counts, namely, Esch.[2] Esch said he had seen Eayrs pass his store in a taxi while he, Esch, stood in the door. The other bookstores had no copies: well, Eayrs could have afforded to send a supply and let them return any unsold balance. However...

Yes, there's the worst of such things as I run across among the College girls of this vaunted age. Unfulfilled desire arises only after it has been fulfilled. Then they can't stop. The horror for promiscuity is gone. So promiscuity it is; and against promiscuity nature protects herself by producing sterility; and thus the race dwindles.[3]

Well...

There is really nothing else to say. Less than a week now. This is Nov[ember] 1st.

So bye-bye

P.

1 E.K. Broadus, who was then Head of tne English Department at the University of Alberta; see letter of October 17, 1928, note 3.

2 An enquiry addressed to the Alberta Provincial Library elicited the following reply: 'We have no material on Esch, bookseller and stationer in Edmonton, except that they have closed operation a few years ago. They were still in operation up to that time.' (April 30, 1973)

3 The prudish tone of this and other passages is in marked contrast with the account Grove gives of his own amorous proclivities in youth, and forms one of the many paradoxes in his personality.

TO CATHERINE GROVE

Melville, Sask.,
November 2, 1928

Here I am on my last week-end stop, with 4 addresses to give – school, teachers' convention (had the same at Biggar), Anglican Men's club, and C[anadian] C[lub].

I got here at 1 in the morning last night, after a gruelling ride on that crack train, the Continental Limited which the C.N.R. runs in competition with the C.P.R., so that it must not be late in Winnipeg. I timed it as the stations flew past: we were going, over a distance of 150 miles, at the rate of 75 miles an hour: the second-fastest going I have had. The fastest was on Vancouver Island: 10 mi[les] in 8 minutes – well, no, that's also at the rate of 75 mi[les] an hour; but though it probably is more dangerous in the car, it *feels* more dangerous in the train. Anyway, I found it nerve-racking. However, I am still alive.

When I get through here, there will only be Kamsack left this side of Winnipeg, for, since Canora has not answered, I am cancelling it – the darn fatheads must be put where they belong.

You talk of a letter from Peace River which is so 'good' – I don't, of course, remember a thing about it.

Ranns[1] antagonises me terribly. So I said all sorts of naughty things to shock him, to discover at last that he was taking notes to use me for a story. I told him I'd never speak a word to him again if a single line appeared anywhere.

However, he confided to me that *he* is out after the money. 'I've never doubted it,' I said. 'Yes,' he said, 'I crave all sorts of luxuries; I wish I were a millionaire.' 'And you,' I said, 'a preacher! *Neither shalt thou take two coats*!'[2] I said several other things that, I hope, stung him.

By the way, the Bishop of Northern Sask[atchewan],[3] at Prince Albert, said to me 'You leave one breathless and gasping for air!' I laughed.

By the way, I left my rain-coat with Ranns, telling him to send it to you, at the expense of the C[anadian] C[lub] – it's the absolutely only expense they had.

Several amusing incidents at Biggar: the pres[ident] of the club – a fat lumber dealer – simply did not know what to do with my address – so he rose the moment I sat down and said, 'We'll close with the National Anthem.'

The Pres[ident] of the Sask[atchewan] club, a Dr. Carrothers,[4] Prof[essor] at the U[niversity], similarly – till Dr. Murray,[5] Pres[ident] of the University came up to ask me whether I could give 3 days to the University – then Dr. Carrothers developed an enthusiasm. These things are very funny to observe.

I enclose another report from Saskatoon which I found last night in the smoker of a sleeping car.

Well, a week from today I'll be speaking at the Men's luncheon in Winnipeg. That'll be interesting. I'm very curious how many will turn out. More than 25? Winnipeg! The chief stronghold of the materialism of the West. No matter! I'll give it to them.

This, I suppose, will be one of the last letters you'll get before leaving – though I'll write again from here. But I won't write again next week, I don't think. No use. You'd get it after we meet. I shall send (perhaps) some dirty laundry from Kamsack. Perhaps not, though. I don't know yet.

When you get this, the last week-end will be gone I suppose.

Bye-bye
P.

1 The Rev. Horace Dixon Ranns (1883–1963). Born in Sheffield, England, and a graduate

of Wesley College, Winnipeg (1915), he held pastorates in several small towns – Craik, Biggar, Humbolt – until 1935, when he became minister of the Metropolitan United Church in Swift Current, where Mrs Grove's family, the Wiens, lived. In 1944, he moved east as minister of the Oak Street United Church (now Regent Street United Church) in Toronto, retiring in 1951. He was, during Grove's visit to Biggar, secretary of the local Canadian Club; and the president of the Club, referred to below, was W.D. Moore.
2 Mark 6:9
3 The Rt. Rev. George Exton Lloyd, DD (1861–1940). He was the Lord Bishop of Saskatchewan from 1922 to 1931.
4 Dr William Alexander Carrothers (1889–1951) was born in Ireland, and educated at the universities of Manitoba and Edinburgh, as well as the London School of Economics. After teaching briefly in Edinburgh, he returned to Canada, and was Professor of Economics at the universities of Saskatchewan (1921–30) and British Columbia (1930–4). He was Chairman of the BC Economic Council (1934–8) and afterwards Chairman of the BC Utilities Commission.
5 Dr Walter Charles Murray (1866–1947) was born in New Brunswick and educated at the universities of New Brunswick, Edinburgh, and Berlin. He taught philosophy at the University of New Brunswick and at Dalhousie University before becoming President of the University of Saskatchewan in 1908, a post he held until 1937. He was active in public life in a number of ways, and acted as a government adviser in several capacities. Several letters from Murray to Grove have survived, but none from Grove to Murray have come to light.

TO CATHERINE GROVE

[Melville, Sask.]
Saturday,
November 3, 1928

Now this is the last week-end. Spoke twice yesterday; again today (teachers' convention) again tomorrow (church). Partly to kill time. Weighed myself. 167 lbs.

Now, coming Wednesday: I'll be at the station – not at the train: they don't allow you to enter the platform. But I'll be downstairs in the subway whence you pass out. I, of course, can't tell what the clubs decree to do with me. But if at all possible, I'll engineer things so as to stay at the Royal Alexandra where, as far as I know, the men's meeting will be held on Friday. No, don't bring any underwear. I've all I need. A week from today we'll be in the train, going home.

Here, I ran into the Deputy Minister of Education yesterday, A.S. Ball.[1] We had quite a chat. This was #34. He was there.

By the way, I fixed things for Mandy.[2] All she will need to do, is to write off her Sup[plementary Papers] and then take 1 month's summer school at Saskatoon in order to get 1st-class standing when she's ready for it. That sounds different from what she thought. She can then, after 2 years, take any position short of principal of High Schools. That will be all she'll want any way I suppose.

This is, as far as the hotel goes, another place like Grande Prairie – no bath, no private closet. Not even hot water for shaving. And the cold water so hard that it won't soften the beard.

I begin to doubt Miller's royalty statements.[3] This is the 25th town at which I have stayed: The *Search* is known everywhere.

As for McClelland and Stewart, I have at last come out into the open and *threatened* to publish my dealings with them.[4] Then have offered them 25c a copy. We'll see.

Eayrs talks a lot; but – if I were the publisher, I'd have seen to it that copies were available even in such places as this – they'd go like hot cakes. But not even in Saskatoon was there a single copy available.

However, what's the use of worrying? One is in the publishers' hands. Enclose a page from Scribner's magazine which shows that the N[ew] Y[ork] firm[5] at least gives the book a moderate amount of publicity. I'm very curious to see what Winnipeg will do.

This, my dear, will probably be the last letter you'll get before you start to meet me. Today is Saturday. If I wrote again on Monday, the letter would hardly get there on Tuesday. I hope you'll receive my raincoat.

So, bye-bye; or rather so long.

P.

1 Augustus Harry Ball (1873–1967). Born in England and educated in Canada, he was Deputy Minister of Education in Saskatchewan from March 1, 1912 to April 30, 1932.

2 Mrs Grove's younger sister, then a student at Regina Normal School

3 See letter of February 12, 1929, note 3. Grove's suspicion was probably unwarranted, for Miller was not accused, even by his worst enemies, of dishonesty. For a further expression of the same doubt by Grove, see letter of February 8, 1929. Miller might best be described as an enthusiastic amateur who over-reached himself.

4 As previously mentioned, the lack of correspondence here makes it impossible to determine the exact threats. The letter of November 8, 1928, from McClelland & Stewart to Grove, reads, in part:

> We do wish that there could be a more kindly feeling between us but somehow your letters to us seem to breathe an atmosphere of threat. Every paragraph of your letter of November 2 contains somewhat of a threat, all without effect as far as we are concerned, but nevertheless we wish that your attitude towards us could be of a different type.

However, Grove's threats, whatever they were, produced results. McClelland & Stewart brought down their price of *The Turn of the Year* and *Over Prairie Trails* in sheets to 50c a copy. Their previous offer, in the letter of October 8, 1928, was 71c for *The Turn of the Year*, and 57c for *Over Prairie Trails*. See also letter of November 19, 1928 II.

5 This is presumably a reference to the US branch of Macmillan.

TO CATHERINE GROVE

The King George Hotel,
Melville, Sask.
November 4, 1928
1 p.m.

Well, I'm sitting around and moping. That's the worst – but I believe I've said that before – sitting around in a 5th rate hotel. Just now a lawyer was in to ask me for dinner tonight. Incidentally he said, 'Quite comfortable here in the hotel?' That happened just after I'd written the first two lines of this letter. So my answer somewhat expressed the true state of my mind with regard to the thing. 'Oh,' I said, 'it's just possible to exist.' He, of course, listened with only one ear. 'That's good,' he said, 'that's good.' And thus it goes.

I haven't shaved yet: for two reasons. 1stly waiting till after dinner, it is just possible to get some hot water from the kitchen – though it is no softer than the cold water in my room. 2ndly – I save it because I can manage to stretch the job out over approximately an hour; and an hour with something to do is that much gained.

I'm going to speak once more, for the 4th time, this afternoon – at the church. Yesterday I addressed a teacher's convention. Oh, how they were bored: they'd so much have preferred to listen to jazz, or to dance, or to see a picture show. Skirts, by the way, averaged about 2 in[ches] above the knee. When they bend down to pick something up from the floor, you see the whole differential. Well...

I had a few hours more with Ball, yesterday, the dep[uty] min[ister] of education: quite an interesting man. Most people I meet are in some way uprooted, transplanted into the wrong soil, etc. etc. That lawyer who wants me to have dinner with him hates his work, would like to fool around with animals etc. But he and his are used to spend so and so much money; and consequently he's got to stick – willy-nilly.

I haven't had a bath since I left Saskatoon – not what I'd call a bath; but when I get my hot water for shaving, I intend to strip and take the sort of thing we've been used to for all our years together. I do hope I'll live long enough to have the real thing for a year or two in my own house. That, apart from a living room 24 by 36 f[ee]t, is my chief ambition in life, I believe: I mean, of course, without moving into a city, or into that American abomination which they call a city.

Well, I think I've now waited long enough since dinner to go up. In two hours or so they'll come for me. Two more *full* days after this one: then I'm in for the last lap.

Bye-bye
P.

TO WATSON KIRKCONNELL

Rapid City, Man.
November 19, 1928

My dear Kirk,

I'm browsing about every now and then in the elegies.[1] I don't know whether they're going or not. But, whether or no, there's nothing to worry about. – I had intended to send you an 'autographed' copy of *O*[*ur*] *D*[*aily*] *B*[*read*]; but I haven't got my contract copies yet. Eayrs writes he's sorry: it was overlooked in the first place; and now the 1st edition is sold out. I'll have to wait for the second printing.

I really sat down to ask you a favour: Could you let me have once more that book on the Homeric poems[2] you loaned me some time a year or so ago? Really, two or three favours: Would you phone to Russell Lang's and give them title, publisher, etc., of Zimmern's book on the *Greek Commonwealth,*[3] with instructions to order it for me and to bill me?

I am working on a slender volume for the next year: 'Addresses Not Delivered.'[4] I don't think I want to publish a novel. Besides, however, I'm working again on that story which I've now rewritten twice: the one I had with me at the hospital last year.[5]

I can't make up my mind about it: it's either great or absolute piffle – I don't know which.

I'll enclose an old poem. Please tell me what you think of it.

Yours
P.

THE SACRED DEATH,

Sacred makes Death him who has done his task,
Forgotten though he be down to his name,
And to the features of his stiffened mask,
His life was seed though unillumed by fame.

They say the gods rule this revolving earth
And send us war and peace, sunshine and rain,
Welcome abundance or the parching dearth,
Perhaps they do. I grudge them not the gain

Of praise and high renown from human lips.
They rule but matter, give the body bread:
They feed our eyes and arms and finger-tips;
But our deep souls are nourished by the dead

By those who lived and strove or sang or thought –
Whose core lies in us as ore in a mine

Which needs but pick and hammer to be wrought
Into pure gold and ornament divine.

What will this[6] mean ten thousand years from now
When we are dead and gone and quite forgotten,
When bones are dust and our firm flesh is rotten,
And this world lives without us anyhow –

(two stanzas which I cannot get together)

When there no longer are grim murder bars
Dividing us from weaker sister-races –
When converse through the intermundane spaces
This planet holds with all the ruling stars?

***

What does it mean to us that long ago,
In the abyss of time where man emerges,
A sorrowing greybeard muttered broken dirges
And stared as blind, on Asia's great plateau?

Or that an inarticulate Eskimo
With wide flung gesture, silent, shrugged his shoulder
As in the ice, so that it would not moulder,
He laid his child upon an arctic floe?

1 *European Elegies* (1928), a book of translations from several languages by Watson Kirkconnell.
2 *The Rise of the Greek Epic* by Gilbert Murray (1866–1957), first published in 1907 and reprinted several times; cf. letter of December 11, 1928.
3 Which Grove had particularly enjoyed reading two years ago; see letter of November 15, 1926, note 3.
4 Published as *It Needs to Be Said* (1929)
5 Grove's next novel, after *Our Daily Bread*, was *The Yoke of Life* (1930) – frequently referred to in these letters as 'Adolescence.'
6 Grove's marginal note: 'antecedent clear from context'

TO MCCLELLAND AND STEWART, TORONTO, ONTARIO

Rapid City, Man.
November 19, 1928 II

Dear Sirs,

I beg to say that I accept your amended offer[1] to sell the remainder of the sheets of my two books *Over Prairie Trails* and *The Turn of the Year* at $.50 a copy, this purchase on my part to cancel the contracts existing between us and bearing dates, respectively of Nove[mber] 1st 1922 and May 14, 1923 in all points.

Will you please deliver the sheets addressed to myself c/o The Macmillan Company of Canada, 70 Bond Street, Toronto and simultaneously bill me for the same, accompanying the invoice by a letter in which you retransfer the copyright in both books to myself. I have not, so far, made any arrangements with regard to republication but hope to do so shortly. Meanwhile Macmillans have agreed to store for me.

On receipt of invoice and advice from Macmillans that the sheets have arrived there, I shall issue cheque for the amount due you.

Yours truly,
F.P. Grove.

1 For the background of the offer, see letter of November 3, 1928, note 4.

TO WATSON KIRKCONNELL

Rapid City, Man.
December 11, 1928

Mein lieber Kirkconnell,

Ich habe das Woerterbuch wie auch Gilbert Murrays 'Wachstum des griechischen Epos' richtig erhalten. Besten Dank. Ich bin so mit Arbeit ueberladen, dass ich kaum Zeit finde zum Lesen. Werden Sie das 'Griechische Epos' bis nach Weihnachten entbehren koennen? Ich habe zwei meiner eignenen Buecher fuer den Druck fertig stellen muessen; und Amann's 'Sun Yatsens Vermaechtnis, Eine Geschichte der Chinesischen Revolution' ist mit dem Kopf bereits unter der Presse, waehrend der Schwanz noch auf meinem Schreibtisch liegt. Dazu habe ich noch ein halb Dutzend Vortraege zu halten: einen, naechsten Montag in Brandon; drei kuerzlich in Saskatoon, fuer die Universitaet. Ende Januar gehe ich wieder nach dem Osten, mit neuen Vortraegen. Zeitschriften verlangen auch Material. Sie bemerken dass dies keine internationale Schreibmaschine ist. Die Diphthonge machen Schwierigkeiten. Nun will ich formell schliessen.

Genehmigen Sie, sehr geehrter Herr, die Versicherung meiner vorzueglichsten Hochachtung.

Ihr sehr ergebener,
F.P. Grove

Meine Interpunktion ist nur schwach wie es scheint.

TO WATSON KIRKCONNELL *translation*

Rapid City, Man.
December 11, 1928

My dear Kirkconnell,

I have received the dictionary as well as Gilbert Murray's *The Rise of the Greek Epic*.[1] Many thanks. I am so over-burdened with work that I hardly find time to read. Will you be able to let me have the *Greek Epic* until after Christmas? I have had to prepare two of my own books for the printer. The head of Amann's *The Legacy of Sun Yatsen, A History of the Chinese Revolution*[2] is already in press while its tail is still lying on my desk. In addition I still have to deliver half a dozen lectures: one in Brandon next Monday; three in Saskatoon shortly, for the University. Towards the end of January I shall again go East with further lectures. Journals also demand material. You will notice that this is no international typewriter. The diphthongs create difficulties. I must now close formally.

Permit me, much-honoured Sir, to assure you of my deepest respect.

Yours most sincerely,
F.P. Grove

My interpunctuation appears to be quite weak.

1 Published in 1907; cf. letter of November 19, 1928, note 2.

2 Grove translated Gustav Amann's *The Legacy of Sun Yatsen: A History of the Chinese Revolution*, which was published by Louis Carrier in 1929. Grove was paid a fee of $295, which included payment for proofreading. A letter from Carrier to Grove reports that Amann himself was greatly pleased with the accuracy and style of Grove's translation.

TO WATSON KIRKCONNELL

[Rapid City, Man.]
January 8, 1929

My dear Kirk,

I have been in such a rush that I have had no time to write. Am on the eve of going to Saskatoon, via Winnipeg. Shall be in a rush at Winnipeg, too.

I hope the parcel of books reached you safely. Thanks very much. The dictionary is the 'real thing.' Why don't other nations have such monumental 'aids'?[1]

Am browsing now and then in the elegies.[2] They grow on

me. Shall be in W[inni]peg again on Monday as you know I suppose. Have I anything to say? Not much.

Yours
F.P.G.

1 Since Grove was, at this time, translating Gustav Amann's book on the Chinese Revolution, this is almost certainly a reference to one of the great German *lexica* – there are several, all of which qualify as 'monumental.'
2 Kirkconnell's *European Elegies* (1928)

TO CATHERINE GROVE

Saskatoon, Sask.
January 10, 1929

Just a word, my dear. Dr. Murray[1] believes in getting value for his money. From the station he took me to a student Club luncheon. Speak. From there to the Normal School and Teachers' Meeting – special leave given by the Board. – Speak. Now, at 5 p.m. he has taken me to the hotel to change clothes – 1/2 h[ou]r. Then he'll call for me for a faculty dinner – Speak. I'm breathless with hurry. Tomorrow mor[ning] Speak – Don't know what next. But Sat[urday] mor[ning] Speak. Then I think I'm through. Back to W[inni]peg in that case on Sat[urday] night. However, I don't know yet.

So bye-bye
Ph.

1 Dr Walter Charles Murray, then President of the University of Saskatchewan; see letter of November 2, note 5. The arrangement for this trip was worked out partly during Grove's visit to Saskatoon (see letter of October 31, 1928 II), and partly through correspondence. Grove's letters to Murray are missing, but it seems, from the letters of Murray, that the University agreed to pay the expenses and an honorarium of $50. The honorarium was doubled in actual payment – see the following letter.

TO CATHERINE GROVE

King George Hotel,
Saskatoon, Sask.
January 11, 1929

My dear,

I am practically through here. This morning, the general U[niversity] meeting was the usual knock-out.

Dr Murray assured the students that this was not the last time they were going to have the priv[ilege] of a visit from me. At the end he handed me a $100 cheque, asking me to give him a statement of expenses re railway, etc. I told him, considering that they pay my expenses here and *doubled* the fee – they being so pleased with what I had done – that there are no railway expenses.

I am going to leave here tomorrow night – nothing left to do but a few conferences with student bodies. So I'll get to W[inni]peg on Sunday morning. Thus I shall have a real night's rest before Monday. It is wiser that way.

Night before last I ran into a stag party at Osborne's.[1] I phoned Phelps[2] up; and he asked me to phone Osborne. Met there a dozen or so U[niversity] men – very interesting. It is almost touching how pleased Osborne is with my progress. Mrs Riddell,[3] he said, is working her head off for that meeting. I am very curious. – Well, I want to go out and get a hair-cut. It is so mild. But a regular blizzard blowing – soft and damp – very beautiful. – Then I'll lie down and rest. Had a very hard morning.

Bye-bye
Ph.

Home on Tuesday for sure now.

1 In Winnipeg, on his way to Saskatoon. William Frederick Osborne (1873–1950) was, at that time, Professor of French at the University of Manitoba. Born in Quyon, Quebec, he was educated in Quebec and Ontario (MA University of Toronto). He travelled to New Zealand and Australia in 1928, and to Greece, Russia, Japan, and China in 1929–32, and wrote *The Genius of Shakespeare and Other Essays* (1908) and *America at War* (1917).

2 Arthur L. Phelps

3 Mrs John Henry Riddell, wife of the President of Wesley College, Winnipeg, where Grove gave two lectures on January 22, 1929, as a guest of the college; Mrs Riddell was responsible for one of the meetings.

TO CATHERINE GROVE

King George Hotel,
Saskatoon, Sask.
January 12, 1929

Well, this is the last day here; so out at 5.30 tonight – 6.30 by your time. And so this will be the last letter which stands a chance of reaching you before I get home. Attended a stag affair last night[1] – university people and 1 judge. Was shocked at the amount of drinking going on among them. Raw whiskey by the half tumbler. Some interesting discussion started – but got nowhere because everybody squatted down on his own opinion and nobody would listen: Mrs P's case you remember.[2] Have one more conference with a few students interested in certain things I have said. At 2 p.m. Then pack; then go.

There's a farmers' convention going on here. 2 speakers from Minneapolis. They were in the audience when I sailed into the U.S.A. That led to some interesting discussion, both at the U[niversity] and here at the hotel. I got them to admit a good many things. It was a lively give and take for a while. Dr. Murray[3] thought I had well defended our cause. It all went off with complete courtesy on both sides. Not a word said at which any one needed to take offence: that's the way I like it, be it ever so tense.

Sent you a pair of wool stockings which I rather liked. Hope you like them, too. You wanted something from Saskatoon, you remember.

Well, bye-bye, or so long.
P.

1 This one was in Saskatoon; the one mentioned in the previous letter took place in Winnipeg.

2 An obscure reference; although elsewhere Grove refers to Mrs Arthur L. Phelps as Mrs P. (cf. letter of January 22, 1929)

3 The University President

TO CATHERINE GROVE

Wesley College,
Winnipeg, Man.
January 22, 1929[1]

My dear,

Sample[2] had forgotten me – so the last moment there was a great rush; I found the old man and caught the train by the skin of my teeth.

Have ordered you the paper. Have done all my shopping and spoken twice at Wesley College. Also had my pants shortened. Am now ready to go back to station. But snatch this minute to drop you a line.

The fire here ran its course. Mrs. P.[3] is all right. A.L.P. in a rush as usual.

And thus it goes. Just this word for today.
Bye-bye
P.

1 The original is written as 1928 – an obvious slip.

2 A local carrier in Rapid City

3 Mrs Arthur L. Phelps

12 Prairie scene, Manitoba. *Photo by Desmond Pacey*

TO CATHERINE GROVE

Chapleau, Ont.
Thursday, January 24, 1929

My dear,

Got here safely and am now waiting for the meeting.[1] Go on to Montreal to-morrow – leave there on Wednesday next week. No news. I believe I mentioned that the brown socks gave out before I reached Winnipeg. If I can, I shall send them back today. I am all right – no cold. So don't worry. This is a miserable little hotel; but lack of heat is no fault of it. Shall add a few more words during the day. They want to show me the place now.

So long
P.

I doubt whether you'll get this for the week-end – though possibly. However...

It's very mild here; but the snow! 3, 4 f[ee]t on the level – in the streets you walk as in trenches.

They are giving me a run for my money all right. Schools, etc. – all the trimmings...

I wonder how you feel by now? Reasonably cheerful? I hope so. I've got to act, of course, as if I'd nothing on my mind.

Well, I'll mail this in going out to the lecture.

Bye-bye
P.

1 This was Grove's third, and last, lecture tour, sponsored as before by the Association of Canadian Clubs.

TO CATHERINE GROVE

Chapleau, Ont.
January 25, 1929

My dear,

I am waiting for the train to Montreal; and it is snowing, snowing – the way it never snows in the west.

I got up late – having got to bed excessively late. The train goes west in 20 minutes; and I'll try to get this off. So I can't write much – nor is there anything to write I am afraid. I am just putting in time here.

Shall speak 3 times at Montreal. $75 – that's all I care about by this time.

Some interesting people here. But a person gets so 'fed up' with them.

There's the baggage van going. So Bye-bye
P.

TO CATHERINE GROVE

En route Chapleau-Montreal
January 25, 1929 II

Snow, snow, snow – We are nearing Cartier and Sudbury. White Pine, bare larch, spruce etc. – all ghostily sketched into the driving snow – with birch, maple etc. barely visible in the universal dimness and murkiness.

Nothing else to say – just a word of where I am and what I am doing. 10 minutes stop soon at Cartier – then I'll get out for a brisk walk and mail this.

Just had a wire from Spry saying I am to be at Montreal till Wednesday – stay at Windsor Hotel – do you remember? We walked along there, looking at the different makes of cars in that swollen gutter of the country's wealth.

Well, bye-bye.
P.

TO CATHERINE GROVE

Montreal, Que.
January 26, 1929.
At night

My dear,

I am in a breathless whirl. So just a word or two. All bookstores have huge displays of my work. All papers welcome me. I enclose one. Carrier report 2300 copies sold;[1] sales steadily increasing. First ed[ition] 3000 copies: second ed[ition][2] *in preparation*. Book-stores say *Our Daily Bread* among *their best sellers*. Am staying with Isles.[3] Expected to leave this minute for a dinner. So this is all I can do today.

Yours
P.

After all, this sort of thing does pay when you strike the big cities.

1 Of *A Search for America*
2 As distinct from the second impression of the first edition, which was issued in June 1928
3 Alan Isles, who was a partner in Louis Carrier and Company. He was born in 1906 in Montreal, and educated at Montreal High School. He attended extension courses at both McGill University and l'Université de Montréal, while serving his apprenticeship with the Mercury Press, an earlier venture of Louis Carrier. In 1928, he was in charge of US sales for Carrier. He moved to Perrault Printing Company as Sales Manager in 1930, and became General Manager of the Canadian Lithographing and Printing Co. in 1934. He died in 1949.

TO CATHERINE GROVE

Montreal, Que.
January 27, 1929

My dear,

I won't find time to write anything like a real letter till I get away from Montreal. A continual whirl. But I know this that the *Search* is slowly selling, with the emphasis on selling rather than on slowly. Carrier is very anxious to get something from me. They consider me the leading man in Canada at last. A word from me placed Regan's[1] book with them. Nobody has ever come to my help like that. Phelps, of course.[2] But he did not have the power which I, after all, have now. I asked to have a copy of the advertising poster sent to you. Got it? I haven't seen any of the local secretaries yet – so have not yet got any word from you. In an hour or so I've got to go to a big reception in my honour.

By the way, my dear, *don't* return heavy socks. I can't stand them here. Shall send underwear tomorrow.

How are you? Keep cheerful.
Bye-bye
P.

Carrier just sends invitation for dinner tonight. Shall also send *Point Counterpoint*[3] – by Aldous Huxley, a *big book*. Return to
Mrs. Sweatman[4]
266 Kingsway
Winnipeg.

1 John Hugh Regan of Victoria BC; see letter of October 9, 1928, note 2.
2 Who had persuaded Lorne Pierce to read the manuscript of *Settlers of the Marsh*; the story is told, from Grove's point of view, in *In Search of Myself* 378–82.
3 Published in October 1928
4 Mrs Constance Travers Sweatman, who wrote some five novels, mostly about young married people or about the relationship between parents and children. Before her marriage she taught music at Brandon College, Manitoba.

TO CATHERINE GROVE

The Windsor,
Montreal, Que.
January 28, 1929

My dear girl,

I am still in a continuous rush. In 1/4 h[ou]r I shall have to speak. 1000 covers have been laid for the luncheon. Tonight again. Tomorrow morning at the University and Women's Club. Have not even had time to stroll through a store or so. This morning had a session with an artist of the camera who wishes to sell my picture. I shall get a few copies in return for my autograph on others.

I am well, how are you. I know there is a letter for me here on Victoria Square. I have spoken to Mr. Webster[1] over the phone. But I simply cannot find time to fetch it before tonight. I do think things are moving here.

Well, I see, its within 5 minutes of the meeting. So I suppose I better meet the executive.

Bye-bye
P.

1 Presumably John Clarence Webster, Jr, the son of the historian. He was born in 1901 in Chicago, and educated at McGill University (B. Comm. 1922). In 1931, he took a plane to England as the first overseas participant in the then annual King's Cup Air Race, and came in second among non-professional pilots. In the same year, he died of a flying accident in Montreal. He shared his father's interest in things Canadian, and was a member of the Montreal Canadian Club.

TO CATHERINE GROVE

The Windsor,
Montreal, Que.
January 28, 1929 II

Another word. Just got through my address. Ca. 500 men. Some of them very fine indeed. Sir Andrew McPhail[1] sat at my right and cheered repeatedly. He wanted to have me at the house. But I escaped. Considerable publicity. Which will help. Am to meet the Pres[ident] of the Women's Club shortly. Am going to go as soon as I've cooled off. I think, Carrier is sending you a few newspaper clippings. I hardly get hold of them. (Damn it, excuse me) It's time for me to be moving.

So bye-bye
P.

1 Andrew Macphail (1864–1938). A native of Prince Edward Island, he graduated in medicine from McGill University and received the LRCP from London in 1893. He was primarily a physician, having been Professor of the History of Medicine at McGill from 1907 to 1937; but he is also remembered for his literary services as an essayist, reviewer, and editor. He was elected a Fellow of the Royal Society of Canada in 1910, knighted in 1918, and awarded the OBE in 1919 and the Lorne Pierce Medal in 1930. His austere and independent outlook, often at variance with contemporary trends, would have appealed to Grove and, presumably, vice versa. His best known work is the biography, *Three Persons* (1929); he also published a translation of the French-Canadian novel, *Maria Chapdelaine* (1921), and was the editor of the *University Magazine* from 1907 until 1920.

TO CATHERINE GROVE

Montreal, Que.
January 29, 1929

My dear,

The whirl continues. I have just an hour between lectures. Spoke this morning in McGill University. I enclose one clipping. There are dozens of them. But I can't hunt them all up. It's the usual story, quite a success, this stay at Montreal. Carrier is, of course, selling his edition here. I connive. He is, at present, selling hundreds of copies a day. I do believe that the *Search* is going to go pretty big in the U.S.A. The second edition is in sight.

Now listen here: there is somewhere a carbon copy, I believe in 4 parts separately bound, of 'Adolescence,'[1] either at home, perhaps on the little table in the front room, or in the parcel of Mss. at Duncan's.[2] Send it to Louis Carrier & Co., 1154 Beaver Hall Square, Montreal, will you? As soon as you can. I am going to play Carrier against Eayrs – Eayrs against Carrier. I am learning a thing or two. So....

The underwear parcel is on the way to the post office. I shall leave tomorrow night.

C.P.R. gives me another pass through the Maritimes: beyond that, I shall not ask. Let them pay; I am tired of begging for other people.

I hope you have been getting my notes. Am going to have more time in the Maritimes I believe. Cheer up. The weeks are rolling off. I am doing my best to bring it about that I won't need to go lecturing any longer like this. And I do believe the time is coming.

Bye-bye.
P.

1 Which was published as *The Yoke of Life* (1930) by Macmillan in Toronto and Richard Smith in New York.

2 Grove stored some of his manuscripts in a granary belonging to the Duncans, who were farmers just outside of Rapid City. The Rev. T.H. Lonsdale gives the following account of a conversation he had with Grove during the latter's visit to Banff:

> he told me he had several finished novels ready for publication, and when I asked where he kept them he said, 'In granaries on the Manitoba prairies.' 'Aren't you afraid they might be lost or burned up due to carelessness?' 'Not a chance,' he said, 'you never heard of a granary being burned up.' (May 11, 1972)

TO CATHERINE GROVE

1154 Beaver Hall Square,
Montreal, Que.
[January 29, 1929 II][1]

My dear,

I have just bought you a birthday present. Parcel will arrive ahead of time; not to be opened till Feb[ruary] 11. From the Morgan Store.[2]

Had an enormous meeting at noon. Some say there were over 800 women. I have had steady publicity here for 4 days now. The *Search* is selling. Have all sorts of enquiries for further lectures here. But, of course, decline to commit myself. Got a pass through the Maritimes, C.P.R.

I'm beginning to feel seedy. Shall catch up on sleep the moment I leave here. Montreal is too important a centre (biggest book-buying town in Canada) for me not to exert myself a bit. They say it's cold here; but I find it wonderfully mild. Am as well as I've ever been during the last few years. Cheer up. It'll soon be over.

Bye
P.

1 Date from postmark
2 A large department store in Montreal, which is still in business

TO CATHERINE GROVE

Montreal, Que.
January 30, 1929

My dear,

Miss Isles, sister of Alan Isles[1] whom you remember, is employed in the Birks offices, here. Last night she showed me a magnificent umbrella at $26.50 and afterwards disclosed the fact that during the Jan[uary] Sale employees get on certain lines 75% off. So I asked her whether she would buy something for me. I have just completed the purchase and am having it mailed to you. There is no cord with it. A brown ribbon will do; we shall get a cord in Winnipeg.

I also am sending 2 photos. One of them I like; the other I don't.

Further, I have last night looked at a furnished apartment of 3 rooms which is for rent every winter from Nov[ember] 1st till May 1st at $55 a month. It would do us nicely. Not a bad idea, eh?

Well, that's about all, except that Carrier sold yesterday

250 copies of the *Search*. Not too bad? Now after this letter there will be a gap – I am off to St. John. In the usual Montreal haste.

Bye, Kiss.
P.

1 See letter of January 26, 1929, note 3.

TO WATSON KIRKCONNELL

Montreal, Que.
January 30, 1929 II

My dear Kirk,

Just a word. If you have anything you want to publish in the near future, will you give Messrs. Louis Carrier & Co., 1154 Beaver Hall Square, Montreal, a chance? I am much impressed with the work they are doing. They are surely putting the *Search* over. They have taste, etc.

Isles (Alan),[1] one of the partners, will be at Winnipeg some time between now and spring and will try to see you and A.L.P.[2] Tell the latter, please. I shall drop him a line when I can. But have so far been in a continuous whirl. Speak tomorrow at St. John. Carrier almost sold the 1st ed[ition][3] of his *Search* out here while I lectured. He distributes in U.S.A. and England as well, you know. I believe them to be 'comers.'[4]

Cordially
F.P.G.

1 See letter of January 26, 1929, note 3.
2 Arthur L. Phelps
3 The Carrier edition was actually the second edition of the book; that by Graphic was the first.
4 We have here another example of a pattern very common in Grove's relationships: initial enthusiasm, followed by disillusionment. The pattern occurs also in his relationship with McClelland & Stewart, Macmillan, Ryerson Press, and Graphic Publishers, and in his attitude to my 1945 book on his work. Even with Arthur Phelps he eventually had a quarrel, according to Leonard Grove.

TO CATHERINE GROVE, CANADIAN PACIFIC TELEGRAM

Saint John, N.B.
Jan[uar]y 31st 1929 5.36 pm

Mrs. F.P. Grove
Rapid City Man.

No certain address till February 9 at Ottawa quite well.
Phil

TO CATHERINE GROVE

Admiral Beatty Hotel,
Saint John, N.B.
January 31, 1929 II

My dear,

Only by being outright rude could I manage to snatch 1/2 h[ou]r from the whirl. I speak at 6:30 and again at 8 tonight. Meanwhile they want to show me all N[ew] B[runswick].

My window overlooks the river and the Bay. It is very mild, 40 above – hard weather, that, for a lecturer. But so far I manage to stand up.

Montreal was really terrific. But I *did* sell books. I must have made $100 in addition to my fees. I enclose some more marked pages – full of nonsense. But. ... I do wish I were at home, going to bed at 9:30, rising at the usual hour. The road-bed from Montreal to St John is almost as bad as in the Peace River. So I did not sleep. They say, it is worse from Truro to Sydney.

My itinerary is exceedingly uncertain. But I shall be at Ottawa on Feb[ruary] 9 to 11. Shall be at Toronto Feb[ruary] 21 or so. Again Feb[ruary] 28. As soon as I have any definite word about intermediate places I shall wire. It will take a letter 4 days to Ontario. Now bye-bye. Have another letter or two to write. Then dress for the performance!

Kiss (Have not yet opened the envelope with the photos)
Bye
P.

TO CATHERINE GROVE

En route St. John-St. Stephen, N.B.
February 1, 1929

My dear,

Received parcels from you and E.S.[1] last night. Also letter. Am worried about you – but you see this is the only method of getting anywhere. And I believe I am getting there. Carrier is very anxious to get 'Adolescence.'[2] Had at St. John the usual success. Both at Montreal and St. John the women went crazy. At Montreal Sir Andrew MacPhail sat next to me at the men's meeting: a very big (physically) man, multimillionaire, and a writer. Every now and then he pinched my leg and grumbled: 'That was *good*!' – while I was speaking.

Am sorry about Alexander.[3] Yet perhaps he is right. It is certainly gratifying to have him say about 'Adolescence' what he says.

Well, this roadbed is too terrible to write in the train – so I'll stop. Bye bye. Hold on to yourself.

P.

1 E.S. Gardiner of Rapid City

2 *The Yoke of Life*

3 W.J. Alexander. Grove had wanted to dedicate *It Needs to Be Said* to Alexander, which the latter declined, saying, 'Of you personally – as you well know – I was absolutely ignorant when I made acquaintance with *Over Prairie Trails* and the *Search for America*. This dedication might seem to the public an indication that one good turn deserves another, "I praise you, you praise me." I strongly suspect that this sort of thing is not unknown in the English literary press.' In the same letter, of January 22, 1929, he went on to praise *The Yoke of Life*, which he had read for Macmillan: 'I congratulate [you] heartily on the outstanding excellence of this remarkable novel – the most powerful and, from the point of view of constructive art, the greatest you have written. You will see doubtless my report to the publisher, and I shall not speak further of it here.' Grove's letter to Alexander, in which the matter of dedication was broached, is missing.

TO CATHERINE GROVE

St Stephen, N.B.
February 2, 1929

My dear,

By a ruse I have almost a whole day to myself. I was supposed to leave here this morning at 7 o'clock for St. Andrews. It takes 5 hours to make it by train, for the road goes almost all the way back to St. John. Yet the distance is only 20 miles: like this:

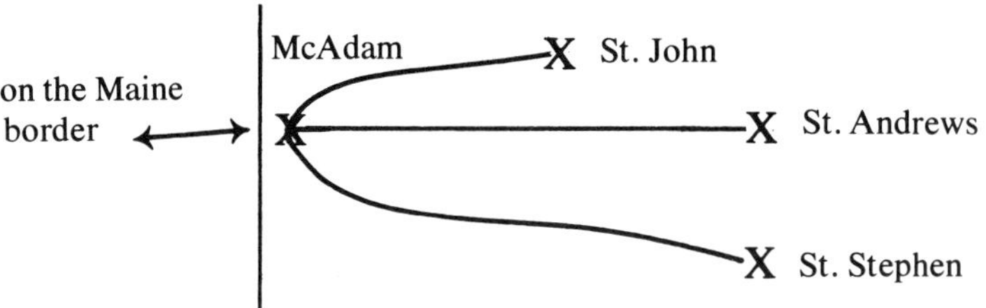

They tell me there is a good direct auto-road which can be covered in about 45 minutes from here. So I slept in, this morning, and am going out at 6:30 tonight instead – to return here after the meeting, letting the car wait. Cost: $20.00. I have a comfortable room with bath here – the inn at St. Andrews[1] is said to be a primitive affair. That will complete the first $200. Moncton and Sydney next.

Could not get a date suitable to both sides with Halifax: so I let Halifax go. Which means that it will be 3 full weeks before I've made $250. Poor pay for this work. But...

I am sending a bunch of books home which I wanted but which I won't have time to read. Carrier books. I shall also get a parcel ready with underwear etc. to be despatched on Monday.

By the time this reaches [letter cut here] I enclose the Birks bill. Doesn't it beat everything? The umbrella, when I enquired for the price was $26.50. Yet it was the only one I could find of that quality of silk. Buying through Miss Isles, I paid $6.75. Don't tell anybody. I asked Miss Isles whether, with this 75% discount to employees, the company was selling below cost. She said, no. On the cost-price they still make about 75c. Though, when 'overhead' etc. is figured in, there is a loss. 'Overhead' means rent of store, salaries of sales people, etc. Strange to say, these most expensive umbrellas were all without cord. The cheaper ones ($10; $15) had cords. But a cord is easily bought.

Have again an offer to go to U.S.A. I said, I might, provided the terms are such that I could take you along. Perhaps next year. They said they would write to me. Carrier is most anxious to get further books from me. But he asked for time on that $295 till spring when the book will appear.[2] Russell Lang owes him over $3000 and many other book-stores don't pay up. Funny business, isn't it?

I dropped Alexander[3] a line.

Montreal was a great success: I am firmly established there: everybody says, I am the only Canadian who counts.

A joke: At the ladies' meeting (800 present) Carrier was invited. When I got through, a woman opposite him said to him, 'Isn't he a *big* man.' '6 f[ee]t 3,' Carrier answered. She, witheringly, 'I didn't mean it physically.' The president bought 3 copies of Carrier's *Search* and sent them up to have them autographed.

Well, by means of my ruse I shall have another day here tomorrow, Sunday. So I better stop. I enclose a few cards[4] which you need. They are all of those missing I have got so far. Shall try to find time to exchange some at Ottawa.

Bye, bye. Kiss.
P.

[bottom of the letter is cut off]

1 Probably a reference to The Shiretown Inn. It is an old, but very comfortable, hotel, and still operates.

2 The fee for the translation of Gustav Amann's *The Legacy of Sun Yatsen*; see letter of December 11, 1928, note 2.

3 The letter to W.J. Alexander is missing.

4 Probably cigarette cards towards a complete set

TO CATHERINE GROVE

Still St. Stephen, N.B.
February 3, 1929

My dear,

And thus the days run by. This is the end of the second week; and it is definitely the last trip I am making alone – I mean the last trip of any extent. However...

You see, Alexander expects a storm of indignation from 'Adolescence'[1] – so do I, and for that reason I should have preferred another book to appear first. Ultimately, of course, it is not going to make any difference. Not a bit. But for the moment. Just now I am distinctly 'popular.' Both at Montreal and at St. John the 'women' went wild over me. I talked it over with Carrier who is very sensitive along those lines. He heard both addresses and said – as I agree – that the second address was hodge-podge as compared with the first. I go even further and call it 'tripe.' But, he said, it seems to have an almost sexual – he used the word 'onanistic' [–] effect on women. I was introduced as 'not only Canada's foremost writer but also Canada's foremost speaker.' 'My fame has gone forth.' It's laughable. At St. John the same. The men were flabbergasted: only a few understand that Nationhood address; the rest, according to Carrier, feel simply worried over it. It strikes like a thorn in their flesh. But the women ... The one who moved the vote of thanks said, 'Nothing should be said. We should quietly disperse. For fear of *treading upon holy ground*!' Imagine! All this, profoundly distasteful as it is to me, helps the sale of my books. And if I brought a book now which they *like*, it would have a big run, I believe. Unfortunately 'Adolescence' will be a slap in their face. Not that I regret that, artistically. It's coming to them; and it would restore my artistic integrity. I don't want to make concessions. I am I. Take me or leave me. That's been my attitude. And it's the only one compatible with my nature – as a writer. But ... How about the money? Carrier thinks that, from what he has heard of 'Adolescence' he can put it over with the Book-of-the-Month Club. I wonder. If Carrier can, Eayrs should be able to, it seems to me.

Well, we'll see.

Went by car, last night, to St. Andrews and came back by midnight. Cost, $16. Not much of a meeting – some 75 or so. And small intelligence. However, it's all grist in my mill. This is a nice little hotel; and I preferred to stay here over Sunday. Had some laundry done here.

Moncton tomorrow; Sydney next. Then Ottawa. I cut Halifax out: no suitable date could be arranged. Let her go. In a way it is too bad. But it can't be helped.

So, on Thursday I'll reach the point farthest east. Then homeward bound. I'm very anxious now to settle down to work again. Have 3, 4 novels in my head. But first of all I must knock 'Abe Spalding'[2] into publishable shape.

This is Sunday. It's 11 here: 9 a.m. at R[apid] C[ity]. And

you feel lonesome, no doubt. Shipping of wine I found impossible. They watch things closely.

I suppose you have by this time received *Point Counter Point* which I loaned to Isles.[3] I sent underwear last night, so as to lighten my grips. I shall soon send some shirts which are not to be returned: I'll replace them I think. With every trip, it seems, my expenses rise: I take more and more all conveniences which the land affords: I'm getting old, it seems. Had a disturbed night: the building next to this hotel burned down at 1 a.m. I can see the smoking ruins now from where I sit. Well, I wish I could get more frequent letters. Bye-bye, old girl. Kiss

P.

1 For Alexander's letter, referred to here, see letter of February 1, 1929, note 3. In that letter, Alexander had said that the book was likely to 'rouse a storm of prejudices' among those who fail to distinguish between a serious treatment of sex and sex merely as a bait for sales.

2 It was published, in 1933, as *Fruits of the Earth*.

3 Alan Isles of Louis Carrier and Company; see letter of January 26, 1929, note 3.

TO CATHERINE GROVE

Hotel Brunswick,
Moncton, N.B.
February 4, 1929

My dear,

Have been travelling all day over such miserable road-beds that it was impossible to write in the train. Now I'll have to speak within an hour or so and there is time only for a few words. Shall write more at length tomorrow when I start for Sydney in the afternoon.

On my way back from there I shall have the 'Ocean Limited,' crack C.N.R. train via Metapedia Valley, Rimouski, Rivière du Loup, Point Levis, Quebec Bridge, etc. – the way we went out last summer. I had to leave my laundry behind at St. Stephen, to be forwarded to Ottawa. It was not ready when I had to leave at 7 this morning. I am still and ever anew amazed to hear how many people have read my books – but borrowed. Today somebody spoke to me in the train, asking whether my name was Grove. 'It is.' 'The author of *A Search for America*?' 'Yes.' – Then he wanted to thank me for the pleasure I had given him. He actually recognized me from Comfort's[1] drawing in Miller's jacket. Rather astonishing, isn't it?

Now, my dear, this is the *3rd* week of the *last* tour. Then no more tours *alone*.

Strange to say, the longer I travel, the more it costs: this time it is $90 for 2 weeks – and no transportation to pay so far. But, of course, the distances have been enormous, and sleepers come high. How do you like that

$26.50 umbrella? That, at least, was a bargain at 6.75 plus 50c postage, wasn't it? I enclosed Gardiner's joke[2] in my last underwear parcel. Pull it out. It telescopes.

I am very travel-weary. Have no itinerary yet. Go from day to day, never knowing where I'll be a week hence. That, too, tends to make it tedious. More so than it would need to be. Because I don't even get letters from home. But I suppose Spry can't help it either.

Well, bye-bye, my dear. Kiss.

P.

1 Presumably the one used by the Association of Canadian Clubs in its folder, and used as an illustration in this volume (p 193).

2 E.S. Gardiner of Rapid City. The reference to 'joke' is obscure; it could have been one of those mechanical contraptions from which, when opened, a funny-face juts out – known as a jack-in-the-box.

TO CATHERINE GROVE

Hotel Brunswick,
Moncton, N.B.
February 5, 1929

Well, my dear, this is Tuesday of week 3. Had quite a good meeting last night. Am amazed again at how many people, after all, like *Settlers of the Marsh* better than the *Search*. Am going to squeeze Eayrs, though. No more 10% for me. 15% first 3000 – 20% thereafter. That's why I want Carrier to read the Ms. before I get to Toronto. I believe that's what he is going to offer me.

Now how are you? Shall reach Ottawa Saturday: and hope I'll find mail there. Just had my first pressing done.

Beautiful weather here. No snow yet. Lots of snow south of St John, though. Shall run up to Sydney this afternoon. It's eleven o'clock. That means you are just getting ready to go to school. 9 a.m. at R[apid] C[ity].

A N[ew] Y[ork] lecture agency wants me to come down to N[ew] Y[ork] at the end of this tour – just to arrange terms for a tour next fall or so. I don't know yet whether to go or not. I am trying to find out what sort of terms I can expect. But I *believe* I could get $200 a week plus expenses. If so, we could go together. After awhile I could no doubt get more. Ludwig – author of *Napoleon*,[1] etc., got $1000 a day – wanted $1500 to come up to Montreal but caught a cold before he started out and so cancelled.

I believe I'll send you a book called *Post Mortem*[2] – just to read one single essay on 'Anne Boleyn' – to give you an idea of Henry VIII of whom you teach. It might be an eye-opener. You will have to return it by book-post to Dr E.V. Sullivan,[3] St Stephen, N.B. from whom I borrowed it.

Had my first real sleep last night in a week. From 11 to

6:30. I, too, suffer a bit from insomnia. Tomorrow, from Sydney, I shall send a shower of post cards. Farthest point east, you know. Shall try to think of everybody.

Enclose a few cards on your list. Not many. Shall try to do better at Ottawa. Bye-bye, old girl. Soon the *second* half of the *last* lonely tour will start.

Kiss
P.

1 Which Grove had read the previous fall; see letter of October 13, 1928, note 2.
2 By Charles MacLaurin (b1872), with the subtitle *Essays, Historical and Medical*, published in 1923 (London). 'The Case of Anne Boleyn' was the first essay in the book.
3 Dr E.V. Sullivan (1874–1947) was a physician in St Stephen. His wife was active in the local Women's Canadian Club.

TO CATHERINE GROVE

Isle Royal Hotel,
Sydney, N.S.
February 6, 1929

Well, my dear, I'm at my farthest point east. Had a rather miserable night in the train: a terrible road-bed, with the car swaying and rolling as badly as in the Peace River. It's amazing. But this is a nice hotel; and I shall make up for it tonight. Tomorrow I shall start on the long, long run to Ottawa: 42 hours. – –

The two dashes mean that callers came. Quite a fuss over my visit. 4 service clubs have cancelled their regular meetings and join the C[anadian] C[lub]. Another 'great honour.' The Cape Breton Radio Broadcasting Station will be opened by myself tonight: with my lecture.

They were ready about a week ago; but they delayed the opening so as to have me give the first talk. It's funny how everybody knows my books. If every reader paid royalty, I'd be a rich man, I'm sure.

I'm waiting for the dining room to open. The train was due to leave Moncton 4:30 and arrive here at 7:45 this morning. But there was a wreck; and we were 3 h[ou]rs late. Unfortunately the dining car was cut off by whatever happened. And so I have not had anything to eat for 24 h[ou]rs except 2 sandwiches, 2 chocolate bars and 2 glasses of iced water.

Marvellous weather. I'm sorry we did not run up here last summer. It is very beautiful. I shall try to get some postcards to send one to everybody who is entitled to be remembered.

There they are opening the dining room. So long ... No, I better mail this so it'll go out tonight. I'll write again.

Bye-bye
P.

TO CATHERINE GROVE

Isle Royal Hotel,
Sydney, N.S.
February 7, 1929

Well, three weeks from today, all going well, I shall speak at Toronto. Last night resulted in a wired order for 5 copies of the *Search*. That adds $1.50 to my fees!!!

Oh, it's all very marvellous! I'm sending you clippings. And thus we burrow on and on. Yet – what are we missing? I might be working on a real book. For I feel, after all, that my real work is to come.

Could not secure lower berth for tonight. Shall have to lie in an upper: hard luck with a road-bed like this. It's somewhat ironical that these commercial travellers should get the lowers and I shall sway. But, of course, what will that mean a year from now? I'm going right through to Ottawa now. Quite a run.

Not much else to be said. I had a good sleep – half past 10 till 6 or thereabouts.

So bye-bye, my dear.
P.

I just notice that, after all the beautiful weather which I've had in the Maritimes, it's snowing at last. But I'll go out for awhile, to have a walk and a little exercise. I wish you were here.

TO CATHERINE GROVE

Isle Royal Hotel,
Sydney, N.S.
February 7, 1929 II
2 p.m., that's noon at R[apid] C[ity]

Just another note with enclosure.[1] It goes to show that they treat me here as elsewhere. One of the 3 local papers just sent around to ask me for the loan of a ms. They want to print my address in full. The whole town is buzzing with it. This is a sleepy sort of place, you know – surroundings very pretty. It seems I woke them up a little last night. I hope they'll buy books, books, books of mine – we do need the money. I have an idea, if Carrier gets 'Adolescence'[2] in time, he'll offer me 25%. If he does, Eayrs will have to come across. There will be a battle when I reach Toronto, that is sure. Well, I'll be armed.

I do wish you were along – and yet, I've earned only $250 so far. Expenses $130 so far. Just got word that I shall have a lower berth, after all. They had to put on an extra car. $8.25 sleeper to Montreal.

Bye-bye, old girl.
P.

1 A card – 'The Royal Cape Breton Yacht Club, Sydney, N.S. / At the request of Mr. E.C. Hanrahan, the Royal Cape Breton Yacht Club extends to Mr. F. Grove, the privileges of the Club for a period of 14 days' – dated February 6, 1929.
2 *The Yoke of Life* (Toronto: Macmillan; New York: Richard Smith 1930)

TO CATHERINE GROVE

En route, Sydney–Ottawa,
West of Truro, N.S.
February 8, 1929, 10 a.m.

Well, my dear, here I am. The first 15 hours of my way back are done; and, I believe, the worst part of the whole. Between Sydney and Truro it would have been impossible to write in the train. I've now hooked on to the crack train of the C.N.R. from the Maritimes to Ontario or rather Quebec – the Ocean Limited. We go via Metapedia (you remember the valley, where we stayed overnight on the fox farm?), Rimouski, Rivière du Loup, Point Levis, etc. Tomorrow at 1:15 p.m. I'm supposed to get to Ottawa.

All night long it poured. The fields are under water. The air is like spring. It's hard on a person, with all the winter clothes. The sap is running in the trees they say.

By the way, I am much disturbed in my mind over my books – I can't make up my mind what to do. I hear so much about Eayrs. He is losing his best salesmen because he puts them on commission. I met one of his crack men who told me he was earning $15 a week – he used to get a salary of $3000 + expenses. The 'trade' hates Eayrs; they say he's stuck up, unapproachable, unfair. And he tells such stories. 'Yes,' he said recently in New York, '*O*[*ur*] *D*[*aily*] *B*[*read*] isn't much. But then I know Grove has some real books; so I took it in order to fix him up. I have all his future work.' Etc. etc. He told Carrier that *O*[*ur*] *D*[*aily*] *B*[*read*] has sold 10,000 copies; but he is still selling the first edition. And surely, he put the Cape contract over on you. Carrier, of course, is only a beginner; but he has done some fine things. And I like both him and Isles. They are very anxious to get another book of mine. They will shortly issue the second edition of the *Search*. Miller, on the other hand, still has copies of the 1st ed[ition], selling them to favoured booksellers at the regular price. A Montreal bookseller told me he had tried to get 1st ed[ition] copies by advertising: a N[ew] Y[ork] firm offered him 5 copies at $25.00 each. A Boston bookstore sold 1 copy for $40.00. Then Miller phoned him up and offered him 5 copies at $3.00 each wholesale – something fishy about that. I saw the copies – they are 1st ed[ition] allright. Is he cheating me? Making a profit of an extra dollar on the side? All that worries me: who is honest? It's an amazing situation. Yet, the books sell. Lots of U.S.A. reviews coming out – mostly luke warm – patronising. N[ew] Y[ork] *Sun* mentions *Search and O*[*ur*] *D*[*aily*] *B*[*read*], saying, 'below mediocrity' – 'not worth reviewing' – but Morley, in the *Sat*[*urday*] *Rev*[*iew*] *of Literature*, mentions me as the only Canadian worth mentioning.[1]

Well, Sydney was a great success. The whole of Cape

Breton 'listened in.' I wrote you, I think, that I was being broadcasted – first lecture over their new station.

That's all I can think of to say without saying things that are better unsaid. Monday's your birthday – this is Friday. I hope I'll find some mail at Ottawa. I suppose I shall.

It is quite a relief to be on a decent road-bed again. Shall mail this at Sackville or Amherst or Moncton – wherever there is a stop long enough to run to the mail car. Bought myself some *Vicks* – have used the other stuff up: it was quite weak towards the end. I use it daily – as a sort of disinfectant: there is so much flu in the east; and people sneeze and cough in the trains, damn them, without using their handkerchiefs.

By-bye, old girl. By the time you get this, half the tour is over. And, as I go west, letters will arrive more regularly.

Kiss
P.

1 These reviews remain untraced. *The New York Sun* ceased publication in the nineteen-fifties, and is not indexed. It did review *Settlers of the Marsh* on November 14, 1925. Christopher Morley (1890–1957), the American author and critic, wrote a weekly feature, 'The Bowling Green,' in the *Saturday Review of Literature*, but the remark attributed to him by Grove does not appear to have been made in 'The Bowling Green' around this time (December 1928 to February 1929). An unsigned review of *A Search for America* appeared in *Saturday Review of Literature* of April 21, 1928, and another review of the same book appeared on March 16, 1929. *Our Daily Bread* does not appear to have been reviewed in that magazine.

TO CATHERINE GROVE

Chateau Laurier,
Ottawa, Ont.
February 9, 1929

Well, here I am, halfway home; and half through this lecture agony.

Ran into a C[anadian] C[lub] meeting here on arrival; met lots of people who profess to be friends. Have, of course, got to make a few calls.

Sir Robert Borden[1] invited me for tea tomorrow. I don't know yet whether I'll go or not. I hate all this snobbery. I'd be looking on at a sort of hypocritical function, conducted on a scale of expense which makes me feel bad. Very flattering, of course, etc. etc.

Miller was at the station, but I managed to get away from him without giving offence. No use getting mad at the man. – So...

Got your two letters and the parcel. Thanks. Well, it'll soon be over, my dear. Yes, *The Peasants*[2] is a pretty big book; and yet it is *too* long; *too* slow. If my pace and its pace were mixed or averaged up, there'd be a book. I'm going to try that with 'Abe Spalding.'[3]

Too bad about Mrs. Westwood[4] – though it was to be expected. Strange to say, I thought of her the other day; and I was wondering, then, when I'd hear this piece of news. I expected it at the time. Yes, the implications of it...

I'm holding on to every cent; but the money simply melts. Have $120 left out of $270 odd. I'm going to try to squeeze some money out of Miller when I see him again.

Apropos of *The Peasants*: the worst, to me, seems that the book leads nowhere: I want a definite *end*: tragic or otherwise.

Am sending home 2 vol[ume]s. Don't read *Adam's Breed*[5] – not a bad book, but nothing outstanding. *Peder Victorious*[6] I have not read myself so far. There's a first vol[ume] which I haven't got yet – *Giants in the Earth*[7] – and I want to read it before I read *Peder*. It was sold out at Montreal. I have two or three more vol[ume]s of French things along.

Shall also, on Monday, send my new underwear. I have not, so far, anything definite in the line of itinerary. But the only address, after this, will be c/o Macmillans, 70 Bond St., Toronto.

One of those photos is good: the other one I dislike, even though it may be good. I hope I'll get one or two prints more. But I don't know.

Carrier expected me to stop over once more at Montreal; but I didn't. I wanted my mail etc. and a day's rest. The which I'll have tomorrow. See *O[ur] D[aily] B[read]* on the news-stands here. Well, bye-bye, old girl.

P.

1 Robert Laird Borden (1854–1937) was Canada's Prime Minister during the First World War. He retired from politics in 1920 with some honour, despite the unpopularity of his war measures, which included conscription. By the time of this letter, he was very much the elder statesman, having just been elected to the Royal Society of Canada, after many other honours and diplomatic assignments.

2 A novel in four parts by Wladyslaw Stanislaw Reymont; see letter of December 14, 1927, note 10.

3 ie, *Fruits of the Earth*

4 Mrs Grove had reported her death – she had been very ill. Some of her children had been at the school where Mrs Grove taught.

5 By Radclyffe Hall (1886–1943), and published in 1926 by Cassell (London) and Doubleday (New York)

6, 7 Two novels by Ole Edvart Rølvaag (Paal Mørck, pseud.) (1876–1931). *Giants in the Earth: A Saga of the Prairie* was translated from the Norwegian by Lincoln Colcord and the author, and published in 1927 by Harper (New York). Another edition, with an introduction by Vernon L. Parrington, was issued by Harper in 1929 in their Modern Classics series. *Peder Victorious* was translated from the Norwegian by Nora O. Solum and the author, and published by Harper in 1928.

TO CATHERINE GROVE

Chateau Laurier,
Ottawa, Ont.
February 10, 1929

Have just sent a night letter for your birthday.

I had a good night's rest. Miller called last night. It is more than amazing to me to see what a mess the man has made of the *Search*. He professes to have sold only ca. 500 copies since last spring.[1] I have asked for his statement by Monday, tomorrow.

The Sydney club wired to Spry saying that my address was the biggest thing they have ever had. *If I came back*, there would be no hall big enough to accommodate the crowd. Well, thus it goes. *If I came back*! It is also astonishing how many people speak to me in trains and elsewhere. All this photographing and lecturing makes my face pretty well known. Went to a skating club last night, about 5 p.m. Had soon a dozen people about me: Mrs. Doughty among them (do you remember my speaking to you of Dr. Doughty, Dominion Archivist?).[2] And yet – 500 copies – total ca. 2100 sold since 1927!

By the way, Senator Hardy[3] has again sent a feeler, asking me whether I'd accept a Dominion job at about $3000 – I have *not* said 'No.' Let them specify first; and then I'll see. We have to make money somehow. I'd prefer some job, after all, to this lecturing: if I went down to New York, from Toronto, I could always get that. But it's too devilish hard work – though, perhaps, at present, I am a little overfed with it on account of the enormous distances I have travelled in the Maritimes. 2 out of every three nights in the train! I am frankly astonished that I do not feel sick. But I don't though I cough a little. But I pack myself every night with Thermogene, even in the train. As a precautionary measure. And I use Vicks all the time, for the same reason.

I met Sir Robert Borden[4] yesterday; and he invited me to come for tea. But I am not going to go. All this expensive living makes me feel badly. I wish I were at home where a week's living for the two of us costs less than a day's hotel bill for myself alone here.

I am getting to be quite callous with regard to certain expenses: laundry, pressing of clothes, etc. I have all that charged on the hotel bill and let others pay that bill. The more time I have to spend in the train, the more I spend on that, of course. A shirt a day barely keeps me clean.

Well, tomorrow afternoon I start for Kemptville by car: 30 miles. From there to Prescott. My total earnings for this tour will not exceed $525. Poor return. And yet: a year ago I'd have jumped at it even if it had been the only sum I could earn. Well...

I figure this way

Fees	$ 525.00
Bank a/c	100.00 – not counting yours

Miller royalty	150.00 – about
Carrier "	250.00 – about
" fee	295.00 – translation[5]
Settlers, royalties	75.00
	$1395.00 min[imum]
– life ins[urance]	100.00
	$1295.00

And that will be what we'll have to live on till other moneys fall due. How much *O*[*ur*] *D*[*aily*] *B*[*read*] will bring, I'll see shortly. But of this sum of 1295, of course, $270 have already been used for the purchase of that bond. So there will be really only ca. $1000 left. It's amazing how little that is, isn't it?

Well, bye-bye, old girl. I am going to make a few calls which I should not neglect: the Grants, Lady Pope,[6] etc.

Kiss P.

1 See letter of February 8, 1929. Grove's doubts were dispelled by the royalty statement which showed a sale of 1036 copies (see letter of February 12, 1929, note 3).
2 Sir Arthur George Doughty (1860–1936). He was born in England, and entered the Quebec Civil Service in 1897, becoming Joint Librarian of the Quebec legislature in 1901, and Dominion Archivist in 1904, a post he held till his death. His publications, mainly histories, ranged from the scholarly to the popular, including history for children.
3 Arthur Charles Hardy; see letter of March 8, 1928, note 2.
4 See the preceding letter, note 1.
5 For his translation of Gustav Amann's *The Legacy of Sun Yatsen: A History of the Chinese Revolution*, published by Carrier in 1929
6 Whom Grove had met during his first lecture tour; for Grant, see letter of March 17, 1928, note 3; and for Lady Pope, letter of March 19, 1928, note 1.

TO CATHERINE GROVE, CANADIAN NATIONAL TELEGRAM

Ottawa, Ont.
February 11, 1929

Mrs. FP Grove
Rapid City Man

Birthday greetings, may the year be light. Next mailing address Care McMillan Toronto, shall be there every week end during this month.

Phil

TO CATHERINE GROVE

Chateau Laurier,
Ottawa, Ont.
February 11, 1929 II

Well, my dear, this is just a word for to-day. I am in a rush and have a slight headache. I spent the morning knocking the initial number of the new *Can[adian] Nation*[1] into shape with Spry. Have to go to a luncheon now, to meet the premier.[2] There is again talk of creating a sinecure for me.

I shall speak here again on Mar[ch] 1st or 2nd.

This afternoon I am off to Southern Ontario.

The tour as such, the executive says, has been an outstanding, unique success. That is gratifying, of course.

Snatched a 1/2 h[ou]r this morning to get to a card exchange.[3] Result enclosed.

Just got your 3rd letter. Thanks.

Well, I must hurry – Toronto next address.

Bye-bye
P.

I count on getting home about March 7, 8, or 9. Toronto has just asked for a meeting on Feb[ruary] 18. I have accepted. Address there Westminster Hotel or c/o Macmillans.

Kiss.

1 The *Canadian Nation* was published by the Association of Canadian Clubs. Altogether six issues were published, beginning with the issue of February 1928 (I, 1) and ceasing publication with the issue of May-June 1929 (II, 2). It was edited by the Association's National Secretary, Graham Spry, who writes:

> The *Canadian Nation* was published on Queen's Street by the Runge Press and was well enough received, but it was costing the Association too much money and was, therefore, dropped at one of the meetings of the annual executive or possibly the annual conference. I suspect that it was a little too arty and probably had no interest for the average person – in sum, leaving aside all political questions, it might be regarded as appealing to the sort of audience which the *Canadian Forum* has served much better.

In February 1929, Grove and Marius Barbeau (1883–1969) joined the staff of the *Canadian Nation* as associate editors, but two issues later the journal was voted out of existence at the annual conference of the Association in Quebec.

The following contributions by Grove appeared in the *Canadian Nation*:

(i) 'Drama at the Crossroads' (April 1928; pp 14–18) – reprinted in *Tales from the Margin* (1971) as 'Saturday Night at the Crossroads.'

(ii) 'Salesmanship: A Story of the Prairies' (May-June 1929; pp 20–2, 31) – reprinted in *Tales from the Margin* (1971) as 'Salesmanship.'
(iii) 'The Meaning of Nationhood' (March-April 1929; pp 8–10, 28) – the 'Nationhood' address, also printed in *It Needs to Be Said* (1929).

2 William Lyon Mackenzie King (1874–1950)

3 Presumably, as has been previously observed, Grove was collecting cigarette cards towards a complete set.

TO CATHERINE GROVE

Prescott, Ont.
February 12, 1929
En route, Kemptville–Gananoque

Well, my dear, another chore done last night. Things are beginning to move a little faster. I have made my first long trip in 'beetles'[1] – I suppose you remember what they are. Quite an experience for a 'hick.'

Well, I was very nice to Miller. Had supper at the house on Sunday – which involved not going to Sir Robert Borden's.[2] Naturally, they felt flattered. Nobody, by the way, knows what to do with *Our Daily Bread* – not even Spry.

However, here is good news. I enclose Miller's royalty statement: 1036 copies sold: not too bad.[3] I secured his cheque – which I shall forward to the bank as soon as I can. I am here only for an hour or so, waiting for a train.

Further, the premier and Senator Hardy were in conference yesterday; and it was resolved to try to create a job for me at $2000, *without work*, except that I shall have to put in an appearance at an office now and then. The very condition is that *I do nothing*, so as not to disturb policies. I am too old for a permanent position – but I am to be appointed temporarily. If ... then I accept.[4] It may not be for long, a few years perhaps. Nor is the pay enough: but it will help. That would mean, of course, living at Ottawa, for appearance's sake. I can get an apartment (3 rooms plus kitchenette) there for $45 a month. That would leave us $100 a month out of that salary. I am also going to receive (if we move east) a salary as editor of the *Canadian Nation*[5] – not much of course; but perhaps $200. And now and then there will be a small tour (a week or so at a time). If this comes about, as, I believe, it will, I think we should be able to leave all royalties untouched and yet to live fairly comfortably. Don't you think? I'd find enough money somehow.

This Miller statement is by $150 better than I had figured with. Not too bad. He begs for another book. Well, we'll see.

Well, I have another night-ride ahead – so I'll go and make reservations.

Bye
P.

Please put the enclosed statement[6] into the *Search* Canadian Ed[ition] envelope: left-hand top drawer, rear compartment.

1 Possibly a reference to the 'Baby Austin' or Austin 7, or to the single-coach trains now known as dayliners.
2 Cf. letters of February 9 and 10, 1929.
3 Grove's previous doubts as to Miller's honesty – cf. letters of November 1928, and of February 8 and 10, 1929 – appear from this to be the product of Grove's tendency to expect the worst, and also, it must be said, of Miller's tendency to muddle things.
4 The whole proposal of a sinecure appears to have fallen through.
5 See the preceding letter, note 1.
6 ie, Miller's royalty statement, referred to in the letter

TO CATHERINE GROVE

The Provincial,
Gananoque, Ont.
[February 12, 1929 II][1]

My dear,

Just a word. Have been here *3* h[ou]rs and have spoken *3* times. *Gratis*.

I have just mailed bank-book and $315.80 in cheques to Bank of Montreal, Winnipeg, with directions to return pass-book to Rapid City.

Please, when you get the pass-book, let me know what our balance is, will you?

Speak at Toronto next Mon[day], Feb[ruary] 18.

Tomorrow at Simcoe,[2] near Lake Erie, after a night-ride. Day after at Sarnia.

Shall write you from Toronto re life-insurance which I want paid up for the year. Sent you a long letter from Prescott this morning, while waiting for a connection.

Am anxious to lie down for an hour or so, before the big meeting.

So bye
P.

1 Date from postmark
2 This was to be Grove's first visit to Simcoe, where he was to spend the last years of his life.

TO CATHERINE GROVE

En route Gananoque–Simcoe, Ont.
February 13, 1929

Well, my dear, my pen is empty. So it is pencil for me.

These 2 days are my two hardest ones on this tour. Left Gananoque 11:40 last night, after having spoken 4 times. The pres[ident] of the club there, a man almost indistinguishable from Argue,[1] was merciless. Then I had to wait at Gananoque Junction for a train that was late till 1 o'clock. Board the Montreal-Toronto train. Get out of bed at 5:15 this morning. Land at Toronto at 6. Leave there at 8:10 for Hamilton. Catch a local there for Simcoe – that's where I am, in the local, I mean. Speak at Simcoe[2] tonight, 8:30, tomorrow morning I must catch a train at 5:26 for Woodstock – thence to Sarnia; and then the agony will be over. After that 8 a.m. is the earliest I shall have to board a train. But on Feb[ruary] 19 I shall speak in 3 different cities: noon, afternoon, night, with 2 bus rides in between. From then on it will all be easy. But I shall have to go back to Ottawa and Montreal, beginning of March. I am trying, after all, to rake in all the money I can get.

From Feb[ruary] 15 till Feb[ruary] 19 I shall be at Toronto – so I can at last get laundry done. Have wired Westminster Hotel to hold room for me – with bath. It's a quiet place. This is a terrific road-bed. Perhaps I had better stop. So long! 11 a.m. I have not yet washed, shaved, brushed my teeth, etc.

10 a.m. February 14, 1929
En route Brantford–Sarnia, Ont.

I was so tired when I arrived at Simcoe yesterday that I could not finish this letter or mail it. I was billeted there with very nice people[3] and was rude, I am afraid; for I went to bed after lunch and slept to within 1/2 h[ou]r of the meeting. This morning they woke me at 4:30, but I turned over and fell asleep again. They let me sleep and meanwhile rustled a car which would take me to Brantford (25 min[utes] away) where I caught this train – so as still to get to Sarnia in ample time. I could sleep till 7:30. That was awfully good of them. These were to be the two hardest days – and here I am, wonderfully rested up, on the mainline from Toronto to Chicago – parlo[u]r car and everything.

Nothing else to report or write about.

Bye-bye

P.

1 Robert Fletcher Argue (1877–1962), for many years on the staff of the English Department at Wesley College (later United College), Winnipeg, Brandon College, and the University of Manitoba. He was born in Stittsville, Ontario, graduated in arts and theology from Wesley College (1911), and was ordained a Methodist minister the same year. He took a Master's degree from the University of Manitoba in 1921, and pursued further study

at the universities of Chicago and Edinburgh. During the First World War he was an instructor in the Khaki College in England, becoming a professor of English at Wesley on his return. In 1923, he moved to the University of Manitoba, and became successively assistant professor (1936), and Dean of Junior Men (1943), retiring in 1949. In 1952, during the 75th anniversary celebrations of the University of Manitoba, he was honoured with a D Litt. He remained active in church circles till his death.

2 Ironically – as Mrs Grove's pencilled exclamation on the envelope notes – this was the first (and last) time Grove lectured in Simcoe.

3 Presumably Mr and Mrs W.D. Powell – see letter of February 15, 1929 II, note 3.

TO CATHERINE GROVE

Hotel Vendome,
Sarnia, Ont.
February 15, 1929

Well, that was another one; and it was quite a success, quite a success. Especially considering that I spoke here for the second time.

And now for the week-end to Toronto. This is an expensive tour; for the work bunches together, with 2, 3 days of waiting in between, when no local club pays for my stay. However...

Now listen here, old girl. Before the 1st of March – that is, so as to reach Winnipeg before that date, make out a cheque on the Bank of Montreal, Winnipeg, for $103.45 (or $105.20 less 5 mo[nth]s interest at 4%; better verify my arithmetic), to the Continental Life Insurance Co., 504 Union Trust B[ui]ld[in]g, Main St[reet], Winnipeg. In a letter state that this is premium #8 on policy ?? 27914 (look up the number), due Aug[ust] 1st 1929, less 4% for 5 mo[nth]s, on your life, in my favour. Then I've got that off my mind.

Re the bond: so long as you have the receipt for $270 sent to the bank, it is all right whether you have the note or not. I'll get the note some time later.

Note of course what balance that leaves at the bank, so we can keep track of it. Miller asserts (whether true who can tell) that the sales for January and February, this year, are keeping up well. If that is right, the second edition should sell out during the year – which would be quite good. Everywhere people bring me *O[ur] D[aily] B[read]* to autograph – so it seems it is still going. In many places people say that 2 weeks ago or so they had never heard my name; now they are reading my books: mostly borrowed, I suppose, but not invariably. So I am still stimulating sales. But I am mighty tired of it. Did I mention that the executive of C[anadian] C[lubs] at Ottawa is planning, through my editorship, to do something for me?[1] It will be a couple of hundred at the most, I suppose; but every little bit helps. Spry told me that he mentioned at the last meeting of the executive that this or that he had done was a good piece of work. Cowan,[2] pres[ident] of the American Bank Note Company, said, 'Your greatest work, Spry, is Grove.' Here, at Sarnia, the club invited me to come back a third time when in Ontario again. I get them, after all. Still, this glory of an hour palls badly. However, my chief aim is to make it possible for you to quit teaching for at least a year or so. The future has ceased to worry me. We are getting there.

I am in a very desirable position today: I might have left at 3:23, or at 6:55, or at 8:20. I do leave at 10:47, getting to Toronto at 4:10. I take the very best train, the International Limited –, Chicago – Montreal; for I have nothing whatever to do at Toronto before Monday. I'll eat oysters and broiled lobster in the train.

My laundry is almost all dirty; but I'll have time for that at Toronto.

Tuesday 3 lectures in 3 cities; Wednesday 2 in 2 cities – then Toronto again for the week-end.

In less than 3 weeks I'll be through. 3 weeks from the time this reaches you, I'll be in the train from Montreal to Winnipeg. Since I have no pass for the C.P.R., I'll have to stay over at W[inni]peg for a whole day: from 10 a.m. to 8:45 a.m. On the C.P.R., I'd have gone straight through to Brandon.

Well, brace up, old girl.
Bye-bye, Kiss
P.

1 See letter of February 11, 1929 II, note 1.
2 Charles Gardiner Cowan (1876–1961). He was Vice-President and Managing Director (1927–47), and later President (1947–51), of the British American Bank Note Company. A native of Hamilton, Ontario, and a graduate of the University of Toronto (BA 1899), he was knighted in 1931, and awarded the King's Medal twice, in 1935 and 1937. In 1929, he was Chairman of the Executive Committee of the Association of Canadian Clubs.

TO CATHERINE GROVE

Hotel Westminster,
Toronto, Ont.
February 15, 1929 II

Well, old girl, I had your three letters here and the parcel. Eayrs had been thoughtful enough to send them around. So I'll answer.

First of all, how about the books. Did Morley Callaghan's *Strange Fugitive*[1] not arrive? I sent it from Chapleau. It is Mrs. Sweatman's. I sent after that 2 vol[ume]s – 1 *Peder Victorious* which I have not read; 1 *Adam's Breed* which I have read; still later, I believe *Post Mortem*[2] which contains the article on Anne Boleyn. Tonight, I sent a French book which I find very good; several others which Carrier gave me I left in trains, hotels, etc. not thinking them worth the postage to send on. [letter cut here]

4thly My chest is quite clear again, thanks to the treatment Mrs. W.D. Powell[3] gave me at Simcoe. It has at no time been bad; but at St. Stephen I called in Dr. Sullivan, just to make sure that it was safe to go on. He fixed me up over Sunday and said, 'No danger of its turning nasty.' But by the time I got to Simcoe there was once more a slight congestion. When I left, next day, in the manner described in another letter, I was quite all right. Today I feel particularly fine.

5thly No, I have not seen Eayrs yet; but just spoke to him over the phone. Mrs. Eayrs is at Palm Beach. I'll see him tomorrow morning at 11 at the office.

Have a letter from Cape, London, c/o Macmillan's (*that* is the spelling, please note), saying that orders on publication[4] have been exceptionally good for an author new to the English public. Don't know, of course, just what that may mean. 200 or 500 copies?

Am glad to hear that the Gardiners are trying to be decent. I'll send them and Duncans another p[ost] c[ard] from here, to keep them in good humour. Ottawa has asked me to give the Assimilation address. Of course, I must go. That is too great an honour to neglect it. I shall speak here on Monday, Feb[ruary] 18; and again on Thur[sday] Feb[ruary] 28 (Empire Club).

Spry feels very badly about it that there are, after all, so comparatively few clubs with which he has succeeded in getting a date. At the best, it seems, there will be $575 or $600. But I am very glad that Sarnia, where I spoke for the second time last night, wants me again – the club as such voted that invitation.

Yes, re Carrier I am disappointed. I believe there was also a royalty statement due on Jan[uary] 31, but, not having my contracts here, I am not positively sure.

I begin to believe that, where money is concerned, Miller is, after all, honest. It hit him pretty hard that he was to part with $310.80. But he did it – provided the cheque is honoured. I keep quite friendly with him.

Yes [letter cut here]

I see you are trying to learn typing. Quite a fair job for a beginner: 75%.

As for wine, we'll get some when I get home. I'll try to bring at least one bottle from here.

By the way, Cape has an ad in the London *Times* which I'll try to get for you.

More tomorrow or day after when I've seen Hughie.[5]
I laughed at the Valentine, of course.
Well, so long
P.

1 Morley Callaghan (b1903) was born and educated in Toronto (BA University of Toronto, 1925; and Osgoode Hall Law School), and has lived there almost continuously. *Strange Fugitive*, his first novel, appeared in 1928, and *Native Argosy*, the first collection of his short stories, in 1929. In the same year he spent several months in Paris in the company of such writers as Ernest Hemingway (whom Callaghan had met earlier as a colleague on the staff of the Toronto *Daily Star*), Scott Fitzgerald, and James Joyce – that experience is recalled in Callaghan's *That Summer in Paris* (1963). Callaghan is the author of many short

stories, the best of which are collected in *Morley Callaghan's Stories* (1959), and of a dozen or so novels – the best perhaps are *Such is My Beloved* (1934), *They Shall Inherit the Earth* (1935), and *The Loved and the Lost* (1951).
2 *Peder Victorious* and *Adam's Breed* with the letter of February 9, 1929, and *Post Mortem* with the letter of February 5, 1929. For bibliographical information, see notes to those letters.
3 Cf. letter of February 13, 1929, note 3. In reply to an enquiry made of Mr Powell, a neighbour, Mr G.K. Higgins, writes on his behalf that he is suffering from failing sight and has no recollection of the visit. A letter from Mrs (Marjorie) Powell to Grove, dated May 31, 1929, does, however, survive in the University of Manitoba Grove Collection. It begins, 'It was such a pleasure to receive your note,' and continues, 'Your visit to Simcoe was far more of a treat and inspiration than you will ever know.'
4 Of *Our Daily Bread*; the sales figures are not available.
5 Hugh S. Eayrs

TO CATHERINE GROVE

En route Sarnia–Toronto
February 15, 1929 III
(neighbourhood of Paris, Ont., you remember?)

Well, this sheet will probably reach you ahead of one or two letters mailed yesterday and today at Sarnia, farther west[,] whence they will have to come back to Toronto for the long run. If my letters don't arrive in the right order, the reason is that I hop about over this province, east and west, never adhering to one direction.

I have really nothing to say. I merely write to relieve your feeling of loneliness. The first few lines were written while we stopped. Now we are hopping: and you can see it in the writing, I suppose. On the whole, we have better road-beds in the west. Next stop Brantford. In a little over 2 h[ou]rs we'll be in Toronto.

By the way, if E.S.G.[1] is silly enough to be disagreeable about that report of yours, why not answer by *resigning*? RESIGNING? We'll manage. Though, of course, the salary would be welcome. But no. I can't write with this train trying to make up for time lost. So bye-bye

P

And this is Brantford whence I started yesterday morning for Sarnia. Hopping like a flea all over the country. Well, bye-bye. She is starting again.

1 E.S. Gardiner, Chairman of the Rapid City School Board – in which capacity, presumably, he would be receiving the report – whatever its contents – from Mrs Grove.

When I visited Rapid City in 1969 and 1970, I was told by various of the older inhabitants that there were a number of controversies during the Groves' stay there, but that the unanimous verdict now is that they were the best teachers the town has ever known.

TO CATHERINE GROVE

Toronto, Ont.
February 16, 1929

At night – The day's work which consisted in shopping, seeing people, dickering with Eayrs, etc., is done; and I am mighty tired. Tomorrow, Sunday, however, I have nothing to do but to have dinner with Alexander and supper, likely, with Pratt. Monday, reception for me at Macmillan's,[1] and an address at night.

I do hope the dress fits; and that you like it. I spent 2 h[ou]rs picking it; and I like it much. It's a very good 'flat crepe.'

Eayrs is trying to cajole me and to treat contracts, etc. as a negligible thing which I can attend to while sipping tea and milling about among 100 guests. But he's mistaken. I'll scan that contract very closely indeed and shall take my time about it.

Did I tell you that I have definitely made up my mind not to bring [out] 'Adolescence'[2] next fall?

And now for a bath and bed. So long
P.

More tomorrow –

Sunday morning. – I had a 'peach' of a sleep; from 10 to 6. It is like spring here: the streets are running with water. Dangerous weather. But I feel fine.

Enquired here at the hotel for price of suites: a nice 2-roomed suite + hall, cloak room, and bath $50 a week + board. Too much; but there are many other small hotels much less expensive. However, the chances are we'll buy a house if we come down here. If I take the job with Macmillans, it will mean that, as far as Canadian things go, I'll be supreme head of the dep[artmen]t.[3] Most of the work I could do at home in the evening. *You* could do a good deal of it: reading mss. etc. I'd get about $200 a month + certain fees: a bread-and-butter job. Royalties would all be extra. I could also go here and there to lecture occasionally. In addition I'd have a few hundred from the *Canadian Nation*.[4] Only if what the Dom[inion] Gov[ernmen]t may offer me is an absolute sinecure – i.e. pay without work – I'll take it.[5] I do consider that Canada owes me a living.

I have just finished reading the proofs of *It Needs to be Said*[6] and am going out now to have dinner with Alexander. In the afternoon I'll drop over to Pratts. Then to bed early. Speak tomorrow.

Bye-bye, old girl, I'll mail this
P.

1 *The Mail and Empire*, February 19, 1929, carried a report of the affair:

Mr. Hugh S. Eayrs, St. Martin's house, Bond Street, was the

> host of an interesting tea yesterday afternoon for Mr. Frederick Philip Grove of Rapid City, Manitoba, the well-known author, whom many of the guests had the pleasure of chatting with. The room with its plum colored hangings and profusion of spring flowers, was attractive. Miss Inrig poured tea and coffee and was assisted by Mrs. Booth, Miss Rooke and Miss Ball. Some of the guests who numbered 60 were Lady Willison, Prof. Alexander, Dean McLay, Mr. W.S. Wallace, Mrs. J.F.B. Livesay, Mrs. George Haddow, Mr. M.O. Hammond, Mr. R. Knister, Mr. and Mrs. Alan Barr, Mr. Clark Locke, Mr. John Garvin, Mr. Arthur Heming, Mr. Barker Fairley, Miss Jean Graham, Miss Marshall Saunders, Miss Lois Osborne, Mr. J. Lennell, Mrs. Horace Parsons, Mr. A.H.C. Proctor, Mr. D.M. LeBourdais, Mr. W.A. Deacon, Mr. J.H. Hodgins, Miss Amy Jacob, Mr. and Mrs. U.W. McLaughlin, Prof. Currelly, Prof. G.M. Jones, Miss Elizabeth Young and Mr. S.B. Watson.

The guest list is an interesting one, indicating those who were regarded as the literary establishment in Toronto at the time. Notice, too, that Grove characteristically exaggerates the number of guests.

2 *The Yoke of Life*

3 This is the first intimation we have of there being some proposal of Grove working for Macmillan. Although he did read manuscripts for them, he was never 'supreme head of the department.'

4 See letter of February 11, 1929 II, note 1. Information on this point is somewhat vague. Graham Spry writes:

> My previous letter said there may have been some discussion about this but I simply do not recall any such offer and certainly not payment, though if he did write a short story, some very modest sum would have been paid over to him. ... there is no trace whatsoever in my memory, even faintly, of his [Grove] being assistant editor or of any proposal being made to him that he should become such... (July 7, 1971)

However, as has been noted previously, Grove was listed as an Associate Editor in the last two issues of the *Canadian Nation*; and Spry's letter to Grove, of March 11, 1929, would indicate that there was a move to provide Grove with a salary for his work with the magazine.

5 This position did not materialize; see also letter of February 12, 1929.

6 The volume of essays which Grove originally conceived of as 'Addresses Not Delivered,' published by Macmillan in 1929

TO CATHERINE GROVE, CANADIAN PACIFIC TELEGRAM

Toronto, Ont.
February 18th, 1929
8.40 AM

Mrs. F.P. Grove
Rapid City, Man

If Riddell[1] makes offer according to Saturdays letter withhold payment till Monday letter arrives Stop Am well.

Phil

1 Presumably the reference is to some financier, and not to the Rev. John Henry Riddell (1863–1952), who was President of Wesley College, Winnipeg, from 1917 to 1938. The Winnipeg City Directory for 1928 lists several Riddells, including a Geo. Riddell, accountant to Traders Trust Company, who may have been the person intended here.

The reference to 'offer' is also obscure. 'Saturdays letter' – that of February 16, immediately preceding – contains no mention of any such offer; and it does not appear to have been excised. However, the letter of February 15 does contain references to financial matters, including the purchase of bonds, but, like 'Monday's letter' (February 18 II), it does not shed much light on the precise nature of the transactions. It appears from the following letter that Grove planned to buy a $1000 bond which was selling below its par value at $970.

TO CATHERINE GROVE

Toronto, Ont.
Monday,
February 18, 1929 II

My dear, I just sent you a wire: this in explanation.[1] I sent you Macmillans cheque for $601.60. I just received word that Carrier has sent you cheque for $295. (This, if made out to me, send on to Can[adian] Bank of Commerce, Brandon, for endorsation when you hear from Riddell, if made out to you, endorse 'for deposit only'); together $896. When Riddell writes you about the price (ca. $970, including accrued interest), you send him the balance + a few dollars to go on by cheque on Bank of Montreal, Winnipeg, so as to pay for the bond in full.

We have at present ca. $300 in the bank at Winnipeg (deducting $100 odd for life insurance) – of that I *shall* need $100 for expenses, and *may* need $150. That leaves $150 for purposes of that second bond purchase.

The two bonds together will give you $45.00 interest on June 1st. Not bad, eh? I had set my heart on $2000 invested + $500 in the bank. I believe we'll get there. We shall have your last cheque + a few trifles to go on for the holidays. After the holidays we'll go east. (+ $500 in the bank).

Dined with Alexander yesterday: he said, 'To find anything to compare with "Adolescence,"[2] I've got to go back to the *great Shakespearean tragedies*.' He added, 'You don't know what you've got there' – (don't I) – 'but that's an immortal book. What's Galsworthy? I can't reread him. I read "Adolescence" 3 times in succession.' Carrier offers *any* sum down that I care to ask ($8000 he mentioned orally) and any contract I care to propose. But I have withdrawn. I am going to write him today or tomorrow.

Well, this will be a rush day for me. I better get busy. So bye-bye

P.

In any case, if you don't hear from Riddell within the week, deposit the cheques before March 1st, so they'll draw interest.

Am sending underwear

1 See the preceding letter, note 1.

2 Which Alexander had read for Macmillan, the publishers of the novel in Canada (see letter of February 1, 1929, note 3); it was published under the title *The Yoke of Life*. The US edition was handled by Richard Smith of New York. The Phelps letters indicate that other tentative titles had been 'The Gate of Life' and 'The Gateway of Life.'

TO CATHERINE GROVE

Toronto, Ont.
February 18, 1929 III

I have just phoned Eayrs refusing point-blank to sign the contract which he was trying to slip over on me. He wanted to bind me hand and foot. In his defence, he says he doesn't want me to go to Carrier. I said, you want to make sure that I cannot even take advantage of the fact that other publishers are bidding for my work. He says, look here, we put you on the map ... Hold on, I said, I put you on the map just as much. We are dealing as equal contracting parties. You made money on *O*[*ur*] *D*[*aily*] *B*[*read*], more than I did. I owe you *no* loyalty ... etc. etc. I'll offer you my future work; but I won't sign even to that; and I'll make my terms. If I can get better terms elsewhere, that's where I'll go. If I deprive myself of that possibility, I make myself your slave. And just get *this*: I will not sign this contract and I withdraw *It Needs to be Said* unless you give me a contract that embodies common decency.

At that we hung up; and there it stands.

More later when I know myself.[1]

Eayrs phoned up, saying 'Don't worry about that contract, I am going to have it redrafted for you.' And there, for the moment, once more, it stands. It's 2 p.m. now. At 4 p.m. I am expected at that reception.

Tomorrow I'll have a hard day – 3 addresses in 3 cities. That means, right after speaking I'll have to take a car to another place. But next week I'll get *through*!!! Then home, I hope. So long. Mail this tonight or tomorrow morning.

Tues[day] 19th
enroute Toronto–Barrie

Eayrs was distinctly cool at the reception – he acted like a dog caught lapping up the cream. Quite amusing – Blizzard blowing today. Looks strange after the spring weather we've been having. Dep[artmen]t of Ed[ucation] is arranging a schoolmen's meeting for Feb[ruary] 27, I to speak on Assimilation.

Alexander was marvellous yesterday. I've never seen him so full of life, spirit, and fire. Quite amazing. He analysed Galsworthy – much as I would do, only much better and more incisively. His thesis was that there is no greatness in Engl[an]d now. Then he turned around, to me, saying, I didn't know it; few others knew it; but *my* work linked up straight with the great tragedies: especially 'Adolescence.' It was quite embarrassing. 80 people there, Deacon among them. It was amazing. A hush fell. He spoke like the old Hebrew prophets. Not that my head swells. It couldn't. It has swollen long ago to its fullest capacity: before anyone else ever praised my work. I also deprecate what he said: he exaggerates my importance to himself: but he sees that there is something in my work which is missing in that of all others.[2] I go down to fundamental things. Well, we'll see if we live.

Bye-bye
P.

This is the day which I rather dreaded – Barrie, Orillia, Midland. But as the days come, they take care of themselves. Was offered a farm of 3 acres, with 2 brooks uniting behind the 8-roomed house, near Port Hope, for $3000. Am much tempted.

P.

Alexander also, by the way, spoke of Allison[3] with supreme contempt. Of all westerners he acknowledges *only* Phelps.

1 Eayrs eventually gave in; see letters III and IV of February 21, 1929.

2 Cf. the preceding letter, note 2. Alexander's comments are comparable to Carleton Stanley's staunch conviction of the greatness of *Our Daily Bread* as tragedy.

3 William Talbot Allison (1874–1941) was born in Ontario and educated at Victoria College, University of Toronto, as well as at Yale. He was ordained as a Presbyterian minister, but after holding some charges in the USA, he returned to Canada in 1910 to be professor of English at Wesley College (later United College), Winnipeg, and from 1920 until his death was professor of English in the University of Manitoba. He published a volume of his poems, *The Amber Army* (1909), edited Milton's *The Tenure of Kings and Magistrates*, and was a frequent reviewer of books for the Winnipeg *Tribune*.

TO CATHERINE GROVE

Orillia, Ont.
February 20, 1929

My dear,

The end is drawing close. Thank the Lord. Get back to Toronto tomorrow and shall have to go out again on Saturday – so I may not get any mail unless you have sent early. This is now $425. As far as I can see, I have 6 more addresses. At any rate, in a little over a week I'll be striking for home. Am being billeted around here, so find very little time for writing. On Feb[ruary] 27 I speak at Toronto to the 'educationists,' auspices of Dep[artmen]t of Ed[ucation] – *free*, of course. Nobody here ever dreams of the possibility of *buying* books: they borrow them at the circulating libraries, etc. It's abominable. If every person that has read my books had had to buy them we'd be rich.

Back at Toronto on Wednesday and Thursday. Unless I go on once more to Ottawa which is still uncertain I'll hit for home next Thur[sday] and shall get to Winnipeg on Sat[urday] morning about 10 o'clock. But there won't be any chance of my getting home before Monday – no train connecting and leaving W[inni]peg late enough for me to catch it. May, however, go on to Brandon Sat[urday] night. What a shame – I almost wish that I'll be delayed here in the east till Fri[day] or Sat[urday] – so as not to sit around so close to home and just kill time. Well, they are waiting for me.

So bye-bye
P.

TO CATHERINE GROVE

Georgian Hotel,
Midland, Ont.
February 20, 1929 II

Just had a wire from Spry. One or two more clubs ask me to repeat. I must accept; for each one means $25; and we need the shekels. It's only $450 so far. But by Saturday night it's going to be $525 – in exactly a month. After that I shall have 3 more lectures as far as I can see + the Empire Club and Schoolmen's Club, Toronto.

It goes without saying that they get me on the wing all the time. Here Y.M.C.A. tonight. You can't get away from it. They are waiting for me *now*. Let them wait. Since Guelph came in, I shall have only a few hours at Toronto this week – and those only if I leave tomorrow morning at 7 instead of 2:35 p.m. as I had planned – so as to have a forenoon to myself without a train-ride. It's rather trying. However ... I'll go to be bed early tonight. This is all I can write. No more time. So bye-bye. Anyway, the end is in sight.

P.

TO CATHERINE GROVE, CANADIAN PACIFIC TELEGRAM

Toronto, Ont.
February 21st, 1929

Mrs. F.P. Grove,
Rapid City, Man.

Am mailing Carriers cheque home week of third.[1]
Phil

1 See following letter.

TO CATHERINE GROVE

Westminster Hotel,
Toronto, Ont.
February 21, 1929 II

My dear,

Just to forward the endorsed cheque. Am in a great hurry – the usual whirl. Carrier had written me that the cheque had gone forward; but it had not.[1]

So the money for the new bond is there.
Bye-bye. Kiss
P.

More tonight.

1 This would be Grove's fee of $295 for translating into English Gustav Amann's *The Legacy of Sun Yatsen: A History of the Chinese Revolution*, published by Carrier in 1929. See also the beginning of the letter of February 18, 1929 II.

TO CATHERINE GROVE

Westminster Hotel,
Toronto, Ont.
February 21, 1929 III

Well, Miss Booth[1] of the Macmillans just sent over, at my request, your 2 letters of Sunday and Monday, 17th and 18th. I see from them that there's at least nothing wrong at home. My itinerary is constantly changing. I don't know from one day to the next where I'll be. I thought I'd get through with Chatham on Feb[ruary] 26. They wired me yesterday that they wish to change to Feb[ruary] 27. But that day and the next I'm tied up here, at Toronto. So I can't do it. Told them that I'd be willing to come any one of the first 3 days of the week beginning Mar[ch] 3, provided they arrange with Spry, so there won't be any collision if I speak again at Ottawa: there they want me, but the date seems to be hard to arrange. Guelph which was not on my itinerary wired to get a date. I hoped I'd be free tomorrow – a day of rest, after Barrie, Orillia, Midland in one day. But I'll run down there and speak to them. It's another $25; i.e. another week of freedom for you. [bottom of the page is torn off]

Eayrs for 3:30. I'll see, then, whether we can come to terms or not. It *may* mean a break; but I shall *not* sign a contract like the one he offered. Rather break. Carrier offers once more *any contract* I care to propose for 'Adolescence.'[2] But, of course, I'd rather stay with Macmillans. I rather think we'll come to terms. I've got Eayrs, in a way. He has printed *It Needs to Be Said*, has even sold it; and he has no contract – on that book I could demand 25%; and he'd have to pay it. But, of course, I won't hold him upon *that*. I want my freedom: I want a *good* contract for 'Adolescence' if he wants it. I think I shall try to get 'Adolescence' out in England before it appears here. However, we'll see about that.

Yes, I do more travelling, more jumping about per lecture than I have ever done. But, thank the Lord, I've done my last but one trip by car. Winter travelling by car is even in Ontario not what it is cracked up to be. In one case I told the driver I'd pay him $1 more than agreed upon if he'd go 10 miles per h[ou]r less fast. He did. I also think I'm through with the terrific branch lines now. Guelph, Brantford, Galt, Chatham, Toronto are all that are left in Ontario, as far as I can see. This morning I came down from Georgian Bay; and for hours I expected every minute that we'd jump the track. There are no roadbeds like that in Manitoba, though the Palmer line in Sask[atchewan], and the Peace River Lines are no better. [bottom of the page is torn off]

1 The present Mrs George M. McKanday (Ellen Elliott of Grove's letters in the forties). She reverted to her maiden name, Ellen Elliott, after the break-up of a marriage which took place in 1927.

She was born in 1900 in Eastleigh, England, and educated in that country. She came to Canada in 1920, and joined The Macmillan Company, serving successively as assistant to the President's secretary, on the staff of the company's library, and, from 1925 to 1937, as secretary to the then President, Hugh S. Eayrs. She was appointed Secretary to the Company in 1937, and a Director in 1942. She retired in 1947. In 1960, she married her business partner and former colleague at Macmillan, George M. McKanday. Mrs McKanday adds: 'We ... are now enjoying our retirement surrounded by the books that have enriched our lives.'

2 *The Yoke of Life*, which Macmillan in Toronto and Richard Smith in New York published in the following year. For the results of Grove's negotiations with Eayrs, see the following letter.

TO CATHERINE GROVE

Westminster Hotel,
Toronto, Ont.
February 21, 1929 IV

This is the third[1] time I write you today; and I shouldn't write again if it were not for the fact that you may worry over the negotiations with Eayrs. Well, the battle is fought and *won*.

It was quite a battle, though. We were sailing close to a break for an hour or so. I repeated and repeated, 'You want me to tie myself down so that I cannot take advantage of the fact that others are bidding for me. You have done nothing for me. At a time when I needed encouragement, you *discouraged* me by steadily declining 4 books. When I came into the lime-light, you accepted a novel which *I* was selling by my lecture-tour and which had behind it the cumulative weight of 4 previous books.'

Then he broke. At last he said, 'Dictate to me what you want.' So I did. *Canadian* Rights *only*: no option on future work. *15%* from the start. 100 free copies (Next book it will be 15% for the 1st 3000; 20% thereafter.) All right, he said. And at 5 o'clock the thing was settled – after a battle of 1½ h[ou]rs.

This darn pen is running dry. I'll go on with pencil.

I enclose a couple of jokes. Just got the *parcel*.

Saw a #37 on Eayrs' mantle-piece and appropriated it. But have no #32 yet.[2]

I have just arranged to leave for home on March *2*; so I'll get there Tues[day] or Wed[nesday], 5th or 6th.

I think this is definite and final; but cannot swear to it. At any rate, I'll get home, all going well, during that week. Have to write to Spry. So

Bye bye
P.

1 Excluding the telegram
2 Cigarette cards, presumably

TO CATHERINE GROVE

Westminster Hotel,
Toronto, Ont.
February 22, 1929

I blew myself to a show last night. The Colbourne Shaw players are here, and, having dodged all engagements, I went to see *Candida*. Cost me $5, including taxi. I wish you'd been with me. It would have cost 8.

Well, I really wrote you all the news last night. About my negotiations with Eayrs, etc.

I'm going to pack up, have lunch with the Curator of the Ontario Provincial Museum,[1] and then leave for Guelph where I am going to speak on Assimilation – a repeat engagement.

The Dominion Chautauqua approached me last night, offering 80 engagements at $50 each, all expenses paid. I was in a hurry and asked the man to repeat his offer in writing: I'd consider it then. So it seems after all that there will be no lack of opportunity of earning some money. Most C[anadian] C[lub]s on the eastern circuit will ask for me again, too, I believe. And though I shall not go out again leaving you alone for months at a stretch, I cannot but come to the conclusion that, what with Ottawa and Macmillans and the C[anadian] C[lub]s, and the Chautauqua – if the worst comes to the worst, we'll always be able to scrape a living together.

I have also agreed to let Macmillans handle *Over Prairie Trails* and *The T[urn] of the Y[ear]*[2] – without royalty till cost is covered; after that 15% – which, on the total stock, will give me ca. $200 royalties, as compared to $240 if I gave them no free sales. In other words, the freedom from McCl[elland] & St[ewart] costs me about $40. Not bad, it seems. The present stock being exhausted, the 2 books are to go into 2 thin-paper pocket editions at $1.00 each.

Having settled all that in one day, seems to be not too bad a day's work – even though I had no speaking engagement.

Ottawa is still uncertain; for I will not consent to waiting a week or so for their convenience. I wired that Mar[ch] 1 or 2 would be the ultimate date. I don't think I'll go back to Montreal. Well, that's where things rest for the moment. If I don't go to Ottawa I may not get any #32 for you.

So long, old girl. It'll soon be over now.

Bye-bye

P.

1 Charles Trick Currelly was curator of the Royal Ontario Museum from 1907 to 1946. Born in Exeter, Ontario, in 1876, and educated at the University of Toronto, he proceeded to train as an archeologist in the field – with Sir Flinders Petrie in Egypt, and with the British School of Archeology in Athens and Crete – and made several notable Egyptological discoveries. He was also for many years professor of archeology in Toronto. He died in 1957.

A letter from Currelly to Grove, dated August 12, 1929, is preserved in the University of Manitoba Grove Collection. He offers to lend Grove his summer cottage: see the next letter.

2 Macmillan reissued the two books in 1929. *The Turn of the Year* has not been reissued since; the New Canadian Library (McClelland & Stewart) edition of *Over Prairie Trails* appeared in 1957.

TO CATHERINE GROVE

New Wellington Hotel
Guelph, Ont.
February 23, 1929

Today the last rush trip. 2 cities to speak in: Brantford and Galt. Tomorrow, Sunday, transfer to London. Gave my assimilation address here last night: result, invitation to address the college.[1] But I engineered it so that, if I accept, I must make a special trip. For I want a fee. If they sponge on me I'm mad afterwards: I've been mad a good many times on this tour. At any rate, tomorrow begins the *last* week; and this is the last but one week-end from home. I begin to feel, too, that it's time to get home.

When I get back to Toronto, next Wed[nesday], I'll find word about that dress, I suppose. I'm worried about it because I liked it and hope it fits.

There'll be a stag party at Eayrs' on Feb[ruary] 28, at night. Fairley,[2] Alexander, and a few others to be there. Yesterday I had dinner with Currelly,[3] the curator of the Royal Ontario Museum. He thinks we can build at Port Hope for about 3000 – to add to the cost as the time goes by. Well, we'll see. He offered us a cottage, 2 rooms and kitchen, for a month or so in summer, we'll see. He, Wrong,[4] and a few other U[niversity] men have their summer homes there and are anxious to secure more people of an intellectual cast there.

Well, bye-bye, old girl. *Auf Wiedersehen.*
P.

1 The Ontario Agricultural College, now part of the University of Guelph

2 Barker Fairley, at that time Professor of German at University College, University of Toronto; see letter of March 26, 1928 II, note 2.

3 See preceding letter, note 1.

4 George MacKinnon Wrong (1860–1948), was born in what was then Canada West (now Ontario), and educated in Toronto, Oxford, and Berlin. Ordained to the Anglican ministry in 1883, he taught history and apologetics at Wycliffe College, University of Toronto, and became head of the history department in that University in 1894, retiring in 1927. He was elected a Fellow of the Royal Society of Canada in 1908. In 1897, he founded the *Review of Historical Publications relating to Canada*, which was succeeded in 1920 by the *Canadian Historical Review*, which he also edited. He was editorial secretary of the Champlain Society from its inception in 1905 till 1922; and he also edited, jointly with Langton, the 32-volume series Chronicles of Canada. He published numerous monographs and historical studies and was largely responsible for establishing the academic study of Canadian history.

TO CATHERINE GROVE

Hotel London,
London, Ont.
February 25, 1929

My dear, I was billeted yesterday at Galt and could not find a minute to write in. When I got here, there was one thing after the other. No mail would have gone out anyway. However, this is early in the morning; and, as far as I can see, this is the last week. I hope nothing will prolong the agony beyond it. I'm sick and tired of it. Here, they have made great preparations. 'Mr. Grove,' the pres[ident] is reported to have said, 'is a big drawing card. Let us use him to increase our membership.' I am going to give them the Nationhood address in the form in which I intend giving it to the Empire Club.

Tomorrow Chatham. Wed[nesday] and Thur[sday] Toronto. After that Guelph or Ottawa or both.

I am sending parcel today – the last one.

Bye-bye, old girl. There's nothing else to write about.

I hope you are all right. I wonder whether the dress fits.

Kiss
P.

TO CATHERINE GROVE

Hotel London,
London, Ont.
February 25, 1929

Your wire reached me today, apparently relayed from Toronto. What a dirty shame! I hope that old coat will be back at Simpson's when I get there day after tomorrow. I won't see them till Thursday, for I get to Toronto on Wed[nesday] 4:10, and the train is usually late. At 6 I shall have to speak. If I could swing thunderbolts, I'd annihilate that store from here, even though I'd lose $35 by it.

Here, there is an enormous to-do about my visit. Banquet in my honour at noon. Had to speak, of course, and set them by the ears. Great publicity for tonight's meeting. Expectancy is keyed up. I am a 'drawing card.' Well, it's time to dress. Car will call for me in an hour.

I'm getting so by this time, again, that it's hard to sleep. But the end is in sight. Hurrah!

It's amazing what a man will do for a few pennies.

Well, I'd worried and worried about that dress. If I can't get *it*, then I'll just take a refund + cost of wire, etc. Bye. Kiss.

P.

TO CATHERINE GROVE

Hotel London,
London, Ont.
February 26, 1929

Pouring rain, my dear, streets look like skating rinks. A veritable terror. Last night, on way home from reception, the car took about 1 1/2 h[ou]rs to cover 10 minutes walk. But I could not walk. The man who left the house in front of me fell on the step and broke his ankle. Rather a terrible closing to what *they* said was a wonderful evening. I myself ... well, I was the performer. Quite a success – quite a success.

In an hour and a half I'm off for Chatham where I was to speak twice. But I have cancelled the second meeting, so as to have time at Toronto to attend to that dress business. Speak on Friday at Ottawa. *Men's* Club. It will be a big thing: hope I'll get it over.

Well, that's that. As far as I can see, I'll leave Ottawa for Winnipeg on Saturday. That would bring me home on Tuesday next week – a week from today. Thank the Lord.

Bye-bye. Kiss
P.

TO CATHERINE GROVE, CANADIAN PACIFIC TELEGRAM

Toronto, Ont.
February 27, 1929
12:06 pm

Mrs. F.P. Grove
Rapid City

Adjusted Simpson purchase goes forward today stop start for west Wednesday March sixth.

Phil

TO CATHERINE GROVE

Westminster Hotel,
Toronto, Ont.
February 27, 1929 II

Well, back at Toronto, my dear. First had a long session at Simpson's. They were very apologetic. Of course, such things will happen. It's only too bad that now you can't fit. In a way I don't regret it. For meanwhile the new spring models had come in; and I don't know but that what I picked is even prettier: though it costs more. Since I have an opportunity of making an unexpected $50 by addressing the Chamber of Commerce, Oshawa, next Wed[nesday] or so, I have incidentally bought a second dress which I liked very, very much. I couldn't resist. That will make up for your disappointment. I shall wire you next Tuesday where I shall be that day; and you wire back whether things fit – just for my satisfaction.

Now the plan is that I start from here, Toronto, next Wed[nesday] 9 p.m. If that comes off correctly, I'll be home on Sat[urday] Mar[ch] 9. If not, I'll start on Mar[ch] 7, Thursday. In that case I'll reach Brandon Sunday morning; and you could meet me there as you suggest. If so, you go to P[rince] Edward Hotel, room with bath for 2 and say you expect your husband on the night train from Winnipeg – that train gets in at 2:15 at night; but the sleeper remains at Brandon; and if I sleep at all, I may not get up till 6 or 7 or 8. So don't wait up for me. But I'll be over for breakfast at the hotel. The train comes in right behind the hotel, you know. Yes, in that case you get Young[1] to substitute for the morning period. But I still hope I'll make it by Wednesday night. It will cost less.

I shall speak here tonight and tomorrow noon; at Ottawa on Fri[day] and on Sat[urday]. Mon[day] Tues[day] shall be back in the peninsula of Ontario – Chatham, Stratford, Brantford. An enormous amount of jumping back and forth. But I am trying to make every penny I can, fagged as I feel.

Well, bye-bye.
Yes, all that about the bond is OK.
Apparently I missed one or more of your letters.
Kiss
P.

Enclose some jokes. I am beginning to be used for advertising.

1 Cannot be identified. None of my Rapid City informants recalled a person of this name.

TO CATHERINE GROVE

Westminster Hotel,
Toronto, Ont.
February 27, 1929 III

Afternoon – Sent you a wire at noon and a letter explaining. Am lying in bed and resting up for the night's meeting: Schoolmen's Club – auspices Dep[artmen]t of Ed[ucation].

Well, the fact that you get 2 dresses should make up for the disappointment over the first. The coat had not yet arrived, nor your letter: they were very decent about it. The mistake was made in the shipping room. [rest of the page is cut off] for *Canadian Nation* article and editorship;[1] payment for an article I intend to give to *Maclean's*,[2] and so on. Even without a job, I think, I could look on.

I have just read the new contracts, re *It Needs to Be Said, Over Prairie Trails*, and *The Turn of the Year*. They are entirely and almost marvellously satisfactory. Eayrs is learning. The battle had to be fought. So I've done it. Shall sign them tomorrow.

The reception committee of the Empire Club has notified me that they will fetch me here tomorrow at 12:20 and take me in state to the ball-room of the King Edward. I'm very curious as to the fee. Re the C[anadian] C[lub] success, people at Ottawa are sitting up: I spoke at Brantford on Monday; yesterday at Chatham: both places wired to Ottawa, asking whether a second meeting could not be arranged before I go west again.

Well, that's all, I suppose. Bye-bye.

P.

[bottom of the page is cut off]

1 See letters of February 11, 1929 II, note 1, and February 16, 1929, note 4.

2 Probably 'Assimilation,' which appeared in *Maclean's Magazine* on September 1, 1929 (XLII, 7).

TO CATHERINE GROVE

Westminster Hotel,
Toronto, Ont.
February 28, 1929
11:45 a.m.

The last day of the month. Within a week I expect to be on the run home. Spoke last night on Assimilation. The usual thing. After that, Principal Grant[1] of Upper Canada College invited me to the house to meet Mrs. Grant. A charming woman, anxious to meet you. She showed me a review of *O*[*ur*] *D*[*aily*] *B*[*read*] in the *Manchester Guardian*,[2] perhaps the second paper in importance in England. Very laudatory. Though the last sentence reads, 'The book misses by a narrow margin being a really great tragedy.' I am inclined to agree.

Within an hour and 1/2 the Empire Club meeting, enormously advertised: largest ball-room in the King Edward Hotel. Tomorrow Ottawa. Tonight big dinner (stag) in my honour. Things are coming. A rather ironical Englishman last night thought it remarkable that a self-styled 'foreigner' should have the command of English and the delivery I had. 'If,' he said, 'all modern orators this side and the other of the Atlantic were joined in a contest, he had no doubt that any audience they cared to assemble would award the palm to me.' Such things to my face I regard as an impertinence and I showed it by the insolent smile with which I bowed, without saying anything.

Just have dropped in at Simpson's, and they assured me that the shipment had gone forward.

Well, old girl, I must dress. So bye-bye

P.

1 William Lawson Grant (1872–1935); see letter of April 2, 1928 II, note 1.

2 In the *Manchester Guardian* of February 8, 1929 (by 'H.B.,' p 7) – an extract is reprinted in my *Frederick Philip Grove* (Critical Views on Canadian Writers, 1970) 139. The review calls the novel 'a book of managed bigness, of many threads held well in hand' and concludes that the characters are 'an improbably unfortunate lot, reducing by that weakness the book's noble ending to something a degree below tragedy.'

TO CATHERINE GROVE

Chateau Laurier,
Ottawa, Ont.
March 1, 1929[1]

My dear,

Back at Ottawa to speak [to the] men at noon. For once I slept [on the] train and don't feel too tired. But there was nobody to meet me, and no room reserved; that made me mad.

The Empire Club is truly Hughie:[2] all talk, no substance. They sent me a cheque for $35.00; but my expenses, not counting personal expenses involved in a ten-day's stay – merely railway, hotel, and taxis – were $31.97 – so that I spoke for the magnificent fee of $3.03. I'm going to stick it to Eayrs. He had a dinner party for me last night; and, I being his guest, I did not feel that I wanted to talk about it. I'll drop him a line about that.

Here Miller would be only too glad to have me; at Montreal I was the guest of Carrier & Co.; at Toronto, I had to pay everything myself. Quite significant. Tomorrow I'll be back there but I don't think I'll have time for anything.

Well, today being Friday, tomorrow and day after will be the last week-end I suppose and hope.

I can't write much just now; must memorise on my talk. Till later, then. I arrived less than an hour ago.

I have just phoned up the Ass[ociation] office; my itinerary is arranged till Tuesday. I shall speak at Guelph tomorrow afternoon. So I must jump all the way back into the peninsula overnight.

But the important point is, I can now definitely say that I shall be on my [way] home by *Wednesday night*.

That means I shall be at Brandon on Saturday morning, a

week from tomorrow. If, therefore, you have business at Brandon, meet me there, taking Fri[day] 3 p.m. train and engaging a room in the Prince Edward, stating that your husband will join you. If I don't find you there, I shall run up to R[apid] C[ity] on the 8 a.m. [train].

Now please, to save wiring *one* way, wire on *Tuesday* to me, care Bodega Tavern, *Brantford*, Ontario, stating whether the dresses have arrived and whether they fit. I shall be at Toronto on Wed[nesday] afternoon and, therefore, be able to pick something else, larger or smaller, as you direct in your wire, to be exchanged when you return one or both dresses: trifling adjustments, I suppose, Mrs. What's-her-name could make?

Well, I'm expecting Miller. So I'll close for this time. May write again later in the day.

Bye-bye
P.

1 A portion from the top right hand corner is cut off. The date is in Mrs Grove's handwriting.

2 Hugh S. Eayrs. He was at that time President of the Empire Club.

TO CATHERINE GROVE

Chateau Laurier,
Ottawa, Ont.
March 1, 1929 II

My dear,

I sent you a letter this morning with directions to wire me on *Tues*[day] to Brantford, Ontario. Meanwhile there has been a change again. Damn these changes!

Wire instead, on Tues[day] to me, care of

Mrs. D.S. Fuller,[1]
233 Douglas St.
Stratford, Ont.
STRATFORD

In a great hurry, as usual.

Noon speech here before the men[,] again quite a success – quite a success.

Bye bye
P.

1 Wife of David Stanley Fuller (1894–1949), who was Principal of the Stratford Collegiate Institute from 1940 until his death. A graduate of the University of Toronto (BA 1917; MA 1918), he had, before becoming Principal, served the Institute as mathematics master for twenty years.

TO CATHERINE GROVE

New Wellington Hotel,
Guelph, Ont.
March 2, 1929

My dear,

Miller and Carrier are sueing each other through me.[1] Bad news, that. That is, Miller, though quite friendly, is sueing me to protect him in Canada; and I shall have to sue Carrier.

That will probably settle Carrier's friendship.

However, nothing to worry over.

This will probably be one of my last notes. Just to show where I am today. What with travelling back and forth, there is very little time for writing. So just this.

Bye-bye
P.

1 Carrier had the US rights to *A Search for America* and was not supposed to distribute his edition in Canada, which was exclusively Miller's (ie, Graphic's) territory. Miller, in the event, did not proceed with his threat of legal action, and he and Carrier came to an out-of-court understanding. For Grove's role in Carrier's unauthorised sales in Canada, see letters of January 29 and 30, 1929. Further light on this affair is shed by the Louis Carrier letters to Grove of April 15 and May 1, 1929, and the Miller letter to Grove of March 16, 1929 (these letters are preserved in the University of Manitoba Grove Collection). It appears, for example, that worry over the affair produced a temporary nervous breakdown in Grove. It further appears that, as Carrier had sold copies of his edition in Canada, so Miller had sold copies of his in the USA.

TO CATHERINE GROVE

Westminster,
Toronto, Ont.
March 4, 1929[1]

Well, my dear,

This is my last full day at Toronto. On Wednesday I shall get in about noon, attend a luncheon of the Toronto Writers' Club in my honour, and board the 9 o'clock night train for Winnipeg.

Yesterday, I lunched with Merrill Denison[2] and his wife. In the evening I went to a party given in my honour by Barker Fairley[3] – and felt bored to death. Most people – women as well as men – drank themselves into a coma. Today, at noon, the leading bookseller, Tyrrell,[4] a very fine man, gave a luncheon in my honour.

In the morning, today, I went to Simpson's; the coat had arrived; and everything seemed to be all right, provided those dresses fit, as I *do* hope they will, for I liked them much. I had to buy myself 2 pairs of socks the last moment: first money I've spent on myself during the tour.

I hope I'll get a wire from you tomorrow at Stratford, telling me about the dresses. If I don't, I'll wire you in the evening. Saw Eayrs for a moment this morning. 'The busy executive.'

Another well-known photographer has had a shot at me.

Tonight I shall pack up – one suitcase definitely – the other I'll take to Stratford. I'm full of material for writing. Fuller than I believe I ever was. Well, I must find time for it.

I'm reading another book by Mrs Mary Quaile Innis[5] – piffle, tripe, trash.

Everybody here thinks I am leaving today for Stratford. So I shall have the whole evening for myself. I intend to dawdle along into bed as soon as I've had my supper. I wish you were here. We could afford for you to give up teaching at Easter, I think. But perhaps it is wise to finish the year. Then a few months at home, and then East – unless some job demands my presence before that time.

I am working myself up to a total condemnation of Galsworthy – strange how that result comes about. But it does.

Had a hair cut today. The callouses of my feet hurt, so I want to operate. Shall leave this letter; perhaps I'll add a word or two later.

IT IS MY LAST LETTER ON THIS TOUR. AFTER THIS, IF NEED BE, WIRES.

Went to sleep when I'd done that. Time for supper now. I'll take this down and mail it.

No use my writing tomorrow. It would have to come back here on the same train with me. I doubt whether you'll get *this* before you leave if you meet me at Brandon.

Bye-bye and so long.
Au revoir (French)
A reviderci (Italian)
Auf Wiedersehen [German]
P.

1 Date inferred from the context and postmark, although in the original letter the year is clearly shown as 1928

2 The Canadian dramatist; see letter of April 2, 1928 II, note 3.

3 Professor of German, University College, Toronto; see letter of March 26, 1928 II, note 2.

4 Born in England in 1866, William Tyrrell came to Canada as a small boy with his parents. After attending public schools in St Catharines, Ontario, he started work as a junior clerk with Hart & Company, booksellers of Toronto. Later he bought out the firm, and the name was changed to William Tyrrell & Company. Under his ownership, it became one of the foremost enterprises of its kind in Canada. William Tyrrell was for a period the president of

the Booksellers' Association of Canada. He was also a member of a number of literary clubs, including the Empire Club and the Arts and Letters Club of Toronto.
5 'Book' is probably an error since Mrs Innis's first book did not appear until much later. Grove's allusion is probably to one of her short stories; she was a regular contributor to a number of Canadian magazines, including the *Canadian Forum*, to which Grove had contributed a few poems. Mrs Innis, whose middle name is spelled Quayle, was born in 1899 and died in 1972. I find Grove's hostility towards her totally inexplicable; one would have expected him to admire the realistic short stories which she was publishing at this time.

TO RAYMOND KNISTER

Rapid City, Man.,
March 21, 1929

My dear Mr. Knister,

I enclose a note from Mr. Dent.[1]

I should like to get one or two short extracts, of about 2500 words each, of some striking *war* scene from that book. I remember a passage where two wounded men emerge from a barrage, under the eyes of an onlooking squad – the men of that squad being unable to bring help, etc.

I am almost certain we shall print at least one of these passages in the *Canadian Nation*.[2] I have offered Mr. Dent $35 for it. If you would kindly copy out, or have copied out, some suitable extract or if you could let me have the Ms. for a day or two (which, including transit, could mean a week) I should be very glad indeed. It goes without saying that we shall be willing to pay any reasonable typist's fee.

Don't forget me, either, with regard to short fiction of your own. Preferred length is 2500 words; but we shall not insist on that. I discussed fees with Mr. Spry when at Ottawa on Mar[ch] 1st; and 1½ cent a word is practically agreed upon – no less, at any rate.

Yours sincerely
F.P. Grove

P.S. – As usual after a tour, I am pretty sick.

1 Walter Redvers Dent, born in Ontario in 1900, a Vancouver free-lance journalist and financial editor, wrote *Show Me Death!*, a novel about Canadian youth and the First World War. It was published in 1930 by Macmillan. How Grove came to know of the manuscript, or how it found its way into Knister's hands is not clear. It seems probable that they had both been asked to appraise the novel by its publisher.
2 See letter of February 11, 1929 II, note 1. Extracts from Dent's book were not printed, but Knister's 'The Fate of Mrs Lucier' appeared in the *Canadian Nation* of May-June 1929 (II, 2 pp 8–10).

TO WATSON KIRKCONNELL

Rapid City, Man.,
March 24, 1929

My dear Kirk,

Thanks for your letter of day before.

The translation scheme[1] is ambitious indeed; but – more power to your elbow. Splendid if it can be carried through. Yet – perhaps it is a good thing for you if you cannot contract for the whole series. It's a bit like selling yourself into slavery, is it not? Suppose the enthusiasm flags ... But to start a series like that is in itself *magnum opus*. It is a great idea.

As for the order – I have no very definite criticism to offer, I ponder over your plan. Is there a *plan*? Geographic or otherwise? First minors – then majors? Suppose a person could get hold of statistics covering the racial contingents of the west. And you worked in the order of the numerical importance of these contingents? Or is the order perhaps dependent on opportunistic considerations? Perhaps, if the plan is ultimately carried through, the order is more or less irrelevant? I don't know. I am too much taken by surprise.

If Carrier takes the first vol[ume], state *the scope of the thing*: a mere statement like that – the mere fact that a westerner projects an idea covering two decades of work – would be valuable in this time of futile hurry. *Ébahissez le bourgeois*[2] – meaning by *le bourgeois* 'don'-dom in Canada. Those people make me tired.

F[or] i[nstance], I sent out, on Mar[ch] 12, 29 copies of my booklet.[3] Apart from your letter, not a response! As if they cowered under a blow. Amusing, eh? Knock them by proclaiming an intention, and then *do it*. Hurrah! ...

As for myself, I had the usual collapse on reaching home – unfortunately with rather serious results. My hearing is pretty well gone. I was out for the first time yesterday and see people shouting at me; but I hear nothing. Indoors, Mrs. G. still can make me hear, as if separated from me by a flight of rooms; but the speech of others reaches me only when relayed. Another step in isolation.

I think I told you that I have withdrawn 'Adolescence.'[4] I shall try to publish it in England, no copies to be imported into Canada and the U.S.A. In the latter country, the reception of *Our Daily Bread* has disgusted me a bit too much. 'Below criticism' – too much of that: 'a degree below mediocrity,' etc. etc. Now you may like the book or not – but the workmanship is not mediocre. The more this seeps into me, the more I am inclined to pull up my stakes and go to Europe to stay.

I am going to submerge myself in work on Abe Spalding – that Twofold Law story I've been wrestling with since 1926:[5] before me, at this writing, lies a stack of 10 200-page booklets in my finest writing: filled with the last draft: #3. #1 was written decades ago. #2, 1926–27; #3 1927–28. Tomorrow I shall begin to rewrite the whole mass, remodelling it all, condensing, turning it inside out: 'The Growth of a Settlement.' It still lives in me, 'with power yet to thrill or to unnerve, And to evoke things felt or heard or seen.'[6]

Have you any original poetry – short, to fill half a page of the *Canadian Nation*? Or some particularly striking translation from the Ukrainian or some other language spoken in some 'foreign' settlement? Has A.L.P.?[7] I am trying to find something. Also, if you run across any book deserving of a 2 or 3 page discussion – with a Canadian bearing – that you – or A.L.P. – would like to 'do,' please keep me in mind.

I've been too troubled with pain to trouble much about that job of mine in connection with the magazine.[8]

Well, so long. Don't forget that trains still run into this district.

Yours
F.P.G.

1 It refers to a projected series, consisting of twenty volumes, of 'Canadian Books of European Verse to be translated by Professor Watson Kirkconnell.' Kirkconnell had envisaged the publication of one book every year, beginning with *The Canadian Book of Icelandic Verse* (1930) and ending with *The Canadian Book of Baltic Verse* (Lithuanian and Lettish) in 1949.

2 Dumfound or bamboozle the middle class

3 Presumably *It Needs to Be Said* (1929); in describing it as a 'booklet' Grove was being very modest, but we know of no other publication at this time.

4 The pre-publication title of *The Yoke of Life* (1930). Among other titles considered by Grove were 'The Gateway of Life' and 'The Gate of Life.' Nothing came of Grove's attempt to secure its publication in England; Macmillan published the book in Canada and Richard Smith of New York in the USA.

5 Which was published in 1933 as *Fruits of the Earth*; other titles considered by Grove were 'The Chronicles of Spalding District' and 'The Growth of a Settlement.' 'Twofold Law' seems the most likely reading of the phrase in the letter, although the handwriting is hard to decipher at that point. If my reading is correct, the law referred to may be that contained in Mark 8: 35 and 36, which is obviously relevant to Spalding's experience.

6 Two lines from Grove's own poem, 'From *The Dirge*,' published in the *Canadian Forum*, XII (April 1932) 257

7 Arthur L. Phelps

8 *The Canadian Nation*

TO RAYMOND KNISTER

Rapid City, Man.,
April 14, 1929

Dear Mr. Knister,

I have received the extract from Mr. Dent's book.[1] It is not exactly what I could wish; I should have preferred the story to begin about 1500 words ahead of its actual beginning, so as to end with that picture of the two wounded men coming out of the barrage. However, I suppose it is too late for that; and I shall see whether I can do anything with this.

I have often thought of our short talk at Toronto. Your letter reminds me again of certain things. It is a marvel to me how you younger people work, impatient to see results, even in that last of all possible ways, the pecuniary one. My books were written because they had to be written, with never any thought, originally, of the remote chance that they might one day be worth money. If I think of such people as Swift, or Fielding, or Flaubert – to mention only those who stood in the second rank – it seems marvellous to me that any book should bring anyone actual cash. I also think that nothing can possibly be worse for a young author than to have an immediate success of any kind. In this I go so far as to say that I should despair of my own work if it were not so consistently misreviewed.* I look at these reviewers of books and I ask myself whether anything they praise can possibly be good; and I do not want to be bought by a public which rushes at the best-sellers. It is true that, from the very day that I published my first volume, I have had the good luck of earning the applause, never broken, of those people in Canada whose applause I coveted – there are only two. One of them wrote me recently, 'I doubt if the "critics" whom I have read really give enough attention to your books to let them grip them.'[2] For instance, to say that 'we are shown the depravity of the "fallen woman" every few pages'[3] – when every appearance of Mrs. Vogel in my *Settlers* marks a new, necessary step in an inevitable tragedy, pondered over for a matter of decades, merely shows me that the critic has not taken the pains to approach the book in that spirit in which every thing must be approached which is 'done.' Not one of my books is published within years of the date when it was written: I have to live with it in order to see whether it 'will stay with me.' Many of my books will never be published.

I have never answered a review and do not intend this to be an answer; but perhaps you will pardon a man twice your age if he says that he is not impressed by any critical acumen displayed.

Which, of course, has nothing whatever to do with my personal relationship to the 'critic.'

$1.50 for the typing will be quite all right.**

Sincerely,

F.P. Grove

*Of course, I have said all I have to say with regard to that in my *It Needs To Be Said*.

**I shall communicate with Mr. Spry.

1 *Show Me Death!*; see letter of March 21, 1929, notes 1 and 2.

2 W.J. Alexander, in a letter to Grove, dated March 24, 1929

3 A reference to a review of *Settlers of the Marsh* by Knister in the *Ontario Library Review*, XIII, 3 (1928). Knister's exact sentence read, 'In some instances it is downright awkward and childish, as when every few pages we are shown the depravity of the "fallen woman" the hero has married by the fact that she plasters her face with powder.' See my *Frederick Philip Grove* (Critical Views on Canadian Writers 1970) 16.

TO RAYMOND KNISTER

Rapid City, Man.,
April 26, 1929

Dear Mr. Knister,

No, we shall pay for the typing. The extract[1] is not quite what I had been thinking of; but I have arranged for it to be used. It is, of course, very difficult to do such things at a distance, without having a Ms. to mark what you want.

As for Mr. Dent having sold a half interest in the book for $5000, it rather illustrates what I had to say about the younger generation of writers. There are remarkable things in his book; but it must at once be capitalised.

I doubt whether you interpreted quite correctly what I meant to say. Thoreau said somewhere, 'Only from the vantage-ground of a voluntary poverty can we arrive at a fair and impartial valuation of life.'[2] Or words to that effect; I am quoting from memory. With that I agree. You mention Shakespeare. Well, Shakespeare did not make money by writing but by acting and by directing a theatre. Swift was a priest. I still doubt whether the highest that has been done or that can be done is ever done for money or with an eye on success. The greatest achievements, as a matter of fact, have been arrived at by those who had worldly ambitions apart from the ambitions they pursued in art. Or by those who knew how to merge their own lives in the lives of works of art. Even truly great inventions have been made by those who today remain nameless. Let us not forget that 'Art for art's sake' is nonsense. It is very hard to explain briefly just what I mean. But I may say that I have made it a rule to make what money I need by other activities rather than by writing. He who writes for money will not find that message with which every human being is born; if every human being found it, this would be a better world to live in and art would perhaps be unnecessary. I have recently been attacked in an unfair way: Grove himself fights for money, it was said; why else autograph books in bookstores; why lecture from coast to coast? Well, exactly; I lecture because I can make a few pennies that way without selling my writing. As for the book-stores, I do autograph a few copies because I cannot withdraw myself from the urgency of the book-sellers. I have never suggested anything like that myself and never shall. I hate to do it.

Well, I don't know whether this puts things right or not. At any rate, I remain,

Sincerely,
F.P.G.

Balzac and Scott – two great geniuses who scattered their unique talents by writing for money at a feverish rate. The wonder is that some of their work does survive. Surely their example is not a good model for us epigonous mortals to be guided by.

1 From Dent's *Show Me Death!*; it was not printed in the *Canadian Nation* – see letter of March 21, 1929, notes 1 and 2.

2 In *Walden* ('Economy,' 19): 'None can be an impartial or wise observer of human life but from the vantage ground of what *we* call voluntary poverty.' Cf. *In Search of Myself* 408.

TO WATSON KIRKCONNELL

Rapid City, Man.
May 15, 1929

My dear Kirk,

You are going through the same experiences with our Canadian publishers which I went through a few years ago. One needs to have

13 Raymond Knister 1929. *Courtesy Mrs Imogen Givens*

patience. Meanwhile, the only thing to do is to go on with the work – as I have done and am still doing.

I believe Carrier is a good bet.

As for Eayrs, well...

I am plugging along – have nearly finished a fourth version of my 'Abe Spalding.'[1] One or two other books are waiting. Cape hesitates over 'Adolescence.'[2]

As for Miller, I don't know. He, personally, is all right, I believe; but *Graphic* I consider as defunct.[3] Miller, as you probably know, is 'The Ottawa Composition Company' – which will pull through, I believe.

No, I did not know about A.L.P.'s[4] going to B[ritish] C[olumbia]. He does not write.

As for my health, I have had 2 very bad spells – pains unexplained and terrible (abdomen).[5] My hearing has readjusted itself at about 1/3 normal: that is, I hear but understand very little. People about me are learning to shout. If they don't, Mrs G. explains to me what the talk was about. Birds I cannot even hear, except an occasional meadow-lark.

We are getting ready to go east in the fall – to stay. I may even decide for Europe.

Yours
F.P.G.

I often think of the youngsters[6] at Lindsay; often see them in my mind.

1 'Chronicles of Spalding District,' the pre-publication title of *Fruits of the Earth*; see the letter to the editor, *Canadian Forum*, May 1933.

2 *The Yoke of Life*

3 It began to fold up officially in May 1932. Meanwhile, Grove had joined the firm from December 1929; see letter of January 13, 1930, note 1.

4 Arthur L. Phelps, who remained the Head of the English Department at the United College, University of Manitoba, till 1945. The trip to British Columbia was made to lecture in the UBC Summer School.

5 Watson Kirkconnell wrote me (May 27, 1972) about similar pains from which Grove had suffered in the 1926–7 period, and about the treatment:

> Grove had been suffering from mysterious body pains and was brought from Rapid City to the Winnipeg General Hospital for observation. On one of my visits to him there, he told me in somewhat disgruntled fashion of the technique employed by one of the specialists – a man whose name, 46 years later, I have forgotten but who seems to have taken postgraduate medical training in Berlin or Vienna. Conversing quietly with Grove in English, he was holding his open hand on Grove's abdomen. He then spoke suddenly, and loudly, to Grove in German; and all of the abdominal muscles suddenly writhed into a quivering spasm. He had apparently suspected that Grove's pains were psychosomatic, and the patient had nothing but admiration for the demonstration that this was indeed the case. Looking back from our knowledge in 1972, however, one may surmise that the

doctor suspected that Grove was actually German and that Grove had been smitten with dismay at the insight of this man who (in Hamlet's phrase to Guildenstern) was about to 'pluck out the heart of his mystery.'

6 Kirkconnell's twin sons, James and Thomas, who were visiting their grandparents in Lindsay

TO WATSON KIRKCONNELL

Rapid City, Man.
June 12, 1929

My dear Kirk,

Congratulations.[1] We'll hope that the series will be a huge success.

As for our visit east, everything is very doubtful. The difficulty is a financial one. I have done well last year; but there seems to be an end to it. I had an offer to go lecturing in the U.S.A. I declined. If in America, I wish to stay in Canada. But I am tired of uncertainties. I am nearly 58 y[ea]rs old and want to look forward to a few y[ea]rs – if they are vouchsafed – of quiet, settled life. It seems that Canada has nothing to offer me. There was talk of a salary in connection with lectures for the Canadian Clubs – of a sinecure at Ottawa – of editorial work for a publishing firm. Of all this nothing has come. I have a few thousand dollars in the bank (don't mention the fact); and I have 2 or 3 books ready for the press. And so we are discussing the advisability of definitely leaving the country and going where I can make a living. Mrs. G. has done her share; but I won't accept that any longer.

It means that I am accepting defeat, of course. And that leaves a bitter taste. But I have, at best, another ten years to expect, to be lived through with my health impaired, my hearing such that I can't listen to the birds any longer. In these ten years I must build anew. Very well, I'll try if I've got to. We are canvassing possibilities in New Zealand, Australia, South Africa, Switzerland – and the pointer of the balance seems to be attracted by the last-named country – though it is too soon to say. I feel convinced, though, that one of the Universities, there, will have use for me – a thing which no Canadian University or college seems inclined to try.

Should we go east during the summer months – and we may, for a last attempt at finding a job for me – I'll let you know. Meanwhile thanks for the invitation.

Best regards from both of us for you and yours as well. I wish I knew of something to send to your boys.

Yours
F.P.G.

1 In view of Kirkconnell's difficulties in finding publishers for his translations – see the previous letter – this must refer to Carrier's acceptance of *The North American Book of Icelandic Verse* (1930). For Grove's recommendation of the firm to Kirkconnell, see letter of January 30, 1929.

TO WATSON KIRKCONNELL

Rapid City, Man.
August 15, 1929

My dear Kirk,

We see our way clear at last. We are selling our furniture here and shall start east by motor end of the second week of September.[1] We plan dropping in on some friends at North Bay, Ottawa, and Simcoe;[2] and, if you will still be at Lindsay during the third or fourth week of September, might possibly drop in there for a day or so. After that I have taken a cottage near Port Hope;[3] and there we shall be through October, I believe. I have a few lectures to deliver[4] and count on doing that before we proceed. From the end of October on all is darkness so far. I shall make one more attempt at securing some sort of a fixed job.[5] Will you let me know how late there might be a chance of finding you at Lindsay?

I look forward to that Icelandic volume of yours;[6] for I don't read Icelandic myself.

As for the date of our call at Lindsay, our plans are quite flexible. We can arrange matters, provided you don't go west before September 21 or 22.[7]

With our best regards for your parents, yourself, and the two boys whose wistful look has haunted me through the year,

As ever,
F.P.G.

1 See the following letter.

2 Probably the Casselmans at North Bay, any of a number of Ottawa friends, and the Powells at Simcoe

3 Presumably the cottage of C.T. Currelly

4 A letter to Grove from C.E. Auger of Victoria College, Toronto, dated June 28, 1929, invites Grove to lecture 'some time during the coming academic year' to the Toronto branch of the English Association; and a letter from Ethel Ritchie, dated July 25, 1929, invites him to lecture to the Montreal Women's Club. (These letters are preserved in the University of Manitoba Grove Collection.) There may, of course, have been other invitations to lecture.

5 There had been suggestions of jobs with Macmillan, with Graphic Publishers, and with the *Canadian Nation*, and even of a sinecure with the federal government, but no definite offer was in sight at this time.

6 *The North American Book of Icelandic Verse*, published in the following year

7 Grove missed Kirkconnell – see the following letter.

TO WATSON KIRKCONNELL

Rapid City, Man.
August 28, 1929

My dear Kirk,

Thanks for your letter. I'm sorry you won't be in the East any longer when we get there. You'll be spinning along north of Lake Superior when we'll be motoring south of it, I suppose.

Our address, for the month of October, will be Canton, Ont[ario].[1] We'll be 9 miles from Port Hope. Naturally, health and weather permitting, we'll motor up one day to Lindsay and drop in on your parents. I am sorry to hear of your mother's indisposition. Nothing serious, I hope?

Always glad to hear of the progress of the good work.

As for myself, I am not optimistic. We are having the worst of luck with our sale. Hardly anything finds a buyer in a year when there is at best 1/4 crop in the country. We have had 3 or 4 sprinkles but not a single *rain* since 1928. Everything is parched. Consequently, I shall have to store the greater part of our furniture, my books, etc., and pay storage. I have given the U[niversity][2] my scientific apparatus (Dep[artmen]t of Botany) and a large stack of books. Some 200 vol[ume]s I have sold in W[inni]peg for $38.00. Many more I am giving away. Remains 5 boxes which, so far, I mean to keep.

Freight and express rates to Ont[ario] being excessive, we are going to take a steamer trunk, 3 suitcases, club-bag, hat box, portfolio, and a huge bundle of bedding in the car. We shall, therefore, not travel *expediti*.[3] These, truly, are *impedimenta*. I wish my library consisted of 20 vol[ume]s, I'd take them, too, in the car. Still rather, I wish I could travel afoot.

I have been putting my 'Tales from the Margin'[4] into order, intending to offer them in England through Curtis Brown.[5] More of them are accumulating for a second vol[ume].

Well, with best regards for yours and your-self from both of us.

As ever
F.P.G.

1 This was a final move to the east on the Groves' part: they never returned west, although they moved around Ontario for a year or two before settling at Simcoe. Hence the sales mentioned below.

2 The University of Manitoba

3 Lightly equipped – a Roman military technical term, used of troops moving at speed, and familiar to any schoolboy educated in the older classical tradition from *Caesar's Gallic Wars*. *Impedimenta* (things that hinder travelling on foot) similarly has technical antecedents, though now, of course, naturalised into English.

4 Grove's own collection of his short stories, which remains unpublished in the University of Manitoba Grove Collection; but the same title was used for a new collection of his short stories, selected and edited by me, and published in 1971 (McGraw-Hill Ryerson).

5 Curtis Brown Limited, literary agents in London, England

C

Hoping for Better Things:

A New Start in Ontario 1929-39

'However, perhaps you are right in what you are going to say, that the sale does not measure merit; and, frankly, I had hoped for better things.'
TO PELHAM EDGAR,
JANUARY 16, 1934

TO WATSON KIRKCONNELL

Canton, Ont.
October 19, 1929

My dear Kirk,

I should have answered your letter before this but have been waiting to go into Toronto for a few days. We came back yesterday; and I can now say that Toronto offers nothing whatever. As for Eayrs, I am through with him, though I may publish another book or so through Macmillans.[1] He has broken every promise he made to me. I offered him 3 novels for $2000 cash, then for $1000. He did not take them. 'Adolescence' among them. I shall go to Ottawa next week. After that, it is probable that my conclusion that a man of letters cannot make a living in Canada will have been confirmed to the point where it will drive me to the necessary action.[2]

Just two questions. (1) I have repeatedly written to A.L.P.[3] but cannot get an answer from him to this question: has he or has he not received certain articles of furniture (desk, 3 chairs, tea wagon) which I have ordered shipped to him. Naturally I am greatly worried about it. Would you mind asking him and letting me know? (2) I enclose the leaf of a tree which people here assert to be a maple; but if my botany is not all wrong, it is a poplar (alternate vernation, laterally compressed leaf stalks, bark of stem, etc.). Do you know it from the leaf? If so, please let me know. Wishing you the best success, I remain, with best regards from both of us,

Phil

1 Macmillan published all but two of Grove's subsequent books, including *The Yoke of Life* (1930), which is referred to in these letters as 'Adolescence.' The American edition of *The Yoke of Life* was handled by Richard Smith, New York.
2 Cf. letter of August 6, 1931.
3 Arthur L. Phelps

TO RAYMOND KNISTER

Bobcaygeon, Ont.
November 15, 1929

Dear Mr. Knister,

I received your letter yesterday. Re 'Rear Road,'[1] you have probably heard by this time that the *Canadian Nation*[2] was, for the moment, voted out of existence at Quebec? We may be able to revive it in some shape or form. Meanwhile I am still holding your story. Should anything further come of the magazine, I think we might make use of it; but if you prefer to have it back, I shall send it as soon as I hear from you.

As for Cape,[3] I don't know. I have not had a single word

from him; nor have I the slightest idea whether he has sold a single copy of *Our Daily Bread*. That is the trouble with all publishing. It is very hard to collect. However, meanwhile we must carry on.

Dent,[4] in my opinion, has done in that book of his what he can do, I am sorry to say. I do not believe that he will ever write another book worth printing; though, of course, if this book of his sells, he will easily get anything printed.

What you say with regard to 'really indigenous work' is quite right. I don't care one particle about any indigenous setting. So long as the work turned out by any Canadian writer is worth its salt, it will be Canadian, no matter whether it deals with Canada or China. The trouble with us is that, so far, I cannot see anything, or perhaps I should say much, that is not imitative in some way or other.

I might say that I have recently read, with much interest, your book *White Narcissus*.[5] May I be absolutely and brutally frank? I was greatly struck with the development of the unique situation and its tragic possibilities. In fact, the first half of the book seemed to me to pave a gradual approach to something that would be enormous. Then the interest scatters. All those farming activities of the quasi-hero (quasi; for the girl is the real heroine) do not interest me; they distract my attention from the fundamental problem confronting the girl. The ending quite disappointed me; it seems to me as if a great knot[6] had been slung, and some little Alexander came to cut it with his sword (which is at best a toy). Or as if a truly great situation were disentangled by a *deus ex machina* who turns it into a joke. Surely if the parents can speak at last, why not at first? That would make the whole book avoidable. But in spite of this criticism I find so much to admire in the setting out of the tragic situation that I came to the conclusion that he who had written the first part can and probably will one day do something that will stand for good and all. Is this book a compromise? Was it first written as a short story? Is not a good deal of really extraneous matter introduced? Should not the ending be tragic? All this troubles and worries me. You may, of course, say, 'Take it or leave it.' Just as I do. But either we cannot see eye to eye in matters literary, or there is something wrong with this book which does not keep its promise. Nevertheless, if this book had been submitted to me by a publisher, for a report, I should have recommended its publication on account of the genuine promise it presents. And there it stands.

Yes, I have been doing some lecturing and some writing; but most of the time I have been looking around for a new home in Ontario; so far without much success, though I have just rented a house here for the winter. I was at Simcoe recently and looked your part of the country over. I liked the western end of Lake Erie; but failed to find any available spot.

Best regards,
F.P. Grove

1 Presumably a manuscript short story which Knister had submitted for publication in the *Canadian Nation*. It is not listed in 'Raymond Knister: A Bibliography of His Works' by Margaret Ray in *Collected Poems of Raymond Knister*, ed. Dorothy Livesay (Toronto

1949), nor found among the Knister papers in the archives of Victoria University in Toronto and Queen's University.
2 See letter of February 11, 1929 II, note 1.
3 Jonathan Cape handled the British publication of *Our Daily Bread* and Knister's *White Narcissus*, and the two books were extensively advertised and reviewed together in Britain (see, eg, Cyril Connolly's review in *New Statesman*, reprinted in my *Frederick Philip Grove* 1970) 139–40.
4 Walter R. Dent, who wrote *Show Me Death!*; see letter of March 21, 1929, note 1.
5 Published in 1929
6 ie, the Gordian knot, cut in two by Alexander the Great with his sword

TO ROY BOTTUM[1]

Locust Lodge Cottage,
Bobcaygeon, Ont.
November 21, 1929

Re pasture land, Kelly Estate.
Dear Sir,

I wish to make three separate and distinct offers re the land comprised in what I understand to be known as the Kelly Estate, limiting these offers in time by the date of December 7 a.c. Beyond that date I may or may not be open for acceptance, since I have other parcels of land in view about which I may have to decide.

1) I am willing to pay for the whole 200 acres, more or less, the sum of two thousand and six hundred (2600) dollars.

2) I am willing to pay for the easternmost thirty or forty (30 or 40) acres, exclusive of lake-front, but with the proviso that I be given a narrow strip, let me say eight feet wide, access to the lake-front, the sum of twenty dollars an acre.

3) I am willing to pay for 10 or fifteen acres, at my choice, north of Front Street, and reaching, from that street, north for forty rods, beginning at a point east about twenty rods west of the south-east corner and reaching thence west, altogether exclusive of lake-front, the sum of forty (40) dollars per acre. This, I might say, would leave all the better pasture land in the eastern portion of the estate untouched.

Hoping to hear from you at your earliest convenience and limiting this offer to the period up to and including December 7 of the current year (for I have a number of other parcels of land in view which I must decide about), I remain,

Yours truly,
F.P. Grove

1 Albert Roy Bottum (1890–1966), a hardware merchant in Bobcaygeon.
Arthur L. Phelps, E.J. Pratt, and Hugh Eayrs had cottages at Bobcaygeon, and Grove presumably meant to build one.

TO MRS M.H.W. CAMERON[1]

211–212 Sparks Chambers,
Ottawa, Ont.,
January 13, 1930

My dear Mrs. Cameron,

I had been in hopes that we could fully discuss the changed situation while Mr. Solmes[2] was here. You know yourself how difficult it is to find you undisturbed at your office. That is the reason why I made up my mind to put my side of it down in writing.

On Thursday last Mr. Solmes made certain suggestions to me with regard to a change in my position within the whole organisation – suggestions which agreed with such conclusions as I had arrived at, though I could not very well broach them myself: it would have looked as if I wished to push myself forward; and nothing was farther from my mind.

However, the fact remains, confirmed by letter after letter from such New York firms as I have written to, that Ariston[3] has nothing to sell. Personally, that makes little difference to me since I want to publish a few books rather than to sell many. But it makes a vast difference to the shareholders of Ariston, for there is no business in sight; and, consequently, I cannot see my way to charging Ariston up with $2400 a year on my account plus from $600 to $1000 of general expense (office, stenographer, etc.).

Mr. Solmes' suggestions apparently did not meet with your approval; for on Saturday morning he had entirely changed his mind.

The following is the only way which *I* can see out of the difficulty:

1) ARISTON proceeds, for the time being, to act as a publishing firm; that is, it tries to get out two or three books for next fall. Meanwhile I shall continue to prepare the way for concluding agency contracts; but for the moment we delay pressing that matter; if we have no more than one or two contracts, we can handle them only at a loss; in my opinion, a minimum of six contracts is needed to produce profits and to warrant the establishment of a sales-force. In other words, as a commission-house, Ariston will remain dormant till next fall. I have one or two small schemes in my mind which may produce a little money (canvassing schemes); but they are still in the planning stage. – For this work, I consider, Ariston cannot afford to pay more than $1200 a year.

2) CANADIAN BIOGRAPHIES.[4] It was proposed that I undertake to edit this. I am willing to do so, provided you agree to my anonymity. That is, I am willing to do the work – hack-work: but my name must not appear in connection with it. – In consideration of this, Canadian Biographies foots the second third ($1200) of my salary.

3) As for GRAPHIC, I am willing to go on reading Mss. and generally assisting as much as I can in such matters as seeing books through the press, etc. – When Mr. Solmes spoke to me on Thursday, I was willing, though

not anxious, to consider a different basis and to lend my name, on condition that I be taken into full confidence and have at least a determining voice in all affairs of Graphic. Since this did not materialise, I cannot give my name; I am content to remain a mere employee, nameless and anonymous, as far as the public is concerned. In fact, it is the only basis on which I can do what I have promised to do. I cannot give assistance in any stock-selling scheme. – In consideration of such services as I can give, Graphic foots the third third ($1200) of my salary.

4) This involves another point. I am, therefore, strictly speaking, an employee of Cameron Solmes. Would it, then, not be much better if Cameron and Solmes handled all accounts directly and I closed out my bank account?

5) Point (4) recommends itself to me all the more since I am told by those who should know that I cannot, legally, sign myself President of Ariston without committing an indictable offence. I have, therefore, with this morning, ceased to use our stationery. This may involve scrapping our letter-heads, I am only sorry that my last suggestion ('Editor' only) was not adopted.

6) I might say that I cannot occupy my office till current bills are paid. I have to meet the people to whom accounts are owing; and I hate to stave them off. But $100.00 would clear that. After which I should like to hand over my accounts.

Hoping that this statement of the way in which I see things agrees with your own, I remain,

Sincerely yours,
F.P. Grove

1 Mrs Marion H.W. Cameron, a widow and member of an old Ottawa family. She was persuaded to invest in the Graphic venture by Miller and her East Indian friend, Carlos Christian, and increasingly the control of the firm fell into her hands. She was vice-president from 1927 to 1931, and general manager from January to May 1932, when control of Graphic passed on to Alfred Trew, CA, the trustee.

Grove joined the firm as a reader in December 1929, at a salary of $3600 a year (to be raised to $6000) at Mrs Cameron's request 'to stand by her in her difficulties; to be, as she expressed it, "a tower of strength to her"' (*In Search of Myself* 410).

Mrs Cameron wrote to Grove on November 28, 1928: 'This is a little matter between just you, your good wife and myself. I have a proposition altogether apart from your Manuscripts that I wish to discuss with you.' She enclosed a cheque for $100 'so that monetary conditions will not delay your visit,' and promised that 'should you decide later to throw in your lot with anyone else, I will consider it no breach of faith on your part.' The letter is preserved in the University of Manitoba Grove Collection.

2 H.L. Solmes, Vice-President of Cameron-Solmes Limited, Investment Bankers and Corporation Underwriters, of which Mrs Cameron was the President. The firm had its executive offices in Ottawa, and branches throughout Canada.

3 An enquiry addressed to Watson Kirkconnell elicited the following information:

> As I recall it, the financial backers of Graphic, when it seemed likely to founder in the late 1920's, decided to put some of their treasure into a second, brand-new vessel, which they incorpo-

rated as Ariston. Miller, the enterprising manager of both, was not too well versed in literature; and Grove was secured as a figure-head president and a working editor. It was found almost impossible to get any substantial new risk capital, and both ships sank in the waters of the Depression. (September 8, 1972)

In addition to Kirkconnell's *The Tide of Life* (1930), Ariston published only one other book, *The Exquisite Gift* (1930), a novel by Ella Bell Wallis.

4 It was, presumably, a Graphic subsidiary; and Erik J. Spicer in his unpublished report, 'The Graphic Publishers Limited' (University of Michigan, Department of Library Science, August 1959), lists only one title under this particular imprint: *Prominent People of the Province of Ontario* (1925). However, it appears that after Grove joined the firm the idea was revived, and a new series called 'The Canada Series' was launched with Grove as the general editor, and an advisory committee consisting of A.G. Doughty, G.M. Wrong, and W.T. Waugh (1884–1932; Professor of History at McGill). A total of three books appeared in this series: A.G. Doughty, ed., *Dr Cheadle's Journal of a Trip Across Canada* (1931); Lawrence Burpee, ed., *The History of Emily Montague* (1931); and Stephen Leacock, ed., *Lahontan's Voyages* (1932).

TO MRS M.H.W. CAMERON

Ottawa, Ont.
April 2, 1930

Dear Mrs. Cameron,

I had expected that everything pending between us would be settled yesterday at the latest.

Several more or less irrevocable decisions have to be made at once, so I will again write to clear matters up.

1) I hesitate over the Harrap contract.[1] If I leave, it would be better not to be involved in it.

2) I hesitate over the Canada series; again, if I leave, it would be best to drop the matter.

3) I shall have to decide by to-morrow night whether I shall be in Ottawa during the summer or not.

I might say that yesterday, when I had received my salary for the current month, I settled all necessary payments and found myself, after providing for the month's living, without a single solitary cent and only three street-car tickets. Instead of making headway, I have steadily been going back since coming to Ottawa. Eayrs[2] whom I saw recently said that, for the work I am doing, I should get $10,000 the first year, with the definite understanding that that sum should be raised from year to year by $2000. I am not asking for that. Nor am I asking for anything except to be released on June 1st. But, if I am to remain beyond that date, I must have at the least $500 a month, and that from April 1st on. If that is not suitable, I must insist that my Saturday's letter constitutes a resignation or a two months' notice. But I shall be quite satisfied to leave; and I don't know whether it would be wise for you to accede to my demand for a higher salary. Financial matters being as they are, it may be wise to retrench in every way. Even if I leave, some way might be found for me to handle the editorial end of Graphic, if that is desired. If not, well and good; I shall go back to Macmillans where things have eased up meanwhile.

The fourth thing that worries me is the fact that the two Ariston books[3] will have to go to press very shortly. I cannot afford to default on my first contracts.

When I came in, in December, I took it for granted that there was no difficulty over the finances. Stock was supposed to be selling steadily and well; and I fully expected that by the middle of January at the latest Ariston would have the $18,000 promised for the first year at its disposal; or I should never have entered on negotiations for books or agency contracts.

Will you please let me know by tomorrow noon what your decision is in the matter? I suppose you will have to consult Mr Burpee;[4] and I shall be quite willing to discuss the matter in his presence; only if that is to be done, let us put nothing else on the order paper. I can present my side of the case in about ten minutes.

Till a definite decision is arrived at, I must act as though I were free to do as I please beginning with June 1st. As I said yesterday, by that time I shall have such matters of Graphic policy as do not involve my staying here cleared up to the point where your shop-staff can go through with it.

Sincerely yours,
F.P.G.

1 An obscure reference. Presumably it was being suggested that Graphic become the Canadian agent for Harrap's of London, England.

2 Hugh S. Eayrs of Macmillan

3 It is impossible to be certain about the books referred to here. Probably one was *The Exquisite Gift* (1930) by Ella Bell Wallis, and the other *The Tide of Life* (1930) by Watson Kirkconnell – they were the only books actually published under Ariston's imprint, but others may have been projected.

Letters from Mrs Wallis to Grove, preserved in the University of Manitoba Grove Collection, make clear that Grove gave her extensive advice and assistance. Biographical information on Mrs Wallis has been hard to obtain. She was the wife of Hamilton L. Wallis of the Canadian Cooperative Wheat Producers Ltd., and moved to Calgary from Ontario in 1912. Her novel, 'Happy Issue,' won the $1000 third prize in the novel contest sponsored by Graphic in 1930. She was last listed in the Calgary directory in 1962. (I am indebted for this note to Mrs Georgeen Barrass, Assistant Archivist of the Glenbow-Alberta Institute in Calgary.)

4 Lawrence Burpee, one of Graphic's directors; see letter of October 4, 1927, note 1.

TO WATSON KIRKCONNELL

Ariston Publishers Limited,
211–212 Sparks Chambers,
Ottawa
April 17, 1930

My dear Kirk,

It just occurs to me that, should you be married early in the summer, you and the bride might spend a few weeks or months on the height overlooking the Ottawa river where our Summer home is located: we have lots of room.[1] I shall try to get Phelps, too, with Mrs. P. and Anne.[2] Lots of room for all my friends; absolute quiet and leisure for work or play. Mrs. G. joins me in the invitation and would write the bride if she knew her name?[3] Think it over. There are a few delightful spots in Ontario; and ours is one of them.

As ever
F.P.G.

1 The Groves lived in an apartment on Somerset Street in Ottawa before moving to their summer cottage on Skead Road, in an old apple orchard overlooking the Ottawa river. The Kirkconnells spent one night of their honeymoon in the Groves' summer cottage.
2 The Phelps' daughter
3 Hope Kitchener of Lindsay, Ontario. This was Kirkconnell's second marriage; his first wife Isabel, née Peel, died in 1925 after only one year of marriage, following complications after giving birth to twin sons.

TO E.H. THISTLETHWAITE[1]

Cummings Bridge P.O., Ont.
November 15, 1930

Dear Mr. Thistlethwaite,

Thanks for the cheque which is more than I meant to charge up to the A[rts] & L[etters] Club.

I can only repeat that I thoroughly enjoyed myself at Windsor and Walkerville: and I hope it won't be my only visit. As for my own little endeavours, I always marvel at the fact that they are appreciated.

Please remember me to Mrs. Thistlethwaite and tell her that I think with pleasure of the evening spent at her house.

With best regards,
Sincerely,
F.P. Grove

1 E.H. Thistlethwaite, born in 1890, was the Business Manager of the Windsor *Star* for over twenty-five years, retiring in 1956. He was a founder of the Art Gallery in Windsor, serving as its treasurer for twenty-five years. He now lives in Victoria, BC.

TO RAYMOND KNISTER

Cummings Bridge P.O., Ont.
December 25, 1930

My dear Mr. Knister,

As far as the length of your Ms.[1] goes, we find that, as a rule, authors underestimate bulk. I did not even rely on my own count but had our factory manager figure on the book.

I must say that I should despair myself of reducing the work to 120,000 words, the maximum length admissible according to the rules of the contest. (By the way, no rights except Canadian book rights are wanted). But your suggestion to split the book into two volumes might solve the difficulty if at least one other judge agrees with me that yours should be one of the three works in line for one of the three prizes: I am amazed to see how much really first-rate work has been going begging in Canada.

You speak of my experience in shortening novels: but, with one exception, while the task was often a heart-breaking one (and still is), I have found that it improves my work (the one notable exception being *Settlers of the Marsh* which has become restless). And my task has sometimes been even more arduous than yours would have to be; most of my novels, when first written, are between 3 and 400,000 words. I am withholding a book from publication, and have withheld it for years, because I believe it should not be more than 100,000 words; and in eight successive revisions, each involving the writing and typing of a complete new manuscript, I have not succeeded in getting it down below 160,000 words. I am at work on the ninth revision at the present moment.[2]

But the main thing is that your attitude is one of willingness; for even if we split the work, it will still have to be shortened.

You understand, of course, that, so far, whatever I may say is only my personal opinion; I am only one of three judges.[3] But, if you can get the book into manageable form (we cannot consider a novel of more than 100,000 words for a two-dollar book; and we cannot publish, in Canada, at a higher price and make expenses) I can almost promise an offer of publication, prize or no prize, provided, of course, that my present connection with Graphic and Ariston does not come to a smash-up before that consummation (which is quite likely, for I fight a lone fight here).

I have not been at the offices since I received your letter; but I will try to find a copy of the rules of the contest to enclose. I must have some here at my house.

Sincerely yours,
F.P. Grove

1 Of *My Star Predominant*, a biographical novel about John Keats. It was Knister's entry in the Canadian Novel Contest sponsored by Graphic in 1930 (for details of the contest, from Grove's point of view, see *In Search of Myself* 413–14). The winners, in order, were

Raymond Knister ($2500), Marcus Adeney ($1500 for 'New Babylon'), and Ella Bell Wallis ($1000 for 'Happy Issue'). Both the second and third prize winners received their prize money, but Knister got only $1500 of his and some of this went for legal collection fees (see letter of August 11, 1931, note 1). Only Knister's novel was ever published, posthumously in 1934 by the Ryerson Press.

2 It is impossible to be certain on this point. 'The Chronicles of Spalding District,' from which *Fruits of the Earth* (1933) was taken, seems likely.

3 The judges were Grove (chairman and convener), Barker Fairley, and W.T. Allison.

TO RAYMOND KNISTER

Cummings Bridge P.O., Ont.,
February 15, 1931

My dear Mr. Knister,

I am very sorry that I ever mentioned the possibility of the prize to you before everything was finally threshed out. The contest committee of Graphic Publishers met the other day; and a majority ruled that no Ms. was to be considered for a prize which did not strictly conform to the rules. Of course, the last word is not yet said. But I should feel very sorry if I had raised hopes which are doomed to disappointment. I assure you that I shall go on fighting strongly; it may come to a resignation of the judges over the question. However, you seem to mention (I am not quite sure that I read the passage correctly) that you actually contemplate cutting the total down to 120,000 words. If you do, please let me know at once. No, the judges have ruled out my proposal to award one prize at least to part of the entry. You speak of the undesirability of a two volume publication; but anything else could not, at present, be considered in the case of your book unless we want to charge $5.00 which would make the book unsaleable.

To summarise, at present the situation is this: the judges refuse to award the prize to part of a novel; the publishers refuse to accept a novel which does not conform to the rules. I, being one of the judges, plead for a compromise; but I am the only one; and, if the publishers and the other judges adhere to their decision, I shall either resign or insist on a minority report in which I shall say that no first prize has really been awarded because the judges found no other book which measured up to the one which was rejected on account of length.

Re the Short Stories,[1] I beg to say that we could not consider paying a straight royalty of 15%. We are beginners in the field and have just weathered a reorganisation. Not one of our authors gets more than 10%. As for advance royalties, as I have already hinted, I believe I could get $200 to 300 for you in March; not before that. We all have had to wait even for salaries because accounts receivable are not being paid up. Graphic owes me over $1400 right now; and for whatever they pay out in advance royalties in March, I shall have to wait till April. Which, by the way, I should be quite willing to do, so long as I get enough for the daily bread.

You criticise Graphic for having arranged the contest the way they did. I criticise them for having held the contest at all. It was done against my advice. I don't believe in that sort of thing and have, therefore never entered a contest.[2] But I agreed to be one of the judges because I wanted to see at least justice done. Usually the prize is awarded on purely commercial principles.

I understand, however, that the intention is to issue cheques on March 31 when the award is to be made.

I believe this answers every point raised in your recent letter.

Sincerely,
F.P.G.

P.S. – As our whole correspondence in this matter, please consider this letter strictly private and confidental.

1 The reference is to a proposed anthology, 'Canadian Short Stories, 1928–31,' a sequel to Knister's *Canadian Short Stories* (Ryerson 1928). It was never published.
2 But see letter of June 26, 1944: Grove did eventually submit *The Master of the Mill* for the Ryerson Fiction Award.

TO WATSON KIRKCONNELL

Cummings Bridge P.O., Ont.,
February 27, 1931

My dear Kirk,

I, too, have been exceedingly busy. A new firm, with unlimited liability, has been formed with a rather peculiar object: all stock, so far, being held by myself and my wife. In brief, the object is to print and produce books and to farm their sale out for limited periods to established publishers and at fixed prices per 1000.[1] The first venture of this company was to acquire the world-rights for *A Search for America* for the purpose of issuing the book at a reasonable price ($1.50); the amazing thing is that the profit of the holding company will be over 300 percent if its estimate of the number saleable is correct; of course, it has, so far, no overhead. The second venture, so far only planned, will be to acquire the rights for all books by F.P.G.; and the third one, to print 'The Chronicles of Spalding District.'[2] This gives the publishers in the old sense nothing but a royalty of about 35 percent on their cost. The retailer remains unaffected. I am very curious to see how it will work out; so far it has proved eminently successful, for the old-style publisher is relieved of risks and does not need to tie money down beyond his immediate needs which, however, in the case of Macmillans who are going to handle the *Search* in Canada was as high as 3000 copies. The book will reappear within two weeks,[3] and Macmillans report pre-publication sales as highly satisfactory. This answers your question with regard to 'Spalding': there will be only one set of plates, made in the U.S.A.; these will be used for three editions, U.S., England, and Canada. The duty question is solved by importing for reexportation when, whatever has been paid, is refunded. A wonder that nobody has ever thought of that simple way before. By-and-by we may take other authors' works and handle them in the same way; though I don't know.

We are all reasonably well and glad to hear that you and yours are. A.L.G.[4] whom, by the way, we call Leonard is 3¾ lbs. ahead of normal weight for his age; and he is, of course, in the eyes of his parents, the cleverest and strongest boy that ever was on sea or land. He is an interesting little chap though, according to present prognostics, he is more likely to develop into a prize-fighter than a leading Canadian author.

Too bad about A.L.P.[5] and 'Towards Criticism':[6] Ariston Publishers have an unusual number of orders for the book. I am sorry I ever let the Ms. go out of my hands again. I am afraid Ariston is not doing much with *The Tide of Life*?[7] I rarely hear anything of them though I read their Mss.

Well, with best regards from the three of us to the four of you. Are you coming east in spring? If so, how about reoccupying that little bedroom in the cottage for awhile?

As ever,
F.P.G.

1 This whole venture, which Grove describes in some detail, does not appear to have gotten off the ground. It is not a reference to Ariston Publishers, a Graphic subsidiary, who published Kirkconnell's *The Tide of Life* (1930).
2 From which *Fruits of the Earth* (1933) was taken
3 As far as is known, no *new* edition of *A Search for America* appeared at this time.
4 Arthur Leonard Grove, the Groves' infant son, presumably named after Arthur Leonard Phelps, one of his godfathers
5 Arthur L. Phelps
6 Phelps' manuscript which Grove was then considering for publication. It was never published. There are a number of references to the projected book in the Phelps letters to Grove.
7 See note 1 *supra*.

TO RAYMOND KNISTER

Cummings Bridge P.O., Ont.,
March 2, 1931

Dear Mr. Knister,

I have had the contract re the Short Stories[1] made out. Nothing is said in it regarding the advance: you can leave that to me. I shall get you $300 which you can expect by March 17 at the latest. In case you get a prize we shall deduct that sum.

I will be quite frank and say that I feel greatly relieved at the fact that you are tightening up the Keats novel.[2] Personally I believe it is going to gain in readability by being cut to 120,000 words. I also feel that I now have a case in my fight for 1st place for that book; and $2500 is, after all, a sum worth doing quite a bit for – as you will agree.

Sincerely
F.P.G.

1 See letter of February 15, 1931, note 1.
2 *My Star Predominant*; see letter of December 25, 1930, note 1.

TO RAYMOND KNISTER

Cummings Bridge P.O., Ont.,
March 16, 1931

Dear Mr. Knister,

I have just returned from Toronto and the judges' meeting. I cannot very well tell you the result of it; but I would ask you to let me have, at once, please, a good photograph of yourself. I have had only a word over the telephone with the Graphic people; and I have asked them whether the $300.00 advance has been forwarded to you. To my dismay they tell me the contract has not yet been completed. I do hope this delay does not seriously embarrass you; if it does, let me have a wire at the above address, via Ottawa, collect; I remember that there was some mistake in the contract, and that Mr. Ashton[1] who handles the business end of it spoke to me about it. I had advised to give you a free hand with regard to the minor points. I did so in order to avoid all delay.

Well, I hope things will look a bit brighter henceforth.

Sincerely,
F.P.G.

1 William E. Ashton, who joined Graphic Publishers in 1931 as manager

TO W.T. ALLISON

Cummings Bridge P.O., Ont.,
March 19, 1931

Dear Professor Allison,

I have your telegram and see with regret that we stand on antipodal grounds.

May I briefly state my case? I do not know whether it is

Fairley's[1] point of view or not; we have not discussed matters of principle in this connection. I merely wrote him at the outset as, I believe, I wrote you that I had undertaken to act as a judge only on condition that none but literary considerations should guide the judges.

The point is that books which offer obvious commercial possibilities find their markets without prize contests. As a publisher's reader I am recommending them for publication all along. This contest was entered into with the avowed purpose of furthering Canadian literature. All over the world prizes are offered with the purpose of helping the young writer – him or her who has something to say but cannot readily find a medium through which to say it. Let me mention merely a few: the Femina prize, the Pulitzer prize, the Goncourt prize. When, a year and a half ago, I was consulted in the matter by Graphic Publishers, it was agreed that contests conducted in the American way, for the purpose of advertising a sales campaign, do more harm than good; and it was also agreed when, six months later, I was approached with the question whether I would undertake to get a judges' committee together, that 'this' (I quote verbatim, for I took special note of it at the time) 'was going to be one contest in which nothing was to be considered but the interests of Canadian literature.' On that understanding I agreed to act and, as you know, I asked Fairley and you to help me, well knowing that I might be outvoted. It so happens that Fairley agrees with me.

Now, while I might grant every one of your arguments in favour of 'Twixt Two Flags,' one or two considerations are sufficient for me to eliminate that book as a serious contender for a prize. 1) It merely rings the changes on old and hackneyed motifs; 2) the author has not even made an attempt to deepen his characters in relation to circumstance.

These two points are the very ones in which *My Star Predominant* and 'New Babylon' excel; and in the latter 'Happy Issue' excels as well. These three works, to put it differently, are creative. So, you might say, is 'Toward the Dawn;' and I shall readily agree. But once it was eliminated from the list of prize-winners, I (and more or less the other judges as well) became again publisher's readers; and I could not recommend it for publication without the enormous publicity of a prize attached to it. 'Toward the Dawn' is a book of 180,000 words, more or less, with practically no action in it: its bulk is, to me, mere coccoon-spinning; much seems morbid to me; much even 'foreign' – as though some continental book had stood model to it. Above all, without the publicity of a prize, it would certainly not sell. It is vastly superior, as a piece of literature, to 'Twixt Two Flags;' but the latter I can recommend as an ordinary commercial venture; the former, much to my regret, I cannot so recommend.

I cannot see any justification for a prize contest other than I have just stated; and when the publishers asked me to act, they were fully aware of the fact.

The essential thing about a prize contest is the enormous opportunity of gaining publicity for the winner. That which would otherwise take years and perhaps decades to be 'put over' is held up before the public eye with a searchlight playing on it.

To the cause of literature no severer blow can be dealt, in

my humble opinion, than an award made on those commercial grounds which you advocate in the last paragraph of your second letter; I, for one, would have to wash my hands of any such undertaking. In the long-run, however, a disregard for what short-sighted people imagine to be commercial considerations is bound to pay even in a money sense.

These, in brief, were my reasons for casting my vote as I did; and I was delighted to see how closely Fairley agreed with me. When I was in Toronto recently, we never discussed the first and second prizes; but we spent two hours or more in threshing out the relative claims of 'Happy Issue' and the 'Ravens of Wodan.' It would be foolish to deny that I felt gratified at my success in convincing Professor Fairley of the greater claim of the former. Now, of course, as you say in your telegram, there is nothing to do but to count votes; and I have reported to Graphic accordingly.

Again regretfully but sincerely,
Yours,
F.P. Grove

1 Barker Fairley, Professor of German at University College, Toronto, who was one of the judges. The other judges were Grove (chairman) and Allison.

TO RAYMOND KNISTER

Cummings Bridge P.O., Ont.,
March 28, 1931

Dear Mr. Knister,

Thanks for your letter of March 25[1] and the sentiments it expresses. But the thing is done,[2] and I feel free and clean again since I have shaken these commercial shackles. I'd rather teach; perhaps I'd rather starve. What you say with regard to the literary fraternity may be true as far as the few go who can do things or who at least attempt to do things. If you had read, and passed on, the ca. 400 Mss. which it has been my lot to read during the last 15 months, you would agree that none too many have reason to thank me, though I believe I have honestly tried to benefit Canadian letters; and a few *have* personally benefited, even when I could not accept their work as a commercial venture. I have handed out encouragement and advice by the bushel, and mostly when I had, in the interests of the shareholders of a commercial enterprise, to decline venturing the latter's money. So long as my word counted for anything, the task was not too distasteful; it became so only with the novel contest of which I had disapproved and to act in which I had refused for over 6 months before at last I gave in. In order to explain this latter statement, I will enclose a copy of my last letter to Professor Allison[3] who, in the committee of judges, represented the opposition. If, as the result of my fight, you are the gainer, you have to thank Professor Fairley just as much as myself, though, in the actual fight, he was able to remain in the background, for I was the chairman of the committee and in touch with the publishers. In fact, without your own willingness to bring the book within the length required, I could not have won out. What you say about the personal element has carried a certain weight with myself, none with Fairley. It is this way. Among the few Mss. which were in line for consideration at all (the one Allison picked, abandoning his first choice, was never considered by myself or Fairley), there was not one as to whose authorship I did not have my shrewd guess. I have not been a publisher's reader for three years for nothing. And it would have weighed with me, in the scales, whether I thought the money to be distributed would benefit Canadian writing in the future or not. As it was, this consideration did not need to be taken into account, Fairley and I being from the start in complete agreement as to 1st and 2nd places. Only about the third prize was there any prolonged discussion; and I am a bit proud of the fact that Fairley yielded completely to my arguments, chief among which was that a winning Ms. must show some trace of *creative* activity. I felt a thrill when, after 2 or 3 hours debate he exclaimed, 'No, I withdraw. You are absolutely right. I agree.' I had gone to this conference with an open mind, willing to let him convince me; I had given him first chance; but when he failed to convince me, I put forward the claims of the other candidate with an almost exultant force; and it won the day.

I can assure you that I am weary of it all; and, I am sorry to say, I am sick. My doctor told me day before yesterday that I am a nervous wreck. So don't grudge me my freedom. I have lived in the past, and though I am sixty years old, I shall live a bit longer in the future, I mean without the opulent salary of a publisher's editor till I can go to the happy hunting grounds. This has been *the* experience of my fighting life; and I feel I can retire, leaving the future to younger folk.

Sincerely,
F.P.G.

Please return copy of my letter to Allison.

1 Which I have not seen; but Knister's letter of February 17, which I *have* seen, deals with his reactions to the results of the Graphic Novel Contest, which forms the main subject of this letter. Knister's *My Star Predominant* (published posthumously in 1934) won the first prize, but a part of the prize money was not paid owing to the liquidation of the firm. See letter of August 11, 1931, note 1.

2 Grove left the Graphic organization about this time as the firm was facing increasing financial difficulties.

3 See the preceding letter.

TO MARCUS ADENEY[1]

Cummings Bridge P.O., Ont.,
April 2, 1931

Dear Mr. Adeney,

May I, as chairman of the committee of judges in the Graphic novel contest, convey to you the congratulations of that committee, not so much on having been awarded second prize in the contest, as rather on having written a book which holds very remarkable promise? We hope that this is only the first of a long line of books which will one day cast lustre on your name.

Your work was the subject of a long and careful consideration and discussion. It ranked very high among the entries and might have been considered for first place, had not the judges felt that it suffers from a lack of unity. About halfway through the Ms. there seems to be a change of hero. The interest shifts from Roddy Chesham to Irwin Harrow.[2] It was chiefly this fact which finally induced them to give the book second place. In giving this decision, however, they charged me to communicate with you and to suggest that you ask Graphic Publishers to return the Ms. to you for a final revision; in making this revision, you could ponder the problem of perhaps strengthening your work by bridging the break: in our opinion there is only one way of doing that, namely by making Irwin more prominent in the first part of the story.

Again permit me to repeat my congratulations.

Sincerely,
F.P. Grove

1 For Marcus Adeney, see letter of June 25, 1931, note 3. Mr Adeney, in forwarding this and the following letter, writes (July 14, 1974):

> Your letter brings back memories of times and events which were exciting, and as it turned out for Raymond Knister, tragic.
>
> F.P. Grove had taken the trouble to look up all of my published writings before he decided to pull an oar in support of my literary potential. The onset of the depression decided all our fates. My novel 'New Babylon' was in the presses when Grove asked us to visit him at his park-like establishment near Ottawa. As I recall he had a summer and a winter home on the same property and everything about the man had that air of amplitude. So convincing was his manner that one missed the overseer and servants proper to such a setting.
>
> Our second visit to F.P.G. was in late spring. He was then established – more rationally – on a farm near Simcoe. Meanwhile we had been corresponding but the messages were brief. He wanted to share with me his almost deferential regard for Greek civilization, lending me his copy of Zimmern's *The Greek Point of View* and recommending J.B. Bury's *Ideas of Progress*. Not only were these books memorable; they helped me to see Grove as he saw himself – a necessary step toward real friendship.
>
> He was very musical, with classical, tending toward baroque, tastes. For the Simcoe visit he asked me to bring my cello and play Bach's unaccompanied Suites, which I did. Practically filling the clothes closet in our room was a row of Harris tweeds – a multi coloured array of costumes suited to an exclusively country gentleman.
>
> As a farmer Grove was, as you might suspect, a pure perfec-

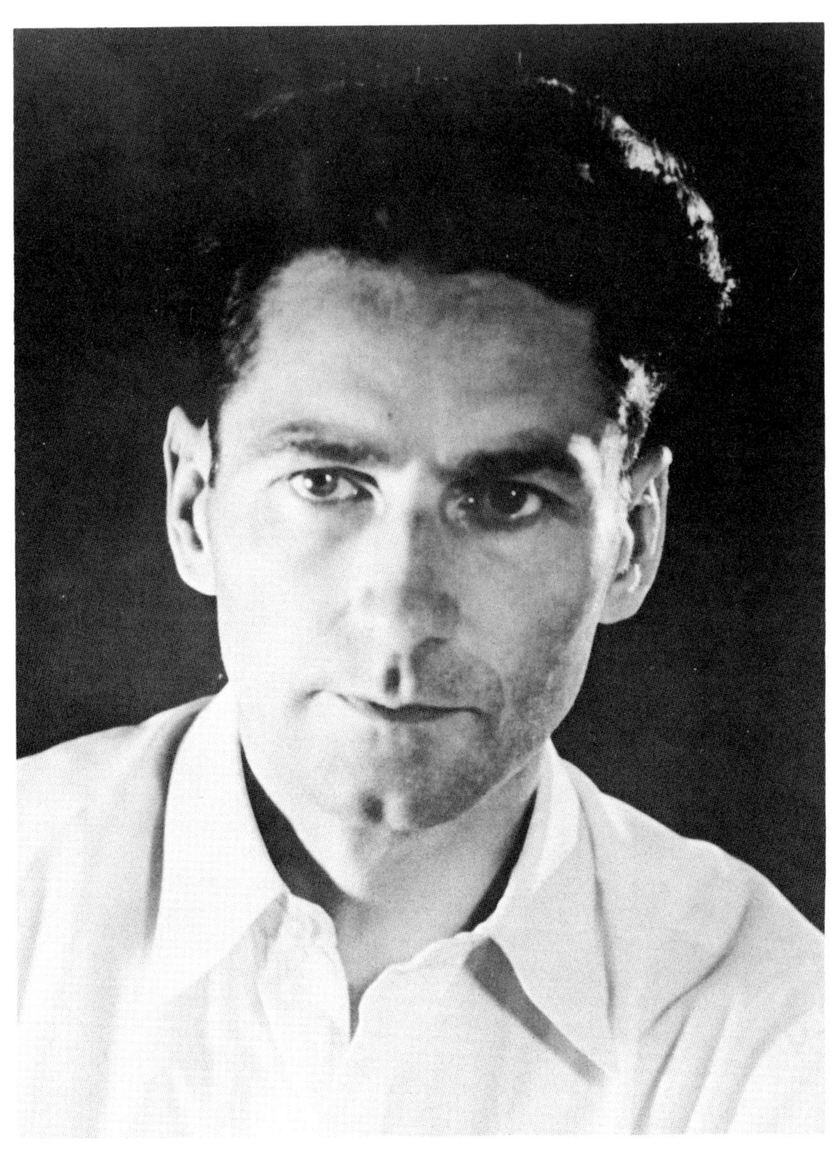

14 Marcus Adeney. *Photo by Marcel Ray c1940, courtesy Marcus Adeney*

> tionist. He claimed to have a personal rapport with his cows, and called one after another by name at milking time. I remember him as a big man of extraordinary sensitivity, whose ego included anything and everything with which it was possible to identify – potentially a Tolstoyan figure. The series of essays beginning with *Over Prairie Trails* was more truly a gauge of the man's imagination than were his novels. Living, as he did, in acute sympathy with nature and figures from the past – especially the literary Greeks – Grove shared Thoreau's distrust of his own kind. It was as though he saw in all our specialization only a cloak for narrow self-interest. So any display of egotism on his part could well be interpreted as exemplary gesture. But alas! Gesture becomes the man. I could not fail to realize that beyond including me in his classical perspective and in his hopes for education (we had similar views), he could get little relief from an inbuilt, perhaps congenital loneliness, from a much younger author-musician.
>
> While we were staying at the Simcoe farm, a large and superbly nurtured strawberry crop ripened. One morning F.P.G. came back from town scowling. He had been offered three or four cents a box for his berries. There and then he decided to plough the whole crop under, offering us as many as we could carry away. His bitterness was terrible to behold. And yet, looking back as we left the place, I could not help recalling the tinge of grandeur in his manner as he announced this great sacrifice. All present day humans, it was plain, shared horribly in Adam's fall....

2 Characters in Adeney's 'New Babylon.' Mr Adeney in the letter just quoted goes on to say:

> The central, somewhat sappy figure of a boy Roddy was part of an unfolding sequence of events within which he was to be included in only a minor way, with the tragedy of Irwin Harrow looming large. In other words, boyhood drama gives way to the imperatives and sanctions of a grown-up and war-torn world. The author's (and readers') view of Roddy and his accidental companions fades, as real life takes over in the person of an (unconsciously) heroic figure.

TO MARCUS ADENEY

Cummings Bridge P.O., Ont.
April 13, 1931

Dear Mr. Adeney,

I shall be glad to discuss the book with you; but I am living out in the country and a bit hard to get at, unless Mr. Pain,[1] of the Graphic

Press, would take you out. I'd take you back to town in my car. Of course, if I knew when you'd come, I could fetch you as well. But I don't get mail every day and am beyond telegraph or telephone.

Sincerely,
F.P.G.

1 Frederick Pain, who was then Graphic's Production Manager. A native of England, he had served his apprenticeship at bookmaking in that country before he emigrated to Canada and joined the Toronto firm of Hunter-Rose. Following Graphic's liquidation, he became a civil servant in Ottawa.

TO RAYMOND KNISTER

Cummings Bridge P.O., Ont.,
June 25, 1931

Dear Mr. Knister,

I have to apologise for not having answered your last letter long ago. The point is that I have lived in great anxieties lately, anxieties which were pressing for momentous decisions. It is now all cut and dried; I am leaving Canada and returning to continental Europe after having wasted forty years of my life here.[1]

I do hope you have received the prize-money by this time? Mrs. Wallis[2] just wrote me that she has received hers; and I was glad to hear it.

I have not changed my opinion about your book; nor about either of the other two to whom Fairley and I awarded the prizes. And I feel that the last piece of work I was destined to do for Canadian letters was a good piece of work, especially under the present conditions prevailing in the country. I sincerely hope that yours and Adeney's[3] will be the future.

Sincerely,
F.P.G.

1 Although from this and the following letters it appears that Grove had seriously considered returning to Europe, he did not of course do so but settled on a farm near Simcoe, Ontario.

2 Ella Bell Wallis, author of *The Exquisite Gift* (Ottawa: Ariston 1930) and winner of the third prize in Graphic's Canadian Novel Contest for her 'Happy Issue'

3 Marcus Adeney, who won the second prize in the Canadian Novel Contest for 'New Babylon.' A native of London, England (born July 1, 1900), he came to Canada in 1904, and trained as a cellist in Toronto under Leo Smith and Boris Hambourg. From 1922 to 1926 he spent varying periods of time successively in Detroit, London, Vienna, and New York studying the cello under Philip Abbas, Arnold Trowell, Wilhelm Jeral, and Percy Such. In 1928 he became a cellist with the Toronto Symphony Orchestra, and later, in 1947, its programme annotator and preview lecturer. He was a member of the CBC

Symphony from 1952 to 1963, and of the Faculty of Music, University of Toronto, from 1953 to 1963. He is the author of one published book, *Tomorrow's Cellist* (McClelland & Stewart 1973), and several unpublished ones. He has published poems, book reviews, and articles on literature and music in *Saturday Night, The Canadian Review of Music and Art, Queen's Quarterly, Canadian Poetry Magazine, The Canadian Bookman* and *Canadian Forum*. The choral from his unpublished 'Mansong' is printed in A.J.M. Smith's *The Book of Canadian Poetry* (Chicago 1943). There is an interesting letter from Adeney to Grove, which in part reads:

> Two and a half years ago I came to Toronto from New York with a cello and a pregnant young wife. I had been away for about five years – Detroit, London, Vienna, New York (young man's folly), then marriage, and, soon after, deportation from the U.S.A. ... You may be interested to know that I, who have little money and again a pregnant wife, recently spent $1.50 on a soiled copy of *A Search for America*. We both danced all over the kitchen when your letter came. (You must know that this is an ideally happy marriage.)

The Adeney letter, dated May 23, 1929, is in the University of Manitoba Grove Collection.

TO RAYMOND KNISTER

Cummings Bridge P.O., Ont.
July 26, 1931

Dear Mr. Knister,

My wife asks me to write you as follows. Won't you and Mrs. Knister, including the baby, run down (or is it up?) here next Saturday, Aug[ust] 1st, early and spend the day and Sunday? We'd have a few common acquaintances in on Sat[urday] night.

This is what we can offer: we give you the little sleeping house by yourselves, with two comfortable beds; and we'd show you this district and have a chat.

Please let us know at once.
Sincerely,
F.P.G.

TO WATSON KIRKCONNELL

Cummings Bridge P.O., Ont.
August 6, 1931

My dear Kirk,

Leonard is fine. He has four teeth now and two more coming; but one hardly notices any difference.

I have not only failed to secure a university berth (though I am promised Coar's[1] chair whenever he resigns at Edmonton; but I cannot wait for that), but anything whatever which would provide bread and butter or even bread without the butter. I am simply one of the 500,000 unemployed; and I am only sorry I did not leave the country in the fall of 1929 when my situation was similar though not quite so urgent and desperate.

I, too, sold my car last night, to convert it into tickets for Europe; and we are selling other things as well. We shall sail within a month or so; and I think this is final; I do not expect to see Canada again.[2] What is more, I do not expect to publish in Canada again and contemplate, in order to save freight, a holocaust of my Mss. as far as they relate exclusively to this country.[3] England, I have found, is simply not interested in Canada; they have their own worries, I suppose. Woodsworth has tried hard to persuade me to go into politics and to stand for election; but I feel that I am too old to change all my adjustments.[4]

As a sort of valedictory to my friends and enemies I published that article in the August *Forum* which you have no doubt seen.[5] Another article with a similar purpose (though few will divine the purpose) will appear in the Jan[uary] number of the new *University of Toronto Quarterly*.[6]

I hope you and yours are well? With best wishes from my wife and myself,

As ever,
F.P.G.

1 John Firman Coar (1863–1939) was born in Germany of American parents, and educated there and at Harvard. After a number of teaching positions, he became Professor of German at the University of Alberta in 1917, a post from which he retired in 1934. He was author of books on political and international issues, notably the question of German reparations, and of *Studies in German Literature of the 19th Century* (1903).

2 The Groves did not, of course, go.

3 An intention which was not carried through, although some manuscripts may have been destroyed

4 Grove was not a candidate that year, but in 1943 he was a CCF candidate in the Ontario provincial election. For Woodsworth, see letter of March 10, 1928, note 7.

5 'Apologia pro Vita et Opere Sua,' *Canadian Forum* XI (August 1931) 420–2

6 'A Writer's Classification of Writers and Their Work,' *University of Toronto Quarterly* I, 2 (January 1932) 236–53

TO RAYMOND KNISTER

Cummings Bridge P.O., Ont.,
August 11, 1931

Dear Mr. Knister,

What a shame about that Graphic cheque.[1] Such things did not happen when I was there; and I am mighty glad that I am out of it. But I have been thinking the situation over since I received your letter; and I have come to the conclusion that you would after all be wise to accept notes, provided you could get them for the full amount. You see, I doubt whether your prize would give you a basis for legal action; whereas a note is directly actionable; but if I held such notes, I should certainly protest them on the date of maturity, which would involve employing a lawyer for the collection. They would somehow rustle the money. And suppose they could not do so: it would clear the air in any case if they were forced to make an assignment. As I have repeatedly intimated, I do not trust that man Ashton[2] across the road. This, of course, is merely an impression I have.

As for the plan of a magazine of the type you mentioned, I really don't know. If you could get the money for it, as a gift, it might be all right. But don't put anything of your own into it; that's my advice.

As for *The Exquisite Gift*,[3] I can't agree with you; and neither do Phelps, Alexander, Stanley, and Fairley, not to mention the nincompoops. We think that, as a piece of writing, it is first-rate. As for its being 'a good novel': just what is a novel? Here is a real problem attacked with psychological insight and power: see the Bible-reading scene. Here is atmosphere, landscape, and genuine life. No doubt the book has its flaws. And among them I count the realistic threshing scene which is out of tone. But the book has astonishing merit in my opinion. As for the dialogue, it is true, it is not realistic in the sense of Dickens and others; but it is poetic and carries me along. I consider the book very nearly a piece of literature; parts of it (as the death of William Botts) perfect little bits of art. There is at least an individuality in the writer; the book has 'style.'

You invite us again. But I am afraid it can't be done. We are living in a complete upset; and I have hardly the composure for a visit at present. However, we may think of it somewhat later, perhaps on our way to the boat.[4]

There is a plan afoot to have me deliver a few lectures before I leave; and something may come of that. I shall see. If so, I shall be rushed to death during the last few weeks. So we must leave this matter open, so far.

With best regards from both of us to you and your wife,
Sincerely,
F.P.G.

1 Presumably it bounced. According to the figures of the official trustee for the Graphic estate, as cited by Erik Spicer in his unpublished paper on Graphic, Knister received $1500 by May 18, 1932. Knister, however, says in a letter of October 19, 1932 (cited by Dorothy Livesay in her *Collected Poems of Raymond Knister*, Toronto 1949, p xxxiii) that he had received only $700. Some of the $1500 undoubtedly went, as Spicer suggests, in legal collection fees. At this stage, presumably, Knister's fight for the money was only beginning.

2 William E. Ashton, who joined Graphic Publishers Limited as manager in 1931

3 A novel (1930) by Ella Bell Wallis; it was published by Ariston, a Graphic subsidiary – for Ariston, see letter of January 13, 1930, note 3.

4 See the preceding letter. The Groves did not go abroad.

TO RICHARD CROUCH

R.R. 4, Simcoe, Ont.
November 15, 1931

My dear Mr. Crouch,

It seems our correspondence is destined to be rather intermittent. We often think and talk of you; but when it comes to sitting down and writing ... well, you know how it is.

Now the occasion of this present letter is business. That is to say, the fact that I am so confoundedly hard up that I don't know where to go in order to turn an honest penny. Illness, the birth of a son, and the depression, I suppose, are to blame. So I have tried, and partially succeeded, to arrange for a recital of unpublished work in Toronto and other places; and I am wondering whether there would be a chance in London; and if, whether perhaps you could indicate to me the proper channels through which to open the matter up. In Toronto, I believe, it is one of the University organizations which is sponsoring the matter. I understand that they are going to charge $1 admission, the whole, after deducting expenses, to go to me. Perhaps, in a smaller town or city, the admission would have to be less. Could you give me a pointer or so?

By the way, why not run over here of a Sunday? My wife joins me in inviting you and the family. We are not, at the present, in a position to put guests up overnight; but the distance is such a trifle that you could easily make it in two hours or less, the way you drive. Follow number 3 to the junction of #3 and #24, at the north end of Simcoe, turn north on #24 for 1½ miles, the white frame house at the corner of a concession road, with spruce and cedar in front, on the left side of the road, coming from Simcoe, is where you'll find us. If you can, call us over long distance the night before or on Sunday morning; so that you'll find us at home.

With best regards for son and wife, from the both of us,
As ever,
F.P. Grove

TO RAYMOND KNISTER

R.R. 4, Simcoe, Ont.
November 15, 1931 II

Dear Mr. Knister,

We are far from settled, and so I must use the Sunday to answer a few letters. You are quite right, I have found the cultural advantages of big cities in Canada conspicuous through their absence; and, as you know, have long since decided that the country (not the small town, either, but the open country) is the place for me. I find that, of true intelligence, farmers have the lion's share on this continent; and the sooner they take the direction of affairs into their hands, the better it will be.

15 Groves' house at Simcoe, Ontario. *Courtesy Leonard Grove*

I am very curious to see the book in print;[1] but I do think that the first of December is an unfortunate date to publish. I had two books appearing as late as that, and both fell flat though they recovered by-and-by.

As for Mrs. Cameron, I am sorry to say that my experience has been the reverse of what you expect. The better she is known at a bank, the less is that bank inclined to discount her paper. I tried in vain to get rid of $1000.00 worth of it before I left Ottawa.

Yes, we have bought a farm, that is, we have assumed the obligation to pay the taxes and the insurance on the place; apart from that we rather owe than own it. However, it is a change for me; and though I am doing very hard work – harder, I fear, than I should be doing – I get a certain amount of stimulus out of a small herd of pure-bred Jersey cows which I have bought, again rather owing than owning it. We have lots to learn from cattle, as you probably know; and I am learning it. So far, to mention the house, we have had to refloor, replaster, repaper, repaint its interior; and we have now lovely rooms, 10 of them, but there is hardly anything in them: our living room boasts that magnificent Chinese rug which you may remember and a set of gorgeous old-gold curtains but nothing else. We spent this afternoon in it, romping with Leonard who enjoys the spaciousness of it all. And the room is beautiful to me even without furniture. Yes, if you were still at Port Dover, we could get together occasionally. We might even make shift to put you up overnight, though that would mean bedding down on the floor which is great fun on occasion.

I hope to hear from you again.

With best regards from us both to the two of you.

Sincerely,

F.P.G.

P.S. Yes, Leonard walks, runs, jumps, and talks a little, understanding everything that is said to him.

1 *My Star Predominant*, published posthumously in 1934

TO THE EDITOR, THE CANADIAN FORUM

Simcoe, Ont.
[May 1933][1]

Fruits of Criticism

Sir:

I have never yet answered reviews, but a plain statement of fact is simply called for in reply to the ill-humoured and ill-mannered effusion which you printed in the last issue of *The Canadian Forum* by way of a notice of my book, *Fruits of The Earth*.[2]

The original title of the book – which I still think it a

mistake on the part of the publishers not to have retained – was 'The Chronicles of Spalding District.' I am not aware that I call the book a novel. My task was to infuse a dramatic interest into agricultural operations and the attendant rural life of an emerging settlement. The only question, therefore, can be whether I have succeeded in that or not. This is the very point in which the present book differs fundamentally from *Our Daily Bread*; but, of course, even after having put close to a decade of labour into this work, it would still be folly to expect so shallow a reading as your reporter has apparently given it to reveal the fact to *him*. Nevertheless, it is amusing to read the last paragraph of that notice in which exactly what the book is meant to give receives praise. In all that precedes this paragraph, your reporter has 'gone' Don Quixote 'one better': he has fought a windmill which has not even the merit that it is there. At no point have I been concerned with Abe Spalding's inner life except where it touches the district or where the district touches it; whereas, in *Our Daily Bread* I was concerned with nothing but the inner life of the hero while the district is not so much as mentioned. In one word, the hero of *Fruits of the Earth* is the Prairie.

The morality? Do these gentlemen of the pen take me for such a tyro as to think that I put anything so uninteresting as my own moral views into a narrative? The morality is that of a majority of the settlers; and, I contend, of a majority of the rural population of the west. If Abe Spalding, in his last gesture, is as ridiculous as your reporter tries to make him out, then, indeed, all traditional morality is ridiculous. I shouldn't like to say off-handedly that it isn't; but in my book I am not concerned with that question. I am not trying to defend Abe, am I? I am merely setting down what, in a similar situation, nine hundred and ninety-nine men out of a thousand would have done if they had dared. As your reporter says, after having swung his arms for awhile, quite unnecessarily, 'The drama of this book is the drama of facts, of events.' If he had said that at the start, and not much else, the notice would not suffer from its air of disingenuousness. *O si tacuisses, philosophus mansisses!*[3]

But enough. Time will judge. I have never been in a hurry.

Meanwhile I should like to set your young man a task. Let him read Shakespeare's *Timon of Athens* and criticize it as a love story or a detective yarn. Shakespeare, as he may not know, is now dead and can afford to smile, from beyond the grave, at such futile efforts.

Yours, etc.,
F.P. Grove

1 The only copy of this letter I have seen is an undated carbon of the original; the letter appeared, also without date, in the *Canadian Forum* of May 1933.

2 The review by Robert Ayre of *Fruits of the Earth* appeared in the *Canadian Forum* of April 1933, and is reprinted in my *Frederick Philip Grove* (Critical Views on Canadian Writers 1970) 153–5. Grove pillories Ayre (as 'Ayr') in *Consider Her Ways* 246.

3 O, if you had been silent, you would have remained a philosopher – Boethius, *Philosophiae Consolationis*, Book II, 7.

TO PELHAM EDGAR

R.R. 4, Simcoe, Ont.
January 16, 1934

Dear Professor Edgar,

It was very good of you to send me the book.[1] I have already dipped into it and know by this time enough about it to say that I shall read it in full with the greatest interest. Since in this course of lectures which I am giving for the Carnegie Foundation (as an 'extension' lecturer for McMaster)[2] I am still exactly 4 weeks from the point where I start on fiction, I am sure, my lectures will be the better for my having in the interval, become acquainted with your work. Tonight I am attempting the impossible: namely to tell a mixed audience (judges to high-school pupils) 'how to analyse a Shakespearean drama' – the subjects are chosen by someone in New York, and I have to make the best of it or them, for the sake of a few dollars.

'Honour,' you say, to me? And 'from high quarters?'[3] You prick my curiosity. As for 'my richly deserving it' – you are very good: my last book *sold*, in Canada, in less than 500 copies – in every other country where it has appeared (3 of which I know) the figure was higher. However, perhaps you are right in what you are going to say, that the sale does not measure merit; and, frankly, I had hoped for better things.

Thanks again.
Sincerely yours,
F.P. Grove

1 *The Art of the Novel* (1933) by Pelham Edgar. For Edgar, see letter of April 2, 1928, note 3.

2 Carnegie Foundation lectures on art and literature, organised by McMaster University. Grove gave a series of five lectures on 'How to Appreciate Literature.' Enquiries to McMaster have failed to elicit any details as to these lectures.

3 The Lorne Pierce Gold Medal of the Royal Society of Canada, which Grove received in June 1934. The medal, established in 1926 by Lorne Pierce, is awarded every two years for 'an achievement of special significance and conspicuous merit in imaginative or critical literature written in either English or French.' The Royal Society has added a cash award of $1000 to the medal since 1966. See also letter of April 1, 1940, note 8.

TO HENRY BUTTON[1]

R.R. 4, Simcoe, Ont.
March 20, 1934

Dear Mr. Button,

I see from your letter that you are worried about my attitude to this decision; so I will answer at once. Let me say first that it held no surprise. It is over two months now since I sent you the Ms.; and since I had not heard a word about it, neither from you nor from London, I knew of course long ago what that decision would be and I had faced it.

It means the end of my writing career; for two reasons. (1) My purely Canadian novels have only landed me in debt. I don't feel any inner compulsion to go back to the struggle. There are half a score of first and second drafts of novels lying about in the drawers of my desk. But why should I take them out when I am better off without trying to publish? Which does not mean that I shall never file them into shape. But, I repeat, why try to publish? (2) I shall shortly be without a roof over my head. You know that I slaved on that 'Antbook' at least partly, last year, because you told me not to worry about that $251.04, which I shall have to pay within a few weeks. I shall not be able to pay it. That means that I shall lose everything I have. In 1930 I put $4000 in cash into the place, the savings of a lifetime; and since 1932 I have, in addition, reduced an indebtedness of $5000 which I had to assume when I bought the place to $3300, in the face of the depression. In addition, I have in the interval, built up a herd of 6 pure-bred Jerseys into one of 15 head; and we, my wife and I, have laid the foundations of a private school. In a year more I should have been safe because both farm and school would have begun to yield revenue. As it is, after canvassing every possibility, I don't see what else I can do but let everything go under the hammer. The proceeds, at present prices, should just about clear me of debt; they won't do more and may do less; for farm property is nowhere today. I might say that I knew what I was about; it was not a wild-goose chase; in Norfolk County, that I had the highest individual cream test in February (8.4%, as compared with the legal minimum of 3.25% or with the next highest of 7.2%), and also the highest average for the herd;[2] but I was converting a small-fruit farm into a dairy farm, and the task is far from finished.

When I am clear of debt, I don't see that I can do anything but try to hire myself out as a herdsman, at an annual figure of, let me say $300. That means manual labour. My friends will say, Why don't you lecture? Why don't you teach moderns or classics in some University? You can do it better than many of the present instructors. The point is that I have, for 40 years, tried to do just that and failed to secure a job, except as a lecturer during 1928 and 1929 when I addressed more Canadian Clubs than any living man has addressed. Add to that the fact that I am 62 years old, that my eye-sight is failing, at least for objects less than 100 yards distant, and that I am very nearly deaf. I know, of course, that in manual labour I shall not last a year. My wife and my little son, I conclude, will be best served if I separate my fortunes from theirs. For I have made one cardinal mistake in my life from which all else has followed; I have tried to publish my writings, at an enormous cost in time, living, while I licked my books into shape, partly on my wife's earnings, partly on savings. Why, in the world, go on with what has so manifestly proved disastrous?

No, my dear Mr. Button, don't for a moment think that this is meant to hold a reproach. If London does not share my opinion that the 'Ant-book' offers all the possibilities of a big popular success, it is their perfect right to do so, and I should be the last one to urge them into a venture which they consider foredoomed. It is not an arguable question.

Don't think, either, that this indicates bitterness; it does not. I am merely trying to face the facts. And one of the facts is that I cannot reconcile it with my own self-respect to take relief and to involve others in my ruin. The school of which you know, I trust, will survive in rented quarters and keep wife and son in bread and butter, provided I free them of that encumbrance which goes by the letter I; I can at least say that I have helped to put it on such feet as it has so far. It cannot bear other burdens; if it could, I would not let it.

You say, get another novel ready. Where should the time come from? To do so would take me a year – 8 months at the least. It took me 8 months to hammer the 'Ant-book' into shape. And I dread the labour. It would mean such a struggle and such a nerve-strain to do it under pressure of time that I simply feel I can't face it. There is nothing to look forward to; for I shall never again huckster my Mss. about as I have cheerfully done in the past.

In conclusion I should like to ask you to let me see the readers' reports if you have them. I should like to see on what grounds they advised declining the book. Not that I mean to quarrel with them. I am simply interested. As I said, the failure of the book to move them is ancient history. And what does it matter? No. I have not set my heart on getting the book out in the fall; I had, but I haven't. I wouldn't let it go out now under any circumstances. I want to read it, instead. So, if you have those reports or any parts of them, slide them along, will you?

Sincerely,
F.P.G.

1 Henry Button (1884–1962), at this time editor of J.M. Dent and Sons, in Toronto, and previously an editor for McClelland & Stewart. Dent published *Fruits of the Earth* in 1933, advancing Grove $500 in June of that year, on that book. Even at that time, however, the London house, in writing to Button in Toronto, had cautioned against accepting further Grove novels in any blanket way, the market being as depressed as it was. Evidently, this letter is in reply to a rejection by Dent of the 'Ant-book' (ie, *Consider Her Ways*).

2 There seems to be an error in punctuation here, or some words omitted, such as 'it is well known in Norfolk County…' The only text of this letter available to me was a typed copy from J.M. Dent and Sons. The same is true of the letters to Button of March 21 and 22, 1934.

TO HENRY BUTTON

R.R. 4, Simcoe, Ont.
March 21, 1934

Dear Mr. Button,

Thanks for copy of Doran's note.[1] No, I don't think I want to try other publishers in the U.S.A. I think we'll just let the matter rest. But you'd oblige me by letting me have the Ms. back. I have a 2nd carbon here; but it is quite illegible to my dim eye-sight. I do know one Canadian publisher who'd print 'like a shot' – he says, anything I'd give him.[2] But I can't give him anything.

And that's that, as the cat said when they shot him because he couldn't catch mice any longer. His teeth were gone, you know. So are mine, and the eyes too, and the ears.

So long,
F.P.G.

1 Evidently Dent had offered the 'Ant-book' (*Consider Her Ways*) to Doran for US publication.
2 This is probably bravado on Grove's part. It is impossible to identify a publisher eager to print Grove's books at this time.

TO HENRY BUTTON

R.R. 4, Simcoe, Ont.
March 22, 1934

Dear Mr. Button,

While the $251.04[1] would not solve all my problems – nothing could do that – I should be enabled, if I had that much by May 1st, to hold on. As I have previously said, if I can hold on for a year, I feel I shall be safe (though not affluent). We have, so far, worried along, occasionally having no more than $2.00 a week; and I believe I could[2] be unwise on my part to assume any liability for current outgo. Spring is coming, and in summer we live largely out of our garden and the product of our hen-house.

But I must warn you even with regard to that $251.04. I may be sick; I may run up against unexpected snags. The river of life does not flow smoothly with me when I'm trying to force a book through the mill. As I've also said, I dread the task; it's a major operation. But I'm willing to try: and, so far, I've always succeeded when I had made up my mind to try – I mean succeeded in more or less satisfying myself. I do think that in 8 or 9 months I could have a new novel ready.

The thing I'd do is this: The Rise and Fall of a Small Western Town:[3] the rise as a consequence of growing industry (flour-milling) – the fall as a consequence of ever-increasing mechanisation (automatic machinery). The thing was started long ago when I first saw two examples of it: Rapid City vs. Keewatin. I know the process as I know the farm. And I do think that if I can get the form (style, etc.) into shape, it will be a big thing; very human, very gripping, and very typical. And it goes without saying but I know the human material in and out. How does it sound?

Sincerely,
F.P. Grove

P.S. Yes, of course, I'd like to meet Mr. Dent.[4] The enclosed was written before your letter arrived.

1 See letter of March 20, 1934. Button presumably offered an advance to cover this sum.

2 'I could' should probably read 'It would.' This letter also is available only as a typed copy, and probably contains typographical errors.
3 Which became *The Master of the Mill* (1944)
4 Hugh Railton Dent. Born in 1874, he became chairman of J.M. Dent and Sons in 1926, which position he held until his death in 1938.

TO HENRY BUTTON

R.R. 4, Simcoe, Ont.
March 28, 1934

Dear Mr. Button,

The MS. received today. I want to read it when I get time. Just now that confounded novel of mine, the one about the Rise and Fall of Langholm,[1] Manitoba, has actually gripped me, and I can't afford to buck that sort of spell that comes over me when I once have started to concentrate.

Yes, of course, if you can swing that $250. or $251.04, (or rather, never mind about that odd $1.04: I'll swing *it*), the 'Ant-book' still remains yours, if you want it, or Dent's.[2] Let me know as soon as you can, of course. For the point is this, if I hold a sale of my belongings, I can withhold what I please: a chair or two, and my few books. If it's a forced sale, I lose all. So, if you don't succeed in persuading London, I'd like to know as far in advance as possible. In any case, I'd repay if I live, even if you don't take another book. Everything looks as though, if I can hold out for one more year, I'll be all right.

Sincerely,
F.P.G.

1 *The Master of the Mill* (1944)
2 Dent did not publish any more of Grove's work; but on April 9, the London house, having seen the three preceding letters, cabled Button to advance Grove $500 on the new novel, without any condition of repayment if it remained uncompleted.

TO WATSON KIRKCONNELL

R.R. 4, Simcoe, Ont.
November 2, 1934

My dear Kirkconnell,

And thus the years go by...[1]

The morning's mail brought your *Quest*;[2] and what little I have had a chance to snatch from it during a day of work, has whetted my appetite. It's encouraging to see that there are still workmen about who do not, apparently, think it a reproach to have taken pains with their work.

We had news of the Winnipeg circles, if not from them, when, a month or two ago, the Riddells[3] stopped at our front yard for a half hour's chat.

But how the years go by!...
With cordial thanks for being remembered.
Sincerely yours,
as ever
F.P.G.

1 This letter is followed by a five-year gap in the correspondence: to what extent this reflects a real absence of letters is difficult to judge. But letters had been becoming less frequent, as will be noted, since 1929–30. Kirkconnell, in a letter to me, warns that 'it would be a mistake to read very much into such a hiatus,' for his 'files got rather demoralized in the middle and late 1930s. ... it was a wonder that *any* personal correspondence was preserved and filed.' He also notes that Grove, 'after the traumatic experience of having the Ottawa Project [ie, Graphic] sink under him,' 'proceeded to encapsulate himself' on the Simcoe property. 'There had been an annual interchange of Christmas greetings, but there had been – to the best of my recollection – no matter that called for elucidation through correspondence' (June 17, 1974). Kirkconnell's contacts with Grove were resumed when he (Kirkconnell) joined the staff of McMaster University in August 1940.

2 Kirkconnell had published *The Eternal Quest* in 1934.

3 The Rev. John Henry Riddell (1863–1952), President of Wesley College, Winnipeg, and his wife

TO RICHARD CROUCH

Simcoe, Ont.
November 12, 1934

My dear Crouch,

We have been anxiously waiting for word about Mrs. Crouch; for we felt worried about the way she left here. We do hope the trip did not do harm?

I am returning today 4 of the 10 vol[umes] lent me and *The Last Adam*[1] which somebody had removed from the little table where I had piled your books. I am retaining the rest a little longer: I have read Eliot's 'Poetry' book,[2] but should like to reread it if I may – also 'Marx.'[3]

The book on Russia[4] I found interesting and sympathetic; *Look Homeward, Angel*,[5] interesting but strangely unsatisfying. Spender,[6] very, very good; though Hammond's *Scott*[7] is perhaps more revealing on the same period. The latter I shall finish within a few days.

Altogether, these books have been a treat: Consommé, entrée, rôti, dessert – a varied fare. Many thanks.

As ever
F.P.G.

1 A novel by James Gould Cozzens (b1903), published in 1933

2 *The Use of Poetry and the Use of Criticism* (1933) by T.S. Eliot (1888–1965)

3 Probably either G.D.H. Cole's *What Marx Really Meant* (1934), or Sidney Hook's *Towards the Understanding of Karl Marx* (1933)
4 There seem to be three possibilities: E.T. Brown's *This Russian Business* (1933); *Russia*-USSR: *A Complete Handbook*, ed. by Peter Nikolaevich Malevskii-Malevich (1934); and *This is Russia* by G.E. Raiguel and W.K. Huff (1932).
5 A novel by Thomas Wolfe (1900–38), published in 1934
6 John Alfred Spender (1862–1942) seems to be intended here. His *Fifty Years of Europe* was published in 1933 and *A Short History of Our Times* in 1934.
7 *C.P. Scott of the Manchester Guardian* by J.L. LeB Hammond (1934), which received high praise in nearly all the reviews of the time

TO RICHARD CROUCH

R.R. 4, Simcoe, Ont.
November 24, 1934

My dear Crouch,

I am returning the balance of the books lent me by concurrent mail: they have given me a few weeks [of] rather fine reading. Perhaps I should give you a note or two

(1) Marx[1] – I do believe this to be the clearest and most accurate definition of Marx's position.

(2) Scott[2] – One of the most interesting – to me – cross-sections of a period of history through which I have lived myself.

(3) Gide[3] – interesting to me chiefly through the evocation of my own youth it occasioned; and you know that, incidentally, I think Gide one of the most revealing men of his time.

(4) Plato[4] – Mr. Fite fights wind-mills of his own erection. Who has ever denied that wherever Socrates speaks of love he means boy-love? Who, i.e., except a few people of the type that assert Solomon's Song to be the expression of the love of the church for Jesus? But does it matter? That Plato's republic was an oligarchy may shock a U.S. professor; but when he proclaims it as a new discovery, we old Platonists can only smile. I am amazed that Scribners should have published the book. It is redolent of Provincialism.

(5) Modern Prose[5] – not bad as a summary of tendencies.

(6) Eliot[6] – most interesting but, to me, profoundly unsatisfying. I'd like to read more of his, especially of his poetry. On a few points, he rouses me to fury: lumping Goethe, f[or] i[nstance], with Wordsworth and Shelley. No, Goethe belongs with the Homers and Shakespeares; but he is not quite so accessible: he has less for the vulgar, more for the student, though I should perhaps say, less of his has so far filtered down to the vulgar; a little has; and there is more where that little came from. *But*, Eliot decidedly is a mind that counts. I won't pass him by again as I have done in the past.

Many thanks –
as ever
F.P.G.

P.S. My last vol[ume]s crossed with Mrs. C's letter, it seems. Hope you are all well again?

1 See the preceding letter, note 3.
2 See the preceding letter, note 7.
3 Several of André Gide's works, in English translation, appeared in the late 1920s and the early 1930s, and these included *The Vatican Swindle* (1925/7), *The Counterfeiters* (1927), *Travels in the Congo* (1929), *The Immoralist* (1930), and *Two Symphonies* (1931).
4 Warner Fite (1867–1955), *Platonic Legend*. The *Times Literary Supplement* concurred in the judgement of this letter and was conclusively destructive (see *TLS*, November 29, 1934).
5 Bonamy Dobrée (b1901), *Modern Prose Style* (1934)
6 T.S. Eliot, *The Use of Poetry and the Use of Criticism* (1933). Eliot's considered view of Goethe was exactly along the lines suggested here. To appreciate Goethe's importance, Eliot says in 'Goethe as the Sage' (1955), we must dissociate him from Wordsworth and Shelley.

TO RICHARD CROUCH

R.R. 4, Simcoe, Ont.
January 13, 1935

My dear Crouch,

Thanks for your letter. Yes, if you can get me that *Cromwell*,[1] some time or other, I'll be glad. Since you offer others, I might say that I am making a study of D.H. Lawrence at present; and it seems there are three books which I can't lay my hands on:

Kangaroo
The Plumed Serpent
and *Lady Chatterley's Lover*

There may be more; I may be putting the number at 3 from ignorance. So, if any of these happens to be available when you send Buchan,[2] please enclose it.

We are glad to hear you are well, all of you. As for Jan[uary] 31st we'd like to awfully; but, after canvassing all possibilities have come to the conclusion that it can't be done.

However, my wife is anxious to have a day or so of shopping some time this winter, perhaps in February; and it does not matter – as far as shops are concerned – whether it's London or Hamilton; and the chance of a chat would, of course, draw us to London rather. Perhaps we could arrange for some Saturday – my wife says just now that finances will forbid it to be before Feb[ruary]. You know our building operations have cost us ca. $800; and we are not quite clear yet; we have to do more now, for the school demands two rooms, and we have to change our present kitchen into a dining room and provide for a new kitchen – all which will cost, cost, cost.

Well, with best wishes and regards to all of you.

As ever,
F.P.G.

P.S. I personally spent Christmas and the New Year in bed, with a terrific cold, the worst I've had in years. But I think I'm over it now.

1 *Oliver Cromwell* (1934) by John Buchan (1875–1940)
2 See above.

TO THE EDITOR, THE SIMCOE REFORMER, SIMCOE, ONT.

R.R. 4, Simcoe, Ont.
April 20, 1935

Sir:

Will you grant me a modicum of space in your valuable paper to explain an essentially private matter which yet holds some slight public interest?[1]

Why, so it has been asked, did I consent to preside over the meeting held at the high school auditorium on April 18; and why, moreover, having consented, did I leave when Mayor Simpson began to speak?

Briefly, Mr. Carter had appealed to me because, according to him, only someone like myself, standing outside of politics, could lend dignity to the proposed meeting. He asked me to introduce the speaker and to be one of the speakers myself.

I hesitated; but I reasoned somewhat as follows. I have close personal friends among the leaders of all three political groups in Canada.[2] While each of these friends seeks for a solution of our present difficulties in his own way, according as he belongs to one or the other of these groups, yet all of those I happen to be acquainted with have, to my certain knowledge, one common aim, namely to serve their country to the best of their ability. Knowing this – which is too often forgotten – I came to the conclusion that perhaps I was not too bad a choice, provided it was the intention to conciliate rather than to provoke. So I consented.

On April 4 I received a letter signed by Mr. T.C. Rogers[3] to confirm the arrangement. Since it is documentary evidence, will you permit me to quote from it?

'If you will undertake to introduce the speaker,' says Mr. Rogers, 'and will yourself deliver one of your exceptionally instructive and interesting talks, this will add in no small measure.' ... etc., etc.

The point is that, unless I was given the chance to speak ever so briefly – and naturally I planned to do so while introducing the chief speaker – my presence in the chair was indeed incongruous.

Had Mr. Carter asked me in the first place to act as a vaudeville announcer and then to introduce him, it goes without saying that I should have politely but firmly declined. Yet that is exactly the part, profoundly distasteful to me, which Mr. Carter and his associates manoeuvred me into playing. The moment I realized this, I had no choice but to leave at once. I left the chair and the meeting when I convinced myself that these gentlemen had no intention of keeping faith with me.

Thanking you,
I remain,
Faithfully yours,
F.P. Grove.

1 The matter referred to concerns a public meeting in Simcoe which was addressed by James Simpson (1873–1960), a close associate of J.S. Woodsworth, the founder of CCF, and himself a prominent labour leader. A native of Lancashire, England, Simpson came to Canada in 1888, and became active in labour causes through his twenty-five years' association with the Toronto *Daily Star* (compositor, reporter, and municipal editor). He won his first election to the Toronto Board of Control in 1914, and in 1935, at the time of the Simcoe meeting, he was mayor of Toronto. Grove, who presided, left the meeting abruptly just when Percy R. Carter (1884–1973), then mayor of Simcoe, began to introduce the main speaker. Grove's reasons for his action are stated in this letter. Carter also issued a statement denying that he had brought 'Mr. Simpson, Mayor of Toronto, to Simcoe to speak for and on behalf of the CCF and thus trick some people.' However, Grove appears to object to the prominent role which Carter assumed in the meeting, especially to his role in introducing the main speaker – a role which Grove had understood to be his (Grove's).
2 From Grove's letters elsewhere, it appears that he knew such Canadian politicians as W.L. Mackenzie King and J.S. Woodsworth – the latter rather intimately.
3 Thomas Campbell Landseer Rogers (1886–1945), a Simcoe resident who was active in civic and political matters.

TO RICHARD CROUCH

R.R. 4, Simcoe, Ont.
October 24, 1935

My dear Mr. Crouch,

I have been indulging in an orgy of reading and again realised how much I miss by my isolation. On the one hand, I find much encouragement: others are thinking as I do; on the other, I become conscious how futile an isolated effort like mine must necessarily be.

Not that my reading was uniformly appreciative. One thing, more than anything else, struck me, especially in the light of Fowler's *The King's English* – namely how slovenly most modern writing is.

Carrel[1] should have written French: he is hardly a master of English idiom. Morris[2] should have submitted his Ms. to some master of prose. Haskell[3] should have gone to school for awhile.

Fowler's *King's English* forms, of course, a notable exception. So does Laski's *Democracy in Crisis*[4] which it was a pleasure to read, both *quant au fond aussi bien qu'à la forme*.[5]

Morris' *50 Years a Surgeon* made me regret the brevity of

our lives: it is such a document of present-day conceptions that I should like to pick it up again 500 years from now, just to read about the things that were possible between 1900 and 1935.

Diaghileff's[6] biography did not impress me.

Carrel's *Man the Unknown* is distinctly interesting in driving home to the reader a possible change in the practise of medicine. It projects an ideal.

I have not yet read Haldane's *Philosophy of a Biologist*.[7] I am merely snatching a half-hour which happened to be unoccupied. I hope, however, I am not keeping these books too long.

Oct[ober] 28

I now have read Haldane and, frankly, can't make out anything of it except that it is an attempt to rehabilitate religion in a sense in which I cannot accept it.

I forgot, it seems, to say a word about Chambers' *Thomas More*.[8] His analysis of the *Utopia*, I think, is good and calculated to correct erroneous views of More as a protestant and a rebel. It is, however, distinctly an ill-managed book, full of repetitions and even dead matter. Roper's little book,[9] historically inaccurate as it [is], makes the man live in quite a different sense.

However, starved as I always am for reading matter, it has been a unique (if, I hope, annual) experience to read improvidently, without saving so-and-so many pages for tomorrow.

One or two things you said impel me to add (which it should be unnecessary to do) that I felt wonderfully refreshed by your visit: I ordinarily dig myself into my peculiar brand of the blues, so that I charge blindly at any unwelcome task, as the traditional bull that charges at a red cloth. I am always reluctant to say anything about my own work; but when I do, the feat invariably helps me to clear up my own ideas. The darn thing is either a great book;[10] or it's piffle – very likely the latter; but there are no *three* ways about it. When, in a casual way, you try to summarise a thing like that, the necessity of sudden and strict simplification imposes, with the force of inspiration, an architectonic arrangement which it is very hard to arrive at in any other way.

Don't forget me when you run across some modern fiction (Lawrence, *Lady Chatterley's Lover*) or Werfel[11] or anything else that you think might serve to keep me in touch with what's going on abroad – abroad being anything outside of Lot 1, Concession 12, Township of Windham, County of Norfolk.

Hope you are all well?
Sincerely
F.P.G.

As usual, I forgot to ask where you want those books sent, to the library or to the house? Since some of them may be your personal property, I am sending to the latter.

1 Alexis Carrel (1873–1944), the French surgeon who won the Nobel Prize in medicine in 1912 for his work on blood vessels, wrote *Man the Unknown* (1933) which is discussed in this letter.
2 R.T. Morris (1857–1945), *Fifty Years a Surgeon* (1935)
3 Arnold Lionel Haskell (b1903). See note 6 below.
4 Harold J. Laski (1893–1950), the English liberal thinker and political economist; his *Democracy in Crisis* appeared in 1933.
5 As good under the surface as on it
6 Sergei Pavlovich Diaghilev (1872–1929), the Russian ballet, art, and music impressario. *Diaghileff: The Secret of His Art and Life* by Arnold Lionel Haskell and Walter Nouvel appeared in 1935.
7 John Scott Haldane (1860–1936), father of J.B.S. Haldane; his *The Philosophy of a Biologist* was published in 1935.
8 Raymond William Chambers (1874–1942), *Thomas More* (1935)
9 William Roper (1496–1578), son-in-law of Sir Thomas More, and his first biographer. His *The Life and Death of Sir Thomas More* (Paris 1626; London 1729), although an eulogy, is still regarded as one of the main sources of information on More.
10 Probably a reference to *Two Generations* (1939); see letter of August 29, 1937.
11 Franz Werfel (1890–1945), the German expressionist poet (he was a Jew from Prague). His *Die vierzig Tage des Musa Dagh*, a novel about the persecution and mass slaughter of Armenian Christians in Turkey during World War I, was translated into English as *Forty Days of Musa Dagh* (1934), which is discussed in the following letter.

TO RICHARD CROUCH

R.R. 4, Simcoe, Ont.
January 5, 1936

My dear Crouch,

It was very good of you to send me those two vol[ume]s just at Christmas time; I have read both of them twice and am returning them now.

Both are great and magnificent conceptions, very different from each other and yet, in a way, complementary to each other; and both have the same weakness, too. Werfel:[1] the very struggle for existence in the mass, the panoramic picture achieved by mass effects; Briffault:[2] the corruption of European high society, internationally seen, the pictures achieved by an almost infinite agglomeration of minute detail, quite individualistic, almost pointillistic; neither, in a strict sense, having a hero or even a central figure (for both Gabriel Bagredian[3] and Julian[4] are the merest sketches, almost schematic points of reference).

Both books are exceedingly instructive to me, for the very reason, perhaps, that their methods are antipodally opposed to my own or to those I have tried to use; perhaps for that reason, too, I find them ultimately unsatisfying – which may be merely a sign of my own limitations. I admire the boldness of the design; I stop at a thousand points, lovingly and almost overwhelmed; and yet, when I finish, I ask myself, Is that the human destiny? Are we all going into the dark? If so, why not grip us and shake us so as to make us start up: wide-eyed, terrified, and yet resolved to cry, It shall not be! for whether revolt is successful or not, whether it is even sensible or not, it remains an attribute of the human spirit as such: it is necessary and fundamentally human. I know that European corruption (or is it merely European?); but there is another Europe; and it is not only that of the revolt of labour against capital; not only that of capital against labour. There is a Europe which has gone more deeply into the essentials: a profoundly pessimistic but also courageous Europe which would always say, '*Quand même!*'[5] In this sense Werfel is more satisfying; but I feel about his book somewhat as I feel about certain of the latest efforts of Shakespeare (*Measure for Measure*): a last crystallisation – almost a last personification – (only the German word *Gestaltung*[6] gives my exact meaning) is missing. One would like to see the struggle of a nation culminating in the struggle of one single mind and figure: Gabriel, after all, remains insignificant; and 'love' has or should have no place in a book like that; especially where it is not made convincing and remains episodic.

And yet I was moved and am moved by both these books; I should put both on my shelves if I could afford to buy books. It was an experience to read them.

Again, thanks.

I hope you and yours are well? We had a very quiet Christmas; I am hard at work.

With our best wishes for a fundamentally fruitful 1936,
As ever
F.P.G.

I am addressing the parcel to the Library, right?

1 See the preceding letter, note 11.

2 Robert Briffault (1876–1948), the English anthropologist, philosopher of history, and novelist, was the son of a French diplomat and a Scots mother. His father became involved in various political intrigues and resigned his post to settle in Britain. The son started life in medicine, but, after serving in the war, turned to the field of social anthropology and published a series of increasingly controversial but well regarded books in that field (*Psyche's Lamp, The Mothers, Rational Evolution*). Later he turned to more overtly economic and political themes, from a Communist viewpoint; and when he turned to the novel, it was largely as a vehicle for his ideas. *Europa*, the novel Grove is discussing, of which Julian Bern is the hero, appeared in 1935.

3 Hero of Werfel's novel, *Forty Days of Musa Dagh*

4 Hero of Briffault's *Europa*

5 'All the same!'

6 Shaping of disparate material; giving form to substance

TO RICHARD CROUCH

R.R. 4, Simcoe, Ont.
March 28, 1936[1]

My dear Crouch,

A few years ago, when we were in London, visiting with you, I mentioned casually that I had once or twice been in danger of losing my place here by the foreclosure of a mortgage; and you replied that, if anything like that happened again, I was to let you know; adding that you knew one or two people who would be willing to help me out by a loan.

Now by a succession of accidents such a situation seems to have arisen. You know what we have done to the house: in two years I have spent three thousand dollars on it; and yet, up to about a month ago, I felt sure that we could swing the thing. Now during the past year I have lost, on the farm, three cows and two horses. I have had to replace the horses, of course; I believe you know that. The loss of the cows – two of them were among my best – has resulted in a diminution of my farm-income, in milk, of close to three hundred dollars for the year. If my farm were clear, this would not cripple me; there is always young stock coming on to replace such as drop out. As it is, I am threatened.

So as to enable you to see just how we stand, I will give a brief statement.

We have been here 4½ years. When I started, we owed, on farm (purchase price $7,000), stock, and equipment, $5,000. Of this we have, within that time, out of earnings – school and farm – paid off $2387.67, so that we still owe, to the Ontario government, $2612.33, on which there is due, in May, a payment of $251.04, which consists of about $120 interest and about $130 capital. The Agricultural Development Board of Ontario, the creditor, has gone out of business and is said to foreclose on any debt on which payments are not kept up as per schedule; they have done so with one of my neighbours. That is where my danger comes in.

In addition to paying off $2387.67, we have invested, in the house, about $3000 or over, making the improvements that you know; and I have improved the farm to the extent of about $1000. My stock has, by careful breeding, also improved; I started with 6 cows, paying an average of $100 a head; I have 14 head today, six of which should be worth twice as much per head. Further, we have worked up a paying business in the school which, during the year, has brought a gross income of over two thousand dollars. Also, I have worked tremendously hard at my literary work, for the last two years; and I should shortly have three volumes ready for publication.

That is the situation. Now I can easily borrow the $250 odd which I need at the bank: my credit is perfect. But a bank loans on short term only. The summer is bare of school income; and I could not definitely promise to repay in less than about ten months. We have, during the past school year, spent about $1700 on the house; we have $300 more to pay, which are provided for in outstanding fees. I shall be quite willing to pay let me say 6% interest and give a note, either demand or ten months. We shall, therefore, be easily able to take care of such a loan during the next school year, especially since we shall not do any building this coming summer. It seems a trifle; and yet, by the combination of unfavourable circumstances, it is apt to trip me up. I was wondering whether you would care to see whether you could, in some way, help me out by finding someone who has that much to spare for the moment and would let me have a loan to take care of the government payment. As I said, the sum needed is $250...

I hope you are all well? We are, reasonably, except that Leonard has a bad cold just now.

Please give our regards to Mrs. Crouch, and don't forget to drop in some time soon.

As ever, yours,
F.P. Grove

P.S. – On reading this over, I find that I should have added another reason why I dislike taking the money at the bank. A farmer is often in a position where he needs temporary accommodation: by taking a bank loan I might impair that standing which enables me to finance from month to month. Right now, f[or] i[nstance], I shall have to spend about $100 on seed, which I cannot pay for till June or July. The seed house gives me 30 days; after that the bank takes care of the amount, and in another month or so I repay the bank. The farm, by the way, comprises, according to my own survey, 42 acres. In 1931, the government evaluator valued it at $6000, for the purpose of fixing the loan; a few months ago, when I wanted $400 from the bank, the bank's evaluator valued it at $9000. I promptly got the 400 and have since repaid it.

1 The original letter has 1946 clearly typed, but Leonard Grove has corrected it to 1936. The circumstances obviously fit that year rather than 1946, and the handwritten insertions are in the firm script characteristic of Grove in the twenties and thirties rather than in the shaky script found in letters of his last years.

TO LORNE PIERCE

R.R. 4, Simcoe, Ont.
June 15, 1936

Dear Dr. Pierce,

A few days ago I was told that somewhere and somewhen you have called my book *The Yoke of Life* a 'pale imitation' of *Jude The Obscure*, and my *Our Daily Bread* an imitation of *Sussex Gorse*.[1] As a mere statement of fact I wish to say that *The Yoke of Life* was known to A.L. Phelps in manuscript as early as 1923; and that I made the acquaintance of *Jude the Obscure* (which I admire tremendously) in 1925. *Sussex Gorse* is unknown to me today.

Don't think for a moment that I am peeved; nobody, as my friends know, can think less of his work than I do; I have to be clubbed into publication. But one day I wish to write the tragedy of a Canadian writer: the tragedy of the man who has something to say and tries to say it but cannot do so for sheer poverty. My personal tragedy has been that I have, throughout the forty-four years of my life in Canada, lived in exile from the realm of literature; rural libraries do not carry what I wish to read; and on an income of a few dollars a week I cannot buy books. Whether I shall ever write that book,[2] is very doubtful; I am getting old.

Sincerely yours,
F.P. Grove

1 A novel by Sheila Kaye Smith (b1887), published in 1916

2 He did, of course, write it: the first mention of the ms as anywhere near completion is in a letter to Pierce, of November 26, 1938; it was submitted to Pierce on March 9, 1940, as 'The Life of a Writer in Canada' (eventually published by Macmillan as *In Search of Myself*). In a letter to Grove, of March 29, 1940, concerning the ms, Pierce wrote: 'I did not mean that you imitated Hardy. I would not say that today, as I said it then, but even at its worst I never imagined you copied him. But let it go.' But the passage in *In Search of Myself* (p 357) appears to have been little altered, although Grove wrote Pierce on April 1, 1940, assuring him that he bore no offence.

TO W.J. ALEXANDER

Simcoe, Ont.
August 29, 1937

My dear Dr. Alexander,

Thanks very much for your kind letter;[1] and I have, accordingly sent the Ms. yesterday.

May I say a word or two?

Firstly, I have never valued *any* appreciation of any thing I have done as I valued yours.

Secondly, what I wish you could tell me is this: Are those people in the novel as much alive as they seem to me? Does this conflict between the two generations carry conviction? Is the epilogue needed? As to the latter, I thought, not; but the few people who have seen the Ms. – not the one I sent you, but the previous (second) draft all exclaimed: 'You cannot leave Abe[2] hanging in the air!' So, against my wish, I added those pages.

Now with regard to the Ms. as such, please do not bother about returning it to me, but ring up Mr. Button,[3] of J.M. Dent & Sons, 224 Bloor St. W. and ask them to call for it. If you think the whole thing 'piffle' – and I am quite prepared for that – just tell *them* to return it to me. If not, they will read it with a view to publication. Any criticism of detail I can attend to after Button is through with it. Personally, I am sorry to part with my own creations; but I have no opinion with regard to their power to interest others.

Nor am I quite sure of having brought the landscape to life. I know I have tried hard; but whether I have succeeded, that is another question.

I might add that this is the second Ontario novel I have written: the other[4] gives the other side: the struggle, the despair, the defeat which the 'depression' has brought: I have failed to interest publishers in it.

Well, permit me to repeat my thanks for your kindness in agreeing to read the Ms. and, please, if you condemn, treat me sufficiently as a friend to tell me so.

With my and my wife's very best wishes,
As ever, yours,
F.P. Grove.

1 Although this is the first letter of Grove to Alexander in this collection, the correspondence seems to have begun in 1928 (see letter of March 24, 1928, note 1; and letter of February 1, 1929, note 3). The earlier letters are missing. For the background to this letter, see *In Search of Myself* 439–41.

2 Since in the letter of September 10, 1937, Grove says that the name Abe would be changed, Abe becomes, in the published version of *Two Generations*, George, who marries Nancy, a professional dancer who leaves him for a career in New York. See also letter of 12 March 1938.

3 See letter of March 20, 1934, note 1.

4 Although Grove's next published novel, *The Master of the Mill* (1944), has an Ontario setting (Langholme-Keewatin in north-western Ontario; see letter of March 22, 1934), the reference here is probably to an unpublished novel, 'Heart's Desire; or, Two Lives' (alternative titles: 'Mortages'; 'Is It Business?'), which is set in rural Ontario, and the typescript of which is in the University of Manitoba Grove Collection.

TO W.J. ALEXANDER

R.R. 4, Simcoe, Ont.
September 4, 1937

My dear Dr. Alexander,

Thanks very much for your note regarding my Ms.[1] I feel much encouraged and shall, therefore, try to secure a publisher, though I am very sceptical with regard to that.

However, I consider it a great honour that you did read the book. I am always so uncertain about my own work unless I have had it lying about for many years. Fairley read a carbon copy and seems equally impressed.

Now, please, don't go to any trouble about the Ms. Button, of J.M. Dent & Sons, 224 Bloor St. W., promised to have it called for if you will be good enough to ring him up.

Once more, many thanks.
As ever,
Most sincerely yours,
F.P. Grove

1 *Two Generations*

TO W.J. ALEXANDER

R.R. 4, Simcoe, Ont.
September 10, 1937

My dear Dr. Alexander,

Many thanks for your second letter re the book.[1] It has helped and encouraged me more than I can tell.

Your criticisms regarding details will all be attended to – I believe you are right in every point but one. I shall change the name Abe; the title is to be found; the verses from 'The Ode to Autumn' deleted; the epilogue will be left out. That epilogue I considered quite unnecessary; but a few lay novel readers to whom I gave the last but final version insisted that I must 'wind' Abe and Nancy 'up.' I had very grave doubts about the wisdom of that. But I wrote that chapter tentatively – with this in mind that I was going to ask you and Fairley to tell me how it struck you. I am glad you agree with me.

The only point I am doubtful about is the blizzard. That scene was in my mind when I wrote the first line of the first draft; and after much careful deliberation I placed it where I left it, for many reasons. I wish I could talk to you and unfold these reasons. But it would take pages of writing, and I do not wish to weary you.

May I repeat that I appreciate tremendously what you have done for me?

With my best and most cordial wishes, I remain,
as ever,
Sincerely yours
F.P. Grove

1 *Two Generations*; see the preceding letters.

TO RICHARD CROUCH

R.R. 4, Simcoe, Ont.
October 18, 1937

My dear Crouch,

How is it that we have drifted apart like this? I haven't seen you for two years.

Is it permissible to post announcements like the enclosed[1] in the Library? If so, will you post this one? I've done something like it here; but I must make pennies by it. The U[niversity] apparently opposes.

Best regards, as ever
F.P. Grove

1 Any enclosure in this letter has not been preserved; possibly Crouch did post it. Grove may well have been advertising lectures; see the following letter, and that of November 15, 1931.

TO RICHARD CROUCH

R.R. 4, Simcoe, Ont.
October 27, 1937

My dear Crouch,

Fine! Only make it as early in the morning as you can and have lunch here, will you?

Now it so happens that I have an appointment with the handful of people who answered my ad[1] for 1:30 at the London Hotel on *Saturday*, Oct[ober] 30. So I'll drop in on you some time for a few minutes in the morning.

I should like to see a number of people, so shall be rushed.

Best regards for you and yours.
As ever
F.P.G.

P.S. I expect to get there around 10 a.m. or half past on Sat[urday].

1 See the preceding letter.

TO RICHARD CROUCH

R.R. 4, Simcoe, Ont.
November 1, 1937

My dear Crouch,

I am deeply immersed in work, revising, remodelling my notes; and the more I work, the more it seems to me I can give something. I have read Lubbock:[1] interesting but inconclusive: very good reading; also Muir,[2] not so stimulating, too professional: sometimes I laugh.

However, I am profoundly conscious of a gap in my knowledge of latter-day fiction. I have never read Virginia Woolf – nor anything

16 Richard E. Crouch 1948. *Courtesy Keith Crouch*

of Gertrude Stein. What more natural than that I should turn to you? Could you help me out? Perhaps – I'm not sure – I can leave Gertrude Stein safely to one side. But Virginia Woolf, from what I have read *about* her?

If so, and a time-limit is desirable, don't hesitate to say so.

I had bad pains when in London. Today I saw the doctor; and he diagnosed a kidney that has gone on travels.

Remember me to Mrs. C., will you?
As ever
F.P.G.

1 Percy Lubbock (1879–1957), *The Craft of Fiction*, published in London 1921, and in New York 1929

2 Edwin Muir (1887–1959), *The Structure of the Novel*, 1928/9

TO RICHARD CROUCH

R.R. 4 Simcoe, Ont.
November 12, 1937

My dear Crouch,

I return, under separate cover, the 2 Virginia Woolf[1] and the Gertrude Stein,[2] fearing they may be asked for. I am very glad to have had an opportunity to see what sort of things these two women do. Neither seems to me of any fundamental importance, such as attaches to Joyce or Lawrence, let me say.

I retain the rest of the books for a few days longer, but shall despatch them, too, next week, unless we hear by that time that you people are coming here.

I am getting my lectures into shape and am just wondering whether anything will come of them.

I can hardly tell you how refreshing I found my recent visit to London. One gets stale sitting in one's burrow.

Please remember me to your wife.
As ever
F.P.G.

1 I can only speculate on the identity of these books. The most recent novels of Virginia Woolf (1882–1941) were *The Years* (1937) and *The Waves* (1931).

2 The following books by Gertrude Stein (1874–1946) appeared in the thirties: *Three Lives* (1933), *The Geographical Lust of America* (1936), and *Everybody's Autobiography* (1937).

TO RICHARD CROUCH

R.R. 4 Simcoe, Ont.
December 10, 1937

My dear Crouch,

I am at last returning the last of the books which I borrowed from you more than a month ago; and I feel I must apologize for the unconscionable delay. I found all but that Gallishaw volume[1] exceedingly helpful in preparing my lectures; in fact I feel I should own them. But...

I don't suppose there is any development re those lectures?

I trust you and yours are well? We are.

With best regards from all of us for you and Mrs. Crouch and Keith.[2]

As ever
F.P.G.

1 Presumably *Advanced Problems of the Fiction Writer: A discussion of basic plot patterns* (London and New York 1931). John Gallishaw's two other books, *The Only Two Ways to Write a Story* (1928) and *Twenty Problems of the Fiction Writer* (1929), may also be considered.

2 Crouch's son, Director of Libraries at McGill University (1967–72).

TO W.J. ALEXANDER

R.R. 4 Simcoe, Ont.,
December 25, 1937

My dear Dr. Alexander,

We are such terribly casual people; and so the very brief note I had written to you had not yet left when your most welcome letter arrived. I replace it by the present sheets.

May I say, first of all, that I wish you a continuance of health and vigour, and that my wife joins me in that wish? We often talk of you; for, may I say this, too, that my contact with you has been one of the most encouraging things with which I have met during the last two decades? I don't know why it is, but I make fewer and fewer friends as the years go by; and, considering the nature of the work which I have tried to do, we live in a very strange isolation.

I was doubly glad to get your letter because you express a number of things which have long worried me. Thus I have always wondered at the success of Miss de la Roche;[1] not, of course, at her success in Canada, but in England and the U.S.A. I, too, have the feeling that her work proceeds, not from a contemplation of life but of books; her inspiration is essentially second-hand. As for my own lack of success, I don't know. I often think that perhaps there is something essential lacking in my endowment. The hostility displayed against my production – for it is not mere indifference – is too unanimous not to be sprung from something that is fundamental; I mean, of course, the hostility shown by the public and its servants, the publishers. In this connection I might say that I have, so far, utterly failed in securing publication for *The Two Generations*; five publishers have declined it; and several literary agents have outright declined even to read it. So there it stands. I have, during the last eight years, written no less than six novels,[2] three of which I consider good; they have all shared the same fate. Before this somewhat discouraging experience with *The Two Generations*, I had started work on a large novel dealing with the very thing you touch on in your letter: the breaking-up of a whole civilization, in the rural parts of Ontario; I am not so sure that I shall go on with it. It seems futile to write and write in order to put manuscripts on my shelves.

In fact, I have tried very hard, of late, to secure some sort of a position in Toronto which would pay for our daily bread. For the clouds of financial disaster that were threatening last spring have meanwhile broken. I do not mean to go into details which are all depressing. But even my attempts at securing some sort of work have been in vain: I applied, for instance, for the position as 'Book-Adviser' at Simpson's – a position which recently became vacant; they asked me to come in for a personal interview; but, the moment they saw I wasn't a young man, they expressed their regret; and I went home. Then I applied for work as a proof-reader with the Ryerson Press; I tried to arrange for a series of lectures on The Technique of the Novel; and everywhere I meet with the same stony hostility. It would be amusing if it were not somewhat disastrous.

However ... I must not trouble you with my personal worries. The mere fact that you read my last book in manuscript has been an encouragement; and even at that I had not been aware of your having gone to the trouble of inserting numerous marginal notes, often in the form of diacritical marks. When the manuscript came back a few days ago, I reread it and found them; and I found most of them helpful and worthy of being attended to.

My wife just now put her head into my door and asked, 'Writing to Dr. Alexander?' On my answering in the affirmative, she said, 'Please give him my best regards and say that, if he at any time feels equal to the fatigue of travelling down here, I should be proud to be his hostess for a week or two; and that I shall do my best to make him feel comfortable.' So there you are; and I do hope you will take this as an invitation meant sincerely and seriously. I could meet you at Brantford or Hamilton any time; and bring Miss Alexander[3] if she cares to come.

Once more, the best wishes from both of us. The little boy is very happy just now, for we were lucky enough to pick up a second-hand electric train for him at negligible cost. When he saw it, he said, 'You're so good to me that I must thank you till next Christmas comes around.'

As ever, yours,
F.P. Grove

1 For Mazo de la Roche, see letter of March 26, 1928II, note 3.
2 Four of which are certain: *Consider Her Ways* (which Dent had apparently offered to Doran in the USA in 1934; see letter of March 21, 1934, note 1), *The Master of the Mill* (mentioned in letter of March 22, 1934 as in preparation), *Two Generations*, and the fourth was the Ontario novel dealing with the effects of the Depression (mentioned in letter of August 29, 1937) – presumably the unpublished 'Heart's Desire.' The remaining two could have been any of his other unpublished manuscripts either in the University of Manitoba Grove Collection or no longer extant. 'The Canyon' and 'Felix Powell's Career' seem the most likely ones.
3 The present Mrs Edith L. McIver of Caledon East, Ontario

TO W.J. ALEXANDER

R.R. 4 Simcoe, Ont.
March 12, 1938

My dear Dr. Alexander,

I was quite touched by your request for a typescript copy of *The Two Generations*; and I almost begin to believe that there must be some merit in that book, although my entire failure to secure even publication, not to say anything about a sale, has long since made me skeptical of my gifts.

Now the two final copies of that book are in New York and London, Eng[land], respectively. But I promptly went to the barn to search in a box in which I keep discarded Mss. I found the original pencil-script and one typescript on onion-skin paper, the third or fourth version which I typed out (I usually have to make 6 or 7 before I leave off).

I looked it over and found that in various respects it differs from the final version: The name 'Abe' for the second brother is still retained (in the final copies it was changed to 'George'); the text is rougher, not having had the last filing; and the final 4 chapters were re-written so as to make it possible to dispense with that awkward 'Epilogue' and yet, by a touch here and there, to 'wind up,' as I call it, George's (Abe's) story.

I am sending you this Ms. which I should gladly correct for you if I had the final version here – sending it in spite of my misgivings: the thin paper makes it hard reading. I cannot afford to use expensive paper except for final versions: 'onion-skin' costs me only 65¢ per 1000 sheets.

I have managed meanwhile to put a 'feature' story or article into the London (Ontario) *Free Press*[1] – and that yields me between $5 and $10 a month (it was $10 only once; and it has been as low as $3.50; but then I rebelled). All which would be amusing enough if it were not partly tragic.

As for any use you may care to make of the typescript, I leave you entirely at liberty. *A Search for America* circulated among friends for decades before it was printed.

I have heard of your interest in my (this) book before this, in a roundabout way; and I always feel as if I must get busy and at last justify your kindness by doing *a real book*. I am trying hard right now: another Ontario novel which I, for identification purposes (not for a title) so far call 'Democracy'[2]: and in which I am trying to present the whole countryside, towns, villages, and rural districts in one broad canvass [sic]. If only I did not mistrust my powers so much!!

The *U[niversity] of T[oronto] Quarterly* will in the July number, bring my answer to Morley Callaghan's 'The Rights of Canadian Fiction' (January issue).[3] Would you care to read that answer in typescript? I have it ready, but shall keep it on my desk for another month or so, to reread and file.

With my most cordial wishes for yourself and yours, I remain,

Most sincerely yours,
F.P. Grove

1 I am not certain what the '"feature" story or article' refers to, but since Grove says that the payment averaged between $5 and $10 a month, it may have been for short book reviews which appeared in the London *Free Press* in 1937 and 1938 and were credited to 'P.G.F.' See, for instance, the *Free Press* of December 3, 1937 p 12 ('Hints Clean-Up of Race is Needed'), December 17, 1937 p 11 ('Put Personality into History of U.S.'), February 5, 1938 p 9 ('Curious English Girl Tells of Baghdad'), March 31, 1938 p 13 ('Woman Reporter Tells About Events'), April 9, 1938 p 9 (review of G. Ward Price's *I Know These Dictators*), April 19, 1938 p 10 ('Bloody Days in History of Kansas'), April 20, 1938 p 13 ('Humanity Closer to Collective Security'), April 21, 1938 p 11 ('Says Duce Long Had Idea of Conquest'), April 25, 1938 p 10 (review of C.E. Rosendahl's *What About the Airship?*), April 27, 1938 p 10 ('Barney Barnato Plunger in Diamonds'), April 28, 1938 p 13 ('Climber Tells of His Vertical Travels'), April 30, 1938 p 11 ('Selfish Politics Blamed for Strife'), May 2, 1938 p 12 ('Excitement in Files of the "Mounties"'), and May 4, 1938 p 10 ('Vanished Life of the Villages is Told'). This is, however, only a guess on my part, and the search in the London *Free Press* is still continuing. In a letter Miss Elizabeth Spicer of the London Public Library and Art Museum writes (July 29, 1974): 'Your "Grove" inquiry presents an intriguing problem especially as correspondence and older personnel of the London *Free Press* of the 1930's seem to be almost non-existent now. I have talked to Mr. John K. Elliott, Editor Emeritus, and to Mr. Les Bronson of the London *Free Press*. Both had considerable experience with the various pages and authors. They both agree that "P.G.F." sounds like a possible anagram for "F.P.G.". Mr. Bronson feels that such a designation sounds like the selection Grove would use. Neither one remembers Grove's connection in any distinctive way. At the time of the late 1930's the correspondence would have been handled directly by Mr. Arthur Ford, the Editor, who is deceased. ... As Grove came to get books fairly often from the Library I suspect he probably left his reviews with Mr. Frederick Ferguson McMartin [Editor of the review page] whose office was close to the Library. I am sorry only to have a "feeling" rather than a proof of this matter. But I think that you are "safe" in assigning "P.G.F." to Frederick Philip Grove.'

For two other references by Grove to his contributions in the London *Free Press*, see letters of October 21, 1939 and February 3, 1943.

2 'The Seasons,' which remained incomplete

3 'The Plight of Canadian Fiction? A Reply,' *University of Toronto Quarterly* VII (July 1938) 451–67

TO RICHARD CROUCH

R.R. 4 Simcoe, Ont.
September 3, 1938

My dear Crouch,

I enclose something that will interest you.[1] Please hand on if you have an opportunity.

I have kept those books of yours an unconscionable time, but shall send them within a week or so.

Having suddenly been seized with the inspiration of working up and consolidating the sequel of *A Search for America*,[2] I have been dead to the world and unable even to read anything but my own text. All day long I write; at night I read what I have written.

In a great hurry,
as ever, yours,
F.P.G.

More copies of enclosed are available if needed.

1 Presumably the announcement of a private printing of *Two Generations*, and order forms therefor
2 Which eventually became *In Search of Myself* (1946)

TO W.J. ALEXANDER

R.R. 4 Simcoe, Ont.
September 24, 1938

My dear Dr. Alexander,

Thanks for your letter. I shall at once send E.K. Brown[1] a supply of circulars, say 50.

Thanks also, very much, for your endeavours, I have received at least 3 subscriptions from people whom I had not circularised, for they are not on my list: MacFarlane,[2] Underhill,[3] N.A. Mackenzie;[4] and I, therefore, trace these to you.

I have now 30 copies sold; but I need a minimum of 388 which will barely cover the cost. However, I cover a new list from day to day; I sent out 133 circulars this morning, to all librarians in Ontario whose names I could get; and to further university men.

One annoying thing is that I must do all this work in bed; I have been laid up with arthritis and a terrific cold for some time.

Many subscribers scribble encouraging words on their blanks; and in spite of the slow response (the total number sent out exceeds 500 now) I feel quite 'bucked.'

No, I don't betray any misgivings to anyone but my closest friends.

Thanks again.
Sincerely yours,
F.P. Grove.

1 Edward Killoran Brown (1905–51) taught English at the University of Toronto from 1929 to 1935, and again from 1937 to 1941 – the intervening years being spent at the University of Manitoba. He became Chairman of the Department of English, Cornell University, in 1941, moving in 1944 to the University of Chicago. His contribution to Canadian criticism is complemented by his studies of Matthew Arnold and E.M. Forster (*Matthew Arnold: A Study in Conflict*, 1948; *Rhythm in the Novel*, 1950). While editor of the *University of Toronto Quarterly* (1932–41), he introduced the section 'Letters in Canada,' an annual survey of Canadian writing. His *On Canadian Poetry* won the Governor-General's Award for 1943.

2 Impossible to identify without initials. At any rate, there does not seem to have been a professor of that name in the University of Toronto at that time. Correspondence with the short story writer Leslie McFarlane (b1902) and the widow of the late R. Oliver MacFarlane (1904–71), who at the time of his death was director of the School of Public Administration, Carleton University, would indicate that it was neither of them.

3 Frank H. Underhill, the historian. Born in 1889 in Ontario, and trained as a classicist at the University of Toronto, he came under the influence of the Fabian movement during the three years he spent at Oxford. In 1914 he joined the University of Saskatchewan as Professor of Political Science, moving in 1927 to the University of Toronto as Professor of History. He was one of the founders of the CCF and author of several political tracts. A collection of his essays, *In Search of Canadian Liberalism* (1960), won the Governor-General's Award. He was elected a Fellow of the Royal Society of Canada in 1949. He died in 1971.

4 The initials in the letter appear to be *M*.A., which would suggest M.A. MacKenzie (b1866) who was then Professor of Actuarial Science at the University of Toronto. However, the more likely person is N(orman) A. MacKenzie (b1894), then Professor of International Law and Canadian Constitution at the University of Toronto and later President of the University of New Brunswick (1940–4), President of the University of British Columbia (1944–62), and a member of the Canadian Senate (1966–9). Dr MacKenzie is retired and lives in Vancouver, BC.

TO W.J. ALEXANDER

R.R. 4 Simcoe, Ont.
September 29, 1938

My dear Dr. Alexander,

Thanks awfully for your kind note. I was afraid that my sending 50 copies to Prof. Brown would look as if I were trying to impose a task upon him. I shall, of course, be only too glad to send him more, and despatch, therefore, an additional supply.

I cannot express my appreciation of your kind endeavours in my behalf; you are, so far, the only person who is doing anything on a considerable scale. I have now a total of 30 subscriptions, for 39 copies, which, I console myself, is over 10% of what is needed to cover the cost (388 copies). I know of ca. 20 more which will come in by-and-by. People are casual about such things.

I have sent 25 blanks to Mrs. Haddow,[1] as you suggest.

Again, many thanks from
Yours sincerely
F.P. Grove

P.S. I enclose 3 blanks as a matter of routine. I do so with every letter I send out.

F.P.G.

1 Presumably, the wife of George Caldwell Haddow; see the following letter, note 2.

TO RICHARD CROUCH

R.R. 4 Simcoe, Ont.
September 30, 1938

My dear Crouch,

The enclosed[1] marks, of course, a move of desperation. However, I mean to put it over.

The Library of Parliament, P[ublic] L[ibrary] of Toronto, P[ublic] L[ibrary] of Hamilton, the university libraries of Western and Toronto are among those that have come through nobly.

A good many libraries are supplying me with names. W.J. Alexander, E.K. Brown, Geo[rge] C. Haddow[2] (McMaster) have constituted themselves into a voluntary brigade of canvassers.

I have a few subscriptions from London, Tamblyn, Spencely[3] – I think that's all.

I know you are rushed. But, can you find a moment to jot down a few names? The need is great. I am still 388 – no 349 – subscriptions short, for there are 39 in the mail.

Hope you are all well. I, like yourself, am in a rush and have been laid up with arthritis and a cold; but am somewhat better.

As ever
F.P.G.

1 Circulars inviting subscription to the privately printed edition of *Two Generations*

2 George Caldwell Haddow taught English at the University of Manitoba from 1922 to 1925, moving to McMaster University in 1926, where he became Head of the Department in 1948. He retired in 1960.

3 William Ferguson Tamblyn (1874–1956) and James A. Spencely (1881–1956), both at the time professors of English at the University of Western Ontario, and friends of the Crouches

TO W.J. ALEXANDER

Simcoe, Ont.
October 10, 1938

Dear Dr. Alexander,

E.K. Brown writes that you wish for some more circulars. I am sending 50.

I have by this time 75 subscriptions; they are coming in very slowly; and among those there is one for 20 copies from the London Public Library. However, I am still hammering away; every day at least a few circulars go out.

I have written to 16 libraries, asking them for lists of people who might be interested; and I have received 3 answers with lists; but no subscriptions have resulted from them.

However, I keep working.

I am somewhat better again, though I find it impossible to get rid of my cough.

Don't be saving with circulars; I have plenty (over 1000) left, though I have sent out ca. 1500 now.

With very best regards,
Yours sincerely
F.P. Grove

TO RICHARD CROUCH

R.R. 4 Simcoe, Ont.
October 24, 1938

My dear Crouch,

The printing of *Two Generations* has meanwhile come within measurable distance of realization, though I still need ca. 200 subscriptions. It strikes me that, if this printing is secured, some regular publisher might strike off perhaps 1000 copies with no additional cost but that of paper, labour and binding, in other words, he might save the expense of setting up the type. I am reluctant to offer this to Macmillans (on account of what you told me),[1] or to the Ryerson Press or McClelland & Stewart (put it down to personal prejudice). Do you think Reg Saunders[2] might be interested? If so, could you jot down his address for me?

I am tremendously busy with a continuation of *A Search for America* – besides planning a trilogy on academic and political life in Ontario.[3]

I feel that the time remaining to me is very short indeed; and so I work feverishly.

As ever
F.P.G.

1 What this matter was, we shall never know.
2 S.J. Reginald Saunders. Born in England in 1898, he settled in Toronto in the publishing trade in 1928, after a brief teaching career in Britain, and worked as an export manager for a British firm, which took him travelling extensively in North America. He started his own publishing business in 1931, retaining business interests in associated fields. He died in 1945, but the firm continued in business.
3 The trilogy was never published, probably never written; the sequel to *A Search for America* is, of course, *In Search of Myself*.

TO FINDLAY WEAVER[1]

R.R. 4 Simcoe, Ont.
October 24, 1938 II

Dear Mr. Weaver,

I am sorry I cannot comply with your request. The book as it *may* be printed, will, if it *is* printed, be distributed *as a manuscript*; and every subscriber is going to be asked to regard it as confidential *till* (if ever) the trade edition appears. After that, of course, I wash my hands of it.

There is another reason: every copy going out *must* bring the $4 if the printing is to be assured.

As for the *University of Toronto Quarterly*, the notice[2] was inserted by Professors E.K. Brown and A.S.P. Woodhouse,[3] *not* by myself. It is an attempt, on *their* part, to secure the printing, for they read the book as a typescript.

In other words, if this printing comes about, it is not to be considered as a *publication*. Publication may or may not follow later on.

Yes, I have seen one or two issues of *The Bookman*, but even if I wanted to, I could not possibly afford to subscribe.

Sincerely,
F.P. Grove

1 Findlay Weaver, then publisher of the *Canadian Bookman* – see letter of November 1, 1938, note 1.
2 Which sought subscriptions for the limited edition of *Two Generations* – see letter of November 1, 1938, and the enclosure.
3 Arthur Sutherland Pigott Woodhouse (1895–1964) was educated at the University of Toronto and Harvard University. For many years a professor of English at the University of Toronto, he contributed literary criticism and scholarship, mainly on Milton and the seventeenth century, to several periodicals. He edited the *University of Toronto Quarterly* (1933–45) and 'Letters in Canada' (1935–45), collaborated with Watson Kirkconnell on *The Humanities in Canada* (1947), and edited *Puritanism and Liberty* (1938). His magnum opus on Milton was incomplete at his death, but, edited by Hugh MacCallum, it appeared in 1972 (University of Toronto Press) as *The Heavenly Muse*.

The letters from Phelps to Grove indicate that Woodhouse met and admired Grove when

Woodhouse was a member of the Department of English at the University of Manitoba in the late nineteen-twenties. If there were letters from Grove to Woodhouse, they appear not to have survived.

TO LORNE PIERCE

R.R. 4 Simcoe, Ont.
November 1, 1938

Dear Dr. Pierce,

Yes, your name is on my list.

Thanks for the complimentary subscription to the *Bookman*. As I said to Mr. Findlay,[1] in my recent letter to him, I am much, much too poor to subscribe to any periodicals, though I receive a few as gifts.

As for the ad which you offer, would something like that in the *U[niversity] of T[oronto] Quarterly* do? I attach a blank of the text as they printed it, also free of charge.

I enclose a few extra blanks. Perhaps you know a person or two who might be interested? I still need ca. 200 subscriptions.

As ever,
F.P.G.

FREDERICK PHILIP GROVE
Will shortly issue, by subscription, a private printing, limited to not more than 500 copies, of the first edition of an Ontario novel
THE TWO GENERATIONS
The edition will be printed on special paper, all copies numbered, autographed and bound in a distinctive binding. It will not be followed by a trade edition inside of six months.

. . . . . .

(*Fill in and return to*)
Mr F.P. Grove, R.R. 4 Simcoe, Ont.
Please reserve for me ______ copies of the above edition of
THE TWO GENERATIONS
at $4.00 the copy, postpaid.

Date______ Signature____________

Address____________

Enclosed find cheque (par at Simcoe).
Or: Please have me billed on delivery.
(*Check off your choice.*)

1 See the preceding letter. Findlay Weaver (Grove was obviously confused by the fact that both names are possible surnames) was publisher of the *Canadian Book Trade Journal* up to February 1922, when it merged with the *Canadian Bookman*. In 1926 Weaver became publisher of the *Bookman*, which he remained until some time shortly after 1936; he was still on the *Bookman* staff in 1938, in an advertising capacity. Frank Flemington, of the Ryerson Press, recalls that he was a frequent visitor in the Ryerson offices in the thirties, which may explain how the preceding letter found its way into Dr Pierce's files.

Weaver was also connected with a small publication called *The Narrator*.

TO W.J. ALEXANDER

R.R. 4 Simcoe, Ont.
November 7, 1938

Dear Dr. Alexander,

I have been wanting to thank you for the consistent endeavour to help me in putting the private edition of *Two Generations* over on a reluctant public. I have received quite a few subscriptions from Toronto people whom I had not circularised and credit for whom must, therefore, be due to you. A very few others have also been active.

It is now 10 weeks since I began the campaign; and I am glad to say that I have come within very little over 100 subscriptions of the goal; but, of course, the more names go down on my lists, the slower the process becomes. However, I am hopeful now.

Among Toronto subscribers whom I do not know is a lady who signs herself Lena Thompson MacAlpine,[1] if I read correctly; but she gives no address; and even that she lives in Toronto I infer merely from the post-office stamp. I was wondering whether you know her and could give me any information as to her address?

I am very hard at work, both on the story of my struggles as a writer and a new Ontario novel.

Not having heard from you for some time, except indirectly, I worry about your health; I do hope you are enjoying this marvellous fall weather. I myself am somewhat better again, though I have developed a painful, chronic cough; but there is a let-up from arthritis; and I am up and doing.

With our very best wishes and kindest regards,
as ever, your
F.P. Grove

1 The wife of Lt. Col. Cyril Douglas Hughes MacAlpine, OBE, a Toronto mining executive

17 W.J. Alexander. *Courtesy Leonard Grove*

TO W.J. ALEXANDER

R.R. 4 Simcoe, Ont.
November 14, 1938

Dear Dr. Alexander,

You gave me genuine pleasure by what you say of your health. As for the recession of powers, we all feel that, of course; I am still 16 years your junior; but I have watched the process in myself for some time. Yet, strangely, I think it has its compensations: a certain detachment arises; a certain elevation of point of view which makes me understand why, in the older civilizations, it was the elders who dominated the state; many things might be better, so I often think, if our senate, instead of being a political machine, were truly an assembly of seniors.

As for the book, I shall continue my fight for a while longer. I had only one subscription last week; but many of those I have received were accompanied by most encouraging notes.

Mr. McFarlane[1] misunderstands the idea of this limited edition. It is not to be a publication in the ordinary sense; though I still hope that publication will follow it.

As for his and your remarks on minor matters (which may be major, after all),[2] I might say that, probably, you have not seen the final version, which, by the way, is itself not final yet; I am going to undertake the last revision this week; and I assure you that all you and Mr. McFarlane have said will be borne in mind in making it. There is only one point which seems irremediable: the opening, of which, I am afraid, I was rather proud. Phil says within the first thirty pages: 'I can't stand the man'; meaning his father. But even in that I shall try to shorten things up, so as to advance that statement if I can.

I might say that the matter of Phil and Alice is a most delicate one. Frankly, in the first conception of these two characters and their relation to each other, there was something which I felt to approach to a feeling transcending that of mere brotherly or sisterly love: as if some creative power had deliberately chosen to split a single personality into two; and since this might give rise to a misconception, I deliberately introduced, at a later stage, that brief reference to their relationship in the scene between the oldest brother and his wife Cathleen; it was intended to kill every suspicion of anything remotely approaching to what Mr. McFarlane calls incest. I shall most carefully ponder the question whether or not this reference is advisable. I feel that I cannot touch the scenes between Alice and Philip without, in Lamb's phrase, falsifying a revelation; they were written down as by dictation; out of an insight into psychologic subtleties entirely beyond the influence of any will of mine.

You may remember that, at first (and perhaps at last as well) you felt that the blizzard should come at an earlier stage; I could not see it; and I still cannot see it; what follows is essentially the resolution of the conflict, in the scene in the kitchen of the house in the hollow in which the father takes part, rapt beyond himself at last, as it were; and somehow I had to give the two young people in conflict with what is quite external to them before I let them face that father with the unconcern with which they do face him, thereby forcing him to his final gesture. I merely mention this in order to make clear that I can take, and listen to, any criticism without necessarily being overwhelmed by it. For in that point I still believe I am right.

But I am no less grateful for the expression of any hesitancy; it is such letters as Mr. McFarlane's and yours that I need; in my writing, as in any writing, there is a great deal that is fortuitous; that is instinctive; and the reasons for which I have painstakingly to unravel ex-post-facto; it is only by this unravelling that I can progress (or advance myself). I am very glad indeed that I had these two criticisms before starting on the final revision.

Believe me
yours most gratefully,
F.P. Grove

1 See letter of September 24, 1938, note 2.
2 Concerning *Two Generations*

TO LORNE PIERCE

R.R. 4 Simcoe, Ont.
November 21, 1938

My dear Dr. Pierce,

The printing of that limited issue of my book *Two Generations* is at last assured since I have a sufficient number of subscriptions to cover the cost.

May I add that the issue will be plainly marked as a private, 'manuscript' printing, in the European fashion; subscribers will be asked, by a slip inserted, to consider it as confidential; no copies will be issued to press or trade. It is very largely my friends who have subscribed, of course.

Now the text will be set up about the turn of the year or a little later; I shall be in Toronto some time next week to make the final arrangements. It has all along been my intention to enter into an arrangement with some Canadian publisher in order to have him take advantage of the fact that the type will be set, so he can strike off 500 or 1000 or 2000 copies of a trade edition to be published next fall; whatever number he thinks advisable. This, of course, reduces the cost of manufacture considerably; for there will be no setting-up to pay for.

My question is, would you consider such a proposition? I am approaching you first, in spite of the fact that I know of several others who would do this, because I know you have the small-library trade. A few of the larger libraries, of which I should furnish you with a list, have subscribed for 1 or 2 copies; and even those have not enough to cover the demand which will arise.

You have read or at least looked into the book; the Ms.

has been read by about 2 dozen people all of whom were enthusiastic, most of all Dr. W.J. Alexander, to whom I can refer you. It is the first of my 'pleasant' books which I offer; and it is the first Ontario novel which I have written, the date of composition being 1931/36. It even has a 'happy ending'; or at least so it will appear to a vast majority of readers. But the book is so exclusively Canadian that, so far, no American publisher has cared to undertake its printing, in spite of the fact that I have received highly flattering letters from half a dozen of them.

Hoping to hear from you at your earliest convenience, I remain,

Sincerely yours,
F.P. Grove

TO LORNE PIERCE

R.R. 4 Simcoe, Ont.
November 26, 1938

Dear Dr. Pierce,

Thanks for your kind letter.

Weather permitting, I shall be in Toronto coming Wednesday, Nov[ember] 30, and shall give myself the pleasure of seeing you first of all – say around 10 a.m., unless I am delayed on the road.[1]

May I mention one matter in advance? The U[niversity] of T[oronto] contemplates putting one of my books on the list for a small, special literature class; from what E.K. Brown says, it will likely be *A Search for America*. The class demand will probably not exceed 40 copies a year, so far. But I have 2000 sets of sheets, folded, not gathered, and, of course, unbound. I have not placed this on the market because I wanted to write a special preface for it, of about 16 pages; this is written now in a 2nd vol[ume], so far entitled (tentatively) 'In Search of Myself,'[2] and dealing with the 26 years following the years treated of in the older book. Now this is the problem: Would you be willing to handle this in a way that the cost, to *students*, would be not exceeding $1.25 – i.e. printing of the preface, gathering, and binding, leaving me a small fee or royalty – putting the price to the general public at perhaps $1.50. There has been, during the last 7 years, since I withdrew the book, a small, trickling demand for it. I also have the plates, and hold all copyrights. With the preface, the copyright would have to be renewed, of course. It would constitute the 4th edition. I believe that, if the book were on display again, the ordinary demand could be considerably increased, especially at a low price. I should, however, want to retain the copyright and make a contract only for, either, a given number of years or a given number of copies.

Whoever brings this reprinting or re-issuing of the older book would, of course, be in the first line for the new book, too.

Macmillans, of course, are anxious; so, I understand, are

Dents; but I feel that Dents have made a mess of it (they handled the *Search* for a while; I gave them ca. 1000 copies, bound, which they disposed of); and Macmillans have tied me down to contracts which I disapprove of. I have, therefore, not published anything for 6 years, although there are plenty of books available.

I will frankly say that I am not looking for a publisher who puts the momentary advantage ahead of my interests as seen over a period of years.

For the moment I am anxious chiefly to secure a Canadian trade edition for *Two Generations*. Then, slowly, I want to re-issue all my older books, revised – while, at the same time, bringing out new books at the rate of one for every year or two. *Two Generations* has roused the enthusiasm of every Canadian who has read it, but does not seem to appeal to either English or U.S.A. publishers: perhaps it is too Ontarian. That was the reason why I at last took the course I did take.

But of all that orally when I see you.
Sincerely yours,
F.P.G.

1 See letter of December 8, 1938, note 1, for the results of this visit.

2 This title, eventually used when the book appeared in 1946, was obviously in Grove's mind at this point; yet when the complete manuscript was first submitted to Pierce in 1940, 'The Life of a Writer in Canada' was used instead (cf. letters of June 15, 1936, February 2 and March 9, 1940). The reference here is probably to the essay which appeared in the *University of Toronto Quarterly* in 1940 under the same title, and is reprinted in the autobiography as 'Prologue.'

Carleton Stanley in a letter to Mrs Grove dated December 11, 1963, blames himself for having persuaded Grove and Ellen Elliott to print the 'Prologue' as it is 'a flat contradiction of the whole book!!! It is pessimistic, and the book, on the whole, is happy.' The Stanley letter is preserved in the University of Manitoba Grove Collection.

TO LORNE PIERCE

R.R. 4 Simcoe, Ont.
December 1, 1938

Dear Dr. Pierce,

I have just written to Dents and Macmillans, in the sense discussed between us.[1]

As for sheets of *Two Generations*, I have most carefully figured everything over once more and find that my guess of $.60 per set was correct within 1¢; it should have been 61 cents, on the basis of 1000 copies, inclusive of royalty; but I am willing to let the price of $.60 stand.

Hoping sincerely that your trouble is subsiding, I remain,
sincerely yours,

P.S. I have put you down for an additional 2 copies of that limited edition.

F.P.G.

1 See letter of December 8, 1938, note 1.

TO W.J. ALEXANDER

R.R. 4 Simcoe, Ont.
December 1, 1938 II

My dear Dr. Alexander,

I was in Toronto yesterday and looked all the time for an opportunity to slip up to Spadina Rd., but every minute was taken, and I drove home in the dark and through a snow-storm; I could not afford to stay over. I felt very sorry.

All arrangements about the printing have been made, and I have sold 1000 copies of a trade edition; it still leaves me short by about 40 copies of the limited edition the cost of which I have to bear; but orders are still dribbling in. May I say that, of the subscriptions I have received, I now trace 67 directly to you; I think that is quite extraordinary. R.E. Crouch, librarian of London, Ont[ario], stands next with 26; Carleton Stanley, third, with 25, i.e. if I can take him seriously when he says that he 'would take 25 copies if necessary.' I shall write to him quite frankly about it. If he means to take them personally, and only in order to help me, I feel I cannot accept it.

I consider myself very lucky in having been able to arrange for a trade edition (which I could not have done without the limited edition which bears the greater part of the cost of setting up type); but the trade edition cuts my cost by about $300. I am printing only 400 copies of the limited edition; and that leaves me without any honorarium; but that is a minor consideration.

I have just received an invitation from University College to address the student body in the near future. The date is still uncertain; it depends on the topic which Dr. Wallace[1] chooses; I submitted two; one on which I can speak any time; another for which I need another three or four weeks; I am such a slow worker.

I might say that I have carefully borne your and Mr. McFarlane's suggestions[2] in mind in making the final revision of *Two Generations*; and I believe, or rather hope, that the new form, with the opening shortened and much lifted out of what you objected to, will meet with your approval.

I do hope you are keeping well. The weather has been marvellous on the whole, and I, for one, am almost free of arthritis now, though I suffer from a chronic cough.

I also hope you will be pleased with the appearance of the

book on which I have spent much thought and considerable time. Type-setting began yesterday, so that I was able to see the first page before I left the city.

I hope to see you on the occasion of my forthcoming visit to University College.

Most sincerely yours,
F.P. Grove

1 Malcolm William Wallace (1873–1960), the biographer of Sir Philip Sidney, was Registrar and Principal of University College, Toronto, from 1928 to 1944.
2 See letter of November 14, 1938; for McFarlane, see letter of September 24, 1938, note 2.

TO LORNE PIERCE

R.R. 4 Simcoe, Ont.
December 8, 1938

Dear Dr. Pierce,

I have, this morning, shipped to you 13 cases containing 2000 sets of sheets, end-papers, and jackets of *A Search for America.*[1]

I made as sure as I could that all were in perfect condition; a single case which had been slightly damaged I opened but found the contents all right.

I am writing once more to Dents, to expedite matters.

Nothing had, by an oversight, been said about the shipping charges; I paid here for the draying, which hit me hard; but shipped otherwise collect.

Thanks for the copy; I had already deposited the original letter with the bank; it saved my skin.

About *Settlers* in a few days.

With best regards,
F.P.G.

1 Pierce's letter to Grove, of December 6, is virtually an outline for a contract – the result of their meeting on November 30 and December 5: Ryerson was to purchase the remaining 2000 sheets of *A Search for America* (thus meeting Grove's reservation concerning copyright in his letter of November 26, 1938) for $300 with a 15% royalty on the list price of $1.50 a copy. Ryerson was also to have the option to buy the standing type within one year. The remainder of *Fruits of the Earth* (about 450 copies), still held by Dent, Ryerson was to purchase, paying Grove $100 plus $135 royalty as a final settlement. A trade edition of *Two Generations* was to be made, at the same time as the private printing, by an over-run of 1000 copies, to be sold to Ryerson for $600 with Ryerson having option on the standing type.

TO LORNE PIERCE

R.R. 4 Simcoe, Ont.
December 10, 1938

Dear Dr. Pierce,

I enclose the nomination blank[1] properly filled in. There are a few other anonymous or pseudonymous publications; and there is, of course, the long list of my lectures, the most important of which I am going to deliver at the University of Toronto during the first week of February 1939. The lectures are, of course, unprinted; and the books published under a mask I do not at present care to divulge.[2] I have added *Two Generations* since it is so nearly ready.

For my wife's sake I sincerely hope you will be successful; it might give her a new lease on life to see that her many sacrifices have not been entirely in vain.

Sincerely yours,
F.P. Grove

1 For election to the Royal Society of Canada. Grove filled one out again in 1939 (October 21). The nomination was resubmitted by Pierce on December 17, 1940, and Grove received notice of his election on April 23, 1941. The sponsors were Sir Charles G.D. Roberts, Duncan Campbell Scott, and Pierce himself. See letter of May 15, 1941 for Grove's announcement of the honour to Willard Holliday.

2 The listing of Grove's publications is included in the letter of October 21, 1939. For 'anonymous or pseudonymous publications,' see the Introduction. The 'mask' is almost certainly that of Felix Paul Greve.

TO LORNE PIERCE

R.R. 4 Simcoe, Ont.
December 15, 1938

Dear Dr. Pierce,

I am sending you 2 photographs, both unique copies. Please let me have the one rejected back; and I wonder whether the one chosen needs necessarily be spoiled? They are my wife's, taken by Hammond[1] who died shortly after.

I've been laid up ever since, last week, I put that deal[2] with Dent's through. Same trouble as yours, very painful. Have Dents delivered?[3] I just received their receipt.

Sincerely yours,
F.P.G.

1 Melvin Ormond Hammond (1876–1934), journalist (with the Toronto *Globe*), author, and amateur photographer. He published two books, *Confederation and Its Leaders* (1917) and *Canadian Footprints* (1926), besides articles on history, travel, and economics in Canadian and US journals. At his death he left a priceless collection of Canadian paintings and an album of photographs of Canadian painters, musicians, and authors.
2 See letter of December 8, 1938, note 1.
3 See the following letter.

TO LORNE PIERCE

R.R. 4 Simcoe, Ont.
December 19, 1938

Dear Dr. Pierce,

I am much worried about things. Have Dents not delivered *Fruits of the Earth*?[1] This stock should have reached you a week ago.

Sincerely yours,
F.P.G.

1 See letter of December 8, 1938, note 1.

TO LORNE PIERCE

R.R. 4 Simcoe, Ont.
December 23, 1938

Dear Dr. Pierce,

I am glad the shipment[1] was located; I was giving it up for lost.

Re other books: Eayrs was in New York for some time and, on his return, was taken to the hospital, with a nervous breakdown.[2] The office staff is shilly-shallying. But I know one thing by this time: there are no bound copies, no sheets of *Settlers* left. There had been a recent sale; I have succeeded in tracing it; but the stock was sold out, there, too (Eaton's). I believe we must talk the whole situation over. Suppose I came to Toronto next week? Will you be at the office? There is a plan developing in my mind which I'd like to discuss with you.

Sincerely yours,
F.P.G.

1 From Dent, of the remainder of *Fruits of the Earth*
2 Eayrs died on April 29, 1940 – but his health had been in a precarious state for several years.

18 Lorne Pierce 1929. *By Sir Wyly Grier, courtesy Art Gallery of Ontario, gift of Dr Lorne Pierce 1960*

TO LORNE PIERCE

R.R. 4 Simcoe, Ont.
December 28, 1938

Dear Dr. Pierce,

I am wondering whether anything has gone wrong to explain the delay in the payment due as to our agreement[1] – a delay which is responsible for the blackest Christmas I have ever lived through.

Yours sincerely,
F.P. Grove

1 See letter of December 8, 1938, note 1.

TO LORNE PIERCE

R.R. 4 Simcoe, Ont.
January 4, 1939

Dear Dr. Pierce,

Since the roads show no kind of improvement, I think I had better write.

1) Re Macmillan stocks. By a little diplomacy I have elicited the information that there is no stock of any kind, bound or sheets, available.[1] Eayrs, before his hospitalisation, wrote angrily that he would reprint or not, as he pleased and when he pleased. In my contracts there is nothing about this matter; I mean in my contracts with Macmillans. However, it is surely not possible for a publisher to keep me off the market and hold the rights? Of course, re *Settlers of the Marsh*, there is not even a contract beyond my contract with the Ryerson Press.

What had I better do about it? Write a registered letter, stating that, unless the books are reprinted within 6 months, I shall resume my copyright and treat any later printing on the part of Macmillans as an infringement of my copyright? That is what a local lawyer, a friend of mine, advises.

If, in that way, I resumed my copyright, something could perhaps be done along the line of what I did with *Two Generations*, in order to get plates.

2) Re *Two Generations*. This is now available in paged proofs, and I have advised the Best[2] people to let you have a set. I think it a good job of printing; though, of course, the proofs you will receive may not yet contain the last corrections.

3) Would you think it advisable to release the title of the next book which I shall have ready? It will be ready sometime late in spring. I have been working at it since 1929; and there are three successive versions. One of these went to England and was read by such people as Church and Pocock;[3]

both of whom called it a book 'in the grand style.' Personally I consider it as one of the two or three really important things which I have written; and that is the reason why I have been so long over it. The present, fourth, version on which I am at work will be the final one. I call it *The Master of the Mill.*[4]

4) If it is still your intention gradually to bring out a definitive edition of F.P. Grove, may I say that I have long dreamt of such an edition bound in plum-coloured cloth, all vol[ume]s alike, each with a monogram on the front cover which an artist-friend designed for me decades ago. The colour of the cloth is that of the collected edition of Thomas Hardy in the India-paper edition.

I think that covers it. Thanks for your endeavours with regard to the R.S.C. I enclose a rough sketch of the monogram.[5] Oh, here comes the cheque.[6] Thanks for that, too.

With best wishes for a prosperous New Year,
Sincerely yours,
F.P. Grove

1 Relations between Grove and Eayrs had deteriorated since the early thirties, as is indicated in the lack of correspondence and the publication of *Fruits of the Earth*, in 1933, by Dent. The trade edition of *Two Generations* was handled by Ryerson. The information re Macmillan's stock is covered in Ellen Elliott's letter of December 23, 1938: 'Thank you for your letter of December 21st. I find that we have no bound stock nor sheet stock of any of your books.'
2 T.H. Best and Company, a Toronto printing firm
3 Probably Richard Church (b1893), the English poet and author of several critical studies, including *Growth of the English Novel*. 'Pocock' would probably be Guy Noel Pocock (1880–1955), the English author and editor, who edited, with Sir Arthur Quiller-Couch, the King's Treasury of Literature series. He was editor of J.M. Dent and Sons in England, and presumably in that capacity read the manuscript. See also letter of May 24, 1939, and note 1 to that letter.
4 Published by Macmillan in 1944
5 This particular enclosure has not survived; but see letter of February 4, 1939.
6 See the preceding letter.

TO LORNE PIERCE

R.R. 4 Simcoe, Ont.
January 10, 1939

Dear Dr Pierce,

The T. Eaton Company notifies me that they bought the last available copies of *Settlers of the Marsh* 'in the fall' – a vague expression, in spite of my request for a definite date. Of what they bought, they say, no copy is left. A friend of mine bought a copy, sometime in October, for $2.50.

And, apart from the statement that no copies, bound or in

sheets, are in the hands of Macmillans, that seems to be the limit of the information I can give.

Sincerely yours,
F.P. Grove

TO LORNE PIERCE

R.R. 4 Simcoe, Ont.
January 11, 1939

Dear Dr. Pierce,

Our Daily Bread is also out of print; Eayrs claims the right to reprint when it suits him – which means when, through some spectacular success, I get into the limelight. The contract says nothing about it. To me, the question is, what does the law say about it, if anything. Unfortunately, Eayrs knows that I and many others believe that that success will come with *Master of the Mill*, because the theme is world-wide, not merely Canadian (Industrial Revolution).

Re *Settlers*: my copies bear no Canadian copyright note, but only Doran's,[1] though the imprint on the title page has the Ryerson Press.

I do hope we'll get it out without a row; though, rather than let Eayrs keep it, I'd risk the row.

Owing to the delays re *Two Generations* I don't think we should sell the trade ed[ition] before end of July. I hope to have the Limited Ed[ition] out next week.

Sincerely yours,
F.P. Grove

P.S. Would you want a Preface for the new ed[ition] of the *Search for America*?[2] If so, please let me know soon. So I can find the time to work it over. I shall lecture at the U[niversity] of T[oronto] on Thursday, Jan[uary] 26.

F.P.G.

1 Who handled the US edition of *Settlers of the Marsh* (1925)

2 The Ryerson edition of *A Search for America* appeared in 1939, with 'Author's Note to the Fourth Edition' – dated February 1939. Ryerson also brought out a 'School Edition,' abridged by J.F. Swayze, in 1947.

TO W.J. ALEXANDER

Simcoe, Ont.
January 15, 1939

Dear Dr. Alexander,

Thanks very much for your letter of day before yesterday, as well as for the invitation for my wife and myself. We shall be very glad indeed to accept.

The book should be out by this time; but, in order to make it a somewhat distinctive volume, I have been adding a few little touches in book-making to it: such as a manuscript title on the front cover, a slip-case, etc. and that has caused delay; also the trade edition – to appear in the fall of the year – had to be printed; and, since I am re-issuing *A Search for America*,[1] uniform with the new book, a binding had to be selected which will do for all my books (the idea is an edition – definitive – of my 'collected works'). All this was an afterthought and took time, time, time. But I think this week will see the book appear.

Hoping, then, to see you overnext week, I remain,
Sincerely yours,
F.P.G.

1 See the preceding letter, note 2.

TO W.J. ALEXANDER

R.R. 4 Simcoe, Ont.
January 17, 1939

Dear Dr. Alexander,

I have your notice[1] and am sending it on to Ryerson's. I think it is entirely admirable; and if there is one regret, it is that you should have been put to this trouble. I think I mentioned in a previous letter that nothing was further from my mind than anything like this. Dr. Pierce has read the manuscript himself and was enthusiastic about it; that was the reason why, when I had so completely failed in securing foreign publication, I offered the book to him, proposing that I would, by means of the limited edition, bear the cost of composition.

I have secured, in addition, a re-issue of *A Search for America*[2] which will appear uniformly with *Two Generations* next fall. Here, too, I was in a position to furnish the Ryerson Press with sheets which I owned, at 12½ cents a copy.

I have already answered your invitation for the evening of January 26. Both my wife and myself accept with sincere thanks.

Till the 26th, therefore.
As ever, yours,
F.P. Grove

1 We cannot be sure what this notice was. The most probable explanation is that Dr Alexander had been asked by the publisher, Ryerson Press, to provide a laudatory notice for publicity purposes.
2 See letter of January 11, 1939, note 2.

TO RICHARD CROUCH

R.R. 4 Simcoe, Ont.
January 30, 1939

My dear Crouch,

I have broken down; but 19 copies go forward to you today by express, 1 by mail.

Three lectures[1] in one afternoon (1, 3, 5 p.m.) at University College 'did' for me; and my wife had to rush me home where I've been in bed ever since Thursday.

I do hope you'll like the book,[2] both as to appearance and contents.

Best wishes for you and yours.
As ever,
F.P.G.

1 In *In Search of Myself* (p 446), Grove mentions receiving fifteen dollars for 'three lectures in Toronto' – presumably these. A review in the *Varsity* of January 27, 1939, headed 'Canadian Novelist Views Writer's Life,' describes him as author of *A Search for America* and *Two Generations*, and quotes him as voicing his desire to write a Canadian book, to place on 'that bookshelf a thousand miles long, from Vancouver to Halifax. On it there is but one book [Louis Hémon's *Maria Chapdelaine*] ... Very likely I shall fail. It does not matter.' His other views, as reported, are familiar and characteristic – the presence of a dormant spirituality in Canada and the need to write being felt as a sort of fate.
2 *Two Generations*

TO LORNE PIERCE

R.R. 4 Simcoe, Ont.
January 31, 1939

Dear Dr. Pierce,

Yes, I had a complete breakdown and was lucky in having my wife along to drive me home; otherwise it would have been the hospital for me. I am in bed.

As for the *Search*, the book is now definitely a textbook in the U[niversity] of T[oronto]. Brown[1] tells me, there will be ca. 60 copies needed the first year, and ca. 250 a year thereafter.

The same news comes from Winnipeg re *Our Daily Bread*.[2] I am to guarantee that it will be available. I am trying to switch them over to the *Search*.

However, what with the state of the roads and of my health (nervous breakdown consequent upon all this worry and excitement), there is no telling when I can get to Toronto.

Sincerely yours,
F.P.G.

Thanks for cheque

1 E.K. Brown
2 That is, the University of Manitoba was proposing to use *Our Daily Bread* as a textbook. It was Grove's characteristic ill luck that that novel was out of print – hence his desire to switch the university authorities to *A Search for America*.

TO LORNE PIERCE

R.R. 4 Simcoe, Ont.
February 4, 1939

Dear Dr. Pierce,

The enclosed[1] is, of course, a mere sketch, done in bed; but any draughtsman, I think, can straighten it out.

Sincerely yours,
F.P.G.

1 A proposed Frederick Philip Grove monogram. See letter of February 15, 1939, for details of how Grove evolved it.

TO LORNE PIERCE

R.R. 4 Simcoe, Ont.
February 11, 1939

Dear Dr. Pierce,

I made a somewhat better drawing of *my* monogram, sitting up at my desk, instead of lying in bed. Then, without saying who made the drawings, I showed them (i.e. mine and Macdonald's)[1] to a number of people. All of them picked my drawing.

But, if it is to be one of the other 3, I choose 1. I don't like the delicate suggestion of woodland scenes and agriculture. And even 1 seems to me rather commonplace.

However, I don't mean to make it a point and leave matters to you.

As ever,
F.P.G.

P.S. I sent Mrs. Haultain[2] a few comments on *Two Generations*, notably one by Lord Tweedsmuir[3] who compliments me on the appearance of the book and is reading with 'great interest.'

F.P.G.

1 These other drawings, presumably enclosed with a letter from Pierce, have not survived. 'Macdonald' is presumably a reference to Thoreau Macdonald (b1901), the painter and illustrator, whose wood-cuts illustrated many Ryerson Press books during the Lorne Pierce régime.

2 Mrs Eleanor Haultain, who succeeded E.J. Moore as Advertising Manager at the Ryerson press

3 John Buchan (1875–1940), first Baron Tweedsmuir, was Governor-General of Canada from 1935 until his death. His letter to Grove is presumably no longer extant.

TO LORNE PIERCE

R.R. 4 Simcoe, Ont.
February 15, 1939

Dear Dr. Pierce,

The following is the evolution of that monogram:

F. P.

F.P. both from script

moved together 

I confess that I have always thought it ingenious; and so has everybody (except my wife) who has ever seen it.

However, as I said, I am not making this a point.
Sincerely yours,
F.P.G.

TO WATSON KIRKCONNELL

R.R. 4 Simcoe, Ont.
February 23, 1939

My dear Kirk,

Thanks for your order[1] which brings my deficit down to 35 copies.

I see you are still pursuing your brilliant career and acquiring honours. The papers had already apprised us of that.

We, on the other hand are, as always, living in our obscurity; and when an opportunity offers to shine a little, as recently, when I was to be the guest of the U[niversity] of T[oronto], lecturing, I broke down.[2] I am getting old (67 last Tuesday a week ago); and my health is failing. If I succeed in bringing out two more books, I'll be satisfied.

Leonard goes up for an examination in music tomorrow, the first time in his young life – Toronto Conservatory of Music. He plays nicely.

As ever,
F.P.G.

P.S. I am sending the copy of *Two Generations* under separate cover. It's a nice-looking book, I think.

1 For *Two Generations* (limited edition). Kirkconnell had written on February 18 to Grove, apologizing for not sending the order sooner, and explaining that he had been, all summer, in Europe – chiefly in Hungary lecturing at the University of Debrecen, which was to confer on him an honorary doctorate in the autumn in connection with its 400th anniversary.

2 See letter of January 30th, 1939.

TO GUSTAV HÜBENER[1]

R.R. 4 Simcoe, Ont.
February 27, 1939

My dear Dr. Huebener,

I have for some time seen your book on England[2] standing on my shelves and felt twinges of my conscience. I think I promised to return it to you last fall.

All the time I was in hopes that I should find time for an experiment in translation. Quite unexpectedly I was deluged with work in

19 Catherine, Leonard, and Frederick Philip Grove. *Courtesy Leonard Grove*

connection with my own books. I postponed and postponed; and I am as busy as ever; for I have promised to have a new volume ready every summer, for several years. So I am now hammering away at *The Master of the Mill*, for 1940, a book I have been working on since 1928.

To cut the Gordian knot, I am therefore returning to you your own book still hoping that, when my own preoccupations subside, I may ask you for it again.

I recently lectured at the University of Toronto and met the whole bunch connected with the *Quarterly* – they are a lively bunch.[3] If I can be of service in that quarter, I shall be delighted. Of course, I have no power; but I do believe that any contribution of yours would be assured of careful consideration if I slipped it along.

Hoping that Mrs. Huebener and you are both as well as you can wish, I remain,

Sincerely yours,
F.P. Grove
P.S. I myself have been rather ill; but I am on the mend.

1 Gustav Hübener, born in Hamburg in 1889, was professor of English successively at Göttingen, Koenigsbert, Basle, and Bonn. He came to Canada in 1937 and was professor of German and Philosophy at Mount Allison University, Sackville, NB, until his death in 1940. He visited Grove in 1938 – Grove probably recalls that visit in his letters of August 26, 1945 and November 28, 1945. Hübener's widow, Jean, was Head of the Department of German at the University of New Brunswick for many years and still (1974) lives in Fredericton.

2 *England und dle Gesittungsgrundlage der europäischen Frühgeschichte, Studien zur Englandkunde* (Frankfurt 1930)

3 The *University of Toronto Quarterly* was established in 1931; its editorial board in 1939 consisted of A.S.P. Woodhouse (Chairman), E.K. Brown, and A. Brady.

TO LORNE PIERCE

R.R. 4 Simcoe, Ont.
May 24, 1939

Dear Dr. Pierce,

I have news.

Throughout the winter I have been at work giving a big novel its final shape, *The Master of the Mill*. Under pressure of financial difficulties I offered it, in 1933, in an unfinished or bungled state, to Dents in London. Mr. Dent had been out here at my place in the spring and offered me, when I outlined the theme to him, $100 a month for the first refusal. I accepted; and – I don't know whether you'll understand this – that spoiled the book on which I had, even then, been at work for four or five years. Nevertheless, I enclose parts of the report on it which Mr. Guy Pollock[1] gave to Dents, leaving out the reasons why he disadvised publication. I have never doubted that, one day, I should rewrite that book. But, about a month ago, I was, as is usual with me, struck with the blues about it all; I had to leave it for the moment, though all but fifty pages, out of 380, are written.

In order to distract myself, I took up an old plan: that of a juvenile[2] which I had planned for years. I had the idea, long before it took place, to weave the king's visit[3] into it. It will be finished in about a month. On account of that visit of the king, it will be imperative, from a commercial point of view, to bring the book out this year, at least in Canada. Do you think that can be done? And would you be interested? Its between 60 and 80,000 words are crammed with action.

My second question is this: Would you consider it too much of a chore to read what is finished, of *The Master of the Mill*, in a manuscript, or typescript, rather, written on onion-skin paper? I could not afford to buy better paper for a Ms. which is, at the best, the last but one. And I cannot afford, now, to buy paper, carbons, and ribbons on an uncertainty. The book must appear internationally; but I want to know whether you are sufficiently impressed with it to put yourself behind it. If not, it can lie for another ten years or so, till after my death.

Please let me know at once, about the juvenile and the novel. The novel, of course, I should not care to see in print till 1940, in the fall. If it comes out, then, I shall be able to furnish a Ms. a year. Otherwise, I believe, I want to give up. It is one of the two or three things which I still have up my sleeve and which I, personally, value.

Sincerely yours,
F.P. Grove

EXTRACT FROM GUY POLLOCK'S LETTER TO HUGH R. DENT RE GROVE'S MASTER OF THE MILL

Grove is undoubtedly a personality. He has tremendous patience, seriousness, and experience. *The Master of the Mill* exemplifies, through the history of a miller, his humble origin, his rise to fortune, and his son's and grandson's rise to colossal economic power, the growth of Canadian industry ... It is monumental. Moreover it presents a considered interpretation of the ethics and economic consequences of the machine age. One cannot withhold admiration from a man who so boldly tackles so vast a social problem, particularly when he has something of Hardy's granite pessimism impelling him instead of the cynical disillusionment of a Sinclair Lewis.

......

It is a book on the grand scale, a book that demands admiration for its scope and its courage in tackling big and contemporary themes ... Its importance in Canadian literature is no doubt considerable.

1 Guy Cameron Pollock (1876–1957), the English journalist and author of two novels, *Hay*

Fever (with W.H. Pollock) and *To See Ourselves* (with Ann Armstrong). However, in the light of the letter of January 4, 1939, Guy Noel Pocock may have been intended here. See letter of January 4, 1939, note 3.
2 'The Adventures of Leonard Broadus,' published in instalments in the United Church monthly magazine, *Canadian Boy*, April 7, 1940–June 23, 1940 (LV, 14–25), under Grove's own name, much to his chagrin; see letter of April 5, 1940.
3 The visit to Canada in the spring of 1939 of King George VI and his consort Queen Elizabeth, now the Queen Mother

TO LORNE PIERCE

R.R. 4 Simcoe, Ont.
May 29, 1939

Dear Dr. Pierce,

I am sending, under separate cover, as much of *The Master of the Mill* as is in type. It is a poor typescript, I warned you; on onion-skin, most of it done with a worn-out ribbon; and with about 50 pages missing at the end: for these the material is there, of course; but not yet in shape. Including final typing in 2 copies, it would take ca. 2 months to finish.

As for the juvenile: 'The Adventures of Leonard Broadus'[1] (provisional title), nothing is in type, so far; but I'll hammer enough of it out to let you get a taste of it within a week or ten days.

As ever,
F.P.G.

1 See the preceding letter, note 2.

TO LORNE PIERCE

R.R. 4 Simcoe, Ont.
June 5, 1939

Dear Dr. Pierce,

I am sending you the first 50 double pages of a preliminary typescript of the juvenile, provisionally called 'The Adventures of Leonard Broadus.'

I am very sorry I have to send you a single-spaced script on yellow paper. But even of that yellow paper I did not have enough to double-space. And I think I have mentioned that I cannot afford any longer to spend money on uncertainties.

Now I have let a very few people read this Ms. as it was being written. Every single one, a youngster among them, pronounced it a thriller. It was written to be one, of course. I set out to write what would have delighted my heart at the age of twelve.

I believe I also mentioned that, since I wove the visit of the king into the yarn, I consider it imperative that the book should appear this fall: that visit makes a selling point.

There is still one chapter to write: it I cannot write till the king has gone through Hamilton day after tomorrow.

The total length of the book will be between 55000 and 60000 words, as near as I can calculate it – a good length for a boy's book, I believe.

I've been working night and day almost to hammer this Ms. out. Can you get it read *at once*? Since time is needed for a U.S.A. canvass of publishers – you know to whom to offer, I suppose – I must get the script back as soon as possible, so I can make a final, double-spaced, and carboned copy – which will take about two weeks. If you are as much taken with the yarn as others, I'll murder a local druggist to get the necessary paper, and the principal of the business college to get the carbons and the ribbons needed. You should countenance that in order to save me from the gallows thereafter; though even the gallows don't matter if the darn thing secures bread for my wife and my kid.

Sincerely yours,
F.P.G.

TO LORNE PIERCE

R.R. 4 Simcoe, Ont.
June 19, 1939

Dear Dr. Pierce,

The note I took of Dr. Wallace's[1] initials has somehow been mislaid. I, therefore, take the liberty of addressing the shortened copy of that juvenile to you. Would you do me a favour to send it down (or up) to Dr. Wallace?

I have complied with all his requests.

By the way, I counted over the copies of the second edition of *A Search for America* when I got home. I am, under separate cover, sending you one. Which leaves 160 copies. As I said to you, I'd be willing to part with them for 25 cents each, or hold them, or destroy them since I wish, above all, to keep faith with your house.[2]

Sincerely yours,
F.P.G.

1 Dr Archer Wallace (1884–1958) was editor of *The Canadian Boy*, a United Church of Canada publication in which Grove's juvenile, 'The Adventures of Leonard Broadus,' appeared serially from April 7, 1940 (LV, 14) to June 23, 1940 (LV, 25). Wallace himself was a prolific writer of inspirational books, stories for boys, and essays.

2 The differences between Grove and Pierce, at this point, seem to have been completely reconciled, but not for very long (see letter of June 26, 1944). *The Master of the Mill* (1944) was published by Macmillan, as were *In Search of Myself* (1946) and *Consider Her Ways* (1947).

TO LORNE PIERCE

R.R. 4 Simcoe, Ont.
June 30, 1939

Dear Dr. Pierce,

As I said before, I am willing to do with that confounded remainder of the second edition[1] whatever you wish. So I'll hold it for the time being.

Could you have my onion-skin copy of the *Master of the Mill* returned to me? I think I shall now have time to ponder it once more and to add the last two or three sections. I still do not feel that I have done all I can do for that book; it is a matter of time. I shall also have to retype the whole thing on decent paper.

Sincerely yours,
F.P.G.

1 Presumably the Carrier edition (1928) of *A Search for America*, 2000 unsold copies of which Grove had sent to Ryerson in December 1938; see letter of December 8, 1938, note 1, and also letter of November 28, 1945, note 3.

TO NORMA MACROSTIE[1]

R.R. 4 Simcoe, Ont.,
July 3, 1939

Dear Miss MacRostie,

Thanks very much for your letter of June 30.

May I trouble you to let Dr. Wallace know that I shall be glad indeed to leave the matter to him? I won't make any secret of the fact that my financial needs are grievous and that I should be glad if he would do what he can, in case there is a chance to get a little more (or, for that matter, much more) for the 'Leonard Broadus' thing; but that, if this is impossible, I shall be glad, too, to accept his offer of $120.00 payable in September – which is the time when my needs will become acute. I myself know nothing of possible markets, besides being extraordinary [sic] reluctant to deal in them.

I am wondering whether you could let me have that draft Ms. of *The Master of the Mill* back. There are some fifty pages missing in that Ms., and I believe I shall have time to fill them in. I also want to revise the whole thing and make a better Ms.

I hope you don't think I'm imposing upon you; please believe me when I say that I appreciate your good offices.

Yours sincerely,
F.P. Grove

1 Dr Pierce's secretary until 1940. Pierce was on holiday.

TO NORMA MACROSTIE

R.R. 4 Simcoe, Ont.
July 27, 1939

Dear Miss MacRostie,

I have allowed myself for so long to be immersed in work that I fear this will find *you* away on your holidays.

This is my point. Dr. Pierce asked me when I saw him earlier in the year for a short story[1] for the *Bookman*. I have looked one out which I think would be suitable. But I should like him to handle it personally. So, would you be good enough to let me know whenever he is back at the office?

Further, a complete and, I hope, final Ms. of *The Master of the Mill* will be available by the end of the second week in August. I had promised this by September and am a little better than my word. It, too, I should like Dr. Pierce to get when he returns. Till then, I should like to keep it handy. One sometimes finds an unexpected improvement. I should merely like Dr. Pierce to know that I am keeping to schedule.

Thanking you again for your personal interest in the various matters pending, I remain,

Very sincerely yours,
F.P. Grove

P.S. The moment I am through with the *Master*, I shall start on a final version of the second of the 3 books of mine which *I* consider important. I have worked at it for exactly 20 y[ea]rs.[2]

1 'The Platinum Watch,' which appeared in the *Canadian Bookman* XXI (October 1939) 5–12

2 Almost certainly *Consider Her Ways* (referred to as 'Go to the Ant' in letter of August 7, 1939)

TO NORMA MACROSTIE

R.R. 4 Simcoe, Ont.
August 4, 1939

Dear Miss MacRostie,

No, indeed, I never received your enquiry re *A Search for America*, or I should have answered it at once, with my usual punctuality.

However, *Brentanos* took over *The Search* for England in 1928, sent out review copies and closed shop. *No copy was ever sold*. I bought the stock back; there were only a few reviews, as far as I know.[1]

Please tell Dr. Pierce that the full Ms. of *The Master of the Mill* will be ready next week. But I should like to keep it for another week or two, to read over and to test the last 2 chapters for unity of effect.

I'll send the short story for the *Bookman* at once.

Very sincerely yours,
F.P.G.

1 Brentano's no longer have an office in London, and their archives in Paris were destroyed during World War II. But reviews of *A Search for America* in England confirm this edition – see my *Frederick Philip Grove* (Critical Views on Canadian Writers 1970) for a list of such reviews, including extracts from *Saturday Review of Literature* (London, August 31, 1929; unsigned), *New Statesman* X (October 12, 1929), and *Punch, or The London Charivari* (February 26, 1930; unsigned).

The Louis Carrier letters to Grove make clear that Brentano's acted as Carrier's English agents.

TO LORNE PIERCE

R.R. 4 Simcoe, Ont.
August 7, 1939

Dear Dr. Pierce,

Since you are back at the office, I am sending today, under separate cover, a small piece of short fiction; I don't know whether one can call it a short story: 'The Platinum Watch.'[1] I hope you will find it suitable for the *Bookman*.

Re the *Search* I have dropped Miss MacRostie a line.

You have no doubt seen Deacon's review of *Two Generations*.[2] On the whole, it seems fair and 'balanced.' What I can't understand about a fellow like Deacon is why he must, for half a column, talk about my private circumstances, setting down, not only statements which are untrue but statements which contradict absolutely such facts as I, on a previous similar offence, conveyed to him. What has that sort of gossip to do with my book? However...

Re *The Master of the Mill* it does seem that I have at last satisfied myself. The new typescript will be completed by the end of this week; and when I have reread the whole, I shall forward it to you: would you like original *and* carbon copy?

By the way, I have not yet seen *Two Generations* of which, as well as of the new *Search*, I was promised 3 copies.

No, I cannot muster hope any longer with regard to anything; but keep plugging away in a sort of desperation.

The moment I have *The Master* off my mind and fingers,

I shall start once more rewriting 'Go to the Ant'[3] which, strange to say, has become topical in more than one sense. I hope to have it ready for 1941. It's one of the three things I should like to finish before I lie down for a long rest.

Sincerely yours,
F.P.G.

1 Published in the *Canadian Bookman* XXI (October 1939) 5–12

2 In *The Globe and Mail*, of August 5, 1939 – an extract from this review, without the biographical portion which Grove here finds offensive, is reprinted in my *Frederick Philip Grove* (Critical Views on Canadian Writers 1970) 157–8.

3 Which was published as *Consider Her Ways* (1947)

TO W.J. ALEXANDER

R.R. 4 Simcoe, Ont.
August 10, 1939

My dear Dr. Alexander,

I have this moment finished the typing of the final manuscript of what I hope will be the next book of mine to appear. On this *Master of the Mill* I have been at work since the early summer of 1929, having, even then, pondered it for almost exactly 30 years. It is one of the three books for which all else has been preparation.

Ever since I began, a year ago, to set down this final version, I have been thinking that, if I have my wish, it should bear your name on the dedication page. Will you grant me that wish?[1]

I have promised to deliver the completed typescript before September, so as to give my Canadian publishers a chance to secure foreign publication without which, as you know, Canadian publication cannot be made.

I have not heard from you for several months. I trust you are well? I am glad to say we are all reasonably so. This piece of work being finished at last, we plan, next week, to go to Georgian Bay for a few days, to visit with friends.

With our joint best wishes for you and yours, I am,
Most sincerely yours,
F.P. Grove

1 Alexander did not live to see the book published; it was dedicated to his memory. See letters of June 16 and July 12, 1944.

TO RICHARD CROUCH

R.R. 4 Simcoe, Ont.
August 17, 1939

My dear Dick,

The *Master*[1] is finished, thank the Lord or whatever or whoever has taken His place for being thanked. Now I am writing an essay on Galsworthy.[2]

We are going to spend next week at Rondeau and I wondered whether I could inconvenience you to the extent of asking you to take down here whatever you can of the following of G[alsworthy]'s work (which I don't know and can't procure):

Villa Rubein
The Island Pharisees
The Dark Flower
Beyond
Saint's Progress
The Burning Spear

Not that, as far as I know, any of these matter; but I'd prefer to *know* that they don't matter. I'd get through with them in short order.

We've had an enjoyable 4 days with the Collins.[3] He is definitely an intellect. I'm looking forward to seeing you at R[ondeau].

As ever,
F.P.G.

1 *The Master of the Mill*
2 Published as 'Morality in the Forsyte Saga' in the *University of Toronto Quarterly* xv (October 1945) 54–64
3 W.E. Collin. Born in England in 1893, and educated at the Universities of Toulouse and Western Ontario, he was Professor of Romance Languages at the University of Western Ontario until 1960. A long-standing contributor to the *Canadian Forum*, his *The White Savannahs* (1936) was one of the first major works in Canadian literary criticism. He became a Fellow of the Royal Society in 1950. See also letter of August 30, 1939, note 2.

TO W.J. ALEXANDER

R.R. 4 Simcoe, Ont.
August 19, 1939

My dear Dr. Alexander,

The news of the disaster[1] that has befallen one of your daughters was a great shock to me. Please permit me to express my profound sympathy. You know that I have not yet got over the death of my daughter in 1927; so I know how you and yours must feel.

As for a holiday, we have spent 4 days on Georgian Bay and are leaving tomorrow for a week at Rondeau. The rest of the summer has been taken up by my getting a final Ms. of *The Master of the Mill* ready.

I don't think I told you that, in spring, I wrote a juvenile and promptly sold it – for $120.00.[2] It will appear next month.

I am glad to hear of your continued good health. If we pass through Toronto, we shall be glad to drop in.

I have seen a few reviews of *Two Generations* which were favourable but rather lukewarm – especially Deacon's.[3]

However, we hope for the best.

Thanks for accepting the dedication[4] of *The Master of the Mill*. You know that I have long wished to inscribe a book for you.

With our very best wishes,
As ever,
F.P. Grove

1 Mrs Beatrice Wheeler, one of Alexander's daughters, in a note on this letter, dated February 4, 1972, adds, 'All his daughters are still living. Perhaps it was the death of a brother-in-law who was drowned.'
2 'The Adventures of Leonard Broadus,' published serially in the *Canadian Boy*; see letter of May 24, 1939, note 2.
3 See letter of August 7, 1939, note 2.
4 See letter of August 10, 1939, note 1.

TO LORNE PIERCE

R.R. 4 Simcoe, Ont.
August 30, 1939

Dear Dr. Pierce,

By separate parcel I am sending you at long last the final typescript of

The Master of the Mill

A carbon copy is available if desired.

I believe you mentioned that you valued the critical work of W.E. Collin[1] (*The White Savannahs*). I spent a week-end with him at Wasaga Beach where I had taken this typescript to correct typing mistakes; and, since he had been asked to write an article on my work for the *University of Toronto Quarterly*,[2] he insisted on my leaving the Ms. with him for a few days. Hence the delay.

In a letter accompanying the Ms. when he returned it he said a few words which might interest you in this connection. So I enclose some extracts from it on a separate sheet.

How are *Two Generations* moving?
Sincerely yours,
F.P.G.

Extracts from letter of W.E. Collin to F.P. Grove re *The Master of the Mill*

......

I think it is a splendid achievement. It held me from first to last...

Such gorgeous dimensions, melodrama and tragic tensions!...

If it doesn't make you a fortune, I lose my bet. Mind you, it is of cosmopolitan significance and should be published in London and New York...

It rises absolutely above the Canadian scene. ...

1 Who was then Professor of Romance Languages at the University of Western Ontario; see letter of August 17, 1939, note 3.

2 Collin appears not to have published anything on Grove in the *University of Toronto Quarterly*, but he did publish an article on Grove in *Gants du Ciel* IV (Winter 1946) 15–40 – 'La Tragique Ironie de Frederick Philip Grove.' He also delivered an address on Grove's unpublished novels before the Royal Society of Canada in Toronto in June 1955.

TO LORNE PIERCE

R.R. 4 Simcoe, Ont.
August 30, 1939 II

Dear Dr. Pierce,

Having just despatched to you the Ms. of *The Master*, I receive the enclosed[1] in my mail and turn it over to you. If you think it advisable, I can send those people a carbon copy.

Sincerely,
F.P.G.

1 There is no further clue in the correspondence, but presumably it was a request for the manuscript of *The Master of the Mill* from some other firm.

20 Willard B. Holliday and Frederick Philip Grove. *Courtesy Leonard Grove*

TO WILLARD B. HOLLIDAY[1]

R.R. 4 Simcoe, Ont.
September 10, 1939

Dear Mr. Holliday,

I have your letter of the 6th and hardly know what to answer.

It is true I own a farm but I do not work it myself; I have a tenant on it. Still, if you were here, I might, in the long-run, be able to do something for you, if only next spring, for the greater part of the season's work is done; and there are said to be twelve thousand men looking for work in this country alone.

However, we have, for a year or so, had a young man in the house to act as a sort of janitor in return for his board;[2] and we have not yet filled the position for this winter. Last year's boy is still working in the tobacco for another week or so. (We conduct a private school here).

I wonder whether you could make it possible to meet me somewhere. Thus, I shall be in Brantford next Thursday, Sept[ember] 14, in the afternoon. If you could make it possible to be there, at the central railway station (there are two), I shall call there at 4:30 p.m. My car is a blue Plymouth license number 62P29; I shall drive up to the platform just west of the station building and remain in or near the car, so I can be easily found. If you could drop me another line to say whether or not I am to expect you, I shall appreciate it.

Hoping for better times, I am,
Sincerely,
F.P. Grove

1 Willard B. Holliday, an aspiring writer who became a friend of the Groves. He spent the winter of 1939–40 on their farm at Simcoe, working in the capacity Grove describes here. Mr Holliday, who was born in 1913 in Toronto, now lives in Kamloops, BC, and is a member of the Dominion Entomological Service. He has described his encounter with Grove in an article, 'Frederick Philip Grove: An Impression,' *Canadian Literature*, 3 (1960) 17–22.

2 Probably the young man featured in Grove's short story, 'The Extra Man,' included in *Tales from the Margin* (1971)

TO LORNE PIERCE

R.R. 4 Simcoe, Ont.
September 15, 1939

Dear Dr. Pierce,

I am extraordinarily well pleased with the review of *Two Generations* by Howe Martyn in the *Bookman*.[1] Apart from the two by Deacon and Milne[2] I have not seen any. Both those were stupidities, though favourable enough.

I think that, if this review of Martyn's were brought to the notice of a wider public – either in toto, or at least the two middle paragraphs – it should have a considerable effect on sales. Couldn't you print a leaflet or something?

This is, of course, only a suggestion, not an attempt at influencing the Ryerson policy.

In view of the outbreak of the war I have once more abandoned work on the 'Antbook.'[3] It would either have to be innocuous, or it would hit below the belt. I prefer to let it rest.

I have, instead, resumed work on 'The Seasons'[4] – another Ontario novel, with a wider canvas and a wider scope than *Two Generations*. It will take a year to finish work on it, provided I can hold out another year.

I understand from Miss MacRostie that Dr. Wallace was going to pay me $120 for that juvenile, in September. Not having heard from him personally, I begin to worry about it. Do you happen to know whether that will be forthcoming?

Sincerely yours,
F.P.G.

1 In the *Canadian Bookman* XX (1939) 43–5. It was entirely laudatory. Howe Martyn was born (1906) in Bowmanville, Ontario, and educated at Victoria College, Toronto (BA 1930), and Christ Church College, Oxford (MA 1932). He was for some time editor of the *Canadian Bookman*, and has contributed reviews to the *Bookman* and the *New York Times Book Review*. He is presently Professor of International Business at American University, Washington, DC.

2 For Deacon's review, see letter of August 7, 1939, note 2. W.S. Milne's appeared in *Saturday Night*, August 5, 1939, p 9, and is reprinted in my *Frederick Philip Grove* (Critical Views on Canadian Writers 1970) 155–7. Milne calls the novel 'substantial and meritorious' in spite of such minor flaws as 'artificial' dialogue and 'unimaginative' descriptions. W.S. Milne (b1902) was a secondary school-teacher who wrote one-act plays, dramatic criticism, and other reviews for a number of periodicals, including the *University of Toronto Quarterly* and *Saturday Night*.

3 *Consider Her Ways*

4 Which remained incomplete; see letter of September 21, 1939, note 3.

TO LORNE PIERCE

R.R. 4 Simcoe, Ont.
September 21, 1939

Dear Dr. Pierce,

Thanks for the bundle of reviews[1] which I am returning. I can't say that I found glancing through them an exhilarating task. In fact, I found it profoundly depressing and discouraging. 'Alas, what boots it...'[2]

However ... Well, I am going on with 'The Seasons.'[3] I am going to try to make it one volume only. If I succeed in that, about one sixth seems to be definitely done; in other words, the knots are very nearly tied.

By the way, those New York people (New York Publishing Service) apparently want potboilers rather than the sort of thing I do. I am not sending them anything, therefore.

Nothing worse could have happened than this cursed war. Thus the gods grind...

Sincerely yours,
F.P.G.

By the way, thanks for phoning Dr. Wallace.[4] The cheque has arrived and saves my life for a month or so.

1 A selection of these reviews of *Two Generations* is reprinted in my *Frederick Philip Grove* (Critical Views on Canadian Writers 1970). W.A. Deacon's in *The Globe and Mail* is enthusiastic, W.S. Milne's (*Saturday Night*) only slightly critical (see the preceding letter, note 2), and Carleton Stanley speaks highly of the novel in the *Dalhousie Review*. Only J.R. MacGillivray, writing in the *University of Toronto Quarterly*, was unfavourable: 'In spite of the fine things in *Two Generations* one feels that the author has for once gone off on a false trail.' But Grove's dissatisfaction with them, as he so often complains in these letters, was with the reviewers' failure to get to the heart of the matter.
2 From 'Lycidas' by John Milton (1608–74)
3 Illness prevented Grove from completing what might have been his magnum opus, a novel on a vast scale about a countryside within the compass of a single year. See Bruce Nesbitt's '"The Seasons": Grove's Unfinished Novel' in *Canadian Literature* XVIII (November 1963) 47–51, for a summary of the plot. The manuscript is in the University of Manitoba Grove Collection.
4 Archer Wallace, editor of *The Canadian Boy*; see letter of June 19, 1939, note 1. Grove sold 'The Adventures of Leonard Broadus' to *The Canadian Boy* for $120.

TO BARKER FAIRLEY

R.R. 4 Simcoe, Ont.
October 9, 1939

My dear Fairley,

Thanks; I take it[1] as another flower in the garland they are sending me, and I am particularly glad of that sentence, beginning, 'How many households...'

May I say one thing? The first thought of the book[2] arose from a question I asked myself: 'What sort of a farmer would my father have made in Ontario?' The child hanging on the tree; the boy accepting the cigar – is myself; and it was not without a sort of sly irony that I named him Philip. So, in a way, there, too, is autobiography. But in the sense that I have wrapped myself in less penetrable disguises, you are right, of course.

21 Barker Fairley. *Courtesy Barker Fairley*

I do hope that your expectation of a greater 'popularity' for this book will be borne out by events. There is no sign of it so far. It seems that, no matter what I release, I am up against a blank wall.

However...

I wish you could come down some time soon. I need tonic contacts. As it is, things are trolling along.

With best regards for you and yours,
As ever,
F.P.G.

1 Barker Fairley's review of *Two Generations* in the *Canadian Forum* of October 1939 – reprinted in my *Frederick Philip Grove* (Critical Views on Canadian Writers 1970) 158–60. The sentence which Grove singles out comments on the book's realism: 'How many households, reading these pages, will be compelled to exclaim – not necessarily at every point, but certainly at many – "This is us, exactly."'

2 *Two Generations*

TO LORNE PIERCE

R.R. 4 Simcoe, Ont.
October 21, 1939

Dear Dr. Pierce,

Enclosed please find nomination paper for the R.S.C.[1] duly filled out. My typewriter being out of commission, I have left it at the one list; I see they want 8 copies. But perhaps someone in the office could make them?

I wish you success in this.

I am writing a pamphlet 'The Case for Democracy.'[2] Interested?

Sincerely yours,
F.P.G.

FREDERICK PHILIP GROVE:

BOOKS:

Over Prairie Trails (1922)
The Turn of the Year (1923)
Settlers of the Marsh (1925)
A Search for America (1927)
Our Daily Bread (1928)
It Needs to be Said (1929)
The Yoke of Life (1930)
Fruits of the Earth (1933)
Two Generations (1939)

PAPERS:

'Writers and their Work' – Jan[uary] 1932 } *University*
'Thomas Hardy' – July 1932 } *of Toronto*
'The Plight of Canadian Fiction' – July 1933 } *Quarterly*
'The Flat Prairie' – July 1932 *Dalhousie Review*
'Snow' – Feb[ruary] 1932 *Queen's Quarterly*

And numerous contributions – short fiction and articles – in magazines (*Maclean's* q.v.) and daily papers (*Winnipeg Tribune*, *London Free Press*, etc.)

1 The Royal Society of Canada. See letters of December 16, 1938, December 17, 1940, and April 23, 1941. The nomination forms, which must be signed by three Fellows, call for a curriculum vitae and list of publications of the nominee. Sometimes, as apparently in this instance, the nominee himself is asked to fill out these portions of the form. Grove's actual election did not occur until 1941, but a year's delay is by no means unusual – in fact a much longer wait often occurs.
2 This was never published as such, although some of the material may have been reworked for the article 'Democracy and Education,' *University of Toronto Quarterly* XII (July 1943) 389–402.

TO LORNE PIERCE

R.R. 4 Simcoe, Ont.
October 28, 1939

Dear Dr. Pierce,

I am glad you express your interest in my pamphlet[1] – I cannot call it a book, for I aim at such condensation that it can be sold very cheaply – perhaps 40, 50, 60 pages.

It does not lay claim to originality but aims at presenting the argument clearly and concisely, basing itself chiefly (though theoretically only; i.e. not in the form of an historical treatise) on the recent history of Europe (including Britain). It summarises the argument against democracy as given by Mussolini, Seipel,[2] Dollfuss,[3] Schuschnigg,[4] Hitler; and then represents the counter argument, proposing changes in the parliamentary system.

I hope to finish the writing by Nov[ember] 4; if, by that time, I can repair my typewriter, a typescript should be ready within a further week.

As ever,
F.P.G.

1 'The Case for Democracy'; see the preceding letter, note 2.
2 Ignaz Seipel (1876–1932), a Roman Catholic priest who became Chancellor of Austria during 1922–4 and 1926–9. Initially a moderate pacifist and advocate of cultural autonomy for the various nationalities in the Austro-Hungarian empire, he became, in 1921, leader of

the Social Christian party and moved steadily to the right. His *Der Kampf um die österreichische Verfassung* (1930) advocated a corporate state, increased centralization of power in the hands of a federal president, and other Fascist ideas.
3 Engelbert Dollfuss (1892–1934) was Prime Minister of Austria during 1932–4, and a member of the Social Christian party. Although opposed to Nazi Germany, he founded the *Vaterländische Front* (Patriotic Front), and remodelled the Austrian constitution, in 1934, along Fascist lines. He was shot during a Nazi raid on the Chancellery.
4 Kurt von Schuschnigg (b1893) became Austrian Chancellor on Dollfuss's death in 1934. During his four years in office, he tried to keep Austria independent of Germany with the help of an Italian guarantee. But Pan-German feelings were strong, and when Hitler invaded Austria in 1938, the invaders were welcomed by a substantial segment of the populace.

TO LORNE PIERCE

R.R. 4 Simcoe, Ont.
November 11, 1939

Dear Dr. Pierce,

I am sending you, under separate cover, a typescript of a pamphlet of ca. 24000 words entitled 'The Case for Democracy.'

Could you look it over, or have it looked over, at your earliest convenience? To let me know whether you think you can do anything with it? I believe it contains a sufficient ballast of ideas to make publication desirable. If it is published shortly and meets with some measure of success, I could produce numbers of other, similar things on all sorts of subjects: especially regarding the European situation: things which, as far as I can see, have not been said and which, at least to my mind, badly need to be said; for ignorance with regard to them is very great in Canada. I have lived in the countries concerned; and *I know Germany* and admire and detest it at the same time. The more I read and study about the present situation, the more I come to see that the Germany which I knew is essentially the same as the Germany of today.

As ever,
F.P.G.

TO LORNE PIERCE

R.R. 4 Simcoe, Ont.
November 16, 1939

Dear Dr. Pierce,

I am laid up with a fierce cold; and I haven't, for the moment, any idea in my head. But I can say that there are two subjects for possible pamphlets which I could write in quick succession: (1) The mentality of the present Reich; (2) The central-European situation as it has developed since 50 years ago.

Both would be partly historical, partly psychological.

As ever,
F.P.G.

TO LORNE PIERCE

R.R. 4 Simcoe, Ont.
November 30, 1939

Dear Dr. Pierce,

I am tremendously worried about things; in spite of superhuman efforts, nothing seems to be forthcoming.

In that connection it occurs to me that last spring, when I mentioned the limited edition of *Two Generations*, you said you would talk the matter over with your wholesale department. I have slightly over 200 copies left; and if I could sell them at full price, I'd be on easy street for the time being, say till next summer or fall. But, of course, I do not expect any longer to get full price. In fact, in order to save the situation for the moment, I'd be willing to let 100 or 150 copies go for half price. Is there any chance of your taking over a block of them?

How is the trade edition doing? Deacon[1] writes me, complaining of lack of advertising.

I have once more taken up that autobiography[2] of mine, trying to soften down such passages as my wife objects to. Friends of mine who have read the typescript call it a 'knock-out' of a book and talk of the Nobel Prize (!!!). I laugh.

As ever,
F.P.G.

1 W.A. Deacon, the journalist and literary critic; see letter of November 10, 1926, note 4.

2 *In Search of Myself* (1946), which won the Governor-General's Award in the non-fiction category. In view of the imaginative way in which Grove re-created his past, it has been suggested that it should have won the award for fiction!

TO LORNE PIERCE

R.R. 4 Simcoe, Ont.
December 8, 1939

Dear Dr. Pierce,

My wife and I were discussing your letter last night when she said that every few days somebody here asks her where *Two Generations*

22 Frederick Philip Grove. *Courtesy Leonard Grove*

can be had. She feels confident that from 2 to 3 dozen could be sold *here* for Christmas presents.

I would suggest that you have them send *6* copies to *E.H. Jackson Ltd* – drugstore – Simcoe, with a covering letter asking them to display in the window, giving them the privilege of returning unsold stock after Christmas. I, too, feel sure there won't be any to return; and possibly there will be repeat orders.

I cannot very well do this myself without loss of dignity. This is a small town, you know; and I must hold my nose high.

Sincerely yours,
F.P.G.

TO LORNE PIERCE

R.R. 4 Simcoe, Ont.
December 15, 1939

Dear Dr. Pierce,

I am bothering you a lot. But here is the point. I just see that my little skit 'A Platinum Watch' has actually appeared in the *Bookman*.[1] Now I have been casting about with might and main for some means of laying my hand on some small sum for Christmas; and I wonder whether you could put in a good word for me with the management to let me have whatever fee is equitable (you mentioned 1¢ a word, I believe, last spring) at once, or in time for me to spend part of it on a few trifles for the boy?

I am working like a hound on 3 books at once,[2] final shapings, of course.

Thanks for your (slightly) encouraging letter, and best wishes for a good Christmas.

As ever,
F.P.G.

1 In the *Bookman* XXI (October 1939) 5–12

2 *The Master of the Mill* is unlikely to be one of them since it was completed around August 17, 1939 (see letter of that date) and the completed ms was sent to Pierce on August 30, 1939. In his letter of September 15, 1939, he informs Pierce that he has 'once more abandoned work' on *Consider Her Ways*. Thus only two of the three books referred to here are certain: 'The Seasons' (see letter of September 21, 1939) and *In Search of Myself* (see letter of November 30, 1939). The third book was probably the unpublished 'Heart's Desire; or, Two Lives' (see letter of August 29, 1937, note 4); but 'Felix Powell's Career' (unpublished and no longer extant) and 'The Canyon' (unpublished, in the University of Manitoba Grove Collection) may also be considered.

TO LORNE PIERCE

R.R. 4 Simcoe, Ont.
December 21, 1939

F.P. Grove wishes
Dr. Lorne Pierce
and all he loves
a pleasant Christmas and
a happy New Year

D

Menaced with Cessation: The Last Years in Simcoe 1940-48

'Feeling menaced with a cessation of things – chronic arthritis and a suspicion of cancer of the throat – I am trying to clear my desk.'
TO LORNE PIERCE,
APRIL 5, 1940

TO LORNE PIERCE

R.R. 4 Simcoe, Ont.
January 4, 1940

Dear Dr. Pierce,

You asked me, with regard to the limited edition of *Two Generations* to wait till after the holiday rush. I cannot wait too long since February 1 is a critical date for me. So here are the facts:

Apart from a few copies which I want to retain (not to sell) there are 288 copies available. Of these 120 are in slip-cases; 14 dozens, or 168 are without them. I had only 300 slip-cases made, at a cost of 6½¢ a piece.

Now, if I could sell the whole stock outright, I should be willing to take $2.00 a copy for those with slip-cases, and to allow a discount of 10¢ a copy for those without them. On that basis the figures would stand thus:

120 copies $2.00	$240.00
168 copies $1.90	$319.20
Total	$559.20

Suppose I shipped you these, which would exhaust the saleable stock, could your house advance me, on that, the sum of $300.00? This sum to be further secured by any royalties that may become due, from books at present in your possession and further books to be published henceforth; sales of the limited edition to be credited to me at the above figures.

Please let me know as soon as possible.

As ever,
F.P.G.

TO NORMA MACROSTIE

R.R. 4 Simcoe, Ont.
January 17, 1940

Dear Miss MacRostie,

Your kind letter of the 5th inst[ant] was received some time ago. I write today to ask you to be good enough to call Dr. Pierce's attention to my note when he gets back. The month is in its second half now; and I'm afraid if nothing can be done within a week or so, I'll be 'in the soup.'

By the way, since I have not heard about that pamphlet of mine 'The Case for Democracy,' I begin to think that Dr. Pierce has no use for it. I have written a number of others since, but I cannot afford to spend money on paper etc. unless something comes out of them. I think, however, that I can place the pamphlet in a periodical, though it would not bring a fee there. Do you happen to know anything about it?

1940 seems to be a tough year all around; may I wish that you live in one of the quieter corners of it?

Sincerely yours,
F.P.G.

TO LORNE PIERCE

R.R. 4 Simcoe, Ont.
February 2, 1940

Dear Dr. Pierce,

I am very sorry to hear of your loss; I know what such things mean.[1]

As for the contents of your letter of yesterday I am disappointed, of course. In fact, I am getting desperate.

I suppose there is, by this time, no chance either for *The Master of the Mill*. I begin to wonder whether I am getting senile.

However, I might say that I have had a little good luck in securing some pupils who, for a short time, give me an income of $5.50 a week. It won't last, though; the teacher wouldn't be doing his duty if he did not eliminate himself.

I have been casting about what to do next. I have four books which I consider to be in shape for publication. Of these, it seems to me 'Life of a Writer in Canada,' or, simply, 'My Life'[2] – for it deals with my childhood in Europe as well – offers the best chances. Yet I hesitate throwing it on the market in war-time. My wife has objected to my publishing the appalling record; but I have worked it over again and omitted the worst things to which she objected. If I type it out, it will be a long book. Would you care to read the first two or three chapters? With a view, not so much of publishing it, but of giving me advice as to the possibility of printing it in some periodical, in the U.S.A. I suppose, for I fully realise that we have no organ in Canada. Here they would want a mild record, with a happy ending, like *A Search for America*. But this thing is grim as death. Not in the writing, but in the contents.

I speak of the first few chapters only; for I cannot afford to buy paper and typewriter ribbons unless I get an immediate return.

Frankly, I cannot quite understand the attitude of the Ryerson Press.[3] For I ask only for an advance of $300.00 which would secure me for a year. Surely, sooner or later there will be a profit of $300 on the sum of my work? However, that is the business of the house; and I must do the best I can with what remains of my time and my work. I came to the Ryerson Press because I thought the house had confidence in me. I feel a bit deserted. It isn't your fault, of course; don't think I am blaming you. It's just my confounded luck. But perhaps I am overestimating my work; I have always been diffident.

Please let me know whether you have the time for reading those first chapters for which I have the paper.

Sincerely yours,
F.P.G.

1 Pierce's reply to Grove's letter of January 4 was not sent until February 1 because he (Pierce) had been in his mother's home during her final illness. Concerning the offer of the limited edition of *Two Generations*, Pierce declined it for financial reasons.

2 *In Search of Myself*
3 See note 1 above, and letter of January 4, 1940. The misunderstanding between Grove and the Ryerson Press probably arose from the fact that Pierce himself was a very enthusiastic man who led Grove to think that he would publish his books, but that Pierce had to convince his Board of their financial viability – and at this time Canadian publishing was still in the doldrums. The revival of the trade began in the immediate post-war years. However, Pierce in a letter to Grove dated December 6, 1938, had virtually promised to undertake the publication of Grove's collected works: 'It is our present purpose to advertise your books collectively as "The Complete Works of Frederick Philip Grove." We are to have refusal of any novel which you may write, and we look forward to a long and happy association.' Grove's reiterated disappointment is thus perfectly understandable.

TO LORNE PIERCE

R.R. 4 Simcoe, Ont.
March 9, 1940

Dear Dr. Pierce,

In desperation I have made up my mind to offer my autobiography for publication, against the wish of my wife and even my own inclination which would be to leave the book till after my death.

Would you be good enough to let me know whether the offer would be welcome to the Ryerson Press? I have the suspicion that it might not be; and I cannot afford to lose time over the matter.

It is rather a long book – ca. 140,000 words; but I believe that, in interest, it should vastly excel *A Search for America*. Tentatively I am giving it the title 'Life of a Writer in Canada.'[1]

Unless the Ryerson Press is very anxious to secure this book, I shall offer it to an agent in the U.S.A. An advance on royalties would be imperative; and so would a prompt decision. I consider it the one asset I have which, I believe, is certain to relieve me of the imminent threat of starvation.

The final manuscript will be finished in two or three days.

Sincerely yours,
F.P.G.

1 The title finally chosen was, of course, *In Search of Myself* (Macmillan 1946).

TO LORNE PIERCE

R.R. 4 Simcoe, Ont.
March 16, 1940

Dear Dr. Pierce,

In compliance with yours of the 13th I am sending you a

completed typescript of the 'Life' from which I have eliminated those parts against the publication of which my wife protested most vehemently.

I had not, so far, considered publication myself, except some 3 years ago when things looked very black for me. My wife's protest then prevailed.

You will understand that there is only one reason why I offer it now. Two Canadian publishers have told me that they'd jump at the chance to get the book, one of them willing to guarantee publication in England as well.

But it is not, in this case, publication in England I seek; it is in the U.S.A.

And, may I say? Unless decision and action come before May 15, it will be useless. I promise to hold to my offer till then. Action, of course, means an advance on royalties. This gives only six weeks – no, eight. But I can't help myself.

There will be a dedication page which I have not inserted.

Sincerely yours,
F.P.G.

TO LORNE PIERCE

R.R. 4 Simcoe, Ont.
March 25, 1940

Dear Dr. Pierce,

Under separate cover I am sending you a Ms. in 4 parts, entitled 'Go to the Ant.'[1]

This is the Ant-Book so often mentioned on which I have been at work since the fall or early winter of 1919. It has had even more rewritings than *A Search for America* or the 'Life'; in fact, I believe it is the most laboriously-produced book of mine, the plan of which reaches back to 1892 or 1893.

I had been in hopes of rewriting it once more; but I find that I cannot do anything more with it. Hitler and Mussolini are sufficiently anticipated anyway. And perhaps there is as much laughter in it as I shall ever evoke.

I should be glad if you could find time to read it; I must clear my mental and metaphorical desk. My physical condition is such that I want to face other than earthly things. From day to day it becomes harder to breathe and to digest food. I am seeing a doctor today.

If you do read it, please let me know what you think of it. It has one merit – that of utter originality. And I think it contains a few things which are important. However...

Sincerely yours,
F.P.G.

The Ms. is the only complete copy of the text.

1 Published by Macmillan in 1947 as *Consider Her Ways*

TO LORNE PIERCE

R.R. 4 Simcoe, Ont.
April 1, 1940

Dear Dr. Pierce,

Thanks for your letter of the 29th March.[1]

Just a few points.

Isn't it the only possible comment on my life as a writer within the period covered that, apart from my very brief time with Graphic, I met none of my contemporaries in the field of letters, arts, or whatnot, except *academic* friends? That, to put it mildly, these contemporaries shunned me? That, when, in 1923 or 24, I joined the C[anadian] A[uthors'] A[ssociation], I was hounded out of it by their lesser lights?

No, my work did not grow out of the milieu of what was being done by others in Canada. I neither knew of it nor cared for it. That a few of them, of late, have sought me out is no matter. I have helped many; nobody has ever helped me. People like Callaghan or de la Roche have gone out of their way *not* to meet me. It is simple charity not to talk about them; apart from the fact that Miss de la Roche, for instance, simply did not count for me. The parallel of Roberts and Carman does not apply. I thought it best to draw the veil. I could have told a few stories – that of the C[anadian] A[uthors'] A[ssociation] convention in Vancouver in 1926; or that of my reception in Winnipeg, early in 1929, when I lectured there for the second time – a reception staged by such as 'Bobby' Watson[2] to whom I had done nothing but kindness.

Even in Ottawa I lived in an isolation comparable only to that of an Antarctic explorer, one afflicted with small-pox at that, lost on the Barrier who, at the best, meets a scavenger gull. How many of the Ottawa writers called on me or my wife? Did Scott?[3] Did Burpee?[4] Did anyone? No, not one. It is true that, as an employee of Graphic, I met a few who expected me to print such of their works as they had failed to place elsewhere – Macdonald,[5] for instance.

Next, as to that remark[6] about Hardy. I put it down just as I read it and as, in my opinion, anyone reading it must interpret it. However, if you prefer, I shall omit it. I have no desire either to offend or to speak, at this late hour, as though I were offended. I am not and have never been.

Re *Settlers*.[7] If there is any inaccuracy which matters, I am willing to make any correction you suggest. The sentence about 'you coming near losing your job over it' is literally what Phelps told me; and, if I remember right, you confirmed it. But my hearing is such that I take anyone else's word for what was said. It is easily omitted.

As for the R[oyal] S[ociety] medal,[8] I have called it the single honour that came to me out of Canada, and I valued it, though it came too late to do me any good. I have pointedly omitted mentioning one or two other honours which came from elsewhere. If you think it wiser, I'll blue-pencil the passage.

For, in any case, I must have the Ms. back for a day or two before it is printed if printing there is to be. This version was typed in a hurry and under tremendous pressure; and a few points were left without that precision which I could have desired; I did not take the time to look through older jottings. Thus the purpose of the trip through Siberia was left rather vague because I could not think of the phrase, 'the Asiatic Focus of the North Magnetic Pole.'

One more word. Should there, against my expectation, result a development, please let me, metaphorically, sit in on the negotiations. Numbers of people, some of them publishers, expect great things from the book. I have made serious sacrifices in order to offer it now. Many passages have been toned down because living people had to be spared; others because certain things would not sound well coming from a writer himself still half alive.

In return, I must expect to be relieved of financial pressure for at least a year. I will put my cards on the table. By the 2nd half of May I must have $675. If I had had half that sum at an earlier date, I should not have made the offer of the book. After May, some modicum will be needed to carry me along.

Little Brown[9] sounds all right; but there is considerable doubt in my mind whether, even if they want the book, they will do this. That is why, in a way, I should have preferred to handle the book through an agent. If I don't get that money, I don't want the book to appear; I could not justify its publication to my wife who is violently opposed to it, though I omitted most of the offending passages, thereby weakening the impact of the book. Any sale *should*, in addition, give us some sort of holiday next summer. Both my wife and I are worn out.

Unless something like that happens, I am faced with losing my place (or $14000 invested in it), to the government for about $2000, and the banks for the sum specified. If I do lose it, I shall have no roof over my head and no bread to put in the mouth of my little son.

That, briefly, is the situation. I know you will do your best and appreciate it. It is a most anxious time; it has been a most anxious time throughout the last few years.

However, enough. A hundred years from now – or, the way it appears to me, day after tomorrow – what will it all matter?

Sincerely yours,
F.P.G.

1 Most of the points in this letter are in reply to those made by Pierce in a long letter in which he acknowledges the ms of the autobiography. He goes on to say that while he was 'deeply moved' by the book, he regretted that Grove made so little mention of his

contemporaries, 'at a time that saw the actual birth of a native arts and letters, such as it is,' adding, 'but I am not urging it. After all, the story centres upon yourself.'

2 Robert Watson, the novelist; see letter of October 9, 1928, note 3.

3 Duncan Campbell Scott, the poet; see letter of March 19, 1928 II, note 2. He was one of Grove's three sponsors for fellowship in the Royal Society of Canada.

4 Lawrence Burpee; see letter of October 4, 1927, note 1.

5 Wilson Macdonald; see letter of March 30, 1928, note 1.

6 In his letter (see note 1 above) Pierce explains his comparison of Grove's work to Hardy's in words already quoted in note 2 to letter of June 15, 1936.

7 Since Pierce's account presents a rather different point of view from Grove's, even as the latter finally appeared in print (*In Search of Myself*, p 381), it may be worth quoting in full:

> The episode about *Settlers* is mainly correct. I went to the lecture unannounced. Phelps spotted me and introduced us. He spoke of your MS, and wanted me to see it. I told him I never read MSS on trips, for it was fair neither to the reader nor the author, so if he would send it in I would read it gladly when I got home. He pressed me the next day, and then finding me adamant, let it go. I had an invitation to Sunday afternoon tea at his home, and to my surprise you came in later, with the MS! It was at this tea, with the four of us, that I promised to take the MS to my room and read what I could before leaving for the west the next day. I read on into the morning and rose late. You called on the phone and asked me if I had breakfast, and might you come down. We had a long and interesting visit, and I remember how tense you were when I suggested that some of the book seemed autobiographical to me. You were very pale and tired, and you were rather vehement in your insistence that you had lived no inconsiderable part of this and other books you had done. I believed you. I don't think I came near losing my job, but I did have a hell of a time with irate agents of moral reform groups and so on.

8 The Lorne Pierce Gold Medal of the Royal Society of Canada, which Grove received in 1934, but sold later to buy a radio set (see *In Search of Myself* 454). The sale distressed Pierce, who remarks, 'You may well have set a style ... I confess it hit me hard. The Society might accompany the medal with a small parchment, stating that the recipient had been awarded the nation's highest honors in Letters. Then if he had to furnish his home or buy a loaf he would still have proof of the award even though the bauble went to the three-balls Uncle!'

9 Pierce in his letter intimates that the ms of the autobiography was being sent to Little, Brown of Boston, with 'a strong letter.' The Little, Brown letter is in the Lorne Pierce Collection at Queen's, and begins: 'We have received the long-awaited autobiography of Frederick Philip Grove, a book which we believe will be of more than ordinary interest to your constituency. Frederick Philip Grove stands among the top three of Canadian novelists, sharing that place with Mazo de la Roche and Morley Callaghan.' The reply from Little, Brown, dated April 5, 1940, is also in the Lorne Pierce Collection. It reads in part: 'Unfortunately I cannot find anyone here who seems familiar with Mr. Grove's work.

Needless to say we know Mazo de la Roche very well and we are also all of us completely familiar with Morley Callaghan. Very likely it is our loss but that is that and we think probably it would be worth your while to try another publisher.'

TO LORNE PIERCE

R.R. 4 Simcoe, Ont.
April 5, 1940

Dear Dr. Pierce,

Glad you like the 'Ant-Book.' How did I come to stumble on to that theme? Well, I have always been a student of ants; and I was an ant myself, was I not, in the great American formicary?

Feeling menaced with a cessation of things – chronic arthritis and a suspicion of cancer of the throat – I am trying to clear my desk. I shall burn scores of manuscripts. But there are a few which I feel reluctant to burn. I am trying to give them the final touch. There are more especially two: 'Felix Powell's Career'[1] – a college story with a multiple sexual theme – and 'Murder in the Quarry'[2] – an analysis of criminal procedure. If I manage to get typescripts – so far I have no paper – I shall send you these, too.

Ultimately I shall try to finish 'The Seasons'[3] – a panoramic novel of Canadian life, with town, city, and open countryside – which I have been at work on for some years.

This does not mean, of course, that I want immediate publication of them all. But you may as well know them and then act as you see fit, provided, of course, you still think of that edition of 'Collected Works.'

Sincerely yours,
F.P.G.

P.S. I see, to my disgust, that Dr. Wallace[4] has attached my full name to that juvenile of mine, of a year ago. That was not what I bargained for.

1 See Grove's letter to me (January 30, 1945), in which he says that because of his wife's 'pronounced hatred of the thing, I have given her the ms., to be kept for 20 years after my death.' The manuscript was apparently destroyed by Mrs Grove – or so her son Leonard believes.

2 Which remains unpublished in the University of Manitoba Grove Collection

3 The unfinished manuscript of 469 pages is in the University of Manitoba Grove Collection; serious illness prevented its completion.

4 Dr Archer Wallace, editor of *The Canadian Boy*, in which Grove's 'Adventures of Leonard Broadus' appeared; see letter of June 19, 1939, note 1. Apparently Grove wished the juvenile to appear under a pseudonym – but there is no other indication of this in any of the correspondence that I have seen.

TO CHARLES E. EATON[1]

R.R. 4, Simcoe, Ont.
April 11, 1940 II

Dear Mr. Eaton,

Complying with your request for a list of my published writings, I give the following.

Books:

Over Prairie Trails 1922 (McClelland and Stewart, Toronto)
The Turn of the Year 1923 (as above)
Settlers of the Marsh 1925 (Ryerson Press, Toronto)
A Search for America 1927 (Graphic Publishers, Ottawa, now Ryerson Press)
Our Daily Bread 1928 (Macmillans in Canada)
It Needs to Be Said, Essays, 1929 (Macmillans in Canada)
The Yoke of Life 1930 (Macmillans in Canada)
Fruits of the Earth 1933 (J.M. Dent and Sons, London, England, and Toronto)
Two Generations 1939 (Ryerson Press, Toronto)

Essays: *University of Toronto Quarterly*, Jan[uary] [19]32, July [19]32, July [19]38.
Dalhousie Review, July [19]31
Queen's Quarterly, Feb[ruary] [19]32.

This is all I have any record of, though there are scores of contributions to daily papers and other periodicals. Perhaps I might also add that the greater number of my books remains unpublished.

I believe that the next book to appear will be my autobiography, under the title of 'Life of a Writer in Canada.' It, together with another book which I call 'Go to the Ant,' I consider as the only two books of any importance which I am likely to publish. I wonder whether, for the purposes of a thesis, you should not be acquainted with the former. If you share that view, I might be able to divert a typescript for a short time – I find I have a bad carbon copy on onion-skin paper, reading matter for good eyes only.

Sincerely yours,
F.P. Grove

1 Charles E. Eaton was born in Edmonton, Alberta, in 1911, and has taught and served in an administrative capacity in schools of the Annapolis Valley, Nova Scotia. He is at present Inspector of Schools of the County of Kings and District of West Hants in that province, and lives in Kentville.

TO LORNE PIERCE

R.R. 4 Simcoe, Ont.
April 11, 1940

Dear Dr. Pierce,

By separate parcel I am sending you a typescript of 'Felix Powell's Career'[1] and would ask you, if it isn't imposing upon you, to read it, sooner or later. I have fixed it up in a convenient form.

I have reread it, with a view towards emasculating it – it has been offered to Macaulay[2] and one agent in New York; the name of the latter I have forgotten; both declined it as 'too strong'; in other words, they put it down as pornography. Well, I found nothing to change; the thing is, psychologically, a *tour de force*; but without such detail as still remains it loses its 'punch'; and I don't see that I can do anything with it. It either stands or falls; and, in my opinion, it stands, of course. Whether to offer it anywhere in New York, I leave to you. The more irons in the fire...

I shall now turn to 'Murder in the Quarry';[3] if I succeed in getting a typescript of that, I shall also send it; and that will, for the moment, finish the list. 'The Seasons' is far from ready.

Sorry to give you so much trouble; but I'm fighting in the last ditch. On Saturday I am going to London to see whether anything can be done to put a stop to the trouble in my throat.

Sincerely yours,
F.P.G.

1 See letter of April 5, 1940.

2 This firm is no longer in business. Their interests in Canada were represented by George J. McLeod Limited of Toronto, but they do not have any record of having negotiated with Grove for 'Felix Powell's Career.'

3 See letter of April 5, 1940.

TO LORNE PIERCE

R.R. 4 Simcoe, Ont.
April 13, 1940

Dear Dr. Pierce,

The Macmillan Company asks me to give them permission to reprint, in a prose anthology, a chapter from the *Search for America*.

I used to own the copyright but don't just know how things stand for the moment. However, considering that they seem to be in a hurry and that such a reprint constitutes something like an advertisement, I have presumed on giving that permission. I hope this is all right with you?[1]

Sincerely yours,
F.P.G.

I also think it wise to keep on a good footing with those people. I stipulate, of course, suitable acknowledgment.

1 Norma MacRostie, Dr Pierce's secretary, replied three days later, saying the Press was agreeable, provided a fee was charged; Macmillan paid $15.00, of which 25% went to Ryerson as commission; see Grove's letter to Pierce, October 29, 1940. The anthology was *Prose of Our Day*, the chapter concerned, 'Riding the Rods' – a showpiece which had appeared, as an advertising gambit, in the Winnipeg *Tribune*.

TO LORNE PIERCE

R.R. 4 Simcoe, Ont.
May 4, 1940

Dear Dr. Pierce,

I see by *The Canadian Author and Bookman* that McDowell[1] got the Governor-General's award. I also understand that I was not elected to the R[oyal] S[ociety of] C[anada].[2] All which is as it should be.

I am, of course, most anxiously waiting for word re one of the Mss. which you are handling.[3] The dead-line date is now only a week and a half away. By that time I shall have finished typing one more book, 'Murder in the Quarry' which I shall send you on completion of the script.

With regard to this latter book, likely to be the last I shall ever offer, I feel that, surely, there is somewhere a magazine which would be glad to have it. May I again suggest that, unless you feel very sure of being able to place it, a literary agent might be able to do so?

Sincerely yours,
F.P.G.

1 Franklin Davey McDowell (1888–1965), Toronto journalist, whose first novel *The Champlain Road* won the Governor-General's Award for 1939

Pierce, in his reply, calls the award 'a frightful decision ... I have already written to the Canadian Authors Association, indicting the whole outfit for such a miscarriage of justice.' The novel was an historical romance, and was thus anathema to Grove.

2 In his reply, Pierce tries to reassure Grove by saying: 'There has been no announcement yet ... You are certain to be elected.' However, Grove was *not* elected in 1940; his election was delayed until 1941. See letters of December 10, 1938, note 1, and October 31, 1939, note 1.

3 May 15 was the deadline set by Grove for Ryerson to make up their mind about publishing *In Search of Myself*; see letter of March 16, 1940.

TO LORNE PIERCE

R.R. 4 Simcoe, Ont.
May 14, 1940

Dear Dr. Pierce,

I am sending you 'Murder in the Quarry,' the last of the Mss. which I consider I have done with what I can.

It was written originally as a pot-boiler and took charge; I believe it is far from being a pot-boiler now.[1] If you could find time to look through it and see whether you think anything could be done in placing it, I'd be much obliged.

As for 'Felix Powell,' I shall think it over; I mean your suggestion as to writing prefaces. I don't suppose there is any hurry about it. I am for the moment in such an upheaval that I cannot concentrate. But I do think that, if I did these prefaces, much misunderstanding might be anticipated, considering that most of our so-called critics need to have their noses tipped on to the important points.

With regard to the third part of 'Felix Powell,' I have already eliminated very large sections of what you call 'Circumstantial evidence.'[2] However, the novelist is in the everlasting dilemma between a novel, which must be living life, and an argument. Every novel, of course, *is* an argument if it is a novel. But ... I should be entirely willing, though, to soften if I thought that the power of the thing would remain unimpaired.

Sincerely yours,
F.P.G.

1 Pierce tried to place it with Dodd, Mead & Co., and the New York agents Brandt & Brandt, but without success. The manuscript is in the University of Manitoba Grove Collection.

2 Pierce, in his letter of May 6 about 'Felix Powell's Career,' had questioned the necessity of 'so much circumstantial evidence.'

TO LORNE PIERCE

R.R. 4 Simcoe, Ont.
May 20, 1940

Dear Dr. Pierce,

I have hesitated, unhappily, over what I am going to say. It is this. Since that confounded 'Life' of mine has not done what I expected it to do when I offered it, namely saved me in my special and present economic troubles, I wish to withdraw it.

If it had done what I hoped it might do, I think I could have justified its publication to my wife who is violently opposed to its publication. Since it didn't, I want to leave it to her to decide whether it is ever going to appear or not. I believe – I almost hope – she will burn the manuscript.

That, if I remember right, leaves 4 Mss.[1] in your hands; and if none of them can be placed, well, please return them to me. I fully realise that these are abnormal times. Nobody in Canada suffers more acutely than do I. But I must face facts.

As for your suggestion that I write prefaces to my novels, I will think about it. But it will take time, for I am in no mood just now to think about such trivialities as my books; and it may well be that it is too late.

Thanks for whatever you have done, in any case.

Sincerely yours,
F.P.G.

1 They were *The Master of the Mill, Consider Her Ways,* 'Felix Powell's Career,' and 'Murder in the Quarry.' Only the first two were published, in 1944 and 1947 respectively, and none of them by the Ryerson Press.

TO LORNE PIERCE

R.R. 4 Simcoe, Ont.
May 30, 1940

Dear Dr. Pierce,

Yes, I expected that Appleton-Century would decline.[1] In fact, I have never had any confidence in them; in spite of the fact that I expected the 'Life' to be snapped up. There are, at least there were, two Canadian publishers who were willing to risk Canadian publication independently of foreign publication; and one of them, I believe, would have relieved my situation.

However, it seems written that my need for a crust of bread is not to be filled by my work. Perhaps it is as well that at least it was not to be through the 'Life' which, in compliance with my wife's desire, I shall hand over to her.

Just what will happen in my present situation is not yet clear. If I were to follow my own inclination, I'd go on the road, in spite of desperately ill health; for most of the time I feel that, if I were my dog, I'd sit down on my haunches and howl with my pains.

The strange thing is that I am convinced I have not yet done my best work. Five minutes ago, since it is raining, I finished re-reading Part I of 'The Seasons.' As a novel, it might well rank among the great works of the age; provided I had leisure and the bare essentials to finish it. I have neither. I must work at manual labour to the point of exhaustion.[2] This goes so far that I become indifferent to what is happening in Europe. And I say to myself that it is all one. In a year and a half, if I live that long, I shall be seventy; which is old age;

and perhaps my own powers of judgment have already suffered a decline. I have lost all confidence; and I have only one desire left, for rest.

As for the European situation, the world has wagged through one disaster after the other; but I wish I could look back upon the outcome from a hundred years hence.

Sincerely yours,
F.P.G.

1 After remarking that 'there is enough variety to the career to make the autobiography more important than a great many life-stories published recently,' Appleton-Century declined because, as they saw it, they could not make a success of it.

2 We know that in 1942 Grove worked in a canning factory; whether he did so also in 1940, or whether he is here referring to some other form of manual labour, is a matter for speculation. See letter of July 8, 1942.

TO LORNE PIERCE

R.R. 4 Simcoe, Ont.
June 9, 1940

Dear Dr. Pierce,

I received the enclosed letter[1] from the Best Printing Company which explains itself.

They are willing to sell the type at the cost of the metal, namely $114.92, incl[usive] of sales tax.

I don't suppose you will feel that a second edition is near enough to warrant the expenditure of that much. Originally, it had been my intention to acquire the type myself, but my financial position puts that out of the question.

Would you, therefore, be good enough to let the Best people know, over the telephone, that they are at liberty to melt the type?

Sincerely yours,
F.P. Grove

P.S. – I am writing them to act according to your instruction.

1 Which asked Grove for his permission to melt down the standing type of *Two Generations*, as 'we do not hold type over the one year period unless we have a second printing' because of the high cost of new material. Pierce replied June 17; Ryerson was taking the type, to hold for six months more, in the hope a new edition might be necessary.

TO RICHARD CROUCH

R.R. 4 Simcoe, Ont.
August 5, 1940

Dear Dick,

Gladiolus time is here, though it does not, so far, seem to be as much of a success as in years gone-by. On the other hand, I have had no bloom so far except from bulbs less than four years old. My 6 to 8-year bulbs were planted a week later.

However, it so works out that I shall have to be in London again on Thursday, August 8; and for three weeks in succession, for treatment by Dr. Wismer,[1] two doors from the library. Like the previous time, I shall arrive in the early afternoon; and I shall try to drop in at the library between 3 and 4, to return some of those French books and to get some more if I can. I am trying to finish the Jules Romains[2] up to vol[ume] 8.

Don't let me keep you from anything important; if, on the other hand, you are free, I shall be delighted to see you.

As ever,
F.P.G.

1 The late Dr Harold St C. Wismer, a graduate of the University of Western Ontario, who died in 1964. His daughter, Mrs Betty Zurbrigg, recalls no mention, by her father, of treating Grove.
2 Jules Romains (pseudonym of Louis Farigoule, b1885), the French poet, dramatist, and essayist, who invented Unanimism and achieved great success on the stage with his farce, *Knock*, was the author of a cyclic novel, *Men of Good Will*, consisting of twenty-seven volumes.

TO LORNE PIERCE

R.R. 4 Simcoe, Ont.
August 27, 1940

Dear Dr. Pierce,

I am wondering whether, if I go to Toronto some time next week, there is a chance of finding you in?

Sincerely yours,
F.P.G.

TO CHARLES E. EATON

R.R. 4, Simcoe, Ont.
September 22, 1940

Dear Mr. Eaton,

Thanks for sending me your thesis. I hope to read it shortly.

Yes, I am afraid I must have the carbon copy of my autobiography back. It is, apart from the original the only copy I have; and these days it is perilous to have the original travelling about overseas.

With best wishes for your continued success,
Sincerely,
F.P. Grove

TO RICHARD CROUCH

R.R. 4 Simcoe, Ont.
October 3, 1940

Dear Dick,

I have been away at Toronto and only just find the card for the Opening.[1] We are sorry that we can't come tomorrow; but we shall be at London on Wed[nesday] Oct[ober] 9, late in the afternoon to fetch Mandy[2] who will be through at the hospital at 7 p.m. We shall have only about an hour to spare but shall drop in at the library where I shall return all the books I still have. If possible, I should like to borrow a few more French books; I have been intensely interested in some of those I got last, especially Guy Mazeline's *Les Loups*[3] which I consider a very great book, head and shoulders above the ruck of the rest.

With best wishes,
As ever,
F.P.G.

1 Of the Elsie Perrin Williams Memorial Building in London, Ontario, on October 4, 1940. The opening ceremony of the cultural centre was attended by Duncan MacArthur, Ontario Minister of Education, and John Adams Lowe, Director of Rochester, NY, Public Library.

2 Amanda (Wiens) Mather, Mrs Grove's younger sister

3 Guy Mazéline (b1901), the popular French novelist, whose *Les Loups* (1933) was translated into English (1935) by Eric Sutton

TO LORNE PIERCE

R.R. 4 Simcoe, Ont.
October 29, 1940

Dear Dr. Pierce,

Miss Elliott, of Macmillans, writes me that the fee for permission to reprint 'Riding the Rods,' from *A Search for America*, was paid to the Ryerson Press on July 5.[1] Surely this fee, or at least all but 10% of it, should have gone to me? They also say that a copy of the anthology was forwarded through the Ryerson Press. I have not seen it.

When I saw you last, I said, I was not going to go home unless I had secured some position. I secured it: as master of Greek at Upper Canada College.[2] To me, there was no doubt about it. So I went home to get some clothes. I had hardly reached it when, by a long-distance telephone call, the engagement was cancelled. Thus it goes.

Sincerely yours,
F.P.G.

1 See letter of April 13, 1940, note 1.
2 Enquiry to the College concerning the incident proved inconclusive – nothing was to be found in the records, and Terence W.L. MacDermot, who as Principal of the College from 1935 to 1942 might have had some knowledge of the incident, is now deceased. This is probably another example of Grove's tendency to jump to conclusions.

TO WATSON KIRKCONNELL

R.R. 4 Simcoe, Ont.
November 16, 1940

Dear Kirkconnell,

I sent that offprint[1] merely to show that I was aware of your having come east. It is a mere trifle, of course.

No, it is Founders Day on which we usually go to McMaster.[2] I don't know whether this year I can afford the gas.

But why don't you get into your bus and run down? It's only an hour's trip; and we are always at home on Sundays. You could be here by 10 a.m. and home again before dark. I enclose a sketch of the road.

Bring Mrs. Kirkconnell, of course; and the children. Leonard is now ten years old and quite a guide around the place, knowing all the exciting spots, exciting for children.

It wouldn't preclude your coming again in spring or summer when things look more cheerful here in the open country.

So, then,
As ever,
F.P.G.

1 Of the article 'In Search of Myself,' *University of Toronto Quarterly* x (October 1940) 60–7

2 Watson Kirkconnell had joined the faculty of McMaster University in Hamilton in August 1940 as Professor and Head of the Department of English.

TO WILLARD HOLLIDAY

R.R. 4 Simcoe, Ont.
December 11, 1940

Dear Willard,

I had been wanting to drop you a line when, this morning, your letter came along.

The skates will go forward at the first opportunity; since they don't weigh much, I shall send them by express, collect.

I am glad to hear that you have a job and feel reasonably happy in it.

Well, yes, farming cannot 'pay'; one either is a farmer or one is not; and you will remember that my first impression of you was that you were not.

And as for that normality of which you speak, naturally, we are anything but 'normal' people; and we hold those that are a bit in horror; at least I do; my wife certainly to a less extent.

I am hard at work on another of those novels[1] which I shall never publish; I have half a dozen such on my shelves. If I published them, the people of Canada would have *me* stoned or call *them* pornography. You see, to me publication means nothing. What matters is solely that the work be done, the book be written, the beauty created. The rest of my work counts for little. But I once published the least 'objectionable' of these novels which comprise my real work (*Settlers of the Marsh*), and the libraries barred me; and my friends cut me in the streets. So why should I even try to publish? Quite apart from the fact that I can't? But that is no reason for not writing those books, to me.

As ever,
F.P.G.

I sent you an offprint of that article of mine in the U[niversity] of T[oronto] Quarterly[2] but don't know whether it arrived.

1 Presumably on a new draft of 'Felix Powell's Career' since Lorne Pierce had objected to 'so much circumstantial evidence' – see letter of May 14, 1940, note 2. 'The Seasons' may also be considered.

2 See the preceding letter, note 1.

TO LORNE PIERCE

R.R. 4 Simcoe, Ont.
December 16, 1940

Dear Dr. Pierce,

I enclose a list of juveniles[1] from the spring catalog.

Could you send this down with instructions to ship to me and bill at the usual trade discount?

I'd like them for the youngster.

I'd be glad, too, if they wouldn't dun me within a few weeks.[2] It's the devil of a job to save out of $2.50 a week for Christmas.

Best wishes of the season,
Yours,
F.P.G.

1 Grove's list runs as follows:
From Spring catalogue 1940
Page 82 – *The Fram*
– *Modern Pirates*
– *The Adventures of Tom Sawyer*
Page 83 – *Deeds of Daring* (Archer Wallace)

2 Pierce, in his reply, assures Grove there is no great urgency over payment. He also notes he has again sent in a nomination for Grove to the Royal Society, with himself, Sir C.G.D. Roberts, and Duncan Campbell Scott as sponsors.

TO ROY ST. GEORGE STUBBS[1]

R.R. 4 Simcoe, Ont.
December 19, 1940

Dear Mr. Stubbs,

Thanks very much for your note of appreciation.

I can only say I wish a few hundred people – say 800 or 900 – in Canada shared your view in some small measure.

I have 6 completed manuscripts lying at my publishers'; and at least two of them are better than anything I have been able to publish. I also know that, if I had the scant leisure needed for production, I could still *write* my best work.

The trouble is that the years go by: in a few weeks I shall begin my 70th year; and my difficulties as to publication are as great as they were in the nineties of the last century; my poverty as grinding as in the days when I tramped the countryside. Just to illustrate: recently we had, for a while, to eliminate butter from our already scanty bill-of-fare. We have since replaced it there, in a reduced ration.

There is no greater curse that can befall a man than to be afflicted with artistic leanings, in Canada.

However, thanks again.
Sincerely yours,
F.P. Grove

1 Roy St George Stubbs (b1907), a graduate in Arts and Law of the University of Manitoba, is presently the Senior Judge of the Winnipeg Family Court. He served with the Royal Canadian Air Force during World War II in Canada, the United Kingdom, and southeast Asia. He is the author of four books: *Lawyers and Laymen of Western Canada* (1939), *Men in Khaki* (1941), *Prairie Portraits* (1954), and *Four Recorders of Rupert's Land* (1967); and of numerous articles. In 1956, he read a paper on Grove at the Festival of the Arts at the University of Manitoba.

TO WATSON KIRKCONNELL

R.R. 4 Simcoe, Ont.
January 6, 1941

Dear Kirk,

Thanks very much for thinking of me in connection with the *Flying Bull.*[1] Since you suggested that these tales be read to Leonard, I promptly sat down and read them myself, giving them precedence over everything else. Unfortunately Leonard is a child blessed with an almost violent imagination and very excitable at night; so that, even where the subject matter does not forbid the stories to be given to him, I must refrain. He is extraordinarily good at sports, but no less good at drawing conclusions and expressing them in a rather amazing vocabulary. He has, by the way, just got over the measles.

May I say a few words about the book as such? I admire your fertility; and I admire your ability to get yourself before the public. I myself have 6 full-length novels[2] ready for the printers; my publishers are enthusiastic about them; but I cannot get them to print, under the present circumstances. My income, from Sept[ember] 1, 1939 to Sept[ember] 1, 1940, has, consequently been exactly $10.80.

I also admire the flow and the power of your verse which are often amazing, and the fluency of your narrative, even where the tale becomes 'tall' and what I call 'steep' – the Steep Gesture and the pathetic word – the baroque in language or emotion. Some of the stories – *qua* stories – held me from beginning to end with a strong grip; others amused me; one or two – guess which – almost repelled me, in spite of the brilliance of the execution, like the *Danse Macabre* of Saint-Saens,[3] or the *Bolero* of Ravel's.[4]

However, enough. I wish you would give us a chance to talk about it; I myself, though a wealthy man, two years ago, gave me a good car, can't afford the gas to travel with. But we have a reasonably large house and can make room, by moving together a bit, for you all. I had, two years ago, to give up farming on my own account; and yet it is the farm which keeps us alive. I am sure your children would enjoy the spaciousness of things here. I have several ponds for skating, and Leonard is very anxious to meet young men of the wider world of arc-lights and crowded thoroughfares – and these young men may even be girls, provided they are not yet too differentiated from the male to enjoy hikes over frozen fields and jumps over shallow streams.

Well, let me close with the best wishes for the year which is still young, both for you and your wife – wishes in which my wife joins me. As for the youngsters, a new year, I suppose, does not yet mean much to them except a chance for repletion and lots of candy; but to them, too, convey my best wishes.

As ever,
F.P.G.

1 Kirkconnell's *The Flying Bull and Other Stories* (1940) is a collection of verse narratives modelled to some degree on Chaucer's *Canterbury Tales*; the story-tellers are snowbound in a prairie hotel.

2 Presumably they were *The Master of the Mill, Consider Her Ways*, 'Felix Powell's Career,' 'Murder in the Quarry,' 'Two Lives' and 'The Canyon.' Only the first two were published in Grove's life-time. 'Felix Powell's Career' is no longer extant, and the remaining three are preserved in the University of Manitoba Grove Collection.

3 Charles Camille Saint-Saëns (1835–1921), French composer, pianist, and organist known for his opera, *Samson et Dalila* (1877), and for several symphonic poems including *Danse Macabre*

4 Maurice Ravel (1875–1937), the French composer known especially for *Daphnis et Chloé* (1909–12) and *Boléro* (1927)

TO DESMOND PACEY

R.R. 4 Simcoe, Ont.
January 20, 1941

Dear Professor Pacey,

In reply to your letter of the 15th inst[ant] I beg to say that I shall be glad to assist you.[1] Would you care to read parts of that Ms. which I originally meant to introduce by the chapter which Woodhouse and E.K. Brown printed as a separate article in the *U[niversity] of T[oronto] Quarterly*?[2] I might look out a few relevant chapters. To answer your questions in a letter would take almost as long as writing that book.

A few of the specific questions you ask I might briefly answer here.

Among my Parisian friends of 1889 to 1891 were Mallarmé, Verlaine, Hérédia, Henri de Regnier, Jules Renard, André Gide. Since some of them are still living, I should, however, prefer to leave them in twilight. Among the Germans stands first Stefan George whom I consider the greatest poet of the last 60 years.

I don't think that any novelist has ever influenced me. My published novels – few of those I have written are published – are mere jottings of what I have seen and felt. But among those whom I admire most stand foremost the Russians, above all Tolstoi.

Neither do I think I have any very definite aims in writing. I try to put down what I see. I have, for two years, been working on a panoramic novel which will require another two years to finish. In it, I aim at replacing the time sequence by an extension in space, giving a whole countryside, with its towns, farms, etc., within the compass of a single year. I call it 'The Seasons.' If I live to finish it;[3] and if, living, I shall find the leisure to work it out as I see it, it will be an enormous book, of course; I mean a book of probably over 1000 pages.

If you care to read parts of that unpublished autobiography of mine, I shall try to pick out some chapters which throw light on my methods; there are two or three chapters dealing with the growth of *Fruits of the Earth* which extends over forty years between conception of the central figure and publication.

On the other hand, an opportunity might offer to publish the 'Life of a Writer in Canada';[4] and I should have to ask you to return the Ms. sections shortly; I have only one copy.

Sincerely yours,
F.P. Grove

1 The questions asked of Grove were in preparation for a radio talk on Grove's novels – see letter of April 2, 1941, note 1. The biographical chapters of my *Frederick Philip Grove* (1945) were based almost entirely on information supplied by Grove in these letters, and in the manuscript of what was to be *In Search of Myself*. At this time I was 23 years old, had just completed my graduate work at Cambridge, and was in my first year as Professor of English in Brandon College, Manitoba.

2 'In Search of Myself,' *University of Toronto Quarterly* x (October 1940) 60–7 – which is, in substance, the introduction to the autobiography of the same title

3 It remained unfinished; see letter of March 11, 1941, note 3.

4 This title was still in Grove's mind at this time for *In Search of Myself*, although the latter title had occurred to him much earlier; see letter of November 26, 1938, note 2.

TO DESMOND PACEY

R.R. 4 Simcoe, Ont.
February 2, 1941

Dear Professor Pacey,

When I received your letter, I tried at once to do what I had said I'd do; but I found it an almost impossible task. I don't know just what would interest you. So, having to go to town yesterday, I despatched the whole of the Ms.[1] as far as it has been typed out. I don't know that it is in shape for publication as it stands; and, of course, since it was typed out over a year ago, it is already slightly out-of-date. However, I thought the best thing would be to let you browse about in it.

Now there is one thing I should not like to see done, namely to see large sections quoted. I don't object to the material being used; but please bear in mind that it is an unpublished book which may be radically altered before I publish it if I ever have a chance to do so.

As for 'The Seasons' – yes, as far as fiction is concerned, I have the deliberate purpose in mind of making it my *magnum opus*, by which I mean that I shall put into it (and have already largely put into it) as much as I can of what I have seen and thought about it, not of course in the form of philosophical expatiation, but brought to life in fictional form, in the thoughts or the fates of the several scores of characters and the hundreds of background figures. It is an undertaking of the scope of a novel like *War and Peace* – though I do not mean to compare my gifts with those of Tolstoi.

Concerning the Paris episode in my life, I might perhaps add that, though both Maupassant and Zola were still living at the time, I had no contact with them except, perhaps, a social one; I don't remember. The figures that stand out in my memory were the poets. Fiction I all but despised as a half-way house to journalism. I myself was dabbling in poetry at the time, now in one language, now in another. The reason why I never amounted to anything, at the time, is probably precisely the fact that I had no language of my own. In everyday life I changed over, with the greatest facility, from French to Italian, from German to English, and even from Spanish to Portuguese. But none of these languages was I rooted in. My native Swedish I had almost completely forgotten even then. The reasons for that you may run across in that manuscript.

If you go to Caledonia[2] in summer, yes, do not hesitate calling, preferably after having given us notice so we shall be at home. We have a large house. If you are married, bring your wife; if you have children, bring them as well; we have put up as many as five grown-ups at a time; and we have all sorts of make-shift ways of putting up youngsters (acrobatic mats make a good improvised bed for young bones) and we have a 10 y[ea]r old boy ourselves. Our house is always open to friends, especially in summer; and occasionally the company is quite international and interesting. Though, since the war, less so, of course. We are poor; but we like to share what we have.

Sincerely yours,
F.P. Grove

1 The manuscript of *In Search of Myself*, then entitled 'The Life of a Writer in Canada'

2 My mother and stepfather lived on a farm near Caledonia, which in turn is near to Simcoe. Out of timidity, I never did visit Grove in Simcoe, an omission which I now deeply regret.

TO LORNE PIERCE

R.R. 4 Simcoe, Ont.
March 10, 1941

Dear Dr. Pierce,

Thanks for the brochure[1] which I think is very well written though I am not sure that I understand its intention fully.

That may be the result of my present condition. I have been very ill since Feb[ruary] 8 when I caught a dangerous cold. There have been days when I was not expected to live. However, I pulled through, it seems: this is only the second day of which I am spending part out of bed.

I am much worried about the outlook, both generally and for myself. I suppose you people (Ryerson) have pretty well given me up. I am at work on my *magnum opus* in fiction;[2] but it seems pretty useless? Yet others (Kirkconnell,[3] f[or] i[nstance], or Pratt[4]) are publishing successfully.

If you agree, I'd like to try some other firm,[5] for it is a miracle I have survived so far, with the help of one or two diminutive wind-falls.

As ever,
F.P.G.

1 The brochure is missing, but it was probably Lorne Pierce's *Armoury in Our Halls* (1941).

2 'The Seasons'; see letters of January 20, 1941 and March 13, 1941.

3 See the second paragraph of the letter to Kirkconnell of January 6, 1941, for another expression of the same complaint. Kirkconnell's publications averaged one book each year; he has published altogether some 170 books and pamphlets.

4 E.J. Pratt; see letter of March 23, 1928, note 1. His *The Fable of Goats, Brébeuf and His Brethren*, and *Dunkirk* were published in 1937, 1940, and 1941 respectively.

5 To which Pierce replied on March 12, 1941: 'It is a mistake for an author to have his books distributed among too many Houses. That is why we went to a good deal of expense in bringing your books under our imprint. Please let me know what we can do for you.' He also advised Grove not to give up work 'on what you call your "*magnum opus* in fiction",' adding, 'We are prepared to do everything humanly possible for you.'

TO DESMOND PACEY

R.R. 4 Simcoe, Ont.
March 11, 1941

Dear Mr. Pacey,

The Ms.[1] arrived safely a few days ago. I have been very ill for a month or so and unable to look after anything; so I have not missed it.

If I can find the time, I hope to re-read it shortly, with a view to determining whether I think it fit for publication.

Yes, if you wish it, I shall be glad to read the script.[2]

Meanwhile I have used the last few days to re-read the first part of my new novel 'The Seasons' – the part entitled 'Summer.' I am not so sure that I really like it – but, I believe, it is by far the best thing I have done, as it is certainly the most ambitious. That first part is in itself the length of a full-sized novel (ca. 80,000 words); and it contains scores of characters; what the completed work will be like, in length and compass, it staggers me to think of. But it is most unlikely that it will ever be finished, though about half of the remainder is written or sketched.[3]

Sincerely yours,
F.P.G.

1 The manuscript of *In Search of Myself*; see letter of February 2, 1941.
2 Of my radio talk on Grove; see letter of April 2, 1941.
3 For a summary of the plot, see Bruce H. Nesbitt's '"The Seasons": Grove's Unfinished Novel' in *Canadian Literature* XVIII (November 1963) 47–51.

TO LORNE PIERCE

R.R. 4 Simcoe, Ont.
March 13, 1941

Dear Dr. Pierce,

Thanks for your letter of yesterday.[1]

With regard to 'The Seasons' I can say this: it consists of four parts: Summer, Fall, Winter, Spring, all these of a single year, very recent, say 1940. The aim is not to spin out a plot in time, but to extend the scene in space, giving a bird's-eye view of all that happens typically within an area thirty miles square, including the (imaginary) town of Rivers and its whole population and all its activities, from the odd-job man to the great industrialist with an income of fifty thousand and over.

Approximately three quarters of it is written, one quarter sketched. But only about one quarter (200 pages) is typed in a form through which anyone but myself can find his way; and, owing to the fact that I have neither typewriter ribbons nor decent paper and cannot afford to buy them, the type is like the one of this letter at its best; and the paper is onion-skin.

And, nothing is final. It will take another year at least to put things into shape; and then it will be a book of 1000 printed pages. So, what?

Personally, I have only one desire: to see it written before I lie down again,[2] and the next time for good. It must be written; 100 years from now it will be read, perhaps somewhat sooner.

Since you have three or four or five books of mine there, I don't see that it can do much good to add another to it. But, if you really wish to see what the thing is like, I am willing to let you have that first quarter of it, provided I get it back within a reasonable time. It goes just to the point where the threads are knit; though, at this moment I see that some three or four pages at the very end have not even been typed yet; but that would be a trifle. Let me know, please.

Yes, I know, I should rather have all my books in the hands of one firm;[3] but as it is I feel condemned to starvation. I have, before my last illness, more than once been on the point of a final despair.

You ask what you can do for me? Well, I don't know. Is there anything that can be done, short of publishing a few of my books? There are a dozen here on my shelves which no-one has ever seen yet.

Sincerely yours,
F.P.G.

1 Referred to in letter of March 10, 1941, note 5
2 A desire he did not live to achieve
3 Cf letter of March 10, 1941, note 5.

TO LORNE PIERCE

R.R. 4 Simcoe, Ont.
March 18, 1941

Dear Dr. Pierce,

Under separate cover I am sending you, conformably with your request,[1] what I must still consider a first draft of Part I of 'The Seasons.'[2]

As you will notice, the main problem has of late been the dovetailing into each other of the many strands of which the book is woven. I am, at present, busy on doing the same thing for Part II. I cannot, so far, say that the result, in the case of Part I, is final; and in order to do the best I can by the whole, vast structure, it is imperative that I have the manuscript of each part at my elbow. So, if you will be good enough to return the Ms. to me at your earliest convenience, no matter what your impression of it is, I shall be glad.

You see, it is this way. I shall be only too glad to let all my books stand under the Ryerson imprint; but I am not prepared to give up because the Ryerson Press declines to handle a given book. I simply cannot afford to do so. My books are all I have; and though *I* won't be needing much more, I have a wife and a son; and I feel convinced that there are two or three manuscripts which will one day be worth something. I hope you see my point.

Sincerely yours,
F.P.G.

1 Made in a very brief letter, dated March 17, 1941
2 See letter of March 11, 1941, note 3.

TO DESMOND PACEY

R.R. 4 Simcoe, Ont.
April 2, 1941

Dear Professor Pacey,

I received your script;[1] and, though I do not agree with every statement, far be it from me to interfere. The mere fact that you mention nobody else seems undeserved honour.

I regret that you could not read *Settlers of the Marsh*. I should gladly have loaned it to you, though I believe I have only a single copy. I consider it the most important of my prairie novels.

I am not sure that I know what dial-number taps CKX or CKY, is it 990?[2] At any rate, I shall try to get the broadcast. Reception is rarely good from the west, I am sorry to say.

May I say that *Fruits of the Earth* was never intended to figure as a novel? I meant it to be taken rather as a piece of pioneer history. Its original title was 'Chronicles of Spalding District.' What I wished to bring out in the book is the slow decay of a great potentiality. The cards are stacked against Spalding, of course. He is slowly being bent into taking the 'slings and arrows' personally. See his reflections on the decay of man's work: the brick dust from his house, etc. However, it is your perfect right to dislike it or to find fault with it. Recently somebody,[3] in discussing with me some of my books, suddenly exclaimed, 'Ah, but *Fruits of the Earth*! There is a book which will begin to live 100 years from now.' I merely smiled. Let's wait and see.

At any rate, many thanks.
Sincerely yours,
F.P.G.

1 Of the radio talk; cf. letter of March 11, 1941. It was broadcast as part of a series, 'The University on the Air,' under the auspices of the University of Manitoba, over stations CKX (Brandon) and CKY (Winnipeg). Brandon College, then an affiliated college of the University of Manitoba, participated in the series with a sub-series 'Manitoba Sketches,' and I was asked to cover the field of Manitoba literature. As the only Manitoba literature I had then read was Grove's novels, I made the novels the subject of my talk.

2 The radio stations which broadcast the talk. Grove was very optimistic in thinking that he could hear those stations at such a distance, no matter how sensitive his receiver may have been.

3 There does not seem to be any clue as to who said this, although Carleton Stanley or W.J. Alexander seem likely.

TO BLANCHE HUME[1]

R.R. 4 Simcoe, Ont.
April 9, 1941

Dear Miss Hume,

I am returning the copy of *A Search for America* which you sent me, duly autographed and marked 'Attention Miss Hume.'

Sincerely yours,
F.P.G.

1 She was Lorne Pierce's secretary for a number of years. She was there when Frank Flemington joined the firm in 1940, and retired 'somewhere about 1955.' She died in her eighties in the late 1960s. Frank Flemington, formerly of the Ryerson Press and now of McGraw-Hill Ryerson, adds:

> She did some little bit of writing during her years with the press, notably three small Canadian History Readers (*Laura Secord*; *The Strickland Sisters*; and *Barbara Heck*). And in 1925 she transcribed and edited five lectures that Bliss Carman delivered before the University of Toronto, entitled *Talks on Poetry and Life*. Dr Pierce always spoke very highly of her as his most trusted secretary. (July 18, 1974)

TO LORNE PIERCE

R.R. 4 Simcoe, Ont.
April 23, 1941

Dear Dr. Pierce,

I have been notified that I have been elected a member of the Royal Society of Canada.

I should like to accept but find that there is a fee of $20.00 to pay, plus $25 or $30 expenses for attending the Introduction of new fellows; and, frankly, I haven't got that money.

Since you were the fellow who proposed me and more or less sponsored the election, I should like to ask your advice as to what to do about it. Decline? Accept provided they will wait for their fees? I am at a loss.

Please let me know.[1] They want my immediate reply.

As ever,
yours,
F.P.G.

1 Pierce replied, on the following day, 'You must accept ... let us think of some way of handling the financial side of it.'

TO LORNE PIERCE

R.R. 4 Simcoe, Ont.
April 25, 1941

Dear Dr. Pierce,

Thanks for your letter.[1] I have accordingly written to Dr. Steacie,[2] saying that I should like to accept, provided they will wait for the fees.

My total income during 1940 has been less than $400. In 1941 it will likely be still less, one item of $2.50 a week having reduced itself already to $1.25 (teaching). You speak slightingly of a $20 bill: to me that is almost a fortune.

If, I add in my letter to Steacie, immediate payment of the fees is imperative, I had rather let the honour go to the next in line.

Personally, I don't think any longer that it matters much. If, through actual death of starvation, I could secure a minimum of safety for wife and child, I should not hesitate. I begin to feel that I am just a dead burden on this earth which, to me, is barren. That may sound bitter; it is not meant so; it is just a statement of fact.

Sincerely yours,
F.P.G.

1 See the previous letter, note 1.
2 Edgar William Richard Steacie (1900–62), the noted chemist. Born in Westmount, Quebec, he was educated at McGill University (PH D 1926), where he taught chemistry from 1926 till 1939, when he was appointed Director of the Division of Chemistry in the National Research Council of Canada. In 1952 he was appointed President of the Council. From 1944 to 1946, he was Deputy Director of the UK-Canadian Atomic Energy Project, and over the years held numerous executive posts in several scientific bodies, both in Canada and abroad. He was a Fellow of the Royal Society of Canada, and, in 1954–5, served as its President. At this time, as appears from this letter, he was acting as Treasurer of the Society. He was awarded the OBE in 1946, and elected a Fellow of the Royal Society in 1948. His name is memorialized by an award open to brilliant young Canadian scientists.

TO LORNE PIERCE

R.R. 4 Simcoe, Ont.
May 5, 1941

Dear Dr. Pierce,

Two or three days ago, in desperation, under pressure from a number of friends, I sent the $20 to the R[oyal] S[ociety of] C[anada]. I ought not to have done this, of course, because it was part of a badly needed small sum of which more in a moment. As for my going to Kingston, it is, as far as

I see, out of the question;[1] and yet I see no sense in belonging to the society unless I go to their meetings.

Now I have for some time been wanting to write to you in order to clear up the, to me, bewildering situation.

You will remember that, a month or more ago, I sent you a first draft of the first part of 'The Seasons,' saying at the time that I could ill spare it, and asking you to return it to me at your earliest convenience. Meanwhile I have laid out the second part and am typing it; but I am constantly embarrassed because I don't have the first part to refer to.

I have not heard from you since – which I interpret as meaning that you are not interested. Would you be good enough to let me have the Ms.?

Apart from that draft, you have the following complete Mss.

1) 'Murder in the Quarry';
2) 'Go to the Ant';
3) *The Master of the Mill*;
4) 'Felix Powell's Career.'

Now I have, by the last week of this month, to meet payments totalling $625.00, of which only $50 is covered. If I squeeze matters to the bleeding point, I may be able to swing another $25. My only assets, apart from my house and farm, are my Mss. If I can meet these payments, I shall be safe for another year; if not...?

You said when I wrote last you would let me know what you can propose by the end of the week.[2] Naturally, I live on needles and pins; and every day that goes by is a torture.

Sincerely yours,
F.P.G.

1 The annual meeting of the Royal Society of Canada was held in Kingston in 1941. Pierce's next letter, of June 4, indicates that Grove did eventually go to Kingston.

2 In the letter referred to, Pierce wrote that he was 'very anxious' to publish one of Grove's manuscripts; and on the first part of 'The Seasons,' he commented: 'It is going to make a very long novel and, in my opinion, falls below *Two Generations*. It will require whittling, and something should be done to heighten the interest of the story.' He goes on: 'I wish you would write me candidly regarding these four manuscripts ['Go to the Ant,' 'Felix Powell's Career,' 'The Master of the Mill,' and 'The Seasons'], and what above all things you would like to have done. I feel that we have got to do something and do it now for you, or find a convincing argument why we should do nothing. Time is going, and we expect to have our fall list lined up within a fortnight. Although we continue to catalogue, advertise and carry your other books among our samples, the sales are negligible, as they are of all Canadian titles practically without exception.'

TO WATSON KIRKCONNELL

R.R. 4 Simcoe, Ont.
May 6, 1941

Dear Kirk,

I am sorry to say that I cannot come for the Thursday meeting,[1] but wish you success.

I have been very ill after my last trip for the initial meeting and am still not quite recovered. I suppose this will be the last meeting this season?

Why not drop down this way shortly?

My tulips will be in bloom in a few days; to my modest eyes they are quite a sight though I have no display to compare with my gladioli which will come later.

Best wishes, and please remember me to Mrs. Kirkconnell who went to so much trouble to make me comfortable.

Sincerely, as ever,
F.P.G.

1 Presumably the meeting of some literary club at McMaster University or in the city of Hamilton. Watson Kirkconnell was at this time on the staff of McMaster University.

TO WILLARD HOLLIDAY

R.R. 4 Simcoe, Ont.
May 15, 1941

Dear Willard,

Thanks for your letter which I will answer at once since I will be away next week. You will probably see through the papers – you read papers, don't you? – that I have been elected a fellow of the Royal Society,[1] the highest honour which can come to a Canadian man of letters; so be sure to put the 'F.R.S.C.' behind my name henceforth. It's as good as a title they tell me.

Well, I have a number of things to say. Jim Landon is merely turning the rope with which he is to be hanged.[2] Think for a moment: a tractor in exchange for two horses! What kind of a tractor that can be? It's a bill of expense. And the debt is growing, growing, growing. The idea is that, if you can't make a toy boat go, perhaps you can run a liner.

As for some sort of enlistment, I quite agree. Many of us have shared your scruples. Yet, were I younger, I should no longer hesitate. We live in a world of insanity. I and my wife recommend to you to read *Out of the Night*,[3] to allay any lingering scruples. I have no sympathy with the author; but essentially what he says is the truth.

I might say that there is many a good opening for a man who can use his hands. We have relatives fighting right now, in England.[4] We have others who are members of ground-crews here. We had a visit from one the other day. He gets his training, board, lodging, and pay; and he does 'his bit.'

I think Leonard[5] has been wanting to write to you. He has a new bike now.

With best regards,
F.P.G.

1 Despite the bitterness he expressed at times over lack of recognition in Canada, Grove valued this honour, and took his responsibility to the Society seriously.
2 An obscure reference, presumably to a farmer getting into difficulties, either in real life or in one of Holliday's stories.
3 The autobiography of Jan Valtin (pseud. of Richard Julius Hermann Krebs, 1904–51), published in 1940. The 841-page book deals with Valtin's involvement in International Communism (Comintern), his capture by the Gestapo, the horrors of Nazi prison camps, and Valtin's eventual escape to the United States, where he wrote the book.
4 Relatives of Mrs Grove
5 Grove's son, then 11 years old

TO LORNE PIERCE

R.R. 4 Simcoe, Ont.
June 5, 1941

Dear Dr. Pierce,

Thanks for your letter of yesterday. I agree that, if the Ryerson Press wants to hold me, it must do something; and I also agree that a book of mine must appear in the near future.

You want my opinion. Frankly, I think it should be the 'Ant-book' or the *Master of the Mill*;[1] but the latter is much longer than the former; and the cost of manufacture would be higher.

As for the 'Seasons,' it will not be ready inside of a year or two. You must not forget that the Ms. which you have – and of which I am in desperate need – is a mere first draft. But the book will be very long; I have some 900 pages of the first draft typed now; and, though it will be condensed, it will ultimately remain a long book – let us say of 720 pages. On the other hand, it will, when I let it go out of my hand, be a panoramic picture of the Ontario scene.

'Felix Powell' had better rest a bit longer. 'Murder in the Quarry' will likely make a short story one day. I have, of course, other Mss.; but they are all of a type that had better wait, notably a volume of short stories;[2] I am still in hopes that I shall be able to place them, or some of them, in magazines, though magazines are perfectly silly in their fiction departments. But I feel that, slowly, slowly, I am putting myself over.

The 'Ant-book' has one great advantage: it is startling.

To publish it is a bold venture; but I believe it would be a successful venture. That, frankly, is my advice.

Now a word regarding the financial situation. On May 29 I boldly went to the bank, renewed all my notes and asked for a loan of $225 on top of my debts. I got it; and I paid the interest and amortisation instalments on my mortgage (government loan). That brings the government loan down to $1800, on a farm normally worth $12,000 to $14,000, the latter figure representing the cost to me. Now I have so far declined to negotiate elsewhere, though advances have been made to me. Suppose the Ryerson Press made up its mind to publish the 'Ant-book,' would they consider making me an advance, perhaps of $300, on all my books, that is those which they have. I should agree to letting such royalties as may accrue, from *any* published books, stand against the advance till it is covered, including the book to be published in the fall. It seems this is a reasonable proposition; for, let me put the initial sale of the new book at 600 copies, by Christmas – which is less than the *total* sale of *Two Generations** – the royalties on them alone (at 15% on a sale-price of $2.50 a copy) would run to $225.00.

Hoping to hear from you at your earliest convenience, I am,

As ever,
F.P.G.

*including the limited edition. I should furnish a list of subscribers for special circularisation.

1 As previously remarked, both were published by Macmillan, in 1947 and 1944 respectively, and not by Ryerson.

2 Entitled 'Tales from the Margin,' this particular book was never published; but a substantial number of these stories, together with others selected by me, appeared under the same title and my editorship in 1971.

TO LORNE PIERCE

R.R. 4 Simcoe, Ont.
July 12, 1941

Dear Dr. Pierce,

Re your letter of the 26th of June,[1] I might say that, if that is the decision of the house, I'll have to make the best of it; it is their perfect right to decline. Yet I feel that, in this case, there has been a certain unfairness;[2] but that feeling refers merely to the time element; and what will it amount to 10 y[ea]rs from now? Yet, if I did not mention it, I'd feel bothered ever after.

I might say that I have since reread *The Master of the Mill*; and I can hardly believe that I have written the thing. I honestly believe it to be a great book. It has since gone to New York.

As for our personal relation, I might say that I am constitutionally unable to bear a grudge. So, don't worry; as I shall not.

Sincerely yours,
F.P.G.

1 Which is, unaccountably, missing from the Lorne Pierce Collection at Queen's University. But the letter immediately preceding, of June 11, is very brief: Pierce returns the manuscript of 'Felix Powell's Career,' keeping 'Go to the Ant' (ie, *Consider Her Ways*) and *The Master of the Mill* because 'I want to have another look at them.' Obviously, in the missing letter he declined both the manuscripts.

2 The manuscript of *The Master of the Mill* was sent to Pierce as far back as August 30, 1939; and those of *Consider Her Ways*, 'Felix Powell's Career,' and 'Murder in the Quarry' were sent on March 25, April 11, and May 14, 1940, respectively. Although Pierce tried to secure US publication for at least one of the manuscripts, his own house was unwilling to publish a Grove book. All this time, Pierce kept promising Grove help in securing publication of his books, and advising him against going to other publishers on his own. See letter of March 10, 1941, note 5.

TO WILLARD HOLLIDAY

R.R. 4 Simcoe, Ont.
November 11, 1941

Dear Willard,

You are right. I don't think very much of that sketch,[1] but chiefly because your Harvey dies in an accident. It would be much more to the point if he deliberately killed himself; and it would be a *story* if that were foreshadowed in the first paragraph.

In that you have also the fundamental principle which a good novel must follow. Express your 'theme' at the earliest possible moment and then work up to the climax. A novel is essentially the road pursued from an idea to an act that bears it out.

Apart from it, there are a few 'rules' as you call them. F[or] i[nstance], be sure your characters live and bring them on the scene, not as mere figures, but as characters within a minimum of pages from the beginning. Never try to surprise; surprise is always arrived at by a break in the characterisation or in the logic of events.

No, I never write out a synopsis; but, before I begin writing I know exactly what I want to say; and I have most carefully surveyed the whole of the book in my mind. No, I don't plunge into Chapter One without further ado; I make very sure that my first chapter really opens the book, that is, broaches the 'theme.' Matter irrelevant to the theme but extraneously necessary I bring in later, perhaps by retrospection. There never is a great deal of that; for, before I finish, the chances are I have found that, while *I* needed it, the reader does not; and so I eliminate it. Give your reader credit for ordinary intelligence. Don't write down to him, rather write up. But of course, I am a very slow worker; and I have never considered a book finished in less than seven or eight years.

But here is a point: work on a long book makes the rest of life seem irrelevant. What difference does it make whether, from day to day, you are dissatisfied with what you are doing; whether, perhaps, you are almost starving; even whether your book progresses satisfactorily; so long as it either is alive or is coming to life; gestation is not a fast process; it demands time, and you can't hurry it. But when the book is born, it is a miracle to you, like every birth.

Apart from these points, I have no 'system.' Every book is unique, at least to me. If it isn't, I refuse to write it.

However, advice is futile; and I don't mean the above as advice. If you read books on writing, you will find that not a masterpiece in the world's literature ever conforms to rules laid down. Turgeniev wrote dozens of short stories that contradict every rule ever culled from Maupassant. Tolstoi wrote novels in the same way; and so did Hardy. Etc. etc.

With best wishes,
as ever,

P.S. The Exhibition,[2] I think, was a disappointment to everyone of us. We went home about 3 p.m.

1 Mr Holliday writes, in a letter to me, that he has 'long forgotten' this piece of writing, although he 'vaguely' remembers 'being ruffled by his [Grove's] reference to ... a "sketch": I preferred to consider it a short story.' (November 5, 1970)
2 The Canadian National Exhibition in Toronto

TO WATSON KIRKCONNELL

R.R. 4 Simcoe, Ont.
November 11, 1941 II

Dear Kirk,

As usual I have to thank you for another book.[1] I have not, so far, had time to do any more than glance into it. But even that cursory glance has made me marvel at the variety of subjects which you command and the power with which you propound principles. I look forward to reading with more leisurely concentration shortly.

I really meant to postpone this note till I had done so; but the announcement of the Friday meeting[2] came along; and I thought I must express my regret at being unable to come.

I am afraid that, after all, within the territory covered by the branch, there are not enough members who are in a position to be at all active.

However, I wish you the best of success.

Please remember me to Mrs. Kirkconnell and the rest of the family,

As ever, yours,
F.P.G.

1 Presumably either *Canadians All: A Primer of Canadian National Unity* (1940) or *Twilight of Liberty* (1941), the two books published by Kirkconnell about this time

2 From the subsequent reference to 'branch,' the meeting may be assumed to have been of the Hamilton branch of the Canadian Institute of International Affairs, the Association of Canadian Clubs, or the Canadian Authors' Association, most probably the last of these.

TO RICHARD CROUCH

R.R. 4 Simcoe, Ont.
November 20, 1941

Dear Dick,

You asked me to let you know my impression of *Barometer Rising*.[1] Well, I don't think I have read a more promising Canadian book.

Yet, the first two thirds raise an expectation: the theme is unfolded, between McCrae and Wain. The explosion comes; and the theme is not pursued. In other words, the problem of the book is brushed aside by a calamity. The various 'piquant' scenes are stuck in without real justification. The whole of Evelyn is an irrelevancy. You know I have no objection to any theme, no matter how daring; but it must be organic in the structure. 'Oh well,' said my wife, 'I suppose he put that sort of thing in for those who like that sort of thing.' I laughed and felt sorry.

Still, there is much in the book which I admire very much: the characters of Penny, f[or] i[nstance], and of Angus Murray; the powerful description of the explosion, and many other things. I am very glad to have read it.

As soon as I am through with the rest, I'll make up a parcel. You wouldn't have a book of Roger Fry's? Let me say the *Cézanne*?[2] I'd be glad to read one.

Too bad we can't talk more frequently. Best regards for you and Mrs. Crouch.

As ever,
F.P.G.

1 The first novel (1941) by Hugh MacLennan (b1907), which is set in Halifax during World War I and which has as its climax the explosion of a munitions ship which severely damaged that port. A native of Glace Bay, Nova Scotia, MacLennan has published five other novels: *Two Solitudes* (1945), *The Precipice* (1948), *Each Man's Son* (1951), *The*

Watch that Ends the Night (1959), and *The Return of the Sphinx* (1967); and three volumes of essays: *Thirty and Three* (1954), *Scotchman's Return and Other Essays* (1960), and *Seven Rivers of Canada* (1961). He has won several Governor-General's awards for both his fiction and non-fiction, and is a Companion of the Order of Canada (1967).
2 *Cézanne* (1927) by Roger E. Fry (1866–1934)

TO HUGH MACLENNAN[1]

R.R. 4 Simcoe, Ont.
November 20, 1941 II

Dear Mr. MacLennan,

Will you forgive me my presumption in writing to you? I have just finished reading your *Barometer Rising*; and I feel impelled to let you know something of my reaction.

May I first say that I certainly should not feel so impelled if I had not been greatly impressed with the promise that book holds. In fact, I have not been so impressed with a Canadian book for many years. From the start I liked its tone and the quiet sureness of touch in the characterisation. Penny, I think, is a triumph; and so is Angus Murray.

Another triumph is the description of the effect of the explosion and the general way in which you make the old town come to life.

And yet I have my criticisms to offer; and I hope you will forgive me for voicing them ruthlessly. Believe me, my purpose is not a destructive one. You are in your thirties; I am seventy; and throughout my life I have been a critical and fastidious reader. I have no objection to any theme as such; I am entirely free of conventional prejudices.

It was my friend R.E. Crouch, librarian of the Public Library in London who, recently, gave me the book, saying, 'I wish you'd let me know what you think of this.' It so happened that for the moment, I was overwhelmed with Mss. which had to be read – I read for publishers to advise them. So I handed the book to my wife.

Now my wife lays no claim to literary knowledge; she follows only her *feeling* for a book. Repeatedly, while she was reading, I asked for her impression; and she praised the book till she was through with it. Then she said, 'I don't like the end.'

Shortly I read the book myself. When about half through, I asked, 'What did you think of pages 101 *sequ[entia]*?' 'Oh well,' she said, 'I suppose the author put that sort of thing in to attract those who are attracted by that sort of thing.' I laughed. When I came to the page where Colonel Wain is found, after the explosion, I asked the same question again; and her answer was the same; but she added, 'It's irrelevant; but it's unimportant.' Again I laughed. When I had finished, last night, while I was drying the dishes which she was washing, I asked, 'Just what was your objection to the end?' She replied, 'The end evades the issue. Up to the explosion we witness the unfolding of a problem, between the two men, McCrae and Wain. That looks like the theme of the book. It raises certain expectations. The explosion comes; and magnificent as that part of the book is, it disappoints us in what we were led to expect.' Again I agreed. 'One of two explanations,' I said. 'Either the author did not know how to solve his problem; or he was so carried away with the calamity that he considered his original problem unimportant as compared with it. Too bad. It spoils the book for me.'

Now that is not entirely true; for, as I found today, there are certain things in it, to which I want to return; f[or] i[nstance] the scene between Penny and Angus in which she tells him that Jean is her daughter; it is a very true and very beautiful scene; and perhaps I should be satisfied that the book contains even one such scene. Perhaps, too, I should not write to you about the rest. I do hope, since, unless I did, I know I could not be satisfied, you will take it as it is meant; I could not pay you a greater compliment than by saying that, while the torso of the Venus de Milo, let me say, is very beautiful and makes me dream, the fact that the arms are lost remains a pity.

Sincerely yours,
F.P. Grove

1 For MacLennan, as well as for the novel discussed in this letter, see the preceding letter and note 1 to that letter.

TO BARKER FAIRLEY

R.R. 4 Simcoe, Ont.
December 1, 1941

Dear Fairley,

It is, of course, very little that I know of Rilke; but, all the more, your profound analysis in the October *Quarterly*[1] interested and delighted me. I wonder to what extent this attitude of – what shall I call it, aloofness? estrangement? has been general in Europe. I have read one or two novels which I ran across; and, brilliantly though they were done, I seemed to scent something of that very thing: they did not seem to be able *sich damit abzufinden*,[2] I believe the Germans would say, or to ignore it, perhaps with anguish, but also with resolution, as Goethe did. So they dig themselves in a contemplation of sex-instincts run wild. That, of course, is not Rilke's case. But he, too, digs himself in. What would he – or Stefan George[3] – have said of the present Germany, with its craving for power gone rampant?

I have been trying hard to bring out a rather subtle novel[4] dealing with what is underlying it all – so far without success. Meanwhile, as most of those who do not serve the hour we are trying to worry along.

You never came, last summer!

Hoping that you and yours are well and as cheerful as one can be these days, I am,

As ever, yours,
F.P.G.

I don't know whether it 'comes out' in these lines, but they are meant as a congratulation and expression of admiration.

1 Barker Fairley, 'Rainer Maria Rilke: An Estimate,' *University of Toronto Quarterly* XI 1 (October 1941) 1–14

2 To come to terms with

3 Stefan George (1868–1933), the German lyric poet; see letter of December 13, 1927, note 3, and letter of January 20, 1941, in which Grove claims Stefan George as first among his German friends. Felix Paul Greve did correspond with George and admired his poetry.

4 Presumably, *The Master of the Mill*

TO RICHARD CROUCH

R.R. 4 Simcoe, Ont.
December 18, 1941

Dear Dick,

I have returned the books kindly lent to me, like a Christmas parcel.

The vol[ume] of verse interested me very much, though I can't say I waxed enthusiastic over it.

Klee-Wyck,[1] too, was interesting, though I found it depressing. This terrific poverty beats even mine; and it is an everlasting reproach to our so-called civilisation.

The 'Fry'[2] is a fine book; and I was glad to have it for a while. I read it twice.

About *Barometer Rising* I have written before I believe.[3]

Well, there you are. And now the Japs.[4]

However, I sincerely hope you and Mrs. Crouch won't let that get you over these holidays for which I send my best wishes to the *three* Crouches.[5]

As ever, yours,
F.P.G.

1 The autobiography of Emily Carr (1871–1945), Canada's leading woman painter, published in 1941. It deals with reminiscences of her sketching trips to Indian villages on the coast of northern British Columbia. Like Grove, Emily Carr had a long, lonely struggle as an artist in Canada, and full recognition came only after her death.

2 Roger Fry's *Cézanne*; see letter of November 20, 1941, note 2.

3 In letter of November 20, 1941

4 The Japanese bombing of Pearl Harbour on December 7, 1941

5 Richard Crouch, his wife, and their son Keith

TO LORNE PIERCE

R.R. 4 Simcoe, Ont.
February 10, 1942

Dear Dr. Pierce,

As you will probably see, I am advertising myself as a literary adviser (*Saturday Night*).[1] I have secured the cooperation of a number of Toronto publishers who have been giving me their outside reading to do.[2] Their unanimous verdict was that, when I report on a manuscript, it settles the matter one way or the other.

The present move is, on my part, one of desperation. In this war-time one source of revenue after the other has dried up; and I can no longer feel sure of the weekly five-dollar bill for bread and butter. Criticism is one thing which I can do; others are doing the same and claim they are doing well at it. So I am going to give it a trial.

I am wondering whether, like other publishers, you sometimes run across a Ms. which, by skilful editing, might be made into something. If you do, would you assist me to the extent of pointing my way? I have done a lot of that sort of thing, mostly gratis, sometimes rearranging whole Mss. for the reading fees the publishers paid me. I believe that all authors whom I have helped in that way have been grateful to me. As for the publishers, if I make a success of this new venture, they will have the advantage of getting *one* expert outside opinion free if the author comes to me in the first place, whether they accept or decline.

Hoping to hear from you, I remain
As ever, your
F.P.G.

1 In *Saturday Night* of February 28, 1942, p 22:

LEADING NOVELIST AND PUBLISHER'S READER
Will read, criticise, edit manuscripts and advise re publication.
For terms write Frederick Philip Grove. RR 4 Simcoe, Ont.

Only one letter of enquiry survives in the University of Manitoba Grove Collection.

2 Grove had been doing some manuscript reading for Macmillan, and was to do some for the Ryerson Press. I am not aware of his reading for any other Toronto publisher.

TO LORNE PIERCE

R.R. 4 Simcoe, Ont.
April 14, 1942

Dear Dr. Pierce,

I think the idea is good.[1] How would you sell the series? In a small portfolio, or bound in a volume?

As for the drawing, others would probably be better judges than I am of any resemblance or non-resemblance. My wife says 'It looks like you all right.' *I* thought the ear is rather larger than my very large ear *is*. However ... I like the look in the eye which is indeed like me. On the whole it's *good* – like the idea, I think.

Sincerely yours,
F.P.G.

P.S. Of course, all these pictures, photos as well as drawings make me look, as a friend recently expressed it, like 'an international banker' rather than the proletarian I am.

F.P.G.

2nd P.S. I see the Royal Society is going to meet in Toronto. I don't think I'll be able to come. I am trying to find a way of giving my son a holiday – and I am a bit discouraged even about that. However...

F.P.G.

1 It is not clear what this refers to; a series of drawings of Canadian authors seems the plausible inference from what is said here.

TO LORNE PIERCE

R.R. 4 Simcoe, Ont.
July 8, 1942

Dear Dr. Pierce,

Being at last reduced to doing the hardest kind of manual labour in a canning factory (12, 13 hours a day) I picked up courage and applied for a position in the *Inspection Board of United Kingdom & Canada*.

I have not been summarily turned down but am asked to furnish 3 personal references. There being hurry about it, I have taken the liberty of giving your name without previously asking for your permission. May I count on your kindness to put in a good word for me if an enquiry reaches you?[1]

Sincerely yours,
F.P. Grove

1 Pierce replied two days later: 'I am terribly sorry over the hardship you have suffered. You may depend on it ... I shall give them [the Board] the very best.' But nothing appears to have come of the application.

Grove's reactions to the experience of working in a canning factory are recorded in 'A Postscript to *A Search for America*,' *Queen's Quarterly* XLIX (Autumn 1942) 197–213.

TO BARKER FAIRLEY

R.R. 4 Simcoe, Ont.
July 12, 1942

Dear Fairley,

By a strange coincidence, the lady who took your off-print[1] along returned it by the same mail which brought your letter. So, don't worry.

Thanks for the papers[2] which I found interesting.

With me things have now reached the stage – that is, my inability to publish books and other things – that I have taken a factory job, in a canning factory where I do the least skilled and therefore least-highly paid and hardest manual labour – lifting things – working for 12 to 13 hours a day and nearly breaking down at the end of every working day. It is the *Search for America* inverted. I end where I began; and I, frankly, look forward to the end. I barely earn enough to keep us going. The interesting thing is that already the rest of the people – those with settled occupations and incomes [–] seem to me to consist of a different race.

Yes, of course, I mean Bill[3] – not John – I seem to be everlastingly getting mixed up. It is a standing joke between myself and my wife. But I am glad to hear he is in Arizona.

John Grube[4] has spent nearly two weeks here with Leonard.[5] Unfortunately the visit ended today – with Leonard falling ill for the second time this summer.

With best regards to your wife and you,
As ever, yours,
F.P. Grove

1 Presumably the offprint of Fairley's article on Rilke in the *University of Toronto Quarterly*; see letter of December 1, 1941, note 1.

2 An obscure allusion

3 Fairley's son. Presumably, Grove was confusing him with John Grube.

4 John D. Grube (b1930), the son of George Maximillian Anthony Grube (the classical scholar and Head of the Classics Department at Trinity College, Toronto), and himself a professor of English, first at the University of New Brunswick in Saint John, later at the University of Windsor, and now at the Ontario College of Art. In a letter dated November 19, 1973 he writes: 'I always had a good time at the Groves, was a precocious and probably intolerable youngster, and enjoyed talking with Grove, who was far from aloof and treated young people as he treated anyone else. He never condescended. ... I recall him telling me that he had met Oscar Wilde.'

5 Leonard Grove, then twelve years old

TO ELLEN ELLIOTT[1]

R.R. 4 Simcoe, Ont.
December 3, 1942

Dear Miss Elliott,

About two weeks ago Mr. Symons[2] wrote me, saying you would welcome it if I wrote a brief introduction to his book. I have done so. Having heard about this only from him, I am sending him the brief script. No doubt he will promptly communicate with you.

I sincerely hope you are well.

My own arm is constantly improving, though I am told that the bones will remain tender for years.[3] Otherwise I keep up to standard.

With best regards, I am,
as ever, sincerely yours,
F.P.G.

1 For Ellen Elliott, see letter of February 21, 1929 III, note 1.

2 Harry Lutz Symons (1893–1962), a real estate consultant and author of *Friendship* (1943), *Ojibway* (1946), *Three Ships West* (1947), *Bored Meeting* (1950), *Orange Belt Special* (1956), and *Fences* (1957). Educated at the University of Toronto (1912–14), he served as a Captain with the Royal Flying Corps (1915–19) during World War I, and later, between 1925 and 1932, as a Major with the Royal Grenadiers. He won the first Leacock Medal for humour, awarded in 1946.

Grove contributed an introduction (entitled 'Just a Word') to *Friendship*, which he had read for Macmillan.

3 Presumably a reference to the accident described in the letter of February 11, 1944

TO RICHARD CROUCH

R.R. 4 Simcoe, Ont.
January 10, 1943

Dear Dick,

Leonard is to be baptized in the Anglican Church. For that ceremony we need 2 'godfathers' and one 'godmother'. I have asked Arthur L. Phelps[1] to be one of the former. Would you be the other? We'd be delighted if you and Hazel[2] could see your way to run over and be present in person. But if that should prove impossible on account of the roads, we could arrange for you to be represented by proxy – a local doctor or lawyer, provided we have your consent.

Would you be good enough to let me know at once? The thing is to be done before the end of the month. Catherine is to join the church – be 'confirmed' on Palm Sunday, at London. I, of course, was baptized and confirmed in the Anglican Church as a child. How we, personally, stand with regard to that, you know.

Please act! And, please, let me know at once.
As ever,
yours,
F.P.G.

1 See letter of April (no date, to Lorne Pierce), 1926, note 4.
2 Mrs Crouch

TO WILLARD HOLLIDAY

R.R. 4 Simcoe, Ont.
January 15, 1943

Dear Willard,

I have been wishing to drop you a line; but I am the third worst correspondent of the world.

Nor have I anything to say. If I do drop you this note, I do so merely to show you that you are not forgotten and that we all often think of you with sympathy. I was glad when I heard that you had entered a branch of the service. Were I a younger man (I shall be 71 a month from now), I should have done so myself; as it is, they don't want me. But I honestly believe that, had you not done so, there would have come a time when you would have felt badly about it; and meanwhile you have, I hope, a sort of life which, physically, will do you good and, mentally, will stock your experience – both ends worth striving for. I feel sure that, what passes before your eyes, will leave its imprint on your heart and mind.

As far as we are concerned, life runs its humdrum course; and only Leonard has so much before him that he still looks for great things. Yes, I keep working; but it is next to impossible to publish my sort of thing.

With best wishes for your continued health and contentment, I remain,

Cordially yours,
F.P.G.

TO DESMOND PACEY

R.R. 4 Simcoe, Ont.
January 18, 1943

Dear Mr. Pacey,

I received your enquiry yesterday and will answer at once.

I believe, on the one hand, that such a book[1] would be

timely and fear, on the other, that there is not enough of my work published to warrant it. It is perhaps natural that the writer should always consider his later work as the more important; and to me it sometimes seems that nothing of any great importance has yet been published. Our purveyors of printed matter are too timid; and not one of them is willing to invest in a future.

However, I am willing to assist you in any way I can; and I shall, therefore, first of all try to find the Ms. of that autobiography. This was not meant to be published till after my death; there are things in it which might hurt people still living. I trust that you will not touch on them.

As for my magazine publications, I have no list; but, apart from early work – before 1928 or 1929 – I can, I believe, put together such a list and shall try to do so.

Miss English[2] I do not remember except as a little girl whom I started on her study of French. But Ernest Birkinshaw[3] – I still call him Ernest – is very vivid in my memory. I have sometimes wished that an opportunity should come my way to go west once more, to lecture or something. I should like to meet him again. Naturally, I often meet former pupils of mine; and a fine lot of young men and women they are.

I am sorry to say that my physical condition is not too good; and my economic condition is wretched.

With best wishes, I remain,
Sincerely yours,
F.P.G.

1 Presumably a reference to my proposed book on him, which was eventually published as *Frederick Philip Grove* in 1945. See letter of January 20, 1941, note 1.

2 Mary Ann English (now Mrs J. Griggs of Toronto) was a student of mine at Brandon College. She had previously studied with Grove in Simcoe, where her family lived before moving to Brandon when the father, Col. S.S. English, became CO of the Artillery Training Centre there.

3 Ernest Birkinshaw was a pupil of Grove in Rapid City. He has been for many years Professor of Mathematics in Brandon College (now Brandon University).

TO RICHARD CROUCH

R.R. 4 Simcoe, Ont.
January 24, 1943[1]

Dear Dick,

I should have answered before this; but there were arrangements to be made which we could not make before I got our long driveway dug out.

The arrangement now is this; the ceremony is to be performed in the afternoon of February 14.

It is not likely, though possible that, by then, the roads

will be open. If not, could not you and Hazel come by train, on Saturday, to Brantford where one of us would meet you, to get here by car if possible, by radial,[2] if not? Of course, we should count on your staying overnight; if possible till Monday morning when I could take you back to Brantford. Just now Highway 24 from here is open, though it would probably take somewhat longer to cover the distance.

One of our proposed godfathers[3] will have to be represented by proxy; but I'd like to have one present in person.

Let me know what you think about it, will you?

As ever, with best regards from us all to you all.

F.P.G.

1 The year, in the original, is given as 1934, but the reference to Leonard's baptism, as Mr Keith Crouch pointed out in forwarding these letters, makes it clear that this was a slip of the pen.

2 A form of electric line developed in southern Ontario to connect urban centres in the Brantford-Hamilton-Toronto-Port Dover area, and so-called presumably because the lines were direct inter-city ones, radiating from each centre.

3 A.L. Phelps, the other godfather, was at the time a professor at United College, Winnipeg, and was not able to attend the baptism in person.

TO RICHARD CROUCH

R.R. 4 Simcoe, Ont.
February 10, 1943

Dear Dick,

For weeks I have been hunting for a book, an old book this time,

Spengler (?) *The Decay of the Occident*?[1] It appeared about 1928. *(Decline?)*

Do you think you have it? Would you throw it into the car? I'd be so much obliged. I am writing a book covering about what the title suggests, but should like to read anything that is pertinent, for I am on thin ice after enormous preparations.

So glad, you and Hazel are coming.

As ever,

F.P.G.

1 A literal translation of the title of Oswald Spengler's magnum opus, *Der Untergang des Abendlandes* (I, 1919; II, 1922); the English translation, which appeared in 1926 (I) and 1928 (II), bears the title, *The Decline of the West*. The influence of Spengler's thought upon Grove may be seen in *The Master of the Mill* and elsewhere.

TO RICHARD CROUCH

R.R. 4 Simcoe, Ont.
February 15, 1943

Dear Dick,

We were so disappointed; and, of course, very sorry indeed for you.[1] We hope you are all right again? It would have been a terrible drive back to London yesterday. The temperature never rose above −2; and late at night, it dropped to −20; even now it stands at −18, with the sun shining brightly.

The ceremony took place yesterday; and I signed the baptismal register for you, giving also your responses which I had all carefully written out for you, while A.O. Grass, K.C.[2] acted for A.L. Phelps, and Mrs. Grass (Gladdy) for Amanda.[3]

Now don't let this mishap stand in the way of your taking a holiday here in the near future, bringing Hazel, of course. Even last night we somehow managed to keep warm; and if you come before April 1st, don't let the gas worry you. I believe Ti[4] is writing to Hazel. We are all well.

With best wishes,
As ever, yours,
F.P.G.

1 Presumably Crouch had been taken ill and was unable to attend the service.
2 The Grasses live in St Catharines, Ontario, where Mr Grass has his practice. Mrs Gladys Grass, who had kept in touch with Mrs Grove, wrote very graciously in response to my enquiry and confirmed that the two families rapidly became good neighbours, and frequently visited each other socially. She recalls the Groves as 'the most agreeable company,' 'especially when Philip could be led into a story of his earlier days. He was a delightful raconteur.' (March 15, 1971)
3 Amanda Wiens (now Mrs Bert Mathers of Calgary), Grove's sister-in-law
4 ie, Mrs Grove – an intimate name Grove usually used only in addressing his wife

TO DESMOND PACEY

R.R. 4 Simcoe, Ont.
February 16, 1943

Dear Professor Pacey,

I think the biographical sketch[1] is all right, I have added one name.

I shall look forward to seeing the complete article.

No, I have not been doing much. It seems all so futile.

I read your short story 'The Hired Man,'[2] if I remember the title correctly. I liked it very much. It is very true indeed.

Please excuse my brevity. I am hunting the dollar to keep the wolf from the door.

Sincerely yours,
F.P. Grove

P.S. No, I have not come across *As for Me and My House*.[3]

1 This refers to the first part of my article, 'Frederick Philip Grove,' which was published in the *Manitoba Arts Review* III 3 (Spring 1943) 24–41. It is reprinted in my *Essays in Canadian Criticism, 1938–1968* (Toronto 1969) 5–21.
2 It appeared first in *Queen's Quarterly* in 1941, and is reprinted in my *The Picnic and Other Stories* (Toronto 1958) 79ff.
3 By Sinclair Ross (b1908), published in 1941. The novel, about a small prairie town, has become a Canadian classic. I had recommended that Grove read it.

TO RICHARD CROUCH

R.R. 4 Simcoe, Ont.
March 5, 1943

Dear Dick,

Thank you very much indeed for sending me Spengler's *Decline*.[1]

When are you going to come? I think Hazel said 'soon.'

I am very busy reading for Macmillans. They seem to rely more and more on my say-so.[2]

Hope you are well? All of you?

As ever.
yours,
F.P.G.

1 See letter of February 10, 1943, note 1.
2 One such reader's report, on Paul-Émile Cloutier's *Idées Générales sur la Guerre et sur l'Après-Guerre*, is preserved in the Macmillan files. The Macmillan letters contain a number of references to small payments for such reports.

The Cloutier report is further evidence of Grove's breadth of learning – he refers knowledgeably to Adam Smith and Euclid and writes: 'For me, a mathematician, there is the same sort of beauty about the conclusions of the author as there is about the demonstration of a theorem in geometry or algebra.'

TO FRANK FLEMINGTON[1]

R.R. 4 Simcoe, Ont.
March 26, 1943

Dear Mr. Flemington,

I am returning the 3 manuscripts[2] which you kindly sent me for my estimate. I have read all three straight through, one twice, and another half again – just to make sure of my opinion.

I suppose I had better delay my reports till I have read all the Mss. which I am to read and am, therefore, looking forward to receiving the second batch.

Sincerely yours,
F.P. Grove

1 Frank Flemington, who is very reticent about revealing the facts of his personal life, was for many years Managing Editor of the Ryerson Press. When Ryerson was acquired by McGraw-Hill, Mr Flemington joined the new amalgamated firm of McGraw-Hill Ryerson and is still in its employment.

2 Entries for the Ryerson Fiction Award, of $1000, which was established in 1942 when it was won by G. Herbert Sallans' *Little Man*. The only restriction imposed as to subject-matter was that spy, detective, and crime stories were ineligible, a condition which jeopardised Philip Child's *Day of Wrath* (1945), and provoked Grove to protest (see letters of May 14 and 31 II, 1943). The judges for the 1943 award were (a) Lorne Pierce, (b) a nominee of the Canadian Authors' Association, and (c) a third agreed on by the Canadian Authors' Association and Pierce – in this case, Grove. No award was made for 1943 and 1944, but in 1945 Child's *Day of Wrath* shared the award with Will R. Bird's *Here Stays Good Yorkshire* (1945).

TO FRANK FLEMINGTON

R.R. 4 Simcoe, Ont.
April 3, 1943

Dear Mr. Flemington,

I am sending, under separate cover, the Ms. of M.P. Marshall's 'This Pillared Dust'[1] and am attaching my report to the other three which I hold.

Sincerely yours,
F.P. Grove

1 Marshall's book was not selected for the Ryerson Fiction Award, and seems never to have been published. The contents of Grove's report, and the identity of the entries, remain unknown; but something may be surmised from the fact that no award was made in 1943.

TO RICHARD CROUCH

R.R. 4 Simcoe, Ont.
April 11, 1943

Dear Dick,

I return Raymond Pearl[1] whom I found very interesting in many ways. I find he confirms rather than contradicts my own conclusions though my approach is very different from his.

If there are any similar books available I shall be glad to read them.

I also found Rice's[2] first half extraordinarily good (dealing with the south); strange to say, in the second half (college teaching) I begin violently to dislike the *author* rather than his book. Julien Green[3] is charming. I shall bring these two books.

But I am still struggling with Spengler whom I dislike.

Best regards to Hazel and yourself.

As ever,
F.P.G.

1 Raymond Pearl (1879–1940), the US geneticist and population biologist, and author of *The Natural History of Population* (1939) as well as a number of highly technical works on the genetics of poultry

2 Elmer L. Reizenstein, afterwards Rice (1892–1967), the distinguished US playwright, whose works include *The Adding Machine*, and who is remembered particularly for the depth and force of social seriousness which underlies his work

3 The latest published novel of Green's available (in translation) was *Then Shall the Dust Return* (1941); but this might, of course, have been any of his earlier ones.

TO THE BOARD OF GOVERNORS, CANADIAN AUTHORS' FOUNDATION,[1] TORONTO, ONTARIO

R.R. 4 Simcoe, Ont.
April 30, 1943

Dear Sirs,

I wish to thank you most sincerely for having remembered me with your cheque for $100.00.[2] The money will ease off matters for me very considerably.

I am,
Faithfully yours,
F.P. Grove

1 The Canadian Authors' Foundation was established in 1931 to support distinguished but indigent Canadian writers. It was incorporated in 1945, and the Board of Governors that

year consisted of Pelham Edgar, D.C. Scott, H.S. Southam, Lawrence Burpee, and Wilfrid Eggleston. Edgar, who was instrumental in launching the project, was chairman of the Board. The Foundation, now known as the Canadian Writers' Foundation, relies on federal grants and private donations.

2 At first on an intermittent basis, then more or less regularly, the Canadian Writers' Foundation voted funds for Grove. This is the first letter in their files which relates to these payments.

TO LORNE PIERCE

R.R. 4 Simcoe, Ont.
May 14, 1943

Dear Dr. Pierce,

Yes, I can readily understand why *Little Man*[1] won the award;[2] I can even think it possible that, had I been one of the 'judges,' I should have given it my vote, from commercial considerations. It is promising, chiefly from the smoothness with which dialogue is handled. The author knows that sort of people. It is, of course, irrelevant to speak of artistic treatment. The public asks for fulness rather than for art; and fulness the book has, in spite of its essential vacuity.

Perhaps it is useless to go into details: the lack of characterisation (I *see* no figure up to page 250); the patness with which things 'happen,' instead of being brought about; the incredibility of *this* career for *this* George who, as an exponent of modern weakness, might have been made into an interesting study but is content to let things happen and to bask in the almost adoration (incomprehensible though it is) with which 3 women and 2 men 'fall for him,' placing him wherever the author wants him to go. The first chapter is far and away the best.

To me, the whole book remains unconvincing, in spite of the purely journalistic skill with which many things are reported; for instance, the championship of the children for their father; or the appearance of Stuart at the meeting.

The Joy episodes are painful. There the author was confronted with an 'either ... or.' He shrank from the 'or,' and so he made best of the 'either' – or the worst. Pitch Black – what a name! – is the only woman who gains my sympathy in the second half of the book; in the first, I didn't 'get' her.

The chief weakness of the book remains George who is a mere nothing, always trying to evade. When I contemplate him, I am doubtful of that word 'promising.'

In the structure of the book, the second anticipation (young Hal at the grave of old Hal, in France) is a grievous mistake; it misleads the reader because it creates the presumption that we are face to face with the main body of the book. Nor do I think the attempt at interweaving the personal record with extended glimpses at world happenings felicitous. The wider outlooks break the mood and are neither new nor profound.

(Why is it that in all American books foreign names and phrases are handled with such painful lack of accuracy? Why not rather leave them out?)

The style is slipshod; the endless repetitions of the 'rakish angle' at which the forage cap was set; the frequency with which 'as' and 'like' are confounded (and not only colloquially); a sentence like this: '... she would reach down into that rich, charged soil of his nature and strike oil'' ... Ouieie!!!. or: '... For of those things he had more a more vivid and precise gift than mere knowledge itself!' (Means? Which things? Fornication?)

But, as I have hinted, the worst is that not a figure, not an idea *interests* me; skillfully as they are shuffled, they remain commonplace or incredible (Clayton, Bo).

These are trifles, you will say. Well, yes. But if the book leads nowhere? If its only asset (and it misleading) is its title? If it relies entirely on its outer garments?

Yet I do understand.
Here I stand. I can no other, as Luther said.
Sincerely yours,
F.P.G.

1 By G. Herbert Sallans (1895–1960). This novel won the Ryerson Fiction Award for 1942, and appeared that year. It is a grim study of a man at the mercy of the historical forces around him, which he does not understand. Grove had entered *The Master of the Mill* for the same award (see letter of June 26, 1944), which may explain the vehemence of his reaction here.

2 ie, the Ryerson Fiction Award; see letter of March 26, 1943, note 2.

TO RICHARD CROUCH

R.R. 4 Simcoe, Ont.
May 31, 1943

Dear Dick,

I must apologize for not having returned Spengler's book[1] much sooner. The fact is it was, in years, the only book I have read which needed *study*.

Whether I agree with Sp[engler]'s main thesis or not, I do not know yet. It will take long for me to define my attitude. But I will say this that I consider the book of the greatest importance. I have learned more from it than from a score or several scores of other books. The man has a grasp of world events which is phenomenal. Wells' *Outline*[2] is a dwarf who could walk upright under Sp[engler]'s bed – on stilts. One can only laugh at the comparison.

Isn't this an awful spring? My man has not yet been in the field. Rain, rain, rain.

Well, forgive me for my dilatoriness.
Best regards to you and yours,
As ever,
F.P.G.

1 *The Decline of the West*; see letter of February 10, 1943, note 1.
2 *The Outline of History* (1920, first issued in fortnightly parts), by H.G. Wells (1866–1946)

TO LORNE PIERCE

R.R. 4 Simcoe, Ont.
May 31, 1943 II

Dear Dr. Pierce,

I was firmly counting on seeing you at the R[oyal] S[ociety of] C[anada] meeting in Hamilton; in fact, it was the only purpose for which I went; and I could ill afford to do so. However, since you were not there, I must once more resort to writing. I cannot let things go.

Naturally, I have given the matter of the Award[1] a great deal of anxious thought; and the more I think about it, the more firmly I am convinced that, by debarring Child,[2] you, or the other two judges (for I do not know what stand Coulter[3] is taking), are on the point of committing not only a monstrous injustice but also a bad blunder (forgive my frankness if you can).

To have sponsored Child's book can, in the long run, bring the publishers only kudos. I repeat, it is the only Canadian book recently written which has depth, power, and beauty. All else, barring none, are piffle.

Now it is to be condemned on a technicality, and a mistaken one at that. One cannot but come to the conclusion that this, like all other contests, is no more than a commercial scheme. The book, if turned down in this award, will, of course, promptly go to another publisher; and I feel sure it would make its way even from a sales point of view.

I must say another thing. If books of a certain type (mystery, detection) were to be debarred; and if Child's book falls under that caption (which it does not), then why did it come to me at all? Among the four I read, it stands leagues ahead; and not only that; it is the one book which, apart from any comparison is of the first order.

Among other things, it has a great theme; namely that, in a democracy, justice will assert itself against any advocacy of injustice. Providence or divine justice will prevail.

Personally, I do not, under present conditions, agree with that. But, if any progress is to be made in this world towards a finer state of affairs, we must steadfastly assert that it will, in order, ultimately, to make it a fact. As Hardy said, the writer must be on the side of the angels.

That theme is worked out with a psychological insight

which is rare even in international literature. Throughout world literature, I know of only one book in which, *in recent years*, something similar in depth has been attempted; and that book is French. I have been fighting for months for the publication, here, of a translation. When we extend our view to the past, Dostoievski is a case in point.

Besides, Smoke and Avery (and others)[4] are figures never to be forgotten by any reader who has surrendered himself.

Child would survive the blow if his book is turned down. Would the Award? For, surely, when a book like Child's is available, the Weekes[5] and Marshalls[6] and Lauristons[7] simply do not count; nor a good many others. Books written because their authors want to be authors never do.

Well, that is what I had to say; and I consider that I have done all I could do; others will now have to do the rest.

With best wishes,
Sincerely yours,
F.P. Grove

1 The Ryerson Fiction Award

2 Philip Child (b1898), whose *Day of Wrath* (1945) shared the Ryerson Fiction Award in 1945. Concerning its ineligibility under the rules of the Ryerson contest, see letter of March 26, 1943, note 2. Philip Child was for many years Professor of English at Trinity College, Toronto, and is the author of several novels and books of verse.

3 John Coulter (b1888), the Irish-Canadian dramatist (author of *The House in the Quiet Glen*, *Family Portrait*, and *The Drums Are Out*, etc.)

4 Characters in *Day of Wrath*

5 Presumably Mary Loretto Weekes (b1885), who wrote a series of books with romanticized Indian settings, of which *Round the Council Fires* (1935), *The Last Buffalo Hunter* (1939) and *Painted Arrows* (1940) had appeared at this time.

6 M.P. Marshall, whose 'This Pillared Dust' had been submitted for the Ryerson Fiction Award (see letter of April 3, 1943, note 1).

7 Victor Lauriston (b1881), author of *The Twenty-First Burr* (1922) and *Inglorious Milton* (1934), etc.

TO DESMOND PACEY

R.R. 4 Simcoe, Ont.
June 1, 1943

Dear Mr. Pacey,

Thank you very much for sending me the essay in the *Manitoba Arts Review*[1] which I enjoyed reading. Not, of course, that I agreed with everything. How could that be? But I feel in it a sincere attempt to come to grips with matters, which I appreciate very much indeed.

May I point out some one or two trifles?

(1) Page 34, the quotation from *Settlers*.[2] Now the intention of that passage was to convey the intoxicating speed of things. I myself, when I read it, involuntarily fall into a chant. Any word added would, to me, break that chant.

It was by the way, *Settlers* which was so ruthlessly cut down, from 3 long volumes to one short one. Hence the dots.

(2) Re *Fruits of The Earth*.[3] This book did end with a tragic climax when first written. I remember talking to a publisher who particularly admired and liked that ending; and it occurred to me *during* that conversation that, considering the conditions in the West, this ending was not true. I told the publisher of my thought. He exclaimed 'No.' I said, 'Abe Spalding, hero though he is in one way, *lies down* under that blow. I shall have to rewrite the ending.' The publisher told me right then and there, 'If you do, you will have to count me out.' 'All right,' I said. 'Let the book lie.' It waited 5 years; but I assert that the ending is true.

However, page 36, bottom:[4] that is a bad sentence, very bad indeed.

It is a disadvantage to let books lie through years and years; one gets used to one's own mannerisms; one does not even notice them in proof-reading.

Does not a 'trap' (page 39)[5] presuppose a trapper? I know of none.

It goes without saying that I did not know Dreiser's *American Tragedy* when I wrote *The Yoke of Life*.[6] The end was suggested by the actual sight of the chattering rocks in Lake Winnepegosis. But the meaning of that ending is, of course, that Len wants something so much that all else falls away (education, etc.): that he will pay *any* price to get it. There is no intention of pessimism there.

However, those are trifles; and I appreciate the intention of the article.

With best wishes,
Sincerely yours
F.P.G.

1 This letter concerns my article in the *Manitoba Arts Review*; see letter of February 16, 1943, note 1. The page references in the following notes are to the article as reprinted in my *Essays in Canadian Criticism* (1969).

2 *Settlers of the Marsh*, 120. I had quoted that passage as an example of the apparently sketchy and unfinished nature of some parts of *Settlers of the Marsh*; see my article, p 12.

3 Which is found inconclusive in the article, pp 14–15

4 The long sentence from *The Yoke of Life* (p 68) quoted in my article, pp 15–16:

> His age, full of enigmatic developments concentrated into a few hours, saturated with what is commonly spread out over years of scarcely perceptible unfolding, was pre-eminently that of the mythic poets who project into nature the procreations of that awe in which they stand of themselves, in the forms of fabulous

concrescences of incongruous parts which they harmonize into imaginable wholes.

5 My exact words were: 'The universe he views as a gigantic sand-trap, in which man must defend himself on all sides against a cosmic attack' (p 19). I am not, in retrospect, proud of the image.

6 I had pointed out the similarity in the tragic climaxes of the two novels; p 13.

TO RICHARD CROUCH

R.R. 4 Simcoe, Ont.
June 14, 1943

Dear Dick,

The time is approaching for Leonard and me to go out on our 2 weeks' (more or less) holiday; and I am wondering which would suit you people best, July 1st or July 15 or any other date? Will you let us know?

We have been planning all sorts of things, hikes, botanizings, bird-studies, swimming, a.s.o.[1]

Leonard was recommended for entrance to H[igh] S[chool] and will, therefore, be free tomorrow. He is taking tennis lessons now, scouting, etc. He is making a little money, caddying on the golf course and cutting lawns. Incidentally, to my surprise, he is writing verse, 'better than Tennyson' a young girl-friend of his says.

Ti[2] and I were at the Royal Society meeting in Hamilton.

We have 75 chicks.

That's all the homely news.

With best regards for Hazel and you and yours,

As ever

F.P.G.

1 and so on. It appears that the Crouchs lent the Groves their summer cottage for a holiday.

2 Mrs Grove; see letter of February 15, 1943, note 4.

TO RICHARD CROUCH

R.R. 4 Simcoe, Ont.
July 14, 1943

My dear Dick,

Had your letter yesterday; and we shall do as you say; stay till Friday about noon. Hope you'll get here in time. I think we should leave about 2 p.m. at the latest. You will find the ice-box full and also some pickerel-fillets (we found some when we arrived). I'll leave the key with the next-door neighbours (north): Mr. Smith. There will also be milk.

Well, it goes without saying that we had a good time. Leonard had 'a whale of a time.' Four times a day in the water. He now swims 25 y[ar]ds, instead of 2 as before.

Both Leonard and I wish to thank you and Hazel most heartily for the holiday we have had and couldn't very well have had in any other way.

As ever, with best wishes,
yours,
F.P.G.

P.S. The day of our arrival, the toilet went wrong. The ball valve would not shut, and then its lever became unhooked in the middle. I opened her up and repaired as best I could. I have had the same thing at home, so should know.

TO FRANK FLEMINGTON

R.R. 4 Simcoe, Ont.
September 23, 1943

Dear Mr. Flemington,

The former Mrs. Knister is married again and living in Toronto.[1] But I know neither her present name nor address. Her mother, however, is a Mrs. Gamble, at Port Dover, Ont[ario]. An enquiry addressed to her should bring the desired information.

Sincerely yours,
F.P. Grove

1 The letter of Frank Flemington is missing. The former Mrs Raymond Knister, now Mrs Myrtle B. Grace, presently lives in Jarvis, Ontario.

TO BARKER FAIRLEY

R.R. 4 Simcoe, Ont.
December 12, 1943

Dear Fairley:

Thanks for the off-print on Doughty.[1] I had already read it in the *Quarterly* which they are good enough to send me with their compliments. But I am glad to have it with your inscription, so I can go back to it when at last I find some of Doughty's writings to read. I have looked for years through neighbouring libraries, especially for *Arabia Deserta*, but none of these little libraries have it. I must write to the University library or to London for it. It has been on my list of *desiderata* for ages, and your essay sharpens my curiosity.

I sincerely hope that you and yours are well.

My own infirmities are 2: increasing age and the inability to place certain books which I should like to see published before I lie down for the long rest.

Best wishes for the coming season.
Yours sincerely,
F.P. Grove

1 Charles Doughty (1843–1926), the author of *Arabia Deserta*; Fairley's essay on him had appeared in the *University of Toronto Quarterly* XIII (October 1943) 14–24.

TO DESMOND PACEY

R.R. 4 Simcoe, Ont.
February 3, 1944

Dear Mr. Pacey,

I have been laid up with the flu; so please excuse the delay in sending you the list[1] of my magazine contributions as far as I can [lay] my hand on them.

U[niversity] of T[oronto] Quarterly:		
	Jan[uary] 1932	'A Writer's Classification of Writers.'
	July 1932	'Thomas Hardy'
	July 1938	'The Plight of Canadian Fiction'
	Oct[ober] 1940	'In Search of Myself'
	July 1943	'Democracy and Education'
Dalhousie Review	July 1931	'The Flat Prairie'
Queen's Quarterly	Feb[ruary] 1932	'Snow'
	Aug[ust] 1941	'The Desert'
	Autumn 1942	'Postscript to A Search for America.'

I seem to have overestimated the number. But there were occasional contributions to *Macleans* (1928), *The Winnipeg Tribune* (1926 or 1927), *Saturday Night* (1932?) *The London Free Press*. That's all I can think of; and I seem to have none of the latter group.

Sincerely yours,
F.P.G.

1 This is not complete; for a fuller list see the bibliography in my *Frederick Philip Grove* (Critical Views on Canadian Writers 1970), which is itself now out of date. To my 1970 list there can now be added:

> Two review articles and a short story in *Saturday Night*: 'The Living Aztec' (October 1, 1927, pp 15–16) on D.H. Lawrence's *Mornings in Mexico*; 'Caveat Emptor' (December 3, 1927, p 212) on Nordahl Grieg's *The Ship Sails On*; and 'The Wedding' (December 19, 1931, pp 13 and 20). Two short stories and an essay in *The Canadian Nation*: 'Drama at the Crossroads' (April 1928, pp 14–18); 'The Meaning of Nationhood' (March–April 1929, p 8ff.); and 'Salesmanship' (May–June 1929, pp 20–2, 31). Two essays in *Maclean's Magazine*: 'Canadians Old and New' (March 15, 1928, pp 3, 75f.); and 'Assimilation' (September 1, 1929, pp 7, 74, 78). An essay in the *Canadian Geographical Journal*: 'The Rockies versus the Alps' (VII, 6, December 1933, pp 261–74).

No signed articles or short stories by Grove seem to have appeared in the *London Free Press*, but the search is not complete. Grove reviewed Arthur Stringer's *Power* and Frederick William Wallace's *Captain Salvation* in *The Canadian Bookman* of June 1925 (p 99) and September 1925 (p 148) respectively.

TO DESMOND PACEY

R.R. 4 Simcoe, Ont.
February 8, 1944

Dear Mr. Pacey,

You can readily imagine that, in a life in which over 20 years are, as it were, taken out and thrown away, chronology gets confused. I am not even sure any longer that I know in what year I was born. The only thing I have to go by is that my mother said to me, in a conversation I remember very distinctly, that the great event happened a year after the Franco-Prussian war.* I have given my age as if I were born anywhere between 1871 and 1873. I believe that the sequence of events as given in my 'Life' is essentially correct; but...? For nearly 22 years no birthday was ever celebrated (1892 or 1893 to 1914 when I married); from then on the years are as it were certified; before that everything is guess work.

So, if you will kindly try to bring some order into the sequences, I will promise to accept it and to govern myself accordingly from now on.[1]

I might add that I am going to Toronto tomorrow, to try to get some arrangement made to publish *The Master of the Mill* which I consider as the most important book I have written. I shall try to have it followed by what

I call the 'Ant' book.[2] There are some 4 or 5 volumes awaiting publication; probably the last I shall finish, at least if the state of my health is any indication.

Sincerely yours,
F.P.G.

*But whether she meant by that 1870 or 1871 I can't tell.

1 I subsequently acted on the assumption that Grove was born in 1871; for my reasons, see my *Frederick Philip Grove* (1945) 1n. Grove also apparently accepted my correction: his son tells me that the 75th birthday was celebrated in 1946.

On June 28, 1947, Mrs Grove wrote to Carleton Stanley: 'As for Phil's date of birth – as I said once before according to our marriage certificate he was born neither '72 nor '71 but 1873. – That's all the help I can be on that question. But some day I'll tell you a funny story.'

If Grove was Greve, however, the correct date is 1879.

2 *Consider Her Ways* (1947)

TO PELHAM EDGAR

R.R. 4 Simcoe, Ont.
February 11, 1944

Dear Dr. Edgar,

Having to go to Toronto to make arrangements for the printing of my new novel,[1] I spent night before last with Ned Pratt.[2] Naturally we talked a good deal about my own circumstances.

I told him that summer before last, to make sure of the daily bread, I worked (at 32c an hour) in a canning factory till, in the 10th week, I was disabled by an accident which permanently injured my left elbow.

I also mentioned that last year my practically only earnings had been reading fees from Macmillans, amounting to a total of $425 for the year, though this sum was augmented by $100 from the Authors' Foundation. Naturally I had found it pretty hard to keep going.

Now I partly own, partly owe a small farm. He asked me, could I not sell it? No. For this reason: I have a young son, now in high school; and I am holding on to the place by the skin of my teeth because one day soon the selling price will have to provide the funds for his education.

That, briefly speaking, is the situation. Perhaps I should add that since 1928 I have not bought any clothes.

Now Pratt urged me to write to you, saying that you and Dr. D.C. Scott[3] controlled certain funds. In fact, he said that you had authorised him to mention this to me in a hopeful sense. I hope I am giving his meaning correctly.

I naturally hate to make the impression as if I were begging. But I have a few more things to say, and worry prevents me from saying them. My connection with Macmillans depends, of course, on the correctness of the guesses with regard to the books submitted to them; and, so far, I am glad to say, my reports or guesses have been lucky. Pratt asked me to give you the full facts. Now I personally keep quite cheerful; but it would indeed make a vast difference if I could look forward to some assistance, be it ever so small. Can you hold out any prospect?

I might say that, in bringing out my new book, I had to promise Macmillans to assist them by selling 250 copies of a limited edition at $4.00 each. Of this I am to get ca. $1.50, perhaps a trifle more. The trade price will be $3.25 to $3.50. Of *Two Generations* I sold ca. 300 copies by subscription. I am not quite ready to solicit subscriptions. The book is scheduled to appear in September or October. In due time I hope to send you a subscription blank.

I shall tremendously appreciate a word from you.[4]
With best wishes,
Sincerely yours,
F.P. Grove

1 *The Master of the Mill*
2 E.J. Pratt, the poet
3 Duncan Campbell Scott, the poet
4 Edgar's reply, of February 14, was warm and courteous: 'It was a hard letter for you to write, but I am glad you wrote it.' He promised that help this time would be more substantial than the $100 given in 1943– 'and the year before,' indicating that some sum was given in 1942. He went on to say: 'You have done noble work, and we are all eager to do everything that lies in our power to emphasize that fact in a tangible way.'

TO LORNE PIERCE

R.R. 4 Simcoe, Ont.
February 19, 1944

Dear Dr. Pierce,

I am so desperately hard of hearing that I am not sure I understood you right when I saw you last. I was under the impression that you promised me to let me know about the abridged edition of the *Search for America*[1] within a week or ten days. If this is not correct, please forgive me. But I promised Dents to let them know within that time. So I am writing.

Now Dents promised to meet your terms, that is, to charge the labour of abridgment up to editorial expense. They promised me a fee of about $100 to $150 for the work.

My financial situation is so desperate that I am not sure from week to week that I can heat my house; apart from other things. This is about as hard a condition as I have ever been up against; and at the moment I see no other way out except that I may collect that fee. If you have decided to bring out that abridged edition yourself, will you let me know at once? Perhaps I can

23 Oscar Pelham Edgar. *Oil painting by Allen Barr c1940. Courtesy Victoria University, Toronto*

borrow against it. If not, please release me, so I can accept Dent's offer. To me, this is a matter almost of life and death. I have, on Dents' demand, reserved the month of March for completing the work, for they want to go to press with it as soon as possible, and that would give me immediate relief.

With best wishes, as ever,
Yours sincerely,
F.P. Grove

1 Pierce replied, on February 24, that he had written Dent proposing the following conditions: Ryerson would license Dent to publish an abridgement of *A Search for America* for five years; the copyright page would show clearly that the copyright is owned by the Ryerson Press; Dent's would pay Grove for the editorial work in preparing the abridgement, and a 10% royalty – 8% to go to Grove and 2% to Ryerson; and the metal would be preserved and the type sold to Ryerson at cost of the metal should Ryerson decline to extend the lease. Dent accepted all the terms except the five-year limit since, according to them, they would 'scarcely have got started in five years.' The arrangement, thus, fell through, and the abridged text did not appear until 1947, when Ryerson brought out their own edition.

TO PELHAM EDGAR

R.R. 4 Simcoe, Ont.
February 27, 1944

Dear Dr. Edgar,

Thank you so much for your letter of the 23rd; it relieved a great deal of anxiety, especially with regard to fuel. We had been anything but comfortable. I know we ought not to complain; and on the whole I believe I don't. Only now and then does bitterness come to the fore. However...

I sincerely hope you and yours are well and will keep so.

Will you be good enough to convey my thanks to the board?[1]

Sincerely yours,
F.P. Grove

1 At a meeting of the Board of Directors of the Canadian Writers' Foundation on February 23, 1944, attended by Pelham Edgar, Duncan Campbell Scott, H.S. Southam, Lawrence Burpee, and Wilfrid Eggleston, a grant of $200 was voted to Grove. Initially, this was moved as $75 (all the Foundation had left, after other demands, of its trust income); but Southam donated $125 to raise this to $200. Grove was not to know of this.

TO RICHARD CROUCH

R.R. 4 Simcoe, Ont.
March 3, 1944

Dear Dick,

I am going to speak to the Hesperian Club[1] on Mar[ch] 25. I am writing chiefly to say that, in view of your forthcoming moving, I would not dream of inflicting myself on Mrs. Crouch. The club pays my expenses; so I shall reserve a room at the London House; it will be a very short visit, for I am rather busy; and there is just the possibility that there will be no time for me to drop in at 291 Huron Street. I know you will forgive me, and I write in advance to avoid any offence.

So, I hear, you have taken the plunge with regard to the house. We are planning something similar. I also heard recently of your accident. Our car is deteriorating fast without any accident. I'll go by train, of course.

Best wishes and best regards to Mrs. Crouch (Hazel, I should say).

Cordially,
F.P.G.

1 Sometime in the 1920s the Hesperian Club was founded by Dr William F. Tamblyn and the students of the English Department at the University of Western Ontario. It met in the homes of members and discussed literary matters. Dr Tamblyn in *These Sixty Years* (London, Ont. 1938) mentions the Club's existence: 'For a few years the Hesperian Club did something in play production. In 1927 they staged a number of scenes from *Hamlet* and *Twelfth Night* ... In 1929 the Players and Hesperian Clubs again collaborated...' (p 128). There is, unfortunately, no record of the meeting of March 3, 1944.

TO LORNE PIERCE

R.R. 4 Simcoe, Ont.
March 8, 1944

Dear Dr. Pierce,

As you probably know, Dents have declined to entertain any contract such as you propose,[1] and I cannot blame them. On the other hand, that leaves me again in the position in which I was before, except that, as time goes by, the necessities increase. Of course, there is still the possibility that Ryersons will do what Dents proposed. Would you be good enough to let me know about that?[2]

I have made up my mind to give a paper at the next Royal Society meeting;[3] always provided that I can get there which is very doubtful.

Sincerely,
F.P. Grove

1 See letter of February 19, 1944, note 1.
2 To which Pierce, on March 15, replied: 'We have been trying to make up our minds regarding your *Search for America*. I do not see what else we could have done in so far as Dents were concerned, for longer than five years, which was the only objection they raised, would have been almost to have parted with our rights in the book'; adding: 'Now that the Dent affair has fallen through we plan to take steps to revive interest in the unabridged edition. I think we shall add it to a popular series to retail for $1.49 and do all we can to get it moving and earning for you.'
3 Grove did not deliver a paper before the Royal Society of Canada that year, and in fact did not attend the meeting. The annual meeting is held in June, and in April 1944 Grove suffered a stroke.

TO ELLEN ELLIOTT

R.R. 4 Simcoe, Ont.
March 9, 1944

Dear Miss Elliott,

Thanks for your letter of day before yesterday[1] which, I believe, makes the financial position regarding *The Master of the Mill* almost painfully clear. However, I have carefully canvassed all possibilities and arrived at the conclusion that, rather than let the matter rest, I shall sell the roof over my head. I think I mentioned something like that in our talk of Feb[ruary] 9. I feel, with regard to this book, somewhat the way Henry George[2] felt with regard to *Progress and Poverty*. In order to meet Appleton's demands, the Georges sold their last rug from the floor; and within ten years the book was one of the most famous and most widely-bought in the world.

The various possibilities seem to me to be as follows:

1) I cannot quite see why *Forges of Freedom*[3] stands so much a better chance than my book; and my book would be much cheaper to produce. A printing of 3000 copies would cover it. But I do not blame you in the least if you decline to take that risk.

2) Suppose we printed the book in a looser style, so as to raise the number of pages rather than reduce it, and then publish in two volumes selling at $5.00 boxed. This would, of course, raise the cost of the paper and of the binding, in addition to adding about 15¢ per copy for the slip-case. It might, then, be wise to print 1250 or even 1500 copies. 250 limited edition, to be taken over by me. One might, in addition, sell a few hundred sheets in the U.S.A. I should, of course, be willing to take 250 copies of the limited edition off your hands, covering as many of that number by subscription as I can. Subscriptions are even now coming in.

I realise that this, for Canada, would be a bold move; but I am not at all sure that it would not be successful.

3) I might print myself, taking on a debt of about $2200, to be covered by the sale of my property which I am willing to risk. I have talked the matter over fully with my wife; and she agrees.

Then, having sold what I can by subscription, I should have anywhere from 750 to 1000 sheets to sell, to be bound up either uniformly with the limited edition of 250 copies, namely in two volumes, or in one volume of perhaps 500 pages @ $3.50 which would net $1650 (750 copies) to $2200. It goes without saying that I should have to waive all profit for myself. That, however, I am willing to do.

While I should want to reread the text once more before starting to print, so as to throw out another two or three thousand words, I should not be willing to perform a major operation. I have been at work on the book for 14 years; and I know that every trifle has been most carefully considered; nothing can be spared apart from a few words here and there. You intimate that this is also your opinion.

Now, please, let me repeat. I shall not blame you if you reject any or all of the above possibilities. Just let me know, the sooner the better. Perhaps this is not a book which, like *Forges of Freedom*, may sell like hot cakes at once. Perhaps it takes more brains to appreciate. I think it important that it appear as soon as possible. But it is a book which will make its way, sooner or later; and it is a book which concerns the whole world, even though U.S.A. publishers do not see it; they have made mistakes before this; and the problem of the book does not yet loom in the immediate future for them, though even for the U.S.A. it is inescapable in the long-run. I shall have, at the best, not much longer to live; and I feel very strongly that, if I go below the sod without having seen this book, I have very largely lived in vain. But I have the most absolute confidence that, whatever I or we do, there will be no loss, provided we have a little patience with regard to the returns. I might add that, if you people think my name may handicap the book – as it possibly may – I have no objection whatever to let it appear under a pseudonym or anonymously. I have no ambition, the important thing is that the book appear. *I* count for nothing.

I am very sorry to give you so much trouble by my obstinacy. Believe me when I say that I am thinking almost as much of Macmillans as of myself in this.

With my most sincere wishes, I am,
Very faithfully yours,
F.P.G.

P.S. – Also, if that facilitates calculation, I am willing to waive all royalties up to so-and-so many copies – you to determine the number.

1 In her letter, Miss Elliott estimated that the manufacturing cost for a single copy of *The Master of the Mill* – in a run of 1000 copies, which both Grove and Macmillan had agreed would be sufficient – would be $1.62. She went on to explain that publishers work on a 3:1 minimum ratio of list price to manufactuing cost, which would set the price of the book at $4.85, an impossible price for fiction in Canada. Even $4.00 was too high to secure reasonable sales. Grove's offer of guaranteeing a sale through subscriptions of some 200–250 copies would not reduce the Macmillan's investment appreciably.

The one problem, she concluded, was the fixed type-setting cost, which would be reduced if the book could be brought down to 300 pages, in which case

$3.50 would be a reasonable price. But she herself realised that it was not practical severely to condense *The Master of the Mill*.

2 Henry George (1839–1897), the American writer on political economy and sociology, author of *Progress and Poverty* (1879), *The Land Question* (1883), *Social Problems* (1884), and *Protection or Free Trade* (1886). He was an early advocate of the nationalization of all land and a single tax based on its increment value.

3 Franklin Davey McDowell's *Forges of Freedom* was published by Macmillan in 1943 at $3.50 a copy which, as Miss Elliott explained, was based on an initial run of 5000 copies. It is, like the author's *The Champlain Road* (1939), which won the Governor-General's Award, a combination of romantic fiction and historical fact. For Grove's laconic comment on McDowell winning the Governor-General's Award, see letter of May 4, 1940; for Lorne Pierce's response to it, see note 1 to the same letter.

TO PELHAM EDGAR

R.R. 4 Simcoe, Ont.
March 10, 1944

Dear Dr. Edgar,

Please do not think for a moment that I am impatient. The point is that, in your letter of the 23rd of February you said that the National Trust Company would send me the sum of $200.[1] in '*the next few days*.' 15 days have gone, and they have not done so. My anxiety arises from the fact that, 2 years ago, a small sum ($5) was lost in the mail, and it took me 6 months to trace it. I am beginning to fear that something similar may have happened to this much larger remittance. If there is any other explanation, please do not trouble to answer. But, if not, I thought you should know. With the best wishes, I remain,

Sincerely yours,
F.P. Grove

1 See letter of February 27, 1944, note 1.

TO PELHAM EDGAR

R.R. 4 Simcoe, Ont.
March 10, 1944 II

Dear Dr. Edgar,

As it usually happens, after I had, this morning, dropped you a worried line regarding the cheque of the National Trust Company of Toronto, the cheque arrived in the noon mail, greatly relieving my anxiety. Will you please consider the other note as replaced by this renewed expression of my thanks?

Sincerely yours,
F.P. Grove

TO ELLEN ELLIOTT

R.R. 4 Simcoe, Ont.
March 17, 1944

Dear Miss Elliott,

Re *The Master of the Mill*, I agree to everything.[1]

Yes, I should have the Ms. back as soon as possible; and would you or Mr. Graves[2] look after those mimeographed circulars we spoke of on Feb[ruary] 9?[3]

I may have to sell here anyway; in fact it is very likely. But, of course, I should use the money I can realise to buy another roof over our heads. Not that I care myself, but I have wife and child.

I hope to be able to arrange for another trip to Toronto, to talk details of production over with Mr. Graves. Meanwhile I want to get busy on collecting subscriptions. I can't very well write letters for the 200-odd addresses which I have. I feel sure I can secure 200 subscriptions; but, what with postage etc., that will hardly quite bring $800.00. However, I shall do the best I can in that respect.

Thank you very much for your kind letter.

In haste, to get this off by today's mail, I am, as always,
Sincerely yours,
F.P.G.

1 Again, in reply to a long letter from Ellen Elliott, which in return replies to Grove's of March 9:

> I think in the long run we shall sell 3,000 copies of this book, but to be quite truthful I don't think it would be advisable for us to take a chance on doing a larger edition than 1,000 copies to begin with.
>
> Mr. Graves does not feel your suggestion of publishing in two volumes, bound, at $5.00, would work out as you think it would. We should run into double binding costs, and in addition might have a great deal of difficulty in getting the binding done at all. Binding is a bottle-neck in the industry as you know just now.
>
> Mr. Huckvale, Mr. Graves and I agree that we cannot agree that you sell your property to take care of the financial risk of this book, and so we have another suggestion to make. We will do an edition of 1,000 copies and make the list price $3.50. By doing so we are eliminating all profit and, indeed, a considerable portion of our overhead. But we think the book is worth it, and we believe the Canadian public in time will appreciate it. It is absolutely true to say that Canadians are more appreciative of good novels today than they were two or three years ago when we were then discussing *The Master of the Mill*. As you know books by Canadian writers have been selling much better during the last year particularly.

If we published on this basis we should like you to get some royalty, but, since we stand only to turn our money over if the whole edition sells out, we do not think we could offer you more than 5%.

On the other hand you would do what you could to secure as large a pre-publication sale as possible at a price of $4.00.

2 Robert Graves, who was in charge of production for Macmillan

3 Circulars inviting subscription

TO WINNIFRED EAYRS[1]

R.R. 4 Simcoe, Ont.
March 28, 1944

Dear Miss Eayrs,

I am returning the Ms. of the *Master* today. May I say that I agree with every suggestion you have made? Thank you for the trouble you have been going to.

Sincerely yours,
F.P. Grove

I found only about 250 words which I could eliminate. But I feel *sure* now.

1 Winnifred Eayrs (b1893), who was in charge of copy-editing and proof-reading at Macmillan until her retirement in 1961. She was a sister of Hugh S. Eayrs.

TO RICHARD CROUCH

R.R. 4 Simcoe, Ont.
March 31, 1944

Dear Dick,

I have Macmillan's answer. Can you get me 1000 sheets of that paper?* The sooner the better. The Circular[1] otherwise is ready; and they are only waiting for the paper now.

Glad I had the chance to see you and Hazel again. Am going to Aurora on April 10 to scout. I think this place is as good as sold. ($10,000.00).[2]

Best wishes, and thanks.
As ever,
Phil

*Address:
The Macmillan Company of Canada
(attention Mrs. A.E. Blochin)
70 Bond St[reet]
Toronto 2, Ont[ario]

1 Inviting subscriptions for a limited edition of *The Master of the Mill* – see following letter.

2 The Simcoe property was not sold – the house, that is; the land was disposed of during Grove's last illness. Mrs Grove lived in the house until her death in 1972; it now belongs to Leonard Grove, who uses it as a year-round country, weekend residence.

TO WINNIFRED EAYRS

R.R. 4 Simcoe, Ont.
April 4, 1944

Dear Miss Eayrs,

I am very grateful to you for all the trouble you are taking with the *Master*. It just goes to show that one is never through with a Ms.

All your suggestions[1] are good; and I have marked them with a '✔' as I pondered them. So as not to put you out with another letter, I return yours enclosed.

Will you be good enough to mention to Mrs. Blochin[2] that I find I cannot manage to go [to] Toronto till Wednesday, April 12. But on that day, *D.V.*,[3] I shall be with you around 10 a.m. or 10:30. I shall motor.

Once more, many thanks.
Sincerely yours,
F.P. Grove

1 Miss Eayrs had made some suggestions concerning women's underwear with regard to Sibyl Carter's 'dismantling' (*The Master of the Mill* 172–9). She questioned the credibility of Edmund Clark's role in the story, and suggested that even in a wealthy Canadian home of the period, there would have been fewer servants than Grove's account implied.

2 Mrs A.E. Blochin, who worked with Ellen Elliott in the Editorial Department at Macmillan

3 *Deo volente* (God willing)

TO BARKER FAIRLEY

R.R. 4 Simcoe, Ont.
June 11, 1944

Dear Fairley,

Thanks for your letter and the subscription.

I know your work demands time, like mine. Don't apologize. I hope to see you in the near future.

I am sorry to say that on April 14 I suffered a 'stroke' and I am paralysed on my right side, but I have made marvellous strides forward since then. It is true, I cannot write except with 1 finger of my left hand, and that very slowly; but I walk with the help of a cane, and, though my speech is impaired, my mind is as active as it ever was. Could you let Malcolm Wallace,[1] Woodhouse,[2] etc. know?

Well, that is as much as I can manage.

By the way, I have not heard from W.J. Alexander for nearly 2 years, though I have written repeatedly. It has worried me; I want to dedicate my new book[3] to him.

Best wishes for you and yours.
F.P.G.

1 Principal of University College, Toronto; see letter of December 1, 1938 II, note 1.
2 A.S.P. Woodhouse, Professor of English at University College, Toronto; see letter of October 24, 1938 II, note 3.
3 *The Master of the Mill*

TO W.J. ALEXANDER

R.R. 4 Simcoe, Ont.
June 16, 1944

Dear Dr. Alexander,

Thank you very much for your subscription and the letter from your daughter.[1]

As you know, I suffered a stroke on April 14, probably from overexertion. I am paralysed on my right side; but am mentally as alert as ever. Speech presents some difficulty, but I am able to dictate. This letter I am typing with one finger of my left hand. One of my two doctors says it will take 15 mo[nth]s for me to recover; the other does not commit himself.

You cannot imagine how much I appreciated hearing from you. Not that I thought for a moment we were 'divided': but momentarily separated. I have been wishing to dedicate my new book to you: the result of 14 years' labour. May I? Subscriptions come in slowly. I have 50, but need 400.

This is about as much as I can manage.

With my very best wishes and in gratitude for all the help and encouragement you have given.

My wife will have to sign for me.
most sincerely yours,
F.P. Grove

1 Edith L. Alexander (now Mrs E.L. MacIver) who, in forwarding this letter, wrote: 'The letter I am enclosing, I found among some old letters of my own, I suppose because it mentions a letter from me, the only one I ever wrote him' (January 10, 1972).

TO LORNE PIERCE

R.R. 4 Simcoe, Ont.
June 26, 1944

Dear Dr. Pierce,

Thank you for your laconic note of the 23rd.[1] Does it mean that you are subscribing for a copy of the limited edition?

No doubt you have heard that on April 14, I had a stroke and am paralyzed on my right side. I am making a reasonable recovery, but the doctors tell me that I shall be disabled for a year to eighteen months. I am meanwhile planning no end of literary work.

Re your enquiry about the trade edition may I say that I offered you the book in 1938, and you declined.[2] I offered it again to you in 1942 for the award; but you preferred *Little Man*.[3] Considering the fact that a prominent and most revered critic[4] called the book 'ultimate and enduring,' and that another, an Englishman,[5] called it 'the most important book to come out of Canada, yes, out of America,' I felt somewhat disappointed; and when another firm not only accepted the trade edition, but also undertook the whole risk of the limited edition, naturally, I was bound to accept. I never expected to get the prize in your award but I rather thought you would make an offer of publication. When you did not, I was, of course, entirely free to make any other arrangement.

Yours sincerely,
F.P. Grove
per C.G.

1 The letter, very brief, asked: 'Is your new novel published? I would like to have you send me a copy. I should also like to inquire whether you would care to have us take a quantity for the trade.' Grove's puzzlement here is explained by the fact that Pierce's secretary neglected to enclose the signed order form for *The Master of the Mill* (limited edition).

2 See letter of July 12, 1941, and note 2 to that letter.

3 By G. Herbert Sallans; see letter of May 14, 1943, note 1.

4 W.J. Alexander; see the following letter.

5 Presumably, one of the readers of the book for J.M. Dent & Sons of London, England; see letters of January 4 and May 24, 1939.

TO RICHARD CROUCH

R.R. 4 Simcoe, Ont.
June 28, 1944

Dear Dick,

I am writing with one finger of my left hand, being paralysed on my right side.[1] Recovery is very slow. One of my two doctors speaks of 15 to 18 months. The other won't commit himself. But mentally I am quite clear and am doing all my work, though by proxy.

Thanks very much for the mysterious apparatus. Will you enlighten me as to how to use it?

Subscriptions for *The Master of the Mill* come in very slowly; and since I promised Macmillans $800, I am beginning to worry. I have not yet heard from any of the big subscribers to *Two Generations*. I am proud, though, of one utterance. Dr. Alexander,[2] speaking to President Stanley[3] of Dalhousie, called it 'ultimate and enduring.' I am reading proof; and I expect the limited edition will be out next month.

I can't go on. So best wishes for Hazel and you.
Cordially yours,
F.P.G.

1 Since April 14, 1944

2 W.J. Alexander; see letter of March 24, 1928, note 1. Alexander's remark was communicated by his son-in-law, Carleton Stanley, in a letter to Mrs Grove, dated June 20, 1944, in which he wrote:

> Will you please say this to your husband for me: that I have never met, anywhere, a person of such critical power and discrimination as Professor Alexander, and that I know from many, many conversations with him that he never wavered in his faith that your husband is writing ultimate and enduring books?

Cf. the preceding and following letters, and also letter of January 4, 1945.

3 Carleton Wellesley Stanley, born on July 6, 1886, was a graduate of the University of Toronto (BA 1911) and Oxford (BA 1913). From 1913 to 1916, he was Canadian correspondent to the *Manchester Guardian*, and lecturer in English at Victoria College, University of Toronto. Then followed a period during which he was engaged in business. From 1925 he was successively Professor of Classics at McGill University (1925–31), President of Dalhousie University (1931–45), and Professor of English at United College (now University of Winnipeg), Winnipeg (1946–53). He wrote two books, *Roots of the Tree* (1936) and *Matthew Arnold* (1938), and was a Fellow of the Royal Society of Canada. He had also prepared a book-length manuscript on Grove – see letter of November 24, 1945, note 2. He died on November 30, 1971.

Stanley wrote to Grove as early as October 4, 1930, when the former was a professor at McGill. He thanked Grove for a review copy of Ella Bell Wallis' *The Exquisite Gift*, writing in part:

> 'I congratulate you on your establishment of a publishing company [Ariston], and I wish you every success in your venture. It's a long while since I've seen so beautifully produced a book...'

TO WINNIFRED EAYRS

R.R. 4 Simcoe, Ont.
July 12, 1944

Dear Miss Eayrs,

I enclose a new dedication[1] page for *The Master of the Mill* which the recipient of the dedication not so long ago had called 'ultimate and enduring.'[2] Since he died before the book was out, the change becomes necessary.

Would you be so very kind as to look after the crippled author?

I might mention that I intend to do the autographing with my left hand. It might be best to have a little slip printed or mimeographed to explain its waviness.

Thanking you in advance,
yours as ever,
F.P.G.

1 As printed in the book:

I dedicate this book
to
the memory
of
W.J. ALEXANDER
whose recent death deprived Canada of its acutest critical mind
and left a void in the hearts of all who loved him.

2 See letter of June 28, 1944, note 2.

TO WINNIFRED EAYRS

R.R. 4 Simcoe, Ont.
July 16, 1944

Dear Miss Eayrs,

Thanks for your letter of the 13th.

Your suggestion re the list of my other books pleases me much. I enclose a list and the Ludwig slip.[1]

I also enclose a sample left-hand signature. Both my doctors say it will be a year to 15 months (if ever) before my right hand will be restored to its natural functions.

I must not run on, or I should add how much I appreciated the courtesy, care, and helpfulness with which you saw me through the galleys.

With best wishes,
as ever,
F.P.G.

1 Miss Eayrs had suggested 'a listing of your other books in a style similar to the enclosed ... If, however, you would prefer them listed in a smaller type...' and Grove's preceding letter has, in Miss Eayrs' handwriting, the annotation 'Other books as Ludwig.' Presumably the reference is to a list of 'other books by Emil Ludwig' in an edition of one of Ludwig's biographies.

TO WINNIFRED EAYRS

R.R. 4 Simcoe, Ont.
August 3, 1944

Dear Miss Eayrs,

Would it be possible to send Mr. or Prof. Desmond Pacey of Brandon College, Brandon Manitoba a complete set of corrected or uncorrected proofs of *The Master of the Mill*. He wants it for the last chapter in a biography of me[1] which he has written and which would appear simultaneously with *The Master*. I believe it would be a great publicity stunt.

Thanking you in advance, I am
Sincerely yours,
F.P. Grove
per C.G.[2]

1 My *Frederick Philip Grove* ('Canadian Men of Letters,' Toronto: Ryerson 1945). The galley proofs of *The Master of the Mill* were indeed sent to me, and the relevant chapter was based on my reading of them.
2 This letter is in Mrs Grove's handwriting.

TO ELLEN ELLIOTT

R.R. 4 Simcoe, Ont.
October 9, 1944

Dear Miss Elliott,

Thanks for letter and cheque.[1] I look forward to your second visit here.

One point re the limited edition of the *Master*. I have sadly fallen down on the sale. In fact I do not see that I can take more than 100 copies off your hand, instead of 200 as I more or less promised. Of these 100 I have collected in advance for 63 copies; 37 need to be billed in 17 batches. Now you mentioned a price to me at which the house would sell to me. This was in February; and I have forgotten. Could you tell me how much I should send you for the 63 copies which I should send out from here? If the house could send out the bills for the remaining 37 copies, it would save me a heart-breaking job, especially since a good many of them would have to go to libraries, to be billed in triplicate.

You have been so good in this matter that I am sort of hopeful. Many have become quite impatient; one lady has written me 3 times enquiring, and I have had the dooce of a time to keep her from cancelling. However...

With best wishes from all of us,
as ever,
F.P.G.

1 Miss Elliott's letter is missing, so we do not know exactly what this payment would be for; but Grove continued, all this time, to read mss for Macmillan, which task provided a small but steady source of income.

TO ELLEN ELLIOTT

R.R. 4 Simcoe, Ont.
October 14, 1944

Dear Miss Elliott,

Thanks very much for your letter of the 11th.[1]

I shall be very glad if you will take care of the wrapping and mailing of the 63 copies @ $2.80., for which I can send the cheque for $176.40 any time.[2]

We have talked the matter of the other 37 copies over, and we agree that perhaps it would be best to let the invoices go out under my name;[3] we could then wait 2 weeks or so for the cheques to come in, whereupon I shall forward the proceeds.

I had hoped to have 200 subscriptions; but as you know I can't move about.

Warner Bro[ther]s is good news.[4] I hope something will come of it.

Of course, there is still the matter of the autographing.

We surely look forward to your next visit. My recovery is slow but, I think, steady. I am trying to write some short stories at the rate of 3 or 4 lines a day.

Very sincerely yours,
F.P.G.

1 In which Miss Elliott had said: 'Please don't feel that you have fallen down on the sale of

the limited edition of *The Master of the Mill*. We don't think you have. As a matter of fact we think you have done remarkably well.' Miss Elliott wrote a steady sequence of encouraging letters to Grove during these final years of his life.

2 Miss Elliott had proposed selling these to Grove at $2.60 (35% off list price of $4.00), plus twenty cents for wrapping and mailing.

3 In reply to Grove's original enquiry of October 9, Miss Elliott had said Macmillan would be glad to take care of invoicing, the only question being whether the invoices should be in Macmillan's name, or Grove's.

4 The film producers; having seen the notices of the book in the catalogues, they had written requesting the proofs. Nothing actually came of this enquiry.

TO ELLEN ELLIOTT

R.R. 4 Simcoe, Ont.
October 17, 1944

Dear Miss Elliott,

I forgot to say that, if the occasion should arise, I am quite willing to let you handle the agency re Warner Bro[ther]s.

My attention is being called to the fact that *Over Prairie Trails* is in demand for supplementary reading but is unavailable. High-school students come to me to borrow the book; but I have only a single copy of the first edition which is getting dog-eared and frayed.

Could not something be done to bring out a cheap edition, perhaps in 1 volume with *The Turn of the Year*?[1]

I now say, *Au Revoir*.
Yours sincerely,
F.P.G.

1 Macmillan reissued *Over Prairie Trails* in 1929, and the New Canadian Library Edition (McClelland & Stewart) appeared in 1957. *The Turn of the Year* was reissued only once, in 1929 by Macmillan.

TO ELLEN ELLIOTT

R.R. 4 Simcoe, Ont.
November 14, 1944

Dear Miss Elliott,

At last I have got around to glancing through the printed copy of *The Romance of Mining*;[1] and I find to my delight that the distinguished author has adopted every one of my suggestions. The book now looks much more like a planned unit.

I enclose in this the list of 100 subscriptions which, in

24 Ellen Elliott. *Courtesy George M. McKanday and Miss Gladys Neale*

spite of my disability I managed to get together. 63 of them (number of copies) were paid for, @ $2.80, including mailing and packing, for which I enclose cheque for $176.40. The remaining 37 copies will have to be billed for, some of them in duplicate (these latter marked with a red pencil). I am anxious to have all this in your hands where I know it will be safe.

My progress is slow but steady. I can now *almost* handle pencil and pen, but not yet quite. It is today 7 months since the appalling surprise.[2] A man's education is not complete till he has had a stroke. My boy insists on my carrying 2 horseshoes when I take my walks.

Best wishes, as ever,
yours sincerely,
F.P.G.

1 By Thomas Arthur Rickard (1864–1953), published in Toronto by Macmillan in 1944. Grove had read the manuscript for Macmillan. Rickard's other books are *Journey of Observation* (San Francisco 1907), *Through the Yukon and Alaska* (San Francisco 1909), *Retrospect: An Autobiography* (Toronto 1937), *Historic Background of British Columbia* (Vancouver 1948), and a volume of verse, *Autumn Leaves* (Vancouver 1948).

2 Since the stroke which he suffered on April 14, 1944

TO ELLEN ELLIOTT

R.R. 4 Simcoe, Ont.
December 27, 1944

Dear Miss Elliott,

Enclosed draft of the required slip. If you prefer to change it, don't hesitate.

I was glad to receive 6 trade-edition copies of the trade edition which I propose to read shortly.

Will you be good enough to add to the list of *paid-up* subscribers

MISS EDITH ALEXANDER,[1] 155 Spadina Road, Toronto, *TEN (10) copies*; for which she has been good enough to canvass friends.

The next time we dig ourselves out, I shall have $28 forwarded to you in payment. On second thought I enclose cheque instead.

Thanks for all the good wishes, which I reciprocate.
With best regards,
as ever, yours,
F.P.G.

[enclosure]

Serious illness has deprived the author of the use of his hand. A facsimile of his signature has therefore been made for the autograph. If at a later date any copies of this edition are sent to him, he will be glad to initial them.

1 The present Mrs McIver of Caledon, Ontario, and a daughter of W.J. Alexander

TO DESMOND PACEY

R.R. 4 Simcoe, Ont.
January 4, 1945

Dear Pacey,

Work on *The Master of the Mill* started on Feb[ruary] 8, 1944, and the printing was finished in August, after many intolerable delays, due to government interference (priorities). Then started the fight for binding cloth which, I have just heard, has at last been won. I believe the book will be out inside of a week.

You, too, will have to be patient.

May I say that W.J. Alexander, in one of his last discussions of my work (with Carleton Stanley, Pres[ident] of Dalhousie U[niversity]) called the book 'ultimate and enduring,' as Stanley wrote my wife. Since I thought the world of Alexander, I was proud of that verdict.[1]

I have half a dozen books in the stocks, but my health is improving so very slowly that I am quite despondent. My doctor says it may take 5 years to get back to something like normal.

I can type about 1/3 of a page a day; nothing when I write a letter.

Sincerely yours,
F.P.G.

1 Cf. letter of June 28, 1944, note 2.

TO ELLEN ELLIOTT

R.R. 4 Simcoe, Ont.
January 6, 1945

Dear Miss Elliott,

Thanks for yours of the 3rd.

As for the weather, it has not only stopped the treatments, but made all exercise impossible except indoors. 5 feet of snow barricade the house. And consequently my walks have been reduced to about 200 feet, from a mile. I am sorry to say that things look bad, but I keep fighting.

The slip looks fine.[1] I hope it will satisfy the subscribers.

Prof[essor] Pacey writes that Pierce has accepted the biography[2] of myself. No telling, of course, when it will be out.

Best wishes from
yours sincerely,
F.P.G.

1 For the limited edition of *The Master of the Mill*

2 My *Frederick Philip Grove* (Ryerson 1945). I had sent the *Manitoba Arts Review* article to Pierce, asking whether he would consider a book-length expansion for publication. After some hesitation, he agreed to consider it, and the book was completed in the summer of 1944 and published in July 1945.

TO ELLEN ELLIOTT

R.R. 4 Simcoe, Ont.
January 9, 1945

Dear Miss Elliott,

I am in an awkward position. Some of my subscribers have received their copies. I ordered 10 or 11 copies to be sent to me, to be distributed from here, personally, all paid for, both to me and Macmillans. But I have not a copy yet; and again they 'dun' me. Could you phone down to the shipping dep[artmen]t to see whether a mistake was made?

I have had some enthusiastic acknowledgements.

Yours, as ever,
F.P.G.

TO ISOBEL SYME[1]

R.R. 4 Simcoe, Ont.
January 15, 1945

Dear Miss Syme,

The shipment arrived Saturday, Jan[uary] 13, safe and sound. I am at once sending out the subscribed and paid for copies.

Best wishes, as ever,
F.P.G.

1 Isobel Syme, one of Miss Elliott's assistants; she had confirmed that eleven copies of *The Master of the Mill* (limited edition) were shipped on January 5. See the preceding letter.

TO DESMOND PACEY

R.R. 4 Simcoe, Ont.
January 20, 1945

Dear Pacey,

I trust that by this time you will have received the copy of *The Master*. I had to leave the distribution to Macmillans, being unable to do anything myself.[1]

I am getting ready for the long rest and looking over my shelves of mss. Most of them I discard and use for fuel.[2] But I had, 40 years ago, 3 mss. which I wished to finish. One is *The Master*. Another, which I have just reread, cancelling the 23-page preface, is the 'Ant-book'; and I am much impressed. It was finished in 1920, and I found only one word which I wished other. I am planning to bring it out. Would you care to read the typescript? If so, I should try to ship it to you as soon as I can. I should like you to answer one question: is it interesting?[3] Otherwise I shall discard it, too.

Please let me know as soon as possible.
Best regards, yours,
F.P.G.

1 The copy – Number 107, with a signature by Grove that appears to have been made with a rubber stamp – did indeed arrive and is still in my possession.

2 This provoked me to reply (on January 24, 1945) in part as follows:

> I am very distressed at the thought of your burning Mss., however imperfect you may feel them to be. We have a very good collection of Canadian literature here – the Hathaway Collection – and if there are some of your manuscripts which you firmly intend not to print, I do wish that you would send them here. They would be treasured, and would be available for the research scholars of the future. The same is true of any letters etc. which could be possibly of interest to posterity. Please do not burn them! I am sure your work will be of interest to future generations of Canadians.

In September 1944 I had moved from Brandon College to the University of New Brunswick, where the Hathaway Collection of Canadiana is located.

3 I did, of course, ask to read the manuscript, and found it most interesting. For my review of *Consider Her Ways*, as published in the *Toronto Daily Star*, see *Frederick Philip Grove* (Critical Views on Canadian Writers 1970) 179–80.

TO HELEN LYONS[1]

R.R. 4 Simcoe, Ont.
January 22, 1945

Dear Miss Lyon,

I have just received a letter from Miss Florence V. Keys[2] whose copy of the limited edition of the *Master* was returned to you.

The new address is:
326 Russell Hill Road,
Toronto.

Thanks for your kindness in holding the book.

Sincerely yours,
F.P.G.

1 Another of the 'third-floor Macmillanites' (as Isobel Syme described them in a letter to Grove). She was a secretary in the Executive Offices, and left the company in the late forties to be married.

2 Florence V. Keys (1869–1951), a graduate of the University of Toronto, was a professor at Vassar College.

TO ELLEN ELLIOTT

R.R. 4 Simcoe, Ont.
January 29, 1945

Dear Miss Elliott,

I have returned to you, at the office, Hardy's *Abraham*.[1] I could not lay my hand on your private address. I hope you'll forgive me. I cannot, at present, see my way to writing that essay on his Biblical books.

Since Dec[ember] 11, the beginning of the snow, I have had a severe set-back. The best I can do in walking, is 200 feet a day; and the snow (5 feet of it around the house, on the level) put a stop to my treatments.

Payments of the limited edition are very slow in coming in; I have only about $30 so far. The moment there is a sum worth mentioning, I shall send it along. So far I have it all in cheques at the house. The 'bulldozer' (is that the name?) has cleared the road for the maildriver, but, of course, left house and private drive-way untouched; so I am still a prisoner.

Have you any reviews of the *Master*? I have seen none.

Leonard, by the way, has not been able to get to school.

With best wishes, as always,
Your
F.P.G.

1 *Father Abraham* (1935), a novel by W.G. Hardy (b1896) who also wrote *Turn Back the*

River (1938), *All the Trumpets Sounded* (1942), *The Unfulfilled* (1951), and *The City of Libertines* (1957). A native of Lindsay, Ontario, and educated at the universities of Toronto and Chicago, Hardy was also the Business Manager of *The Rebel* (now the *Canadian Forum*) and for many years Professor of Classics at the University of Alberta.

TO DESMOND PACEY

R.R. 4 Simcoe, Ont.
January 30, 1945

Dear Pacey,

I have yours of Jan[uary] 24 and shall, therefore, at the first opportunity, when someone goes to town, send a ms. of the 'Ant-book' along. It is a carbon copy; but a good one, and the only one which still contains the preface. I hope you'll enjoy its 'envergure.'

As for other mss., my boy and I weighed what there is: 135 lbs., without duplications. I have reread 3 complete novels:[1] one which my wife hates, the last word I have to say about sex, very powerful, in fact, I believe, the most powerful thing I have written; but, on account of her pronounced hatred of the thing, I have given her the ms., to be kept for 20 years after my death which, considering the severe set-back I have had since we were snowed in, I consider imminent; no. 2, one which struck me as important, Art v[ersu]s Life, with art conquering; decades ago I put it aside because a friend, the only person who has read the ms. called it 'cocoon spinning,' but I think it good; no. 3, another prairie novel, not bad, but unimportant. Years ago, the U[niversity] of Toronto made me the same offer that you (Hathaway Collection) make now.[2] I can't make up my mind. Certain things, no doubt, are so weak, though I haven't met with them yet, that I'd rather see them done away with. Hardly any bear a date. But, in fifty years, one is bound to produce a lot of piffle. The 'Ant-book,' however, was, after 20 y[ea]rs of study, written in 1920.

I very much hope that you omitted, or deleted the 1926 passages,[3] which would give my wife a nervous breakdown. We are now, as always, locally surrounded by meanness and ill-will. We live the most retired life possible; but for a person not born in Canada, it is the greatest crime imaginable to have done something in life. The local paper gives a notice of the *Master* as a book published by the Swedish-Scotch novelist who lives in Wingham township. To call me a Canadian author, after 53 y[ea]rs of my stay in this country, goes so much against the grain of the editor that he'd rather die. This, of course, is only local, though I see Phelps, too, cannot get around the 'incomer Canadian,' though I feel more like an 'outgoer Canadian' just now. However,

With best wishes, yours,
F.P.G.

1 Which probably were, from Grove's description here, 'Felix Powell's Career,' 'The Canyon,' and 'Jane Atkinson.' All but 'Felix Powell's Career' are preserved in the

University of Manitoba Grove Collection. 'Felix Powell's Career' is no longer extant.
2 See letter of January 20, 1945, note 1.
3 These passages in his autobiography were concerned with Rapid City matters. In 1926, a petition was circulated in an attempt to remove Mrs Grove from the school, but a counter-petition to the school board brought the movement to an end.

TO CARLETON STANLEY

R.R. 4 Simcoe, Ont.
February 15, 1945[1]

Dear Stanley,

Thanks for the *Globe and Mail*. All this comes too late, of course. I can't write any longer; otherwise it might inspire me to finish 'The Seasons.' However...

We are debating about the best time to invite you and Mrs. Stanley to come down. The house is not so empty any longer, of course. My wife lost two pupils, though, through medical interference; this loss is welcome, from one point of view; but rather disastrous from another. However...

It is very cold here and fuel is scarce.

Well, I must stop. I have already written a letter to my boy whom I miss very much.[2]

Best wishes to you and all the Alexanders, including your wife.

As ever, yours,
F.P.G.

1 In the original, the month is clearly shown as January, but since Grove refers to the review of *The Master of the Mill* in *The Globe and Mail*, which appeared on February 10, it must have been an error. The review by William Arthur Deacon – on the whole highly favourable – is reprinted in my *Frederick Philip Grove* (Critical Views on Canadian Writers 1970) 163–6.
2 Leonard was a boarder at St Andrew's College, Aurora, Ont., at this time, having won a Leonard Foundation Scholarship.

TO DESMOND PACEY

R.R. 4 Simcoe, Ont.
February 28, 1945

Dear Pacey,

I have the ms. of the ant-book (which is hardly a title, is it?), still unopened, but...

25 Carleton Stanley. *Courtesy Mrs C.W. Stanley*

I shall make an attempt to place it. Macmillans are afraid of it.[1] Ryersons I no longer trust.[2]

I have now reread some 50 or 60 essays and short stories, condemning some, putting the others back into their drawers. Also 8 novels, of which I have fed 4 into the fire, leaving

'The Canyon'
'Jane Atkinson' (western stories)
'Two Lives' (Ontario, good in the skeleton, doubtful in the flesh)
'Felix Powell's Career' (college youth; ms. belonging to my wife, to do with as she pleases; the extreme of sex)

apart from the ant-book, and autobiography which I may destroy, at least partly, for I don't think anybody would be interested in the European part; I am not.

There are still two drawers unexplored, in my desk. Since you are my biographer, apart from Eaton's 'Thesis,'[3] I thought it well to let you know these facts. The above novels I do not intend to offer.

Re ant-book: do you think I should leave the introduction (24 pages) or start with Wawa-quee's narrative? There is also a 4-vol[ume] novel: 'The Seasons' (Ontario) which I have not yet run across.

Sincerely yours,
F.P.G.

1 They did publish it two years later as *Consider Her Ways*.
2 Relations between Grove and Pierce had cooled over what Grove considered the latter's procrastination over his manuscripts, especially *The Master of the Mill*. See letters of July 12, 1941, and March 8 and June 26, 1944.
3 See the letter of March 18, 1945.

TO DESMOND PACEY

R.R. 4 Simcoe, Ont.
March 18, 1945

Dear Pacey,

The title is,

THE LIFE AND WORKS
OF
FREDERICK PHILIP GROVE
BY
CHARLES E. EATON
WOLFVILLE 1940
(In partial fulfilment of requirements for
the Master in Arts degree)
Acadia University

This in hurry to fulfil your wish.[1] More another time.
Sincerely,
F.P.G.

1 Grove had mentioned this thesis in his letter of February 28, 1945, and I was anxious to include it in the bibliography of my *Frederick Philip Grove* (1945), then in press.

TO ELLEN ELLIOTT

R.R. 4 Simcoe, Ont.
May 3, 1945

Dear Miss Elliott,

The case of *A Search for America* stands as follows:[1]

The book is not out of print (Ryerson Press, 4th edition, $1.50). They bought the copyright in 1938, meaning to bring out a collected ed[ition] of all my works. *But* I have the copperplates for which, after Montreal litigation, I paid $300. This is the fine U.S.A. edition. Ryersons bought sheets which I owned; but not the plates.

No doubt it would be possible to produce a very cheap edition with their help. I am willing to sell the plates for what they cost me, though I should still be ca. $1500 out on the total transactions.

I am most anxious to do something about it, being desperately hard up for money. Can you help me by advice if not by action? Give me, f[or] i[nstance] names and addresses of committee members?[2]

Thanks for enquiry after my health. The winter has set me back very badly. But...

With best wishes, as ever,
Yours,
F.P. Grove

1 Miss Elliott had written, on May 2, about *A Search for America*, saying, 'I believe that you own the copyright.'
2 ie, the Committee for Grades X and XI English texts in Ontario, who had selected *A Search for America* as a required text provided that the book was kept in print. At the bottom of this letter Miss Elliott wrote: 'Hate to pass the business on to Ryers. – but they'd never relinquish copyright to us.'

TO PELHAM EDGAR

R.R. 4 Simcoe, Ont.
May 27, 1945

Dear Dr. Edgar,

I must thank you most heartily for your letter of the 23rd[1] which relieved me very much, the more so since I have just had to borrow $125 to complete a mortgage payment of $225, toward which I had been able to save only $100 during the past year.

Thanks also for your enquiry re my health. The terrible winter had set me back sorely. My daily walk, which had reached 1 mile by December 10, dwindled in February to zero and has not yet exceeded 750 feet, in 3 instalments; it is even now more difficult than 7 times that much in the fall; yet my doctor says that there is progress. If I could afford a stenographer, I should be writing a new book. As it is, I must be satisfied with waking up from day to day.

My wife thanks you for remembering her and reciprocates your greeting. We quite recently talked of our last meeting at Maud Grant's[2] house in Toronto.

With my best wishes,
Yours sincerely,
F.P. Grove

1 Which explained the delay in remitting 'the balance of ... $100 for this month,' and assured Grove of $100 for each of the months of May, June, and July.
2 Wife of William Lawson Grant; see letter of April 2, 1928 II, note 1.

TO WINNIFRED EAYRS

R.R. 4 Simcoe, Ont.
May 31, 1945

Dear Miss Eayrs,

Your note of March 26 re the ms. of the *Master of the Mill* reached me promptly; but apparently my answer, as prompt, did not reach you. I said that I should be much obliged if you would return the Ms. to me.

Thank you very much for clearing this up.
Sincerely yours,
F.P.G.

TO WILFRID EGGLESTON[1]

R.R. 4 Simcoe, Ont.
June 25, 1945

Dear Mr. Eggleston,

Thanks for your letter of the 10th.

I can't reply so fully; just a line or so.

We remember you and Mrs. Eggleston quite well and have occasionally thought and talked of you.

No; I have no copies of the prairie essays left except my own. But no doubt they'll come out again some time. *The Master of the Mill* is sold out. But I get only $100 out of it, in November; and that was spent before I heard of its success. I had to borrow more than that to avoid foreclosure on my place.

Excuse my brevity. It cost me an hour to do that much.
Best regards for you and Mrs. Eggleston,
Sincerely,
F.P.G.

1 Wilfrid Eggleston, a graduate of Queen's University (BA 1926), was born in England in 1901. After some four years of high-school teaching, he began his journalistic career in 1924 with the *Lethbridge Herald*. In 1926, he joined the staff of the Toronto *Star*, becoming its Ottawa Correspondent in 1929. During the War, he served as Chief Press Censor (1940–3) and Director of Censorship (1944) in Canada. He has published a volume of his verse (*Prairie Moonlight and Other Lyrics*, 1927), a novel (*The High Plains*, 1938), a book of literary criticism (*The Frontier and Canadian Letters*, 1957), a book of reminiscences (*While I Still Remember*, 1968), and several books on current affairs, and has edited *The Green Gables Letters, from L.M. Montgomery to Ephraim Weber* (1960). He is a past president of the Parliamentary Press Gallery and professor emeritus of journalism at Carleton University.

He and his wife were close friends of the Groves during the Groves' stay in Ottawa (1929–31). This letter, the only one Grove wrote to Eggleston, was in response to an enquiry about copies of *Over Prairie Trails* and *The Turn of the Year*.

Eggleston participated in the Grove Symposium held at the University of Ottawa in May 1973, and his reminiscences of Grove's Ottawa years are published in *Inscape* XI (Spring 1974) 101–10.

TO LORNE PIERCE

R.R. 4 Simcoe, Ont.
July 29, 1945

Dear Dr. Pierce,

Thanks for sending me the monograph.[1] I like its appearance very much.

My wife read the first few chapters and approved of them. I read a few critical passages. I did not agree and thought that the author did not get my intention; but, as I wrote him perhaps a year ago, anything I have written and published is fair game; and I do not intend to interfere with impressions or opinions. On the whole, I think it a workmanlike performance. It appropriately buries me or embalms me.

Thanks again.
Sincerely yours,
F.P.G.

1 *My Frederick Philip Grove* (Ryerson 1945). For Grove's comments to me on the book, see the following letter.

TO DESMOND PACEY

R.R. 4 Simcoe, Ont.
August 26, 1945

Dear Pacey,

I had recently a second stroke which, for the time being, deprived me of my speech and generally set me back.

I know my wife wrote to you, but don't know what.[1] She is not at home just now; so I can't ask her. I should like to say a few things; so I struggle with the typewriter.

Suppose I had had your criticisms while writing my books and had adopted them all; then my books would have been your books, not mine. I therefore welcome your criticisms, with some of which I agree; with others, not. Occasionally I feel that out of my strength you have made my weakness; but that does not matter. On the whole I feel rather flattered that you should have felt the books to be of sufficient importance to discuss them, for I feel somehow that your book is very honest; though I also feel occasionally that you overestimate my importance, flatteringly. But I wish to thank you. I hope the book will find many readers. I hear that something is being translated into French (*Gants du Ciel*).[2] My wife feels 'bucked.' Poor girl. I shall likely have to give up my fellowship in the Royal Society, for I can't afford the fees. However ... Will you be in our neighbourhood? It is over a year since I have seen any visitor. The last one, strange, was a Swede; the last but one, a German Professor of English (1938)[3] who told me that all my works were in the libraries of Berlin and Munich. No Canadian has come since W.J. Alexander (1932).

Sincerely,
F.P.G.[4]

1 The reference is to Mrs Grove's letter of August 3, 1945, in which she wrote: 'I think you have done the author justice as no other critic has. I agree entirely with your criticism of his women. I used to argue with him over that – also over his treatment of sex. In fact I once got him started to write a novel dealing with a normal, happy marriage, but he did not finish. I tried very hard to keep Nancy out of *Two Generations*, but without success.'

2 *Gants du Ciel* was a literary magazine, founded in 1943 and edited by Guy Sylvestre (b1918), now the National Librarian. It ran till 1946. W.E. Collin wrote an article on Grove, which Sylvestre translated, and it appeared as 'La Tragique Ironie de Frederick Philip Grove' in the Winter 1946 (no. 10) issue of the magazine.

3 Gustav Hübener; see letter of February 27, 1939, note 1.

4 My August 29 reply to this letter is preserved in the University of Manitoba Grove Collection. It said in part: 'I should very much like to see you, but do not expect to be in Ontario before next summer at the earliest. I am very pleased that the book seems to you honest. ... You think I was too flattering – I think on the whole I was too severe. Who can tell? All I know is that your books interest me even when I think they are at fault, that my instinct or taste ... tells me they have staying power.'

TO DESMOND PACEY

R.R. 4 Simcoe, Ont.
September 3, 1945

Dear Pacey,

Just a word in answer to yours of Aug[ust] 29. *The Master* sold out within two months, in 1000 copies; that was all Macmillans would risk. I had a limited edition of 400 copies most of which remain on my hands. As usual, to me the book is a loss. Perhaps it is lucky that I have nothing that can be taken from me.

What they are translating into French, I don't know, except that they asked me, through Ed Collin,[1] for *Fruits of the Earth*.

'Who is there?'[2] Well, there is E.J. Pratt. As for the 'Ant book,' I intend to offer it to Reg Saunders.[3] Macmillans don't want it.

Sorry, that's all I can write.
Sincerely,
F.P.G.

1 See the preceding letter, note 2.
2 The context of this quotation is my letter to Grove of August 29, in which I had said: 'I should like to write another book on another Canadian writer. But who is there?'
3 S.J. Reginald Saunders & Co. of Toronto, who declined, but Macmillan, as has been noted before, did publish the 'Ant-book' (ie, *Consider Her Ways*) in 1947.

TO CARLETON STANLEY

R.R. 4 Simcoe, Ont.
November 3, 1945

Dear Stanley,

For several months I have been wanting to drop you a line; but I did not know where to address and hesitated about making use of the university against which I now bear a grudge, especially since they want to shut up the review.[1]

Yesterday I received your most welcome letter and should have answered it at once but that I am unable, after the first hour or so of the day, to use the one finger which I need to pound the typewriter. I will, therefore, answer first the one question which I am very anxious to settle. Would you be in Toronto between Dec[ember] 20 and Jan[uary] 6? You would be most welcome any time; but between those dates we should be very glad to have you at the house for a few days. The house will at that time be empty apart from my boy and ourselves. Plenty of beds etc. available. My wife says she'll be delighted. At any other time you'd have to stay in town, though, of course, we'd be glad to have you take your meals with me in my room. Best way to reach us from Toronto: C.P.R. to Galt; at Galt, next track, Radial to P[or]t Dover, takes you in 1 hour to Simcoe. Get off, before you get to Simcoe, at Windham Road which is 500 steps east of my house. Ask the conductor for Old Windham Church which is directly north of my farm. Anybody in that neighbourhood knows me. If we know the time of your arrival, somebody will be there to meet you. It is a flag station.

Now a word about Pacey. I don't know him. About 5 years ago, he wrote me; and I have since answered a score of letters of his; but refused to read the critical part of his book till it was printed. Ryerson's asked me for names of people who might be interested. Among those I sent them no doubt was yours. As for that critical part of the book, there is much with which I disagree, and I wrote Pacey this, adding that, of course, anybody had the right to his own opinion, and adding also that, on the whole, I feel that too great an importance is attributed to anything I may have done.

I shall be very glad to send you the Ms. of my autobiography, enclosing your copy of the *Dalhousie Review*. I have at present no intention of publishing that autobiography during my life time. So you can return it at your convenience.

Re your review of *The Master of the Mill*,[2] I again feel, as I did in the case of 'Len Sterner,'[3] that you read out of it more than I wrote into it, though I will say this that the first version (1934) was straight narrative, in 1300 pages, and that, during the five years following, while I put it into its present form, I reduced it, through that form, to 400 pages. It sold out, by the way, apart from the limited edition which was a flop, within 2 months. It so happens that this morning I received $109 as my royalty. If the publishers had had the courage to print 5000 copies, they would have sold them, giving me 5 times as much. However, I never wrote for money in my life. And never made money.

To write this, took 2 hours, so you must excuse me. I should have liked to ask you many questions about yourself; but I must postpone them. I shall have to lie down.

Best wishes. As ever, yours,
F.P.G.

1 In his letter of October 24, 1945, Carleton Stanley had hinted that the *Dalhousie Review* was to be discontinued. Stanley took a special interest in the *Review* during the fourteen years he was at Dalhousie, and might have been discouraged about its future because he himself was leaving that university. But so far as can be ascertained, the *Review* did not face any special problem at this time, and it survives to this day.

2 It appeared in the *Dalhousie Review* xxv (1945) 173–81, and extracts from it are reprinted in my *Frederick Philip Grove* (Critical Views on Canadian Writers 1970) 116–17.

3 ie, *The Yoke of Life*

TO CHARLES CLAY[1]

R.R. 4 Simcoe, Ont.
November 6, 1945

Dear Sir,

I wish to thank you for your kind letter of the 1st inst[ant], telling me that I can look forward to the receipt of the Foundation's November grant.[2] You probably know that I have been ill for nearly two years and am unable to use my hands, except one finger, even for signing my name.

Sincerely yours,
F.P.G.

1 Charles Gray (b1906), author of such novels as *Young Voyageur* (1938), *Fur Trade Apprentice* (1940), and *Muskrat Man* (1946), and collector of Indian folk tales (*Swampy Cree Legends*, 1938), was the secretary of the Canadian Writers Foundation from April 12, 1945 to March 12, 1946.

2 The payments had continued, in the meanwhile, every month at $100: Clay's letter had apologised that there would be a few days' delay over the November cheque.

TO PELHAM EDGAR

R.R. 4 Simcoe, Ont.
November 15, 1945

Dear Dr. Edgar,

Thank you for your charming letter[1] of the 9th inst[ant].

Indeed, I do not object in any way to my name's being used in your drive for funds. I can only say that without your grants, in my present helpless state, I don't know what would have happened to me; and while I personally blame only myself for my poverty and feel that I should have written in such a way as to compel a material success which would rather have enabled me to be one of your donors than one of your beneficiaries, still I am very grateful to you and your collaborators and, yes, honoured by your interest in my plight.

Sincerely yours,
Frederick Philip Grove
F.P.G.[2]

1 Edgar had written: 'I hope you will be without all worry about your monthly cheque ... We are very proud to be able to be of use to you, and I hope that you will get some satisfaction from the fact that your noble work is appreciated and recognized. It would make our financial drive more simple if we had your permission to tell prospective donors that you are one of the beneficiaries. ... If I were such I think I should consider it an honour. ...' He concludes by saying that, naturally, the Foundation will not do anything of this kind without Grove's permission.

2 The initials have been added in Grove's handwriting to the typescript letter.

TO CARLETON STANLEY

R.R. 4 Simcoe, Ont.
November 19, 1945

Dear Stanley,

When I answered your first recent letter to me, I wished to tell you of a coincidence; but before I got around to it, I was exhausted and left it. Your second letter made me think that it *would* interest you after all.

I have only a few books (perhaps 500); and so I read them over and over again, they being the best of 4 or 5 literatures. Alongside my typrwriter lay 2 volumes: 1 of Thucydides, open at the page of the plague. In taking it down from my shelves, I had taken the volume next to it, not knowing what it was; when, after writing my answer to you, I sat down in my chair and opened it, I found it to be your *Roots*.[1] My impulse was to return to my letter. But, as I said, I was too tired and let it go. I have since reread it, to my great delight, especially Thucydides, Science, and Lucretius. I thought it might please you; so here is the coincidence.

With best wishes, as ever, yours,
F.P.G.

1 *Roots of the Tree* (1936), a book of essays on classical literature and culture by Carleton Stanley

TO FRANK FLEMINGTON

R.R. 4 Simcoe, Ont.
November 22, 1945

Dear Mr. Flemington,

Of course, there is nobody who can give more information[1] about Graphic than myself; and since I manoeuvred to get Knister the prize (at least the award, if not all the money), and he came here at my suggestion and worked part of the time on my farm, there is perhaps nobody who knew him more intimately during the last two years of his life than did I.

But you know I am paralysed and cannot write. This little note costs me many hours and unbelievable effort.

So you will have to excuse me.
Sincerely yours,
F.P. Grove

1 The letter from Flemington, of November 19, had asked (1) about the Graphic Press and (2) about Raymond Knister's biographical novel on John Keats, *My Star Predominant*, which won the award in a novel contest sponsored by Graphic in 1930. The Ryerson editors were, at this time, considering publication of a collection of Knister's poems with a memoir, which they eventually published in 1949 (edited by Dorothy Livesay).

TO DESMOND PACEY

R.R. 4 Simcoe, Ont.
November 24, 1945

Dear Pacey,

Thanks for the off-print.[1]

I am getting worse. I don't believe any longer that I'll recover. But...

I've been wanting to tell you that Carleton Stanley applauds your book, though he disagrees with your criticism. He (as did W.J. Alexander) places *The Yoke of Life* first, as a novel and calls it 'great.' As for the philosophy, he says, 'When will North-Americans begin to catch up with the thought of F.P. Grove?' I believe he would like to write another book;[2] he announces his prospective visit. Since I am fond of him, I look forward to it (probably in Jan[uary]).

I am sorry; this exhausts me.

Sincerely,
F.P.G.

1 I am not now sure what this offprint was, but it probably was my article, 'The Novel in Canada,' *Queen's Quarterly* LII (1945) 322–31.

2 Carleton Stanley did, indeed, write a book on Grove, for I read the typescript for the Humanities Research Council, from whom a grant in aid of publication was sought. It stressed the classical influences on Grove. Unfortunately it was turned down by various publishers, including Macmillan and the Ryerson Press. An enquiry made of Dr Stanley by me on April 21, 1969 – 'I remember hearing rumours some twenty years ago that you were writing a book on Frederick Philip Grove ... if a manuscript is available, I should like to examine it' – elicited the following reply: 'Dear Dr Pacey: Please excuse this scribble. The rumour is incorrect. Yours faithfully, Carleton Stanley.' However, a copy of the manuscript has apparently survived, and is now in the possession of Stanley's sister-in-law, Mrs Edith McIver of Caledon East, Ontario.

TO FRANK FLEMINGTON

R.R. 4 Simcoe, Ont.
November 26, 1945

Dear Mr. Flemington,

It so happens that it would be inconvenient this week.[1] After Dec[ember] 3 it will be all right if the stenographer can understand me. I think I have quite a story to tell.

Sincerely,
F.P.G.

1 See letter of November 22 to Flemington, who had replied, on November 24, suggesting that Pierce and he would visit Grove, accompanied by a stenographer, to get Grove's version of the Graphic story.

TO CARLETON STANLEY

R.R. 4 Simcoe, Ont.
November 28, 1945

Dear Stanley,

No, I am sorry, I cannot find a carbon copy of my autobiography. No doubt it was destroyed together with the scores of Mss. which I have burned in the last seven years. There were trunks full; there still are suitcases full. For I cannot restrain myself from glancing at them as I feed them to the flames.

I spent a sleepless night over your remark about all my books being classics. For I do not see it that way, though when I wrote them I thought so: and up to a few years ago I still had the hope that there was something good and valuable in them. But just consider these facts: till Alexander's death, there were perhaps half a dozen men who thought somewhat as you do; that number has now dwindled to yourself, Pacey, and Sandwell, of the *Saturday Night*. In 7 years one person has called on me; and he a German engaged in writing a book on Empire literature.[1] As for success in the ordinary sense, I have a pension of $100 from the Canadian Writers' Foundation. If it were not for that, I'd long ago have starved were it not for the fact that my wife feeds me. When I need a haircut or a box of matches, I sometimes wait for weeks before I can manage it. Fortunately I have a little library which I read over and over, being unable to go to the public library. During two years I made a little money: by lecturing and editorial work (1928 and 1930). Fortunately again, I saved every penny and bought the place where I live, paying cash all but $3000 which I owe; this debt takes $225 a year. My little boy (15 years old) is at St. Andrews College, largely on a Leonard Scholarship[2] which I was lucky enough to secure on my reputation. As for my books, all but 2 vol[ume]s are out of print, the stocks having been sold as remainders. Even *A Search for America* has cost me about $1500 to date, though 34000 copies were sold.[3] No book except *Our Daily Bread* has ever brought me more than $100; it brought $500, because I was lecturing at the time. My income in fifty years has averaged $150 as I figured out recently. Most of it was earned by hard physical labour; which I should be doing now if I had not had my strokes which no doubt are the direct consequence of it, because I always had to work beyond my strength. My wife now keeps boarders (what I call idiot children, sent her by a U.S.A. psychiatrist, a thing I hate.[)]

As for the *Search for America*, one word of explanation: the Canadian publishers went bankrupt; the American publishers the same; and next the English publishers (Brentanos). In every case, fool that I was, I bought back the rights from the receivers. The present publishers, Ryersons, bought 2000 copies from me for $300,[4] and my total royalties on all my books are less than $2.00 a year.

This has wormed me for so many years, that here I have burst out, for the first time in my life. That is why I don't take comfort any longer from 'immortality.' Excuse and forgive me; but I simply don't believe it any longer. My wife simply laughs. If Sandwell had written his article two years ago,[5] she said when she read it, I'd never have had the strokes.

Well, as I said, forgive me. I am, as usual, at the end of my strength.

Don't let this disturb you. No, *Ça vous amuse, la vie?*[6] is just something I used to say when I still liked to speak French. I still say it today. I could go on for days and weeks. Better not.

With best wishes,
as ever, yours,
F.P.G.

1 Gustav Hübener; see letter of February 27, 1939.
2 Offered by the Leonard Foundation, created by Lt Col. and Mrs R.W. Leonard, of St Catharines, Ontario, and reserved for Anglicans
3 Its failure to bring in a good return, as Grove explains later in this letter, was due to the heavy personal investment he made in the book. For example, in October 1947, his wife offered 200 copies of *A Search for America* to Lorne Pierce at 25c a copy, which the latter declined. Evidently, Grove had bought the entire unsold stock at cost price when Graphic went into liquidation. The copper plates of the Carrier edition, bought for $300, were sold in 1947 as scrap-metal for $100. Investments like these may account for the net deficit of some $1500.
4 For details of that particular sale, see letter of December 8, 1938, note 1.
5 B.K. Sandwell's review article on my book on Grove appeared in *Saturday Night* LXI (November 24, 1945), 18, and is reprinted in my *Frederick Philip Grove* (Critical Views on Canadian Writers 1970) 56–9.
6 Isn't life funny? – the motto on the title-page of *In Search of Myself*

TO CARLETON STANLEY

R.R. 4 Simcoe, Ont.
November 29, 1945

Dear Stanley,

I am sorry I wrote yesterday's letter, the more so as, in another sleepless night, it occurred to me that it was liable to misinterpretation. Of course, I did not mean to suggest that those who ascribe a considerable importance to my work were not perfectly sincere but rather that they are mistaken through a hidden similarity of their minds to my own. My belief is that, as my books have fought their way against an ever increasing resistance, they will gradually succumb and disappear as if they had never been written. I see their shortcomings more clearly than anyone else, than, let me say, Mrs. Skelton;[1] and I fully expect that they will prevail more and more.

Keep the Ms. as long as you like. There is no ghost of a chance anyway of any publisher's wanting to print it. I believe there are a few things in it which are good; but I also believe that, the 3 or 4 people who have read it, having approved, it has served its purpose. Who else would want to hear about me? I have still 8 vol[ume]s unpublished, and for my wife's sake and my boy's, I have forced myself to offer them. No; nobody wants them. They come back to me with amazing speed.

But I must not neglect any possibility; I have no life insurance; and I see the time coming when my wife will be as penurious as I have been.

Forget and forgive. As ever,
F.P.G.

1 A reference to Isabel Skelton's 'Frederick Philip Grove' in the *Dalhousie Review* XIX (July 1939), 147–63 – reprinted in my *Frederick Philip Grove* (Critical Views on Canadian Writers 1970) 24–44

TO FRANK FLEMINGTON

R.R. 4 Simcoe, Ont.
December 6, 1945

Dear Mr. Flemington,[1]

Directions;

1) by rail (a) Toronto-Galt (immediate connection, radial[2] waiting). Radial to Port Dover. After passing Waterford, watch. Get off at Windham Road. Straight west to church (afoot). Next house south is mine. (b) Toronto-Brantford (Radial station a mile from CNR station). Taxi. Take radial as above.

2) By car (A) Brantford. SW corner of city, HW#24 to south to Waterford-Bloomsberg. 2 more miles. Watch for small church to right. Next house (immediately beyond church). (B) Hamilton. South via #6 to Jarvis. #3 west to Simcoe ... Don't enter town. North on #24 for ca. 2 miles. Cedar-spruce grove with cream-coloured house brown trimmings. Mine. Church just beyond. Total drive 3 h[ou]rs.

Excuse brevity.
Sincerely,
F.P.G.

1 Flemington had written again, on December 4, reiterating his suggestion of a stenographer. See letter of November 26, 1945.
2 An electric railway system; see note 2 to letter of January 24, 1943.

TO ELLEN ELLIOTT

R.R. 4 Simcoe, Ont.
December 7, 1945

Dear Miss Elliott,

I believe it is the moment to make use of the sudden burst of fame that has come upon me. Dr. Pierce announces his forthcoming visit here. I should like to say to him that he [comes] too late.

Would you consider the 'Ant-book'[1] now? It is only 300 pages. Several critics are clamouring for it. I believe it would be the literary event of the year. I should follow it up with my autobiography which, however[,] is a long book. Dr. Stanley tells me that he considers it my greatest work.

Ryersons are making capital out of what is happening. I have before me an offer of 'Collected Works.'[2] I have never trusted them, however. Yet....

Please let me know about
'Ants, A Novel'
With best regards,
as ever, yours,
F.P.G.

1 ie, *Consider Her Ways*, first mentioned in a letter to Watson Kirkconnell (January 11, 1927), and intermittently thereafter; offered to several publishers including Ryerson. The 'burst of fame' was occasioned by the appearance of *The Master of the Mill* and my first book on Grove. Canadian books of merit were far more infrequent in those days, and my study of Grove was given feature-length reviews in all major newspapers and occasioned review articles in such magazines as *Queen's Quarterly*, *Dalhousie Review*, *Saturday Night*, and the *Canadian Forum*. *The Master of the Mill* also received a very good press and Grove was once more in the public eye.

2 No offer for a collected edition of Grove's works appears to have been made at this time, although Grove and Pierce had corresponded about such an edition in the late thirties and very early in the forties.

TO ELLEN ELLIOTT

R.R. 4 Simcoe, Ont.
December 10, 1945

Dear Miss Elliott,

Thank you so much for your letter of the 7th. If anything can put me on my feet again, it is the fact that you will publish the 'Ant-book' and the autobiography.[1]

The latter, by the way, was finished in 1939. Dr. Carleton Stanley and the Alexander girls have just read it. They say, 'We hardly know where to begin about the Autobiography. It is so big, so moving and noble, so Aeschylean ... no, when you do remind me of books, my mind goes back to Thucydides, Job, Tolstoi ...

We consider it greater than any of your published books...'

Let us talk again of 'Collected Works' two years from now. So far, with regard to both books, I shall indeed say, 'It is too late.'[2]

I enclose Sandwell's article[3] which is the only thing I can lay my hand on just now for advertising purposes; but I also consider it the best.

I'll send the 'Ants' in two or 3 days. I had cancelled the preface; and I want to add, instead, an appendix (not more than 3 pages). If I find that I cannot do the latter in a day or 2 I'll leave it to follow later.

Personally I feel sure that the ant-book will be a big success, now. Sandwell has set everybody talking – more than Pacey.

I must close and rest.
As ever, yours,
F.P.G.

1 Miss Elliott had written: 'Now, with *The Master of the Mill* at last on the market and fame at last in your lap, we ought to do the 'Ant' book, and I think we should be failing you if we didn't ... Ibby and I are thrilled to know that you are working on your autobiography, and we'll publish that too just as soon as you tell us it is ready.' Ibby (Mrs. Blochin) was Miss Elliott's assistant.

2 To Lorne Pierce; see also letter of December 7, 1945. Miss Elliott in her letter referred to above had written: 'I do hope that you will tell Lorne Pierce that it is too late ... and I'd give almost anything to be there with you and hear you say it.'

3 B.K. Sandwell's 'Frederick Philip Grove and the Culture of Canada' in *Saturday Night* LXI (November 24, 1945), a review article devoted to my 1945 monograph on Grove. It is a very sympathetic critique of Grove's intentions and shortcomings, explained in terms of 'the immaturity of Canadian culture.' The article is reprinted in my *Frederick Philip Grove* (Critical Views on Canadian Writers 1970) 56ff.

TO CARLETON STANLEY

R.R. 4 Simcoe, Ont.
December 11, 1945

Dear Stanley,

Just a word to say that, to my surprise, Macmillans have offered to print my 'Ants, A Novel' in 1946 and my autobiography a year later. Shall I cancel the European part in the latter?

Sincerely,
F.P.G.

TO PELHAM EDGAR

R.R. 4 Simcoe, Ont.
December 11, 1945 11

Dear Dr. Edgar,

The National Trust cheque arrived together with your note of the 8th. Thanks very much. A further windfall came through 109 dollars royalty on *The Master of the Mill*. It seems a paltry sum for 14 years of work. Yet, for the first time, it enables me to have a small reserve.

Will you take and hand on to your associates of the Foundation, my heartiest thanks for the help given me during the year? I might also mention that my son, last fall, won a scholarship for a year at St. Andrew's. If now I could feel sure that my wife would look forward to a competence, I might die in peace, though I am not ready to die, in spite of all my disabilities.

Please take my best greetings of the season.

Sincerely yours,
F.P.G.

TO DESMOND PACEY

R.R. 4 Simcoe, Ont.
December 14, 1945

Dear Pacey,

We cannot afford Christmas cards, So here are our best wishes of the season.

No, I am not aware of a new printing of the *Master*.[1] As for *Fruits of the Earth*, Ryersons bought the remainder in 1938. I get nothing out of it. Someone sent me the *Saturday Night* of Nov[ember] 24.[2] Stanley is reviewing your book in the Jan[uary] *Dalhousie Review*,[3] so he writes me. My total royalty on the *Master* was $109 for 14 y[ea]rs work. But I have sold the 'Ants.'[4] That's something. Macmillans want the autobiography.[5] I don't know.

However...

Sincerely yours,
F.P.G.

I had yesterday the most painful day since my illness: hands and mouth. Horrible. Do you know that my boy won a scholarship for a year at St. Andrew's. I expect him home next Wednesday. First in Latin, French, and Greek, so far.

1 The second impression; see letter of February 1, 1946, note 1.

2 I had offered to send him B.K. Sandwell's review article (see letter of November 28, 1945, note 5) if he had not already seen it.

3 The review appeared in the *Dalhousie Review* xxv (1946) 433–41.
4 *Consider Her Ways* (Macmillan 1947)
5 *In Search of Myself* (Macmillan 1946)

TO ELLEN ELLIOTT

R.R. 4 Simcoe, Ont.
December 14, 1945 II

Dear Miss Elliott,

Thanks for your letter of the 12th.

My wife would be very happy to have the contracts. As for 'Ants,' a complete Ms. has gone forward. The 'Autobiography'[1] is with Dr. Carleton Stanley. I shall send when it gets back. He is preparing an article about me for the *Dalhousie Review*.[2]

Pierce has not yet been here but announces that he will bring his assistant – which makes me laugh. I know he wants a Collected Works. He won't get it. Hurrah!

Let me give you and Mrs. Blochin the best greetings of the season. But I look forward to the contracts. Pierce, by the way, says I should have 15%, which also makes me laugh since he is selling *Fruits of the Earth*, having bought the whole remainder, 459 copies, for $135. But, no doubt, says Stanley, there will be money made out of my books when I'm dead. I am saving up for my funeral.

As ever, sincerely yours,
F.P.G.

P.S. Somewhere I have drawings for jacket etc. but can't find them.

1 Published as *In Search of Myself* (1946)
2 See the preceding letter, note 3. Grove seems to have had difficulty in realizing that Stanley's article about him and his review of my monograph were one and the same thing: see letter of March 29, 1946, and notes 1 and 3 to that letter.

TO CARLETON STANLEY

R.R. 4 Simcoe, Ont.
December 20, 1945

Dear Stanley,

Just a word to send you and yours the best greetings of the season for Christmas and the best wishes for the coming year.

For myself I merely desire less pain.

I have reread 7 of my books and liked 1 of them and outright disliked 2.

Hoping to see you in the near future, I am,
Sincerely yours,
F.P.G.

TO ELLEN ELLIOTT

R.R. 4 Simcoe, Ont.
December 24, 1945

Dear Miss Elliott,

Thanks, thanks, thanks!

Should I not have a copy [of] each of the contracts?[1]

Some Christmas!

I am searching for the drawings for 'Ants.' If I find them before mailing this, I'll enclose them. If not, they'll follow as soon as possible. The Ms. of 'My Life' will follow as soon as I get it back. I did find a carbon copy, but it is very bad; and it is without the corrections of the last five years. It is 367 typed pages of my usual typing.

Many thanks also for the fruit to 'ALL THE MACMILLANS.'

As for the Mss. for reading, you are quite mistaken.[2] I have welcomed even the worst, because every one has meant sugar in my coffee.

Now the happiest New Year for you, Ibby,[3] and all of you.

As ever, yours,
F.P.G.

NB. The other party[4] has not yet turned up, though I get a letter every few days, telling me of the rush which will soon be over now. I'd like a copy of the contracts so as merely to show them, instead of saying anything.

1 Macmillan offered, for *Consider Her Ways*, 10% up to 1500 copies, 12½% up to 2500 copies, and 15% thereafter. On the autobiography, they offered a straight 15% with an advance of $500.

2 Miss Elliott had expressed the fear that at times 'the sight of another manuscript must have irritated you beyond words' – a reference to Grove's reading of manuscripts for Macmillan.

3 Mrs Blochin, Miss Elliott's second-in-command

4 Lorne Pierce; see letter of December 10, 1945, note 2.

TO ELLEN ELLIOTT

R.R. 4 Simcoe, Ont.
December 31, 1945

Dear Miss Elliott,

Tomorrow is 1946. Best luck.

I have had here Dr. Carleton Stanley for the last three days. He will bring you the Ms. of 'My Life.'

As for the drawings, I simply cannot find them and must presume them lost in the upset of my illness. I have not yet said anything about bindings. I should like: *plum-coloured cloth*, quite plain, with a monogram as enclosed.[1] The 'Ant-book,' if possible, with many ants in the background of the monogram; if you can secure Wheeler, *Ants*,[2] page 17, number 1 would do. A very heavy book; but I could not send it to you. I want to cancel the appendix of the ant-book and replace the first 23 pages with a few changes, for which I need another few days.

Many thanks for that ten-spot. As for the 500 advance,[3] it paid for 200 debt and leaves 300 reserve to which I shall try to hold on.

As ever, yours sincerely
F.P.G.

1 A rather shaky drawing of the same design that was enclosed in the letter to Pierce, of February 15, 1939.
2 W.M. Wheeler, *Ants: Their Structure, Development and Behaviour*, 1910 (reprinted 1913) – referred to in *Consider Her Ways*
3 See the previous letter, note 1.

TO ELLEN ELLIOTT

R.R. 4 Simcoe, Ont.
January 5, 1946

Dear Miss Elliott,

I have yours of January 2 and wish to thank you. I agree with Dr. Stanley that the off-print 'In Search of Myself'[1] would make a very fine prologue for 'My Life' and I am sending you therefore a second copy. As for the manuscript, Stanley tells me that there are many pencil marks of mine and of his in the text. Would it not be best to return it to me for a few days? I'll try to hurry it up.

As ever
Yours sincerely,
F.P.G.

1 Which had appeared in the *University of Toronto Quarterly* x (October 1940) 60–7. It is reprinted as a 'Prologue' to his autobiography, which had not yet been given its final title.

TO CARLETON STANLEY

R.R. 4 Simcoe, Ont.
January 5, 1946 II[1]

Dear Stanley,

Thanks for yours of January 3. I agree with all your suggestions and have asked Miss Elliott to return me the manuscript[2] so there won't be too many corrections in the proofs which are expensive. Thanks also for the Duhamel.[3] Unfortunately I have a big editorial job on for Macmillans. So it will be a few days before I get around to the *Défense des Lettres*. I have a bad case of pink eye and can hardly see.

Best wishes for you and all of yours.
Sincerely,
F.P.G.

1 In the original, the year is shown as 1945, but the matters covered belong to January 1946.
2 Of *In Search of Myself*
3 Georges Duhamel (b1884), the French novelist (and incidentally poet, essayist, and dramatist), who was named perpetual secretary of the French Academy. His *Défense des lettres* was published in 1937. An English translation by E.F. Bozman appeared in 1938.

TO ELLEN ELLIOTT

R.R. 4 Simcoe, Ont.
January 7, 1946

Dear Miss Elliott,

Having just written the enclosed brief report,[1] I receive yours of the 5th. I believe I have answered all your questions before this.[2] Yes, I believe, in order to save proof corrections, I had better look over the text of the autobiography before letting it go to press.

Yes, by all means, if you can manage, come down and cheer me up.

As ever, yours,
F.P.G.

1 Reader's report on W.G. Hardy's *Our Path Emerges*. For Hardy, see letter of January 29, 1945, note 1.
2 See letter of January 5, 1946.

TO CARLETON STANLEY

R.R. 4 Simcoe, Ont.
January 9, 1946[1]

Dear Stanley,

I should and would have written you sooner had I not had to make an important decision for Macmillans. Then I read Duhamel,[2] once completely, the second time leaving out the parts dealing with the cinema and *la radiophonie*.[3] Meanwhile Leonard was still at home. He leaves this morning for school, somewhat strengthened, I hope, in algebra. So I am again, as usually, very lonesome. Glad to hear that you don't think all those short things mere trash. I had pretty well come to regard them such. But it is many years since I wrote or even read them. This morning something you said about Ellen in the haystack in *Settlers* sent me at 3 a.m. to look for the book; and I read the two chapters 'Niels and Ellen' [–] melting at my own coals.

Duhamel I found better than several other books of his I have read. Yet I thought it somewhat disjointed.

This minute came your letter of the 8th. Too bad to give you so much trouble about the autobiography. I should never have thought of publishing it in my lifetime if it had not been for you. I wonder how Miss Elliott heard of it. Would you accept dedication of the book to you? For, since Macmillans paid me an advance on royalties (the enormous sum of $500), I suppose they are really going to publish. I have struck out another ca. 3 pages to please my wife which brings the bulk down to that of the *Master*. Miss Elliott is in New York. Do you think 'Tales from the Margin'[4] would make another not too discreditable book? (no. 13.) I wish to leave enough to bring the total number up to 15, for my wife's sake. I intend rereading Mss of 'The Canyon' and 'Murder,' though I still consider 'Felix Powell's Career' one of the best things I have done.[5]

Best wishes, sincerely yours,
F.P.G.

1 Georges Duhamel's *Défense des lettres* (1937)

2 Broadcasting

3 It was never published, but a substantial number of stories from this collection together with some others selected by me was published under the same title in 1971 (McGraw-Hill Ryerson).

4 The manuscripts of 'The Canyon' and 'Murder in the Quarry' are preserved in the University of Manitoba Grove Collection; that of 'Felix Powell's Career' is missing, and is probably no longer extant.

5 The year, in the original, is shown as 1945, but the matters covered in this letter clearly belong to 1946.

TO CARLETON STANLEY

R.R. 4 Simcoe, Ont.
January 16, 1946[1]

Dear Stanley,

I hardly remember any of the short things, though occasionally I have sold one when I had the chance, for the sake of a few pennies. Usually Dr. Clarke[2] of Queen's picked it out.

Now re the dedication. Twice I have offered and sold a ms. of mine on someone else's say-so: 1) *Settlers*; for this Phelps was responsible, and I dedicated the book to him; 2) 'My Life'; for which you are responsible. You probably know that I am very diffident and cannot imagine why anyone should want to read what *I* have written. Who am I! It is quite true that on rare occasions I am seized with megalomania, mostly after I have been dreaming of something I have done. So I recently thought *The Master* was a great book. It is quite true that I thought of that book in 1912, when a farm hand, but in my own estimation it is mostly just piffle. I, a farmhand, to talk of world conditions! What nonsense, all this talk of great art: Pacey, Sandwell, Deacon etc. So it is just a question whether you will accept the dedication. It is I who am honoured.

Yes, Miss Elliott wants the book, much to my surprise; and since they sent me $500 for it, they can have it. The 500 means too much for me.

When you get through with the 'Tales,'[3] I'll reread them. So far nobody has wanted them, and I have not looked into them for 17 years. *Macleans* have many times tried to teach me how to write (Napier Moore[4]); and I have tried, but proved to be unteachable; they have never printed any of my fiction.

Best wishes.
Yours,
F.P.G.

1 In the original, the year is shown as 1945, but Stanley acknowledges this letter in his letter to Grove of January 19, 1946, sent from Toronto. In January 1945, Stanley was still in Halifax, NS.

2 Dr George Herbert Clarke (1873–1953) was professor of English at Queen's University and for many years editor of *Queen's Quarterly*.

3 'Tales from the Margin'; see the preceding letter, note 4.

4 Henry Napier Moore was born in Newcastle-on-Tyne, England, and began his career as a reporter with *The Newcastle Daily Journal*. He joined the news staff of the *Montreal Daily Mail* in 1915, later becoming its news editor. From 1917 to 1926, he served on the editorial staff of the Montreal *Star*. In 1926, he became editor of *Maclean's Magazine*, and at the time of his retirement in 1955 he was editorial director of Maclean-Hunter Company. He died in Nassau, the Bahamas, on March 25, 1963.

He was the author of many short stories and plays, a syndicated writer for the United Press, and Canadian correspondent to the London *Daily Express*.

TO CARLETON STANLEY

R.R. 4 Simcoe, Ont.
January 20, 1946[1]

Dear Stanley,

I enclose clipping from *Winnipeg Free Press* of the beginning of November. Daniells[2] is, of course, a close friend of Pacey's, but, on the whole, I think he is right, though the article sounds ... I don't know ... grudging? I had heard that Daniells was agitating for a D.Litt. for me; but to that sort of thing I never pay any attention till it is an accomplished fact.

A few minutes ago I finished reading Meredith, *Beauchamp's Career.*[3] Surely, I have never done anything to compare with that.

Everything fine with you? I'm as usual since 1944.

Best regards from us to you and yours,
F.P.G.

The three pages of the Autobiography are a few words here and there, all concerning my wife and objected to by her. She cannot see herself historically. Totally ca. 60 lines.

1 The year, shown as 1945 in the original, is in error, for the enclosure, which has survived, was Roy Daniells' review of my book in the *Winnipeg Free Press* of October 24, 1945.

2 Roy Daniells was born in London, England, in 1902, and educated at the universities of British Columbia and Toronto. He was, at the time of this letter, Head of the English Department at the University of Manitoba, and he actively campaigned for the D. Litt. which was conferred on Grove in June 1946, by the University of Manitoba. Later he moved to the University of British Columbia as Head of the English Department there. His publications include two volumes of verse, *Deeper into the Forest* (1948) and *The Chequered Shade* (1963), and a book of criticism, *Milton, Mannerism and Baroque* (1963). He was a lecturer in English at Victoria College, Toronto, when I was a student there, and we have remained close friends.

I cannot understand why Grove described Daniells' review as 'grudging.' It is true that he admits that Grove has faults as a writer, but his theme is that 'Grove's virtues are enduring and his place in the history of Canadian letters is assured. ... It is a fair guess that Grove, when the history of the Canadian novel comes to be set down, will be found in a place corresponding to that of Hardy and Gissing in English letters.'

3 A novel by George Meredith (1828–1909). It was serialized in 1875, and published in book form in 1876.

TO CARLETON STANLEY

R.R. 4 Simcoe, Ont.
January 22, 1946[1]

Dear Stanley,

Just a few words. I am not feeling well.

So sorry to hear that Mrs. Stanley has been ill. Give her my best wishes for full and speedy recovery.

Thanks for your acceptance of the dedication.

I wish I could read about the *Master*. I am so discouraged. I am almost indignant about Pacey and could wish to write a paragraph against him myself.[2]

Yesterday I reread 'Murder'; and though it excited me, I agree with my wife that it would be best not to publish it unless there is a real call for more of my work.

As for short stories, there are hundreds, but with them too, it will be best to let them lie, I think. Perhaps my wife can one day get a few pennies out of them.

Best wishes, as ever,
F.P.G.

PS. By the way, we hear that we are to be evicted here. The province intends to build a straight highway through our house.

1 In the original, the year is shown as 1945 – clearly a slip, for the matters covered here are in reply to Stanley's letter of January 19, 1946.

2 It is not clear whether he refers to my book or my review of *The Master of the Mill* in the *Toronto Star* of January 19, 1945. Since the review was largely favourable, it is difficult to understand Grove's indignation. Probably the reference is to my book, about which Stanley had complained to Grove for not coming to terms with his (Grove's) genius, and particularly to the chapter on *The Master of the Mill*, which is somewhat inept. That chapter had to be written in haste, after a reading of the galley proofs of the novel in 1944; I should now be prepared to commend the novel much more warmly; and to note complexities in it which completely eluded me at that time.

TO ELLEN ELLIOTT

R.R. 4 Simcoe, Ont.
February 1, 1946

Dear Miss Elliott,

I enclose a dedication page for the autobiography.[1]

By the way. Several people, Pacey included, tell me of a new edition of *The Master*.[2] I know nothing about it. Dr. Stanley writes me that he will read the autobiography over once more. Which means that I shall have to read it again. It will take 2 or 3 days.

I hope Mrs. Blochin is better and back on the job?[3]

Best wishes for you and all my Macmillan friends.

As ever,

F.P.G.

1 As printed in *In Search of Myself*:

TO
MY FRIEND
CARLETON STANLEY

2 Miss Elliott replied, on February 5: 'No, there is no new edition of *The Master of the Mill*, but of course a new printing is now in stock. It is exactly the same as the earlier one; I send you a copy for your library.' My own letter, of January 2, 1946, reads: 'It is strange that you have not been informed of the reprinting of the *Master*. I know it has been reprinted, for I saw a copy recently in a local bookstore which was so inscribed.'

3 Her illness turned out to be quite serious, however, and she had to retire from her work.

TO ELLEN ELLIOTT

R.R. 4 Simcoe, Ont.
February 4, 1946

Dear Miss Elliott,

Thanks for kind letter of the 2nd.

All right, let it be, then, *In Search of Myself*,[1] if that does not sound presumptuous: for who am I? That anyone should search for me? I believe I have done some honest work; but on the whole, as my wife says, I have done what I wished to do; and therefore, she says, I should be satisfied. The trouble is, I have not been able to provide for her in even the smallest measure.

Well, when the Ms. comes back, I'll get at it at once. It shall not take me longer than to 'read' another's ms. for you.

Well, I look forward to your long promised visit. Yes, wire or phone; and my wife will put the kettle on to boil.

As ever, yours,

F.P.G.

1 Miss Elliott, impressed by the article so entitled, had suggested the title for the autobiography. But this was not the first time Grove had thought of using it for his autobiography; see letter of November 26, 1938, note 3. For the first mention of the projected book, see letter of June 15, 1936 – although some material was already there in the notes for *A Search for America* – and also letter of September 3, 1938, where it is described as 'a sequel to *A Search for America*.'

TO CARLETON STANLEY

R.R. 4 Simcoe, Ont.
February 5, 1946[1]

Dear Stanley,

I am very sorry to hear (through Miss Elliott) that you have been and perhaps still are ill. Best wishes.

She also sends me your '500 words.' It seems they are getting ready to print. But I am still to reread the script. I'll do so with a view towards discovering what its superlative merits are. Pacey certainly has not discovered them. It is his advice to cut Europe out or at least down.[2] However, I am now committed, having accepted the $500 which I needed so badly. My wife also read your 500 words and said, 'Well, it looks as if you had arrived; and now you should be satisfied.' The trouble is, I never am and never shall be. Macmillans seem to want to print the autobiography before 'Ants' which I don't quite like. However...

Let me know how you are.
As ever,
F.P.G.

1 Although the date as given in the original is January 5, 1945, the reference to Stanley's '500 words' makes it clear that it must have been a mistake. They were not written until January 30, 1946, and Miss Elliott enclosed the write-up with her letter of February 2, 1946. It was printed (unsigned) on the back of the dust jacket of *In Search of Myself*.

2 I do not recall having given this advice – but as is clear from other letters Grove himself often suggested that the European part of his autobiography might be eliminated or abbreviated, and I may have said I agreed with him. I am at a loss to explain the often antagonistic tone which Grove adopts when speaking of me to others: in his letters to me he was always most cordial.

TO ELLEN ELLIOTT

R.R. 4 Simcoe, Ont.
February 7, 1946[1]

Dear Miss Elliott,

Having now had 2 or 3 days to mull over those pages[2] you sent me re the autobiography (Feb[ruary] 2), I cannot let them go without thanking you once more and congratulating you upon them. I don't know that I deserve them; but I think they are marvellous, both yours and Stanley's. The latter, I think, should be printed as a leaflet, separately; it is a piece of art for which I have merely given the occasion.

By the way, is there, as Pacey writes, a reprint of *The Master*? Do come, will you? I believe I won't be here much longer, no matter what the doctors say.

Both of you, hurry up and get well!
As ever, yours,
F.P.G.

1 The original has 'Jan' clearly typed, but it is certainly a slip for February since Grove himself refers to Miss Elliott's letter of February 2.
2 See the preceding letter, note 1. Miss Elliott had enclosed her own '1000 words' on the autobiography along with Stanley's '500.'

TO CARLETON STANLEY

R.R. 4 Simcoe, Ont.
February 8, 1946[1]

Dear Stanley,

I am so sorry to hear of all your illness in the house and hope it will speedily end.

I will try to answer if I can.

'Ants'[2] was finished during the winter 1920/1921 but has, as is my custom, repeatedly been nibbled at since. The script you read was made about 10 years ago.

No, I read *Erewhon*[3] only after you had mentioned it when here, though I had the book, since 1923 when a man who figures in *The Master*, named Horatio White gave it to me. But, knowing *The Way of all Flesh*,[4] I had no desire to know more of Butler. Such a desire has even yet failed to result, though the 4 volumes[5] you mention, re evolution, will now stick in my flesh like thorns till (if) I read them.

You speak of my 'learning.' It is so small that I spread it out thinly and husband it.

By the way, I must thank you very much for revising the autobiography. I have last night finished rereading it. Having, from your 500 words, some idea of it in my head, I was so much disappointed with it, that I was sorely tempted to burn it. If I didn't, you are the only one to blame or praise. I have adopted all your suggestions except one where, in a causal reference to Goethe which I cannot now remember, I intentionally used the word 'scan' with regard to his lyrics. He uses that word in a verse which I cannot lay my tongue on, in *Venetianische Elegien*.[6] The mixup in the reference to yourself I have now rectified according to your suggestion.

Well, let me know how the battle with the flu germs sways.

Yes, I offered 'Ants' to Ellen Elliott in 1938, but...
Best wishes,
yours,
F.P.G.

1 The month, typed 'Jan' in the original, is again a slip, this being a reply to Carleton

Stanley's letter of February 5, 1946, in which Stanley discusses Samuel Butler's books, and asks in a PS, 'When did you finish the "Ant-Book"?'

2 *Consider Her Ways*

3 A satirical romance by Samuel Butler (1835–1902), published in 1872. The title is an anagram of 'nowhere.'

4 Published a year after Butler's death

5 *Life and Habit* (1877), *Evolution Old and New* (1879), *Unconscious Memory* (1880), and *Luck or Cunning* (1887) – Stanley had preferred them over Butler's novels.

6 Either the *Venetianische Epigramme* (1796), or more likely the *Römische Elegien* (1788), is intended here. They were the products of Goethe's Italian journey (1786–8).

TO CARLETON STANLEY

R.R. 4 Simcoe, Ont.
February 12, 1946

Dear Stanley,

Thank you so much for letting me know about that inadvertence.[1] How to explain it, I don't know. There is some mistake which I somehow must straighten out in the proofs. If I remember right, the name Furtwaengler occurs only once; and probably I shall be able simply to leave it out or switch it into the Berlin period. Of course I am now, 6 y[ea]rs after writing the autobiography, still more hazy about dates and names than I was then; and I do not succeed in making things clear to myself. But, of course, in any case I'd accept the authority of *Brockhaus* and the *Britannica*. As for Pacey, I'm sorry to have misled him.[2] It is entirely my fault. I do remember F[urtwaengler] and I should like to have him in the right place. But...

Glad to hear that you've been out again. I'm not very well. Birthday on Thursday. Have to decline invitations. Rest is the only thing. Leonard will be home last week end of month.

With the usual best wishes,
Yours,
F.P.G.

1 This concerned the presence of Adolf Furtwaengler (1853–1907), the noted archaeologist, at Munich, at the time Grove claimed to have studied there. Since Furtwaengler went to Munich only in 1894, two years after Grove's supposed emigration to North America, Stanley had pointed out this error in chronology. Cf. *In Search of Myself*, 172, for the emended text, and letter of March 1, 1946. Felix Paul Greve was enrolled in Maximiliens University, Munich, in 1901–2, when Furtwaengler was a professor there.

2 The biographical section of my *Frederick Philip Grove* (1945) was based on Grove's then unpublished autobiography. I had said that in 1891–2, Grove studied at the University of Munich. 'attracted there by a leading archaeologist in the person of Furtwaengler' (p 7). In retrospect, I appear to have been a very credulous young man!

TO CARLETON STANLEY

R.R. 4 Simcoe, Ont.
February 14, 1946

Dear Stanley,

Just a word on this, my 75th birthday. Thanks so much for all the trouble you go to on my account.[1] The *Brockhaus* excerpt[2] calls before my mental vision the picture of Loeschke[3] whom I met in Rome and Athens and liked very much. I believe he was teaching at Bonn; but I dare no longer feel sure, having been tripped up on Furtwaengler, of whom, in 1939, I would have felt that I could have taken oath. I have not yet succeeded in clearing up that mixup and believe I shall have to give it up; though, during the last few days I have struggled to find *met' amousias*[4] in my memory. The *Hercules Furens* keeps rising up in my mind. But, as I told you, I have no Euripides. Strange how such a thing bothers one, even at my age. By the way, in trying to locate Furtwaengler in the autobiography, I have reread quite a bit and have, *passim*, not been too dissatisfied. Keep your mind open for a young Albertan; W.O. Mitchell, whose first novel[5] I have just most strongly recommended to Ellen Elliott. There is all of Saskatchewan in it. Glad to see him coming along. To me he seems much better than myself.

Leonard wrote a very poor ode on my 75th birthday.[6] I am quite disgusted with him.

Well, I am getting tired; and I still have the envelope to do.

So, as ever, yours,
F.P.G.

1 In tidying up parts of *In Search of Myself*

2 Concerned with Furtwaengler, which Stanley had copied and enclosed with his letter to Grove. See note to the preceding letter.

3 Georg Loeschcke (1852–1915). He was a professor of archaeology at the University of Bonn from 1889 to 1912, and at Berlin from 1912 till his death. Frau Assunta Loeschcke, widow of George Loeschcke's youngest son Walter, wrote me that although her father-in-law made several trips to Rome and Athens, there was no way of confirming if he actually knew Grove.

3 The phrase, meaning 'amid barbarism,' occurs at line 676 of Euripides' tragedy, *Hercules Furens*, in an ode sung by the chorus. The full context of *Met' amousias* is:

μὴ ζώην μετ' ἀμουσίας,
αἰεὶ δ' ἐν στεφάνοισιν εἴην.

It is a kind of poetic manifesto, meaning (roughly):

Let me not live amid barbarism,
But ever bear the laurel crown.

Its precise relevance in Grove's letter is not clear. Presumably Grove was trying to remember its original context.

5 *Who Has Seen the Wind* (1947). Set in a small prairie town, it traces the development of a boy from childhood to early maturity, and portrays the prairie scenes from the child's eye view. William Ormond Mitchell was born in Weyburn, Saskatchewan, in 1914, and educated at the universities of Manitoba and Alberta. A collection of his short stories, *Jake and the Kid* (1961), won the Leacock Medal for humour. He has published two other novels, *The Kite* (1962) and *The Vanishing Point* (1973).
6 According to the 1871 birth year

TO ELLEN ELLIOTT ET AL

R.R. 4 Simcoe, Ont.
February 18, 1946

Dear Miss Elliott,
Dear Mrs. Blochin,
Dear Misses Lyon & Syme,

Thanks for the Valentine and birthday greetings.[1]

I am worried about a passage in the autob[iography]. It contains a chronological error which I can't correct. It is a complete puzzle to me, excavated by Dr. Stanley.[2] If I succeed in straightening it out in my mind, can I correct it in the proofs? At most 12 words. If not, can we let an error stand? It's just one date; but it worries me. Could you phone Dr. S[tanley]? I mean about this thing, whether to cancel a paragraph or let it stand?

I still don't see how, by a very simple narrative, I deserve so much praise.

I am very tired, so will stop.
As ever,
yours, F.P.G.

1 Grove's birthday was, according to his reckoning, on February 14. This was also the date Leonard was christened.
2 Presumably a reference to the error about Furtwaengler's professorship at Munich; see letter of February 12, 1946, note 1.

TO CARLETON STANLEY

R.R. 4 Simcoe, Ont.
February 19, 1946

Dear Stanley,

I have reread the short things[1] which you had (about 1/2 of the total available, I should say); and while they are not on the same plane with my novels, I do think they compare favourably with the average in Canada.

Since there are 2 books coming, I'll let them rest for another 2 years. It is 16 years ago that I had read them last.

Re Furtwaengler,[2] I am still in the same muddle. I may have to leave things as they stand. I remember his lectures distinctly, also walks with him, in the Englischen Garten, *not* the Tiergarten, which, in my muddle head, means in Munich. However, if there's a mistake, there's a mistake. As you say, I've admitted the possibility in the text.

I hope you and Mrs. Stanley are well. Miss Elliott promises to come here shortly. I hope so, because I have very definite desires re binding etc. of the books. *The Master* I disliked.[3]

However, best regards from both of us.
As ever, yours,
F.P.G.

1 Grove's short stories
2 See letter of February 12, 1946, note 1. If Grove actually studied under Furtwaengler in Munich, his emigration to North America must have taken place some time after 1894. Felix Paul Greve was enrolled at Maximiliens University, Munich, in 1901–2.
3 Probably because of war-time shortages, *The Master of the Mill* was bound in a singularly unattractive cover – a vivid blue which quickly faded.

TO CARLETON STANLEY

R.R. 4 Simcoe, Ont.
February 21, 1946

Dear Stanley,

Since you did not mark what I considered some of the best short stories ('Snow,' 'Water' etc.) I had already placed some such explanation upon the marks as you now give me.

And, as for adding a paragraph or two to the autob[iography], that also I had been pondering and shall do so if I can get hold of a stenographer who won't charge too much; for I certainly cannot write that much. However ... Thanks in any case for all the thought you give me and my work. I have almost daily reread your 500 words; and if I could write, they would be an inspiration to me.

I started this at 9 a.m. It is now half past ten; and I feel all in. I am getting weaker from week to week.

I was very glad to hear, indirectly, from Gilbert Norwood.[1] I wrote him a few years ago, because something he had written struck me as particularly good. He very graciously thanked me, saying, '*Laudari a laudato*.'[2] The *laudato* touched me to tears.

Well,
Ever yours,
F.P.G.

1 Gilbert Norwood (1880–1954) was born in Sheffield, England, and taught classics at the University of Manchester (1903–8) and at University College, Cardiff (1908–26), before coming to the University of Toronto, where he was Professor of Latin (1926–8), and Director of Classical Studies (1928–51). He became a Fellow of the Royal Society of Canada in 1943. Besides books on Classical literature, he published two books of essays, *The Wooden Man* (1926) and *Spoken in Jest* (1938).
2 To receive praise from one already praised [by others] – the remark occurs in Norwood's letter to Grove of July 29, 1940.

TO FRANK FLEMINGTON

R.R. 4 Simcoe, Ont.
February 28, 1946

Dear Mr. Flemington,

Since I don't know who the French publisher[1] is, I can't tell whether I'd want to appear under his imprint. There will shortly be numbers of them who will want my books. Perhaps you have a line on him?

I am of course quite willing to publish in France. I think that I should have $100 for, let us say 2000 first copies. After that a percentage, how much?

If you come in the near future, we could discuss it.
I am very ill and hardly able to write.
Sincerely yours,
F.P.G.

1 The Éditions Athené, who had enquired about translation rights to *Two Generations*

TO ELLEN ELLIOTT

R.R. 4 Simcoe, Ont.
March 1, 1946

Dear Miss Elliott,

I am so sorry to hear of all the bad luck you are having with regard to health and the loss of Mrs. Blochin's help.[1] Please let her know that I sympathize with her.

I enclose a short Postscript to the 'Autobiography' and the carbon copy of Page 129 with a necessary change which will straighten out Dr. Stanley's objection to chronological error – by inserting the one word 'expected'[2] toward the bottom of the page.

As ever,
F.P.G.

1 Mrs Blochin, Miss Elliott's assistant during the War years, became seriously ill and left the company in January 1946. She died shortly thereafter.
2 See letter of February 12, 1946, note 1.

TO ELLEN ELLIOTT

R.R. 4 Simcoe, Ont.
March 10, 1946

Dear Miss Elliott,

The page[1] looks good and prosperous. I propose a slight change for page 1. I think some acknowledgment is due to the quarterly,[2] and my name, being on the title page, should not be repeated here. However, as you think best.

I am far from well, had a terrible week of the flu.
As ever, yours,
F.P.G.

1 A sample page, sent to Grove to give him an idea of the general appearance of the book (*In Search of Myself*)
2 *University of Toronto Quarterly*, from which the 'Prologue' to *In Search of Myself* was reprinted. Page 1 of the book bears a footnote to this effect.

TO CARLETON STANLEY

R.R. 4 Simcoe, Ont.
March 12, 1946

Dear Stanley,

Thanks for yours of the 9th. Yes, I have read and reread the review[1] almost every day, always marvelling that it should be largely about such an insignificant person as myself. Not that I mean to be immoderately modest. I know that, writing my books, I always felt raised high. When I didn't, I burnt the ms.

No. I have never seen your article about Hardy.[2] I should like to, for I rank your critical insight very high, from your *Roots*.[3] Otherwise, you could never have persuaded me to let Macmillans have the Auto[biography]. Many people had tried to persuade me, though they had never read it; Pacey and you, as far as I remember, were the only ones; no, a young Nova Scotian asked me for it, 6 years ago, and wrote a thesis on me, a quite unimportant thing.[4] I'm glad, Pierce had the sagacity to write you.

You say you are a poor correspondent. Well, apart from Ellen Elliott, you are my only one who thinks it worth his while.[5] My wife says I am to see you shortly. I'll then tell you about Rutherford.[6]

Thanks, the cold is better.

Yes, apart from the Canadian, Siberia was my deepest experience.

Well, *au revoir*,
as ever,
yours,
F.P.G.

1 The reference is either to Stanley's review of *The Master of the Mill* (*Dalhousie Review*, XXV, 1945, pp 173–81) or to his review article on my *Frederick Philip Grove* (1945) (*Dalhousie Review* XXV, 1946, pp 433–41), although the postscript to the letter of March 29, 1946 would seem to rule out the latter.
2 'The Poetry of Thomas Hardy,' *Nineteenth Century* CVIII (August 1930) 266–80
3 *Roots of the Tree* (1936)
4 Charles E. Eaton's thesis (1940) at Acadia University – see letter of March 18, 1945.
5 Another instance of Grove's tendency to exaggerate, since I for one was writing to him regularly at this time.
6 His 'great-uncle Rutherford'; see *In Search of Myself* 145. Nothing more is known about him. What a pity that Grove did not attempt a written explanation! See also the Introduction, where it is suggested that the name may have come from Lord Rutherford-Clark, an eminent Scottish jurist and grandfather of Felix Paul Greve's friend, H.F.C. Kilian.

TO ELLEN ELLIOTT

R.R. 4 Simcoe, Ont.
March 14, 1946

Dear Miss Elliott,

I send you under separate cover a copy of the only book[1] which I had a chance to design as I wished it to look. It is my only copy, too; could you therefore be good enough to return it? Of course, it has not the monogram. Pierce rejected that. But format, cloth etc. are what I wished.

I have had a terrific cold and am still weak; so let this be all.

As ever, yours,
F.P.G.

1 *Two Generations*

TO ELLEN ELLIOTT

R.R. 4 Simcoe, Ont.
March 18, 1946

Dear Miss Elliott,

Here is my report on the Pratt appraisal.[1] I'll repeat, I should be mighty proud if such a book had appeared on myself (it will when somebody is as indignant as I am about the Pacey book).[2] Yet, as I make clear, I doubt whether Wells will appeal to any but university readers.

My cold is better. There is no reason why I should not read mss. My worst enemy is boredom. I have reread the books I have at least 4 times, and many begin to be tedious. Those that do not (Greek lyrics, etc.) as Stanley can tell you I know by heart, have known by heart for over 50 years.

With my best wishes, as ever,
yours,
F.P.G.

PS. – Have you a copy of the Barnard book[3] of short stories lying around loose?

1 *Edwin J. Pratt: The Man and His Poetry* by Henry Willis Wells and Carl Frederick Klinck, which Grove read for Macmillan – it was published in 1947 by Ryerson.
2 In view of Grove's early commendation of my book, this remark is rather hard to understand. He never took kindly to adverse criticism of any kind, and he did not suffer fools gladly.
3 Leslie Gordon Barnard (1890–1961) was born in Montreal and educated at Westmount Academy. His short stories appeared in leading periodicals in Canada and the United States. The book of short stories referred to here is Barnard's second such collection, *So Near is Grandeur* (1945); his first, *One Generation Away*, had appeared in 1931. He also wrote two light romantic novels: *Jancis* (1935) and *Winter Road* (1939).

TO ELLEN ELLIOTT

R.R. 4 Simcoe, Ont.
March 26, 1946

Dear Miss Elliott,

Just a word to thank you for the two books.[1] As for Werfel, I am much interested, even though I don't seem to understand him. He is enough of a name that one should have read him.

I am sending Miss Blackstock[2] my first report to her. Glad to say, it's favourable.

Glad to hear, too, of your impending visit here.

By the way, the binding of *Search for America* I asked Hugh S. Eayrs for in 1928, for *Our Daily Bread*. However...

As ever, yours,

F.P.G.

1 Miss Elliott had sent Franz Werfel's *Star of the Unborn* with Barnard's *So Near is Grandeur*, the latter book having been specifically asked for by Grove in his previous letter. For Grove's comments on Werfel's *Forty Days of Musa Dagh*, see letters of October 24, 1935 and January 5, 1936.

2 Of Macmillan's advertising department, who was filling in for Mrs Blochin till a permanent replacement was found

TO CARLETON STANLEY

R.R. 4 Simcoe, Ont.
March 29, 1946

Dear Stanley,

It is weeks since I have been wishing to write to you. I have felt too weak and unable.

All I have to say is that your visit has been an oasis in the last 15 years, and I very much wish that, before leaving Toronto, you could see your way to come back here once more. I might not, during what is left of my life, feel quite so alone in this world for a few months or years, or whatever there may be. Whenever I reread your article,[1] it seems greater to me, much greater than its subject. I have just finished rereading *The Yoke of Life* and *Settlers of the Marsh* with your comments at hand. They have shattered me.

By the way, Pacey's 'strange and unearthly.'[2] Why didn't the man take a boat from the nearest point (Leifur) on L[ake] Manitoba and row across to the outlet into L[ake] Winnepegosis, where he would have found the capes and covers of which my descriptions are pale photographs.

Well come if you can. If not, this must be my good-bye.

As ever, yours,

F.P.G.

P.S. Yes, top inspiration *Settlers of the Marsh*. Have not seen yet your review of Pacey's book.[3]

F.P.G.

1 Presumably 'Frederick Philip Grove' in *Dalhousie Review* XXV (January 1946) 433–41 – a review article on my *Frederick Philip Grove* (1945)

2 In commenting on *The Yoke of Life* in my 1945 book on Grove, I had found the whole final sequence, in which Len and Lydia 'drift about the lake chanting Shelley's odes,' straining our 'powers of belief to the breaking point.' Grove's specific comment applies to the following sentence in my book: '...from the real and tangible world of a pioneer district

we are whisked to a strange unearthly lake which might have graced the pages of a novel by Mrs. Radcliffe or Monk Lewis.' See my *Frederick Philip Grove* (1945) 61–3. Further study has confirmed my belief in strong Gothic influences on Grove's fiction.
3 See note 1 above. Grove appears to be under the impression that Stanley was to write another review of my book. Perhaps Grove regarded the review article to be an article on himself. See also note 1 to the letter of March 12, 1946. As far as is known, this was the only article Stanley published on Grove in 1946.

TO CARLETON STANLEY

R.R. 4 Simcoe, Ont.
April 14, 1946

Dear Stanley,

You had just gone out of sight on Monday, when I went for your *Arnold*.[1] By night I had read it. On Tuesday I started reading *On Translating Homer*,[2] etc. etc.

At ten a.m. I received a letter from Dr. Trueman[3] of Winnipeg. The senate offered me a D. Lit. for May 15. I have accepted. Quite some news. Leonard is at home and says he does not want to go back to St. Andrew's. Lots of fun, he says; but no chance for work. I rather respect him for it.

I sincerely hope you will stay in Toronto.
I feel lonesome since you have gone.
As ever, yours,
F.P.G.

By chance I met a Simcoe *reader*. I mentioned your article of the *Dalhousie Review*.[4] I must read that, he said. Stanley is a critic. My wife gave it to him.

1 *Matthew Arnold* (1938) by Carleton Stanley, a book of essays originally delivered as the Alexander Lectures at the University of Toronto in 1937
2 By Matthew Arnold, published in 1861
3 Albert W. Trueman (b1902) came to Canada from the United States in 1913, and was educated at Mount Allison (BA 1927) and Oxford (MA 1932). After several years of teaching, mostly at Mount Allison University, he served successively as Superintendent of Public Schools in Saint John, NB (1942–5); President, University of Manitoba (1945–8); President, University of New Brunswick (1948–53); Commissioner, National Film Board (1953–7); Director of the Canada Council (1957–65); and Principal, University College, University of Western Ontario (1965–7).
4 Presumably the review article, 'Voices in the Wilderness' (*Dalhousie Review* XXV, 1945, pp 173–81), on *The Master of the Mill* and Gwethalyn Graham's *Earth and High Heaven*. Stanley's review of my book on Grove in the same journal (XXV, 1946, pp 433–41) may also be considered.

TO ELLEN ELLIOTT

R.R. 4 Simcoe, Ont.
April 15, 1946

Dear Miss Elliott,

Thank you so much for sending me McCowan's *Naturalist in Canada.*[1] I had been wishing to read it for some time. Dealing as it does very largely with the extreme west, it contains much that is new to me; and a great deal that I find very interesting. Dr. Stanley was here a week ago (not you); he is writing a book about myself[2] which promises to be very excellent, vastly superior to Pacey; he is a real critic. By the way, the University of Manitoba is going to make me a Doctor of Letters on May 15; but this is to remain a secret till a few days before that date. They want to make the announcement themselves.

As ever, yours,
F.P.G.

1 Daniel McCowan (1882–1956), whose *A Naturalist in Canada* appeared in 1941, was born in Scotland. He was widely travelled in the Canadian Rockies, accumulating 25,000 photographic negatives of the flora and fauna of the region. One of the foremost Canadian naturalists, he wrote several books including *Animals of the Canadian Rockies* and *Outdoors With a Camera.* Besides lecturing and writing for newspapers and radio, he wrote *Hill-Top Tales* (1948), a book of stories about men and women who came to the Rocky Mountain area during the opening of the West.
2 See letter of November 24, 1945, note 2.

TO CARLETON STANLEY

R.R. 4 Simcoe, Ont.
April 18, 1946

Dear Stanley,

Thanks for yours of the 15th. I am rereading *Fruits.* So far I don't like it overly well.

Agree with you re *Little Man*[1] and *Cakes and Ale.*[2]

'Jane Atkinson'[3] I haven't read for 15 years; but neither have I burned it; but I fear I shall. I hope to read it shortly. It is all so difficult; especially reading a ms.

Since *Fruits* is one of my *slow* things, it should be all right; but as usual I search for what you praise in it. But I agree, there is quite a gallery of characters in it. *You* see them, Pacey doesn't. Maybe it condemns Pacey. I hope so. *I* like Nicoll,[4] only one I have met so far.

Regards from my wife and Leonard whom I like particularly well this time: he has done badly in exams; and he feels it.

Well, as ever, Yours,
F.P.G.

Don't give up Toronto just yet.

1 *Little Man* (1942) by G. Herbert Sallans (1895–1960)
2 *Cakes and Ale* (1930), a novel by Somerset Maugham (1874–1966)
3 The manuscript, with a western setting, remains unpublished in the University of Manitoba Grove Collection.
4 A character in *Fruits of the Earth*

TO WINNIFRED EAYRS

R.R. 4 Simcoe, Ont.
April 21, 1946

Dear Miss Eayrs,

Forgive me for being very brief.

Re 'Autobiography.' I have had the first galleys which you say did not come back to you. I returned them the day after having received them. The trouble is I cannot register such things except as by chance somebody offers to go to town. Nor have I ever found it necessary for printed matter. Could we insure? Insured parcels are delivered. Or send at letter rate? Anything you say except registration.

Re 'Ants.' The sample page is good. I return it, uncorrected since it is sample only.

With best wishes, Yours as ever,
F.P.G.

TO CARLETON STANLEY

R.R. 4 Simcoe, Ont.
April 24, 1946

Dear Stanley,

I cannot tell you how sorry I am that you are going to go west, though I don't wish to say anything against Winnipeg.[1] Only I am so alone.

I finished reading *Fruits* the other day. When I threw it down, I said, 'no matter what anybody else says, that's a great book.' I am glad I wrote it.

I am very sick just now and feel I am not long for this world. Am typing in bed.

Anyway, thanks for your two visits and everything else. Let me know address etc.

Good-bye. As ever, yours.
F.P.G.

1 In 1946, Carleton Stanley moved west to become Professor of English at United College, Winnipeg.

TO WINNIFRED EAYRS

R.R. 4 Simcoe, Ont.
[April 24, 1946] 11[1]

Dear Miss Eayrs,

Receiving or sending registrations is equally difficult, but receiving or sending letters or printed matter is easy. These proofs I shall send by letter rate which perhaps is safer than printed matter. I'm sorry to be so much trouble.

Best regards,
F.P. Grove

P.S. It is not necessary to return the Ms. I have the carbon copy here. But I should like to have it back after the printing is completed. You would help me if here and there you could put the Ms. page on the galley.
F.P.G.

1 No date is given; but it is in reply to a letter from Miss Eayrs, dated April 23, and was attached to her next letter, in reply to this, of April 26. The letter is in Mrs Grove's handwriting.

TO CARLETON STANLEY

R.R. 4 Simcoe, Ont.
May 14, 1946

Dear Stanley,

Trois mois de patience...[1]

It is impossible for Winnipeg to hesitate...

I am very sick. Hardly able to be up. In fact, lying down most of the day.

Pacey is certainly wrong with incest. Phil and Alice are much too decent to go so far; if they were not ... it is *Geschwisterliebe*[2]...

I am glad you defend me against Dreiser.[3] I can't stand the man. Nor Sinclair Lewis.[4] The more I dislike them, the less I say about them.

Very much good wishes from my wife. She goes to Aurora tomorrow. I can't.

Good bye. You don't weary me.
Write again. Soon. Yours ever…
F.P.G.

1 Three months of patience – the context, however, is not clear. In view of the sentence that follows, it may be a reference to the delay which Stanley was presumably experiencing in getting confirmation of his appointment as professor of English at United College, Winnipeg. Stanley's term as president of Dalhousie University expired in 1945.
2 Love between brothers and sisters – without of course any suggestion of impropriety. That I was not so far wrong, however, is clear from the November 14, 1938 letter to Alexander, where Grove says that in his first conception of the relations between Phil and Alice there was 'a feeling transcending that of merely brotherly or sisterly love.'
3 Theodore (Herman Albert) Dreiser (1871–1945), US novelist, known particularly for his austere, humourless realism and rugged style, exemplified in such novels as *Sister Carrie* (1900), *The Financier* (1912), and *An American Tragedy* (1925). Northrop Frye's obituary tribute to Grove, published in the *Canadian Forum* of September 1948, and reprinted in my *Frederick Philip Grove* (Critical Views of Canadian Writers 1970) 186–7, is entitled 'Canadian Dreiser.'
4 Sinclair Lewis (1885–1951), US novelist, author of *Main Street* (1920), *Babbitt* (1922), *Martin Arrowsmith* (1925), *Elmer Gantry* (1927), *Dodsworth* (1929), etc. He was awarded the Nobel Prize in 1930.

TO PELHAM EDGAR

R.R. 4 Simcoe, Ont.
May 14, 1946 II

Dear Dr. Edgar,

I received $100 for May from the National Trust Co. today, for which, thank you. I wonder whether there has been a mistake since I did not receive anything for April.[1] This is particularly unfortunate since I have a payment of $225. to make on my property May 31. However, I appreciate what the Foundation is doing for me.

Very sincerely,
F.P. Grove
per C.G.

P.S. You will be sorry to hear that my husband had a serious set-back a week ago Sunday. The doctor says it's a clot forming. I can now understand very little he says.

Catherine Grove

1 Edgar replied on May 16, expressing his deep distress over the news of Grove's health, and emphasizing '*Your April payment will of course be made good to you*' (italics Edgar's). The delay was due to the ill health of the Foundation's Executive Secretary, Charles Clay,

who had to resign suddenly, in consequence of which normal payment authorization procedure was disrupted.

Edgar also added, in a kindly way, that Mrs Grove might be assured she and Leonard would not be forgotten by the Association in the future.

TO WINNIFRED EAYRS

R.R. 4 Simcoe, Ont.
May 16, 1946

Dear Miss Eayrs,

Thank you so much for being so helpful to me in this matter of proof-reading. It does make things easier for me.

As ever,
F.P. Grove

TO ALEX. J. PHILIP[1]

[Simcoe, Ont.
October 1946]

Dear Sir,

Since I wrote to you last week, I have a letter from my Can[adian] publishers, Macmillans, telling me that their London House will release my autobiography *In Search of Myself*. I can now offer you the book for Eng[lish] pub[lication] under the same terms as my Can[adian] contract with Macmillans, namely, 15% royalty and a $500 advance. An early reply is important since the Macmillan House in London wishes to import copies if you do not undertake to publish the book. I am sending you a copy of the book under separate cover.

1 This letter, in Mrs Grove's handwriting, is doubtless a draft. It is written at the bottom of a letter to Grove, dated October 15, 1946, from Alex. J. Philip, 'Lodgewood,' Gravesend, England, who had requested a copy of Grove's autobiography for possible publication in England.

TO ELLEN ELLIOTT

[Simcoe, Ont.
November 28, 1946][1]

It is not often that a person gets a book as beautifully bound as the copy I received from you of *Consider Her Ways*. I wish to thank you very much indeed.

Yours sincerely,
F.P. Grove.

1 This letter, presumably a draft, was found among the miscellaneous letters in the University of Manitoba Grove Collection; the date is deduced from the fact that Macmillan (ie, Ellen Elliott) sent author's copies of *Consider Her Ways* to Grove on November 26, 1946.

TO LORNE PIERCE

R.R. 4 Simcoe, Ont.
March 17, 1947

Dear Dr. Pierce,

Thank you for the copies of the school edition of *A Search*. I think Mr. Swayze[1] has done a good job. I like the book.

I accept the conditions as proposed in your letter of Mar[ch] 12 though the royalties on the other edition are 15%. But if you will kindly fill out a new contract for the school edition and send it to me I shall sign it and return it to you without delay.

Sincerely,
F.P. Grove
per C.G.

1 James Frederick Swayze (1907–67), who abridged *A Search for America* for the school edition, was a writer of children's books, primarily romanticized biographies – *Tonty of the Iron Hand* (story of Henri de Tonty) (1957), *The Fighting Le Moynes* (1958), *Frontenac and the Iroquois* (1959) – and one historical novel for children, *Run For Your Life* (1960).

TO THE RYERSON PRESS

R.R. 4 Simcoe, Ont.
August 26, 1947

Dear Sirs,

I am wondering whether you would be interested to take over the remainder of the limited edition of *Two Generations* which I own. There are about 230 copies left.

I should appreciate an early reply.

Yours very truly,
F.P. Grove
per C.G.[1]

1 This letter is in Mrs Grove's handwriting. In the first week of May 1946, Grove had a serious setback, and his mental powers and speech suffered noticeably. The correspondence with Macmillan and, later in 1947, with the Ryerson Press was carried on by Mrs Grove. There is a group of very sad letters from Mrs Grove to Carleton Stanley, which recount the steady deterioration of Grove's health and his increasing disability. On August 11, 1948, she wrote: 'Phil is in a nursing home in Simcoe. He is very feeble and has almost entirely lost his speech. ... My only hope now is that the end may not be too far away and that he will not suffer.' Grove died eight days later, on August 19, 1948, and was buried in the Rapid City cemetery, next to the grave of his daughter, Phyllis May. Mrs Grove survived her husband by twenty-four years, dying on January 9, 1972.

Sources of the Letters

LETTERS TO:	SOURCE:
Isaak J. Warkentin,* McClelland & Stewart Ltd.,* Carleton Stanley,* Graphic Publishers Ltd., Henry Miller, M.H.W. Cameron, Alex J. Philip, W.J. Alexander, Roy Bottum, Willard Holliday,* and Catherine Grove*	The University of Manitoba Grove Collection, Elizabeth Dafoe Library, The University of Manitoba, Winnipeg, Man.
The Ryerson Press, E.J. Moore, Norma McRostie, Blanche Hume, Lorne Pierce, Findlay Weaver, and Frank Flemington	The Lorne Pierce Collection, Douglas Library, Queen's University, Kingston, Ont.
The Canadian Authors' Foundation, Pelham Edgar, and Charles Clay	The Public Archives of Canada, Ottawa, Ont.
Richard E. Crouch	Keith Crouch,[1] Toronto, Ont.
Barker Fairley and E.H. Thistlethwaite	Thomas Fisher Rare Book Library, The University of Toronto, Toronto, Ont.

The Macmillan Co. of Canada, Ellen Elliott, Winnifred Eayrs, Isobel Syme, and Helen Lyons	The Macmillan Co. of Canada,[2] Toronto, Ont.
Gustav Hübener	Mrs Jean Hübener, Fredericton, NB
J.M. Dent & Sons and Henry Button	J.M. Dent & Sons, London, England
Watson Kirkconnell and Desmond Pacey	Desmond Pacey, Fredericton, NB
Austin Bothwell	The University of Saskatchewan Library, Regina, Sask.
Roy St George Stubbs	Roy St George Stubbs, Winnipeg, Man.
Mary Jean McMahon	Mrs Mary Jean McMahon, Weston, Ont.
Hugh MacLennan	The University of Calgary Library, Calgary, Alta.
William Reid	Edward Phelps, Librarian, The University of Western Ontario, London, Ont.
Raymond Knister	Mrs Myrtle Grace,[3] Jarvis, Ont.
W.J. Alexander (June 16, 1944)	Mrs Edith L. McIver, Caledon East, Ont.
Pelham Edgar (January 16, 1934)	Victoria University Library, Toronto, Ont.
The *Canadian Forum*[4]	
Charles E. Eaton	Charles E. Eaton, Kentville, NS
W.T. Allison	Dr F.G. Allison, Vancouver, BC

The Rapid City Reporter	Dr Margaret Stobie, Winnipeg, Man.
The Simcoe Reformer	Simcoe Public Library, Simcoe, Ont.
Wilfrid Eggleston	Wilfrid Eggleston, Ottawa, Ont.
The Canadian Bookman[5]	
Marcus Adeney	Marcus Adeney, Scarborough, Ont.

*These letters were originally supplied by Mrs Grove, but have since been deposited in the University of Manitoba Grove Collection.

1/Mr Crouch has since given these letters to the University of Manitoba Grove Collection.
2/These letters are published by arrangement with the Macmillan Company of Canada Limited, Toronto, Ont.
3/The University of Manitoba has now acquired Grove's letters to Knister, and has provided me with copies of seven Grove letters to Knister not included in the group supplied by Mrs Grace.
4/To the best of my recollection, a copy of this letter came to me with letters to Mrs Grove from Mrs Grove herself, but this particular letter is apparently not among the letters which the University of Manitoba acquired from her.
5/The letter of November 3, 1925 is copied directly from the *Bookman*, and that of April 30, 1926 was an enclosure to Grove's letter to Watson Kirkconnell of the same date.

Appendix A

Introduction

Although the case that Frederick Philip Grove of Canada was Felix Paul Greve of Germany is still not conclusively proven, the circumstantial evidence for their identity is so strong* that it has seemed wise to include as an appendix those letters by Greve which have so far come into my possession. I have also included a letter from Anton Kippenberg of Insel-Verlag to Else Greve, as it sheds some light on Greve's 1909 disappearance. I know that there are a number of additional letters to André Gide still in existence, and letters also to Stefan George and Friedrich Gundolf. Additional letters will almost certainly come to light. In all probability, the quantity of Greve letters will eventually be such as to warrant a separate volume. In the meantime, this group of letters will give Canadian scholars an opportunity to assess the likelihood of Grove's identity with Greve.

For the acquisition of these letters I am indebted to the Deutsche Staatsbibliothek in Berlin, Schiller Nationalmuseum in Marbach, Nationale Forschunsund Gedensktätten der klassischen deutschen Literatur in Weimar, and Mme Catherine Gide.

For the free translations of the letters I am indebted, in varying degrees, to Dr Harold Lusher, Dr Franz Eppert, Dr Jean Hübener, Mrs Maria Kaiser, and Dr Anthony Pugh of the University of New Brunswick. In the interest of those who are familiar with German and French, the original German and French texts are reproduced.

Desmond Pacey

* See D.O. Spettigue: *FPG: The European Years* (Ottawa: Oberon 1973); and Desmond Pacey and J.C. Mahanti, 'Frederick Philip Grove: An International Novelist,' *International Fiction Review* 1 1 (January 1974) 17–26.

Gardone-Riviera
August 2, 1902

Sehr geehrter Herr!

Durch meinen Freund Karl Wolfskehl hörte ich vor einiger Zeit, dass sich Ihr gesch. Verlag ev. für moderne englische Litteratur interessieren würde. Ich möchte mir daher gestaten, Ihnen eine Übertragung von:

Ernest Dowson, *Dilemmas,*

zum Verlage anzubieten. Ich habe für den Verlag Bruns in Minden die Hauptwerke Oscar Wildes übertragen und im Anschluss daran mehrere Werke der Kreise, die mit Wilde gleichzeitig oder gemeinsam schufen. Von ihnen ist das Ihnen angebotene das erste, das druckfertig vorliegt. Der Einfachheit halber gestatte ich mir, das Manuscript gleich an Ihre werte Adresse abzusenden, damit Sie Sich ein Urteil bilden können.

Im Fall der Ablehnung bitte ich, es einfach unfrankiert an meine Münchener Adresse zurücksenden zu wollen.

Für den Fall, dass Sie meiner Offerte nährer zu treten wünschen, darf ich wohl gleich meine Bedingungen mitteilen:

ich erhalte als Honorar:

40.M. pro Bogen für die ersten 1000 Exemplare davon zahlbar 150 M. bei Übernahme des Manuscripts, der Rest bei Erscheinen des Buches, von jeden weiteren 1000 Ex. 20% des Reingewinns; ausserdem von der ersten Auflage 10 Freiexemplare, von jeder weiteren Auflage 5. Würden Sie die Liebenswürdigkeit haben, mir nach München, Giselastrasse 15^{iii}, an meine ständige Adresse zu antworten?

Indem ich Ihrer freundlichen Antwort entgegensehe, zeichne ich hochachtungsvoll.

Felix Paul Greve

TO INSEL-VERLAG[1]

Gardone-Riviera
August 2, 1902

Dear Sir,

Through my friend Karl Wolfskehl[2] I heard some time ago that your esteemed publishing house might possibly be interested in modern English literature. I therefore take the liberty of offering you for publication a translation of Ernest Dowson,[3] *Dilemmas*.

For the Bruns Publishing Co.[4] in Minden I have translated the principal works of Oscar Wilde, and, in connection with that, several works of those authors who either worked with him or were his contemporaries. What is (being) offered you is the first of them to hand and ready to print. For the sake of simplifying matters, I am taking the liberty of forwarding the manuscript to your valued address directly, so that you may form your (own) opinion.

In the event of rejection, may I request that you return it C.O.D. to my Munich address.

In the event that you wish to consider my offer more closely, may I inform you of my conditions immediately:
as a fee I receive:
40 M[arks] per sheet for the first 1000 copies, of which 150 M[arks] is payable on acceptance of the manuscript, the balance when the book appears; of every further 1000 copies, 20% of the net profit; furthermore, 10 free copies of the first edition, 5 of every further edition.

Would you be kind enough to reply to my permanent address in Munich, Giselastrasse 15^{iii}?

Looking forward to your friendly reply, I remain
Sincerely yours
Felix Paul Greve

1 A publishing firm in Leipzig, established in 1902 and still in business. The West German section of the house is situated in Frankfurt am Main.
2 Karl Wolfskehl (1869–1948), the German lyric poet who emigrated to New Zealand
2 Ernest Dowson (1867–1900), the English 'Decadent' poet and novelist. Greve's translation of his *Dilemmas* was published in 1903 (Leipzig: Insel-Verlag).
4 J.C.C. Bruns, a publishing house in Minden

Giselastr. 15^{iii}
Munchen
September 19, 1902

Sehr geehrter Herr von Poellnitz,

ich fühlc das dringende Bedürfnis, Ihnen ein Wort über das Ernstsche Buch zu sagen, das mich während der ganzen Fahrt hierher erstaunlich wach gehalten hat. Dass Herr Ernst auf das 'Was' nicht allzu viel Gewicht legt, zeigt schon die Wahl der zum grossen Teil entlehnten Stoffe. Übrigens war mir dies besonders erfreulich. In ihrer Gesamtform, das heisst, als Kunstwerke der Erzähling erschienen mir drei der Novellen: Warum leben denn nur die Menschen? die Buhlerin, der Gefangene – also die besten. Si sind wirklich kleine Meisterstücke, die zeigen, wie viel Herr Ernst von Italienern und Franzosen (vielleicht auch von Spätlateinern?) gelernt hat. Aber was mich am meisten interessierte, war die Behandlung der Prosa. Diese Periodenbildung ist in der That 'ein Weg.' Soweit ich sehe, ist Herr Ernst der erste, der sie versucht hat (mein Marius ist ähnlich gebaut), und da bleibt es natürlich nicht aus, dass der Autor hie und da übers Ziel hinaus schiesst.

Was ich ganz ausgezeichnet finde, das ist die sozusagen pragmatische Schachtelung der Sätze. Ich nehme die ersten, vielleicht die besten Beispiele, die mir momentan aufstossen: 'Aber damals kam in ihre Gegend ein glänzender junger Herr, welcher der vertrauteste Freund des benachbarten jungen Erzbischofs wurde und an dessen Hofe, *denn der war Reichsfürst*, eine hohe Stelle erhielt.' (S. 254 unten)

'...und wiewwohl er in seiner grossen Angst zuerst gar nicht das Mägdlein erkannte, welches ihn so liebreich angeblickt hatte auf seinem bösen Wege *und hatte ihm damals der Liebesgott seinen Pfeil ins Herz geschossen*, sah er doch...' (S. 228 unten) So etwas wirkt vorläufig noch als Anakoluth. Aber das Anakoluth führt zur Periode (Beisp. Herodot), genau wie die Periode wieder im Anakoluth endet (Beisp. Plato, Pater). Und gerade das ist der Weg, auf dem die Kunstprosa bisher immer noch zu Stande gekommen ist. Pater sagt: Wir müssen versuchen, unsere Sprache zu schreiben, wie der Römer Latein, wie der Franzose französisch schreibt. Das ist bei Herrn Ernst aus einem Grunde noch nicht erreicht: er hat den Weg über die Rhetorik nicht gemacht, d.h. er schreibt noch nicht fürs Ohr, sondern für den Verstand. Aber ich persönlich halte seinen Weg für DEN Weg, genau wie in der Dichtung Georges Weg für den vorwärtsführenden halte.

Dann ist noch ein Punkt, über den man an der Hand des Ernstschen Buches viel Fruchtbringenden und Nützliches sagen könnte, nämlich: das 'Figürliche.' Es gelingt ihm bisweilen, mit ein, zwei glücklichen Worten eine Figure wie ein Schwarzweissbild hinzustellen: '...der Saum des Mantels stand auf der Erde, und so hatte der Mantel einen leichten Querknick.' (S. 264) Ähnlicher Sachen finden sich viele.

Im Ganzen ist das Buch ausserordentlich erfreulich und sicher ein Symptom.

Über die Ausstattung sage ich nichts. Sie ist wundervoll. –

Morgen früh werde ich die Wildeschen Märchen engl[isch] und deutsch an Ihre w. Adresse senden. In einigen Tagen folgen einige Kapitel Pater. Das Patermanuscript ist nämlich aus Versehen unter die zu bindenden Sachen geraten, und ich müsste Ihnen also das ganze Manuscript senden, wenn ich es sofort schicken wollte. Das wäre mir unangenehm, da ich dann eine Zeit lang nicht daran arbeiten könnte. Ich lasse einige Kapitel abschreiben.

Inzwischen bin ich in ausgezeichneter Hochachtung Ihr sehr ergebener

Felix Paul Greve

TO R. VON POELLNITZ[1]

Giselastr. 15^{iii}
Munich
September 19, 1902

Dear Mr. Poellnitz,

I feel impelled to say a few words about the book by Ernst,[2] which held my attention remarkably during my journey here. It is obvious that Mr. Ernst did not consider the 'what' important, as shown in his choice of borrowed subjects for the most part. On the whole, I liked this, i.e. three of his novellas appeared to me to be masterpieces of narration: 'Warum leben denn nur die Menschen!' 'die Buhlerin,' 'der Gefangene' – are the best. They are, indeed, minor masterpieces that show how much Mr. Ernst has learned from the Italians and the French (and perhaps also from the late Latins?). But what interested me most was his handling of prose. His structuring of sentences has indeed 'one way.' As far as I know, Mr. Ernst is the first (my *Marius*[3] is structured similarly) who has tried this, and it is thus understandable that here and there the author has gone too far.

What I find particularly excellent is, so to speak, the pragmatic interweaving of the periods. Let me take the first, and perhaps the best, examples that strike me at the moment:

'Aber damals kam in ihre Gegend ein glänzender junger Herr, welcher der vertrauteste Freund des benachbarten jungen Erzbischofs wurde und an dessen Hofe, *denn der war Reichsfürst*, eine hohe Stelle erhielt.' (cf. p. 254 below)

'...und wiewohl er in seiner grossen Angst zuerst gar nicht das Mägdlein erkannte, welches ihn so liebereich angeblickt hatte auf seinem bosen Wege und *hatte ihm damals der Liebesgott seinen Pfeil ins Herz geschossen*, sah er doch...' (Cf. p. 228 below)

Something like this still has provisionally the effect of anacoluthon. But the anacoluthon leads to the period (e.g. Herodotus), just as the period ends up again in the anacoluthon (e.g. Plato, Pater). And this is precisely the way in which rhythmic prose has always come into being. Pater says: We have to try to write our language as the Romans wrote Latin and Frenchmen French. Mr. Ernst has not quite succeeded in this for one reason: he did not make his way via rhetoric, i.e., he does not yet write for the ear, but for the intellect. But personally I consider his to be *the* way, just as I consider George's[4] way to be the one which points ahead in poetry.

Then there is one further point, about which one could say much that is fruitful and useful with the aid of Ernst's book, and that is: his 'figures of speech.' Occasionally he manages to present a figure like a black-and-white image with only one or two words: '...der Saum des Mantels stand auf der Erde, und so hatte der Mantel einen leichten Querknick.' (p. 264) One can find many similar examples.

On the whole, the book is extraordinarily pleasing and certainly original.

I shall say nothing about the format. It is wonderful.

Tomorrow morning I shall send the fairy tales[5] by Oscar Wilde in English and German to you. In a few days some Pater chapters will follow. The Pater manuscript accidentally got mixed up with the books to be bound, and I should therefore have to send the complete manuscript, if I wanted to send it now. That would be an inconvenience for me, since I would then not be able to work on it for a while. I shall have some chapters copied.

In the meantime, I remain
Yours very faithfully
Felix Paul Greve

1 Rudolf von Poellnitz. He was a relative of Eugen Diederichs, the publisher, and had worked for him before he joined the Insel-Verlag firm in 1901 as business manager. He died

at the end of 1904 after a short illness. During his management of the affairs of Insel-Verlag, the house launched the Grossherzog-Wilhelm-Ernst-Ausgabe series of German classics, which included the works of Goethe (in 16 vols) and Schiller (in 6 vols).

2 Paul Ernst (1866–1933), in whose *Die Prinzessin des Ostens und andere Novellen* (1903) the stories discussed in this letter appeared. A second edition of the same book was issued in 1918 as the fourth volume in Ernst's *Gesammelte Werke* (Munich: G. Müller).

3 *Marius der Epikureer* von Walter Pater, translated from the English by Felix Paul Greve, was published in 1908 (Leipzig: Insel-Verlag).

4 Stefan George (1868–1933), the German lyric poet and leader of a literary movement which he himself launched. There are five extant letters from Greve to George in the George archives, the first of which is dated May 9, 1902 and the last December 8, 1902.

5 Presumably, Greve's translation of *The House of Pomegranates* (*Das Granatapfelhaus*), published in 1904 (Leipzig: Insel-Verlag)

Giselastr. 15^{iii}
München
October 9, 1902

Sehr geehrter Herr von Poellnitz!

Endlich glaube ich, nach fast sechsmonatlicher Arbeit, am ersten Bande des Marius alles gethan zu haben, was ich überhaupt thun kann, und sende Ihnen ein Druckmanuscript gleichzeitig ein. Ich glaube nunmehr, den Ton Paters getroffen zu haben, was mir eine Vorlesung von Teilen aus dem Buch bestätigt hat. Ob dieser Ton im Deutschen möglich, ob er wünschbar ist, weiss ich nicht zu sagen. Ich hielt mich – ausser in zwei bis drei Fällen – nicht für berechtigt, als Übersetzer zu vereinfachen. Der englische Text ist dem Engländer genau so schwer, wie meiner dem Deutschen. Ich weiss das zu beurteilen, da ich das Englische mindestens so gut beherrsche wie das Deutsche. Es wurde mir auch vielfach von Engländern bestätigt. Um jener Forderung der Vereinfachung von vornherein zu begegnen, habe ich ein Vorwort geschrieben, in dem ich mit Paters eigenen Worten meine Übersetzungsprinzipien auseinandergesetzt habe. Vielleicht werfen Sie einen Blick hinein. Den zweiten Band werde ich in etwa einem Monat beenden. Mit ihm werde ich Ihnen wahrscheinlich ein Manuscript von: 'In a Balcony' (aus *Men and Women*) von Robert Browning (Versübertragung) zu geneigter Einsichtnahme senden, dem aber noch die letzte Feile fehlt. Vielleicht, dass Sie es drucken würden. Nun habe ich noch eine grosse, etwas seltsame Bitte. Mir wurde dieser Tage eine Kollektion sehr seltener englischer Dekadenzwerke zu relativ geringem Preise angeboten. Da ich aber mein kleines Vermögen, das mir meine Unabhängigkeit sichern soll, nicht angreifen darf, wollte ich Sie fragen, ob es Ihnen im Fall der Annahme des Marius möglich wäre, mich durch einen Vorschuss auf die drei Bände, die dann in Ihren Händen sind, in der Höhe von ca. 800 M. zu dieser Erwerbung, die für meine Studien sehr wichtig ist, in Stand zu setzen. Ich würde Sie in dem Falle bitten, mir umgehend zu antworten, da ich das Recht an die Sachen nur bis Sonntag früh reserviert habe. Sonst gehen sie in andere Hände. Mit der Bitte, mir meine Anfrage nicht übel zu nehmen, verbleibe ich in vorzüglicher Hochachtung Ihr sehr ergebener

Felix Paul Greve

TO R. VON POELLNITZ

Giselastr. 15^{iii}
Munich
October 19, 1902

Dear Mr. von Poellnitz!

At last, after nearly 6 months of work on the first volume of the *Marius*, I believe I have done everything [with it] that I can do, and I am herewith sending you the manuscript to be published. By this time I think I have managed to capture Pater's tone, a fact confirmed for me by having had parts of the book read aloud. Whether this tone is possible in German I dare not venture to say. Except in two or three cases, I did not consider myself justified in simplifying as a translator. The English text is precisely as difficult for an Englishman as mine is for a German. I can judge that, because I know English at least as well as I do German. That has been confirmed for me on many occasions by Englishmen. To meet that demand for simplification head on, I have written a Foreword in which I have explained my principles of translation in Pater's own words. Perhaps you can take a look at it. In about one month I shall complete the second volume. With it I shall probably send you a manuscript of 'In a Balcony' (from *Men and Women*) by Robert Browning[1] (verse translation) for your favourable consideration, but the final polishing still has to be done. Perhaps you would print it. And now I have another large, but somewhat strange, request. Recently I was offered a collection of very rare English decadent literature at a relatively low price. Since I dare not touch, however, the little money I have, which has to ensure my independence, I wanted to ask you whether it would be possible, in case the *Marius* is accepted, to advance 800 M[arks] on the three volumes which will then be in your hands, so that I can acquire the collection, which is very important for my studies. If so, I would request an immediate reply, since I have reserved an option on the books only until Sunday morning. Otherwise they will pass into other hands. Hoping that you will not be offended by my enquiry, I remain

Yours truly
Felix Paul Greve

1 The following works of Browning, translated by Greve, were published by Insel-Verlag: *Auf einem Balkon: In einer Gondel* (1903), *Die Tragödie einer Seele* (1903), and *Paracelsus* (1904). The first two appeared under his pseudonum of F.C. Gerden, and the last under his own name.

Königin Augustastr. 3[i]
Berlin W.
November 19, 1902

Sehr geehrter Herr von Poellnitz,

gestern gestattete ich mir, Ihnen ein Exemplar meiner Übertragung von Oscar Wildes *Intentions* zuzusenden

Dass ich Ihren ausführlichen Brief, für den ich nachträglich danke, nicht eher beantwortete, lag zum Teil daran, dass ich mich schlecht befand, zum Teil an allerlei erneuten Aufregungen. Ich kann mir allerlei abenteuerliche Gerüchte, die über mich in Umlauf sind, nur erklären, indem ich annehme, dass irgend jemand ein Interesse daran hat, mir die unglaublichsten Dinge und Aussagen in die Schuhe zu schieben. Ich kann zum Beispiel aufs bestimmteste versichern, dass ich niemals von einem 'unglaublichen opulenten Diner,' zu dem Sie mich eingeladen hatten, geredet habe. Ich entsinne mich genau, dass ich über meinen Aufenthalt in Leipzig gesprochen habe. Aber in ganz anderem Sinne, als Sie andeuten. Mir selbst erschien meine erste Zusammenkunft mit Ihnen wegen der Eile, in der alles abgemacht wurde, ausserordentlich komisch und als einige Freunde von mir nach München zurückkamen, habe ich in einer lustigen Stunde meinen Besuch bei Ihnen, in der angedeuteten Richtung hin mit den groteskesten Übertreibungen, erzählt. Doch bezog sich meine Erzählung nicht nur darauf, sondern auf all das, was ich an jenem Vormittag in Leipzig ausrichtete. Ob ich überhaupt Ihren Namen dabei erwähnte, kann ich nicht mehr sagen. Wenn es geschah, so bedaure ich es lebhaft, zumal es für die Geschichte, wie ich sie erzählen wollte, ganz gleichgültig war. Was meine Bücher angeht, so stand ich allerdings unter einem Missverständnis. Ich glaubte nämlich, aus einem Brief von Ihnen über die Ricketsschen Zeichnungen Ihre Zusage herauslesen zu dürfen. Ich habe auch wohl erwähnt, als ich aus Paters *Marius* einmal vorlas, dass er wahrscheinlich im Insel-Verlage erscheinen wurde.

Wie daraus die Erzählungen werden konnten, die Ihnen zu Ohren kamen, verstehe ich nicht. Aber ich soll auch über andere Bekannte von mir, deren Namen zu erwähnen mir nie beifiel, die tollsten Gerüchte ausgestreut haben, und, wie mir mein Freund August Endell erzählt, gehen auch über mich die unmöglichsten Gerüchte um. Man behauptet, mir allabendlich in einem verrufenen Hotel zu sehen, wo ich dem 'jeu' obliege u.d.m. Ich erzähle Ihnen das alles, um Ihnen die von Ihnen vernommenen Gerüchte begreiflicher erscheinen zu lassen.

Wenn von meiner Seite eine Schuld vorhanden ist, so ist es die, dass ich das Bedürfnis habe, mit anderen über Pläne und Hoffnungen zu reden, die noch im Ungewissen schweben.

Ich werde jedenfalls daraus die Lehre ziehen, dass ich künftig erst von den Dingen rede, wenn sie faits accomplis sind.

Es sollte mir furchtbar leid thun, wenn ich durch Unvorsichtigkeit und Böswilligkeit die Verbindung mit Ihnen, die mir besonders wertvoll war, verscherzt hätte.

Wenn Sie Sich doch noch entschliessen wollten, den Wilde zu bringen, so könnte ich nunmehr auch einen Vorschlag über den Buchschmuck machen. Doch möchte ich zunächst ein Wort von Ihnen erwarten.

Ich bin inzwischen mit vorzüglicher Hochachtung
Ihr sehr ergebener
Felix Paul Greve

TO R. VON POELLNITZ

Königin Augustastr. 3[i]
Berlin W.
November 19, 1902

Dear Mr. von Poellnitz,

Yesterday I took the liberty of sending you a copy of my translation of Oscar Wilde's *Intentions*.[1]

The reason for my not replying sooner to your detailed letter, for which I thank you belatedly, was partly because I was not well and partly owing to all kinds of renewed agitations. I can only explain the many kinds of fantastic rumours circulating about me by assuming that someone is interested in ruining me with the most incredible things I am supposed to have done or said. I can assure you most emphatically, for instance, that I have never talked about an invitation from you to an 'unbelievably opulent dinner.' I recall very clearly that I talked about my stay in Leipzig. In a completely different sense, however, than you indicate. My first meeting with you appeared to me very comical because of the haste in which everything was agreed upon; and when some friends of mine returned from Munich, I told them, in a burst of good humour and in the sense indicated above, about my visit to you, exaggerating grotesquely. However, my story was not limited to that alone, but to everything I did in Leipzig that morning. I can no longer even say whether I mentioned your name. If I did so, I regret it profoundly, especially as it was unimportant for the story I wanted to tell. In so far as my books are concerned, I was labouring, to be sure, under a delusion. That is to say, I gathered from your letter that I was permitted to take your approval for granted concerning the drawings by Rickets.[2] I probably also mentioned, when I once read aloud from Pater's *Marius*, that it would probably be published by the Insel-Verlag.

How this developed into the rumours that reached you I do not understand. But I am also supposed to have spread the wildest rumours about other acquaintances of mine, whose names it would never occur to me to mention, and, as my friend August Endell[3] tells me, the most incredible rumours are circulating about me too. People claim to see me every evening in a disreputable hotel, where I am supposed to be gambling, and so on. I am telling you all this to make the rumours you may have heard about me more comprehensible to you.

If I am to blame in any way, it is because I have the urge to talk to others about hopes and plans which are still uncertain.

In any case, I shall learn from this that in future I shall only talk about things, when they are *faits accomplis*.

I should be terribly sorry, if I had forfeited, through ill-will or carelessness, my connection with you, which was always particularly valuable to me.

If you should still decide to publish Wilde,[4] I could now make a recommendation about the illustrations too. But I shall wait for a word from you first.

In the meantime I remain,
Yours truly,
Felix Paul Greve

1 The German translation by Greve bore the title *Fingerzeige* (Minden: J.C.C. Bruns 1903).

2 Charles Ricketts (1866–1931), British painter, sculptor, engraver, author, designer for the stage, founder of the Vale Press and designer of the Vale Books. He lived for many years with his fellow-artist Charles Shannon (1863–1937), and was a joint editor, with Shannon, of *The Dial* from 1889 to 1904. He was elected RA in 1928, Shannon in 1921. They jointly designed and decorated Oscar Wilde's *A House of Pomegranates* (1891), and Ricketts designed and decorated *The Picture of Dorian Gray* (1891), *Intentions* (1891), *Lord Arthur Savile's Crime* (1891), *The Sphinx* (1894), the limited edition of Wilde's *Poems* (1892), and the Collected Edition of 1908. According to Rupert Croft-Cooke (see his *The Unrecorded Life of Oscar Wilde*, 1972), Ricketts met Oscar Wilde in 1889, and visited him in Reading jail. Apparently the principal characters in *The Picture of Dorian Gray* had their counterparts in real life, and 'Basil Hallward ... was Charles Shannon, the artist who lived for many years in marital bliss with Charles Ricketts' (Rupert Croft-Cooke, *op. cit.* 112).

3 August Endell (1871–1925), self-taught German architect and designer noted for his Art Nouveau decorations. His most famous work is the Studio Elvira (1897–98) in Munich. He was married twice, in 1901 and 1909. It was presumably his first wife, Else Hildegard Ploetz, who eloped with Greve in 1902.

4 *Das Granatapfelhaus*

Bonn a/Rh.
May 12, 1903

Sehr geehrter Herr von Poellnitz!

Ihren werten Brief, für den ich bestens danke, empfing ich gestern. 'In a Gondola,' 'A Blot,' und ein paar Zeilen über 'Brownings Stil' als eventuelle Vorbemerkung vor den ersten Band, sind unterwegs. Die Übersetzung des *Paracelsus* übernehme ich mit Vergnügen. Die Briefe habe ich bereits liegen (in Palermo). Ein Teil daraus erscheint demnächst in der Neuen Deutschen Rundschau.

Von Dowson kann ich nicht sehr viel sagen. Äusseres:

Bohémien-Caffé-leben. Beständige Not. Des Verlegers (Smithers) Checks halten ihn eben über Wasser. Paris: Quartier Latin, London: Soho-Square. Absinthtrinker. Unmässiger Zigarettenraucher (man erzählt: 120 pro Tag). Starb sehr jung (ich glaube, mit 27 Jahren) an der Schwindsucht. Besuchte Wilde im Gefänginis. – Als Künstler: feiner Lyriker, sehr zart, sehr duftig, oft dünn, selten stark, dann freilich erschütternd. Von Verlaine beeinflusst. Unendlich müde, aber von einer letzten, schönen Müdigkeit. Als Erzähler gilt ziemlich das Gleiche von ihm. Eine Neigung, Lebens*schlüsse* zu erzählen.

Das ist ziemlich alles, was ich weiss, ohne spekulative Kritik zu treiben und mich in meine Psychologie der Dekadenz zu verirren (von der übrigens ein Stück in Gestalt eines Büchleins über Wilde erscheint oder schon erschienen ist.)

Ich hoffe, über meine anderen Einsendungen von Ihnen zu hören, und Sie auch demnächst persönlich aufsuchen zu können. Inzwischen verbleibe ich mit vorzüglicher Hochachtung

Ihr sehr ergebener
Felix Paul Greve

TO R. VON POELLNITZ

Bonn on the Rhine
May 12, 1903

Dear Mr. von Poellnitz!

Thank you very much for your kind letter that I received yesterday. 'In a Gondola,' 'A Blot,' and a few lines on 'Browning's Style' as a possible foreword to the first volume are on their way. I shall be delighted to do the translation of *Paracelsus*. The letters are already completed (in Palermo).[1] Parts of them will appear soon in *Neue Deutsche Rundschau*.[2]

I cannot say very much about Dowson. Outward appearance: Bohémian life in café houses. In constant need of money. Cheques of his publisher (Smithers) keep him just above water. Paris: Quartier Latin, London: Soho Square. Absinthe drinker. Heavy cigarette smoker (they say: 120 a day). Died very young (I believe at age 27) of tuberculosis. Visited Wilde in prison. – As artist: fine lyricist, very delicate, very fragrant, often weak, seldom strong, but then profoundly moving. Influenced by Verlaine. Extremely weary, but of a final beautiful weariness. More or less the same applies to him as a prose writer. A tendency to dwell on the *final* phases of life.

That is about all I know without indulging in speculative criticism and getting lost in my psychology of decadence (of which by the way a bit in the form of a booklet about Wilde is going to be, or has been, published).[3]

I hope to hear from you about the other things I mailed to you and to be able to visit you personally very soon. In the meantime I remain with highest regards,

Yours very sincerely
Felix Paul Greve

1 The Browning letters, translated by Greve, were published by S. Fischer of Berlin in 1905, under the title *Briefe von Robert Browning und Elizabeth Barrett Browning*.
2 If a selection of these letters was published in the *Neue Deutsche Rundschau*, I have been unable to find it.
3 Greve published two monographs on Oscar Wilde in 1903: *Oscar Wilde* (Moderne Essays, Nr. 29. Berlin: Verlag Gose u. Tetzlaff), and *Randarabesken zu Oskar Wilde* (Minden: J.C.C. Bruns). The latter book, however, was not published until October 1903.

Wilhelmstr. 19
Bonn a/Rh.
Juni 6, 1903

Sehr geehrter Herr von Poellnitz,

Ich schreibe Ihnen heute sozusagen persönlich, da ich es bei geschäftlichen Beziehungen wie den unseren für absolut notwendig halte, dass Klarheit zwischen beiden Parteien herrsche. Sie werden vermutlich aus den Zeitungen über die Katastrophe erfahren haben, die mich getroffen hat. Ich kann von Ihnen nicht erwarten, dass Sie Sich (!) eine mir günstige Auffassung in dieser Sache gebildet hätten, viel weniger, dass Sie unmittelbar den richtigen Zusammenhang errieten, den auch eine Gerichtsverhandlung nicht klarlegen konnte – wie ich es von meinen Freunden verlange. Ich hoffe, einmal in aller Ruhe mit Ihnen über die Sache reden zu können.

Nun aber möchte ich Sie herzlichst bitten, darum Ihre Beziehungen zu mir nicht abbrechen zu wollen, sondern sowohl den Browning wie auch Wilde und Pater (?) weiterzubringen: erstens, um der Sache willen; zweitens, weil ein Bruch für mich gleichbedeutend wäre mit vollständigem Ruin.

Um Ihnen aber nach außen hin die Sache zu erleichtern, wäre ich einverstanden, wenn wir ein Pseudonym (Friedrich Karl Gerden) wählten, ja, ich bin sogar zu vollständiger Anonymität bereit. Ich überlasse das Ihnen.

Ich bitte nochmals um der Sache und um meinetwillen, sich dieses Arrangement zu überlegen. Besonders dankbar wäre ich auch für eine baldige Entscheidung über den *Marius*. Sie wissen, dass ich nicht mehr für mich allein zu sorgen habe, und deshalb selbst im Voraus rechnen muß.

Inzwischen verbleibe ich mit ausgezeichneter Hochachtung

Ihr sehr ergebener
Felix Paul Greve

TO R. VON POELLNITZ

Wilhlmstr. 19
Bonn on the Rhine
June 6, 1903

Dear Mr. von Poellnitz,

Today I write to you – so to speak – privately, since I deem it absolutely necessary in business connections such as ours that there be clarity on both sides.

You have presumably read in the newspapers about the disaster which has overtaken me.[1] I cannot expect from you – as I demand from my friends – that you should have formed in this matter an opinion favourable to me, much less that you would guess immediately the true circumstance, which even a court trial could not elucidate. I hope in the future to be able to talk with you about this matter calmly and uninterruptedly.

Now, however, I would like to ask you most sincerely not to wish to break off relations with me, but to continue with Browning as well as Wilde and Pater (?): firstly for the sake of the project itself, and secondly because a break would be for me the same as complete ruin.

But in order to make things easier for you with respect to the public, I would agree, if we were to choose a pseudonym (Friederich Carl Gerden), in fact, I even agree to complete anonymity. I leave that to you.

Again I ask you for the sake of the project and for my own sake to consider this arrangement. I would also be especially grateful for an early decision about the *Marius*. You know that I no longer have to support only myself and must therefore make calculations in advance.

In the meantime I remain with the highest regards
Yours truly
Felix Paul Greve

1 The 'disaster' is obviously a reference to Greve's trial and conviction on charges of fraud. On May 29, 1903 he was sentenced to one year's imprisonment which he served in the Bonn jail – which was, and still is, located at 19 Wilhelmstrasse (Greve's address in this and the following three letters).

Wilhelmstr. 19
Bonn a/Rh.
Juni 14, 1903

Sehr geehrter Herr von Poellnitz,

ich danke Ihnen für Ihren werten Brief vom 11.vi. Ich habe nun heute eine grosse Bitte an Sie und wäre Ihnen sehr dankbar, wenn Sie derselben gelegentlich denken würden.

Wie Sie wissen, habe ich nicht nur für mich allein zu sorgen, und infolgedessen stehen jetzt die pekuniären Fragen bei mir im Vordergrunde des Interesses. Ich wäre ohne weiteres bereit, jede Arbeit, die ich leisten kann, zu übernehmen, um dadurch Geld zu verdienen, selbst, wenn sie mir nicht so nahe liegen sollte, wie die Dinge, die ich bisher getrieben habe. Ich beherrsche ausser dem Deutschen drei Sprachen vollständig: Englisch, Französisch und Italienisch. Meine Bitte nun ist die, dass wenn Sie gelegentlich selbst irgend ein Werk der betreffenden Sprachen herauszugeben beabsichtigen, ober etwa unter Ihren Bekannten, vielleicht von Herrn Diederichs davon hören, dass Sie Sich dann meiner erinnern möchten, oder ein Wort der Empfehlung sagten. Dass die gelieferte Arbeit an Sorgfalt und Genauigkeit nichts zu wünschen lassen würde, brauche ich nicht erst zu versichern. Auch aus den alten Sprachen würde ich als studierter Altphilologe natürlich mit Vergnügen übersetzen.

Ich habe grosse Lust, die 'Contes' von Flaubert zu übertragen; wäre das nicht etwas für Sie? Ferner dachte ich an den Engländer Wells, der in England und Frankreich neben Kipling eine grosse Rolle spielt und bei uns ganz unbekannt ist. Auch der Italiener Verga fände sicher sein Publikum, zumal er der Antipode von d'Annunzio ist und ihm an wirklicher Bedeutung doch wohl überlegen. –

Dass der *Marius* also gar keine Aussichten hat, ist natürlich äusserst deprimierend für mich, zumal er mich fast dreiviertel Jahr Arbeit gekostet hat. Wissen Sie vielleicht irgend einen Verlag, der ihn eventuell bringen würde? Ich hatte ziemlich fest auf die Einnahme zum Winter gerechnet.

Schliesslich noch ein Wort über den *Paracelsus*. Die Arbeit daran schreitet rüstig fort, und zwar schneller, als ich gedacht hatte. Sie werden das Manuskript bald in Händen haben. Aber das Honorar! Der Umfang ist fast de vierfache (der Paracelsus enthält 4500 Verse) der beiden anderen Dramen. Es werden in dem kleinen Format ca. 220 Seiten! Und mir scheint da doch die Summe etwas zu klein, selbst wenn ich die Hauptsache eben um der Sache willen thue. Könnten wir nicht in diesem Falle wenigstens die doppelte Summe, also 200 M ansetzen? Ich hatte ursprünglich auf 400 M. dafür, auf 300 M. für jedes der anderen grösseren Dramen, und 200 M. für die kleinen gerechnet. Es wird doch vermutlich auch im Buchhandel den doppelten Preis bringen! – Schliesslich habe ich noch eine Bitte: würden Sie mir eventuell die 'Altitalienischen Novellen' senden? Ich entbehre sehr eine derartige Lektüre.

Für eine Antwort auf all meine Fragen wäre ich Ihnen sehr dankbar. Inzwischen verbleibe ich mit vorzüglicher Hochachtung

Felix Paul Greve

Sollte man nicht einmal Balzac übertragen?

TO R. VON POELLNITZ

Wilhelmstr. 19
Bonn on the Rhine
June 14, 1903

Dear Mr. von Poellnitz,

Thank you for your kind letter of June 11th. Today I have a great favour to ask of you, and I would be very grateful if you would give it some thought at your leisure.

As you know, it is not only for myself that I have to provide, and consequently questions of money are of prime interest to me at the moment. I would be prepared without further ado to undertake any kind of work I can do in order to make money, even if such work were not to suit me as well as the things which I have pursued up to now. I am completely in command of three languages besides German: English, French and Italian. My request now is that if by chance you should intend to publish anything in one of these respective languages, or if you hear about [such intentions] among your acquaintances, perhaps Mr. Diederichs,[1] you might keep me in mind or pass along a word of recommendation. I do not need to assure you that the finished work would leave nothing to be desired in point of care and exactitude. I would be happy to translate from the classical languages also as I am a trained classical scholar.

I have a great desire to translate the *Tales* of Flaubert.[2] Would that not be something for you? I also thought about the Englishman Wells,[3] who is famous in England and France on a par with Kipling and here practically unknown. The Italian Verga would find a public, especially since he is the exact opposite of d'Annunzio and yet superior to him in real significance.[4]

That the *Marius* has no prospects is, of course, extremely depressing to me, especially since it cost me three quarters of a year of work. Would you perhaps know of a publishing house that might possibly publish it? I had been counting rather heavily on the income for the winter.

Finally a further word about *Paracelsus*. Work on it is proceeding well and faster than I had thought. You will get the manuscript very soon. But the honorarium! The scope is almost four times that of the two other plays (the *Paracelsus* contains 4500 lines). There will be about 220 pages in that small format! And the sum to be paid does seem rather too small, even though I do the job mainly for the sake of the subject. Couldn't we at least double the sum in this case, to 200 M[arks]? Originally I had counted on 400 M[arks], 300 M[arks] for each of the longer plays and 200 M[arks] for the shorter ones. I presume that it will still bring twice the price in the book trade! – Finally I have one more request: would you perhaps send me the *Altitalienischen Novellen*?[5] I miss reading matters like that.

I would be thankful for a reply to all my questions.
In the meantime I remain,
Yours truly
Felix Paul Greve

P.S. Should one not try to translate Balzac sometime?[6]

1 Eugen Diedrichs (1867–1930), a German publisher

2 Greve translated Flaubert's *La Tentation de Saint-Antoine* (*Die Versuchung des heiligen Antonius*, Minden: J.C.C. Bruns 1905) and a volume of letters (*Briefe an Zeit- und Zunftgenossen*, Minden: J.C.C. Bruns 1907), edited Flaubert's *Reiseblätter* (Minden: J.C.C. Bruns 1906), which was translated by E. Greve, and provided commentary for Flaubert's *Briefe über seine Werke* (Minden: J.C.C. Bruns 1904), also translated by E. Greve. These translations were included in Flaubert's *Gesammelte Werke* in 10 volumes (Minden: J.C.C. Bruns 1906–7).

3 Greve translated several works of H.G. Wells, all published by J.C.C. Bruns of Minden: *Ausblicke auf die Folgen d. techn. u. wiss. Fortschritt f. Leben und Denken d. Menschen* (1905), *Doktor Moreaus Insel* (1904), *Die ersten Menschen im Mond* (1905), *Die Riesen kommen!* (1904), and *Die Zeitmaschine* (1904). *Die Zeitmaschine* has remained continuously in print since its publication.

4 I am not aware of any tranlations by Greve of Verga's or d'Annunzio's works.

5 By Paul Ernst (1866–1933), published in 1902

6 Greve did translate several sections of Balzac's *Menschliche Komödie* (Leipzig: Insel-Verlag 1908–9).

Wilhelmstr. 19
Bonn, Rh.
Oktober 26, 1903

Sehr geehrter Herr von Poellnitz,

Ich möchte zunächst um eine Änderung im Titel des Wildebandes bitten. Ich weiss, dass ich damals bei der Übersetzung lange suchte und mit dem, was ich schliesslich schrieb, keineswegs zufrieden war. Jetzt ist mir eine Verbesserung eingefallen: 'Das Granatapfelhaus'. – Ich hoffe, der Titel wird noch danach gedruckt werden können.

Ferner sind mir in letzter Zeit mehrfach Kritiken früherer Wildebände von mir und einer kleinen Broschüre über Wilde (die ich, wenn ich mich recht entsinne, so frei war, Ihnen senden zu lassen) zugegangen, in denen auf den bei Ihnen erscheinenden Band hingewiesen wird. Auch habe ich in eben dieser Broschüre (die im Frühjahr erschienen ist) bereits den in Frage stehenden Band als in 'Vorbereitung' angekündit: ich möchte also zur Erwägung stellen, ob es nicht geraten sein dürfte, den Übersetzernamen statt des Pseudonym zu drucken oder aber eine Notiz über die Übersetzung ganz bei Seite zu lassen, da sonst mein Pseudonym sofort aufgedeckt ist.

Schliesslich möchte ich noch ein Wort über den Bühnenvertrieb der kleinen Browningschen Dramen hinzufügen. Herr v. Langen, Berlin, hat sich mir gegenüber in Sachen der Dramen Wildes so unkulant gezeigt, (un keinen stärkeren Ausdruck zu gebrauchen: die Sache eignet sich zu gelegentlicher Veröffentlichung) dass ich sehr wenig Lust verspüre, in irgend welche

Beziehungen zu seinem Institut zu treten: Nur um so weniger, wenn, wie Sie schreiben, der Insel-Verlag in freundschaftlichen Beziehungen zu ihm steht – denn das beweist, dass ein Arrangement möglich war. Ich dagegen habe die Druckkosten für 2 Bände in je 2000 Exempl. tragen müssen, weil besagter Herr das Arrangement als unmöglich hinstellte. Die Einzelheiten, die die Sache erst pikant machen, kann ich leider so kurz nicht schildern. Mir ist dunkel, als hätte ich Ihnen seiner Zeit davon gesprochen. Auch dürfte Herr v. L. kaum geneigt sein, den Bühnenvertrieb zu übernehmen: denn längst, ehe von der jetzigen Ausgabe die Rede war, haben ihm die Dramen im Manuskript vorgelegen; er aber lehnte sie ab, indem er mir schrieb, Georg (sic!) Browning eigne sich leider nicht für seine Anstalt. Ich könnte weitere Einwände gegen die Vermittlung durch diesen Herrn häufen, aber, wie gesagt, erst die Einzelheiten machen die Sache interessant. – Mir persönlich wäre Fischer zehnmal lieber, da ich sowohl mit dem Verlag wie mit der Bühnenabteilung in den besten Beziehungen stehe, und zweifellos auch die übrigen Dramen Brownings durch seine Vermittlung vertreiben lasse. Ich muss gestehen, dass ich lieber auf jede Bühnen- [sic] verzichten würde, als gerade mit H.v.L. in Verbindung trete, zumal es doch nur durch persönlichen Einfluss gelingen dürfte, vielleicht eins von den kleinen Dramen ('Auf einem Balkon') an einer oder zwei uneigennützigen Bühnen anzubringen.

Natürlich kommt das nur dann in Frage, wenn das Aufführungsrecht ausschliesslich *mir* gehört, was ich glaube – jedenfalls war es meine Absicht, es mir zu reservieren – und auch dann werde ich den Bühnenvertrieb nicht an S. Fischer geben, wenn Sie Einwände dagegen haben sollten.

Noch eins: ich fragte Sie im Januar in Berlin persönlich, ob es Ihnen recht sei, wenn ich aus dem Dowson und dem Wildebande vielleicht je eine Erzählung in die Neue Deutsche Rundschau brächte, was Sie bejahten. Leider konnte ich es bei Dowson nicht arrangieren, weil die N.D.R. gerade eine ganze Reihe von Sachen von mir brachte und auf mehrere Nummern hinaus versehen war. Ich möchte dagegen jetzt sehr gern eine der Wildeschen Erzählungen mit einem Hinweis auf das Buch dort publizieren. Ich hoffe, Sie haben auch jetzt nichts dagegen.

Der Dowsonband wird auf meine Veranlassung an einigen Stellen (Magazin etc) besprochen werden: ich werde es auch für die Browningbändchen arrangieren. Wenn es Sie interessiert, werde ich Ihnen die Rezensionen zugehen lassen.

Ich verbleibe mit ausgezeichneter Hochachtung
Ihr sehr ergebener
Felix Paul Greve

TO R. VON POELLNITZ

Wilhelmstr. 19
Bonn on the Rhine
October 26, 1903

Dear Mr. von Poellnitz,

First I would request a change in the title of the Wilde volume. I remember how I searched when I translated, and I was not at all satisfied with the one I finally hit upon. An improvement has just now occurred to me: *Das Granatapfelhaus* – I hope this title can still be printed.

Also I received recently reviews of my earlier Wilde volumes and a little booklet about Wilde (which, if I remember correctly, I took the liberty of having sent to you) in which reference is made to the volume you are publishing. I also announced in that very booklet (which was published in the spring) that the book in question was 'in preparation': I wonder, therefore, whether it might not be advisable to print the name of the translator instead of the pseudonym, or else leave out the note about the translation altogether, since otherwise my pseudonym would be instantly disclosed.

Finally I should like to add a further word about the stage sale of the short Browning plays. Mr. von Langen,[1] Berlin, has shown himself to be so unkind about me in the matter of the Wilde plays[2] (not to use a stronger expression: the matter would be suitable for publication at an opportune time) that I have very little desire to establish any kind of connection with his institute: even less so, if, as you write, he is on friendly terms with the Insel-Verlag – for that proves that an arrangement was possible. On the contrary, however, I had to bear the cost of printing 2 volumes of 2,000 copies each, because the gentleman mentioned stated that the arrangement was impossible. Unfortunately I cannot describe so briefly the details which make the matter so piquant. I have the feeling that I talked to you about this at one time. Mr. von L[angen] would hardly be inclined to take over the stage sale, because even before there was any talk about the current edition, the dramas were submitted to him in manuscript and he refused them, writing to me that Georg (sic!) Browning was unfortunately not suitable for his publishing company. I could add further objections to the mediation of this gentleman, but, as I mentioned before, only the details make the matter interesting. – I would prefer Fischer[3] ten times over, since I am on the best possible footing with the publisher and the stage department and shall doubtless sell also the other plays by Browning with their help. I must admit that I would rather give up stage-performance altogether than ask Mr. von L[angen]'s help, especially since it would be possible only through personal influence to dispose of perhaps one of the small plays ('Auf einem Balkon') to one or two independent stages.

Of course that question only arises when the right of performance, as I believe it does, belongs to me exclusively – in any case it was my intention to reserve it for myself – and even then I shall not give S. Fischer the right to sell, if you should raise objections to it.

One more point: I asked you in January in Berlin personally if it were all right with you, if I published one story each from the Dowson and Wilde volumes in the *Neue Deutsche Rundschau*,[4] to which you agreed. Unfortunately I could not arrange to do so in the case of the Dowson, as the *N.D.R.* was just then publishing several of my pieces and was booked for a number of issues. Now I would very much like to publish one of the Wilde stories in it to advertise the book itself. I hope you have nothing to object to this matter either.

On my suggestion the Dowson volume will be reviewed in a few places (*Magazin*[5] etc.). I shall arrange the same for the short Browning volumes. If you are interested I shall have the reviews sent to you.

I remain
Yours very truly
Felix Paul Greve

1 Arthur von Langen, who from Greve's description here appears to have been either a publisher or a producer of plays, probably the latter. Herr Klähn, Verlagleiter with Insel-Verlag Anton Kippenberg, Leipzig, wrote (June 11, 1974) in response to an enquiry that he was unable to identify the man. The reference is not apparently to Albert Langen (1869–1909), whose publishing house, established in 1894, was located in Munich, not Berlin.

2 It is not clear whether this is a reference to the stage production in Berlin of some of Oscar Wilde's plays in Greve's translation, or to their publication in Germany. According to a bibliography prepared for me by Dr Reinhard Tgahrt of the Deutsche Literaturarchiv Schiller-Nationalmuseum, Marbach am Neckar, the following plays in Oscar Wilde, *Sämtliche Werke in deutscher Sprache* (Wien: Wiener Verlag, Berlin: Globus Verlag), are in Greve's translation: 'Vera oder die Nihilisten' (*Vera; or, The Nihilist*) Mit e. Essay: Oscar Wilde und das Drama von Felix Paul Greve (Bd. 7, 1908), 'Eine Frau ohne Bedeutung' (*A Woman of No Importance*) (Bd. 9, 1908); and 'Bunbury' (ie, *The Importance of Being Earnest*) (Bd. 10, 1908). It is not certain whether this was their first publication, for some of these as well as some others not so far identified as being Greve's translations may have been issued earlier in single volumes. For example, Kayser's *Bücherlexikon 1907–1910* (p 1251) records the publication in 1907 of *Ernst sein! (Bunbury)* in Herman Frhrn. von Teschenberg's translation (Leipzig: M. Spohr). Although it has not been established that this translation and that used in the *Sämtliche Werke* are identical, Greve's known propensity for pseudonyms makes one wonder.

3 Samuel Fischer (1859–1934), who in 1886 established the publishing firm, S. Fischer Verlag, in Berlin. The firm has since prospered with branches in several countries.

4 In the index volume of the *Rundschau* covering the period between 1890 and 1909, there is no mention of Greve. However, several reviews and articles signed 'F.P.' or 'F.Pg.' and a chapter from Greve's translation of *The Picture of Dorian Gray* (unsigned, 1903) had appeared in the *Rundschau* between 1901 and 1905.

5 It is still not known what articles, if any, either by Greve or about him had appeared in *Magazin*.

Wilhelmstr. 19
Bonn a. Rh.
November 16, 1903

Herrn R. von Poellnitz, Leipzig, Insel-Verlag,

Sehr geehrter Herr, Ihren werten Brief vom 10. XI habe ich dankend erhalten. Ich sehe mich gezwungen, einige Worte darauf zu erwidern, um ev. Missverständnissen vorzubeugen, resp. sie rückgängig zu machen. Denn mir scheint ja, es ist sicher, dass Sie mich in mehreren Punkten missverstanden haben.

Zunächst habe ich ausdrücklich gesagt, dass ich den Bühnenvertrieb der Browningschen Dramen nur dann vergeben würde, wenn Sie absolut nichts dagegen einzuwenden hätten. Ich ersehe aus Ihrem Brief, dass Sie nicht nur gegen die Vergebung an Fischer Einwände haben, sonden dass auch mein Wunsch inbetreff einer ev. Vermittlung durch die 'Deutsche Bühne,' Berlin (der doch begreiflich genug war) Ihr höchstes Missfallen erregt hat. Ich bedaure das in höchstem Grade, – jedenfalls aber wird von meiner Seite aus in Bezug auf irgendwelche Vermittlung *nichts* mehr erfolgen. Ich verzichte darauf umso leichter, als ich vertraue, bei den ganz wenigen Bühnen, die überhaupt in Frage kommen dürften, durch persönliche Verbindungen mehr auszurichten als durch irgend welche geschäftliche Vermittlung. Trotzdem kann ich nicht umhin, eine Frage zu stellen. Sie bedauern, für eine Vermittlung durch S. Fischer keine Bühnenexemplare abgeben zu können – wie wollten Sie diese Sache mit Herrn von Langen regeln, da sich doch dort die gleiche Schwierigkeit erhoben hätte? – Da ich doch denke, dass ich die mir in einem Brief vom 21.X. in Aussicht gestellten Autorenexemplare erhalten werde, so werde ich für meine Zwecke auch kaum weitere Ex. benötigen... Was den Abdruck einer Novelle von Dowson oder eines Märchens von Wilde anlangt, so versteht sich von selbst, dass ich damit nicht nach dem Erscheinen der Bücher kommen wollte, weshalb ich ausdrücklich nur von Wilde sprach. Aber auch da erhebt sich für mich eine Frage. Sie erboten Sich damals (im Januar 1903, in Berlin), die Fähnchen an die N.D.R. zu senden. Das hiess mit anderen Worten: 'lassen Sie den Abdruck machen, während wir das Buch vorbereiten.' Anders war es auch gar nicht möglich, da das Manuskript in Ihren Händen war. Entweder musste diese Erlaubnis bedeuten: 'Sie können den Abdruck kurz vor Erscheinen des Buches bringen' – oder sie bedeutete gar nichts: denn ehe ich Korrekturen hatte, konnte ich der N.D.R. keinen Text geben. Ich würde mich also für vollkommen berechtigt gehalten haben, auch ohne nochmalige Einwilligung den Abdruck zu veranlassen. Dass ich nochmals anfragte, war für mich nur eine Höflichkeitsform. Wäre darauf eine sofortige Antwort erfolge, dass Ihnen entgegen Ihrer früheren Zustimmung ein Abdruck aus irgend welchen Gründen jetzt nicht mehr angenehm sei, so hätten Sie mir reichliche Unannehmlichkeiten, vielleicht sogar Kosten erspart. Ich bezweifle zwar, ob das Buch am ersten Dez[ember] heraus sein kann, und also käme der Abdruck auf jeden Fall vor Erscheinen, und da ich fast drei Wochen vergebens auf eine Antwort gewartet habe, so ist das erste Märchen gerade drei Tage vor Empfang Ihrer

Absage in die Druckerei gewandert. Ich werde trotzdem mein Möglichstes thun, das Erscheinen zu hindern und die entstehende Lücke durch etwas anderes zu füllen... Was Besprechungen im *Magazin* angeht, so ist von meiner Seite nichts geschehen, sie zu provozieren. Ich bedaure, dass meine Unkenntnis dieses Blattes Sie hat reizen können. Ein Bekannter von mir, der anderweitig recht gescheite Dinge über englische Literatur gesagt hat, erbot sich, meine Ausgaben zu besprechen, und erwähnte dabei, glaube ich, unter anderen Blättern das M. Ich meinte Ihnen einen Gefallen zu thun, wenn ich ein wenig für die Verbreitung der Bücher mit sorgte, wie ich auch über Browning eine längere Anzeige in der Zukunft plante und noch nachträglich an einem Artikel über Paters 'Imaginary Portraits' arbeitete. Natürlich würde ich schon aus Höflichkeitsrücksichten niemals gegen die Wünsche meines Verlegers 'thun und lassen, was ich will,' da es schliesslich nicht so sehr darauf ankommt, 'was einem freisteht.' Jedenfalls sehe ich mich durch die Form Ihres Briefs gedrängt, Ihnen ausdrücklich zu versichern, dass ich von nun nichts wieder in der Hinsicht unternehmen werde, weder Besprechungen anregen, noch meine Exemplare an Leute senden, durch die eine Besprechung zu Stande kommen könnte, noch endlich selber meine Bücher anzeigen. ...

Schliesslich möchte ich wegen weiterer ev. Publikationen noch eignige Bemerkungen anfügen.

Da sowohl Wildes Märchen wie auch Dowsons Novellen in je einem Bande bei Ihnen erschienen sind, resp. erscheinen, so werde ich einen zweiten Band von beiden vorläufig nicht anderweitig vergeben, sondern liegen lassen, falls Sie ev. daran denken, wenn die beiden vorliegenden Bände Absatz und Beifall finden, auch die anderen folgen zu lassen (vielleicht in einem Jahr oder so). Vielleicht geben Sie mir darüber eine gelegentliche Antwort, da ich sie für den Fall, dass Sie diese Publikationen prinzipiell ausschliessen, Bruns oder Fischer geben möchte. – Auch Paters *Marius* werde ich liegen lassen, da einige Monate eifriger Bemühungen, jemanden dafür zu interessieren, erfolglos geblieben sind. Sollten Sie wider Erwarten noch einmal auf Parer zurückkommen, so bitte ich dann an mich zu denken. Das Manuskript steht jederzeit zu jedem nur annehmbaren Honorar zur Verfügung.

Inzwischen verbleibe ich mit vorzüglicher Hochachtung
Ihr sehr ergebener
Felix Paul Greve

TO R. VON POELLNITZ, LEIPZIG, INSEL-VERLAG

Wilhelmstr. 19
Bonn on the Rhine
November 11, 1903

Dear Sir,

Thank you for your kind letter of November 10th. I find myself compelled to answer it briefly in order to prevent possible misunderstandings or to put an end to them, for it seems to me – indeed, it is certain – that you have misunderstood me in several respects.

First of all, I expressly emphasized that I would only sell the stage rights to the Browning plays, if you had absolutely nothing against it. I gather from your letter that you not only object to my giving it to Fischer, but also that my wish regarding a possible negotiation with the Deutsche Bühne, Berlin,[1] (which was certainly understandable enough) has aroused your deepest displeasure. I regret that infinitely – in the future I, in any case, shall *not* ask anyone for help or negotiation on my behalf. I renounce it all the more easily as I believe I shall accomplish more with the very few stages in question by personal connection than by any kind of business connection. Nevertheless I cannot help but ask a question. You regret not being able to provide stage copies in the event of an arrangement with S. Fischer – how did you expect to arrange this matter with von Langen, since the same problem would have arisen there too? Since I have every reason to believe that I shall receive the author's copies promised in your letter of October 21st, I shall hardly need further copies for my own purposes. As far as the printing of a novella by Dowson or a fairy tale by Wilde is concerned, it goes without saying that I shall not come with my request after the books have appeared, which is why I expressly talked only about Wilde. But there too another question arises. You offered (in January 1903, in Berlin) to send the proofs to the *N[eue] D[eutsche] R[undschau]*. That meant, in other words: 'You go ahead with the printing [of the story] while we [ie, Insel-Verlag] prepare the book.' Otherwise it was not at all possible, as the manuscript was in your hands. This permission must either have meant: 'You publish the announcement shortly before the appearance of the book' – or it did not mean anything at all, for I could not give the text to *N.D.R.*, before I had the proofs. I would therefore have felt completely justified in having it printed without asking you again for permission. The fact that I asked you again was only a matter of courtesy on my part. Had you replied immediately that contrary to your earlier agreement you would now object to a copy for some reason or other, you would have spared me a lot of unpleasantness, perhaps even costs. I doubt indeed that the book will be out by the first of Dec[ember], and therefore the publication will in any case come before the appearance of the book! and since I waited in vain for your reply for nearly three weeks, the first fairy-tale went to the printing company just three days before receiving your refusal. I shall, however, do what I can to prevent publication and try to fill the gap with something else. ... So far as reviews in the *Magazin*[2] are concerned, I for my part did not do anything to provoke them. I regret that my ignorance of this publication was able to irritate you. An acquaintance of mine who has elsewhere published some very clever things about English literature has offered to review my publications and, I believe, also mentioned the *M[agazin]* among other journals. I thought I was doing you a favour by helping a little to promote the circulation of the books, just as I planned a longer review on Browning in the future and, in addition, was working on an article on Pater's *Imaginary Portraits*. Naturally, out of considerations of courtesy I would never 'do and omit whatever I wish to' against the wishes of my publisher, since ultimately it does not depend so much on what one is free to do. In any case, the tone of your letter impels me to assure you explicitly that in future I shall never do anything in this regard again, neither asking for reviews nor sending copies to people so that reviews could be written nor announcing my own books. ...

Finally I wish to add a few remarks concerning eventual future publications. Since both Wilde's fairy-tales and Dowson's stories have each appeared (or are about to appear) with you so far, I shall not pass along the second volume of both to anyone else for the time being. I prefer to wait in case you eventually decide to let the others follow (maybe in a year or so), ie if these first volumes sell well. Perhaps you could let me know about this soon, since I might like to give them to Bruns or Fischer in the event that you decide definitely against their publication, – I shall also let Pater's *Marius* rest, since months of eager effort have been unsuccessful in arousing anyone's interest in it. Should you, contrary to expectations, come back to Pater, I ask you to keep me in mind. The manuscript is available to anyone at any time for an acceptable honorarium.

In the meantime I remain
Yours very truly
Felix Paul Greve

1 Deutsche Bühne (literally 'German Theatre') may refer either to a theatre company or to Genossenschaft Deutscher BühnenAngehoriger, a theatre-workers' guild established in 1871.

2 See the preceding letter, note 5.

Wollerau, Kanton Schwyz
Schweiz
März 21, 1905

Sehr geehrter Herr Doktor,

ich gestatte mir, Ihnen mit gleicher Post ein Exemplar meiner Übersetzung von André Gides *Immoralisten* zu übersenden, das ich bitte, als ein Zeichen der Huldigung für den trefflichen Essayisten ansehen zu wollen. Dürfte ich vielleicht nebenbei eine Frage einfliessen lassen? Haben vielleicht Sie, wenn die Zukunft inzwischen das von mir übersetzte kleine Fragment aus Gides *Nourritures Terrestres* gebracht hat, Belegexemplare erhalten? Herr Harden kennt zwar, glaube ich, meine Adresse, aber er hat mir keine geschickt. Sollten Sie welche erhalten haben – ich hörte von M. Gide, Sie haben die Freundlichkeit gehabt, die Korrektur zu lesen, wofür ich Ihnen noch danke – so würden Sie mich sehr verpflichten, wenn Sie mir eines davon schickten. Es dürfte Sie interessieren, dass ich die Veröffentlichung zweier weiterer Bücher von Gide vorbereite: die der *Paludes* und der *Nourritures Terrestres*.

Genehmigen Sie, bitte, den Ausdruck meiner besten Wertschätzung.

Ihr sehr ergebener
Felix P. Greve

TO FRANZ BLEI[1]

Wollerau, Kanton Schwyz
Switzerland[2]
March 21, 1905

Dear Doctor,

I take the liberty of enclosing a copy of my translation of André Gide's *Immoraliste*,[3] which I wish to be regarded as a token of my reverence for the superb essayist. By the way, might I be permitted to ask a question? Did you by any chance receive complimentary copies, if in the meantime *Die Zukunft* has brought out the little fragment from Gide's *Nourritures Terrestres* which I translated?[4] Mr. Harden,[5] I believe, knows my address, but he did not send me any. If you have received any, – I learned from Mr. Gide that you were kind enough to read the proofs, for which I thank you – then you would oblige me very much if you were to send me one of them. It might be of interest to you that I am preparing for publication two more books by Gide: the *Paludes*[6] and the *Nourritures Terrestres*.[7]

Please allow me to express my best regards
Yours very sincerely
Felix Paul Greve

1 Franz Blei (1871–1948), Austrian novelist, essayist, and translator

2 This is the only indication I have that following his release from jail, Greve actually lived in Switzerland. In André Gide's 'Conversation avec un Allemand,' Greve speaks of his intention of so doing.

3 *Der Immoralist* (Minden: J.C.C. Bruns 1905)

4 I am not aware of this particular article, but several articles by Greve were published in *Die Zukunft*, including '*Der Immoralist*, von André Gide' in vol. LII (1905) 305–6.

5 Maximilian Harden (1861–1927), essayist and publicist, was editor of *Die Zukunft*.

6 *Die Sümpfe* (Minden: J.C.C. Bruns 1905)

7 This particular translation by Greve does not appear to have been published.

Felix Paul Greve
Nachodstr. 24
Berlin W. 15
März 6, 1907

Sehr geehrter Herr,

Wollen Sie bitte entschuldigen, wenn ich Ihre mir seinerzeit gesandte Aufforderung, Ihnen Daten für Ihr Lexikon anzugeben, so lange unbeantwortet liess. Ich war mit Arbeiten überhäuft. Beifolgend sende ich Ihnen einige biographische Notizen.

Hochachtungsvoll
Ihr sehr ergebener
Felix P. Greve

Ich wurde geboren am 14.11. 1879 zu Radomno, einem deutsch-russischen Grenzort, als Sohn mecklemburgischer Eltern, die dort vorübergehend ein Gut besassen. Meine frühere Jugend verlebte ich dann auf einem pommerschen Gutshof, die Jahre meines geistigen Erwachens in Hamburg. Dort absolvirte ich die lateinlose Realschule St. Pauli, da ich zunächst nach eigener Neigung und nach dem Wunsche meiner Eltern für den Kaufmannsberuf bestimmt war. Eigentlich erst, als ich schon in die Lehre treten sollte, kam mir der Gedanke an die Möglichkeit des Studirens: und zwar, wenn ich aufrichtig sein soll, lediglich aus einer Art Grössenwahn heraus. Ich war nämlich fest davon überzeugt, dass ich irgendwie einmal in der Welt einen Mittelpunkt abgeben müsste: ich hatte die Absicht, allerlei aus den Angeln zu heben: Mittel und Wege waren mir gleichgültig. Es folgten ein paar Jahre fieberhafter Vorbereitung auf das Abiturientenexamen. In den alten Sprachen bin ich fast vollständig Autodidakt. Da mir trotz der ungünstigsten Umstände dieser Versuch glänzend gelang – ich machte mein Abiturientenexamen am Johanneum mit Auszeichnung – so war ich in meinen weiten, aber noch sehr ungestimmten Plänen bestärkt. Wenn ich wiederum aufrichtig sein soll, so richteten sich meine Pläne, wenn sie überhapt Gestalt annahmen, eher aufs Technische als aufs Schönwissenschaftliche. Ich stellte mir vor, ich werd eines Tages Luftschiffe bauen oder ein leichtes Automobil erfinden, das mit zwei Pferdekräften so viel zu leisten imstand wäre wie heute eins mit fünfzig Pferdekräften. Von solchen Gedanken bin ich noch heute nicht frei. Trotzdem studierte ich Archäologie und alte Sprachen. Das Studium führte mich, bald eifrig, bald lässig betrieben, nach Bonn, Paris, London, Rom, Neapel, Griechenland und schliesslich nach München. In München begann ich, veranlasst durch einen blossen Zufall, zu übersetzen und – zunächst in parodistischer Absicht – zu dichten. Aus Lässigkeit und Verachtung der landesüblichen Karrieren gab ich mein Studium auf, überzeugt, dass ich auf jedem Wege durchs Leben und an meine Ziele gelangen werde. Dieser Ueberzeugung bin ich noch heute. Mit dreiundzwanzig Jahren heiratete ich. Etwa gleichzeitig veröffentlichte ich zwei Bändchen Verse, die schlecht sind, sobald man ihre parodistische Absicht ausser acht lässt. Seither lebte ich abwechselnd in Süditalien, der Schweiz, Nordfrankreich und jetzt in Berlin. Während der vier Jahre meiner Ehe schrieb ich zwei Romane und eine Komödie. Ich habe die Absicht, in den nächsten Jahren ein paar Werke zu schreiben, die ich für wichtiger halte, als alles, was ich bisher geschrieben habe, obgleich auch in ihnen allerlei Beachtenswertes stecken dürfte.

Verzeichnis meiner Schriften:
Wanderungen (Gedichte) – München, 1902
Helena und Damon, Ein Spiel in Versen – ebnda. 1902
Oscar Wilde, eine Studie – Berlin, 1903.
Randarabesken zu Oscar Wilde – Minden, 1903
Fanny Essler, Ein Berliner Roman – Stuttgart, 1905
Maurermeister Ihles Haus, Roman – Berlin 1907
Der Heimliche Adel, Komödie – (erscheint vorläufig nicht im Buchhandel, da ich zuvor eine Aufführung abwarte.)

TO FRANZ BRÜMMER,[1] NAUEN

Felix Paul Greve
Nachodstr. 24
Berlin W. 15
March 6, 1907

Dear Sir,

Please excuse me for having left unanswered so long your earlier request to give you data for your dictionary. I was overloaded with work. Enclosed I am sending you some biographical notes.

Yours very sincerely
Felix Paul Greve

I was born on 14.11.1879 in Radomno, a village on the border of Germany and Russia, a son of Mecklenburg parents who owned a farm-estate there for a short time. I spent my early youth on a Pomeranian farm-estate, and the years of my intellectual awakening in Hamburg. There I attended the St. Pauli Realschule, which did not teach Latin, because at first, according to my own desire and the wish of my parents, I was trained for the mercantile profession. In fact, just as I was about to start my apprenticeship, the idea of the possibility of study entered my mind, and indeed, speaking honestly, solely due to a kind of megalomania. That is to say, I was firmly convinced that in the future I would somehow, somewhere in the world, be a centre. I intended to bring about radical changes – the ways and means of achieving this were all the same to me. Then followed a few years of feverish preparation for the *Abiturientenexamen*. In classical languages, I am almost completely self-taught. Since I succeeded in this venture in spite of the most unfavourable circumstances – I graduated from the Johanneum with distinction – I was confirmed in my ambitious, but as yet indefinite, plans. If I were to speak the truth again, my plans were directed – if they were taking shape at all – more towards the technical side than towards the belletristic. I dreamed that I would one day build airships or invent a small automobile with two horse-power which would perform as well as the present-day cars of 50 horsepower. Even today I am not free of such thoughts. Nevertheless I studied archaeology and classical languages. Studies, which were pursued eagerly at some times and lazily at others, took me to Bonn, Paris, London, Rome, Naples, Greece and finally to Munich. In Munich, motivated by a mere accident, I started to translate and to write verse, at first with parodistic intent. Because of my *laissezfaire* attitude towards, and contempt for, conventional careers, I gave up my studies, convinced that I could go through life and attain my goals in any way. I still have the same conviction today. I married when I was twenty-three. At about the same time I published two thin volumes of verse, which are bad if one fails to take their parodistic intent into account. Since then I have lived in turn in southern Italy, Switzerland, northern France, and now I am living in Berlin. During the four years of my marriage, I wrote two novels and one comedy. In the years ahead I intend to write a couple of works which I regard as far more important than everything I have written so far, although my works up to now also might well contain all sorts of things worthy of consideration.

List of my works:
Wanderungen (verse) – Munich, 1902.
Helena und Damon, a play in verse – ebnda. 1902.
Oscar Wilde, a study – Berlin, 1903.
Randarabesken zu Oscar Wilde – Minden, 1903.
Fanny Essler, a Berlin novel – Stuttgart, 1905.
Maurermeister Ihles Haus, novel – Berlin, 1907.
Der Heimliche Adel, comedy – (presently not being offered for sale, pending stage-performance).

1 Franz Brümmer (1836–1923), German bibliographer and compiler of *Lexikon der deutschen Dichter und Prosaisten vom Beginn des 19. Jahrhunderts bis zur Gegenwart* (Leipzig 1910). On page 439 of the *Lexicon* (Vol. II) the entry on Greve summarizes the substance of this letter. The outline of this autobiography substantially agrees with what Frederick Philip Grove was later to say about his early life, although Grove claimed Swedish nationality and said that he was born sometime between 1871 and 1873.

Nachodstrasse 24
Berlin W. 15
April 15, 1907

Sehr geehrter Herr Doktor,

Was das Zuviel angeht, das Sie mir 'aufbürden', so können Sie darüber ohn Sorge sein. Ich habe meine ganz bestimmte Tagesleistung, die ich selten überschreite und fast nie nicht erreiche. Wenn, was ich ohne weiteres als möglich anerkenne, in den Nächten zuweilen Ungeschicklichkeiten oder Gleichförmigkeiten im Satzbau stehen bleiben (die [?] nach einem Vierteljahr niemanden unangenehmer im Ohr klingen als mir), so liegt das auch daran, dass ich bisher selbst bei den Korrekturen noch den ganzen Text, wie ich ihn übersetzte, aus dem Gedächtnis hersagen konnte (denn bei der ersten Arbeit wiederhole ich jeden Satz solange laut, bis er mir 'rund' genug scheint) – und das übt begreiflicherweise eine suggestive Gewalt, die blind macht. Ich folge gern Ihrer Anregung, noch einen dritten zur Lektüre heranzuziehen, einen Herrn, der früher schon für mich Korrekturen gelesen hat. Sie werden von selber sehen, dass ich etwas 'wirksamer' Korrektur lese, sobald zwischen der Übersetzung und der Lektüre mehr Zeit liegt: soviel Zeit, dass ich meinen Text inzwischen vergesse, was bei meinem Gedächtnis nicht ganz leicht ist.

Auf den Cervantes verwende ich ganz besondere Mühe, und ich glaube, er wird gut. Ich hatte übrigens, wie ich schon fürchtete, die Keller-Nottersche Übersetzung über-, und meine Arbeit unterschätzt. Ich halte diese Art der Modernisierung alter Texte nicht für praktisch und glaube fast, sie macht mehr Arbeit, als neu zu übertragen. Die Schwierigkeit liegt darin, dass man unbedingt den komplizierten Satzbau wahren muss, will man nicht das Gepräge des Originals verlieren. Dabei eine annähernd gleiche Klarheit zu bewahren, wie das Spanische sie hat, ist äusserst schwer, und Keller & Notter haben es sich sehr leicht gemacht: zudem sind sie doch, wie übrigens auch Förster und Müller, sehr ungenau. Das war nach der ersten Probe nicht zu beurteilen; jetzt sehe ich, dass dieser Novellenband mich *mehr* Arbeit, und, da es Korrekturarbeit ist, unerfreulichere Arbeit kostet als ein Band der Nächte. Das Hübscheste ist für mich einerseits die Kulturepoche (die des *Gil Blas*), und zweitens die Wiederbelebung meiner spanischen Kenntnisse, die solange vernachlässigt waren. Eins ist, wie mir scheint, unvermeidlich: ein wenig Korrekturkosten: es scheint mir physisch unmöglich, alles im gedruckten Text [Teil?] zu streichen, wofür ich geschriebens an den Rand setze. Wenn ich eine Stelle viermal durchlese und lasse sie liegen, entdecke ich am Tage darauf plötzlich noch ein Wort, das ich hätte streichen müssen und nicht gestrichen habe.

Da nun von Ihnen der Punkt des Zuviel-Arbeitens einmal berührt worden ist, so möchte ich diese Gelegenheit benutzen, um Ihnen ganz privatim eine Kleinigkeit zu sagen, die ein Verleger, der soviel mit mir arbeitet, vielleicht wissen sollte. Ich arbeite unter ganz ungesunden und anormalen Verhältnissen. Meine Arbeit leidet eigentlich nur unter *einem*: unter Geldsorgen. Wenn ich nicht auf eine Weile ruhig und sicher in die Zukunft blicken kann, überwältigen mich die Lasten, die auf mir liegen, und die, zum Teil ohne meine Schuld, z.T. durch meine Schuld auf mich gefallen sind. Dann leidet, wie ich wohl weiss, meine Arbeit in ihrer Qualität. Ich weiss nicht, ob ich Ihnen einmal erzählt habe, dass ich von meinem 16. Lebensjahr an meine Mutter und mich ernähren musste. Zum Teil noch aus jener Periode schreiben sich auch gewisse Lasten her, an denen ich noch auf Jahre hinaus zu tragen habe, und um Ihnen einen Begriff von ihnen zu machen, nenne ich die Summe von über 4000 M. jährlich. Da ich nun immer bestrebt bin, zunächst diesen alten Verpflichtungen – auch später um ihretwillen wieder übernommenen – nachzukommen, so bleibt *mir* von meinem Einkommen mitunter so gut wie nichts übrig, und es kommt vor, dass ich trotz meiner Erfolge mit meiner Frau einfach hungere. Ich spreche darüber nicht gern. Aber es erklärt Ihnen vielleicht, weshalb ich so oft um Geld bitte, obgleich ich ganz gut verdiene. Und ich sage es Ihnen auch, un Ihnen dies deutlich zu machen: Meine Arbeit is dann zuverlässig gut, und ich vertraue ihr am meisten, wenn ich auf eine Weile hinaus genügend Aufträge vor mir sehe, um vor Not gesichert zu sein. Ich habe jetzt in letzter Zeit ein wenig versäumt, andere Beziehungen zu suchen oder aufrecht zu erhalten, und bin ein wenig auf die Insel angewiesen. Und damit komme ich eigentlich zu einem Punkt, den ich berühren möchte: Haben Sie den *Don Quijote* schon vergeben? Oder würden Sie eventuell in Erwägung ziehen, ob Sie mir auch diese Arbeit anvertrauen könnten?

Wie schon gesagt, bitte ich diesen Brief als einen rein privaten anzusehen.

Mit den besten Empfehlungen
Ihr sehr ergebener
Felix P. Greve

TO ANTON KIPPENBERG[1]

Nachodstrasse 24
Berlin W. 15
April 15, 1907

Dear Doctor,

You should not worry about giving me too heavy a work load. I have a definite daily goal, which I seldom exceed and hardly ever reach. I realise that, as I work at night, sometimes clumsy and monotonous constructions remain unchanged in my sentence structure (three months later they sound to no-one more unpleasant than to me). The reason for this is that as I translated I memorized the complete text (while doing the work for the first time I usually repeat each sentence aloud to myself until it seems perfect) and understandably that excercises a suggestive power which creates blind spots. I accept your suggestion that there should be a third reader, a gentleman who has already read proofs for me before. You will discover that I read proofs somewhat more effectively as soon as there is more time between translation and proof-reading: a long enough interval for me to forget the text, which is not very easy with my memory.

I put a lot of effort into Cervantes[2] and I believe it will be good work. Moreover, as I feared, I had overestimated the Keller-Notter translation[3] and underestimated my own. I do not consider this method of modernising old texts practical, and I almost believe it requires more work than a new translation. The difficulty lies in the fact that it is absolutely necessary to preserve the original complicated sentence structure, if one does not wish to lose the impact of the original work. To do this and to make it as plain as the Spanish is, is extremely difficult, and Keller and Notter made it too easy for themselves: on the top of which they are also, like Förster and Müller,[4] very imprecise. That could not be judged after the first examination, but now I realise that this collection of *Novellen* is costing me more work, and as it is proof-reading, more unpleasant work than [?]. On the one hand, the nicest thing for me is the cultural period (that of *Gil Blas*[5]), and secondly thc brushing up of my knowledge of Spanish which I had neglected for so long. One thing, it appears to me, is inevitable: some expenses for proof-reading: it seems to me physically impossible to cross out everything in the printed text and make written comments in the margin. If I read a passage four times and leave it, the next day I suddenly discover another word I should have crossed out and didn't.

As you touched upon the problem of my working too hard, I should like to take this opportunity to confess very privately a detail that a publisher who works with me as much as you do should perhaps know. I work under very unhealthy and abnormal conditions. My work actually suffers from only one thing: financial worries. If I cannot for a while look to the future calmly and securely, I cannot bear the burdens which overwhelm me partly through my own fault, and partly not. I know then very well that my work suffers in its quality. I cannot remember whether I ever told you that I had to support my mother and myself from the time I was 16 years old. Certain of the debts can still be partly ascribed to that period, and it will take me years to pay them off! To give you an idea of them, I need about 4000 M(arks) annually. Since I make constant efforts to fulfil these old obligations, there is not much left of my own income, and it sometimes happens that in spite of my successes my wife and I simply starve. I do not like to talk about this. But perhaps it explains to you why I am so often asking for money, although I earn a good amount. I am also telling you this, so you can understand: my work is good and reliable, and I trust it best, when I have enough lined up ahead of me to feel secure. Lately I neglected keeping or looking for other connections and I depend somewhat on the Insel. And that leads me to one point I should like to touch upon: have you already promised the *Don Quixote* to someone else or would you possibly consider entrusting me with this job too?

As I mentioned before, I would appreciate if you would keep this letter confidential.

Yours very truly
Felix Paul Greve

1 Anton Kippenberg (1874–1950), publisher, Goethe scholar and collector, and friend of the poet Rainer Maria Rilke. Under his leadership Insel-Verlag became one of the most successful publishing enterprises of its kind, in recognition of which the firm is now known as Insel-Verlag Anton Kippenberg.

2 *Die Novellen* (1907) and *Don Quixote* (1908), in Greve's translation, were published by Insel-Verlag, but under one of his pseudonyms, Konrad Thorer.

3 *Cervantes' Sämtliche Romane und Novellen*, from the Spanish by Adelbert Keller and Friedrich Notter, 12 vols (Stuttgart 1839–42)

4 The Müller translation is obviously *Cervantes' Ausgewählte Werke*, translated by Hieronymus Müller, 6 vols (Stuttgart 1889–94). I have not been able to find any reference to the Förster translation.

5 Greve's translation of Le Sage's *Gil Blas* appeared in 1908 (Leipzig: Insel-Verlag), but under his pseudonym Konrad Thorer.

Nachodstrasse 24
Berlin W. 15
Mai 3, 1908

Sehr geehrter Herr Doktor,

Zunächst möchte ich mit bestem Dank den richtigen Eingang Ihrer zwei Sendungen von zusammen 566.60 M (fünfhundertsechsundsechzig Mark 60 Pf.) bestätigen.

Dann der Balzacbogen. Ich will nicht verhehlen, dass mir Ihr Brief eine rechte Enttäuschung bereitet hat, denn ich meinerseits finde den 2. Band, dem ich ja schliesslich jetzt wieder fern genug stehe, um ihn ein wenig beurteilen zu können, besser, um nicht zu sagen, noch besser als den ersten. Ich habe den Satzbau im ganzen ein wenig freier behandelt, was mir nicht wenig Arbeit machte. So habe ich denn heute, und zwar nicht allein, den Bogen 4 aufs genaueste noch einmal durchgesehen und mit dem Original verglichen. Ich habe mir erlaubt, meine Bemerkungen direkt in den Bogen einzutragen. Im Grunde finde ich nur eine wirkliche Verbesserung, Seite 58. In etwa 10 Fällen scheint mir die Aenderung eine Verschlechterung. In etwa ebenso viel Fällen ist die Aenderung annehmbar, aber vollständig unwesentlich; und nochmals in ungefähr ebenso viel Fällen ist, wenigstens wie mir scheint, nur ein Wort für ein anderes gesetzt, so dass ich bei jedem anderen als Ihnen einfach annehmen würde, dass es sich wirklich um nichts als eine Schulmeisterei handelt. Ich kann beim besten Willen nicht einsehn, weshalb Seite 49 'entgegenkam' besser sein sollte als das genauere 'entsprach'; oder Seite 58 'auf etwas zählen' schlechter als 'mit etwas rechnen'; oder Seite 62 'erheuchelter' besser als 'gespielter.'

Ich hatte schon während der Korrektur des 1. Bandes einmal die Absicht, auf die Tätigkeit des Korrektors zurückzukommen. Es waren da mehrmals umfangreiche Aenderungen in den Fahnen vorgenommen, die den Sinn vollständig entstellten; die zwar ein scheinbar flüssigeres Deutsch ergaben, aber eben an die Stelle des Richtigen etwas arg Falsches setzen, so dass ich einfach meinen Text wiederherzustellen hatte. Ich habe es damals noch nicht getan, weil der Korrektor in einer Kleinigkeit, in der ich mich versehen hatte, wirklich das Richtige traf, ich weiss nicht, ob in Kenntnis des Originals; aber den anderen Stellen gegenüber fällt die eine kaum ins Gewicht, und ich stehe noch jetzt unter dem entscheidenden Eindruck, dass der betr. Herr seine Befugnisse überschreitet und mir unnütze Arbeit macht, da ich mich bei Band I zum Schluss einfach genötigt sah, die Revisionsbogen noch einmal mit den Fahnen zu vergleichen. Dadurch bekomme ich zudem ein grosses Gefühl der Unsicherheit: ich fürchte mich zum Beispiel im *Don Quixote* mitunter da, wo ich ganz sicher bin, richtig zu übersetzen, vor einer von allen anderen Uebersetzungen abweichenden Version; fürchte mich in der Besorgnis, nachher doch diese einzig richtige Version nicht im gedruckten Band zu finden, während ich doch bisher im ersten Band bereits vier Stellen habe, die vor mir *noch nie richtig übersetzt* worden sind. Ich habe auch hin und wieder schon in den Nächten einmal eine kleine unliebsame Ueberraschung dieser Art erlebt, wo mir nichts weiter übrig blieb, als mir die Stellen für spätere Ausgaben vorzumerken.

Ich bitte, mir diese Bemerkungen nicht zu verargen; Sie werden verstehen, dass sie aus keiner 'Rechthaberei' fliessen, sondern lediglich aus dem Wunsch, nur noch Bücher herauszugeben, für die ich volle Verantwortung übernehmen kann: was bei manchen früheren Arbeiten meiner Lehrzeit naturgemäss nicht der Fall ist. Natürlich bleibt man fehlbar, und eine wirkliche Verbesserung wie auf Seite 58 nehme ich stets dankbar an.

Mit den besten Empfehlungen
Ihr sehr ergebener
Felix P. Greve

P.S. – Zu entschuldigen bitte ich die langsame Erledigung der Pater-Korrekturen: da ich sie sehr genau mit dem Original vergleiche, so ist es kaum anders möglich. Gleichzeitig schicke ich *Don Quixote*- und Balzac-MS., wenn auch noch nicht sehr viel, da ich unter Frühjahrsdepressionen leide.

d.O.

TO ANTON KIPPENBERG

Nachodstrasse 24
Berlin W. 15
May 3, 1908

Dear Doctor,

First of all I would like to acknowledge with many thanks the receipt of two sums of money totalling 566.60 M[arks].

Then the Balzac proofs. I shall not conceal the fact that your letter was a real disappointment to me, because I for my part consider the 2nd volume, – from which, after all, I am now far enough away to be able to judge – better, if not indeed much better, than the first. On the whole, I treated the sentence structure a little more freely, which cost me quite a lot of work. So today I checked sheet 4 again extremely carefully and compared it with the original. I took the liberty of entering my remarks directly on the sheet. Properly speaking, I found only *one* actual improvement, on page 58. In about 10 cases the change seems to me to make it worse. In about just as many cases, the change is acceptable but completely immaterial, and again in approximately the same number of cases, at least so it seems to me, one word is only replaced by another, so that if it were anyone else but you, I would simply assume that it is really nothing but schoolmasterly pedantry. With the best will in the world, I cannot see at all why on page 49 'entgegenkam' should be better than the more exact 'entsprach'; or on page 58 why 'auf etwas zählen' is poorer than 'mit etwas rechnen'; or on page 62 'erheuchelter' better than 'gespielter.'

I had already planned to discuss the work of the proof-reader with you while doing the proof-reading of vol. 1. Several times extensive corrections had been made in the proofs that completely changed the meaning; indeed, although they apparently resulted in a more fluent German, they still replaced what was right with something very wrong, so that I simply had to restore my text. I did not do so at the time because the proof-reader indeed proved to be right in a small detail where I had made a mistake. I do not know whether this was due to his knowledge of the original. However, compared to all the other corrections this one was scarcely of importance, and I am still under the definite impression that the person concerned is going beyond his authorization and causing a lot of needless work for me, since I finally found myself simply forced to compare the revision sheets at the end of vol[ume] 1 once more with the proofs. As a consequence of this I have developed an intense feeling of uncertainty: for example, when translating *Don Quixote* I am at times afraid to translate correctly, even where I feel absolutely certain; afraid of a version which may differ from all other translations; afraid out of sheer anxiety that subsequently I may still not find this uniquely correct version in the printed volume, whereas I nevertheless already have four passages in vol[ume] 1, which have never been translated *correctly* before I came along. From time to time I have experienced little unpleasant surprises of this kind while working at night, when I had no other alternative but to make a note of these passages for later editions.

I beg you not to hold these remarks against me. You will understand that they do not emanate from any dogmatism or obstinacy on my part, but arise solely from the desire to publish books for which I can assume full responsibility, which naturally was not the case with many earlier works during my term of apprenticeship. Naturally one remains fallible; I always gratefully accept a genuine correction like the one on page 58.

With best regards
Yours very truly
Felix Paul Greve

P.S. Please excuse my tardy completion of the Pater corrections; since I am very carefully comparing them with the original, it is otherwise scarcely possible. I am also forwarding the *Don Quixote* and Balzac manuscripts, even if there is not very much of them yet, as I am suffering from depression caused by the spring.

Nachodstrasse 24
Berlin W. 15
22 juin 1908

Cher Monsieur Gide,

Je vous remercie vivement de votre essai et les poèmes d'Emmanuel Signoret. J'ai été terriblement malade, des mois entiers – . Maintenant je me sauve en Norvège. Mon départ: le 1er juillet. Je vous envoie tome X des 1001 nuits. Ça court sa routine. Mais il y aura une grande lacune dans quelques mois. Encore une nouvelle: je serai divorcé!

Quant à Saül, il sera imprimé prochainement, monté probablement l'hiver 08/09. Moi aussi, j'aurai une comédie montée. Où en est votre roman?

Amicalement
votre
Felix P. Greve

TO ANDRÉ GIDE

Nachodstrasse 24
Berlin W. 15
June 22, 1908

Dear M. Gide,

Thank you very much for your essay and for the poems of Emmanuel Signoret.[1] I have been very sick, for months on end – . Now I'm off to Norway. I leave on 1st July. I send you volume x of *The 1001 Nights*.[2] Everything as usual. But there will be a great gap in a few months. Here is another bit of news: I shall be divorced.

As for *Saul*,[3] it will be published soon, probably in the winter of 08/09. I too will have a comedy staged.[4] How is your novel going?

In friendship
Felix P. Greve

1 Emmanuel Signoret (1872–1900), French poet whose poems were collected in one volume by André Gide in 1908

2 Which Greve translated in twelve volumes (Leipzig: Insel-Verlag 1907–8)

3 A play by André Gide published in 1903; the German translation by Greve appeared in 1909 (Berlin: Erich Reiss).

4 This may be a reference to *Der Heimliche Adel*, which Greve mentions in his letter to Brümmer. But it is not known if it was ever published.

September 21, 1909

Frau Else Greve, Berlin
Sehr geehrte gnädige Frau!

Ihr Brief vom Freitag voriger Woche bestätigt den Inhalt Ihres Telegramms, wonach Ihr Herr Gemakl nicht mehr unter den Lebenden weilt. Ich möchte, bevor mir nicht eine authentische Nachricht über seinen Tod zugeht, zunächst noch daran zweifeln und für Ihren Gemahl, für Sie und für mich hoffen, dass er noch lebt.

Sollte das indessen nicht der Fall sein und Ihr Gemahl freiwillig den Tod gesucht haben, so kann ich mir doch irgendeine indirekte

Mitschuld daran keineswegs zumessen, und muss daher den Inhalt Ihres Briefes in seiner Gesamtheit, soweit er sich gegen mich wendet, unbedingt ablehnen. Ich bin mir im Gegenteil bewusst, Ihrem Herrn Gemahl von dem nicht gerade erfreulichen und zur Fortsetzung reizenden Anfang unserer Verbindung an stets das *allerdenkbarste Entgegenkommen* gezeigt, ihn zeitweilig sogar über Wasser gehalten zu haben, wofür genug briefliche Beweise von seiner Hand sich bei mir befinden. Sie wissen, dass ich ihm stets in der liberalsten Weise Vorschüsse gewährt, ja, sie ihm zu Zeiten, wo ich das Gefühl hatte, dass er ihrer besonders bedürfe, freiwillig angeboten habe. Abgeschlagen habe ich ihm die Hilfe niemals, und auch in seiner letzten Not würde er sie nicht vergeblich bei mir gesucht haben. Wenn ich darauf hinweise, dass das Vorschusskonto Ihres Gatten sur Zeit mit nahezu 4000 Mark belastet ist, so beweist das wohl mehr als irgend welche weiteren Worte die Richtigkeit dessen, was ich sage. Wenn Ihr Gatte in seinem letzten Briefe dies Gefühl der Dankbarkeit, das er mir wiederholt ausgedrückt, ins Gegenteil verkehrt hat, so muss ich das einem unnormalen geistigen Zustande zuschreiben, der ihn die Dinge verzerrt hat sehen und ungerecht werden lassen.

Ebensowenig aber haben Ihr Gatte und Sie, da Sie sich in dieser Beziehung zu seinem Sprachrohr machen, ein Recht, darüber ungehalten zu sein, dass ich ihm in verschiedenen Fälle ernste Bedenken über die Qualität seiner Arbeit aussprechen musste. Ich habe stets durchaus anerkannt, dass viele seiner Leistungen, und ich kann sagen die meisten, vortrefflich waren und seiner hohen Begabung entsprachen. Andere dagegen waren es durchaus nicht, und ich bin nicht der einzige, der etwa darauf hingewiesen hat, sondern in vielen, an sich ganz uninteressierten Besprechungen und brieflichen Aeusserungen an uns ist das zum Ausdruck gekommen: Ihr Gatte hat das fast immer selbst eingesehen, oft auch unumwunden zugegeben. Wenn z.B. in der zweiten Auflage von Murger's *Boheme* gegenüber der ersten kein Stein auf dem andern geblieben ist, wenn der zweite Druck der ersten beiden Bände von *1001 Nacht* vollkommen umgestaltet wurde, wenn Ihr Gatte Manuskripte oder Revisionsbogen, die ich ihm mit Bemerkungen zurücksandte, durchaus änderte, so liegt darin wohl der Beweis, dass er selbst fühlte, in diesen Fällen nicht genügt zu haben. Das lag nicht en einem Mangel an Können – die Begabung Ihres Gatten hat niemand höher geschätzt als ich – sondern daran, dass Geldmangel und die Notwendigkeit, eine alte Schuld – wie er mir oft sagte – abtragen zu müssen, ihn zwangen, viel mehr Arbeiten zu übernehmen, als er trotz enormer Arbeitskraft in guter Qualität auszuführen fähig war. Dies liegt so klar auf der Hand, dass ich mich auch da auf die einfachste Feststellung beschränken kann: gerade heute noch habe ich gehört, wieviel Arbeiten er in letzter Zeit auch für andere Verleger gleichzeitig in Angriff genommen hatte. Meine *Pflicht* aber als Verleger ist es, auf die Qualität unserer Verlagswerke unermüdlich, aber auch ohne Rücksicht auf falsche Empfindlichkeit, zu achten. Die Annahme, dass ein sehr in Anspruch genommener Geschäftsmann zu seinen Vergnügen die Arbeiten selbst prüft, um dann zu nörgeln, ist absurd. Wenn ich Bedenken äusserte, so geschah es nicht so 'wie man einen dummen Jungen abkanzelt', – wie Sie sich audrücken, sondern in Form freundschaftlicher Mahnung: Du übernimmst zu viel.

Wenn also wirklich Ihr Gatte den Tod gesucht haben sollte, so ist es trotz des Inhaltes seines letzten Briefes nicht der Grund, den Sie aus diesem Briefe zitieren – denn vor dem eigenen Gewissen Ihres Gatten hätte er nicht bestehen können – sondern die Tatsache seines wirtschaftlichen Zusammenbruchs. Ich weiss, dass wir nicht der einzige Verleger sind, der grosse Forderungen an ihn hatte; die Einsicht, dass er sie niemals durch Arbeit würde begleichen können, wird das eigentlich Motiv seines Entschlusses gewesen sein, und die Tatsache, dass er in der jüngsten Zeit dieselbe Arbeit zwei Verlegern gegeben und sich von beiden hat honorieren lassen, vielleicht dazu beigetragen haben.

Ich habe niemals damit gerechnet, dass Ihr Gatte die hohen Vorschüsse, die er von uns hatte, jemals ganz abarbeiten würde, habe vielmahr einen Teil davon stillschweigend als besondere Honorierung betrachtet, und ebensowenig bin ich geneigt, Ihnen jetzt irgendwelche Schwierigkeiten zu machen. Voraussetzung dafür ist indessen, dass mir die Manuskripte und sonstiges Verlagseigentum an Büchern, was sich noch bei Ihnen befindet, sofort zur Verfügung gestellt werden. Wenn Ihr Gatte mich richtig berichtet hat, woran ich nicht zweifle, so muss sich bei Ihnen befinden: das fertige Manuskript von *1001 Tag* Band 3 und 4, die Druckvorlage zur Jugendausgabe von *1001 Nacht*, und das Manuskript der Uebertragung des Copperfield. Ich habe einen meiner Mitarbeiter, Herrn Dr. Buchwald, gebeten, am Mittwoch nach Berlin zu fahren; er wird Sie gegen Mittag aufsuchen und in meinem Auftrage die genannten Manuskripte und diejenigen Bücher, die Ihr Gatte von uns zur Bearbeitung von *1001 Tag* erhalten hat, in Empfang nehmen, auch etwaiges weitere mit Ihnen besprechen. Ich würde bereitssein, für den genannten Fall auf alle Ansprüche zu verzichten, die der Insel-Verlag an die Hinterlassenschaft Ihres Mannes zu stellen hat und würde dann auch für den erwünschten Fall, dass Ihr Gatte nicht tot ist, dem Lebenden gegenüber dieselben Ansprücke fallen lassen, un ihm, soviel an mir ist, die weitere Existenz zu ermöglichen.

Der Ton Ihres Briefes hätte mich von einer so ausführlichen Antwort eigentlich zurückhalten sollen, aber ich habe mir gesagt, dass die begreifliche Erregung, in der Sie sich befinden, Sie in Ihrem Gefühl für die Tragweite Ihrer Worte gehindert hat. Sollte ich mich darin nicht getäuscht haben, so würden Sie mich auch zu weiterer Hilfe Ihnen persönlich gegenüber bereit finden.

Mit vorzüglicher Hochachtung

FROM ANTON KIPPENBERG TO MRS ELSE GREVE, BERLIN[1]

September 21, 1909

Dear Madam!

Your letter of Friday last week confirms the contents of your telegram, according to which your husband has passed away. I would still like to doubt it, until I receive authentic news of his death, and hope, for your husband's sake and yours and mine, that he is still alive.

Should this not be true, and should your husband have committed suicide, I cannot attach any degree of indirect blame to myself in any way, and must therefore reject completely the contents of your letter in its entirety, in so far as it is directed against me. On the contrary, I am conscious of always having been extremely generous to your husband from the very start of our connection, which was not very pleasant and did not invite continuation; from time to time I kept him from sinking, for which I still have enough letters in his own handwriting that confirm this. You must be aware that I always advanced money to him in the most liberal way; I even offered it to him voluntarily at times, when I had the impression that he needed it particularly. I never refused my help, and he would not have looked for it in vain in his last distress. When I point out to you that the account of your husband is at the moment charged with 4,000 Marks in advances, it will prove more than any further words the truth of what I am saying. If your husband in his last letter transformed the feeling of gratitude that he repeatedly expressed to me into the opposite, I can only attribute it to his abnormal mental condition, which made him see things distortedly and be unjust.

Your husband and you, speaking for him, also have no right to be indignant about the fact that on different occasions I had to express my doubts about the quality of his work. I have always completely acknowledged that a lot of his work, and I can say most of it, was excellent and in accordance with his great talents. Some of it, on the contrary, was not at all that way, and I am not the only one who pointed that out, but in many discussions and written remarks contained in letters to us this became obvious. Your husband almost always realized and candidly admitted this himself. For example, when the second edition of Murger's *Bohème*,[2] as compared to the first, had to be changed completely, when the second impression of the first two volumes of *1001 Nights* had to be entirely done over, when your husband revised and altered completely manuscripts that I returned to him with annotations – in all of this is proof that he himself admitted his inadequacy in these cases. The reason was not a lack of ability – nobody could have appreciated the talent of your husband more than I – but rather that he felt forced to take on more work than he could cope with adequately, in spite of his tremendous energy, as he needed the money to pay off an old debt, as he often told me. This is so obvious that in this respect too I can limit myself to a simple fact: only today I was told how much work he recently took on simultaneously for other publishers. However, it is my duty as a publisher to pay ceaseless attention to the quality of our publications without regard to false sentimentality. Your assumption that a very busy businessman checks the work for his own amusement, just to have a chance to nag about it, is absurd. If I expressed doubts it was not, as you see it, a rebuke to a foolish person, but in the form of a friendly warning: you are taking on too much.

Should your husband really have committed suicide, the reason was not, in spite of the contents of his last letter, the one you cite from this letter – for your husband's own conscience would not have permitted this – but the fact of his financial ruin. I know that we are not the only publishing company which had sizable claims on him: the real motive for his decision was his realization that he would never be able to pay them off, and the fact that he recently sent the same work to two publishers and was paid an honorarium by both perhaps also contributed to his decision.

I never reckoned with the possibility that your husband would ever be able to work off the large advances which he had from us, and I silently considered a part of them as a special honorarium. I am just as little inclined to cause you any difficulties now, provided that you immediately return the manuscripts and books that must still be in your hands and which belong to the company.

If your husband reported correctly, and this I do not doubt, you must still have in your possession the completed manuscript of *1001 Days*,[3] volumes 3 and 4, the manuscript of the 'youth edition' of *1001 Nights*,[4] and the manuscript of the translation of *Copperfield*.[5] I have asked one of my colleagues, Dr. Buchwald, to go to Berlin on Wednesday. He will visit you at noon and, in accordance with my instructions, pick up the manuscripts I have mentioned and those books which your husband received from us for his work on *1001 Days*. He might also discuss a few other things with you. I would in this case be willing to forego all claims that the Insel-Verlag has on your husband's estate, and I would relinquish the same claims in the event that, as I hope, your husband is still alive, in order to help him carry on in the future.

The tone of your letter should have restrained me from replying at such length, but I told myself that the understandable agitation under which you are writing prevented you from exercising control over your words and feelings. Should I not be wrong in this, I would be glad if I could personally be of any help to you in the future.

With respectful regards

This letter, although not by Greve, is included here because of the light it sheds on the circumstances of Greve's 1909/10 'death.'

1 If my speculation about her identity is correct, she was Else Hildegard Ploetz, the daughter of a master mason (Maurermeister) of Swinemünde and herself an artist. She married the architect August Endell on August 22, 1901, but eloped with Greve towards the end of 1902. The marriage with Endell was annulled in Berlin on January 23, 1904, when Greve was presumably still serving his sentence in Bonn. Sometime after his release in the summer of 1904, Greve and Else apparently settled in Switzerland, and they may have been married that year.

2 *Die Bohème* (Leipzig: Insel-Verlag 1906), German translation by Felix Paul Greve

3 *Tausend und ein Tag* (Leipzig: Insel-Verlag 1909–10) – only the first two volumes were translated by Greve, and volumes III and IV were translated by Paul Hansmann.

4 This may refer to either *Die schönsten Geschichten aus 1001 Nacht* (1914) or *Die Abenteurer Sinbads des Seefahrers* (1914) – both, in Greve's translation, were published by Insel-Verlag.

5 Presumably the anonymous translation of *David Copperfield* (Leipzig: Insel-Verlag 1912)

Sources of the Letters

To Insel-Verlag, R. von Poellnitz, and Anton Kippenberg	Nationale Forschungs- und Gedenkstätten der Klassischen Deutschen Literatur in Weimar
To R. von Poellnitz, June 6, 1903	Schiller-Nationalmuseum, Marbach am Neckar
To Franz Blei and Franz Brümmer	Deutsche Staatsbibliothek, Berlin
To André Gide	Mme Catherine Gide, 92 Neuilly sur Seine, France

Appendix B

Felix Paul Greve to Anton Kippenberg, dated April 15, 1907, courtesy of Nationale Forschungs- und Gedenkstätten der klassischen deutschen Literatur in Weimar

Frederick Philip Grove to Isaak J. Warkentin, dated September 7, 1913, courtesy of Elizabeth Dafoe Library, The University of Manitoba, Winnipeg

Nachodstraße 24
Berlin W. 15.
d. 15. V. - 07

Sehr geehrter Herr Doktor,

Was das Zuviel angeht, das Sie mir „aufbürden", so können Sie darüber ohne Sorge sein. Ich habe meine ganz bestimmte Tagesleistung, die ich selten überschreite und fast nie nicht erreiche. Wenn, was ich ohne weiteres als möglich anerkenne, in den Nächsten zuweilen Ungeschicklichkeiten oder Gleichförmigkeiten im Satzbau stehen bleiben (die SB nach einem Vierteljahr niemandem unangenehmer im Ohr klingen als mir), so liegt das daran, dass ich früher selbst bei der Korrektur noch den ganzen Text, wie ich ihn übersetzte, aus dem Gedächtnis hersagen konnte (denn bei der ersten Arbeit wiederhole ich jeden Satz solange laut, bis er mir „rund" genug scheint) – und das übt begreiflicherweise eine suggestive Gewalt, die blind macht. Ich folge gern Ihrer Anregung, noch einen dritten zur Lektüre heranzuziehen, einen Herrn, der früher schon für mich Korrekturen gelesen hat. Sie werden von selber sehen, dass ich etwas „wirksamer" Korrektur lese, sobald zwischen der Übersetzung und der Lektüre mehr Zeit liegt: soviel Zeit, dass ich meinen Text inzwischen vergesse, was bei meinem Gedächtnis nicht ganz leicht ist.

Auf den Cervantes verwende ich ganz besondere Mühe, und ich glaube, er wird gut. Ich habe übrigens, wie ich schon fürchtete, die Keller & Notter'sche Übersetzung über- und meine Arbeit unterschätzt. Ich halte diese Art der Modernisierung alter Texte nicht für praktisch und glaube fast, sie macht mehr Arbeit, als neu zu übertragen. Die Schwierigkeit liegt darin, dass man unbedingt den komplizierten Satzbau wahren muss, will man nicht das Gepräge des Originals verlieren. Dabei eine annähernd gleiche Klarheit zu bewahren, wie das Spanische giebt, ist äusserst schwer, und Keller & Notter haben es sich sehr leicht gemacht: zudem sind sie doch, wie übrigens auch Förster und Müller, sehr ungenau. Das war nach der ersten Probe nicht zu beurteilen; jetzt sehe ich, dass dieser Novellenband mich mehr Arbeit, und, da es Korrekturarbeit ist, unerfreulichere Arbeit kostet als ein Band der Nächte. Das Hübscheste ist für mich einerseits die Kulturepoche (die des Gil Blas), und zweitens die Wiederbelebung meiner spanischen Kenntnisse, die solange vernachlässigt waren. Eins ist, wie mir scheint, unvermeidlich: ein wenig Korrekturkosten: es scheint mir physisch unmöglich, alles im gedruckten Text zu streichen, wofür ich geschriebenes an den Rand setze. Wenn ich eine Stelle viermal durchlese und lasse sie liegen, entdecke ich am Tage darauf plötzlich noch ein Wort, das ich hätte streichen müssen und nicht gestrichen habe.

Da nun von Ihnen der Punkt des Zuviel-Arbeitens einmal berührt worden ist, so möchte ich diese Gelegenheit benutzen,

26 Felix Paul Greve to Anton Kippenberg, April 15, 1907. *Courtesy Nationale Forschungs- und Gedenkstätten der klassichen deutschen Literatur in Weimar*

um Ihnen ganz privatim eine Kleinigkeit zu sagen, die ein Verleger, der soviel mit mir arbeitet, vielleicht wissen sollte. Ich arbeite unter ganz ungesunden und anormalen Verhältnissen. Meine Arbeit leidet eigentlich nur unter einem: unter Geldsorgen. Wenn ich nicht auf eine Weile ruhig und sicher in die Zukunft blicken kann, überwältigen mich die Lasten, die auf mir liegen, und die, zum Teil ohne meine Schuld, z.T. durch meine Schuld auf mich gefallen sind. Dann leidet, wie ich wohl weiss, meine Arbeit in ihrer Qualität.
Ich weiss nicht, ob ich Ihnen einmal erzählt habe, dass ich von meinem 16. Lebensjahr an meine Mutter ernähren musste. Zum Teil noch aus jener Periode schreiben sich auch gewisse Lasten her, an denen ich noch auf (und nicht) Jahre hinaus zu tragen habe, und um Ihnen einen Begriff von ihnen zu machen, nenne ich die Summe von über 4000 M. jährlich. Da ich nun immer bestrebt bin, zunächst diesen alten Verpflichtungen – auch später neu freiwillig wieder übernommenen – nachzukommen, so bleibt mir von meinem Einkommen mitunter so gut wie nichts übrig, und es kommt vor, dass ich trotz meiner Erfolge mit meiner Frau einfach hungere.
Ich spreche darüber nicht gern. Aber es erklärt Ihnen vielleicht, weshalb ich so oft um Geld bitte, obgleich ich ganz gut verdiene. Und ich sage es Ihnen auch, um Ihnen dies deutlich zu machen: Meine Arbeit ist dann zuverlässig gut, und ich vertraue ihr am meisten, wenn ich auf eine Weile hinaus genügend Aufträge vor mir sehe, um vor Not gesichert zu sein. Ich habe jetzt in letzter Zeit ein wenig versäumt, andere Beziehungen zu suchen oder aufrecht zu erhalten, und bin ein wenig auf die Insel angewiesen. Und damit komme

ich eigentlich zu einem Punkt, den ich berühren möchte: Haben Sie den Don Quijote schon vergeben? Oder würden Sie eventuell in Erwägung ziehen, ob Sie mir auch diese Arbeit anvertrauen könnten?

Wie schon gesagt, bitte ich diesen Brief als einen rein privaten anzusehen.

Mit den besten Empfehlungen

Ihr sehr ergebener

Felix P. Greve

Winkler, Man.
7/IV 13

Lieber Herr Warkentin,

Ich bin so froh, jemanden in Steinbach zu haben der mir vielleicht behilflich sein kann, dass ich Ihnen möglicherweise lästig fallen werde. Vielleicht wird es Ihnen zur Genugtuung gereichen dass Sie ja schliesslich Ihrer Heimat helfen.

Ich habe 3 weitere Büchertitel über die ich gern Auskunft hätte:

Fitzga, Die leitenden Grundsätze für den Elementarunterricht ~~im~~ Rechnen und Geometrie (Wien 1897)

Knilling, Die Naturgemässe Methode des Rechenunterrichts (München 1899)

Rein Pickel, Volksschulunterricht (Leipzig 1879)

Petersen, Methoden und Theorien für die Lösung geometrischer Konstruktionsprobleme (Kopenhagen 1879)

Wenn Sie noch nicht bankerott („broke") sind, kaufen Sie mir doch, bitte, den Rein Pickel; ich werde Ihnen, ich eigentlich zu einem Punkt, den ich berühren möchte: Haben Sie den Don Quijote schon vergeben? Oder würden Sie eventuell in Erwägung ziehen, ob Sie mir auch diese Arbeit anvertrauen könnten?

Wie schon gesagt, bitte ich diesen Brief als einen rein privaten anzusehen.

Mit den besten Empfehlungen

Ihr sehr ergebener

Felix P. Greve

Winkler, Man.
7/IV 13

Lieber Herr Warkentin,

Ich bin so froh, jemanden in Dtschld zu haben der mir vielleicht behilflich sein kann, dass ich Ihnen möglicherweise lästig fallen werde. Vielleicht wird es Ihnen zur Genugtuung gereichen dass Sie ja schliesslich Ihrer Heimat helfen.

Ich habe 3 weitere Büchertitel über die ich gern Auskunft hätte:

Fitzga, Die leitenden Grundsätze für den Elementarunterricht im Rechnen und Geometrie (Wien 1897)

Knilling, Die Naturgemässe Methode des Rechenunterrichts (München 1899)

Rein Pickel, Volksschulunterricht (Leipzig 1889)

Petersen, Methoden und Theorien für die Lösung geometrischer Konstruktionsprobleme (Kopenhagen 1879)

Wenn Sie noch nicht bankrott („broke") sind, kaufen Sie mir doch, bitte, den Rein Pickel; ich werde Ihnen, sowie ich Nachricht über den Preis erhalte, den Betrag schicken.

Vielen Dank im voraus

Ihr

F. Grove

NB. Wir erregen Aufsehen hier durch die Neuerungen, die ich in Winkler eingeführt habe, Sie werden wohl davon hören. A. W. ist starr und sieht staunenden Auges zu.

27 Frederick Philip Grove to Isaak J. Warkentin, September 7, 1913. *Courtesy Elizabeth Dafoe Library, The University of Manitoba, Winnipeg*

Index

Titles of books and articles etc. are listed under their authors. Only the English versions of the letters in Appendix A are indexed. Main biographical entries are indicated in bold type.